Claws of the Bear

Also by Brian Moynahan

Airport International
The Tourist Trap

Claws of the Bear

The History of the Red Army
from the Revolution to the Present

———•———

BRIAN MOYNAHAN

A MARC JAFFE BOOK

HOUGHTON MIFFLIN COMPANY

Boston • 1989

FIRST AMERICAN EDITION

Copyright © 1989 by Brian Moynahan

ALL RIGHTS RESERVED

For information about permission to reproduce selections
from this book, write to Permissions, Houghton Mifflin
Company, 2 Park Street, Boston, Massachusetts 02108.

Library of Congress Cataloging-in-Publication Data
Moynahan, Brian.
Claws of the bear : the history of the Red Army from the
Revolution to the present / Brian Moynahan — 1st American ed.
p.   cm.
"A Marc Jaffe book."
Bibliography: p.
Includes index.
ISBN 0-395-51076-7
1. Soviet Union — Armed Forces — History — 20th century. 2. Soviet
Union — History, Military — 1917–   I. Title.
UA770.M78   1989   89-31004
355'.00947 — dc19   CIP

Printed in the United States of America

P 10 9 8 7 6 5 4 3 2 1

For my father

Contents

Introduction: The Greatest Show on Earth   ix

FROM TSAR TO STALIN: BY WAY OF WAR, CIVIL WAR AND SIBERIA

1. Red October   3
2. Flawed Titan   7
3. 1917   20
4. Trotsky: The Prophet Armed   28
5. Kronstadt: Assault on The Citadel   44
6. The Steel Monster   50
7. Stalinism   59
8. The Great Terror: A Trench at Khodynka   68
9. The Beneficiaries   77
10. The Winter War   82

BARBAROSSA: THE GERMAN WAR

11. 'Can we open fire?'   91
12. Die in Kiev   99
13. The *Taifun* Blows Out   109
14. 'I want a child, soon'   118
15. The Forge   123
16. To the Volga   130
17. The Pit   143
18. To Berlin: Citadel at Kursk   150
19. *Perelom* and the Great Pursuit   158
20. *Dosvidania*, Ukraine   163
21. Centre Fold   171
22. The Satellites Change Sides   181
23. The House of Cards   187
24. To the Zoo Station   194
25. Victory's End   205
26. Plus Ça Change   208

CURTAIN FALL

27. A Lunch at the Lubianka   215

THE MOUTH OF THE CANNON: KHRUSHCHEV AND
THE BOMB

28. Armageddon: The Bomb   241
29. Nikita: The Rocket Man   247
30. In Uncle Sam's Backyard: Crisis in Cuba   256

INVASIONS: THE FOUR SEASONS

31. Hungarian Autumn   265
32. Berlin Summer   277
33. Prague Spring   285
34. Polish Winter   298
35. Afghanistan: The Bear Trap   306

THE VIEW FROM THE FRUNSKAYA EMBANKMENT:
PRESENT STRENGTH

36. Red Elite   323
37. The Three Million   337
38. Army Audit   352
39. Red Navy: Blue-water Build Up   361
40. Air: Floggers, Flankers and the Wild Red Yonder   370
41. Senior Service: Nuclear Attack Forces   376
42. The Spies: Run Silent   386
43. Warsaw Pact: The Uneasy Alliance   393
44. The Metal Eaters: Defence Industry   398
45. The Rival General: Secretary Gorbachev   406

FUTURE WAR

46. *Voyna*   419

Notes   429
Index   459

Introduction

THE GREATEST SHOW ON EARTH

The Red army, the world's most powerful institution, is on view in Moscow. It looks accessible and reassuring.

Troops from show divisions parade in Red Square, gloved, helmets suspended motionless as boots hit the cobblestones outside the waxen body of Lenin in his mausoleum. By St Basil's Cathedral, an officer with staff tabs parks his car and carefully puts its windscreen wipers in his issue briefcase as an insurance against theft. Under the Kremlin Wall, a bride in a thin white dress throws her posy of roses on the granite blocks at the Tomb of the Unknown Soldier.

The defence ministry lies a short distance downstream on the Moscow River along the Frunskaya Embankment. It is a four-rouble ride from the Kremlin by cab, a few seconds in the little Cessna in which a teenage German pilot came calling and so ensured that an obscure general named Dmitry Yazov became its minister.

It has fine views to Gorky Park and the Lenin Hills. A ferris wheel, edge on, revolves in blue and red and cream. Summer queues in check shirts wait for beer and ice cream. A gingerbread church upstream reminds of past loyalties to Tsar and Christ. In winter, a plume of steam rises from the open-air bath.

Yazov, the controller of the Red army, orders the daily rounds of 5,096,000 servicemen, a figure that he can swell to 11,313,000 in a fortnight with the call-up of active reserves. In the Soviet Union itself, they are scattered through eleven time zones and behind ten borders from Norway to North Korea.

As the Red flag is lowered at dusk at the divisional headquarters in Kaliningrad, in former German East Prussia, the sun is already rising from out of Alaska over the garrisons of Kamchatka.

Others of his units are stationed in Eastern Europe, in Vietnam, Mongolia, Cuba, Angola, Libya, Mozambique, Syria, Yemen, Ethiopia, Laos, in nuclear bombardment submarines off the American seaboards, in long-range reconnaissance aircraft in international airspace.

From here is decided the targeting of 1,386 intercontinental ballistic missiles and 978 sea-launched missiles. A rocket from a 'boomer', one of the four or so bombardment submarines on permanent station off the US east coast, could vaporize Washington within five minutes of the order being sent from the Frunskaya Embankment. The ICBMs would take a further twenty-five minutes to arrive.

Add in the 53,000 tanks, the four surface Fleets, the fighters with their curious Western codenames, Foxbats, Floggers, Flagons, Fiddlers, Firebars, the satellites, and the factories that feed it, and this is a colossus. Against Yazov, the Americans have 2.1 million men and 1.6 million active reserves.

Seen in Moscow, it appears bound to its desks and its parade grounds. A giant, in terms of size, but a being with recognizably the same temperament and tastes as its Western counterparts. It fits a familiar pattern that is made comforting by the fact that Gorbachev and *glasnost* now rule and that arms cuts seem the order of the day.

Only the slightest of ruffles, of names, play at its bloody memories and remind how fraught is Yazov's office how perilous the search for *glasnost*.

Mikhail Frunze, doctor's son turned Bolshevik revolutionary and commissar for defence, has a city and the main military academy named for him as well as the embankment. He died under an operation in 1925.

The operation was not ordered by a surgeon. It was decided on by the Politburo, the supreme political body whose anonymous black limousines and bulky figures are on view within the Kremlin. The prompting came from a predecessor of Gorbachev as party general secretary, Joseph Stalin. Frunze's death under the knife was almost certainly state-instructed murder. His predecessor as defence commissar, Leon Trotsky, the founder of the Red army, died with an ice-pick in his brain in exile in Mexico in 1940.

That, too, was murder ordered by the general secretary whose authority is now enjoyed in unbroken line of succession by Mikhail Gorbachev.

Spend an evening wrapped in the athletic sensuality of the Kirov ballet, and the nagging doubts of Frunze are lanced. The officers in the audience seem abnormal only in their unmilitary and laudable passion for the dance. Millions of Red army men[1] seem to stand easy, seventy-seven boomers submerge beneath distant icecaps, covers slam over 1,951 missile silos, orders go out to ground five Air Armies.

But Sergei Kirov was murdered, too, by a system that then honoured him with three major cities, countless lakes and factories, a 23,000-ton cruiser class, and the ballet. His death unleashed on the Red army and the blocks along the Frunskaya a terror that *glasnost* has not fully dispersed. Khrushchev alone of Lenin's heirs, not Gorbachev, not the vain Brezhnev, not the secret policeman Andropov, complained of the inhumanity of his inheritance.

Beneath the style, away from the Moscow parade grounds and the known terrain of the general secretary and the stars and bit-part players of disarmament talks, there is a different substance. Little is truly familiar in the modern power of the Red army and in the awesome and often ghastly sweep of its history.

At its birth, within living memory, it fought and won a civil war and created the world's first communist state. Its leadership then subjected it to a terror which, like the scale of the German invasion that swiftly followed, was on a scale unknown to any previous army.

Engulfing Eastern Europe, it underpinned Russia as it turned into a superpower with an ideology that raced into the poor parts of the world. The Soviet Union is not a superpower because of its trade, its economic strength or the cultural dynamic of its people. There are no worldwide Chicken Kiev franchises, no Ro-Ro ships packed with export Zils and Zims. Its best-known writer lives in exile.

It maintains its empire and its superpower status thanks to military power alone.

To the long burden of history, which contains so much of this violent century within it, Yazov must add the present. What responsibility this man bears!

The Soviet Union has 22.3 million square kilometres of territory, half of Eurasia and one sixth of the land surface of the planet. It traverses most of the meridians of the eastern hemisphere. On the Chukotka peninsula and Wrangel Island, it scrapes over the edge of the western.

Yazov's men must guard it from 19 degrees 38 minutes east on the Polish border to 169 degrees 59 minutes west at Cape Dezhnev across the strait from Alaska. He knows it well enough. His last posting before Moscow was 8,333 kilometres away at Khabarovsk in the Far East, a westward journey of six days on the Rossiya express. He also has the advantage of having accurate military maps. The head of the Soviet Cartography Administration admitted in 1988 that all maps for public use had been deliberately distorted on secret police orders for more than fifty years. 'Almost everything' was changed, 'roads and rivers moved, streets tilted.'[2]

In latitude, the most southerly town is dusty Kushka with its peeling yellow buildings and dirt roads on the Afghan border at 35 degrees north, below Gibraltar in European terms, at a level with Memphis in American. The frozen rock of Cape Chelyuskin huddles at the extremity of the landmass at 77 degrees 4 minutes north in Siberia. The archipelagos extend further north, to the 82nd parallel at Cape Fligeli in Franz Josef Land.

Its vastness, and its proven ability to soak up enemies, Swedes, French, German or White, is both a strategic blessing and a logistical and manning

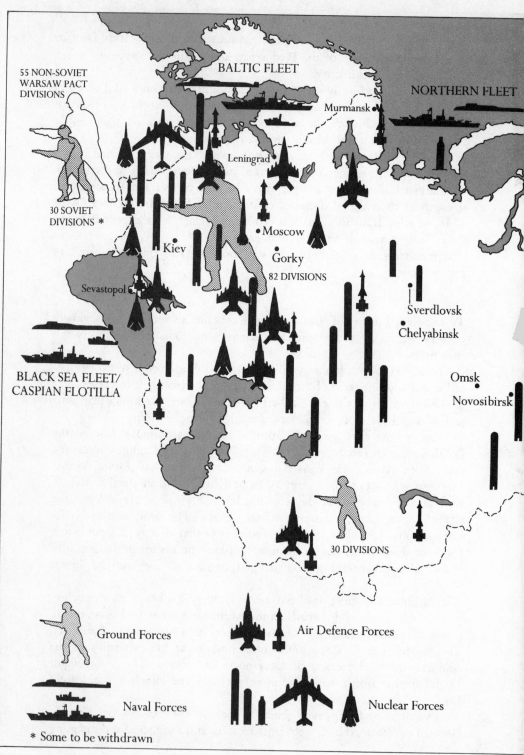

55 NON-SOVIET
WARSAW PACT
DIVISIONS

30 SOVIET
DIVISIONS *

BALTIC FLEET

NORTHERN FLEET

Murmansk

Leningrad

Moscow

Gorky

82 DIVISIONS

Kiev

Sevastopol

BLACK SEA FLEET/
CASPIAN FLOTILLA

Sverdlovsk

Chelyabinsk

Omsk

Novosibirsk

30 DIVISIONS

Ground Forces

Air Defence Forces

Naval Forces

Nuclear Forces

* Some to be withdrawn

The Armed Forces of the Soviet Union and the Warsaw Pact

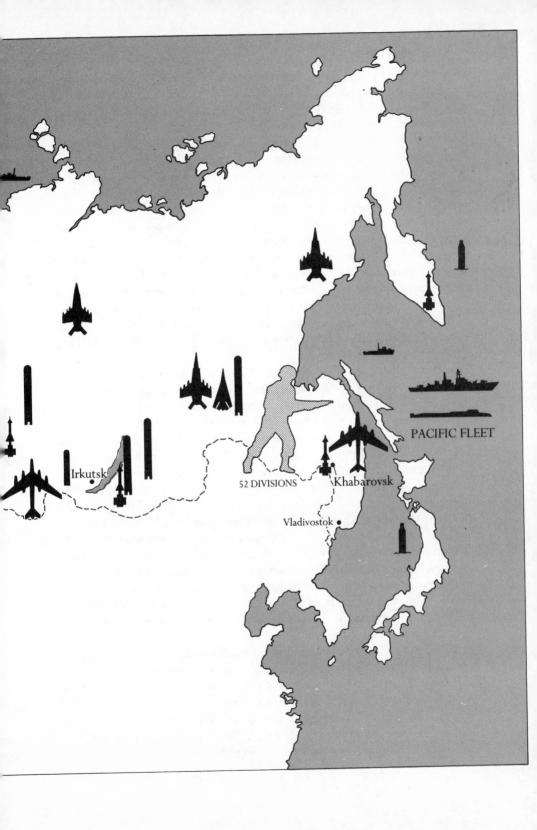

Irkutsk

52 DIVISIONS   Khabarovsk

Vladivostok

PACIFIC FLEET

nightmare for Yazov. Through routes from Poland to the Pacific exist only by air and rail. There is no transnational highway.

The climate is another strategic ally, for long also a military secret so jealously guarded that Soviet newspapers did not begin publishing weather maps until the 1970s. This, despite the US satellites that were equipped to deal with the immensity of climatic change. From their lofty orbit, the satellites see weather patterns that are affected by both the Icelandic and Aleutian lows as well as the Iranian minimum. Western Russia is influenced by the Azores high. South-easterly winds blown off the periphery of the Hawaiian high reach aircraft flying over the coasts of the Far East. At the poles of cold, Oimyakon and Verkhoyansk, in a depression where the coldest air concentrates on the upper reaches of the Yana and Indigirka rivers in Siberia, the average January temperature is below minus 50 degrees Centigrade and on some days drops to minus 70. The rivers freeze to their beds of rock. Most of the country has average winter temperatures below freezing and the average summer temperature of the entire landmass is only marginally above zero Centigrade. It is only in the Colchis, eastern Transcaucasia and the southern fringes of Central Asia that January temperatures stay above freezing.

In the western part of the country, along the traditional invasion routes, severe cold can start in November and persist in waves until late March. The average snow depth in which Yazov's mechanized units must operate is above thirty centimetres. Only in the Baltic area and south of the Pripyat marshes are temperatures above freezing for more than six months of the year. January and February see the most severe cold, with temperatures dropping to minus 37 degrees Centigrade as arctic air advances across the central plains from the Kara Sea. This cold is normally windless with brilliant clarity to the days, dawns with bands of palest salmon pink and the sharp drop in temperature the Wehrmacht so feared hurrying in with the rapid nightfall. The interceptors, radar and missile systems of the Western air defence commands play complex manoeuvres with pre-heat and low-temperature lubricants. The snowstorms that build heavy cloud in the centre and north in November and December sweep into European Russia with winds that produce a chill factor more dangerous than the steeper cold of pure winter. In winter, the frozen rivers bring a vulnerability that only the Mongols exploited.

The crews of Yazov's attack and bombardment submarines are snugger in their bases on the Kola peninsula than their northern latitude gives them any reason to expect. The warmth of the North Atlantic Current and the Atlantic air masses give the strategic north-western corner of Russia a mild winter. The January temperatures in Murmansk are 18 degrees Centigrade higher than the average for this latitude. The Barents and Murmansk seas never freeze, though they are beyond the polar circle.

For campaigning, 'March is a month without water and April is a month without grass.' The rivers are too thinly frozen in March to be used for transport but too thickly for the ice to be broken for navigation. With the April rainstorms comes the mud as soft as dough that sucked German panzers and half-tracks into its maw.

Spring comes late. When it gets going in the steppelands in May, it has traditionally provided the best campaigning weather. The grass is so thick that the leading regiments in the great expansionary drives of the nineteenth century marched barefoot to trample it down for the mass of animals and men moving behind them to the sound of kettledrums. With snowmelt and light rain, the grass is rich enough to forage but too wet to burn and there is winter wheat on the arable land. Tanks are less concerned with grass. For their crews the mildness of spring, the firm going and the absence of telltale plumes of dust from their tracks make it the ideal fighting season.

Summer heat is intense and reaches 37 degrees Centigrade on the steppelands. Wood and water are short and the steppe can burn from bursting shells. Tartars would fire the steppe against the advancing Russians, forcing them to dig firebreaks around the perimeter of their camps and to march along riverbanks. Dust gives away the line of march and dirt roads corrugate into washboards, shaking motorized infantry and straining tank tracks. Sudden rainstorms, as cyclones pass from west to east, mire trucks before the drying sun releases them. Visibility is clear across the long landscapes, making offensives easy to follow. Temperatures rise deeper into the country and in the last century the Russians 'lost great numbers by fatigue, want of water, travelling through these scorching deserts, and by the plague'.

The garrisons in Verkhoyansk and Oimyakon whom Yazov equips to survive winter must now cope with temperatures above 30 degrees Centigrade. In Kazakhstan the temperatures can exceed 37 degrees Centigrade for more than a month, and that in the few scraps of shade, as rivers exhaust themselves and disappear into the dunes.

In autumn, the polar and arctic fronts move south. Their cyclones produce the autumnal rain and mud that frustrated Guderian and the cloud that protected the Red Square parade of the first November of the last war.

Size and climate do Yazov better than terrain. It is a land of great plains, particularly in the west. Yazov deploys a few mountain specialists who unfurl their banners for propaganda pictures on the highest point of the country, the Peak of Communism at 7,495 metres in the Pamirs. The southern frontier is bounded by a mountain ring running from the Carpathians, the Crimea and the Caucasus to the soaring Pamirs and

Tyan-Shan and the lake-laced Altai in Asia. Neither the invasion threat nor the bulk of Yazov's men come from here.

Most of his country-boy troops are plainsmen, tank and truck riders for whom river crossings and forests are the main obstacles, descendants of the traditional infantryman described a century ago as 'sallow in complexion, lank in figure, with straight yellow hair and a heavy expression of face'. Though Yazov depends increasingly on city Slavs and Central Asians, such plainsmen are still the backbone of his forces. In the moments when his armies think of what they serve, it will be an emotional picture of the old Rus, a wooden village with an ochre domed church, ponds fringed with stands of silver birch and small oaks, and a morning mist giving intimacy in place of the dull immensity of the curving horizon.

The Russian, Turan and West Siberian plains are seldom over 180 metres high, with few natural choke points for invading armour. The Russian plain, with the Siberian taiga spilling into it on the north, is flat with no barriers beyond the rivers and huge marshlands of the Pripyat Polesye. It includes the Karelian taiga of lakes and pines and the oak forests of central Russia. As Napoleon found on the Borodino, and the Germans throughout their retreat, the rivers and water are barriers, a reason why Yazov's engineers and amphibious-tank crews are important. The Volga, on whose banks the Germans spent themselves, is the greatest waterway in Europe but its 3,690 kilometres make it only the fifth river of the Soviet Union. The Volga basin is a million and a half square kilometres, almost a third of the Russian plain. Its canals, some built by slave labour, make it the 'river of the Five Seas', emptying into the Caspian and linked to the Baltic, to the Sea of Azov and the Black Sea by the Volga–Don canal and to the White Sea by the northern Dvina canal. So prevalent are waterways, lakes and rivers that Yazov is obliged to maintain special flotillas. The Caspian Sea is the world's largest lake, five times greater than Lake Superior, and Baikal is its deepest. In Siberia, the Ob runs for 5,570 kilometres to the Arctic and the Lena 4,269 kilometres to the Laptev Sea. They are so long and the summers so late that they do not disgorge at flood levels into the ice-clogged northern seas until August.

Cold tundra lies to the north of the Russian plain and fertile grass steppelands to the south. Though the Urals stand to the east, with craggy valleys and mountain tundra, in their middle section the Urals are almost flat and can be crossed without difficulty. They would not have held the Germans for long. Beyond the Urals lies Siberia, running east through the forest, steppe and tundra. It does not appear on Yazov's maps, for it is not a political or military entity. There is no place or district called Siberia except in the soul, a place of ultimate retreat and resupply to the Russian, a wilderness of cold and cruelty to the invader.

There are many punishment postings far from Gorky Park for those who fall foul of Yazov, or for himself if he goes the way of his predecessor Sokolov. The thought helps discipline. The arctic islands, with their naval and radar stations, are ice-covered deserts where an officer will find only the arctic bear, sea-lion, seal and beluga and those who hunt them. Further south, the tundra covers a seventh of the national territory. This is Gulag and reindeer territory of moss, lichen and low shrubs and the keening howl of the snowy owl. In the summer, the swamps and lakes melt above the permafrost and mosquitoes breed in the thin mud. Below it, the forest zone is as much as 1,930 kilometres deep and eats two fifths of the Soviet land area with its larch, pine, spruce and fir. An officer, like Lenin before him, can console himself by hunting elk, wolf, bear, lynx, hare and fox. This taiga of coniferous trees slowly gives way to deciduous forests in the south.

Into the steppelands, the next belt of 15 per cent of area, are concentrated the cities, the big farms, the training grounds and major garrisons and the old invasion routes. Nothing else is Moscow or Leningrad, but anywhere here is preferable to the sand, loam and stone deserts east of the Caspian in Kazakhstan and Central Asia. Anywhere, except the dream posting for the officer tired of Moscow politics and yearning for the red and yellow soils, the fruit and cotton plantations and coasts of the subtropical corner of Georgia and the Crimea.

The loneliest postings are on the borders, 48,000 kilometres long – 29,000 kilometres of coastline and the rest abutting on eleven countries. These are the responsibility, though, of the KGB border guards. Yazov need not worry overmuch about them, beyond regretting that the coastline, for all its length, does not give easy access to the oceans and splits his fleets into four. The coast has a necklace of seas, Barents, Kara, Laptev, East Siberian, Bering, Okhotsk, Japan, Black and Baltic. It is short on warm water and, apart from the Arctic, lacks ocean frontage.

Missile attack nags at Yazov most. He may *believe* that the West Germans could invade again from the west, this time accompanied by NATO, that the Chinese could debouch over the Ussuri whilst the Americans and Japanese attacked the Pacific coast. He has been exposed to a lifetime of such propaganda. As a military professional, he *knows* that this rates low on the scale of possibilities. He has the *glacis* of eastern Europe and the eighty-two divisions of reserves in the western military districts and forty-four divisions on the Chinese border to protect him against conventional invasion.

History, however, has taught him to expect Russian cities to be razed to the ground. Minsk has been flattened eight times, the Germans simply taking rather longer and doing a more thorough job than Napoleon had done in 1812. Kiev has been put to the sword ten times, by Vikings, Mongols, Poles, Lithuanians, Swedes, White Russians and Germans. Yazov has only to go on the most mundane inspection trip, to Stalingrad/Volgograd, to Rostov, to Kharkov, to Brest to be reminded why the streets are so wide and the faceless blocks that line them are so new. The old ones went under tank and artillery rounds and high explosives. Next time, it would be missiles.

His first concern is his own missile sites. His ICBMs are in twenty main areas. The bulk are in the western part of the country, within a circle extending for 2,400 kilometres from Moscow. Dombarovsky, on the border of Kazakhstan beyond Orsk, marks the southern point, Derazhnya the west, Yedrovo the north close to the Barents Sea, Perm the east on the edge of the Urals. A belt of sites then runs well above the southern frontiers to the east, from Zhangiz Toba above Sinkiang to Svobodnyy north of Manchuria. He also thinks of the Tyuratam, Plesetsk and Nenoska missile and space test centres, his submarine bases in the Arctic and the Far East. Though the Americans can reach the lot, and the British and French can throw their tuppence worth in deep, it is as good a spread as he could hope for.

Besides Moscow and Leningrad with their eleven million population total, there are fourteen cities and conglomerations that exceed the million mark. Yazov can be grateful to geography again. The population is better scattered than the American, or the West Europeans and Japanese at that, and Yazov and his civil defence commanders have less to fear from a city-busting attack. There is not the same concentration of targets that his rocket force and submarine staffs find on the US east coast, in California and the Great Lakes.

The dangerous concentration of industry in the west, that so nearly tipped the scales for the *Barbarossa* invasion in 1941, has gone. Key defence plants are spread deep and wide, on the Black Sea, in the Donetz, behind the Urals, in Sverdlovsk, Tashkent, Novosibirsk and a score of cities. Tanks are produced at Nizhniy Tagil in the Urals, 320 kilometres south at Chelyabinsk, 800 kilometres east at Omsk and 1,600 kilometres south-west at Kharkov. Missiles, of course, can penetrate the whole of Soviet airspace. But there is nothing on offer as tempting as the California defence industry or the Detroit tank complex.

No danger, either, in being cut off by war from vital strategic minerals. The Soviet Union is self-sufficient in metals like titanium, aluminium and beryllium and in nuclear and conventional fuels. It is the only major industrial power that is energy independent. It needs no vulnerable tanker fleets like the West. It is the world's largest oil producer and its proven oil reserves are second only to the Persian Gulf area. It is a larger natural-gas producer than the US.

One fierce reaction will come from Yazov as he looks at the map. It is *all* Soviet territory. The insistence that *every last scrap* is Soviet, in a territory bigger than South America, may seem odd. It is because some parts of the Soviet Union are recent acquisitions and are claimed by some not to be Soviet at all.

In the west, a large slice of land, including Brest but running well to the west of the present border city, was Poland until 1939. Yazov will not wish to dwell on the Molotov-Ribbentrop deal under which it was then acquired. The Soviet city of Kaliningrad on the Baltic was the Reich city of Konigsberg in East Prussia. Meddling foreign-based Balts still claim independence for Lithuania, Latvia and Estonia and the fact that this was once ceded to them under Lenin does not improve Soviet sensitivity.

The Chinese have an unfraternal claim on 1.5 million square kilometres of Soviet territory. They may not be able to do much about it, but Yazov will not have forgotten Mao's outburst in 1963. 'About a hundred years ago, the area to the east of Baikal became Soviet territory, and since then Vladivostock, Khabarovsk, Kamchatka and other areas have been Soviet territory,' the troublesome Chinese said. 'We have not yet presented our account for this list.' Some day, they may.

The Japanese are no better. They have a claim on the island of Sakhalin and the Kurile Islands stretching from Hokkaido to the Kamchatka peninsula. Although only an irredentist fringe want the northern and central islands back, mainstream Japanese regard the Soviet presence in the southern ones, Kunashiri, Etorofu, Shikotan and the Habomai archipelago, as foreign occupation.

As a former Far East commander, a resident of Khabarovsk until 1986, Yazov is well aware of his submarine and air assets in these regions. His political masters know that, if empires start giving up scraps of disputed territory, things can unravel quickly. They have, after all, themselves invested in the process to wind up the older European empires, the British, the French, the Portuguese.

Do Yazov's peers think of the withdrawal from Afghanistan as just such a scrap? Do they reckon arms reductions and *glasnost* to be a fraying of will that can unravel the seam of their power?

For all their mutual fascination, direct contact between the Red and Western armies remains negligible. It is restricted to the odd exercise and visit, to military attachés, glimpses in Berlin and parrying in Geneva, the exchange of electronic signatures between submarines and of information between agents and their spymasters.

One contact at the close of the last war remains a moment of absolute insight.

Soviet tanks came to a POW camp in Prussia in early evening, the weak spring sun setting into the drivers' eyes. The German guards had fled and the Western prisoners, British and US aircrew, had prepared gifts for their liberators. A reception committee stood by the open gates of the camp with presents of hoarded chocolate and carvings of squadron crests. The lead tank ignored them and the gate. It clattered through the perimeter wire. The cheers died and the prisoners scattered as it moved at speed through the huts. It headed for a further compound where gaunt and sick Red army prisoners waited in silence.

A sub-machine gunner was sitting on the front of the tank, braced against the turret with his boots splayed on the deck. 'He rode on the tank as if it was a horse,' says Kenneth Pearson, a captured Royal Navy pilot. 'His face was Asian, yellow and black with oil and an utter indifference to us. He was wearing sunglasses, with little hexagonal frames and pink rims.'

The tank burst into the Russian compound and stopped. Red army men, in scraps of greatcoats, gathered round it quietly. That night, the British and Americans roamed their compound, lighting fires and singing. The Russians stayed without noise in their huts. At dawn, the sky red over the forests to the east, the Russians were marched off under guard back along the route their liberators had taken.

'They went with the same sort of dull resignation that we had when we were marched into captivity,' says Pearson. 'I knew instantly, we all did, that the half-rumoured stuff about the regime, those echoes about show trials and purges and *kulaks*, the way they treated their own people, I knew they were true.

'And those sunglasses on that Mongol face, taken from some fashionable German woman and worn with that strange nonchalance. We sensed that something was happening far beyond the end of yet another war in Europe. The Russians weren't in any way like us. And they were here to stay.'

Thirty-three years later, Pearson returned to the site of his Prussian captivity. The huts, wire and wooden watch towers were intact. The camp inmates were now a battalion of Russian motorized infantry, part of the Group of Soviet Forces in East Germany, a symbol of the imbalance of conventional forces to the West and a vital front-line asset to Yazov.

This is the story of his inheritance, shot through with the achievement and suspicion and suffering, much of it self-inflicted, that stamps the Soviet soul.

From Tsar to Stalin

By Way of War, Civil War and Siberia

I
RED OCTOBER

September and October are the worst months of the Russian year. The skies over Petrograd in 1917 were dull and grey, the days shortening and the rain drenching and incessant. 'The mud underfoot,' wrote the American eyewitness John Reed, 'was deep, slippery and clinging, tracked everywhere by heavy boots.' Damp winds blew in off the Gulf of Finland. It was dark from three in the afternoon to ten in the morning and, for fear of German airships and economy of coal, there were few street lights. Robbery and housebreaking were rife. Food was scarce and the queues were lengthening.[1] Inflation reached 1,000 per cent, and bank customers were expected to cut individual notes from printed sheets of currency.

In the countryside, smoke trails marked the burning of landlords' forests and their houses. At an estate in Tambov province in September, the *muzhiks* burned everything flammable and slaughtered the breeding cattle, 'drunk to madness'.[2] In Tauride province the peasants took the work animals, the machinery, the grain. They tore the doors from their frames in the estate houses, the floors from the rooms and the zinc roofs and carried them away. Near Minsk the wagonloads of plunder were so dense that there was no room to pass on the roads. The peasants 'just dragged and carried things off, beginning at twelve o'clock noon, for two days and two nights without a stop'. The destruction of the great estates around Ryazan, south of Moscow, took four days. When they had taken all they could get, they broke up the stoves, taking the flue-plates, ripping up the floors and planks and dragging it all home. Behind it, said Trotsky, was the thousand-year-old strategy of all peasant wars, to leave the enemy no place to cover his head.

Respectable Petrograd tried to cling to some normality, even gaiety. Alexander Kerensky, the head of the Provisional Government that had replaced the Tsar seven months before, swept round with Caucasian cavalrymen as his bodyguards in bright red cloaks, tall fur hats and naked swords. Cossacks, the 'veritable heroes of bourgeois Petrograd' according to Trotsky, were applauded in restaurants and benefit evenings were held for their wounded in theatres and cinemas.

The daughters of noblemen and rich *maradiors*, ghouls or speculators, came in from the provinces to study at the conservatoire or trawl for husbands. The ex-Tsar and his family were still alive, though they had been moved from palace arrest at Tsarskoe Selo to humbler house arrest in the Siberian province of Tobolsk, dead Rasputin's birthplace. Chaliapin was singing and the ballerina Karsavina was appearing to packed houses in a new ballet. Although electricity was cut off at midnight, to save coal in the power stations, gambling clubs were 'champagne sparkles by candle-light' and stayed open until the early hours. Officers wore their gold-trimmed crimson *bashliki* and Caucasian swords in brothels and around the hotel lobbies. The red banners, draped on palaces and ministries in the February Revolution that had overthrown Nicholas II, faded in the autumn rains.

But the issue of power was about to be decided. Each night crowds packed the gloomy amphitheatre of the Cirque Moderne, to listen to haranguing speeches, and each day tons of propaganda were sent out by the carload from the Smolny, the girls' school used as an HQ by the Soviets. The reports reaching Kerensky from the front were chilling: '126th Division, disintegration ... IVth Army, morale sinking ... IIIrd Army, disintegrating.'

The Empire was cracking. Nationalist movements were rolling in the Ukraine, Finland, Poland and White Russia. The Finnish Senate refused to loan money to the Provisional Government, declared Finland auton-omous and demanded the withdrawal of Russian troops. The Ukrainians were beginning to form a national army. Strikes and lock-outs paralysed the Don coal mines. The Germans had taken Reval (now Tallin) and were less than 300 kilometres from Petrograd with little to stop them. There was talk of moving the capital to Moscow.

On 20 October the Petrograd Soviet elected a Military Revolutionary Committee for the defence and garrisoning of the city. Trotsky was its chairman. It was to become the chief instrument of the insurrection, as Trotsky was its chief character. Commissars were appointed for each regiment by the Committee as the Bolsheviks reached for a direct strike for power. Kerensky provided the spark. Using the German advance as an excuse, he proposed to rid the capital of its Bolshevized troops by sending them to the front. On 24 October Lenin, a wig covering his baldness and his beard shaved, slipped back into Petrograd. For ten hours a secret session of the Bolshevik Central Committee argued whether the time had come for a coup. Supported by Trotsky, Stalin wavering, Lenin won. A declaration, written on squared paper in a child's exercise book, was passed that 'an armed uprising has become inevitable and acute'.

The Bolsheviks accused Kerensky of being set on the destruction of the country. At the Cirque Moderne, Trotsky swayed crowds of workers and soldiers, in dirty uniforms, greatcoats and tunics unbuttoned, faces upturned in the acrid haze of tobacco smoke. Bolshevik newspapers demanded an immediate truce on all fronts, landlord estates to be given to the peasants without compensation, and workers' control in industry.

It was easy for the Bolsheviks to get supplies of arms. The Soviet was accepted as the effective authority in many factories, workers at the

Sestroretsk Arms Factory handing over 5,000 rifles to a delegation from the Military Revolutionary Committee. The Committee had sounded out the Petrograd regiments about a rising and only one, the 9th Cavalry, was opposed.

On 29 October the Petrograd regiments refused to obey Kerensky's orders to move to the front. Trotsky signed orders the same day to the arsenals to issue rifles to the Red Guards. Three months before, rifles had been distributed to reliable party members and machineguns smeared with tallow had been buried in the ground. These were now recovered.

The regimental committees adopted Trotsky's resolution of revolt early in November:* 'The Petrograd garrison solemnly pledges itself to put at the disposal of the All-Russia Congress all its forces, to the last man ... We are at our posts, ready to conquer or die.' Mass meetings were held throughout the city that day, a Sunday, in 'a mood very near to ecstasy'. On Monday 5 November Kerensky declared a state of emergency and placed all forces in the city under the military governor, Colonel Polkovnikov. The Military Revolutionary Committee was outlawed and the arrest of Trotsky and other Bolshevik leaders was ordered. Cossack patrols reappeared on the streets. Artillery was drawn up in the Winter Palace. Polkovnikov issued a stream of orders to repress all insubordination with the 'utmost energy'. He had fewer and fewer troops to listen to them. Trotsky had persuaded the garrison of the Peter and Paul Fortress to join the rebellion.

Early on the morning of 6 November a group of cadets sealed the doors of the *Pravda* offices. Trotsky ordered troops of the Litovsky Regiment to reopen the plant. They obeyed. The Provisional Government ordered the cruiser *Aurora*, lying at anchor in the Neva, to sea. Trotsky told the sailors to stay where they were. The day was cold and raw. The Petrograd Soviet was in continuous session at the Smolny, a 'monstrous dun mass' of debaters among the furniture of the girls' school, the ballroom and classrooms thick with sweat.

The Bolsheviks struck that night. 'We're moving!' a Bolshevik told Reed in the Smolny at four in the morning. 'We pinched the Assistant Minister of Justice and the Minister of Religions. They're down the cellar now. One regiment is on the march to capture the Telephone Exchange, another the Telegraph Agency, another the State bank. The Red Guard is out...' Outside, Reed saw his first Red Guards, a 'huddled group of boys in workmen's clothes, carrying guns with bayonets, talking nervously together'.

The city was divided up into districts, patrolled by troops and Red Guards. All night the targets fell, railway stations, telephone exchanges,

* Still October in the old-style Russian calendar, hence Red October.

newspaper offices, banks and barracks. Nowhere was there much resistance. A smart group of officers at the Military Hotel allowed themselves to be detained by a small group of sailors.

Kerensky fled the Winter Palace the next morning, Wednesday 7 November.[3] He left in an open-topped Pierce-Arrow tourer, with petrol borrowed from a hospital's supplies, driving south in a fruitless attempt to raise the army at the front. The remaining members of the Provisional Government stayed in the Malachite hall of the Winter Palace, defended by a women's battalion and a troop of military cadets from the *yunker* schools. The ministers doodled, the troops lounged in a litter of cigarette butts, bits of bread and bottles with expensive French labels. The women's battalion remained in rooms at the rear of the palace.

At 10 a.m. Trotsky issued a proclamation saying that the Provisional Government had fallen and that all power had passed to the Soviet and to his Military Revolutionary Committee. The rest of Russia had yet to declare itself. The position of the army at the front was unclear and the government clung to some form of life in the Winter Palace. 'In order to get complete possession of power,' Trotsky explained, 'it was necessary to act as a power.'

By 6 p.m. the Winter Palace was surrounded. Seven warships from the Baltic fleet had arrived in the Neva and their sailors added to the Red forces. The ministers were warned that the palace would be shelled if they did not surrender. They declined, moving deeper into the building. They wandered, as one of them recalled, 'through the gigantic mousetrap, meeting occasionally, either all together or in small groups ... condemned people, lonely, abandoned by all'. At 9 p.m. the cruiser *Aurora* fired a first shell, a blank. At ten the women's battalion surrendered. At eleven, a barrage was loosed from the batteries in the Peter and Paul Fortress. Two shells hit the palace, damaging the plasterwork and little else.

At the Smolny, Reed found a 'dun herd of armoured cars ... under the trees in the courtyard, engines going'.[4] Crowds poured down the staircases, workers in black blouses and round black fur hats, guns slung over their shoulders, and soldiers in rough dirt-coloured coats.

The scene at the Winter Palace was less frenetic, almost calm. Red Guards and soldiers infiltrated the building. Loot in plenty lay about, porcelain, glassware, gold-handled swords, bedspreads worked with the Imperial monogram. It was deemed 'property of the people' to prevent ransacking. Old palace servants in blue and red and gold uniforms tried to prevent the Red Guards penetrating deeper into the building but eventually they burst in on the room in which the ministers were abjectly waiting for them.

It was not the wild and bloody struggle of present-day mythology. Little blood was spilt in the few skirmishes. Life in the city continued almost normally. Shops and theatres were open, restaurants served the famished revolutionaries and charged them, the trams ran. It was a coup, in which the Bolsheviks relied on the support of other groups they would soon suppress.

It was, however, decisive. At 2.10 a.m. on Thursday 8 November 1917, the Provisional Government was arrested in the Winter Palace. The ministers were hustled away to the Peter and Paul Fortress. The Bolsheviks had Petrograd and the government, though they needed a further three and a half years of civil war to master Russia.

2

FLAWED TITAN

It had taken a world war to finish off what Count Witte, who served Tsarism well, had called 'this insane regime ... this tangle of cowardice, blindness, craftiness and stupidity'.

On 2 August 1914, with loyal crowds cheering 'For Faith, Tsar and Country', the army had gone light-heartedly to war. Guards officers, foreseeing a victory parade down the Unter den Linden in Berlin, asked whether they should pack their dress uniforms.[1] Mobs spontaneously sacked the German embassy in St Petersburg and the name of the city, founded by Peter the Great on the swamps of the Neva river in 1703, was changed to the Slavonic Petrograd.

The Russian army was comfortably the largest in the world, numbering 114.5 infantry divisions to the Germans' 96. Mobilization added 3.1 million reserves to the prewar regular strength of 1.4 million within a few weeks. More than 15 million men would eventually be harnessed to what her Western allies called the Russian steamroller.

Most of the millions who were to be tested in the coming slaughter were peasant *muzhiks*. They were born in log huts thatched with straw, above a single room with a large flat stove on which the family slept in winter. 'To pass to leeward of a Russian peasant,' wrote an English traveller, 'is so terrible an event I always avoid it if possible.' The land their families worked was a flat and rolling plain with few features beyond the great rivers and their occasional bluffs. The soldier's disposition and character, the American military attaché F. V. Greene noted, 'are determined by these dull, sombre surroundings, a cheerless climate, monotonous village life and a superstitious religion'.

The infantry recruit was subject to a constant and harsh discipline that found its most savage expression in the knout, a length of raw elkhide that could cut through a back to the intestines. It was accepted as part of the natural order of things that the Russian needed to be driven. 'It is scarcely possible for a people to be as fitted for slavery as the Muscovites,' a Westerner had noted in 1706. 'They are so corrupt by nature that they will do nothing of their own free will but must be driven by hard and cruel blows.' Despite the emancipation of the serfs by Alexander II in 1861, the serflike treatment of soldiers continued under his grandson Nicholas II in 1914. A recruit first learnt unquestioning obedience. His NCOs beat him on parade with incessant flicks of their swagger sticks, a ritual that was compared with a valet beating dust from a curtain. He stood at attention, his hand at his cap, through any conversation with an officer. He did not answer with a direct yes or no, but with a *t'otchen* or a *ne kak nyet*, a 'quite so' or a 'not exactly so'.

He was illiterate. The Russians compensated for this with grand manoeuvres and repetitive training, essential for large armies of men less educated than their enemies. Discipline made him at first dull and slow in initiative. It was only after he had passed through several battles, Greene observed, that he learned through terrible experience 'the knack of looking after himself, of taking advantage of every shelter, of quickly protecting himself by entrenching'. A slow but deep-blooded ability to learn amid suffering, to overhaul an initially superior enemy, obvious under Stalin, was already characteristic.

So was courage and endurance. The Russian ability to absorb heavy casualties so impressed the Prussians that they found at Zorndorf in 1758 'the vision of a kind of battle they had never seen before. Even a shot through the body was not sufficient to bring the Russians to the ground.'[2]

Russian self-denial and cheerfulness under physical hardship were held to be 'excelled by nothing in history'. In peace, he lived off *kahsha*, a buckwheat gruel, with heavy black bread and cabbage and onions. His barracks were cold and filthy. At war, he lived off the land, without supply columns, scouring the fields for vegetables and livestock. His ability to move with indifference to logistics, a sack slung across his back with a twist of salt and scavenged potatoes, would still astonish the Germans in 1944 when, rations eked out with American-supplied Spam, he thought himself in luxury.

The cooperative life of peasant villages made it easy for him to fit into a unit. Each unit had *artels*, cooperatives which took in the soldier's assets, booty, spare pay, the possessions of the dead, and then paid out for a feast of meat or for a horse and cart for transport. This strong sense of shared possessions was one part of the communist doctrine, the brew that would be brought to them by Lenin in a sealed train from behind enemy lines in 1917, to which the troops responded naturally.

For the moment, the army was still intensely religious. The first recognizable Russian state, Kievian Rus, adopted the Greek Orthodox faith a millenium ago under the Grand Prince Vladimir. This, and the Mongol invasion, cut Russia off from Catholic Europe. It denied Russia both Renaissance and Reformation and gave the country and its army a deep feeling of religious exclusivity. On its battlefields, such as Zürich in 1799, its dying soldiers almost to a man 'clutched at the image of the patron saint he wore about his neck, and pressed it to his lips before drawing his last breath'. Religious ceremonial continued to consume an amount of time Western attachés found 'almost incredible. The best part of the day is given up to one or another of them four days a week.' Its faith served then, as the Lenin Rooms and political officers who have replaced its ikons and priests serve now, to isolate it from other armies. For the soldier's service of his deity 'had not much to do with morals, but a great deal to do with hatred of foreigners'.

His xenophobia was sharpened by isolation and invasion. A total of 245 attacks were counted on the territory of Rus, by Tartars, Swedes, Poles and Lithuanians between 1055 and 1462. Of the 550 years that had passed since 1364, Russia had been at war for 306.★

He already exhibited 'child-like' changes of temper that were to terrify later generations in Europe. Billeted in a house, he often left it wrecked and plundered 'as if in the time of the Tartar raids'. Attacking Warsaw in 1794, the banks of the Vistula were 'piled with heaps of the bodies of the dead or dying, warriors, townspeople, Jews, monks, women and lads'. French prisoners during the retreat from Moscow in 1812 were stripped naked and their necks laid on a felled tree whilst Russians 'singing in chorus and hopping round, struck out their brains'. Yet he could behave with exemplary kindness, the Swiss during the Napoleonic wars finding that he was 'most restrained and pious, and did not the slightest violence to clergy, sacred property or women'.

There were exotics in the army of so vast an empire. Cossacks, in red and purple cloaks, were the freebooting descendants of Russians who had fled from serfdom in Muscovy to the lands of the lower Don and Dnieper. Bound to military service in return for their relative independence, these horsemen had become specialists in repression, breaking strikes and sabreing Jews in pogroms. An Englishman had noted the influx of Mongols into the army, so significant today with the decline in the Russian birthrate,

---

★ After 1914, apart from Russian fighting Russian in civil war, German, Austrian, Czech, American, British, French, Japanese, Hungarian, Rumanian, Italian, Finnish, Spanish and Chinese troops fought on Russian soil. The Spanish might amount to a division, the British and Americans to small units, the Chinese to a few border squads but all join the Russian roll call of invaders.

in 1782: bowlegged men, 'their faces broad and flat, with a flat nose and little black eyes, distant from each other like the Chinese'.

But the ethnic Russian was the backbone of the army. 'Gentle, even timorous' as an individual, when massed in a battalion he had a 'herd-like cohesion which makes him redoubtable and sometimes unbeatable'.

He existed in plenty for, despite the recent exodus of Jews and Poles to America, the population of the empire had reached 155 million by 1914. The impact of manpower, however, was being offset by quick-firing artillery and the machinegun. The essence was how it was handled in battle and the omens were not good.

A meanness hung in the chasm between officers and men. Soldiers were beneath society, forbidden to enter first- and second-class compartments on trains, restricted to the lower decks on steamers, barred from theatre stalls, and not allowed to enter restaurants and cafés. Civilians addressed them in the familiar, *thou*, as they would a child or a pet. Officers called their men fool, idiot, pig or dog to their faces.

Russian officers were notorious for their addiction to idleness, alcohol and cards – 'when they have run out of money, they continue to gamble on their pledged word, making over their horses, their porcelain, their carriages'.[3] A cavalry officer would show more interest in his saddle horses than in his men. Whilst the men lived on gruel, officers sat at ritual dinners of caviar, pâté de foie gras, cheeses, filèt of beef with mushrooms, a 'gigantic sturgeon weighing over ninety pounds and about five feet in length', washed down with Château Yquem and 'a dozen varieties of native and foreign whiskies, brandies and cordials'.

There were strong elements of a show army. The magnificently plumed officers of the imperial bodyguard, whose 600-man regiments cost as much to keep as a 10,000-strong infantry division, had been called on to fight only once in the century since Napoleon's invasion. The higher echelons of the officer corps were stuffed with over-age generals, kept on the active list regardless of performance. In the infantry, two fifths of the poorly paid officers below the rank of colonel were themselves of peasant origin.

Many of the best officers were foreigners, Germans or Balts. The relationship with the Germans was so intimate that a Manteuffel commanded a Russian brigade in Prussia in 1757, whilst Hitler's General Hasso von Manteuffel commanded 7th Panzer Division in 1941 going in the opposite direction. Seven of the sixteen men who commanded armies in the 1914 fighting had German names.[4] The artillery was the 'one branch of the military art to which Russians apply themselves industriously and in which they have able native-born officers', wrote the Prussian Christoph von Manstein, whose own family would create standards of prowess in tank warfare.

The campaigns and great commanders who had beaten Western armies were a century and more in the past. Napoleon's Grande Armée had lured itself to annihilation in Russia in 1812. The finest troops in Europe retreated from Moscow as a rabble in winter, dressed in the rags of their summer uniforms and looted coats, their feet bound in cloth and parchment. No more than 30,000 of the half million men who crossed the Niemen in June 1812 returned in December. Three years later, the Russian army bivouacked in the Bois de Boulogne in Paris.

Since then, it had been beaten on its own turf by the British and the French in the Crimea. Its victories were against Turks in the drive into the Caucasus or against the descendants of the Mongol Golden Horde, Kazan Tartars, Bashkirs, Irtysh, the Kalmyks of the Astrakhan steppes. The great spring campaigns across the steppes were picturesque but had little to do with modern warfare.

In that, the Imperial army had been badly beaten by the Japanese in Manchuria barely ten years before. The ambitious Japanese, foreshadowing Pearl Harbor, attacked the Pacific fleet in Port Arthur in February 1904 and laid siege to the town. With the garrison still holding out, Nicholas ordered the Baltic fleet to steam to the Pacific in October.

Few naval enterprises have been so riddled with incompetence. The commander, Vice Admiral Zinovy Rozhdestvensky, referred to his number two as a 'sack of shit' and the equally obese commander of cruisers was known as 'the vast space'.[5] Obsessively frightened of a fresh Japanese surprise attack, they opened fire on British fishing smacks in the North Sea, thinking them to be Japanese torpedo boats. Before Christmas the Japanese took a high point above Port Arthur, which brought the thinly armoured decks of the trapped Russian ships within heavy mortar range. The Pacific fleet which Rozhdestvensky was steaming to reinforce ceased to exist as he rounded the Cape of Good Hope.

He put in to Madagascar and got news from home for the first time since leaving the Baltic. It was uniformly bad. Port Arthur had surrendered and revolt had struck St Petersburg. On the morning of 'Bloody Sunday', 22 January 1905, workers and their families had marched to the Winter Palace in St Petersburg. They petitioned the Tsar to deliver them from the 'capitalist exploiters, crooks and robbers of the Russian people'. Nicholas' Cossacks and Hussars answered by opening fire, killing ninety-two by official count and staining the snow of the Nevsky Prospekt. The revolutionaries Lenin and Trotsky prepared to return to Russia from their exile in Europe. An even more obscure revolutionary, Joseph Djugashvili, later Stalin, wrote excitedly: 'The Tsarist autocracy is losing its main prop, its reliable warriors.'

Lost to the world, Rozhdestvensky sailed on. The Russian columns appeared in the Strait of Tsushima between Japan and Korea on 27 May. Admiral Togo was waiting. Tsushima was the greatest naval battle since Trafalgar. All twelve Russian battleships were lost, eight sunk and four captured, together with seven out of twelve cruisers and six out of nine destroyers. The Japanese suffered 117 dead. Nicholas was on a tennis court when the telegram announcing the destruction of his fleet was given to him. He stuffed it in the pocket of his flannels and went on playing.

Revolution rode the coat tails of humiliation. Strikes and demonstrations broke out from Warsaw to the Urals. In the Polish city of Lodz, 300 were killed in rioting. In the Black Sea port of Odessa, police, Cossacks and the anti-Semitic gangs of the Black Hundreds fought against strikers. The city was put under martial law on 15 June. That day the battle cruiser *Potemkin*, the pride of the Black Sea fleet, put into Odessa with the Red flag flying. Her crew had mutinied and her officers had been shot, thrown overboard or locked in cells. As fighting continued ashore, the sailors turned the big guns on the city. Their range-finding was so inaccurate that they abandoned the bombardment and steamed out to sea, eventually scuttling the ship at Constanza in Rumania.

The naval mutinies spread to Kronstadt, the big base off St Petersburg. By October a general strike had spread throughout the empire with railways and factories at a standstill. Fortunately for the regime, the heaving unrest was leaderless. The revolutionary elite was abroad, unprepared, indulging in internecine émigré squabbles. Lenin read of the events in foreign newspapers.

He had been born Vladimir Ulyanov, the son of a senior civil servant, in 1870 in the pretty provincial town of Simbirsk on a bluff above the Volga. Once a model student, 'very gifted, always neat and assiduous', he was soon attracted by the ideas of Georgi Plekhanov, an exiled former terrorist who had formed the first Russian Marxist party. Plekhanov had modified Marx's gloomy view that a proletarian revolution was only possible after a long period of industrialization in which full-blown capitalism and a bourgeoisie would develop. This imposed a huge time lag on backward Russia. Plekhanov held that this could be short-circuited by workers leading their own revolution regardless of the bourgeoisie. 'In Russia,' he wrote, 'political freedom will be gained by the working class or it will not exist at all.' Plekhanov also held that individual terrorism, of the sort planned by Lenin's brother, a student who had been hanged in 1887 for plotting to assassinate the Tsar with a bomb concealed in a medical dictionary, was useless. Organization, planning, agitation were the keys.

Lenin* had journeyed to Switzerland to see Plekhanov in 1895, returning with the bottom of his trunk stuffed with revolutionary propaganda. He was arrested and exiled to Siberia for three years. He then began a long and impoverished circuit of those cities in Europe that would tolerate him, Paris, Brussels, Zürich, London, where he worked in the British Museum and saw the sights from a double-decker bus. Dogmatic, ferociously self-confident, Lenin was soon at loggerheads with Plekhanov. A party congress was called in a rat-infested flour warehouse in Brussels in 1903. There were bitter arguments over the nature of the movement. Plekhanov accepted varied views in a broad membership. Lenin insisted that the party should be a small, highly disciplined elite. Expelled by Belgian police, the delegates took ship to London to continue their arguments in a church. Lenin narrowly won the vote, claiming his group to be *Bolsheviks*, of the majority. The other splinter became known as the minority, *Mensheviks*. The names were a reversal of philosophical positions, since the Bolsheviks favoured a ruthless minority and the Mensheviks a more tolerant majority.

Lenin was still consumed with this vitriolic in-fighting as Bloody Sunday and Tsushima rolled out their afterbirth. The only exile of note to return swiftly to St Petersburg was the young Menshevik, Leon Trotsky. He was active among the *Soviets*, the councils that organized the strikes within the various factories. These councils in turn elected delegates to a coordinating St Petersburg Soviet.

The Soviets would eventually lend their name to the country. Not in 1905, for the army continued to prop up Tsardom. Revolution could not succeed without the support of the army, or at the least its disinterest. For the moment, the army generally obeyed its officers. After troops had put down the revolts, executions followed swiftly. The strikes withered. Trotsky and many members of the Soviets were arrested.

The army had won Tsardom a reprieve.

The humiliations of 1905 seemed an aberration when, in 1913, the Romanovs celebrated their tercentenary.

True, a vast and venal bureaucracy, mixing centralized clumsiness and petty tyranny to a degree 'which defies all belief and comprehension' continued to keep Russia grindingly poor. The income per head was one sixth that of the US, a quarter of Britain and a third of Germany.[6] But a vigorous class of land-owning peasants had emerged as a counterweight to revolution. Nine million peasant families owned their own land by 1913. In the southern oilfields the agitator Stalin, later to take a grisly revenge on these *kulak* peasants, felt that the tide was flowing against revolution. The harvest of 1913 was a record, not to be repeated until the

* He adopted the name later during his European exile.

1960s. Russia had become the fifth industrial producer in the world, pouring more steel than France, second only to the US in oil, rich in coal, iron ore, gold and platinum. Overall industrial production was up 74 per cent since the beginning of the century.

It was thus with confidence that Nicholas presented his Empress Alexandra with a Fabergé egg to commemorate 300 years of Romanov rule. It enclosed a globe of blue steel with two maps of the Russian Empire engraved in gold.

The map for 1613 showed Russia as a narrow and barren compression between Europe and Asia. The first Romanov, Michael, had been crowned in the Kremlin that year a few months after Moscow had been sacked by rampaging Poles. Swedes held the Baltic coast. In the east, Russian fur traders had penetrated past the Urals into Siberia in their search for the sable, but the Tartar descendants of the Golden Horde still clung to the lands east of the Caspian and the Crimea. The engraving for 1913 extended 193 kilometres west of Warsaw, south to the Black Sea and along the Persian and Chinese borders in the east until it reached Vladivostok on the Sea of Japan and the Bering Strait 65 kilometres from Alaska. Poland, the Baltic States and Finland were Romanov possessions. The last three major khanates had been defeated under Nicholas' grandfather, Alexander II. Treaties forced on weakened China had transferred the north shore of the Amur and the Maritime Province east of the Ussuri river to the Tsar.[7]

The Tsar was Emperor and Autocrat of all the Russias, a title that, like much else, echoed the Mongols who had subjugated Russia for twelve generations.* The system could flourish under a gifted autocrat, like

---

*Batu, a grandson of Genghis Khan, captured and destroyed Kiev in 1240. The Mongols or Tartars of the Golden Horde established a khanate on the Volga, keeping the river as a barrier and ruling to the west through petty princes, entering in force only to punish. The princes of Moscow, a small frontier outpost, became the major collectors of taxes and tribute for the Horde. The Tartars decayed slowly. They suffered their first defeat at Russian hands in 1380, retaking and burning Moscow two years later. They did not lose their control of European Russia until Ivan the Great a century later. To the east, the Russian conquest of the lands of the Horde was only completed under Nicholas' grandfather.

There were many military parallels between the Russians and Mongols. 'To scratch a Russian is to find a Tartar.' Napoleon claimed. Patience was an important Mongol military virtue. Unlike Napoleon himself, Charles XII of Sweden and Hitler, Batu did not try to finish off Russia in one campaign. He took four years. The Mongols were fine winter campaigners, and Batu's first attack came when the frozen ground and rivers made good going for the tough Mongol horses. His emphasis on the weight of missilry by arrow is mirrored in the Russian passion for *ognevoye prevskhodstvo*, fire superiority. The Mongols' system of spies, often sent as diplomats and traders, was unequalled. They were skilful at dividing the enemy and flattering and tricking him. The manner in which they took Moscow in 1382, first offering a truce, slipping a small

Peter the Great, who had burned his courtiers' caftans and transformed backward, half-Mongol Russia into a force with modern Guards regiments like the Preobrazhensky and Semonovsky and the most powerful artillery of the early eighteenth century. It survived under one as ruthless as Ivan IV, the Terrible, who had sat on his throne in the open air whilst the people of Novgorod were executed in front of him.

Nicholas II had neither of these qualities. He was, the demon-monk Rasputin said, a man who 'lacked insides'. The German Kaiser, Wilhelm II, found him 'only fit to live in a country house and grow turnips'. Even his virtues turned against him, for he was that most lethal companion in war, a man without luck.

The army marched off to the guns of August 1914 cocooned in the confidence of its own size, its columns spilling off the roads into the fields, and its conviction that the war would be over within two months. But the flaws ran deep.

The minister of war, General Vladimir Sukhomlinov, was described by the French ambassador Paléologue: 'With his sly look, his eyes always gleaming watchfully under the heavy folds of his eyelids, I know few men who inspire more distrust at first sight.' This 'drawing-room soldier, scented, pomaded', had spent much of his duty time exploiting his official mileage allowance by making round trips by train to Vladivostok. In this way he kept his wife, thirty-two years younger than himself, in parties and clothes. He had last fought against the Turks in 1878. Although he correctly foresaw that fortresses were becoming outdated, he thought that machineguns and rapid-firing artillery were cowardly. The Russians thus went to war with half as much field artillery as the Germans. Sukhomlinov was despised by the Commander-in-Chief, the Grand Duke Nicholas. A magnificent figure, six feet six inches high in boots which reached to his horse's belly, a cavalryman with the traditional bias against the infantry, he was at least percipient. He burst into tears when his second cousin, the Tsar, appointed him.

The government arms factories, set up under Peter the Great, were grossly inadequate. A chronic shortage of shells developed almost immediately. Reservists reporting to their depots found only enough .299-inch rifles for two men in three. Some were not issued with boots. Lack of machineguns meant that there was little mobile firepower to deploy against German attacks. Signals units had no telephone wire, and communications, never a Russian strong point, were forced on to radio. Because there was

---

force into the city and invading it whilst negotiations continued, differs little in essentials from the crushing of Budapest in 1956. The use of the Volga as a barrier is similar to the buffer the Russians instinctively seek between themselves and the West.

also a shortage of code books, many radio messages, to the delight of German intelligence, were in clear.

This might not have been serious if the steamroller had been directed solely at Austro-Hungary, as expected. But, having been drawn into a war in which they had no vital interest, the Russians had drawn two short straws. Besides the Austro-Hungarians, whom they consistently outfought, they were also to face German forces with a brilliant General Staff and a sound appreciation of modern tactics. And frequently they were obliged to face them, not at their own time and pace but in a manner dictated by the weaknesses and promptings of their distant British and French allies. Less than a month after crossing the French frontier, the Germans were forty-eight kilometres north of Paris. To lance that pressure on their allies, the Russians agreed to attack into East Prussia with two armies.

It turned into self-sacrifice through incompetence. The Russian army outnumbered the German in manpower, guns and budget even before the Germans had sent the bulk of their forces against the French. But too many of the men were cavalry, who, with their horses and fodder, needed four times as much precious rolling stock as infantry.[8] There were too few light field guns and the commands were widely split.

The 1st Army with 200,000 men under General Rennenkampf was to drive south-west parallel to the Baltic coast, drawing the bulk of the German force, whilst the 2nd under General Samsonov advanced north out of Poland. The coordination of the Russian armies went seriously astray. Samsonov made heavy weather of his advance through the wild country north of the Polish border. The formidable pair of German generals in East Prussia, Ludendorff and Hindenburg, gambled by leaving only a light cavalry screen to check Rennenkampf. The bulk of their forces was sent against Samsonov.

Early on 25 August the Germans intercepted Russian wireless messages, sent in clear and giving the exact orders of both Rennenkampf and Samsonov. This information was so priceless that the suspicious Germans kept asking 'anxiously over and over if we should believe them'. Rennenkampf's host hung over Ludendorff 'like a threatening thunder cloud' since, as Ludendorff wrote, 'he need only have closed with us and we should have been beaten'. But amid confusion, poor staff work and worse transport, the Russian forces remained apart.

The Calvary of 2nd Army lasted four days as it gradually disintegrated under German artillery barrages, trapped amid the lakes and forests with German machinegunners covering the escape routes. Only 50 officers and 2,100 men of the Russian 13th and 15th Corps extricated themselves. The Russians had lost 110,000 men when Samsonov, saying that 'the enemy has luck one day, we will have luck another', rode off into the forest and shot himself. The Germans named their victory Tannenberg, in revenge for the defeat suffered by the Teutonic Knights in the battle of the same name against the Slavs in 1410. With 2nd Army wiped away, the Germans turned on Rennenkampf, who fled back over the East Prussian border in a motor car.

The Russians had better luck against the Austro-Hungarians, Russian cavalry streaming across the Carpathians and riding out across the Danubian plain towards Budapest and Vienna. But the Russian advance stopped of its own accord. Russian generals who sensed a chance to knock the Austro-Hungarians directly out of the war were overruled. The influence of Paléologue and the French was felt again as they insisted on direct Russian pressure against the Germans. A fruitless attack was launched on German Silesia.

By the end of 1914 the Russians had lost 1.5 million men, dead, wounded, missing or captured, a quarter of the army. The casualty rate for officers was appalling, since they would make their men crawl forward whilst they themselves stood erect. The 18th Division had only 40 of its original 370 officers left. 'These people play at war,' said the British attaché General Knox.

Recruits brought the strength back to over four million men in early 1915. A further Russian offensive rolled on against the Austrians in Galicia. Przemysl, the strongest Austro-Hungarian fortress, fell in March with 120,000 prisoners. The Carpathian passes were taken in mid April and General Brusilov's 8th Army again debouched on to the Danubian plain.

The Germans chose this moment to unleash a massive blow, trying to knock the Russians out of the war with one stroke as they had tried and failed against the French a year before. On 2 May 1,500 German guns opened up on a single section of the Russian line in southern Poland, firing 70,000 shells in four hours. 'The elementary Russian trenches were completely wiped out and so, to all intents and purposes, was human life in that area,' wrote the British observer, Sir Bernard Pares. 'The Russian division stationed at this point was reduced from a normal 16,000 to five hundred.'[9] The Russians were forced back in Galicia and Poland, suffering hideously from the lack of supplies and ammunition. 'You know, Sir, we have no weapons except the soldiers' breast,' a private said to Pares. 'This is not war, Sir, it is slaughter.'

The army, the 'bulwark of Tsardom', was lacerated. 'The spring of 1915 I shall remember all my life,' wrote General Anton Denikin, later a leader in the civil war that the bloodshed of 1915 helped to precipitate. 'The retreat from Galicia was one vast tragedy for the Russian army ...'[10] Censors dealing with field mail were convinced that the references to losses were hysterical. Checking a sample regiment, the 226th Grazovetsky, they found that its strength had fallen from 2,389 to 665 in less than ten days.[11]

The Russians failed to learn from the Germans. An Allied observer found their trench systems 'poorly built and badly planned'. Rifles were in 'very poor condition' and the cavalry still had lances. Officers 'gave the impression of being lazy and hard drinkers.' The artillery batteries were 'frequently unconcealed, without pits or shelters for the men'. Artillery rarely supported infantry, even though shell production in July reached 900,000, about the same as the Germans had available in the East.

The Germans drove deep into Poland. At Opatow, Russian artillery fired on its own troops to prevent them surrendering. Men said simply: 'We throw away our rifles and give up, because things are dreadful in our army, and so are the officers.'[12] Although casualties made it rare for a front-line regiment to have more than a dozen officers after 1915, NCOs were rarely promoted. Without any of the status of the German NCOs in the opposite trenches, they would often be the first to go Bolshevik.

Warsaw fell on 5 August 1915. Grand Duke Nicholas was reduced simply to trying to keep his army in being, until in late August Tsar Nicholas replaced him as C-in-C. Sukhomlinov had already been disgraced and ousted. In the spring and summer of 1915 half the Russian army was destroyed, with 1.4 million men killed or wounded and another 976,000 taken prisoner. By September the German offensive began to lose impetus. The Russians, fighting now on Russian soil, gave ground slowly. By November, when winter closed the front, they had stabilized the front but Russian Poland and the Baltic states had fallen.

The army was not yet broken. 'Religious belief is a power in the Russian army,' wrote Knox. He told of 'officers crowding round, with serious, bearded faces, in the little dug-out' to tell of the power of prayer.[13] During the winter of 1915–16, it recovered some of its strength as ammunition stocks were built up and conscripts were trained. Russian industry showed its potential. Shell production climbed twenty-fold, guns and rifles ten times. By 1916 the army 'was not suffering from material shortages of any significance'. But distribution was chaotic, and war profiteering and inflation were rife.

As the siege of Verdun reached its climax in France in June, the Russians again attacked in the east to relieve the pressure. The offensives planned by General Brusilov were highly successful in the south-west. The Austrian commander, Archduke Josef Ferdinand, was shelled in the middle of his birthday party. Thousands of prisoners were taken in breakthroughs. Brusilov had planned that the Russians should follow this up with an attack against the Germans in Lithuania. The *Stavka*, or HQ, instead sent troops to reinforce the Austrian front.

Freed from immediate Russian threat, the Germans were able to send reinforcements to stave off Austrian collapse. The Russian offensive turned into retreat.

The cumulative Russian casualties were so grotesque that they remain incalculable. 'In the Great War ledger, the page on which the Russian losses were written has been torn out,' Hindenburg was to write. 'No one knows the figure. Five millions or eight millions? We too have no idea. All we know is that sometimes in our battles with the Russians we had to remove the mounds of enemy corpses in order to get a clear field of fire against fresh assaulting waves.'

The punishment the country suffered was made more intolerable when, with Nicholas at the *Stavka* hundreds of kilometres distant from Petrograd, its government fell into the hands of the Empress Alexandra and her Friend, Rasputin.

Gregory Rasputin was born in a village hut in a Siberian backwater in 1872. He was a drunkard and a lecher, with a reputation as a *starets*, a peasant holy man, touched by God and with powers of healing. His hair was long and greased in strands, his beard a napkin for the food he wolfed. It was his eyes that, according to Paléologue, concentrated his personality. 'They were pale blue, of exceptional brilliance, depth and attraction,' he wrote. 'His gaze was at once piercing and caressing, naive and cunning, far-off and intent. He carried with him a strong animal scent, like the smell of a goat.'

The *starets* was lionized by Petrograd society. His life became 'a continual revel', said Prince Felix Yussupov, his murderer, 'the drunken debauch of a galley slave who had come into an unexpected fortune'. The Empress was infatuated by Rasputin, who was able to ease the haemorrhaging and pain of the Tsarevich Alexis' haemophilia. Modern medicine has shown that hypnosis, his 'piercing and caressing' gaze, is able to stem internal bleeding. She would hear no word against her 'Friend', as she called him. 'They accuse Rasputin of kissing women, etc,', she stormed. 'Read the apostles; they kissed everyone as a form of greeting.' The Tsar being equally besotted, the Siberian acquired extraordinary influence at court.

Rasputin and the Empress became the effective rulers of civilian Russia. Ministers were sacked, appointments to high office made at the whim of the *starets*. 'Bring your fist down on the table,' Alexandra wrote to her husband. 'Don't yield. Be the boss. Obey your firm little wife and our Friend.'

Disaster closing and scandal rife, Prince Yussupov invited Rasputin to supper in his palace on 29 December 1916. Drink and cakes laced with potassium cyanide had no visible effect on his sturdy frame. As his co-conspirators cranked out 'Yankee Doodle' on a gramophone, Yussupov shot him. Rasputin opened his eyes, grasped the Prince's shoulder and pursued him upstairs on all fours, bellowing. Two more shots were fired into him before his body was pushed beneath the ice of the Neva. When the corpse was recovered three days later, it was found that Rasputin had died of drowning. The Empress wept beside the grave and Nicholas hurried back from the front. The rise of Rasputin had revealed the rottenness of the dynasty more vividly than Bloody Sunday. The loyal regulars of 1905 lay dead in the forests of Tannenberg, the flat Polish plain and the Carpathians.

The discovery of the body in the Neva ushered in 1917.

3

1917

Russia did not crack because the front collapsed and demoralization spread inward from it, but because the state and its capital disintegrated and took the country and the front with them.

Bread had to be rationed in Petrograd on 1 March 1917. The war had taken millions of men off the farms and overstrained the railway system. The number of locomotives in service had fallen by more than half since 1914. Heavy snowfalls and frosts in February further reduced the flow of food and fuel to the capital.

Apathy, hunger and the war seemed to have bitten out revolt. In Zürich, in cheap lodgings far from the convulsions of the fronts, Lenin admitted drearily that 'we older men may not live to see the decisive battles of the approaching revolution'. He had no plans for speeding it. The shrewd British ambassador in Petrograd, Sir George Buchanan, reckoned the city docile enough for him to take a holiday in Finland. The Tsar shared the feeling. On 8 March Nicholas left his capital for the front.

The revolution started that day, a Thursday. Russian workers were concentrated in large plants, thrown in on each other and easy to organize and whip up into revolt. Peter the Great had set the industrial style two centuries before, seeing factories in military terms. Workshops in Russia had grown as colossal civilian barracks where the workers lived in bunks in cavernous, echoing rooms. While only 17 per cent of American labour worked in factories with more than a thousand workers, half the Russian workforce did so. The Putilov engineering works in Petrograd had 10,000 workers and on 8 March women textile workers persuaded the Putilov men to strike and march with them.

The strike continued to grow on Friday and the demonstrators were applauded by richer onlookers as they marched down the Nevsky Prospekt. Towards evening the first attacks began on the police, the 'Pharaohs'. Lumps of ice and stones were hurled at them and the Cossacks looked on indifferently, a squadron riding quietly through the crowds. 'Some of them smiled,' a demonstrator said. 'And one of them gave the workers a good wink.'[1]

On Saturday 10 March almost a quarter of a million workers crossed the Neva bridges from the Vyborg slums and took to the wide streets of the centre. Students and lawyers began to join them. The Cabinet, rattled, telegrammed Nicholas at the front, pleading with him to return. He cabled General Khabalov, the military governor of Petrograd: 'I order that the disorders in the capital, intolerable during these difficult times of war with Germany and Austria, be ended tomorrow. Nicholas.'[2] Petrograd could not be put down by telegrams. The garrison was large enough, 170,000 strong, but the flower of the army was either dead or at the front. It was made up of recruits, poorly trained, very young or already middle-aged, sweepings whom the Staff did not want at the front.

Khabalov did his best. He forbade all public meetings on Sunday 11 March and warned that strikers who did not go back to work the next day would be sent to the front. He was ignored. Police opened fire on illegal meetings but people in the crowd fired back at them. The Cossacks were the next line of defence for the government, but they 'glanced at each other in some special way', an onlooker noted.[3] Police stations throughout the city were being wrecked and rifles, revolvers and ammunition were passed out among the crowds.

The troops were the last element of authority. Some did shoot to kill, mainly the regimental training squads. More than two hundred people died on the Sunday. Russia remained a Romanov fief on the morning of Monday 12 March.[4] Buchanan's daughter looked out of the windows of the British embassy and saw 'the same wide streets, the same great palaces, the same gold spires and domes rising out of the pearl-coloured morning mists . . .'[5] A crowd that gathered in the early morning outside the barracks of the Moscow Regiment was scattered by machineguns manned by officers.

The number of troops in Petrograd was tiny in comparison to the army as a whole, about two per cent. But the capital and not the trench was the fulcrum of power. An incident at 6 a.m. brought on the final convulsion, provided by a sergeant in the Volinsky Regiment, Timofeyev Kirpichnikov. As the Moscow Regiment fired on the crowd, Kirpichnikov shot dead a captain who had struck him the day before. Kirpichnikov rallied his company to the revolution. The officers fled from the barracks. The Volinsky Regiment flooded out on to the streets, marching in order with its band playing. It called on the other regiments to join them.

All morning, the once proud regiments mutinied, the Litovsky, the Ismailovsky, even those original creations of Peter the Great, the Preobrazhensky and Semonovsky Guards. The three Don Cossack regiments went over to the revolution together with the Konvoi, a Cossack imperial household regiment.

Armoured cars with red banners began appearing in the streets. Companies of soldiers stormed police stations, freeing prisoners and handing out weapons. The headquarters of the Okhrana secret police was torched. New field guns brought up in the embrasures of the Peter and Paul Fortress remained silent. At noon the fortress was surrendered to the revolutionaries, after an assurance that the officers would not be killed. Elsewhere in the city, officers tore the epaulettes off their uniforms and went into hiding.

The crack Battalion of St George, its discipline intact, was held outside the city. But the position had deteriorated beyond recall. 'The rest of the troops have gone over to the revolutionists. The whole city is in the hands of the revolutionists,' General Khabalov reported under siege in the Admiralty, west of the Winter Palace. The Battalion of St George stayed put.

Khabalov and his men marched out of the Admiralty building in the afternoon of Tuesday, 13 March. Triumphant mobs sacked the mansions of the rich. Firemen were prevented from dousing the burning buildings. In Kronstadt, sailors murdered their officers, forcing some below the ice and burying others alive. On Wednesday, Paléologue watched the regiments pay their respects to the revolution, regimental standards surrounded by Red Flags, led by 'a few officers ... wearing a large red cockade in their caps, a knot of red ribbon on their shoulders and red stripes on their sleeves'. The Marine Guard, many of whom had served aboard the imperial yacht and knew Nicholas personally, were led by their commanding officer Grand Duke Cyril. He became the first Romanov to formally break his oath of allegiance to the Tsar.

Nicholas had tried to move back from the front to rejoin his family at his country home, Tsarskoe Selo, near Petrograd. Railway workers refused to let the train pass and it was re-routed back to the military headquarters at Pskov. A straw poll was taken of military commanders. They were unanimous that they could not rely on their troops to put down the revolution and that Nicholas should abdicate. Their telegrams were brought to the imperial train and laid before the Tsar on Thursday morning, 15 March. The Tsar 'became white ... and walked to the window. Absentmindedly, he lifted the shade and peeped out.'[6] At nine that evening Nicholas abdicated. For the first time since Ivan the Terrible had taken the title 370 years before, there was no Tsar in Russia.

The revolution had been cheap, bought by little more than a thousand dead, a few hours' worth of casualties at the front. It had, however, been largely unplanned and leaderless. Power, as Trotsky put it, had fallen into the street. Having wrested it, the street, not knowing what to do with it, allowed it to be shared.

The Provisional Government, led by the Cadets, constitutional democrats, and the Soviet of workers' and soldiers' deputies were effectively two separate governments, representing different classes and sharply different policies. The Soviet wanted an eight-hour day, land hand-outs, an army with elected leaders and voluntary discipline, and a negotiated end to the war. The Provisional Government wished to continue the war and to minimize social change.

The differences quickly focused on the army. The soldiers in the Soviet forced through the famous 'Order Number One'. All units were to elect their own committees from the lower ranks to control weapons. Off-duty salutes were abolished. Units were only to obey the orders of the Provisional Government if these were sanctioned by the Soviet. At the front, the Russians began to fraternize with the Germans. They shouted from their lines: 'Germani nicht Feind. Feind hinten.' The Germans were no longer the enemy. The enemy was 'behind'.

Few were Bolsheviks at this stage, and Lenin's presence in Russia was essential to prevent the revolution drifting permanently beyond their grasp. The British and French had no intention of helping him. The Russian army might no longer be a steamroller, but it was still pinning down German and Austrian divisions. The position of the German General Staff was different. Lenin might collapse the Russian war effort. 'It was with a sense of awe,' wrote Winston Churchill, 'that they turned upon Russia the most grisly of all weapons. They transported Lenin in a sealed truck like a plague bacillus from Switzerland into Russia.' The train left Zürich on 9 April, a month after the revolution had taken place without him. It crossed Sweden and Finland, where Lenin's wife Krupskaya noted in a telling phrase that 'everything was already familiar and dear to us: the wretched third-class cars, the Russian soldiers ...' Without wretchedness and soldiers, Bolshevism was nothing.

Lenin arrived at Petrograd's Finland Station late at night on 16 April. The Soviet and the Provisional Government had sent representatives to meet him. He was given an ungainly bouquet of red roses. To the crowd, 'Lenin's voice, heard straight from the train, was a "voice from the outside". There had broken in on us in the revolution a note that was ... novel, harsh and somewhat deafening.'

He was carried off on the shoulders of the crowd and lifted on to an armoured car. The spotlights of the Peter and Paul Fortress played on him as he was driven to the Bolshevik headquarters, the palace of Kshesinskaya, a former prima ballerina. He listened to speeches by other Bolsheviks, with the weary air of 'a pedestrian sheltering in a doorway from the rain', before embarking on his own two-hour downpour. He ridiculed the Provisional Government. He scorned democracy. 'We don't need any parliamentary republic,' he said. 'We don't need any bourgeois democracy.

We don't need any government except the Soviet of Workers', Soldiers' and Peasants' deputies!'

The Provisional Government's continuation of the war was deeply unpopular. The first crisis came from a note sent to Allied governments on 1 May promising that Russia would keep fighting to the end on the basis of the Allied treaties. Once its contents were known, the April Days followed.[7] Soldiers led demonstrators who 'had but one face, the stunned ecstatic face of the early Christian monks. Implacable, pitiless, ready for murder, inquisition and death.'[8] They demanded the removal of Alexander Guchkov, the war minister, who typified the chronic instability of the Provisional Government. He had dismissed all officers he considered to be reactionary, including about seventy divisional commanders. This speeded the disintegration of the army without in any way improving his popularity.

Mob pressure worked and he was excluded from a new Provisional Government whose Cabinet now included six socialists as well as ten surviving liberals. Its problems increased when Trotsky returned to Petrograd from exile in New York. Though the note to the Allies was disavowed, the new government decided on a summer offensive. Alexander Kerensky, the socialist lawyer who had become war minister and was emerging as the head of the government, was a fine if flowery orator but no judge of war.

Kerensky gave rousing speeches to the troops at the front, urging them to fight for the revolution instead of the Tsar. Some listened, but the Bolsheviks were increasingly active. The editorial offices of *Pravda* had a soldiers' canteen where they could get spiritual and actual sustenance. Men from the Kronstadt naval base off Petrograd were active in harrying the Provisional Government. Mikhail Frunze raised Bolshevik cells among the troops of the Western front.

The offensive was a disaster. An initial advance led the emotional Kerensky to claim 'the great triumph of the revolution'. Within two weeks it had petered out. Chronic supply shortages had resurfaced. One division, the 506th Infantry, lost 2,513 men killed or wounded out of 3,000 due to a German artillery superiority of twelve to one.[9] Infantry refused to follow up the assault units. They called on troops still advancing to halt and dragged away field kitchens to stop others from moving up. Commissars of the Provisional Government reported soldiers streaming away from the front 'armed and unarmed, in good health and high spirits, certain they will not be punished'.[10]

On 16 July the German counter-offensive began and the Russian front fell to pieces amid panic and flight. Officers, divisions decomposing about them, were humiliated and attacked by mobs of soldiers. 'Under such circumstances the army constitutes a colossal danger...',[11] wrote Guchkov.

The disaster at the front, however, spurred the Bolsheviks into a premature rising. When it became impossible for the government to conceal news of the débâcle any longer, the Cadets resigned en masse. This triggered the July Days. The 1st Machine-Gun Regiment, a particular target for Bolshevik infiltration because of its firepower, decided on armed demonstrations. On 16 July, led by regiments and armed factory workers of the new Red Guards, the mobs marched on the Soviet HQ in the Tauride Palace to demand: 'All Power to the Soviets!' and 'Down with the War!'

Cars full of 'delegates, agitators, reconnoitrers, telephone men', the same cargo that the Reds would meet in the streets of Budapest forty-one years later, sped through the streets. The cockades of Tsarist officials, the shiny buttons of students and the hats of lady sympathizers, prominent in the original revolution, were missing now. In July 'only the common slaves of the capital were marching'.

The rising was not planned. It had little purpose, a demonstrator at the Tauride shrieking to the Menshevik leader Victor Chernov: 'Take the power, you son of a bitch, when they give it to you!'[12] Russia was at the stage of a revolution where the vacuum of departed power remained intimidating enough for only fools to rush to fill it. Chernov was no fool. He declined and so did the Bolshevik leadership. They could not deny the passion of the machinegunners, but neither could they channel it. Bourgeois Petrograd was frightened by the 'insane, dumb, beastlike faces' in the streets. Regiments loyal to the government were drafted into the city from the front and re-established order. On 19 July the city was quiet again.

The attempt to force an issue had failed. The Bolsheviks were discredited by their ambivalence and Kerensky had a chance to stop the drift to the left. His government announced that it had proof that Lenin and Trotsky were German agents, paid to create chaos in Petrograd and so aid the German advance.[13] Lenin fled, hiding up in a haystack with the orator Zinoviev[14] before crossing back into Finland disguised as a locomotive fireman. Soldiers loyal to the government took over the *Pravda* offices, ripping out the telephones and smashing the rotary presses. Trotsky was arrested and sent to the Kresty prison.

Kerensky formed a new government. Feeling himself strong enough to put an end to continuing revolution, he now played as surely into Bolshevik hands as they had into his. The death penalty was reintroduced into the army. It was rarely invoked and even more rarely carried out, but for the troops it smacked of a return to Tsardom. Attempts were made to restore saluting and the prestige of officers. An officer in the 10th Army Corps told a private who stepped out of the ranks: 'Shut up, don't answer back, there's been enough liberty. That's finished. Now it's back to work.'[15]

Nine hundred troopers of the 5th Army were transported to the east.

But it was, as one general remarked, impossible to lock up the entire army.

The front-line troops had not ridden in triumph through Petrograd in automobiles with red banners. They had not seen midnight scenes on the Nevsky. They lived in trenches in alder-grown marshes, in wet sheet-iron observation posts, in freezing slush behind barbed-wire entanglements.[16] Their mistrusted officers, not Lenin in his perennial exile, were the best Bolshevik propaganda. The officers told them that all their ills came from Bolsheviks. 'Who are these Bolsheviks? What party do they belong to?' the troops asked plaintively.[17] 'A short time ago we were against them as the revolutionary government asked us to be, but now we are slowly going over to the Bolsheviks' side. But send us information.' The American military attaché in Petrograd saw that final collapse was close. The army 'has been so undermined by Bolshevik propaganda that it has lost all fighting value', he told Washington. 'The regular officers in Russia are rapidly losing their morale, and if these officers are lost to the army, the latter will be beyond any possibility of regeneration . . .'[18]

It was this army that General Lavr Kornilov, the new C-in-C appointed by Kerensky, now tried to turn against Petrograd and the revolution. Kerensky weakened the Bolshevik-dominated regiments in Petrograd by transferring men to the front. He was confident. The Bolshevik leaders were safely in prison or in Finland. The meetings of the Soviets were slackly attended and the Petrograd Soviet was removed from the elegance of the Tauride Palace in the city centre further out to the Smolny Institute, a former girls' school for the daughters of the nobility. But Kerensky's choice of C-in-C was disastrous. Kornilov was a bluff man, the son of a Siberian Cossack, described by a fellow general as 'a man with the heart of a lion and the brain of a sheep'. Kornilov considered that the revolution, Kerensky included, had already gone too far. He had no intention of using the troops he was gathering to reinforce the position of the Provisional Government. He meant to overthrow it.

Kornilov assembled a force of units he considered loyal within striking distance of Petrograd. He transferred the 3rd Cavalry Corps from the South-western front, together with the Caucasians of the Savage Division, 'mountaineers who don't care who they slaughter'. He collected Cossack units, military cadets and disaffected officers. Within Petrograd itself, conservative 'patriotic societies' claimed to have 2,000 well-armed men who would rise within the city as Kornilov, surrounded by bodyguards in long bright red coats, advanced on it. Boxes of hand grenades were ordered for street fighting.

Kerensky got wind of what was afoot. On 9 September he ordered his C-in-C to hand over control of his armies and report to Petrograd. Kornilov refused, claiming that the Provisional Government 'under pressure from the Bolsheviks ... is acting in full accord with the plans of the German general staff'. He said that he preferred 'to die upon the field of honour and battle', a wish granted the following year, when he fell in the civil war proper he was now helping to unleash.

There was an instant resurgence of revolutionary fervour in Petrograd. Kerensky, relying on the city to halt his mutinous C-in-C, was in no position to dampen it. The regiments in the city prepared for action and the sailors returned from Kronstadt. Forty thousand Red Guards poured into the streets. These were the Bolsheviks' private militia, trained in factories, city squares and streets, armed with the plunder from police stations and barracks or with staves and pikes. Bizarrely, they included Chinese who had been brought to Russia for railway-building.

Kornilov never reached the capital. Railway workers blocked tracks, diverted trains and paralysed his divisions. Telegraph messages were sent astray. It was as though, Trotsky wrote, Kornilov was 'playing at blind man's buff on the railway lines'.[19] Supplies went to the wrong stations, units were separated from their artillery and all the time agitators worked on the men. 'Almost everywhere we saw one and the same picture,' admitted General Krasnov, a future civil war leader. 'On the lines or in the cars, or in the saddles of their black or bay horses, dragoons would be sitting or standing, and in the midst of them was some lively personality in a soldier's long coat.'[20] The propaganda, that this was a revolt of generals in which the men had no part, was effective. Even the murderous mountaineers of the Savage Division heard out the agitators in full, hoisted a red banner, arrested their officers and came out against Kornilov.

The commander of the 3rd Cavalry Corps, General Krymov, was arrested by his men and shot himself. Kornilov was imprisoned in a monastery. Kerensky's failure to have him shot as a traitor to the revolution was bitterly resented by the troops. The Bolshevization of the army accelerated. The Germans continued to advance.

Although Kerensky continued to govern, indeed declared himself C-in-C as well as Prime Minister, his authority was all but shattered. He was forced to release the Bolsheviks from prison. Within a few days Trotsky was elected president of the Petrograd Soviet. He had 'no treasury, no newspapers, no secretarial apparatus ... no pen and no pencil'. But the Bolsheviks had the Red Guards, the support of the Petrograd regiments and in Lenin, though he was still in Finland, they had a catalyst. In a 'Letter from Afar' on 28 September Lenin urged: 'We should at once begin to plan the practical details of a second revolution.'

Red October followed.

4

TROTSKY: THE PROPHET ARMED

The October Rising was the achievement, Trotsky said, of 'hardly more than 25,000 or 30,000 at most', far from the mass movement that had swept away the Tsar. Peasants and soldiers wanted land and peace, not a pubescent Bolshevism they ill understood. Kerensky was vowing to return to Petrograd at the head of loyal Cossacks and White generals were moving south to rally anti-revolutionary units.

Many of the troops who had taken part in the coup were 'infected with the drinking madness' as they looted the well-stocked cellars of the Winter Palace. 'The Preobrazhensky Regiment, which had hitherto maintained discipline, got completely drunk while it was doing guard duty at the Palace,' wrote Antonov-Ovseenko.[1] 'The Pavolovsky Regiment, our revolutionary rampart, did not withstand the temptation either.... Men of the armoured brigades ... paraded to and fro a bit, and then began to sway suspiciously on their feet.'

The Petrograd garrison was in danger of disintegration by the time the commissars ordered the contents of the cellars to be pumped into the Neva. The Bolsheviks had invested much of their energy in destroying the army. They now needed to create a disciplined force of their own, a task Trotsky took for himself.

An army is, through its constraints, early to shed its revolutionary skin. It marches on its stomach, feeding on orderly logistical support. It devours weapons and machines and must plan and cooperate with industry to get them. Discipline and regimentation are imposed on it by the complex manoeuvres it must perform to survive in war. It faces external enemies and it must adapt its professional skills to match theirs. A brief loiter in central Moscow confirms that the modern Red army is a conventional force, no matter what horrors it has gone through, bourgeois in its distinctions of rank and its spruce respectability. The Tsarist past is clear in the shoulder boards of rank, the black staff cars with generals' stars above the mudguards, the saluting conscripts in their long greatcoats, the backdrop of the Kremlin.

The Red army had only a brief encounter with revolution in its fever sense, when rank and direct orders were abolished and soldiers elected command committees amid the sweaty haranguing of the barracks. Trotsky is personally remarkable for the depth and lucidity of his revolutionary passion. He is professionally remarkable for his speed in junking such thought from the Red forces.

Tsarist officers and specialists, the *voenspets*, organized and protected by

Trotsky, formed the cutting edge of the Red army throughout the civil war. It would have been lost had Trotsky not relied on these despised relics of the old regime, who link the Tsarist tradition with the coming generation of Stalinist generals. No Trotsky Prospekt, no Order of Trotsky commemorates his name. He remains a non-person in modern Russia.

It is not his real name. He was born Leon Bronstein, the son of a rarity, a landowning Jew with a small estate in the southern Ukraine, in 1879. He was schooled in Odessa, with its light seascapes of the Black Sea, intelligent, confident and precocious – 'for several months I was in love with a coloratura soprano'. He entered Odessa university in 1897, his passions the theatre and pure maths. The following year politics joined them. He was arrested in 1898 for founding an illegal union.[2]

He was never tried and was seldom interrogated, as though the Tsarist authorities thought that boredom and discomfort would get the rebellion out of him. In 1899 he was sentenced to be deported to Siberia for four years. Waiting for deportation in a Moscow prison, he married Alexandra Sokolovskaya, a Marxist several years his senior. The Bronsteins were sent to Ust-Kust, an old gold-diggers' village of squalid wooden huts in eastern Siberia. He later worked as a book-keeper to a rich merchant further east, made an error in his accounting and was returned to Ust-Kust by sledge in midwinter with a wife and ten-month-old daughter. His revolutionary shell was hardening and, at least under the Tsars, a determined man could broaden his mind. He read hungrily, a gluttonous diet that included the future Fascist heroes Nietzsche and D'Annunzio as well as the socialists' Zola. 'The spiritual estate of man is so enormous and so inexhaustible in its diversity,' he wrote, that one should 'stand on the shoulders of great predecessors.' It was a principle he applied to the imperial past when he created the Red army.

He escaped, for no Gulag wire surrounded him. Bronstein hid under the hayload of a peasant cart and boarded the Trans-Siberian express at Irkutsk. He had a false internal passport and he wrote the name of one of his Odessa gaolers in it. Bronstein became Trotsky. He relaxed on the westbound train by reading Homer's hexameters.[3] In the autumn of 1902 the Siberian fugitive arrived at 10 Holford Square near King's Cross Station in London. Here Lenin lived in a one-room-and-kitchen apartment with his wife. His relations with Trotsky were volatile. As a Menshevik, Trotsky attacked Lenin after the split with the Bolsheviks as 'hideous ... dissolute ... malicious and morally repulsive'.

He moved on to Paris, a city that more suited his vivacity and style. He met his second wife, Natalia Sedova, a radical Russian student at the Sorbonne. He became interested in military affairs, deeply influenced by a series of articles on 'War and Revolution' published in the revolutionary paper *Iskra* by a Russian émigré, Helfand. Helfand held Russia to be a military-bureaucratic regime whose purpose was to withstand pressure from the more civilized and advanced West. Reluctant tsars since Peter the Great had been forced to introduce some parts of European civilization into Russia. They had done this notably in the army and for defensive reasons. 'Thus the Russian state organism came into existence,' Helfand wrote. 'An Asian absolutism buttressed by a European type of army.' It takes little to extend that past Helfand to Gorbachev.

Trotsky returned to Russia after Bloody Sunday in 1905, fleeing from the secret police to Finland disguised as a landowner, back in St Petersburg for the series of strikes in mid October. He spoke to a group of Guards officers at a political soirée in the house of a baroness – 'the butler waited for my visiting card but, woe is me, what visiting card should a man with a cover name produce?' That Guards officers should listen to Trotsky showed the rot in the regime. It showed, too, that Trotsky, witty, literary in the cascade of his speeches, a revolutionary who could pass as a landowner, had no fear or instinctive hatred of officers.

Whatever amusement their officers got from flirting with Trotsky, the infantrymen stayed loyal and Trotsky was back in prison in December 1905, lying on his cot reading French novels, with 'the same physical delight with which the gourmet sips choice wine or inhales the fragrant smoke of a fine cigar'.

He realized the absolute importance of the army. 'The unarmed heroism of the crowd,' he wrote, 'could not face the armed idiocy of the barracks.' If the revolution did not cooperate with it, there would be no revolution. He saw the barricade not as an object to be taken or defended, but as the interface between the people and the soldier. The barricade was vital because 'by hampering the movement of the troops it brings them into close contact with the people. Here on the barricade, for the first time in his life, the soldier hears honest, courageous words, a fraternal appeal ... In the atmosphere of revolutionary enthusiasm, the bands of the old military discipline snap.' He grasped with clarity the phenomenon that had done for Louis XVI as it would do for the Romanovs and, later, the Pahlevis of Iran.

He was bound for Siberia again, this time sentenced for life. His destination was the penal colony at Obdorsk, on the Arctic Circle in empty *taiga* a thousand miles from the nearest railhead. He did not escape from the train, despite the false passport and money hidden in the sole of his boot. In those genteel days it was not done for prisoners to flee en route. It would have got the escort into trouble.

An evening spent watching an amateur production of a Chekhov play in the colony gave him his chance. The guard was lax. February is a blizzard month in the taiga and his escape route took him across roadless wilderness to a goldmining settlement in the Urals with a single-track railway. A local Zyrian guided his reindeer-drawn sledge, so drunk that Trotsky had to kick him to keep him awake. The odd couple, the drunken native and the liquid-eyed revolutionary, scribbling notes on the tracks of animals as he passed, ermine, wolf, fox, and on the social habits of the few raw-fish-eating inhabitants, sped for a week over a landscape 'which nobody had measured except for the archangel Michael'. They reached the railway at Bogoslovsk, where Trotsky explained variously that he was a polar explorer or a merchant.

A train returned him westward to St Petersburg. From there, his restless itinerary took him to Finland, London, Berlin and, later in 1907, to Vienna. Trotsky remained in Vienna until 1914, doubtless unaware of the close proximity of Adolf Hitler but conscious of the petty jealousies and futilities of émigré society. After the First World War broke out, he became a war correspondent for the underground journal *Slovo* (*Our Word*), run by a former Tsarist officer, Antonov-Ovseenko. Trotsky was deported from France after the French had reacted to Russian pressure and banned the paper in September 1916. Arriving in Spain, he was shipped out to the US from Barcelona with a boatload of rich deserters from the Western front and other undesirables.

The ship docked in New York on a wet Sunday in January 1917. Trotsky, with wife and two children, took an $18 a month apartment on 164th Street in the Bronx. For the first time in his life, he had a telephone. He worked on the Russian émigré daily *Novy Mir* (*New World*). He was in the US for two months, regretting that he had 'only a glimpse into the foundry in which the fate of men is to be forged', aware of growing American might. 'It is a fact that the economic life of Europe is being shattered to its very foundations, while American wealth is growing,' he told a meeting. 'As I look enviously at New York – I who have not ceased to be a European – I wonder anxiously: "Will Europe be able to stand all this? Will it not decay and become little better than a graveyard? And will not the world's economic and cultural centres of gravity shift to America?"'

He was in New York, dreaming that America would ultimately make as great a contribution to Marxism as it had to capitalism (not a hope that persists in Moscow) when news of the Petrograd rising came through in March. Trotsky sailed from New York for Europe on 27 March. The ship called at Halifax, Nova Scotia, and British naval police put him in a camp for captured German U-boat crews. He at once got to work to convert them to socialism, doing well enough for the German officers to ask the camp commandant to ban him from giving talks. 'The English colonel,' Trotsky noted sarcastically, 'immediately sided with Hohenzollern imperialism.' Released to the cheers of the U-boat men, he sailed to Finland. He arrived in St Petersburg by train on 17 May (4 May old calendar), ten weeks after the start of the revolution.

He was back in the Kresty prison after the failure of the July Days. Had Kornilov reached the city, Trotsky would probably have been shot. As it was, he was released on bail on 17 September, free to take up his crucial leadership of the Military Revolutionary Committee. He later claimed that 'compromisers of all shades' had tried to fob off Bolshevism 'as a soldier movement'. He said that 'the fundamental political force of the October revolution was the proletariat'. Trotsky admitted that 'longing for land and peace was the colossal programme which the peasant and soldier intended to carry out', but added 'under the leadership of the workers'. This is nonsense. Neither the soldiers nor the peasants showed any desire to be led by the workers. In any event, it was not the workers who led but the Party, the Bolsheviks, who, as Trotsky said, 'saw it as their mission to stand at the head of the people'. The act of revolution was more a *coup d'état* in which a ruthless party of intellectuals – Trotsky himself, apart from his brief spell as a Siberian book-keeper, had never had a conventional job, let alone been a 'toiler' – took advantage of the exhaustion of the army to seize a power it has never relinquished. As to the offers of land and peace, the land would be forcibly taken into state *kholkozes* and some ten million would be killed in the interval between the civil and the next German war.

He was franker at the time. During October, he held the army to be the key and said that 'the last task of the revolution', namely winning, was 'purely military in character'. What was to follow was equally military, Trotsky's part in it equally essential.

Kerensky was easily enough dealt with. His Cossacks proving disloyal, he was turned away outside Petrograd and fled Russia for good, disguised as a seaman. The murder by rebellious troops of General Dukhonin, his last C-in-C, turned many officers and NCOs decisively against the Bolsheviks. They drifted south to the valleys of the Don country and the Kuban, to rally to the counter-revolutionary White cause.

The Germans remained. Peace negotiations started in the burned-out town of Brest-Litovsk, the delegations put up in huts inside the compound of the old Russian frontier fortress. Trotsky, passing through the Russian trenches on his way, was astounded to see that they were almost unmanned. Nevertheless, he refused to sign a peace treaty accepting German demands whilst simultaneously confirming that the Russians would demobilize. '*Unerhört*', protested the Germans. To cede a war whilst not accepting a peace was 'unheard of'.

German troops were ordered to advance to persuade the Bolsheviks to sign. Resistance was as ghostly as the army. 'This is the most comic war I have ever experienced,' wrote a German officer. 'It is waged almost exclusively in trains and cars. One puts on the train a handful of infantry with machineguns and one artillery piece and one rushes to the next station. One seizes the station, arrests the Bolsheviks . . . and travels further.' On 19 February 1918 the Bolsheviks formally sued for peace. Russia was to cede Latvia and Estonia and to evacuate the Ukraine and Finland.

The infant communist state, born prematurely to an underdeveloped country, was ringed by hostility. The Germans, in a first run of 1941, occupied the Ukraine, the Crimea and the coasts of the Black and Azov seas. Cut off from the Ukrainian wheatlands, hunger soon struck Moscow and the northern cities. The Japanese attacked Siberia and took Vladivostok. British, French and American troops landed, for their countries had yet to reach the climax of their war against the Germans, and their Russian ex-allies had vast quantities of aid supplies that could fall to the Germans.

The Bolsheviks needed terror and armed force to survive. The Cheka secret police were formed under the Pole Felix Dzerzhinsky, whose statue today graces the square outside the Moscow headquarters of his KGB descendants. Lenin signed a decree establishing the Red army on 28 January 1918, with Trotsky becoming commissar of war in March. The twin props of the regime were in place. Trotsky's formidable task was to 'arm the revolution', living at first in one room, 'partitioned off like a poor artist's attic studio' with a desk and a couple of cheap wooden chairs, on the top floor of the Smolny. The new army had to be built from scratch. A single division, of Latvian riflemen, passed intact into the Red army from the eerie remnants of the imperial steamroller.

The shortage of commanders was acute. Only a few former officers volunteered to join the Reds. Trotsky conscripted them on a huge scale. The Red army was to employ 41,000 bourgeois officers and *voenspets*, more than it was able to create itself from workers and peasants, and 250,000 former Tsarist NCOs. 'Some came over to our side out of fear, some came for the novelty; others came because they had no alternative – they had to earn a living,' wrote Nikita Khrushchev, then a humble Red rifleman. 'And some came out of treachery.'[4] Stalin and others regarded them as untrustworthy class enemies, and they were finally accepted only on the basis that the Party would 'squeeze them like lemons and then throw them away'. Stalin was never convinced, remaining, as Khrushchev put it, 'a specialist eater all his life'. Treason was checked by dual controls. Lists were drawn up of their families and relations, to be held hostage against their good behaviour. The system of political commissars, first used by Kerensky, was broadened. Every professional officer from the C-in-C to company commander was accompanied by a commissar. No order was valid unless it was signed by both. The commissar had the right to execute his commander if the latter showed signs of treason. Officers had no insignia and no official rank but disciplinary powers and the death penalty were reintroduced. The brief, heady days when soldiers' committees had run their units and elected their officers had gone.

By the summer of 1918 only the inner core of European Russia, roughly the area of the medieval Grand Duchy of Moscow, was under firm Bolshevik control. The Germans had moved through the Baltic states and landed a contingent in Finland to help the nationalist Gustav Mannerheim, a former Tsarist general, in his defeat of the Finnish Communists. German and Austrian troops remained in the Ukraine. The Cossacks of the Don under General Krasnov were linking with White Volunteers in the northern Caucasus. In the Kuban, south of Rostov, Kornilov had been killed by a shell in April. The Reds, finding his body, had hung it from a tree and kicked it round the streets before burning it in the slaughterhouse of Ekaterinodar, modern Krasnodar. His volunteers survived under General Anton Denikin, virtuous and orderly but lacking like all White generals a fervour of ideas to sustain his men through the incestuous ferocity of civil war.

Groups of Whites set up provisional governments in Siberia, where a corps of anti-Communist Czech legionnaires was on the loose. The Czechs were ex-POWs and deserters taken on the Austrian front and released and equipped to fight for Czech independence. Trotsky had agreed that they could travel to France to resume fighting the Germans, by way of the Trans-Siberian railway and the Pacific. The Germans objected to this and the Bolsheviks blocked their passage and tried to disarm them. The Czechs seized part of the railway in May and linked with Admiral Kolchak's White Guards. The Western Allies aided the Whites, hoping to re-create the Russian front against the Germans. British, French, American and Japanese troops landed on the Russian periphery, near Archangel in the north, around Vladivostok in the east, on the Black Sea and in the Caucasus to the south.

A small force could advance through huge swathes of the toppled empire, transport ruined, towns starving and packs of deserters roaming the countryside. The Bolshevik writ expanded and contracted like a gypsy accordion and the horse and the armoured train were king. The Czechs made a formidable striking force amongst the incoherent Russian units. Former colonels served as platoon commanders and *Yunker* cadets as infantrymen in White all-officer battalions and factory workers mixed uneasily with conscripted peasants in Red units. Only the five-pointed Red stars or the epaulettes of White officers distinguished revolutionary from reactionary. Joined by White officers and troops, the Czechs steamed west along the Trans-Siberian.

Their success was fatal to Nicholas and the imperial family. The Bolsheviks had taken them in April for safekeeping to Ekaterinburg, 1,450 kilometres east of Moscow on the far slope of the Urals. The Czechs captured Omsk at the beginning of June and moved rapidly on Tyumen. That was 320 kilometres east of Ekaterinburg, but on their good days the Czechs would steam 160 kilometres. By mid July the Czechs had outflanked the town. The Bolsheviks had hoped to give Nicholas a show trial, but, with liberation imminent, his execution was urgently brought forward. Towards midnight on 16 July the family were awoken in the merchant's house where Cheka men were guarding them. They were told that they were to be moved away from the approaching Czechs and Whites, and led into the basement to wait for motor cars. The Chekists opened fire on them with revolvers, finishing their task with bayonets and rifle butts. The bodies of Nicholas, his Empress Alexandra, their four daughters Olga, Tatiana, Maria and Anastasia and the fourteen-year-old Tsarevich Alexis were taken by lorry to an abandoned mineshaft. The Chekists dismembered them, fed them into a fire of petrol, and dissolved the residue in sulphuric acid before raking the ashes into the mine. Ekaterinburg fell eight days later. White officers who came to the merchant's house found that, though the blood had been carefully scrubbed from the basement, the walls were pocked from the impact of bullets.

Thus, after 305 years, without trial and with its children, the Romanov dynasty departed Russia. Ekaterinburg was renamed Sverdlovsk, to commemorate Jacob Sverdlov, the intimate of Lenin who handled the Moscow end of the decision to murder the family.

On 6 August the retreating Reds fled Kazan, the last important town on the east bank of the Volga. As added bounty, the Whites and Czechs captured the gold and platinum reserves of the imperial government, which were stored there. Open plain lay between the Whites and Moscow.

Trotsky steamed off to do battle in his armoured train, which mounted machineguns and light guns, a printing press, radio for direct contact with Moscow, a sleeping car, horse boxes, ammunition wagons and a flat-bed for his Rolls-Royce command car. A nucleus of handpicked officers was carried on it, to organize new units or to replace poor commanders on the spot. 'In the train of the People's Commissar for War,' Trotsky wrote, 'a military revolutionary tribunal is in session ... which has unlimited powers within the zone of this railway line. A State of Siege is proclaimed ... The Republic is in danger!' His train pulled in to Svyazhsk, a small town on the western bank of the Volga opposite Kazan. The Reds were streaming away from the river, dishevelled, rifles and uniforms filthy, eyeing their commanders with a view to murder. Trotsky rallied them, intense in leather coat and pince-nez, his shock of black hair trembling with the violence of his gestures. 'I issue this warning,' he cried. 'If any detachment retreats without orders, the first to be shot will be the commissar, the next the commander.' The joint leaders of a regiment that pulled out of the line were court martialled and shot. He could encourage too, sending for a brass band and a popular poet to perk up morale, carrying large amounts of tobacco on his train to hand out to the troops.

The scattered Red forces in the Volga valley were rounded up into five 'armies', though these numbered only a few thousand ill-equipped men each. Command of 1st Army was given to Mikhail Tukhachevsky, a young aristocrat who had distinguished himself as a tsarist lieutenant with escape attempts from German POW camps. He counter-attacked on 12 August. Trotsky was so short of troops that his escort was forced to join the fighting, leaving him near deserted on his train. Sailors from Kronstadt were important stiffening, for the navy had escaped the war without the traumas suffered by the army, and its revolutionary fervour was high. Over the next month the Whites and Czechs were forced out of the Volga valley and withdrew into the western foothills of the Urals. The Reds stormed Kazan on 10 September and two days later Tukhachevsky took Simbirsk.

The victory on the Volga eased the pressure on Moscow, where an attempt on Lenin's life had unleashed a Red Terror.* There was an ubiquity to the terror, for amid the regulations of War Communism and the social collapse, 'everyone had some reason to feel that he was guilty of everything, that he was an imposter, an undetected criminal . . . People slandered and accused themselves, not only out of terror but of their own free will, from a morbidly destructive impulse . . . carried away by that passion for self-condemnation which cannot be checked once it has been given free rein.'[5]

In 'dumb, dark, hungry Moscow', people were dependent on the black market to live. Men and women of the old regime offered artificial flowers, black net evening dresses and uniforms of offices that had been abolished for sale. Simpler people traded in more useful things, 'spiky crusts of stale rationed black bread, damp, dirty chunks of sugar and ounce packets of coarse tobacco . . .'

---

* The decree proclaiming the terror, on 5 September 1918, stated that 'all persons involved in White Guard organizations, plots and insurrections are to be shot'. No proof was needed to condemn a man. 'We are not waging war against individuals,' the Chekist commander on the Eastern front told his men. 'We are exterminating the bourgeoisie as a class. Do not look for evidence that the accused acted in deed or thought against Soviet power. The first questions that you ought to put are: To what class does he belong? What is his origin? What is his education or profession?' It was on such a basis that a Cheka detachment led by a future prime minister of the Soviet Union, N. A. Bulganin, had already shot fifty-seven people, most of them ex-officers, in Yaroslavl.

Trotsky's stock was sent soaring by Kazan, to the open disgust of the Reds in Tsaritsyn, downstream on the Volga. The local commander, Voroshilov, and his commissar Stalin had driven off a White attack and effectively controlled the Southern front. They resented interference from the new capital, Moscow, and mistrusted Trotsky's use of the *voenspets*. Trotsky recalled Stalin to Moscow and appointed a former general to command the front. These humiliations were not forgiven. In time, Trotsky and his favourites paid with their lives and Tsaritsyn was renamed Stalingrad.

The Germans and Austrians pulled out of Russia and the Ukraine after the armistice in November 1918, selling their rifles to the Reds for a mark each and their field guns for 150,[6] but Allied support for the Whites continued.

A lull set in over winter. 'Glaciers, mammoths, wastes' infected Petrograd. 'Black nocturnal cliffs, somehow resembling houses; in the cliffs, caves ... Cave men, wrapped in hides, blankets, wraps, retreated from cave to cave.' Typhus added to the horrors of starvation, for millions of acres of grain had been left to rot during the autumn. The rye turned 'so ominously rusty brown, the colour of old, dimmed gold ... fields silently proclaiming their distress' amid a plague of mice. Industry collapsed under enforced nationalization and regulations that were 'ever more lifeless, meaningless and unfulfillable as time went by'. Survival depended on the black market and its *meshochniki*, its bagmen.

The issue was decided in 1919. The Whites launched three major offensives which, untimed and uncoordinated, compressed Red resistance. The Whites in southern Russia, the Volunteer Army and the Armies of the Don and the Caucasus, were loosely grouped under General Denikin. Admiral Kolchak, the former commander of the Black Sea fleet, ruled in Siberia. Kolchak was also recognized by a White force assembling under General Yudenich in Estonia and by the British-backed troops of General Miller, a Baltic Russian, in Archangel. They operated externally, driving into the Red heartland from the east, south and west without mutual communications or support, each advance bringing with it a nightmare of logistics and desertion as it left its base area behind it.

The Reds operated in internal space, able to switch troops between fronts. They became inured to long retreats, a lesson invaluable in 1941, their strength growing as lines of communication became shorter. Discipline was whipped in by Trotsky, by idealism and by the risk of being shot if they lost. Some troops were given the choice of changing sides when they were captured, but often both Red and White prisoners were killed out of hand. The writer Mikhail Sholokhov, who witnessed the

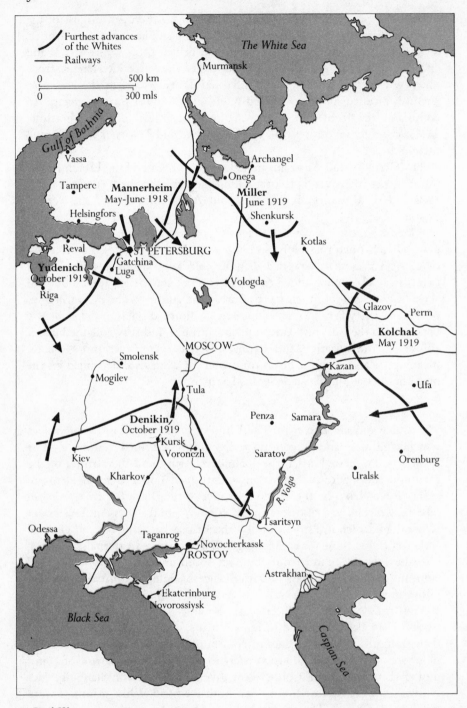

Furthest advances
of the Whites
Railways

0   500 km
0   300 mls

The White Sea

Murmansk

Gulf of Bothnia

Vassa

Archangel

Tampere

Onega

Mannerheim
May-June 1918

Miller
June 1919

Helsingfors

Shenkursk

Reval

Kotlas

Yudenich
October 1919

ST PETERSBURG
Gatchina
Luga

Vologda

Glazov

Perm

Riga

Kolchak
May 1919

MOSCOW

Kazan

Smolensk

Ufa

Mogilev

Tula

Denikin
October 1919

Penza

Samara

Kiev

Kursk
Voronezh

Saratov

Orenburg

Kharkov

Uralsk

R. Volga

Odessa

Taganrog

Tsaritsyn

Novocherkassk
ROSTOV

Astrakhan

Ekaterinburg
Novorossiysk

Black Sea

Caspian Sea

Civil War

civil war in the Don country, described how an escort of Red Cossacks murdered its officer prisoners. After a cry of 'Cut them down ... Damn them! All of them! We take no prisoners!' an officer fell on his knees while 'flying blades played over his face'. Another was shot through the back, 'running with his coat flapping in the wind', then 'squatted down and grabbled with his fingers at his breast until he died...'[7] At Kharkov, the Reds nailed the epaulettes of captured officers into their shoulders. In a massacre by the Whites, Sholokhov related how 'fresh groups of barefoot and unclothed Red Guards were brought up ... volleys spurted out, and single shots drily shook the air as the half-dead were finished off. Hurriedly earth was shovelled over the first group of bodies in the trench...'

Admiral Kolchak's Whites advanced out of Siberia early in 1919, cracking the Red 3rd Army, whose exhausted soldiers lay in the snow and begged their commissars to shoot them: 'We have not enough strength to stand up, we are worn out, finish with us, Comrades.' Ufa in the western Urals fell as the Reds scattered back towards the Volga. Denikin's forces in the northern Caucasus broke the Red 9th Army, whose *voenspets* commander was executed for treachery. The collapse of 9th Army ripped a wide breach in the Southern front, the Whites of the Volunteer and Don armies advancing on the Donets basin. In April and May the army of newly independent Poland moved into western Russia, taking Vilna and pushing the Reds back on Minsk. Yudenich advanced from Estonia and took Pskov on the road to Petrograd. Far to the north, Miller moved down slowly from Archangel with his British allies.

Trotsky thought the most acute threat to be Kolchak in the east. He toured the battlefields, returning to Moscow briefly at the beginning of March for the founding congress of the Communist International. Trotsky was convinced that the ancient divisions of Europe would be swept away by a continental federation of Soviet republics. His appearance, in full uniform straight off his train, was dramatic but the Comintern was a sideshow. A rising in Berlin had recently been crushed, its leaders Rosa Luxemburg and Karl Liebknecht murdered, and attempts at revolution in Bavaria and Hungary failed through apathy and White terror.

The Bolshevik hold in Russia was a different matter, sturdier than it seemed. The Whites had advanced up to 400 kilometres on a 1,100-kilometre front and were overextended against Red armies under Frunze and Tukhachevsky. Frunze broke through in late April and the Reds were back in Ufa at the beginning of June, helped by the mutiny of a Ukrainian regiment which murdered its officers. Tukhachevsky outflanked the Whites to seize the passes through the Urals. The Reds consolidated their positions with trenches dug by forced labour gangs. Trainloads of these labourers were sent off to the front, 'rich, smart lawyers and stockbrokers from Petrograd side by side with cabbies, floor polishers, bath attendants,

Tartar rag and bone merchants, escaped lunatics, shopkeepers and monks, all lumped together with the exploiting classes'.[8]

Kolchak no longer had any hope of advancing on Moscow and retreated into Siberia, pursued by Tukhachevsky. At Ufa, almost 100,000 tons of Allied wheat fell into Red hands as Kolchak's ragged soldiers began to starve. Though huge quantities of Allied supplies were landed in Vladivostok, corruption on the railways had so firm a hold that whole trains were diverted and their supplies sold off.[9]

'Twenty or thirty thousand resolute, comprehending, well-armed Europeans could, without any serious difficulty or loss, have made their way very swiftly along any of the great railroads which converged on Moscow,' Winston Churchill claimed. But Kolchak commanded a force that was disintegrating through typhus, hunger and its own lack of will. What uniforms the Whites had were British-supplied, Kolchak himself wearing one with a Russian admiral's epaulettes. A British officer noted sadly: 'The uniforms walked over to the Reds, thousands at a time, with the Whites inside them.'[10]

Trotsky was free to turn to the Southern front, where the Whites were streaming through the Ukraine. Kharkov fell to White cavalry in June. A Red counter-offensive failed and Moscow was again threatened. The Whites sliced behind the Red lines, where Red Guards and deserters roamed, selling their rifles to *kulaks*. Trotsky complained that neither oratory nor terror 'can make battleworthy a barefoot, naked, hungry, lice-ridden army'. He himself should have been killed at a meeting in Tsaritsyn, which was successfully bombed by a British pilot flying a de Havilland bomber. The commissar was not in the town that day.[11] Wrangel broke into the future Stalingrad on 30 June, supported by British-supplied tanks and armoured cars. A victory *Te Deum* was held in the cathedral, which the Reds had used as a food dump. In the villages, the peasants greeted the Whites with gifts of salt, singing 'Christ is risen'. On 13 October, Denikin took Orel, less than 300 kilometres from Moscow. British pilots, eagerly volunteering for the White air force, strafed Red artillery and broke up cavalry units.

Yudenich, armed by the British and with Royal Navy support, was closing on the outskirts of Petrograd. Though the British were not formally at war with the Soviet government, a British torpedo boat, commanded by a Royal Navy lieutenant who was acting under the direct orders of the British officer commanding in the Baltic, sank the Red cruiser *Oleg*. Two forts guarding the western approaches to Petrograd went over to the Whites. Stalin, the senior Bolshevik in the city, had sixty-seven officers of the Kronstadt garrison executed as an example. British torpedo boats attacked the Red fleet in Kronstadt under cover of an RAF bombing raid, sinking two battleships and a destroyer for the loss of six officers and nine ratings killed. On land, the Whites pressed on the city. Trotsky was haunted 'by the image of half-naked soldiers trembling in the frost and of the wounded dying en masse' but still confident that a last effort would break the Whites.

At a meeting of the Politburo on 15 October Lenin proposed abandoning Petrograd to concentrate the remaining Red strength round Moscow. The possibility of a Bolshevik withdrawal from Moscow to the Urals was also discussed. Trotsky argued vigorously that Petrograd, cradle of the revolution, could not be given up to the Whites. He set off to Petrograd by train the following day, with Stalin replacing him on the Southern front. 'In the pale sunlight of the early winter morning, down a long avenue strewn with yellow trees', the Whites entered the huge Imperial Palace at Gatchina, 36 kilometres south-west of the city. They found the 'air soaked not merely with the melancholy scent of autumn but with crowding tragic memories'. Half-starved dogs tore at the carcass of a horse and a dead soldier lay face up in the street.

The appearance of Yudenich's British-built tanks on the outskirts of the city on 20 October panicked the defenders. The Whites could see 'the whole panorama of the city ... even trains pulling out of the Nikolai Station, the white plumes of their steam trailing across the brown landscape as they hurried towards Moscow'. Trotsky rallied the defenders from horseback. 'This beautiful Red Petrograd remains what it has been,' he said. 'The torch of revolution.' Troops and Red Guards fought with what Yudenich called 'heroic madness'. After three days he was back in Gatchina. The second anniversary of the revolution coincided with Trotsky's fortieth birthday. He celebrated it by returning to Moscow to announce victory.

The Whites were collapsing in the south. A newly formed Red cavalry brigade under Semyon Budenny, a former cavalryman in the Imperial army and a survivor of the Japanese war, defeated the White cavalry outside Voronezh, retaking the city on 24 October. The Reds streamed past Orel. Kursk was taken in early November as Denikin fell back towards the Black Sea. The defeats were as much moral as military. 'The inner sores festered in an atmosphere of hatred,' Denikin said of the pogroms that had haunted regions under White control. 'They affected the spirit of the troops, warped their minds and destroyed discipline.' He realized that 'our liberation of enormous areas should have brought about a rising of all elements hostile to Soviet power'. It did not, a lesson that was to escape the Nazis. Another White general, Wrangel, said that, although Allied munitions and Cossack bread still reached his men, their 'moral bases had already been destroyed'. A British correspondent noted that none of the 15,000 nurses' uniforms sent to Denikin ever reached a nurse, but 'I have seen girls, who were emphatically not nurses, walking the streets of Novorossisk wearing regulation British hospital skirts and stockings.'

Prostitutes rated higher than the sick. There was grotesque speculation in estates as men gambled on the return of the landlord. In the night clubs, the Soviet propagandist Ilya Ehrenburg wrote, drinking bouts often ended with White officers 'shooting at fellow customers, at mirrors, or in the air: the officers saw partisans, underground workers and Bolsheviks every- where. The more they shouted about their strong nerves, the more it was clear that their nerves were giving way; and the goal was vanishing behind a fog of alcohol, hatred, fear and blood.' Pillage and violence turned the peasants against the Whites as the front collapsed. The returning White commander May-Maevsky and his officers seemed more concerned to protect their trainload of women and booty than their men. The cavalry force pursuing them, dragging machineguns on light carts, was to benefit later from Stalin's presence on the Southern front. Three of its members would become Soviet marshals, Budenny himself, Timoshenko and the young Georgy Zhukov.

The British had already given Kolchak up as a lost cause. At a banquet in the Guildhall in London on 8 November David Lloyd George said that anti-Bolshevism in Russia faced at best a 'prolonged and sanguinary struggle' in which the British should play no further part. His judgement was soon justified. On 14 November, to the east, Kolchak abandoned Omsk. He, his mistress and the imperial gold reserve moved east on the *magistral*, the rail line, a slow progress since it was choked with trains filled with Czech booty. Firefights broke out between Czechs and Whites over the pumps where water had to be unfrozen over fires before it could be transferred into the locomotives. On the *trakt*, the trail beside the line, refugees and soldiers toiled as typhus and the bitter cold thinned out their ranks. The advancing Reds captured the rearmost trains. Three days after the loss of Omsk, on the Southern front Denikin was forced out of Kursk. Kharkov followed within a month, the troops who fled it riddled with typhus, leaving armoured trains and artillery behind them. By the end of the year, with Kiev also gone, the Whites were streaming back on Odessa.

On 15 January 1920 the Reds caught up with Kolchak at Irkutsk, on an inlet of Lake Baikal. When his train drew into the station, the admiral saw that there were Red Guards on the platforms as well as the Czechs who were supposedly safeguarding him. The Czechs were theoretically under the command of the French C-in-C of Allied troops in Siberia, General Janin, but neither he nor the Japanese soldiers who were in the town played any part in what happened. The Czechs wished only to get out of Russia. For their safe conduct to move east, they handed the Reds Kolchak, his mistress and staff officers and what remained of the gold reserve. After nightfall, the little party of exhausted Whites was taken from the train and marched across the frozen Angara river to Irkutsk prison. The following day, as the Czech trains began to steam on for Vladivostok, the Allies lifted their trade blockade of Soviet Russia.

Like his Tsar before him, Kolchak was denied a show trial for fear that counter-attacking Whites would free him. In the pre-dawn gloom of 7 February Kolchak was taken from prison and shot by the headlights of a lorry on the banks of the Angara. His body was pushed into a hole in the ice. There was no White counter-attack. Twelve days later, far to the north-west, the White front at Archangel collapsed and General Miller escaped the city on an icebreaker. The Whites in Murmansk struggled over the border into Finland.

In the south, Odessa fell on 7 February, the Allied evacuation ships steaming out of the port with Whites clinging to their gangplanks. Denikin's forces in the Kuban fell back on Novorossisk, hoping to be evacuated by sea to the Crimea. They struggled through the mountain defiles above the port in a human tide 'infected with fear and panic . . . Cossacks, nomad families with their black tents, Caucasian tribesmen . . . Their route was marked by bodies, stripped naked and frozen; dead horses, mules and camels; abandoned guns, field-kitchens and vehicles.'[12] As they waited for Royal Navy ships, Cossacks shot their horses on the dockside and refugees tore at them for food. Red artillery was shelling the port as men trying to board overcrowded destroyers were clubbed off with rifle butts. White officers abandoned on the quays shot themselves as the ships sailed for the Crimea with 50,000 aboard, many of them women and children. The Reds took 22,000 prisoners when they seized the town on 27 March.

Denikin was landed in the Crimea but the Royal Navy soon carried him on to Britain. The remnants of his army fought on from the Crimea under Wrangel, tall in his high Cossack hat, aristocratic, the 'Black Baron' to Bolshevik propaganda. At the end of April 1920 the Whites were given a lease of life when the newly independent Poles attacked the Bolsheviks. They advanced into the Ukraine rapidly, taking Kiev on 7 May. Trotsky was forced to divert the bulk of the Red army to the west.

The Poles lost ground as rapidly as they had gained it, evacuating Kiev on 10 June. Wrangel took advantage of the Soviet involvement with the Poles to move into the country of the lower Don, a threat which merited Trotsky's personal attention to check it.

Red armies numbering three quarters of a million men pushed forward against the Poles. Pilsudski, the Polish leader, thought of Tukhachevsky's advance as 'something irresistible, a monstrous and heavy cloud which no obstacle could halt . . . Men trembled and the hearts of our soldiers began to yield.' To the part-Tartar, part-Italian Tukhachevsky, all of Europe was on the verge of revolution and 'a rapid and victorious offensive would hypnotize the peoples and draw them eastward'. He closed on Warsaw as

Budenny's cavalry streamed on Lvov. Foreign diplomats left the city with the Red army less than twenty-five kilometres away on 14 August. The following day Pilsudski counter-attacked. To his own astonishment, the Poles quickly outflanked the Russians and created panic and confusion in the rear. With Tukhachevsky himself 480 kilometres away in Minsk, Russian cohesion disintegrated and three Red armies broke up in shock, units caught up in a miasma of desertion and chaos as they fled east, whilst the ragged Poles advanced for tens of kilometres without firing a shot. By the time the Red armies of the west reached Brest-Litovsk, they had lost 150,000 men.

Ironically, this Bolshevik catastrophe was the end of the Whites. The Poles realized the dangers of becoming as overextended and exhausted in advance as Tukhachevsky had been. Driving the Reds back to Minsk during September, Pilsudski negotiated an armistice on 12 October. The eastern frontier of Poland was fixed along the Minsk line the following year and remained so until the Soviets had their revenge in 1939.

The full weight of the Red army was now used against Wrangel. The first troops transferred from the west arrived at the end of October, the Whites shivering with cold on the steppes, their shirts stuffed with straw and moss. They were forced back to the Crimea and their defence lines on the narrow isthmus at Perekop. The assault began on the third anniversary of Red October. Blücher's Reds crossed the frozen marshes east of the isthmus after a frontal assault by shock troops under Frunze had been bloodily repulsed. Although White machineguns firing on fixed lines took a terrible toll, the Reds broke through into the Crimea after four days. French warships and the White navy stood offshore at Sevastapol to evacuate Wrangel's forces as the White air force flew its last sorties against the advancing Reds.

On the afternoon of 4 November Wrangel climbed aboard a motor boat from the Sevastapol quayside for a waiting warship. Trotsky had won the civil war. Waiting in ambush for him were two of his own, Stalin and his spearheads of revolution, the sailors of Kronstadt.

5

KRONSTADT:
ASSAULT ON THE CITADEL

Kronstadt is the walled and fortified city on the eastern tip of the island of Kotlin in the Gulf of Finland, lying 32 kilometres west of Leningrad.

To the south of the city lie the docks and workshops of the Baltic fleet. The island shores are protected by forts and artillery batteries.

The island remains a major base for the Baltic fleet, with its forty-seven major fighting ships and thirty-four submarines. It saw in 1921 an act of repression that marked the final subjugation to the Party of the Red military and of the industrial and rural poor in whose interests the island mutinied. After Kronstadt, the concept of the 'Soldiers', Workers' and Peasants'' state was ruined. If Soviet rule is in essence the elevation of force into a moral system, Kronstadt is the beginning.

At Kronstadt Red sailors, the 'shock force of the revolution', rebelled because 'life under the yoke of the communist dictatorship has become more terrible than death'. In the countryside, 'food detachments' of the Red army seized grain and the horses and carts to transport it to the cities and to their barracks. The peasants reacted by revolt and by sowing less, so that food output by 1921 had fallen to less than half the 1913 level. Disbanded Red army men, armed with axes, bludgeons and pistols, roamed for food and plunder, setting up camps by railway lines 'amid old tree stumps overgrown with wild strawberries'.

The situation was worse in the towns. Industrial production in 1920 was a fifth of pre-war levels, despite the drafting of troops into Trotsky's 'labour armies'. Transport was chaotic, bridges destroyed in the fighting, locomotives spoiled through being run on wood instead of rare coal. Skilled workers in Leningrad metals plants were thought pampered on a ration of 800 grammes of black bread a day. Other workers were on 200 grammes, a starvation diet. Inflation and the black market destroyed the money economy.

Cities were depopulated as people left for the countryside in search of food. Abandoned houses were dismembered for logs. Trains were crammed with families moving out to forage for food. It was said that all Russia was waiting for trains. When a train stopped, the noise of the crowds outside 'rose to the pitch of a storm at sea' as people rolled down the banks 'like marbles' and jumped on the buffers or clambered in through the windows. Between the October revolution and the high summer of 1920, the population of Moscow halved and in Leningrad it dropped from 2.5 million to 750,000, down by two thirds.

Severe weather in the early months of 1921 disrupted freight trains of food and the government announced a cut of one third in the bread ration. In Leningrad, factories closed for lack of fuel. Checkpoints to stop 'speculators' bringing in food increased tension. Tsarlike, Zinoviev, the party boss in the city, used military cadets to break up food demonstrations. These *kursanty* were called in to patrol the streets since large numbers of regular troops were considered unreliable and were disarmed and confined to their barracks.

On 26 February 1921 the crews of the dreadnoughts *Petropavlovsk* and *Sevastopol* sent a delegation to Petrograd to report. The sailors were shocked by conditions: 'One might have thought that these were not factories but the forced labour prisons of Tsarist times.'

Two days later, a packed squadron meeting was held on the *Petropavlovsk*, a name now as blank in Soviet memory as the *Potemkin* is cherished. The men demanded freedom of speech and the press, free trade unions, the liberation of political prisoners. A further mass meeting was called for 1 March in Anchor Square.

The sailors had a history of revolt and mutiny. They had been crucial during the revolution when Anchor Square, a huge open space in the centre of the city by the Seaman's Cathedral, was known as the 'Free University'. In the July Days, they had sailed to Petrograd and earned the title 'pride and glory of the revolution' from Trotsky. They had defended the city against General Kornilov in August. It was, ironically, the crew of the *Petropavlovsk* who, the purest of the pure, had murdered four of their officers who protested at their call for the execution of Kornilov.

They developed, however, a *Partizanshchina*, an ill-disciplined, free-booting spirit, that ran counter to Trotsky's restoration of order and obedience. They were against the *voenspets* and resisted the replacement of ship's committees by commissars. With the civil war won, discipline irked the more. Their own grim conditions, barracks unheated, warships idle and icebound, and the riots and misery in 'Red Peter', as they affectionately called Petrograd, combined in a fresh rush of 'navy fever'.

Kalinin, the president of the Soviet Republic, was shouted down by a crowd of sailors and artillerymen in Anchor Square at the mass meeting on 1 March. By midnight the following day, the rebels had taken full control of the city and the docks. A new provisional revolutionary committee was set up on the *Petropavlovsk*, led by Stephan Petrichenko, a seaman. The committee included a telegrapher, a senior clerk and a navigator.

The Bolsheviks reacted to the grave crisis, this internal Prague with its heretical demands for free elections and secret ballots, with the utmost speed. The chance of contagion, of ideas coming across the ice to the mainland, was high. A deprived and half-subdued population had reason to join and turn against the Party. The revolt was labelled a White plot, directed from Paris and abetted by officers in Kronstadt. There was little evidence of this, but proof was not needed at a time when scepticism had been debilitated by a decade of false claim and real disaster on all sides.[1]

A three-man delegation from the 1st Naval Air Squadron at Oranienbaum on the mainland crossed the ice to Kronstadt to make contact with the mutineers and the Squadron elected its own provisional revolutionary committee. In the early hours of 3 March a trainload of reliable communist military cadets was sent to Oranienbaum. The barracks were surrounded, taken and forty-five men were led out and shot. The first precedent of a post-civil war liquidation of Red military men was set.

The mutineers in Kronstadt contained themselves within the thick city walls and the twin fortresses of Peter and Paul, confident that their armory would protect them from the brooding landmass across the ice. Trotsky was far absent, attending to the suppression of peasants in western Siberia. The city had 135 cannon and 68 machineguns. The two main battleships had a dozen 12-inch guns and 16 120-mm guns apiece. Three heavy cruisers and fifteen gunboats were also in port. Attacking infantry would have to advance across eight kilometres of ice against artillery and automatic weapons in positions that had been built to withstand a long siege more than a century in advance.

The ice was the key, an open line to transmit the demand for freedoms outward, or for repression to move inward. Attempts to use it outward were desultory, a few volunteer propagandists who were quickly arrested when they reached the mainland shore. Artillery *voenspets* had advised Petrichenko to shell it to create a moat that would keep off any invading force. Nothing was done. The ice remained thick and firm to the shore. The warships stayed icelocked.

Militarily inactive, the rebels sealed their fate with their ideas. They created a free trade union and scrapped the political officers. They had their own radio station and started a daily paper, the *Kronstadt Izvestia*. It poured contempt on the 'nightmare rule of communist dictatorship' and the 'commissarocracy'. 'Lenin said that "Communism is Soviet power and electrification,"' ran an article. 'But the people are convinced that the Bolshevik form of communism is commissarocracy plus firing squads.' There were few plans, more a vague sense that things would turn out well.

The sailors had a backbone of anarchists. A violent and dreamlike haze of anarchism had run through the civil war.[2] 'Black Guards' of anarchists roamed to a marching song of the 'new Age of dynamite' that would kill off all oppressors, Red and White. In Kharkov, the NABAT, the 'Alarm Confederation', called for 'Death to world civilization'. Peter Kropotkin, the grand old man of Russian anarchism, died of pneumonia and old age (an achievement in such a bellicose movement) in Moscow the month before the Kronstadt rising. Thousands had marched, black flags in the cold air, to the burial place of the Kropotkin princes at the Novodevichi monastery.[3]

The forces that were building on the mainland, in contrast, were wholly uncomplicated and purposeful. Trotsky trained into Petrograd on 5 March and signed a leaflet that was airdropped over the island. He warned the sailors, who had once devotedly 'followed him to the Tauride Palace, to his prison cell at Kresty, to the walls of Kazan on the Volga, always taking his advice, always almost blindly following his orders'[4] that, if they failed to capitulate within twenty-four hours, they would 'be shot like partridges'. The families of Kronstadt men in Petrograd were rounded up as hostages. The 7th Army and the troops in Petrograd were put under the command of Tukhachevsky, with military cadets, communist fighting units and Cheka forces as stiffening.

When his ultimatum expired, Trotsky attacked. Mainland batteries opened fire on Kronstadt after dark on the evening of 6 March, bringing counter-fire from the 12-inch guns of the *Sevastopol*. Early the next morning Tukhachevsky ordered the military cadets, their uniforms covered in white linen sheets to blend with the ice and snow, to assault across the Gulf of Finland. They were followed by Red army units. Cheka machinegunners brought up the rear to discourage deserters. 'Distant rumbling reaches my ears as I cross the Nevsky Prospekt,' wrote the anarchist Alexander Berkman.[5] 'It sounds again, stronger and nearer, as if rolling toward me.'

The assault failed. Men froze to death in the water where the ice cracked under shellfire. Some threw away their weapons and scrambled to the Kronstadt shore to join the rebels. Despite the Chekists, only a few neared the outer forts of Kronstadt. The rest withdrew, sliding some 2,000 wounded with them and leaving 500 dead on the ice.

Morale on Kronstadt was low, the mutineers short of ammunition and food, flour exhausted, each man rationed to a can of condensed milk each and a few cans of meat. But Tukhachevsky had to achieve a victory before the ice broke into floes and then slushed back into sea. Once ice-free, the Gulf of Finland would prevent any assault from the mainland whilst loosing the battleships and cruisers for an attack on Petrograd.

Tukhachevsky gathered a force of 50,000, alarmed by deteriorating discipline in a rifle division and by the discovery of an anti-Bolshevik conspiracy among the cadets in the Peterhof Command School. He drew on Chekists and units from the Ukraine and the Polish front stiffened with Tartars, Bakshirs and Letts who had little sentiment for the predominantly Russian rebels. An accurate artillery barrage started after noon on 16 March and continued throughout the day, despite a smokescreen laid by the *Petropavlovsk*. Both battleships were hit. Aircraft were sent on bombing runs over the city.

The second assault began in a pincer movement to north and south before dawn on 17 March, helped by a freezing fog that dissipated and confused the Kronstadt searchlights. The attackers half froze in the dark, melt water soaking through their white coveralls. During the morning the fog lifted into a brilliant March day. Shells again pierced the ice to increase the toll of the drowned. 'Days of anguish and cannonading,' wrote Berkman. 'My heart is numb with despair. Something has died within me. The people on the streets look bowed with grief, bewildered. No-one trusts himself to speak. The thunder of heavy guns rends the air.'

The northern group took heavy casualties attacking the outlying forts. There were only eighteen survivors in one communist battalion. It took until 1 a.m. on 18 March, twenty-two hours from their start-lines on the mainland, before these troops finally took the forts. The southern group, attacking over the ice from Oranienbaum, broke into the city before daylight on 17 March. Fighting in the dense Kronstadt streets was intense, with more than half one brigade killed or wounded. The defenders were inhibited by the families in their midst and demoralized by the flight of their leaders across the ice to Finland. The battleship crews refused to blow up their ships as Tukhachevsky's men fought their way closer, claiming victory over these 'counterrevolutionary nests' shortly before midnight. Sporadic fighting in the city lasted until the afternoon of 18 March.

The attackers paid a high price for a direct assault on a defensive showpiece, though in terms of preserving Soviet rule it was cheap enough. So many corpses lay on the ice that the Finnish government, fearing epidemics if they washed ashore during the icemelt, officially asked that they be removed. Out of 50,000, Tukhachevsky's force is thought to have lost 20,000 killed and wounded. A mass funeral was held in Petrograd on 24 March. The rebels suffered 600 killed and 1,000 wounded. About 2,500 were taken prisoner and 8,000 escaped to Finland. Amongst the dead were fifteen delegates to the 10th Party Congress, then meeting in Petrograd, who had volunteered to join the Tukhachevsky force.

It was ironic that the congress had, before the final assault began, already begun to dismantle the War Communism that had inflamed the revolt. Trotsky's labour armies were given notice to disband, along with the roadblocks against food speculation, and private commerce was re-established in the New Economic Policy.

The memory of the sailors was obliterated root and branch. The *Petropavlovsk* was renamed the *Marat* and the *Sevastopol* became the *Paris Commune*. Difficult to know whether these names represent an infection of the mind, a humour of ebony blackness or a confidence as cold as the iceflows by those who chose them. Marat, the French Jacobin, the man easing the putrefying skin of his prurigo in his bath when Charlotte Corday murdered him in 1793 – why select him if not to crow of one's own expertise in terror? And the Paris Commune, that symbol of a brave city rising suppressed by the troops and artillery of reaction, a veritable Kronstadt – what can that be if not the joke of an executioner? As to Anchor Square, it became and remains the Square of the Revolution.

The sailor prisoners did not taint the public. Thirteen alleged ringleaders were tried, in camera, and executed. Several hundred are thought to have been summarily shot on the island. The remainder were ferried to Cheka prisons on the mainland. Some were shot in batches, others were dispatched to the prison camps of the Gulag, the *Glavnoye Upravleniye Lagerei*, the Chief Directorate of Camps. Most went to the Solovetsky camps on the islands of the White Sea. Petrichenko was returned by the Finns in 1945 and perished in a camp.

The anarchists were also done for, their poet Lev Cherny executed without trial by the Cheka in September. Berkman wrote in his diary on 30 September: 'The shadow of today hangs like a black pall over the country. Dictatorship is trampling the masses under foot. The revolution is dead. Its spirit cries out in the wilderness . . .'

The assault troops were sent to remote postings. Within a month Tukhachevsky was fighting peasants in the black-earth Tambov province.

Kronstadt was Trotsky's affair. Stalin was distant from it, a fact that would later aid the death or disappearance of virtually every principal involved in it, party congress delegates, Tukhachevsky, Zinoviev, Trotsky. But nightmares do not signal themselves in advance, and neither Trotsky nor his Red army anticipated their Stalinist futures.

6

THE STEEL MONSTER

Whatever limbo he is cast into now, in his plain granite grave, no figure in Russian history compares with Stalin. He outdid Ivan the Terrible in terror, deporting, imprisoning and killing his subjects on an unmatched scale. He excelled Peter the Great in the grandeur of his political and economic achievement, for where Peter honed the existing principles of imperial absolutism, under Stalin a new state and a new economic system were defined. As many thousands of Russians still bear his face, tattooed in admiration on their arms and chests during the long years of his power, he continues to ink the Soviet Union.

Stalin was born Joseph Vissarionovich Djugashvili, in a hut, to a former serf. He was the first of four children to survive infancy, in a hick town in a deep-south province, Gori, on the banks of the tumbling Kura river in Georgia. His cobbler father died when he was eleven, a heavy drinker and probably killed in a brawl. His home was a *domik* by the main cathedral in Gori, with two brick-floored rooms, the main room 4.5 metres square with a single window, a table, stools, a samovar, a plank bed with a straw mattress and a rough trunk for their few possessions. It was rented for 1.5 roubles a month. His secret police chief Beria would later erect a marble pavilion over it.

His mother, devout and devoted, took in washing to send young 'Soso' to a church school in Gori. She was anxious for her son to get on. When he had, though she moved into an old palace with a park in Tblisi, she retained her modesty and morality, her room small and dark with windows giving on to the courtyard. 'The room was full of old women wearing black, as old women do in Georgia, and a little old lady was half-seated on the narrow iron cot,' Stalin's daughter Svetlana recalled.[1] She spoke Georgian, and Stalin, though he learned Russian at school, never lost his accent. He brought a particular intensity to his adopted nationality, becoming what Lenin called an 'assimilated Great Russian chauvinist'.

Georgia was backward, indolent, considered oriental, dominated by a lethargic and impoverished gentry that clung to a system of 'temporary serfdom' until 1912. Feuds and long-hatching retribution were deep in the Georgian soul. The land was un-Russian, lush and easily farmed, with vineyards and orchards. Georgians match this with over-ripeness of character, an eye for intricate corruption and the fast rouble. Lunch now at the National Hotel off Red Square in Moscow, and Georgian black marketeers are there to celebrate the sale of a crop of fruit, swarthy men in Cuban boots and shiny black shirts, with bloodshot and sometimes black eyes, eating salted salmon and dilled cucumber and drinking Georgian champagne and vodka chasers through the dull northern afternoons. It is his mother Yekaterina who, according to Svetlana, set Stalin apart from the Georgian norm. 'She passed on all her stubbornness and firmness, her puritanical standards, her unbending, masculine character and her high requirements for herself,' wrote Svetlana. 'He was much more like her than like his father.'

School and then the theological seminary at Tiflis, the Georgian capital, added to the maternal discipline and capacity for work. He was a hardy small boy who survived smallpox and blood poisoning that gave him a minor withering of his left arm. He was frequently punished at the seminary for reading books that had not been sanctioned by the monks. The school principal ordered: 'Confine him to the punishment cell for a prolonged period. I have already warned him once about an unsanctioned book, *Ninety-three* by Victor Hugo.'

The seminary prepared young Georgians for the priesthood, and Djugashvili for austerity and prison. It gave him no sympathy with those who later read books he had proscribed, for he knew how dangerous subversives like himself could be. The routine was inflexible, each day starting with an Orthodox service at seven. At five each evening, the gates were locked. 'Shut up within barrack walls we felt like prisoners, innocent of any crime, who were forced to spend a long time in jail,' wrote a fellow pupil. His interest in long and intricate work was at odds with Tiflis, its Russian squares and oriental bazaars awash with Turks, Armenians and Persians. The seminary suited him for, like Bolshevism, it was 'half monastery and half barracks'.[2]

Quick and self-confident, he was soon involved in politics. Revolution had worked its way to the south. He was expelled in 1899, on paper because he had failed to sit exams, more probably on suspicion of political disloyalty. After a stint as a clerk at Tiflis Observatory, a job as brief as Trotsky's Siberian book-keeping, he went underground as a socialist militant in 1901. The police were moving in on him. He used almost twenty aliases over the next fifteen years. He did not emerge from clandestinity until a few weeks before he was named a member of the first Soviet cabinet in 1917.

'Illegals' like Djugashvili were the in-country core of the revolution. At their high points, when the population was restless and the police demoralized or off guard, they agitated in run-down halls and on the streets. The millennium would loom until a good harvest and an upturn in industry, common in the early 1900s with the French-backed growth of Russian railways and, in Djugashvili's area, the expansion of the oil industry, put food on tables and roubles in pockets. They then rode out the apathy of the 'masses', preserving a nucleus at secret meetings, publishing papers and pamphlets on crude presses, hand-setting the type in ill-lit cellars and waiting for informers to come calling with the police. It was the same drabness faced a few decades later and a few miles south by the Moslem fundamentalists working the slums of imperial Iran, and again in the name of an émigré prophet comfortably installed in the West.

Djugashvili's landscape was the lodging house and the railway station. He required constant subterfuge and movement, the ability to blend into greyness and never to dazzle, to keep suspicion well oiled and close. Tsardom was squeamish when it came to intellectuals, rebels with a background identifiable within Russia and abroad, men who could play on its developing sense of shame. It had sentenced Lenin's brother with embarrassment and had allowed his mother to attend the execution. For fifteen formative years, Djugashvili was a tiny irritation that a provincial governor and his hangman could deal with at will.

Djugashvili, under the name Koba,[3] helped organize the first May Day, *Mayevka*, organized outside Tiflis in 1900. He set up a battered flat-bed press for pamphlets in the Moslem quarter of Baku, short of type and ink, dangerously noisy to operate.

He moved on to Batum, a hot, grimy half-Turkish city on the Black Sea where Rothschild and Nobel had oil refineries, and set up another printing press. The Okhrana secret police noted: 'As a result of Djugashvili's activities ... organizations began to spring up in all the factories of Batum.' In February 1902 a mob of workers marched on the head-quarters of the military governor during a strike at the Rothschild refinery. Fifteen were killed when police opened fire. Police searched for the inflammatory printing press and Djugashvili concealed it in a house in the tangled streets of a Moslem village on the outskirts. Oil workers dressed as women in the *chadra* veil collected leaflets from it.

The police caught up with him for the first time in April 1902, in a house in Batum. The Okhrana had not only surrounded the house but had informers within it. Stalin, calmly smoking, was led away. A police file described him: 'Height: 5 ft 4 ins. Body: medium. Age: 23. Second and third toes of the left foot fused. Appearance: ordinary. Hair: dark brown. Beard and moustache: brown. Nose: straight and long. Forehead: straight and low. Face: long, swarthy and pockmarked.' The police nicknamed him *Ryaboi*, the pockmarked.

He was imprisoned for eighteen months in 1902. Whilst the Bolsheviks and Mensheviks were having their emotional and historic split in Brussels in 1903, Djugashvili-Koba was in a Caucasian gaol. On his release he was deported to the Irkutsk province of eastern Siberia. Like Trotsky and Lenin, he escaped without much difficulty, in a peasant cart in midwinter. A southerner unused to the cold, he suffered frostbite to his face and ears before making his way back to Tiflis in February 1904. He was told of the Brussels meeting and opted for Bolshevism.

He met Lenin at the Bolshevik national conference in Tammerfors in Finland. It was his first contact with the high echelons of the Party. Several of the delegates introduced to the rough Georgian ex-cleric – Lozovsky, Borodin – he would later put to death. He met Trotsky for the first time in May 1907 at the party congress held at a church in Whitechapel in London's East End. On his return to Baku, he described the polished man he later had murdered by ice-pick as 'beautifully useless'.

Lenin needed funds and the restless, turbulent Caucasus was the easiest place to raise them. 'Fighting squads' were formed, a quixotic mix of idealists, crooks, adventurers and assassins, who attacked banks and armoured cash transports and murdered Tsarist officials. A bank raid in the main square of Tiflis in June 1907 netted a quarter of a million roubles. Much of it was in high-denomination notes which Bolsheviks, including the future foreign affairs commissar Litvinov, were arrested for trying to change into more manageable notes in Western Europe. Three armed escorts taking cash to the State Bank in Erivan Square were killed by bombs and fifty bystanders were hurt.

Djugashvili was the link-man between the Caucasian party and the fighting squads, moving between Tiflis and Baku, planning and approving terror raids and hold-ups, developing his skills in logistics and concealment.

His time in the oilfields of Baku, on the hot shores of the Caspian, was productive. He lived in the Moslem quarter of the shambling city, printing crude and effective strike calls. He kept up unrest among the oil workers at a time when revolution had again dimmed in most of Russia. 'Two years of revolutionary work among the oil workers of Baku hardened me as a practical figure and as one of the practical leaders,' he wrote later with characteristic contempt for mere theorists. 'I first learnt what it meant to lead big masses of workers.' Lenin was impressed by the Baku men, 'Our last Mohicans of the political mass strike'.

Betrayed again to the Okhrana in 1908, Djugashvili was gaoled in Bailov prison. It had been designed for 400 but held 1,500 prisoners, among them police informers and provocateurs who were murdered if they were discovered. It was harsh for a Tsarist prison, though gentle enough by the later standards of Stalinism. Deported to Vologda province, he escaped and was back in Baku by July 1910. Under another false name, Zakhar Gregorian Melikyants, he was picked up and banished again after ten months. By mid 1911 he had served out his banishment. He was re-arrested by the Okhrana after the murder that year of the Tsarist Premier Peter Stolypin, part of the long cat-and-mouse game the Tsarist secret police played with him.

This time his imprisonment was brief. In 1912 Lenin, who admired his persistence and administrative competence, placed him on the Central Committee. Djugashvili became co-editor of the Russian newspaper *Pravda*, its name poached from Trotsky's foreign published version. Lenin asked him to write a paper on the Russian nationalities, a problem the Georgian knew well. Signing it, the man known variously as Djugashvili-Koba-Ivanoivh-Nisharadze-Melikyants-Chizhikov first used the name 'Stalin', the 'man of steel'. He was thirty-three.

Researching his work on minorities further, Stalin went to Vienna in 1913. He again met Trotsky, who later wrote of the 'glint of animosity' in Stalin's 'yellow eyes'. Stalin himself described Trotsky that year as 'a common noisy champion with faked muscles'. The most savage feud in Russian history was under way.

Stalin was taken within a week of returning to St Petersburg from Vienna, arrested at a Bolshevik musical matinee to raise funds for *Pravda*. He was exiled for four years to northern Siberia. When the war broke out, he was in a settlement of wooden huts on the Yenissey river that flows into the Kara Sea on the fringes of the Arctic Ocean. The native Ostyaks lived in reindeer tents during the brief summer and in the long winter withdrew into pits dug into the soil with timber and skin roofs. His spirit left him. Escape was foolhardy, since martial law had been declared with the war. Other Bolsheviks travelled scores of miles by reindeer or dog sled to a settlement for a debate. Stalin ignored them. He wrote a rare non-political letter to his future wife Alliluyeva. He asked for picture postcards: 'I have been overcome by a silly longing to see some landscape, if only on paper.'

The slaughter on the distant fronts in the west was so great that, at the end of 1916, the government was forced to scrape up the political deportees from Siberia. Stalin was ordered to Krasnoyarsk, on the headwaters of the Yenissey. Because of the childhood stiffening of his left arm, the future warlord and Generalissimo was declared unfit for military service. After Nicholas abdicated, he was freed.

Stalin arrived in St Petersburg on 12 March 1917. With the main leadership still abroad, Lenin in Switzerland, Trotsky trying to cross the Atlantic from New York, he was the *de facto* head of the Party until Lenin's return on 3 April. He remained on hand for Lenin, faithful and uncomplaining, through the summer of swirling fortunes. During the July Days, with many baying for his master's blood as a German spy, he led Lenin to the safety of the Maritime Station and flight to Finland.

On 10 October, with Lenin returned and insisting on an armed and immediate coup, Stalin voted in his favour at the Central Committee meeting. After the vote, a Political Bureau was elected 'for the purpose of political guidance during the immediate future'. This, the foundation of the Politburo, was done at the proposal of Felix Dzerzhinsky, soon the head of the Bolshevik secret police and the spiritual father of the KGB. Stalin was one of its seven original members.[4]

Cautious, he played little part in the coup, hovering in Bolshevik newspaper offices. He showed a deepening streak of spite, ridiculing the ancestors of Russian revolution, Plekhanov and Kropotkin, as 'remarkable only because they are old'. Trotsky was contemptuous. 'The greater the sweep of events the smaller was Stalin's place in it,' he claimed.

Small or not, Stalin wove himself into the new power. He was appointed commissar for nationalities in the first Soviet government. Working with Lenin, he drew up a 'Declaration of the Rights of the Peoples of Russia' which gave them 'the right to free self-determination, even to the point of separating and forming independent states'. In fact, with the Germans occupying most of the borderlands, and Turks and Germans in his native Caucasus, Stalin had little effective control of the key nationalities. The secession of the Ukraine led promptly to the reversal of the ideal.

As the civil war developed, Stalin was sent to Tsaritsyn as political commissar. He responded to the attempt on Lenin's life with a whiff of terror. 'Answer this base attack from ambush with the organization of open and systematic mass terror against the bourgeoisie and its agents,' ran an order under his signature and that of Kliment Voroshilov, the commander of the Tsaritsyn army, a former colleague from the Baku oilfields and long to be a crony. Tsaritsyn, midway between the northern points of the Black Sea and the Caspian, became the centre of intrigue against Trotsky's command of the Red army. Trotsky did not try to hide his low opinion of Stalin, Voroshilov and Budenny and the Tsaritsyn group. He tried to get Lenin to recall Stalin. As to Voroshilov, he said in a judgement proved valid in 1941, he 'is capable of commanding a regiment, not an army of fifty thousand'.

When the Whites were finally driven back in October 1918, Stalin grasped the credit for the victory. With the danger to Moscow from the east finished by the withdrawal of the Czech legion beyond the Urals, Trotsky was free to concentrate on the south. He succeeded in having Stalin relieved. Lenin treated Stalin with tact, sending a special train to bring him back to Moscow, but Stalin's hatred for Trotsky had set. The jealousy increased the following year. Stalin was in charge of the first successful defence of Petrograd against Yudenich's Whites in May. In the critical month of October 1919, with the Whites close to taking Moscow as well, it was Trotsky who drove Yudenich out of the Petrograd suburbs.

Both men were awarded Orders of the Red Banner for their part in the civil war. But it was Trotsky who was the unrivalled hero and master of the Red army. Stalin was, as Trotsky put it, 'soporific' in public, too monotone and flat to make impact. Trotsky underestimated the Georgian's watchful ambition and capacity for administration. Bolshevik bureaucracy sprouted after the civil war. Apparently no rival, a dull party workhorse, Stalin slowly emerged at the top. He had three key power bases.

As commissar of nationalities, he dealt with the lives of 65 million non-Russians, a mix that whirled from bitter, westward-looking Ukrainians to oriental Turkmen shepherds and Ostyak fur hunters. From 1919 Stalin was also commissar of the workers' and peasants' inspectorate, the *Rabkrin*. Theoretically made up of 'toilers' who could check at will on the work of Soviet civil servants, the *Rabkrin* was in effect a force that could pry into the whole buraucracy. It gave Stalin, as commissar, a wide brief to supervise the functioning of government. And, within the Politburo, Stalin was responsible for the daily running of the Party. He was the link between the Politburo and the Ogburo, which commanded party personnel.

Stalin had an unequalled grasp on the party organization and its shifting alliances, of dull routine and the dull people who performed it. He was far from the brilliant heights where Trotsky strolled his tongue but he ran the engine room of Bolshevism. Trotsky's armoured train, that 'vital shovelful of coal that kept a dying fire alive', was now in a museum. The Red army had been demobilized. Its strength had been reduced by two thirds by the beginning of 1922, and with it had gone much of Trotsky's power base. He was unable to protect the *voenspets* from the contempt of

Stalin, Voroshilov and Budenny now that the war was over. Fitfully, he railed against the 'infectious pacifist mood' in the country. He drafted new Regulations, in which the Soviet infantryman was to fight 'not only with the rifle, the bayonet and the machinegun but also with the word of truth'. He perfected the May Day parade, riding out through the Kremlin's Spasky Gate to review the troops on Red Square. Whilst peace extended Stalin's workrate and influence, it left the commissar for war half unemployed.

On 3 April 1922 Stalin was appointed general secretary of the Central Committee. The secretariat gave him extensive and detailed power. It prepared the agenda for the Politburo, supplied the documents for debates, held sway over the careers of the functionaries. It was the general secretary who, according to his own feelings, saw Politburo decisions acted on, altered or ignored. He was also the link between the Central Committee and the Central Control Commission. This had been set up the year before to 'audit party morals', holding forums where party members could be accused of careerism, defeatism and all the other *isms* in the list of party crimes. The forums later became the purge trials and Stalin's immense knowledge of the Party made it easy enough for him to produce members to go before them.

Lenin had a stroke at the end of May 1922, with Stalin hardly behind his desk as general secretary. Lenin returned briefly from resting in the country in mid autumn, before a second stroke and then a third in March 1923 removed him from influence. Stalin's emergence above Trotsky was a close-run thing. In a brief political Testament at the end of 1922, Lenin had said that Trotsky and Stalin were 'the two most able leaders of the present Central Committee'. It was a surprising verdict, given that Trotsky was clearly the more imaginative and mercurial, but Lenin found him to have 'too far-reaching a self-confidence'.

Lenin also had misgivings over Stalin. He found Stalin 'too rude', a fault that 'becomes unbearable in the office of general secretary. Therefore I propose to the comrades to find a way to remove Stalin from that position and appoint to it another man ... more patient, more loyal, more polite and more attentive to comrades, less capricious.'

This hostility, which might have ruined Stalin, was burned out by the third stroke in March 1923. With Lenin now literally speechless, Stalin fixed deeper his control of the administrative machine and its spiralling patronage. Within the Politburo, he formed a triumvirate with G. E. Zinoviev, the head of the Comintern, and Lev Kamenev, the party boss in Moscow. Its main purpose was to block Trotsky, neither of his allies anticipating that the workaday Stalin would emerge above them. He was already listening in to his colleagues' conversations on the Kremlin's internal telephone system.

His apparent reticence worked in his favour. Often silent, 'he was unique in a country where everybody talked far too much,' said his secretary, Boris Bazhanov. Pulling contentedly on his pipe, he was a good listener, sensitive to gusts of opinion and bending with them. He was modest, a man who 'loves neither money, nor pleasure, neither sport nor women', who lived quietly with his wife in small lodgings in the servants' quarters in the Kremlin. Trotsky had the worst of all worlds. Though he did not enjoy the comfort, he lived in more luxurious quarters in the Kremlin, served by an old court butler on plates still bearing the Tsar's coat of arms. He was seen as Lenin's heir, and was thus envied and mistrusted, whilst failing to undertake the manoeuvres necessary to gain his inheritance. He was publicly associated with opposition to the triumvirs, without taking decisive action against them. In the army, cavalrymen were closely associated with Stalin and were emerging as a new elite, critical of Trotsky's defensive ideas and his emphasis on a territorial militia.

Lenin died on 21 January 1924. His Testament was never published, merely read out to a Central Committee plenum. This was enough to rattle Stalin, who 'felt himself small and pitiable. In spite of his self-control and enforced calm one could clearly see from his face that his fate was in the balance.' His future victims allowed the moment to pass. Zinoviev and Kamenev urged the Central Committee to allow their ally to remain in his post, confident that he was a mere understudy. Trotsky, 'as though numb and frozen with detestation', kept his silence. It was Stalin who had dominated Lenin's emotional funeral. Trotsky, suffering from exhaustion and persistent fever, had been on a slow train journey to the Black Sea to take a health cure when he received a coded message from Stalin telling him of the death. Lying, Stalin told him that the funeral would take place before he would have time to return to Moscow, so Trotsky carried on his journey to the palm trees and camellias of Sukhumi.

Stalin, the boy from the Georgian seminary, had an instinctive grasp of the importance of liturgy and faith in the Russian soul. He urged the preparation of the red granite Mausoleum in Red Square.[5] He called on the Party to collect relics of Lenin. He stood in the guard of honour at the bier. He read out his Oath to Lenin, a communist catechism that drew heavily on his days in the seminary: 'In leaving us, Comrade Lenin ordained us to hold high and keep pure the great title of member of the Party. We vow to thee, Comrade Lenin, that we shall honourably fulfill this thy commandment ... In leaving us, Comrade Lenin ordained us to guard and strengthen the dictatorship of the proletariat. We vow to thee, Comrade Lenin, that we shall honourably fulfill this thy commandment ...' Put an initial capital letter on the pronoun, and it is clear what Stalin was creating with his Oath.[6]

Mussolini and Hitler, who copied much from Stalin, enshrined themselves as messiahs. Stalin was subtly content to be the Great Disciple. The public humility shielded the private power-lust in his stalking of Trotsky.

His skilful shuffling of key appointments in the army left Trotsky increasingly isolated in 1924. A quarter of the command staff were now party members, owing allegiance to Stalin and aware that the general secretary's personnel department kept detailed records on them in its files. In March the Politburo dismissed Trotsky's deputy at the Commissariat of War and appointed the hostile Mikhail Frunze in his place. Stalin's protégé Voroshilov was named commander of the Moscow garrison. Troubled by malaria, which left him soaked with sweat after a speech 'as if from a rainstorm', Trotsky was undermined. A conference of political commissars held at the end of the year demanded his dismissal.

Had Trotsky chosen to appeal to the army he had built and directed for seven years, he might still have defeated the triumvirs. He did not. In January 1925 he resigned. For the coming quarter century, Stalin would dominate the Red army.

7

STALINISM

Frunze became the new commissar and commander-in-chief. Seven military districts were established, with two independent armies still operating against rebels and nationalists in the Caucasus and Central Asia. The peacetime strength of the regular 'cadre' Red army was fixed at 560,000 men. There were 77 infantry divisions, 31 of them with regular troops and 46 with territorials.

Major operational or mobilization orders were still signed by both commanders and commissars, but commanders were released from the day-to-day supervision of their commissars by a decree in March 1925. Additional political control over the army was ensured by the Political Administration, which came directly under the Party. It had party cells, which operated in every unit from the general staff to individual companies. It also controlled the constant propaganda effort in the army, running cinemas and 'Lenin rooms', selecting the books for unit libraries. A Special Section, *Osobyi Otdel* or OO, of the Cheka injected a network of informers and secret police into the army.[1]

The military cells were intended to prevent the development of an officer class.[2] Workers and peasants were eased through to command positions on the basis of social origin. In the early days of peace, there were few social or financial distinctions between commanders and men. In 1924 divisional commanders were paid 100 roubles a month and a company commander 43 roubles, when a metal worker could earn 150. Officers would sometimes refuse to ride on the new motor buses that appeared in Moscow in 1925, on the ground that they were too grand for proletarian commanders. Officers and men ate in the same mess. Plays were commissioned for army units on the war against capitalism where officers played bit parts and the main roles went to privates.

Frunze died in 1925 from an operation for gall-stones, which he did not want but which was forced on him by Stalin.[3] Voroshilov, a former miner and farm worker, a fine rider and marksman, but ill educated and no strategist, succeeded him as commissar. In 1928 he removed the energetic and incisive Tukhachevsky from his key position as Chief of Staff and posted him to the provinces. Trotsky acknowledged the 'undeniable courage' Voroshilov had shown in the Civil War, but found him a 'backwoodsman' with a 'complete lack of military and administrative ability'.

Not that there was much to administer in the reduced Red army. The mass of territorials were unwilling peasants and half-trained workers and the half million men of the regular army were poorly equipped. There were not enough uniforms to go round. The whole Siberian military district, which extended from the Urals to the Pacific, had thirty light tanks and twenty-one armoured cars.

Relations with that other international pariah, Germany, were already close and Voroshilov eagerly expanded them in talks with the Reichswehr General Werner von Blomberg. Senior Soviet officers travelled to General Staff courses in Berlin, masquerading as 'Bulgarians', and their opposite numbers were invited to the Red army's autumn manoeuvres in the Ukraine. A joint tank training school was set up at Kazan on the Volga, and British tanks were bought for testing. German pilots trained with Russians at Lipetsk, south of Moscow. Blomberg watched German pilots and Russian artillerymen exercising together in Voronezh, finding that 'the knowledge of German military literature is frequently astonishing'. German technicians worked in Soviet ammunition plants in Leningrad, Sverdlovsk and Kharkov.

The army consolidated and extended its privileges. Officers' pay increased and their messes were reintroduced. In a 'mass phenomenon', many divorced their first wives, daughters of peasants and workers, and remarried to girls from the old aristocracy and bourgeoisie. They were protected for the time being from the violent winds that were again tossing outside the barracks. But the Red army, with its Political Administration, its commissars and its Special Section, never has more than temporary shelter from politics.

★

Zinoviev and Kamenev had tardily realized that Stalin, having toppled Trotsky from his military pedestal in January 1925, was no longer their junior partner. They joined with Trotsky as the 'left opposition', dedicated to international socialism against a 'right' which believed together with Stalin in 'socialism in one country'. The immediate past was like a horror film, played jerkily at unnatural speed, and the country yearned for stability. Stalin was backed by Bukharin, Rykov and Tomsky. In time, two would be executed and Tomsky would commit suicide, but for the moment they suited Stalin well enough. They supported the moderate New Economic Policy and incentives for peasants against the crash industrialization and foreign meddling demanded by the left. Why should the despised Russian *muzhik*, who had already won more for socialism than all the Communists of Berlin, Bavaria and Budapest combined, be cajoled into more foreign adventures?

Trotsky, the 'adventurer ... the player of revolution', would have none of it. The problems of a 'backward country with an overwhelming peasant population' could only be solved 'on an international scale, in the arena of the world proletarian revolution'. He ignored the profound indifference of the Western proletariat to the Soviet experiment. There was almost full employment in the US, Britain and France at this period. Germany was recovering. Fewer than 800 motor cars were being crafted each year in Russia, where 15 million Model T Fords had rolled off US production lines by 1927. Nevertheless, Zinoviev insisted: 'The theory of final victory in one country is wrong. We are building and will build socialism in the USSR with the aid of the world proletariat ...'

Stalin, listening, quietly pipe-sucking, massaged Russian egos and amassed his 'internal forces of the revolution'. Trotsky declared himself repelled by 'exchanging visits, assiduously attending the ballet, the collective sessions with the gossip about those absent'.[4] These were the stuff of politics and his aloofness cost the left dear. Zinoviev was thrown off the Politburo in July 1926, whilst Stalin's nominee Kirov took over his old power base in Leningrad. Trotsky followed in October, the same month that Kamenev lost his status as a candidate member.

The rout was completed the following year, aided by a rise in international tension. Britain broke off relations with Moscow, the Soviet ambassador in Warsaw was murdered by an émigré. In China, Chiang Kai-shek massacred Communists whom Stalin had urged to support him. Communists were tracked down and shot by Chiang's troops in Shanghai and Canton, though they had offered no resistance. On the night of 1 August, a date which is now the official birthday of the Chinese National Liberation Army, communist insurgents attempted to seize Nanchang. The rising was brutally crushed within a week.

Trotsky blamed Stalin for the setbacks. On 7 November 1927, the day of the official celebration of the tenth anniversary of the revolution, he and Zinoviev called for street demonstrations in Moscow and Leningrad, as Petrograd had been renamed. Both men were immediately expelled from the Party. Zinoviev and Kamenev recanted but Trotsky was exiled to Alma Ata on the Chinese frontier.[5]

The left was broken, but Bukharin, Rykov and Tomsky had little time to savour the victory. Stalin retained his control of the Politburo and set about liquidating the right and the NEP. Seventy years out from the revolution, change is laborious in the Soviet Union, a wearisome affair that has Gorbachev clawing at hard-set attitudes with his fingernails. Stalin was able from 1928 to impose a blinding lurch in course. Within a year of their triumph, Tomsky had resigned as head of the unions and Bukharin had gone from the *Pravda* editor's office. Rykov survived a little longer before he, too, was thrown off the Central Committee.

Stalin then set out to recast Russia and her soul on the lines of the defeated left, driving peasants into collectives, and forcing through a vast programme of industrialization that transformed the Red army. One Trotskyite element was missing. There was no internationalist feeling to deflect the process. To Stalin, Russia was not a backward outpost on the borders of a more advanced world. She was the one country of socialism, a huge laboratory where he could experiment on living flesh with the forms of the future. Five years after laying Lenin to rest in the granite Mausoleum on Red Square, Stalin let loose a second revolution that was more radical, bloody and intrusive into life than the first.

The country floated beyond the limits of reason as Stalin poured out statistics and plans. After his fiftieth birthday in December 1929 the cult of his personality permeated the nation and the walls of public buildings were covered with his portrait and the slogan of his obsessive belief: 'There are no fortresses that Bolsheviks cannot storm.' The man who had sneered at Trotsky and Zinoviev as 'superindustrializers', and shelved plans for the Dnieprostroy hydro station on the ground that it was like a *muzhik* buying a gramophone instead of a cow, now demanded an industrial investment five times greater than his finance commissar had allowed.

Russia was to become the second America. The first Five Year Plan of 1928 aimed at boosting pig-iron production from 3.5 million tons to 10 million. That was not enough. In 1930 Stalin said: 'We must at all costs get to seventeen million tons in 1932.' That year, he ordered industry to increase its output by 50 per cent in a year. The fantasy targets were unachievable, even by a workforce that squandered its own overworked and underfed present for the future. Stalin refused to slow. 'No, comrades, it is not possible,' he told workers in 1931. 'The pace must not be slackened! On the contrary, we must quicken it . . .'

The cost of the crash transformation from a peasant to an industrial country was compared with a war. Labour was conscripted from the farms, industries signing contracts with collective farms to provide set numbers of men and women for factories. An American, who volunteered to help build the blast furnaces in Magnitogorsk, reckoned that 'the battle of ferrous metallurgy alone involved more casualties than the battle of the Marne'.[6] On the railways, a report on thirty-five engine-drivers involved in collisions found that 80 per cent had tuberculosis and that all were exhausted and undernourished. They were fortunate to be examined before disappearing into the Gulag. Failure to meet norms, caused by shortages, by lack of experience, by the teething problems of a new society, by the ignorance of ex-peasants working new machinery, by the miasma of exhaustion and abnormal demands, was put down to 'wrecking'. The imperialists, having failed to strangle Bolshevism at birth in the civil war, were now trying to kill it off by sabotaging its industry. 'Our class enemies do exist,' Stalin told young Communists in 1928. 'And they not only exist but are growing and trying to act against Soviet power.'

To excuse itself for power cuts, the Moscow Electric Power System found wreckers within its ranks. When the Donbass industrial belt fell behind target, a large-scale conspiracy of engineers was uncovered. The trial of the Shakhty engineers in the Donbass in 1928, with its written confessions, its defendants driven insane or to suicide, was the forerunner of the coming Show Trials. By 1931 half the engineers and technicians in this vital area had been arrested. Mass trials of engineers working for 'foreign powers' were held. Foreigners, who played a vital role in industrialization, were not exempt and themselves appeared in the Metro–Vickers trial in the desperate year of 1933. Even Stalin's nerve was tested. His wife committed suicide, suffering because of 'the famine and the Terror, because of her own comfortable life in the Kremlin . . . worn down by fits of melancholy'.

The results, though they could never match the awesome human input, were remarkable in the key defence, power and heavy industries. New cities like Magnitogorsk were built on virgin land, whilst young Communists volunteered to pioneer industry in the wilderness of Kazakhstan. Giant new industrial zones were created in the Urals, Kuznetsk basin and the Volga. The colossal Dnieper hydro-electric project went on stream. Kharkov and Stalingrad (the ex-Tsaritsyn, renamed in 1925) were sites for new tractor plants, easily converted to tank production. A new automotive industry was centred at Dnepropetrovsk. During the first Five Year Plan, from 1928 to 1932, electricity output trebled, and coal, oil and iron-ore production doubled. The Red army began to suck in new equipment. Where 860 military aircraft had been delivered in 1930, the 1932 figure was 2,500. Tank production, based on copies of British Vickers and

American Christie machines, swelled from 740 to 3,300. Artillery and rifle production doubled.

What was happening in the factories saved Russia in the coming war. Defence production began to match that of Germany. What took place in the countryside half destroyed Soviet society. The keening sadness and inefficiency that remains on the farms is known well to Gorbachev, an agricultural expert whose grandparents were pioneers of the collective movement.

Industrialization had to be financed and manned. Agriculture was the only reservoir of surpluses and labour. Original proposals to transform small family holdings into large collectives were modest and involved a ten to fifteen-year time span. Since only 2.7 per cent of arable land was in collective or state farms in 1928, and the richer peasants were producing enough grain to feed the cities, sense dictated a cautious approach. In 1929 Stalin determined on immediate and mass collectivization. Russia had some twenty-five million peasant farmers with their own land. Some five million were semi-destitute, working small plots with wooden ploughs, hiring out their labour to richer neighbours. The richest, who may have numbered two million, were prosperous, the backbone of the NEP, with their own livestock, horses and machinery. To these Stalin attached the word for the village usurer and crooked rural trader, *kulak*. Between them was the great bulk of 'middle peasants', perhaps eighteen million strong, holding their own well enough.

The *kulaks* were, as Stalin put it in brute simplicity, to be 'liquidated as a class'. No conscience or sentiment would be allowed to protect them, for 'when the head is off, one does not grieve for the hair'. No attempt was made to explain the policy to peasants, perhaps because it was inexplicable. Tens of thousands of party officials were dispatched to the countryside, with orders to deport and liquidate the *kulaks* and to herd the rest into collectives. It was easy enough to declare that a couple of villages had become a *kolkhoz*. The effort of forcing peasants to collectivize their property, their livestock and implements, degenerated into warfare. Peasants slaughtered their livestock, smashed machines and burned crops rather than let the state take them. They gorged themselves on the slaughtered meat so that 'everyone had a greasy mouth ... everyone blinked like an owl, as if drunk from eating'. Slaughter was protest, even if it was also the harbinger of starvation. In three years the number of sheep and goats was reduced by two thirds, of horses by half, of cattle by 45 per cent. The death penalty, applied to the theft of collective farm property, meant that a peasant could be executed for repossessing an animal or a utensil that the state had taken from him.

The process became a military operation, with villages surrounded and machinegunned. Red army morale slumped, for 'in every unit there was a mass desertion of peasant soldiers, who hastened to their native villages, with or without their rifles, to wreak vengeance on the executives of the collectives'.[7] A GPU colonel, broken in spirit by his experience in the countryside, almost sobbed on a train between Moscow and Kharkov: 'I am an old Bolshevik. I worked in the underground against the Tsar and then I fought in the civil war. Did I do all that in order that I should now surround villages with machineguns and order my men to fire indiscriminately into crowds of peasants? Oh, no no!'[8]

Peasants wrote to sons serving in the army, bidding them to go to 'Stalin, the chief of the townsfolk' and demand the restoration of their rights. The *kulaks*, men who had returned from the Red army just nine years before to claim their land, suffered an 'ethnic catastrophe'. Stalin's agents, like 'raging beasts', rounded up the best farmers and their families and drove them, 'stripped of their possessions, naked, into the northern wastes, into the tundra and the taiga'.[9] Those too poor to be classified even under the catch-all label of *kulak* were sentenced as *podkulachniks*, people aiding the *kulaks*.

This extermination pre-dates the rise of Hitler.[10] Hitler became German Chancellor in January 1933. Cooperation with the Reichswehr was broken. The new German threat increased the priority given to the Red army.

Defence plants flourished under the second Five Year Plan. The defence budget, 1.4 billion roubles in 1933, reached 23 billion roubles in 1938. The number of regular troops more than doubled to 1.3 million between 1933 and 1936 as the territorial system was run down. Military engineers were making a deep impact. Langemak and Pobedonostsev were working on the predecessors of the Katyusha rocket missile. Aircraft designers, whose names survive through the design bureaux they established, were feeding the Red air force with new machines, Tupolev and Ilyushin in bombers and transports, Yakovlev and Mikoyan in fighters, Mil in the auto-gyro antecedent of the helicopter. Tupolev startled the world with new records including a flight over the North Pole to North America. The aircraft industry was reported to be making 4,000 airframes and 20,000 aero engines a year.

Soviet tank technology was growing rapidly. In 1932 the Kharkov tank plant 'completed two tanks with difficulty, but in 1935 whole companies of the machines rolled off its conveyors daily'.[11] By 1935 the Red army was easily the largest armoured force in the world, with 10,000 tanks. At the start of collectivization there were 7,000 tractors in the whole of Russia. Within seven years the intensity of effort in tracked vehicles had spawned Koshkin, Morozov and Kucherenko, designers whose product, the T-34 tank, influences modern history as surely as the Spitfire. The new weapons appeared on the proving grounds in the Ukraine and White Russia. The British observer, General Martel, who saw more than a thousand tanks on manoeuvres in the Ukraine in 1935 and 1936, was 'immensely impressed by the general enthusiasm and efficiency ... Nearly all their mechanical equipment is new and excellent in design. What they have done is to get sample machines from every country, take the best of each and design composite machines.'[12] Martel also witnessed an early mass parachute drop, where 1,200 troops were dropped from 48 aircraft to seize an airfield in 7.5 minutes. The first US military attaché in the Soviet Union, Colonel Philip R. Faymondville, was equally impressed by a 'powerful, loyal and intelligent military force thoroughly indoctrinated in the Socialist ideas'.[13] Ironically, in view of what was about to happen, he found that the 'relation between the Army and the Government in the Soviet Union is as close as in any country in the world and the loyalty of the Army to the Government appears to be beyond doubt.'

In defence, at least, the Soviet system had already shown its ability to release the latent energies of the nation to an effect inconceivable under the Tsars.[14]

A warming shift in status went with the new muscle in equipment. Commissars were renamed political leaders, *politruks*, and acted only as advisers in morale and discipline. Personal ranks were restored in 1935. Stalin still gagged on generals, calling his army commanders Komandarms, but lieutenants, captains, majors and colonels reappeared. The rank of Marshal was created for the five most senior officers. Pay and housing improved. No longer embarrassed to ride on a motor bus, officers played polo and danced the mazurka with their former-regime wives. Cossack units, despite their freebooting, White traditions, reappeared in 1936.

Academies were opened for the General Staff, artillery, air engineering, military engineering, mechanization and motorization. Senior officers of insight reinforced this intelligence: Tukhachevsky; the Jewish commander of the Ukrainian district, Yakir; the Latvian head of the air force, Alksnis; the artilleryman Sedyakin. They grasped the concept of a coming war in which mobile offence, driven by tank and aero engines, would overwhelm static defence in slicing encirclements. What cavalry had lost to the machinegun and rapid-fire artillery, oil and armour would win back.

The most valued new perk was immunity from arrest by civil organs like the NKVD without the specific agreement of the defence commissar.

Politicians and party men joined the *kulaks*. On a December afternoon in 1934 Sergei Kirov, the party leader in Leningrad for whom the Ballet is named, was shot dead. Stalin reacted violently and directly, leaving Moscow for Leningrad on the night train. He was met at the Moscow

Station by the head of the Leningrad police, and struck him in the face. Stalin took personal charge of the investigation at the Smolny Institute, from which Lenin had launched the Red October, and where Kirov had been shot as he strolled without a bodyguard.[15] The assassin, Nikolaev, appears to have acted on his own, but thirteen alleged accomplices were shot with him on charges of organizing a 'Leningrad Centre' of assassination.

The Kirov affair was sweetly timed for Stalin to rid himself of senior party members, the Old Bolsheviks he suspected of being Trotskyites. Wipe them out, replace them with younger men who would owe their power to him, and the easier would rest his crown. In the spring of 1935 thousands of party members from Leningrad were sent to the Gulag as accessories to Kirov's murder. The prey became grander. Zinoviev and Kamenev, triumvirs with Stalin a decade before, were arrested. In July 1936 a secret circular 'On the terrorist activity of the Trotskyite-Zinovievite counterrevolutionary bloc' ordered the Party to denounce enemies of the regime. The following month, the showpiece inquisition known as the 'Trial of the Sixteen' opened in Moscow to a hysterical press campaign. Zinoviev and Kamenev, hauled from prison, were accused with fourteen other Old Bolsheviks of setting up a terrorist centre under Trotsky's orders. These old comrades of Lenin were accused of planning the murder of Kirov and of plotting against Stalin. All pleaded guilty, despite the naked absurdity of the charges, and were shot. In their 'confessions', they implicated other senior figures, including Bukharin, Rykov and Tomsky. Tomsky committed suicide.

The terror took new strength when Nikolai Ezhov replaced G. G. Yagoda as head of the NKVD on 26 September 1936. The *Ezhovschina*, the name given to the psychotic purges that now engulfed the country, broke in January 1937. A second great show trial opened in Moscow, the 'Trial of the Seventeen', in which the accused parroted admissions of sabotaging the economy, and of conspiring with Trotsky, the Germans and the Japanese. A fever, with hallucinations of spies and traitors, engulfed the country. There were queues outside NKVD offices as people waited patiently to register denunciations. When a wave of arrests was at its height, prisoners came into the prisons by truck, passenger car, Black Maria and open hansom cab, causing traffic jams at the gates and in the courtyards.

Morale in the Red forces remained high, but the arrest of Bukharin and Rykov brought the terror closer. Senior officers were thought to be sympathetic to Bukharin. When the names of Tukhachevsky and General Putna, the former military attaché in London, were mentioned during the Trial of the Seventeen, colleagues began to shun them.

On 3 March 1937 Stalin warned the Central Committee of the harm that could be caused by a few spies on the army staff. Tukhachevsky had visited Germany, as well as Paris and the funeral of King George V in London. It would not be difficult to concoct a plot against him, perhaps with the help of the Gestapo and its agent General Skoblin, who also had links with the NKVD. In May the political commissar system was reintroduced at the top command levels. The dual command had been scrapped entirely in 1934. Its return smacked of crisis.

So, more ominously, did the treatment of the head of the army's Main Political Administration, I. B. Gamarnik. He had held the post since 1929. MPA political officers had conducted earlier, minor purges of the military.[16] In 1937 the task of 'unmasking enemies' in the armed forces was being performed by the eager NKVD.

Gamarnik was sick in bed with diabetes for most of May 1937, dragging himself out only for the May Day parade, where he had an emotional farewell with Tukhachevsky, who stood next to Stalin on the Lenin Mausoleum, apparently at the height of his power. On 10 May Gamarnik was dismissed as deputy defence commissar.

On the morning of 31 May Marshal Blucher visited him at home, telling him of spreading arrests in the army. Tukhachevsky had been demoted to command the Volga military district. Later in the day, Gamarnik was told that the NKVD had sealed his office and that he had been sacked as the head of the MPA. When NKVD agents came calling at his flat, and his daughter opened the door to them, he shot himself. *Pravda*'s note on his suicide the next day said that he had been 'entangled with anti-Soviet elements and evidently in fear of exposure'. His removal meant that there was nothing to spare the army from NKVD terror. Articles praising the NKVD and its chief, the lame-legged Ezhov, began to appear in the military press at the beginning of June.

Senior officers began to fear that 'some great misfortune was moving towards us'. They had not long to wait.

8

THE GREAT TERROR:
A TRENCH AT KHODYNKA

Sharp at 10 a.m. on 11 June 1937 the cream of the Red army met in an unimposing, three-storey building on October 25 Street, not far from the Kremlin. The entire command attended, the Chief of the General Staff, the deputy defence commissars, military district commanders, all four

Army Commanders First Class, naval flag officers, and four of the five new Marshals of the Soviet Union. Only Marshal K. E. Voroshilov, the defence commissar, was absent.

A group in full uniform was seated at a long table. At their head sat Military Jurist of the Army First Class V. Ulrikh, a man with considerable if perverted experience of show trials. The other seven military judges, who included two marshals and all but two of whom were soon to die themselves,[1] had no legal training.

An even more distinguished group of eight officers, stripped of their insignia and medals, faced them from behind a barrier. Marshal Tukhachevsky sat with the head of the Frunze Academy, the former military attaché in London, the chief of the army's central administration and the commanders of military districts.[2]

This was the flower of the Red army, still young, a challenge to Stalin and a reminder of Trotsky's domination of the civil war. Tukhachevsky was forty-four. The former Tsarist cadet had commanded the Soviet forces against Poland in 1920 when he was twenty-seven, destroyed the Kronstadt uprising with Trotsky at twenty-eight, become chief of the Red army staff at thirty-one. He was handsome, a lover of music who had supported the young Shostakovich. It was said that he could do a pull-up whilst in the saddle, horse and all. Such myths were dangerous, for Stalin was in the business of destroying other men's legends. Uborevich was another young civil war hero who had commanded armies against Denikin and Wrangel in 1919 and 1920. Primakov had been a Red Cossack. Yakir, a former chemistry student who was an outstanding civil war commander at twenty-one, had played a vital role in the development of the Kharkov tractor-tank plant.

They had been taken silently and without fuss. Tukhachevsky had been arrested, without struggle, between sessions of a party conference in his military district. Uborevich was seized as he travelled from Smolensk to Moscow, either on the train or on the platform in Moscow. Yakir was ordered by Voroshilov to leave the Ukraine immediately for a meeting of the military council in Moscow on 30 May. The last Moscow train had left and Yakir used the personal train that was available to him as a commander. During the night, his private sleeping car was uncoupled at Bryansk. He was seized in his berth by NKVD officers, transferred to a car and driven directly to the Lubianka. Primakov had also set off on an urgent summons to Moscow in his personal train.[3] The NKVD tried to arrest him en route but his personal guard drove them off. He telephoned Voroshilov, a common error. The defence commissar told him: 'There has been a misunderstanding. Some people are coming who will explain everything.' A reinforced detachment of NKVD duly arrived. Primakov surrendered his Mauser and was taken to the Lubianka.[4]

All were accused of working for German intelligence and with deliberately weakening the combat strength of the Red army. No documents or material evidence were introduced. It was different from the civilian trials, with no show element, and no false confessions. None pleaded guilty, although in the surviving typed report of the trial their 'noes' were changed in ink to 'yeses', with the exception of Tukhachevsky, who refused to answer questions.[5]

The judges were uneasy. Marshal Blucher claimed to be ill and excused himself. The Chief of the General Staff, B. M. Shaposhnikov, looked agitated and unwell as Ion Yakir shouted at his former colleagues: 'Look me in the eyes! Can you really not understand that this is all lies?' 'Give it up, Ion. Don't you see who we are dealing with here?' said his co-defendant Primakov, referring to Stalin.

The trial was finished by 2 p.m. The convicted men were condemned without right of appeal and were led off to the Lubianka. Yakir was shot the same day, the others at dawn on 12 June. Their bodies were taken to a construction site at Khodynka, thrown into a trench, strewn with quicklime and covered with soil.[6]

Stalin, the 'Kremlin mountaineer, the murderer'[7] with a 'cockroach whistler's leer', was pointing his 'fingers fat as grubs' at the military.

Military disappearances gathered pace. Trials were held by *troikas*, groups of three NKVD men constituted as a tribunal, who accused, arrested and sentenced without publicity. Arrests were carried out by a pair of young NKVD men★ with their purple ID cards. The prisoner was then taken to a crowded cell in a gaol, in Moscow the Lubianka, the Butyrka or the Lefortovo, in Leningrad the Kresty or the Shlaperny. In the smaller provincial cities, which ran to only one prison, it was known simply as the *Bolshoi Dom*, the Big House.

Men were taken from classrooms. General Vatsetis, the former Tsarist

---

★ The Soviet secret police, known today as the KGB, started out life as the Cheka, the Extraordinary Commission for Struggle against Counterrevolution, Sabotage and Speculation, in 1917. It was renamed the OGPU, the United State Political Administration, in 1922. It was rechristened the NKVD, the People's Commissariat of Internal Affairs, in 1934 and became the NKGB, the People's Commissariat of State Security, in 1943. From 1946 to 1953 it was known as the MGB, the Ministry of State Security. After a brief period in 1953 when the secret police were known simply as MVD, for the Ministry of the Interior, they became and remain known as the KGB, the acronym for the State Security Committee.

As a Western child might learn the dates of Kings, then, the Russian secret police are: Cheka 1917–22, OGPU 1922–34, NKVD 1934–43, NKGB 1943–6, MGB 1946–53, MVD 1953, KGB 1953 – present day. And indeed it is its own dynasty, of repression, that has yet to suffer an interregnum.

colonel who had been the first C-in-C of the Red army, was lecturing on military history at the Frunze Academy. 'We listened to him for an hour,' a student said.[8] 'After the break the lecture was not resumed. The commissar of our class announced: "Comrades! The lecture will not continue. Lecturer Vatsetis has been arrested as an enemy of the people." '

A VIP would[9] be given a holiday ticket to a Sochi sanatorium where 'the geraniums cascade down to a perfumed sea and the soul unwinds from the overloaded springs of the arrests'. As he waited for the train, he would be hailed by a young man who knew him and whom he did not know. A navy captain was arrested while buying a cake for a young lady. A man was invited to the fancy food counter in the Gastronome food store and was taken.[10] Pobeda sedans took men off the pavement.

Few tried to escape.

One who did thought his arrest was a mistake. G. D. Gai, a corps commander, broke a floorboard on a train after his arrest by the NKVD and jumped out. He hurt his leg but managed to hide up in a haystack. He slept through a search by young Communists and NKVD men and then took refuge in a peasant hut. He decided to go to Moscow, thinking that his arrest had been carried out illegally by the NKVD. The peasant tried to dissuade him from going to the local railway station. Gai demanded: 'Are the pictures of Lenin and Stalin still hanging there?' They were. 'That proves Soviet authority still exists,' said Gai, who walked on to the platform. Gai, as trusting as Primakov, telephoned Voroshilov in Moscow to explain his situation. Voroshilov told him to wait where he was. People would come to explain everything to him. They did. They took him to the Lubianka.[11]

Rumours of sanctuaries abounded, until news arrived on the swift grapevine that the arrests had reached there. The Far East was envied and untouched throughout 1937. Its luck held in the first half of 1938, until there arrived at the end of May, on separate trains on the Trans-Siberian, the deputy head of the NKVD and General Mekhlis, the new head of the MPA, a man 'whose sickly vanity overshadowed everything else ... Soon thereafter commanders were seized by the hundreds.'[12]

By the end, nowhere was safe in the Soviet Union. Neither was a foreign posting. Those who had been abroad faced specially high odds of arrest on their return. This applied to the 'volunteers' in Spain as much as to military attachés on diplomatic posting, like Putna, shot after the June trial on his return from the Soviet embassy in London. Despite this, there were few defections.

The feeling of inevitability corroded personal outrage. Stalin could not have done it all alone. 'Many of us were guilty,' wrote Admiral N. G.

Kuznetsov, who, filling the shoes of the purged, advanced from a lowly posting on a cruiser to navy commissar in a few months.[13] 'Even if only for remaining silent when the situation demanded that we speak our minds. Many paid themselves for such passivity when their turns came.'

Stalin's daughter explained her father's role in the terror, in which 'people disappeared like shadows in the night', through the suicide of his wife on the night of 9 November 1932 and the murder of Kirov two years later.* These events, Svetlana Alliluyeva maintains, shattered him. 'Maybe he never trusted people very much, but after this he stopped trusting them at all,' she wrote.[14]

Some chose to try to wipe out others. Instead of drifting with the tide, they sought their defence in urging it on. They pestered NKVD men to record on grey issue paper their denunciations of their colleagues. Family ties, chance encounters or scraps of conversation with those already taken became treason. Breakdown of equipment, unhealthy horses in a cavalry unit, defective piston rings in aircraft engines were evidence of wrecking. The commandant of the Zhitomir military hospital denounced every hospital official who had ever criticized the hospital.[15] Change in status was abrupt. One day, Karl Radek, a journalist who had played an important part in the early military cooperation between Germany and Soviet Russia, was writing about Trotsky in *Izvestia* as the 'fascist *ober*-bandit'. The next day, the lead article in *Izvestia* described Radek as 'that cringing, hypocritical, fornicating scum'. A new crime of 'supervigilance' was introduced in 1938, which condemned careerists striving for promotion 'by means of unfounded acts of repression against party members'.

There were rare examples where denial brought release. Lieutenant General Andrei Vedenin vigorously denied charges that his family had been Whites and that he had bought unhealthy horses for a garrison in Central Asia. Both charges were enough to have had him shot. He was allowed to travel to produce evidence of his innocence and survived to become, in sweet irony, commandant of the Kremlin.

Budenny himself claimed to have outwitted the executioners.[16] Seeing how others were being taken, he set up machineguns in his dacha and deployed soldiers on guard. He only slept at the dacha. When the NKVD came for him, he warned them that he would open fire. He then telephoned

* Though, as her daughter wrote, 'people shot themselves fairly often in those days', and millions of other deaths in peacetime Russia were inflicted by the state, her suicide has a tragic flavour of its own. It followed a 'minor falling out at a banquet in honour of the fifteenth anniversary of the October Revolution. My father merely said to her: "Hey, you. Have a drink!" And she screamed: "Don't you dare talk to me that way!" And in front of everyone she got up and ran from the table.' The next morning, Nadezhda Sergeyevna Alliluyeva was found lying in a pool of blood beside her bed in the Kremlin apartment overlooking the Alexandrovsky Garden and the Troitsky Gates. A Walther pistol was in her hand. Alliluyeva, op. cit., p. 117 et seq.

Stalin. Stalin said that he had no better idea of what the NKVD was up to than Budenny, and that they might come for him next. Budenny said that he would shoot if they closed on him, to which Stalin replied: 'Go ahead, give it to them.'[17]

Mute, aggressively sycophantic or occasionally defiant, the vulnerable sat out the terror as it fed upon itself. The paranoia and fear were ubiquitous and constant, the violence of language and thought matching the events in the execution cellars and the camps. The half-mad reaction to the Tukhachevsky trial mingled in the press in June 1937 with more normal fare, the visit of a Basque football team to Moscow, the first flight by Soviet pilots from Moscow over the North Pole to America. 'Tremble, you scum!' screamed the workers of the Second Clinical Hospital. 'Their destruction is our sacred duty,' said Academician I. Orbeli, the normally cultured director of the Hermitage museum. Traditional Russian xenophobia ran high: 'The bloody Marlboroughs of fascism cannot set one foot on Soviet soil.'

Interrogation preceded confession and sentence. Most interrogations took place at night. The interrogators kept the same hours as Stalin himself, who would awaken late, eat his first meal 'at two or three in the afternoon'[18] and work into the early hours.

Starvation was a commonplace. So were beatings, with rubber truncheons, wooden mallets, small sandbags and the edge of rulers. Richard Ohola, a Finnish Red Guard who had been a company commander during the attack on the Kronstadt rebels, was lifted off the floor by pliers attached to the ends of his moustache and held like that for ten minutes. With 'bridling', or the 'swan dive', a long piece of towelling was put between the prisoner's jaws like a bridle. The ends were pulled back over his shoulders and tied to his heels so that he lay like a wheel, breaking his back.

Conditions bore no relation to Tsarist prisons. In the Kresty prison in 1938, the former Tsarist political prisoner Zelensky was whipped half naked. Afterwards he cried in his cell: 'My Tsarist interrogator didn't even dare address me rudely.'[19] The sense of helplessness was a particular horror to military inmates, trained to accept death but in the utterly different context of war. 'Death in battle is not frightening,' said a temporary survivor of the Soviet death cell, Filipp Mironov.[20] 'One moment and it is all over. But the consciousness of close, inevitable death is horrifying, when there is no hope, when you know that nothing can halt the approaching grave, when until the frightful moment there remains less and less time, and finally when they say to you, "Your pit is ready".'

Confession was a point of release, almost of privilege. 'The accused may not yet have known that he would be killed,' explained Jakub Berman, most of whose Polish communist colleagues died during the purges.[21] 'It was only a question of a trial, a public confession – and so often he agreed to perform a service for the Party if the Party demanded it ... because serving the Party was, for old communists, not just a goal in life but also an inner need.'

Inevitability was all and the discipline of the military mind accentuated it. The authority of Tukhachevsky, Yakir and Primakov in the Red army had been enormous. 'Many line commanders would have followed them with their regiments and divisions. They had only to call. But they didn't.'[22] Neither did Berman argue. 'I didn't try to justify what was happening. I accepted it as a tragic turn of events that involved the sacrifice of enormous numbers of people. I tried desperately to cling to the thought that you can't make omelettes without breaking eggs – not a profound saying but one that made its rounds among us.'[23]

The average period between arrest and sentence and transportation was three months. For those shot, by a pistol in the back of the neck, in a prison courtyard or an execution cell, the process was normally shorter. Sentences were based on Article 58 of the Criminal Code of 1926 which listed fourteen crimes against the state, 'failure to make a denunciation', 'intentionally careless execution' of duties, 'subversion of industry' (wrecking), suspicion of espionage and even 'contacts leading to suspicion of espionage'. Proof of an action was not necessary. Mere 'intention' was enough to convict.

'We draw no distinction between *intention* and the *crime* itself,' the Criminal Policy Institute had said in 1934, adding with a sneer: 'This is an instance of the superiority of Soviet legislation over bourgeois legislation.'[24] The most common sentences were death or ten years in a camp.

The Lubianka, a few yards from downtown Moscow, had a reception 'kennel' where three prisoners were stuffed into each square yard of space. There was no ventilation and the temperature rose to 40–50 degrees Centigrade. The prisoners squatted together half naked and got eczema from each other's sweat.[25] From prison, the prisoners were taken to goods yards and herded on freight trucks, the rusty, ochre-red wagons on the rattling wide-gauge tracks that give a swaying, clackety-clack, a permanent background noise, almost comforting, to the mute horrors of Soviet history.

The worst camps had been on the islands of the White Sea. By the 1930s the hutments supplying labour for the Baltic Sea to White Sea canal gained that title. Here, a survivor, D. P. Vitkovsky, recalled that: 'At the end of the workday there were corpses left on the work site. The snow powdered their faces ... At night the sledges went out and collected them. The drivers threw the corpses onto the sledges with a dull clonk.'[26] By the time the military were purged, the gold mines of Kolyma were the 'pole of cold and cruelty', more truly a 'supreme penalty' than execution.

It could take forty-seven days for a wagonload of sentenced officers to grind its way from European Russia to the transit camps for North-east Siberia outside Vladivostok and Nakhoda. There was no light, apart from cracks in the timber of the wagons, and little food. When they were let off the train, for a few minutes each day, guards ordered them to squat.

In the transit camps, the 'disappeared' met each other. 'I met Ushakov, the former commander of the 9th Division,' recalled General A. V. Gorbatov.[27] 'Ushakov had once been thought a man of culture, the best of the divisional commanders. Here he was the foreman in charge of camp kitchens [until] he was demoted and put on heavy physical labour.'

Kolyma lies at 70 degrees north on the East Siberian Sea. The NKVD had its own fleet of ships, their funnels painted blue and white to represent 'hope', to transport prisoners to a wild land where temperatures on the coast dropped to minus 50 degrees Centigrade in winter, and in the interior to minus 70 degrees Centigrade. In the summer of 1937 Stalin criticized the 'coddling' of prisoners at a meeting of the Central Committee. The following winter, fur clothing was banned, felt boots were replaced by canvas shoes and many froze to death. Others died in the gold mines of pneumonia and meningitis. Their lungs were destroyed by ammonal blasting and by toiling with wheelbarrows from areas where the frozen sand was being softened with steam heat to spoil tips where the temperature was minus 50 degrees Centigrade. General I. S. Karpunich-Braven described men removing frozen earth and rock in these temperatures, 'transporting it on sledges to which were harnessed four prisoners, beaten as they hauled'.

In the language of the zeks, the convicts, those who were too exhausted to live were dokhodyagas, 'goners'. A man loading a barrow would sink to the ground, blood would gush from his mouth, and it was over. Work stopped only at minus 60 degrees Centigrade, and even then woodcutting continued. Rock had to be dynamited for the graves. Near starvation added to the cold. General Karpunich-Braven described how prisoners 'stood on all fours, growling and rooting about' in the filthy garbage near the tents and, especially near the kitchens, looking for anything remotely edible and devouring it on the spot. 'They had become semi-idiots whom no amount of beating could drive from the refuse heaps.'[28] The katorzhniki, those on special forced labour, worked in special camps, in chains, without blankets or mattresses.

Troikas, the three-man NKVD courts, dealt with malingerers. At the Serpantinka death camp, between thirty and fifty zeks a day were shot. Sometimes tractor engines were run to hide the screams, and the corpses were dragged away on motorized sledges. Other zeks were led to a trench and shot in the ear or the back of the neck. About 26,000 were shot at Serpantinka in 1938, a year when 40,000 were executed in the northern camps as a whole, and five to ten times that number died of cold, hunger and overwork. The poet Yevtushenko demanded for the nameless dead in 1987:

> Free them with pickaxes, now frozen sculptures, from Siberian graves;
> And then with woodman's gloves, near-frozen, almost marble,
> Go rapping at all the doors where they have been forgotten.

No comparison can be made with the exile suffered by Stalin, or Trotsky and Lenin, under the Tsars. Not in numbers, let alone in treatment. From 1938 there were more prisoners in Kolyma, probably twice as many, as the maximum number held in Tsarist prisons of all types in the whole of Russia. The highest number recorded under the Tsars was 183,949 in 1912. More prisoners were executed in the Serpantinka camp than the total number of executions throughout the Russian Empire in the last century of Russian rule. The official *Small Soviet Encyclopaedia* gives 94 executions between 1866 and 1900, and a total of 14,000 in the final half century of Tsardom. In this period some 4,000 assassinations were carried out by the revolutionary left. During the Stalinist age, there was just one assassination, of Kirov, and that may have been ordered by Stalin himself.[29] Only one comparison can be made with the treatment of Red army officers under Stalin. It is the fate of those who were soon to be taken prisoner by the Germans.

Some Red army men survived the camps.

The future Marshal Rokossovky, who was subjected to two mock executions, was the best known of about four thousand officers who were released in 1940 from imprisonment or the camps to take up command in the Red army.[30] With nine missing teeth and three broken ribs as a reminder, he took over command of a mechanized corps a few months after being freed.

Another future Marshal, Meretskov, was released in even more bizarre circumstances. He had been broken by the NKVD and forced to sign a confession admitting that he was a British agent. Beria told Khrushchev that he had summoned Meretskov from prison to his office and told him that what was written in his confession was nonsense. Meretskov looked forlornly at the NKVD chief and said: 'I've got nothing more to say. You have a confession written in my own handwriting. I don't know why you're interrogating me again.'

Beria told him: 'Go back to your cell and think it over. Sleep on it.'

The next day, Beria asked him: 'Well, have you thought it over?'

Beria described Meretskov as 'weeping and thanking me, saying. "How could I be a spy? I'm a good Russian. I love my people. I believe in my people." ' At which, the NKVD 'let him out of jail, dressed him in a general's uniform, and off he went to be a commander at the Front.'[31]

The most extraordinary *zeks* were the 'prisoner specialists', condemned military engineers and designers, brought to the Red army proving grounds under heavy escort to perfect the weapon systems that kept their tormentors in power. 'Not all valuable specialists were sent to dig gold in Kolyma or to build brushwood roads in the swamps of Siberia,' Colonel Starinov recalled.* 'Some were permitted to work in prison too. These "lucky ones" worked and perfected their projects in solitary cells, cut off from the world.' It was an uneasy life, since any design setback could be labelled 'sabotage', with Kolyma beckoning.

In 1939 a prisoner and his guards arrived at Starinov's proving ground. The prisoner was housed in a small forest clearing surrounded by a high double barbed-wire fence. Here the convict, V. M. Petliakov, designed and tested the Pe-2 dive bomber, the Soviet answer to the Stuka.

9

THE BENEFICIARIES

Awesome in their sweep, the purges were enough to convince both Hitler and the Western Allies that the Red army was all but finished as a fighting force. The impact is seen in the miniature of a graduate from the Frunze academy arriving to take up a new staff appointment with a rifle division.

S. S. Biriuzov was assigned to the 30th Irkutsk Red-Banner Division where a 'stupefying picture' unfolded before him. He was posted to division headquarters at Dnepropetrovsk. He was told on arrival at the railway station that the division had no leadership 'strictly speaking'. The commanding officer, the political officers, the chief of staff and the service chiefs had all been arrested. The driver who picked him up at the station said: 'In corps headquarters, every last chief from the lowest to highest was swept out. What bastards these enemies of the people are! They had everything in their control.'

Biriuzov, in a 'cold sweat', asked him: 'Who commands the division, then?' 'Nobody,' the driver answered. 'Except the chief of the first section. Major Etsov is still kicking.'

An entire rifle division had been purged down to the rank of major. 'It

* An artillery officer, Starinov was appointed director of a major Red army experimental proving ground. Bialer, op. cit., p. 75 et seq.

was,' Biriuzov said with understatement, 'a situation which defied the imagination.' And, something that places an equal strain on the imagination, Biriuzov did not turn with revulsion against the whole concept of purges. As a general and Soviet representative on the Allied Control Commission in Bulgaria after the war, he oversaw a purge in the Bulgarian army and was present in Sofia when opposition leaders were hanged in 1947 after a series of show trials. Purges remain in the continuity of the Red army to the present day, unbroken by any formal, real rejection.

Even Voroshilov was astonished at the turnover of officers caused by the terror. He complained at a meeting of senior corps commissars in August 1938: 'You are all new, unfamiliar faces!' One third of the total officer corps of the Red army was shot, imprisoned or sent to labour camps. The carnage at the top, where arrest was most likely to lead to execution, was far worse.

For the second time in twenty years, Russia was faced with rebuilding an officer corps. Three of the five Soviet marshals, the post created with such apparent generosity by Stalin barely two years before, were shot. All eleven deputy people's commissars of defence and thirteen out of fifteen generals of the army received '8 grammes of lead in the back of the head'. The commander of the Red artillery, traditionally the finest of Russian arms, was liquidated. All those commanding military districts in May 1937 were shot or disappeared. Out of 85 corps commanders, 57 disappeared within a year. Of 406 brigade commanders, 220 were dead by the autumn of 1938 and others were to follow them. Five of the 80 members of the higher military council survived.

In all, 93 per cent of those at lieutenant-general level or above were shot. Between major general and colonel, the attrition rate was 58.5 per cent.[1] The general staffs of the regions and of armies, corps and divisions were, as the phrase went, 'cleaned out'. There were rather more than 100,000 officers on active duty in the Red army in 1937 and 1938. The number of those purged may have reached 50,000. By contrast, in Hitler's purge early in 1938, sixteen generals were dismissed, but neither imprisoned nor shot, and forty-four others were transferred to new posts.

The purges affected all arms of the services. Alksnis and A. I. Sedyakin, the head of air defence, were merely the most senior air force officers to be shot. The navy lost more senior officers than the army. The commander in chief, Admiral Orlov, was shot. Admiral Muklevich, the highest-ranking officer and the main backer of the 'new school' of a small defensive navy focusing on submarines, mine-laying and aircraft, was shot. Only one of the four fleet commanders, Admiral Viktorov, in the Pacific, escaped death. He probably owed his life to his sympathy with Stalin's preference for an ocean-going fleet over the Muklevich school of defence. The fleet admirals commanding in the Black Sea, White Sea and Baltic[2] were liquidated along with the three senior men at the naval academy and the former chief of the naval staff. In addition, 'many captains of ships and shore bases, and hundreds or possibly thousands of officers of lower rank simply disappeared, fate unknown'.[3]

The bulk of the killings took place in 1937 and 1938. The Tukhachevsky trial marked the beginning of the most vicious phase. They did not end with the squalid death of Ezhov in December 1939.* The last known peacetime execution of a senior officer took place in June 1941, only two weeks before the German invasion, when the new head of the air force, General Shmushkevich, was shot.

The deterioration in morale, expertise and stability was shattering. By the spring of 1940 the Red army was riddled with command vacancies which the military schools could not fill. The level of training was dangerously low. Two thirds of company-level officers had only a five-month course for junior lieutenants behind them. At the time of *Barbarossa*, the German invasion, only 7 per cent of Red army officers had had any higher military education and 37 per cent had not even completed intermediate training.[4]

It can be said that the purge was Russian in its soul, that the oppression and its acceptance had been bred by the Hordes and by the Tsars. Or the events can be said to be revolutionary. Stalin seems to share two habits common to revolutionary leaders, the nervous desire to finish off the old system root and branch, under the easy slogan of a new society, and the need to kill or imprison any competitors riding in the same bandwagon. Men were executed for their connections with the Whites, and with the Trotskyites, and sometimes, neatly, for both: as Mekhlis advertised it in April 1938, this was 'the final cleansing of hostile filth'.

Yet it was not Russian. The past slaughter in the hamlets of Rus and the killings still three years off in European Russia were the result of Mongol and German invasion. No Russian persecution ever approached Stalin's scale. Never have the officers of an undefeated and unrebellious army been thus slaughtered in their own country and at a time of supposed peace. Neither was it revolution, in the sense that a Jacobin or an Iranian mullah would recognize. To first hang aristocrats and the Shah's 'puppets', and then move on to eliminate rivals, Girondins or *mujaheddin*, is familiar

---

* In March 1939 Stalin had called him a 'fool'. In July of that year L. P. Beria was appointed as his deputy. On 9 November Ezhov carried out what may have been the last execution he attended to personally. He shot Marshal Blucher in his office. He was later taken to his dacha under house arrest where he spent most of the time still allotted to him drinking. At the beginning of December the guards were told to leave the dacha and other NKVD men came to arrest him. Ezhov was charged, apparently for deceiving the Party and the people, tortured, a 'confession' extracted, and shot in the last days of 1939. Rappoport and Alexeev, op. cit., p. 414, note 36.

ground. But the interval between the two is brief, three years at most. In Russia, sixteen years had passed since the civil war.

Those who died were not an ethnic minority, political rivals or dangerous equals, as the Jews, Communists and Roehm's slaughtered Brown Shirts were in Germany. They were aircraft designers, tank commanders, pen pushers, doctors, a hero of long-distance aviation, a keeper of cavalry horses in Central Asia, a navigator on an icebreaker, an ex-cook who was the head of army catering on the Pacific coast, the conductor of an army band.

To those who survived, particularly young officers, the terror led to opportunity and promotion on a colossal scale. In war, deaths in action speed promotion but a logjam develops at the level of lieutenant colonel and above. The purges opened the heights of the profession.

The sense of elation and young blood helped the Red army to survive the shock of the slaughter. Konstantin Rokossovsky, returning to command his mechanized corps in 1940, found officers around him who 'had risen to heights they had never dreamt of'. They owed their position and their loyalty to Stalin in a way that the older men who had gone had not. This applied equally to civilians, for the killings had embraced the entire Soviet elite. Only two of the hundred and fifty delegates who had attended the 17th Party Congress from Leningrad survived.

The purges were the launching pad for those who were to rule Russia after Stalin's death. Georgy Malenkov, the senior figure in the Soviet Union between 1953 and 1956, was the chief purger in White Russia and Armenia. Khrushchev, who dominated the country between 1956 and 1964, was involved in the purges in both Moscow and the Ukraine. An unknown director of a textile factory at the start of the purges, Alexei Kosygin was deputy prime minister of the Russian Republic in three years. In the 1970s he became Soviet premier. Leonid Brezhnev rose in thirty months from junior engineer in a metal-working plant to party overlord of a province. At thirty-three he was party secretary of a major industrial region in the Ukraine. His successor as Soviet leader, Andropov, had become first secretary of the communist youth organization in the Karelo-Finnish republic at twenty-six. And his successor, Chernenko, was thirty when he became secretary of the party committee in Krasnoyarsk, an area as big as the British Isles, in 1940. Dead men's shoes had lifts in the heels. Gorbachev is the first Soviet leader to be too young to have needed them.

In the army Georgy Zhukov, a division commander, became chief of the Soviet General Staff in three years. In six months, Brigade Commander Kriukov rose from command of a railway regiment to chief of military communications for the entire Red army. In May 1937 Pavel Rychagov was a test pilot and the captain of his unit hockey team. In April 1940 he had advanced six ranks to become head of the air force.[5]

In the navy, Admiral N. G. Kuznetsov went from assistant commander of a cruiser to head of the Red navy in three years. He has described[6] how he was summoned from a posting in Vladivostok to Moscow in March 1939 for the party congress. Unexpectedly, Stalin told him to make a speech to the congress, which he did, 'trying with all my strength to master my emotion'. Sleeping in a Moscow hotel room after the speech, he was woken late at night and taken to the Kremlin by car. Stalin was looked at him 'fixedly', tapping his pipe on the rim of an ashtray. The dictator would break Herzegovina Flor cigarettes in two, carefully remove the paper and tamp the tobacco into his English-made Dunhill pipe. Stalin asked how he would feel about working in Moscow. 'I haven't thought about it . . .' said Kuznetsov.

He was taken back to his hotel at 3 a.m. The same day, he received the official red envelope containing his appointment as first deputy commissar of the navy. Kuznetsov set up a brief trip back to the Soviet Far East. On his return in April, he was again summoned to the Kremlin. Another red package awaited him. He had become commissar of the navy in place of a former commander of NKVD frontier units who had bizarrely held the post after his predecessor had been shot.

'I read the document with a mixture of joy and anxiety,' Kuznetsov said. He was thirty-seven years old. 'Too fast an elevation is dangerous for a man. That applies not only to skindivers and pilots. Many dangers lurk in too fast a rise up the service ladder.'[7]

The aircraft designer A. S. Yakovlev was thirty-five when his summons to the Kremlin came over the special telephone line in January 1940. Stalin was on the line: 'Are you very busy? Would it be possible for you to come here immediately?' Yakovlev was in the Kremlin in fifteen minutes. Stalin told him that the commissar of the aviation industry, M. M. Kaganovich, had failed in his duties and was being replaced. Kaganovich was, in fact, to disappear without trace. 'Astonished, prepared for anything but such a proposal', Yakovlev was told of his appointment as deputy commissar. Yakovlev tried to turn the job down but Stalin was macabrely jovial. 'Are you a Communist? Do you acknowledge party discipline?' he asked. Yakovlev said that he would have to obey, in the ultimate, but that this would be 'coercion'.

'We are not afraid of coercion,' said Stalin, bursting into laughter. 'Sometimes, coercion is necessary. Without coercion, there would have been no revolution. After all, coercion is the midwife of revolution.'[8] Yakovlev accepted the post.[9]

The coerced, the new officers and the survivors were about to be tested.

Whilst the Red army underwent its terror, Europe slid towards war as Hitler destroyed the post-1918 peace settlement. This had left a 'middle zone' of small states between the temporarily prostrate Russian and German giants. Poland, Czechoslovakia, Finland, Estonia, Latvia and Lithuania had not existed in the pre-1914 imperial order. They were bitterly resented by both Russians and Germans and were riddled with internal cross-hatreds.

Poland was a semi-dictatorship under Marshal Pilsudski, Rumania and Yugoslavia royalist dictatorships. Hungary languished under Admiral Horthy, gutted, dismembered and humiliated at Versailles, with a shabby anti-Semitic oligarchy of landowners, officers, functionaries and financiers.[1] A brief experiment in peasant democracy in Bulgaria had ended in a coup. Czechoslovakia was a democracy but lacked strength as the arch of the post-Habsburg settlement. Czechs numbered only a fraction over half of a population that was 23.4 per cent German and had numbers of resentful Hungarians and Poles. The Germans and Hungarians called it a *Saisonstaat*, a country which existed only through an aberration in the political climate, a hothouse that would wither in the harshness of the natural world. It depended for its security on distant Great Power support from France and Britain.

The British had drifted into appeasing Hitler by 1935, accepting a restoration of German naval strength to 35 per cent of their own. In 1936 Hitler remilitarized the Rhineland, laid the basis of the Axis with Italy and signed an anti-Comintern Pact. In February 1938 the British foreign minister Anthony Eden resigned over appeasement. A month later, Hitler incorporated Austria into the Reich in the *Anschluss*.

Czechoslovakia was next. The Sudeten Germans demanded autonomy in the spring of 1938. A Soviet suggestion in March, that the British, French and Americans should confer with the Russians to prevent future aggression, foundered on appeasement and suspicion of the Soviets. Hitler demanded the annexation of the Sudeten territories in September, threatening to use force if this 'final territorial claim' was not settled. The Russians might have been willing to stand by their treaty obligations to Czechoslovakia. This was dependent on French action, which itself depended on the British. In this circle of indecision, appeasement won. At Munich on 29 September 1938, Britain and France agreed to the German takeover of the Sudetenland.

Though President Beneš resigned in protest, the Czechs accepted the diktat and the transfer of a population of 3.6 million within ten days. The Poles also feasted on the Czechs, as the Germans and Russians were soon to feast on them. On 2 October Poland seized the Teschen region, gaining 80,000 Poles and 120,000 Czechs, Slovaks and Germans in the process. The Hungarians joined in a month later, regaining 100,000 of their own and acquiring 300,000 Slovaks, Germans and Rumanians in a bargain struck with Hitler and Mussolini. Munich was a tocsin for the world. For Central Europe, it was a death ride marked by cannibalism.

With Czechoslovakia a Nazi 'protectorate', Hitler went at Poland. In March 1939 he demanded the return of the Free City of Danzig to the Reich. In April he denounced the German–Polish non-aggression pact which the Poles, more worried by their disputes with Russia than with Germany, had signed in 1934. By May, Winston Churchill was asking: 'If we are ready to be an ally of Russia in time of war, why should we shrink from becoming an ally of Russia now, when we might by that very fact prevent the breaking out of war?'

Munich had already sapped cooperation between the West and Russia, and Nazi–Communist links were becoming closer. Britain and France extended a guarantee to Poland in April, which could only be effective in harmony with Russia. Long negotiations with the Russians during the spring and summer failed, the Soviets accurately complaining that, whereas the British and French Premiers had attended Hitler at Munich, they had sent Stalin no more than an 'Admiral Nobody and a General Inconnu'.

A Nazi–Soviet pact was signed by the German foreign minister, Joachim von Ribbentrop, and the Soviet foreign affairs commissar, Vyacheslav Molotov, in Moscow on 23 August 1939. On 1 September, Hitler invaded Poland.

A secret protocol to the pact gave the Kremlin an immense prize in the return of territories lost during the revolution. For the simple price of remaining neutral over the war in the West, the Germans permitted the Soviets to reabsorb eastern Poland. Together with the Baltic States[2] and parts of Rumania annexed without firing a shot in June 1940, about twenty million people in a slice from the Baltic to the Black Sea became Soviet subjects.

Polish resistance had been crushed by the Germans and the Polish army was already beaten by the time the Red army began concentrating along the border on 15 September 1939. It was emphasized that there should be no fighting against German troops. 'We were told that we were not conquerors, but only liberators and that an honourable task had been allotted to us,' said Colonel G. I. Antonov.[3] 'To free our own class brothers

who were suffering under the yoke of Polish landowners and capitalists.'
Mechanized cavalry moved over the frontier at dawn on 17 September.
There was little resistance by the Polish frontier troops, since the mass of
Polish forces had been sent to the Western front against the Germans. By
nightfall, Red units had penetrated sixty miles with light casualties.

The invasion became a shopping spree as the Russians liberated the
contents of Polish shops. The short jackets of the Russian troops, with
their cotton wool linings, bulged with parcels. 'When we had the chance
to slip into a shop without being observed we bought everything, as much
as our money could buy – watches, clothes and shoes,' said Antonov. 'It
was curious to watch some combatant officer running out from a shop,
pushing his purchases under his shirt, trying to catch up with his unit.'

Though Polish resistance stiffened on the second day, the Russians
reached the demarcation line with the Wehrmacht by 21 September. There
were a few incidents. A 'misunderstanding' between a Russian cavalry
squadron and a German infantry company resulted in two dead Soviet
troopers and a cavalry charge with drawn sabres that left fifteen Germans
dead. A German major and a Soviet colonel arrived, 'apologized, shook
hands and, considering the incident as having been due to a misunderstanding, departed'.

The territory taken by the Red army was immediately purged. 'Polish
citizens were arrested nightly, in thousands and immediately transported
to the East,' wrote Antonov. 'People woke in the morning to find that
their neighbours had disappeared ... The officials of the NKVD worked
skilfully, efficiently and silently.' Polish officers taken prisoner were sent
to camps in the Soviet Union.

Eastern Poland was 'openly and quickly pauperized'. Carpets, pictures,
furniture and china were crammed on Russian-bound railway wagons and
and lorries. 'Closed cooperative stores' appeared to serve the Red army,
and government and party officials. They were barred to the general
population. Leaflets were scattered at night: 'You deprived us of bread,
sugar and meat and have given us prisons and concentration camps, and
German friendship.' Elections were held to the new Supreme Council of
the Polish Socialist Soviet Republic. Cossacks were stationed near the
voting booths to ensure that 99.8 per cent voted for Stalin.

The ease with which Poland was dismembered strengthened ambitions
in the Kremlin, already strong after successes against the Japanese in the
Far East. The future Marshal Zhukov had won a series of bloody clashes
against the Japanese Kwantung army in August 1939 at Khalkin-Gol on
the Mongolian–Chinese border.

Finland was next. The Russians were worried by its closeness to Leningrad
and Kronstadt. They wanted the Bjorko region and its islands ceded to

them, to place Leningrad beyond Finnish artillery range, and a lease on the Hangoe peninsula near Helsinki for a base capable of blocking German access to the Gulf of Finland. In return, the Kremlin proposed ceding the Finns a wooded slice of country north-west of the Onega Lake.

Feelers in 1938 became demands after the seizure of eastern Poland. The Finnish Marshal Mannerheim felt it militarily necessary to accept but national pride ran against a deal. The Soviets manufactured a 'provocation' on 26 November 1939, claiming that Finnish artillery had fired on a Russian border village. Four days later, the Red army attacked with overwhelming force, preparation and choice of time. The Russians still claim that the 'Winter War' was 'provoked by the White Finns'.

The attacking formations were concentrated on the Karelian isthmus, where twelve rifle divisions, an armoured corps and several armoured brigades with massed artillery support were grouped into the 7th Army. They were intended to overrun the Finnish frontier fortifications, the Mannerheim Line, and thrust up via Viipuri to Helsinki. A second Red Army, the 8th, with seven rifle divisions and an armoured brigade, attacked north of Lake Lagoda along the exposed flank of the main Finnish forces on the Karelian isthmus. The 9th Army with five rifle divisions was to advance towards the northern part of the Gulf of Bothnia to cut land communications between Finland and Sweden. Yet another Army, the 14th with two rifle divisions, was ordered to occupy the Petsamo region to foil any foreign intervention via the Arctic Sea.

The Finns should not have lasted a fortnight. Indeed, General N. N. Voronov, the senior artillery officer in the Red army, was told that 'between ten and twelve days' had been allotted for the operation. The Russians rapidly had to tear up their timetable. On the Isthmus, Voronov records,[4] 'our forces encountered for the first time deep zones of anti-tank obstacles, granite posts, anti-tank ditches and mighty log barriers. Tanks had difficulty pushing through. Finnish infantry, well adapted to the terrain, showered our troops with a hail of lead.' Despite committing 1,000 tanks, with air and artillery support, the Red army failed to break through the Mannerheim Line.

The 8th Army, operating north of Lake Ladoga against weak Finnish forces, made better gains. The central group of the 9th Army penetrated to Suomussalmi after its two divisions linked up in mid-December after moving through the frontier zone. Mannerheim was forced to call on scant reserves, scraping together a division, the 9th. Only one of its regiments contained regular army troops, although all its regimental commanders, and the divisional commander Colonel Hjalmar Siilasvuo, were veterans of a *Jäger* volunteer battalion that had fought with the Germans against the Russians in the First World War.

The 44th Motorized Infantry Division of the Soviet 9th Army had been
sent from Ukhta towards the Bothnian port of Oulu to cut Finland in half
at its narrow waist. The division was intended to help the 163rd Infantry
Division which had been checked at the hamlet of Suomussalmi, about
forty kilometres from the Soviet border.

The battle area lay 160 kilometres south of the Arctic Circle. Daylight
is limited to five hours in December. Towards the end of that month in
1939, the snow was a metre deep and temperatures fell to minus 40 degrees
Centigrade.[5] Colonel Siilasvuo's Finnish division numbered only 11,500
men. On 27 December he counter-attacked the Soviet 163rd Division and
shattered it. By New Year's Eve, its survivors were fleeing back to the
frontier in disorder.

The Soviet 44th Division was strung out as it advanced to help the
163rd, its troops Ukrainians who had no experience of the northern forests
and the cold. Many froze to death in snow holes or in lean-tos made with
branches in ditches. Finnish patrols concentrated on destroying the Russian
field kitchens.

The first effort to cut up the 44th came on New Year's night. A Finnish
battalion overran the most advanced elements of the 44th, capturing an
artillery battalion and establishing a road block of mines and felled trees
that cut off the Russian spearhead. At dawn, when the Russians counter-
attacked with tanks and infantry, the Finns brought up anti-tank guns on
sledges. They destroyed seven tanks in fifteen minutes.

A second attack was launched by Colonel Siilasvuo on 5 January. The
decisive battles took place from before dawn the following day, the Finns
advancing on skis against Russians floundering in snowdrifts. The 44th
degenerated into bands of stragglers. Late that evening Commander Vinogradov, the divisional commander, authorized those who could escape to
do so. A final attempt to rescue the 44th was beaten off during the morning
darkness on 7 January. The last organized resistance came from bunkers
by a frozen lake which were overrun by a Finnish company. Vinogradov
escaped across the border in a tank, later to be shot on orders from Moscow.
Snow shrouded the Russian dead and dying. The Finns estimated Russian
losses at 22,500 men. Their own were 2,700.

Mass infantry attacks 'presented the Finnish machinegunners with
such persistent and generous targets'[6] that the Red army was forced to
reorganize its operational command. Marshal Mannerheim found 'signs
of inertia' amongst the higher ranks of his enemy. 'The Russians based
their art of war on the weight of material, and were clumsy, ruthless and
extravagant.'[7] The purges had taken their toll.

The Russians used January for preparation. Infantry sledges and electric
digging machines were moved up to the front. Fresh divisions were given
time to get used to the extreme conditions. Artillery was sighted on Finnish

firepoints instead of generalized bombardment. Clearer skies favoured Soviet reconnaissance flights.

The second Soviet assault started in February. The Finns, never more than 200,000 strong, could not resist the pressure of 1.2 million men, five Armies, supported by 3,000 aircraft and an overwhelming weight of armour. Although the French and British considered sending an expeditionary force to help the Finns, they did not have time to dispatch one.[8] Voronov witnessed from a forward observation post the 'hurricane of our bombs and shells' descend on Finnish positions. Nevertheless, the Kremlin was so reluctant to believe the change in fortune that Voronov had to repeat his news of the advance three times during a telephone call to Moscow.

The Finnish forces on the Isthmus were slowly overrun. Red army units crossed the ice of Viipuri Bay despite bombing and strafing attacks by the remaining Finnish bombers. A Soviet bridgehead was taken close to Viipuri and reinforced by columns of tanks, infantry and sledges crossing the ice. On 3 March 1940 Finland sued for peace.

Dangerous conclusions were drawn from the poor Soviet performance in the Winter War.

The Russians, worried by their initial failures, made too much of the eventual storming of the Mannerheim Line. It became an operational model where troops were taught to overcome enemy defences by a build-up of supplies and the patient gnawing through of breaches. 'We ceased to deal seriously with mobile combat and with the struggle against highly mobile mechanized units of great striking and firing power,' complained Biriuzov.[9] 'We relegated to oblivion the fundamentals of combat-in-depth tactics and of combined arms manoeuvres which had been widespread before the Finnish campaign.' It was the Germans who, in the Tukhachevsky spirit, were about to let loose mass air attacks, tank breakthroughs and encirclements on the British and French armies in the West. The Russians were left with the ponderous spirit of the Mannerheim Line. 'We had to retrain ourselves under [German] fire,' Biriuzov wrote bitterly.

Others drew a false picture of Soviet weakness, Churchill speaking openly of the 'military incapacity of the Red army and Red air force'. More ominous was the German view. A General Staff evaluation of the Red army stated: 'In quantity a gigantic military instrument ... Organization, equipment and means of leadership unsatisfactory ... Communication system bad, transportation system bad, no personalities.' The assessment concluded: 'Fighting qualities of the troops in a *heavy* fight, dubious. The Russian "mass" is *no* match for an army with modern equipment and superior leadership.' Neither did the Germans gain respect for Russian ability in winter warfare.

This sense of contented superiority, reinforced by the overrunning of France and the Low Countries in the early summer of 1940, led to *Barbarossa*.

Barbarossa

The German War

II

'CAN WE OPEN FIRE?'

In the border fortress town of Brest, the Russians spent the afternoon of Saturday 21 June 1941 drilling to the music of a military band. No extra guards were posted to check on the German positions on the other side of the river Bug. At the Minsk Officers' Club, Red army officers spent a relaxed evening watching the popular comedy *The Wedding at Malinkovka*. In Moscow, Stalin gave orders that a German deserter, who had crossed the lines to warn of an impending attack within hours, should be shot forthwith for false provocation. Soviet frontier guards passed the Berlin–Moscow express through to Brest shortly after midnight.[1]

There was more urgency on the German side of the border running through dismembered Poland.

Helmut Pabst, a signals NCO with the German 9th Army, spent the evening digging into a potato field near the banks of the Bug. General Heinz Guderian, commander of a German panzer group in Pabst's sector, hurried his way to an observation tower nine miles north-west of the Brest fortress. Hitler was in his *Wolfsschanze*, the wolf's lair headquarters in East Prussia, writing to Mussolini of feeling 'spiritually free' now that the 'mental agonies' of the unnatural partnership with the Soviet Union were about to end.

Thirty minutes after midnight on Sunday 22 June a reluctant Stalin was persuaded to authorize a vague warning of a 'possible surprise attack' across the immense border stretching from the Baltic flatlands to the Carpathians. The spy Richard Sorge, who had access to the secrets of the German embassy in Tokyo, had warned of this as early as April.

The British added their warning of 'an early military attack on Russia' on 13 June. On 18 June a German deserter who had struck an officer whilst drunk fled to the Russian lines. He was interrogated by General Fediuninsky on the frontier, a 'tall, rather ungainly fellow' whose 'big, red hands trembled perceptibly' as he told the general that Hitler would attack along the whole length of the front at 4 a.m. on 22 June. 'At 5 a.m. you can have me shot if I have lied to you,' he said.[2] Soviet forward units reported that the Germans opposite them appeared to be taking their start-up positions. Tank engines were heard at night and German reconnaissance aircraft were violating Soviet air space in groups of twenty.

Stalin was still anxious to give Hitler the benefit of any doubts. He stressed that the Red army should 'not give way to provocative actions of any kind'.

It was anyway too late. Half an hour later, the German army commands in the East transmitted their call-signs confirming their full and final readiness. The assault troops went forward to their start-lines. German troops were already in Brest, having been smuggled in under loads of gravel in railway wagons on Saturday. The telephone lines to the fortress had been cut.

Shortly after 3 a.m. a Soviet steamer was shelled by German torpedo boats off Gotland in the Baltic. In the Black Sea, 2,000 kilometres to the south, German aircraft dropped parachute mines into the harbour at Sevastopol, guided by lit Russian navigation marks. Other Luftwaffe bombers were making high-altitude approaches to Soviet airfields where fighters remained neatly lined up on the ground. At 3.15 a.m., in the pre-dawn dark, the land forces joined in. Pabst wrote: 'The first salvo! At the same moment everything sprang to life. Firing along the whole front – infantry guns, mortars. The Russian watch-towers vanished in a flash. In file and in line, the infantry swarmed forward. Bog, ditches; boots full of water and mud. Ahead of us the barrage crept forward from line to line. Flame-throwers advanced against the strong-points. The fire of machine-guns, and the high-pitched whip of rifle bullets.'[3]

Along a front of 1,600 kilometres, 3,200,000 Germans drove to the east in 148 divisions, in 3,350 tanks and in the 2,000 aircraft of three air fleets. They had 7,184 artillery pieces, 600,000 trucks, many looted from France, and as many horses. They were backed by Rumanians and soon by Hungarians, Slovaks, Italians and Spaniards.[4]

On the Soviet side of the frontier was massed 54 per cent of the strength of the Red army, 170 divisions. There were 56 divisions and 2 brigades in the first echelon, deployed to a depth of 56 kilometres. The second echelon was at a depth of 56 to 96 kilometres and reserves were held up to 380 kilometres back from the frontier.

Though the Russians still maintain that they were outnumbered by the Germans, the Red army on the frontier had at least the same strength in infantry. The Germans were numerically inferior by seven to one in tanks and by four to one in aircraft. They relied entirely on superior quality of men and machines and on the shock effect of *Blitzkrieg*.

Hitler thought that massive Russian losses in the first few weeks would cause the Soviet Union to collapse from within. The pessimists among the Germans realized that their front would soon stretch the 2,100 kilometres from northern Finland to the Black Sea. They anticipated that they might be forced to penetrate to Gorki, 400 kilometres east of Moscow and 1,600 kilometres from their start-lines, before the Russians would capitulate. As it was, they achieved a similar depth at Stalingrad. At that point their front was 3,200 kilometres wide.*

* To give some idea of scale, the penetration was equivalent to getting to Minneapolis from New York, and the 22 June front would have extended from Minneapolis to the

The Germans were divided into three army groups, each under a field marshal. Army Group North was to attack from East Prussia through the Baltic states towards Leningrad under von Leeb. The more powerful Centre Group under Bock was to move along the Moscow highway from the Warsaw staging area to Minsk and Smolensk. Army Group South under Rundstedt was to drive into the Ukraine and the Caucasus with Kiev and the Dnieper as its targets.

As in Poland and France, the seventeen panzer divisions were split from the infantry and concentrated in four independent groups under brilliant, driving commanders, Kleist with 1st Panzer in the South, Guderian and Hoth with 2nd and 3rd in the Centre and Hoeppner with 4th Panzer in the North.[5] Hitler's Directive said: 'The mass of the Russian army in western Russia is to be destroyed in daring operations by driving four deep wedges with tanks, and the retreat of the enemy's battle-ready forces into the wide spaces of Russia is to be prevented.' The panzer groups were to penetrate the flanks of Russian forces marked down for liquidation and then wheel inwards to cut them off from their supply routes and paralyse their commands. German infantry would thrust in on the enemy flanks at the same time to achieve an inner encirclement.

Even before the artillery had started, the Germans in the Centre sector had seized vital bridges across the Bug. Russian frontier guards were lured from their positions by German shouts and machinegunned as they moved forward. German assault troops shot down the guards on the railway bridge across the river at Brest and ripped out the demolition charges from the central span.

The lead tanks of Guderian's 2nd *Panzergruppe*, waterproofed for the cancelled invasion of England, had forded the Bug by 4.45 a.m. In the weird, post-purge atmosphere of the Red army, fear replacing initiative, Russian officers at all levels were asking plaintively: 'Can we open fire?' By then, the German ambassador in Moscow, von Schulenburg, had delivered the German declaration of war to Molotov. Stalin, informed of it, 'sank down into his chair and lost himself in thought'. Two hours later Guderian crossed the Bug in a rubber assault boat.

As the blows of combined arms, tanks, artillery, aircraft, slammed into the body of the Red army, its head jerked in a reflex action. German radio operators caught repeated appeals, not for help, but for orders from Moscow. 'We are being fired on, what shall we do?' One reply was: 'You must be insane. And why is your signal not in code?'[6]

General Boldin in Minsk, the next major point on Guderian's itinerary,

---

Gulf of Mexico. The eventual front would stretch from New York to Mexico City. In European terms, the original front was the equivalent of London to the Algerian coast, later swelling from London almost to Timbuctou in Mali.

reported that the Luftwaffe was strafing troops and civilians well behind the frontier. Marshal Timoshenko, the defence commissar, telephoned him from Moscow: 'Comrade Boldin, remember that no action is to be taken against the Germans without our knowledge ... Comrade Stalin has forbidden to open artillery fire against the Germans.'

'How is it possible?' Boldin yelled into the receiver. 'Our troops are in full retreat. Whole towns are in flames, people are being killed all over the place ...'

'No,' said Timoshenko.[7]

Moscow Radio was broadcasting keep-fit exercises, the Young Pioneers' reveille and news of the weather and the good prospects for the harvest. Colonel Starinov was in the 4th Army HQ at Kobrin near Brest. It had just been bombed. 'Thick black pillars of smoke billowed up,' he said. 'A newly felled tree lay across the street. Part of the HQ building was in ruins. Somewhere a high-pitched, hysterical female voice was crying out a desperate, inconsolable "Aaaaaa!"'[8] Starinov heard the radio speak of German bombing raids, on cities in Scotland.

On a hot, sultry morning in Berlin, with crowds getting ready to leave the city to swim in the Wannsee, the staff of the Soviet embassy listened in similar disbelief as the news was followed by jolly folk music. It was already five hours since, blinded by spotlights and flashbulbs, the Soviet ambassador had been driven to the Foreign Affairs Ministry of the Reich to be told by a slurring, apparently drunken Ribbentrop that German troops had crossed the Soviet border.

Admiral N.G. Kuznetsov reported to the Kremlin at 10 a.m. that Sunday. The city was 'resting peacefully. As always on holidays there were few people in the centre, and the occasional passers-by looked festive ... In the Kremlin, everything looked as it did on a normal day off. The sentry at the Borovitsky Gates saluted smartly ... Everything was silent and deserted.'[9]

By midday, when Molotov finally told the Russians in a halting voice that they were at war with Germany, the Red air force had lost 1,200 aircraft, 900 on the ground and 300 in the air. Returning Luftwaffe pilots half-apologized to their groundcrews about the 'infanticide' wrought amongst the ill-trained Russians in their obsolete aircraft. Guderian's 800 tanks had torn into gaping holes the points in the Central front pierced by the assault troops. The general himself followed their progress by motoring in their tracks in a wireless truck. The more humble Corporal Pabst, with his signals unit, was moving 'fast, sometimes flat on the ground, but irresistibly. Ditches, water, sand, sun. Always changing position. Thirsty. No time to eat. By ten o'clock we were already old soldiers and had seen a great deal: abandoned positions, knocked out armoured cars, the first prisoners, the first dead Russians.'

Deeper into the Soviet Union, the Luftwaffe was flying low enough for General Boldin to 'clearly see the spiders of the swastika'. Dawn raids on airfields had already crippled the Red air force. Confused civilians milled about the roads near Bialystok. There were a few cars, led by a Zis belonging to a party official with the broad leaves of an aspidistra flapping from a window. Boldin's truck was strafed by German aircraft. The Zis was hit, killing the two women and two children in it. 'Only the evergreen leaves of the aspidistra were still sticking out of the window.'[10]

The Brest fortress, Guderian noted, was continuing to hold out 'with remarkable stubbornness'. But by the evening the lead panzer elements were lulling a few hours' rest fifty-five kilometres east of Brest, the sounds of the fortress battle fading behind them.

To the north, von Leeb's Army Group with 600 tanks in three panzer divisions had attacked on a narrow, 40-kilometre front and was chopping up the single rifle division opposed to them piecemeal. It was rolling fast into Russian-occupied Lithuania. In the south Rundstedt had a similar number of tanks and six infantry divisions to fall on two Soviet infantry divisions. He surged into Galicia, the Russian defences no better than 'a row of glass-houses'.

By nightfall on the first day of the Russian war, exhilarated radio operators in the vanguards of each German Army Group were reporting that they were driving fast and free clear of the frontier zone, dust spuming behind them.

Operation *Barbarossa*, the German invasion of Russia, was perhaps the most critical decision of the century.

The drive to the East had long obsessed Hitler. It was inhabited by his hate objects, Jews, Slavs, Communists, *Untermenschen* incapable of resisting a Teutonic onslaught. 'This colossal Empire in the East is ripe for dissolution,' he had written in *Mein Kampf*.[11] 'We put an end to the perpetual Germanic march towards the South and West of Europe and turn our eyes towards the lands of the East.' The threat from the Slav masses would be destroyed finally, and with the booty of space and a glut of rich farmland.

The first German conference on an invasion of Russia was held on 19 July 1940. The army had deep misgivings. Fear of a war on two fronts ran strong even if Hitler could by now argue that the Western front, with France defeated and Britain isolated, was no longer a threat. The 'Prussian' school favoured continued alliance with Russia. General Franz Halder wrote in his war diary on 30 July that, far from first waging war on Russia in order to defeat England, 'we should do better to keep friendship with Russia'.

The Germans feared a repeat of 1812 when Napoleon, frustrated by the

Europe in 1941

English Channel, had also turned on Moscow.[12] If the Germans knew that *Gotterdämmerung* could lurk in the Napoleonic example, they were vulnerable to its attractions. In any event, the Wehrmacht was more successful than the Grande Armée at its height.

It was a disciplined force with an unchallenged grasp of tactics and technology, at the height of its powers. It had won its stunning victories in the West with little toil and less blood – 27,000 dead, 18,000 missing, the toll of a few days' trench fighting in the First World War. The speed of Hitler's conquests has no parallel in history. Poland fell in 27 days, Denmark in 1, Norway in 23, Holland in 5, Belgium in 18 and France in 39.[13] The Red army had taken over 100 days to impose a peace on Finland.

On 18 December Hitler detailed the strategic objectives of an invasion of Russia and gave the plan its name, Operation *Barbarossa*.[14] He expected to break the back of the Red army and to advance to the line of the Volga–Archangel in three or four months.

Barbarossa overextended the Wehrmacht. By June 1941 it was holding back 8 divisions in Norway and Denmark, 38 in France and 8 in the Balkans. Outside Europe, two Afrika Korps divisions were fighting the British. Mussolini's invasion of Greece, started without consulting Hitler, was a disaster that had left the Italians fighting and losing on two fronts. It dragged the Germans into the Balkans and North Africa, where the British had routed the Italians in Egypt. Though Hitler had overrun Yugoslavia in less than two weeks in the early spring, and Greece in three, he needed to extricate his tanks from there before he could attack Russia. That led to the postponement of *Barbarossa* from mid-May to the second half of June.

The time schedule for the invasion, always optimistic, got tighter and tighter. The first estimate was for five months. This was pared by General Marcks, the CoS for the East, to seventeen weeks. His successor, the ill-fated General Paulus, reduced this to ten weeks. Even the cautious General Brauchitsch was anticipating: 'Massive frontier battles to be expected; duration up to four weeks. But in further development only minor resistance is still to be reckoned with.'

The Germans were acutely short of reserves and dependent on the panzer divisions. Their 3,350 tanks were faced in western Russia by more than half the total Soviet tank strength of 24,000. The Luftwaffe was also weakened since it was in action against the RAF over Britain and in the Mediterranean. It had 1,150 combat aircraft facing the RAF in June 1941, leaving only 2,770 for the Eastern front.[15]

Further, the Russians were spared a war on two fronts. On 13 April 1941 a Soviet–Japanese neutrality pact was signed in Moscow. It suited both sides – it freed Japan for war in the Pacific as well as easing the dangers for the Russians in the East – and it saw Stalin at his most eager to please. 'We are both Asiatics,' he told Matsuoka, the Japanese foreign minister. Matsuoka replied that he himself was a 'moral Communist'. The day that Matsuoka left Moscow, 18 April, Stalin emerged from his normal seclusion in the Kremlin to see him off on the Trans-Siberian. The Germans had failed to set the Japanese, still mindful of their sharp defeat by Zhukov at Khalkin-Gol twenty months earlier, against the Russians.

They grossly underestimated the strength of Soviet industry, particularly east of the Ukraine and the Moscow and Leningrad areas. The vast new Urals–Kuznetsk Basin Combine, for example, lay far beyond the anticipated limit of the German advance, using the iron ores of Magnitogorsk in the Urals and the coal of the Kuzbas 2,000 kilometres to the east. Where the German economy was not on a proper war footing, with more consumer goods produced in the Reich in 1941 than in 1940, draconian labour discipline was already enforced in the Soviet Union.

Germany was, moreover, dependent on Russia to provide or to transport from the Far East large quantities of grain, bauxite, lead, nickel, rubber and tin. As to oil, the lifeblood of *Blitzkrieg*, more than 40 per cent of German imports in 1940 came from Russia.★

Most critical of all, the Germans had little real idea of why they were invading the world's greatest landmass. General Halder said of *Barbarossa* that: 'The *purpose* is not clear. We do not strike at the British and our economic potential will not be improved.'[16] It was a theme that came to haunt the men on the Eastern front.

There were deep veins of hatred for the Germans to mine within the Soviet Union. Anger at the collectives and the suppression of Christianity infected the countryside. In the dusty villages of eastern Poland and the Ukraine, peasants stroked the black crosses on the tanks, thinking the panzer crews their allies in Christ. Church bells greeted them as they plunged into the Baltic states.

But the German officers had known as they stood on their start-lines that *Barbarossa* was not to be normal warfare. The rules had been scrapped. Hitler told a meeting of 200 senior Wehrmacht officers on 30 March 1941 that the restraints of previous campaigns would not apply in Russia. All 'Bolshevik bosses and commissars', the 'Jewish-Bolshevik intelligentsia' and all inhabitants opposing the Wehrmacht were to be shot out of hand. The 'Commissar Order' made it clear that this was to be a war of

★ The German dependence on Russian supplies after the Nazi–Soviet Pact makes a nonsense of the excuses given by British traitors, such as Blunt, that they provided British secrets to the Soviets between 1939 and 1941 because the Soviet Union was a bulwark against the common Nazi enemy. Fuel for German bombers in the Battle of Britain came from Soviet oilfields in Baku. In April 1941, for example, 90,000 tons of oil, 6,400 tons of copper, steel, nickel and other metals, and 4,000 tons of rubber were supplied.

annihilation. The Russians themselves had not signed the Geneva Convention and did not recognize the International Red Cross.

Vaguely, the Germans planned 'settlements of privileged soldier-peasants, dominating such indigenous inhabitants as remained to do the menial work'.[17] The collective farms, which might have won support if they had been handed out to the peasants, were to become fortified estates for German *Herrenmenschen*.

Barbarossa was not the result of detailed planning but of opportunistic hopes of a cheap victory. So cheap, indeed, that as late as the autumn of 1941 the Germans were proposing to move sixty to eighty divisions back to the Reich at the onset of winter, reckoning that what was left would be enough to control Russia until the spring campaigning weather came.[18]

Kick on the door, Hitler said, and the whole rotten Soviet edifice would come crashing down. With clear goals, adequate reserves and an anti-Soviet but not anti-Slav policy in the conquered areas, the Germans might have succeeded. Coming as slave-makers sapped with over-confidence, they riddled themselves with vulnerability.

12

DIE IN KIEV

Not that it seemed so as the German momentum picked up speed. Two Soviet fronts, the North-western and the Western, had been unhinged on the first day. *Blitzkrieg* stuns by its concentration of assault and its rapid vitality. The Red army was losing its equilibrium, dizzy from constant bombing that left its headquarters and supply dumps blazing, tortured by rumour and ignorance of enemy positions, its defensive shell pierced by the four panzer groups that were motoring deep in its rear.

After dive bombers had blasted the Russian positions, scattering men and weapons in the gun pits, a distant plume of dust marked the approach of the panzers. The reconnaissance groups at the head were motoring at up to forty kilometres per hour.

Dust blew off the corrugations in the dirt roads from the eight wheels of the leading armoured cars, festooned with tow ropes, picks and shovels. Motorcyclists with stick grenades in their belts and a machinegunner in the sidecar hastily chalked signs for the line of advance, sometimes on the wings of shot-down Russian aircraft. The lead elements, stiffened by light tanks, flowed round the centres of Red army resistance.

The main tank strength followed the reconnaissance groups, keeping in constant radio touch, ready to deploy into attack formation in the fields if the head of the column was held up. Behind that was a 'sandwich' of lorried infantry and divisional artillery.[1] The commanders were driven furiously between the forward divisions and the Group command posts. On Tuesday afternoon, Guderian found himself in the middle of an enemy infantry unit. 'I ordered my driver to go full-speed ahead and we drove straight through the Russians,' he wrote. 'They were so surprised that they did not even have time to fire their guns.'

The panzer groups snapped forward on the operations maps like lizard tongues, narrow, black penetrations, long and vulnerable but for their speed, seizing the next objective at the tip. They were leaving huge pockets of Russians in their rear to be dealt with by artillery and infantry. In Poland and France, surrounded pockets would tidy themselves up, sniff at the possibility of a break-out, professionalism *oblige*, contract into as neat a circle as they could manage and then surrender. The Russians floundered but fought. Divisions marched into the sights of German bombers, and artillery and tank brigades fuelled up and headed blindly west.

Guderian's armour, the right wing of Bock's Army Group Centre, was through Kobryn, sixty-five kilometres from Brest, on the second day. The left wing took the fortress and rail centre at Grodno. The Russian salient in northern Poland was being pinched off into the Bialystok pocket. But the German infantry was slow in sealing the inner pincers around the two Russian armies trapped 160 kilometres deep at Slonim. Almost half escaped as the German infantry cursed its broken-down French trucks or, like Corporal Pabst, marched 'till my knees were shaking' with horses pulling his wireless cart. The Luftwaffe and the panzers and the intricate combination of their attacks were at the forward edge of machinery and military thought. Much that followed was Napoleonic, horse-drawn and road-bound. The Germans used 2.5 million horses on the Russian front, relying on them more and more as their ragtag collection of trucks wore out. One artillery regiment, for example, had sixty-nine different types of lorry, many of them captured in France and the Low Countries.

German infantry found mopping up to be exhausting and dangerous. They were constantly on the march as the Russians sought to break free. A German wrote of 'uncanny, unbelievable, inhuman' sights in which whole sections of a first wave of Russians vanished under machinegun fire, and 'new waves of men advanced across their own dead without hesitation ... The fury of the attacks exhausted and numbed us completely.'[2]

The Germans marched 'into a dark hole, the landscape pale and bare', sand and dust caking their light camouflage jackets, singing to keep awake:

Zicke-Zacke
Juppheidi
das ist Deutsche
Infanterie

The armoured wings wheeled inwards beyond Minsk, which was taken on the ninth day, 30 June. That night one of Guderian's reconnaissance groups on the left wing reached the Beresina, 145 kilometres south-east of Minsk.

General Pavlov's Western Army Group fell into the first of two gigantic German encirclements. At Bialystok, the Germans captured 150,000 prisoners, 1,200 tanks and 600 guns. In the Minsk pocket, the Russians lost 287,704 men as POWs, 2,585 tanks and 1,400 guns. Pavlov's clumsy and desperate counter-attacks only speeded the disintegration. In these two pockets the Red army lost more tanks than the Germans possessed.

But the Germans had failed to trap the bulk of the Western Army west of the Dnieper river as they had intended. They were drawn deeper into Russia and forced to reopen their panzer pincers to close in on the Russians again on the line of the Dnieper beyond Smolensk. The frustration made Guderian fear that the campaign would not be done by the autumn.

Bypassing the main Russian defences on the Dnieper, his operation hanging 'by a thread', his panzers crossed the slow-flowing river on 10 July and raced for Smolensk. Rainstorms turned the roads into quicksands and, although the tanks could move on their tracks, the trucks were stuck and strung out in columns of 150 kilometres until the drying sun released them. On 16 July Guderian's 2nd Panzer Group captured Smolensk.

In little more than three weeks the Germans had got within 320 kilometres of Moscow and captured Smolensk, the largest and the last big city directly west of the capital.[3]

The northern pincer, Hoth's 3rd Panzer Group, was slowed by rainstorms and swampy ground. At Vitebsk, as it hooked south-east to join up with Guderian, it ran into the 19th Army of General I. S. Koniev, a name to become familiar to it.* There was fierce street fighting as Koniev struggled to hold the town.

Vitebsk was devastated when Pabst entered it. Traffic lights hung 'like bats' in the torn tramway wires. The population, mainly women, moved among the ruins looking for charred timber for a fire or any remaining

---

* A former lumberjack, and the commissar of an armoured train during the civil war, the future Marshal was forty-four. Like Zhukov, he had served in the Far East and escaped the purge. After 19th Army, he took over command of the Western Army Group for the battle of Moscow. Later he commanded the Steppe and 2nd and 1st Army Groups in the Red army offensives in the Ukraine, Poland and against Berlin.

loot. Then he marched south towards Smolensk for the link-up with Guderian's men, through cornfields and scented fields of clover with huddles of thatched, weather-worn cottages in the villages.

Reducing the Smolensk *Kesselschlacht* was a bloody business for the panzers. Their machinery was clogged with dust and mud, tank engines worn by the long advance, their depots now hundreds of kilometres away across a ravaged landscape still seething with cut-off Russian units. The men were exhausted. 'We have had our turret hatches closed for ten days,' a panzer sergeant wrote. 'My tank has been hit seven times and the inside stinks to heaven.'[4]

The surrounded Red army units fought with bitter courage. A wounded captain, an eye lost, squatted for ten days in his knocked-out tank, with a corpse for company, in order to report German movements back on his radio. The Russians burnt their own villages, which reflected against slate-grey skies. 'From now on the fighting became visibly more embittered and merciless on our side too,' Pabst reported as the ring closed in on 4 August. 'Only those who were there will understand why.'

For the first time the Russians used their *Katyusha* – the Stalin Organ to the Germans – a multi-barrelled rocket launcher. Instead of husbanding them, they were forced to throw in four fresh tank brigades, all equipped with the new T-34.

Guderian called this 'the best tank in any army up to 1943'. It was cramped, the gun recoiling 35 centimetres into the noisy crew compartment where the commander served as gunner. The transmission often broke down and crews went into battle with spare sets roped to the decks. But it was small, 26 metric tons, with a low profile and a 500-hp diesel that was full of heart. Its wide tracks kept it going in mud and snow that cost the narrower-tracked German tanks manoeuvrability. In time, as its numbers grew, it became mule as much as charger, hauling artillery and carrying weary infantry forward.

In these early stages, the more experienced panzer crews had the measure of the T-34 as they drew in more Red army units. From Velikie Luki 160 kilometres north of Smolensk to Gomel 260 kilometres south, eleven Russian Armies were flung into the cauldron by Marshal Timoshenko, the C-in-C of the Western Strategic Sector. In the German rear, at Mogilev, the Soviet 13th Army was finally liquidated after successfully beating off the SS *Das Reich* division. The Smolensk cauldron yielded the Germans a further 300,000 prisoners.

To the south Rundstedt's Army Group South was grossly outnumbered by the Soviet forces, soon placed under Marshal Budenny. The old civil war cavalryman, one of the charmed circle who had been at Tsaritsyn with Stalin, had almost 5,000 tanks against the 600 of Rundstedt's 1st Panzer Group, commanded by Kleist. Budenny was described by one of his own officers as 'a man with an immense moustache but a very small brain'.

Rundstedt battered his way into Lvov at the end of the first week, the future turncoat General Vlasov fighting his way out of encirclement with the remnants of the Soviet 4th Army. General Kirponos, the commander of the Soviet South-Western Army Group, was unable to hold Kleist's armour as it broke into the Ukraine. General Zhukov* arrived to bolster Kirponos' HQ. Counter-attacks by Kirponos became weaker and weaker. He had little left to block the developing German drive on Kiev.

In the north, von Leeb split apart the two Russian fronts facing him. He had 4th Panzer Group under Hoeppner, two armies and powerful Luftwaffe support, in all twenty-nine divisions, including three armoured and three motorized.[5] He rapidly overran the Baltic states, welcomed with summer flowers thrown by girls in national dress.

In a vast catchment area, now stretching from Tallinn to the southern-most reaches of the Ukraine, Red army men were hauled into captivity.

Soviet prisoners were not spared. Before they were marched off in long dun lines, cotton bags slung over their shoulders, German security units searched for those who would be shot on the spot. 'Commissars, Communists, Jews – forward!' rang the orders.[6] Those who escaped the Germans were not safe from their own, from Stalin, his crony Lev Mekhlis, the former editor of *Pravda* turned political boss of the Red army, and Beria and his ubiquitous NKVD.

Front, corps, army, divisional and unit commanders were put before firing squads.[7] The commander of the Western Army Group, General Pavlov, was the first scapegoat to be shot. He was followed by the Army Group's Chief of Staff, Major General Klimovskikh, and its artillery commander, Lieutenant General Klich. 'All remembered 1937 too well,' said Colonel Starinov. He described what happened when men in the green caps of the NKVD came calling at the HQ. 'The commander lifted his head and paled. His chin started to shake in a nervous tic ... He suddenly started to mumble some pitiful excuses. "I was with the troops, and I did everything – I am not guilty of anything ..."'[8]

On the South-western front, cracking under Rundstedt's blows, the chief political commissar, N. N. Vashugin, terrorized the commanders.

---

* Son of a shoemaker and a highly decorated Tsarist cavalry sergeant, he was a Red cavalry squadron commander in the civil war. After his successful offensive against the Japanese at Khalkin-Gol in Mongolia in 1939, he became CoGS. Commander of the Reserve Army Group in the Smolensk fighting, he organized the defence of Leningrad in September 1941 before commanding the Red army in the battle of Moscow. A beneficiary of the purge, he was forty-five when he joined Kirponos.

On 27 June he drove to the command post of 8th Mechanized Corps which, exhausted and dispersed by a 250-mile forced march and two days of heavy fighting, was unable to assemble its divisions for an attack ordered by the South-western Army Group. The corps commander, Lieutenant General Riabyshev, stood at attention in front of the small, moustached Vashugin.

'How much did you get to sell out, Judas?' shouted Vashugin. 'The field tribunal will listen to you, traitor. Here under the pine trees we will listen to you and under the pines we will shoot you . . .' He gave Riabyshev twenty minutes to start his attack. Predictably, it was cut up. Three days later Vashugin led a division of tanks into a swamp where they had to be abandoned. He committed suicide in the swamp.[9]

Political prisoners were shot in their cells as the Red army retreated. At Lvov, the NKVD massacred its Ukranian nationalist prisoners or herded them east in columns, killing any who lagged. Those who broke out of German encirclement were interrogated: 'How did *you* escape when so many did not?' Those who retreated without permission were sent under Stalin's Order No. 227 into punishment battalions and were 'soaked up in the red sand of advanced positions, leaving not a trace'.*

Such was the early fate of the 'twins of October', the draftees born in 1917, and those other younger men born after Russia had become Red.

The tally of prisoners and conquered territory, so impressive by mid July, failed to dissipate the miasma that infected the Germans of every rank as they penetrated into Russia proper. To a general, 'the spaces seemed endless, the horizons nebulous'.[10] The immensity of the forests, marsh and plain numbed him. The villages, with their straw-thatched wooden huts, were wretched and melancholy. And the Russians were as hard as Nature,

---

* One who did survive, to become a member of the Supreme Soviet and a foreign affairs commission colleague of Mikhail Gorbachev, was the writer Vladimir Karpov. Arrested before the war for a slighting remark about Stalin, he was sent to a penal battalion in 1942. 'All we could expect was to win back our good names, and you had to pay in blood for that,' he said. 'For most of us the only relief was wounds or death . . . Our job was to go behind enemy lines and bring back "tongues", prisoners for interrogation.'

'There was an unwritten rule. Pilots had to shoot down twenty enemy planes. We had to bring back at least twenty "tongues" . . .' *The Guardian*, 30 March 1986.

Karpov was eventually decorated and became a regular army officer. He was lucky. Solzhenitsyn cites a Lieutenant Semyonov, captured and then liberated from a German concentration camp in 1945. He was forced to join the penal unit of tank-borne infantry and took part in the capture of Berlin seated atop a tank. He was awarded the Order of the Red Star. After all that, he was imprisoned and sentenced on his return to the Soviet Union.

'indifferent to weather, hunger and thirst and almost as indifferent to life and losses, pestilence and famine'.

The Red army, at a stage where it should by rights have keeled over and submitted, was still in being. As one new unit after another was identified on German intelligence reports, replacing others that had been scratched off, a collective shudder ran through the Wehrmacht. A colonel[11] likened the German army in Russia to an elephant attacking a host of ants: 'The elephant will kill thousands, perhaps even millions, of ants, but in the end their numbers will overcome him and he will be eaten to the bone.'

A Russian captain said: 'You cannot imagine the hatred the Germans have stirred up among our people. We are easy-going, good-natured people but I assure you they have turned our people into spiteful *muzhiks*. *Zlyie mujiki* – that's what we've got in the Red army now. We officers sometimes have a job keeping our soldiers from killing German prisoners.' He pointed to the red glow over Smolensk. 'Think of all the torture and degradation these people are made to suffer.'[12]

The attitude of the civilians was changing. At first, Guderian reported, women 'came out from their villages on to the very edge of the battlefield bringing wooden platters of bread and butter and eggs'. Pabst remembered passing an old man in a fur coat, his schnapps-reddened nose shining in the wild scrub of his beard, 'grinning at us happily'.

This did not last. Behind the combat troops came the Reich commissars, fulfilling Hitler's orders that after conquest should come exploitation, men like Erich Koch in the Ukraine who let the SS loose in public whippings and executions. As Guderian drily noted, they soon 'managed to alienate all sympathy from the Germans and thus to prepare the ground for all the horrors of partisan warfare'.[13]

Men went off into the woods 'in the hope that they may murder a German some time'. A shellshocked woman wandered barefoot round a shattered village near Smolensk, 'with a few dirty rags and a tattered sheepskin, and one recognizable word in her vocabulary: *Cherti*, the devils.'[14] The barbarities guaranteed that the supply troops, vulnerable and strung out over hundreds of miles of railway track and roads, would be bled constantly by partisan attacks.

Slowly, the Soviet nerve began to collect itself.

Stalin had been silent since the invasion had started, seemingly suffering a nervous collapse. The first person to try to get through to Stalin's office on 22 June, Admiral Kuznetsov, was told by the duty officer: 'Comrade Stalin is not here, and I don't know where he is.' Khrushchev claimed that Stalin sobbed: 'All that Lenin created we have lost forever.' Ivan Maisky, then Soviet ambassador in London, said that Stalin locked himself in his office and refused to see anyone, showing 'no signs of life'.[15]

It was not until 3 July, at the off-peak hour of 6.30 a.m., that Stalin finally spoke to the public by radio. He spoke in 'a toneless, slow voice with a strong Georgian accent. . . . You could hear a glass click as he drank water. His voice was low and soft, and might have seemed perfectly calm, but for his heavy, tired breathing and that water he kept drinking.'[16]

He gave orders for partisan units to be formed, for scorched-earth retreats where 'the enemy must not be left a single engine, or a single railway truck, and not a pound of bread nor a pint of oil'. The most remarkable part of the speech was its opening: 'Brothers and sisters, my dear friends.' Stalin had never been so intimate with his people before, nor was he to be so again. But the speech reassured the Russians that the 'boss' was still alive and defiant and it began to cement patriotism into the war. Where Hitler was abandoning the last vestiges of humanity, Stalin was acquiring at least its mask.

The position as he spoke was desperate. Guderian's advance in the Centre was beginning to threaten Moscow. In the North, the Germans were breaking through the Stalin Line around Lake Peipus and were set to take Pskov and Porkhov before advancing on Novgorod to cut off Leningrad from the east. Army Group South was thrusting towards Kiev.

Hitler was, however, about to finalize a historic error. On 19 July 1941, with the battle of Smolensk at its height, he issued Directive 33. He ordered the panzer groups in the Centre to peel apart.

Punching close from its own body, the balance of a *Blitzkrieg* force is maintained by the proximity to its own source of strength, its reserves, fuel dumps, airfields. As the Germans drew away from their bases, they had less body weight behind each blow. Balance was delicate, with three lines of advance, in the North on Leningrad, to the South on Kiev and, most successfully, with Army Group Centre where the panzer groups of Guderian and Hoth were preparing to roll on Moscow before winter closed down the front.

It was essential to maintain momentum. By now, German intelligence had already identified 360 Russian divisions instead of the maximum of 200 originally allowed for. The Germans were taking heavy casualties, obliged, as Halder put it, to 'fight according to their combat manuals. In Poland and the West they could take liberties, but here they cannot get away with it.'

Yet Hitler decided not to concentrate his draining strength in the Centre. Directive 33, an incomprehensible 'miracle' to the Russians, split the panzer groups in the Centre. Guderian was to swing south, linking up with Army Group South to encircle the Russian forces around Kiev. Hoth's tanks were to move north to cut the Moscow–Leningrad lines of communication and aid Army Group North in its attack on Leningrad.

Timoshenko managed to get almost 500,000 men out of the Smolensk

Kesselschlact and withdrew them to a defensive line in front of Moscow. On 26 July Guderian was ordered to start the southern operation by helping to round up Russian units at Gomel, 280 kilometres south of Smolensk. German strength was now being fed into a front expanding in width at the sacrifice of depth. This was a negation of *Blitzkrieg* and could, as Halder noted, end up in position warfare where the Germans would gradually be worn down.

By mid August the Germans were at a critical stage of their advance. Guderian was anxious to advance at once on Moscow. He wanted to move up both sides of the Smolensk to Moscow road. Visiting the front east of Roslavl on 13 August, he saw that his troops had put up many signposts marked 'To Moscow'.

These wasted German days were priceless to the Russians. As the Red army recovered balance and nerve, the Germans squandered the brilliant tank weather in front of Smolensk. Napoleon reached Smolensk on 16 August and started his move on Moscow from it on 25 August, reaching the Kremlin on 14 September. The Germans were in Smolensk on 16 July and did not start for Moscow until 2 October.

The stall was fatal. It led inevitably to a winter campaign and it confirmed that Hitler had no single clear objective. Moscow was of no great importance to him. 'Only completely ossified brains, absorbed in the ideas of past centuries,' he said, 'could see any worthwhile objective in taking the capital.' He wanted Leningrad for its industrial area, the Ukraine for a colony, the Crimea to protect the Rumanian oilfields against Soviet air attack.

On 23 August Guderian attended a conference at Army Group HQ, convinced that Moscow must be the prime and immediate target. It was the great Russian road, rail and communications centre, the political 'solar plexus', a place of incalculable emotional importance and his troops were psyched up to take it. Field Marshal Kesselring agreed that the capital could have been taken before winter after 'a reasonable breather' to recover from the Smolensk encirclement battle. 'The capture of Moscow would have been decisive in that the whole of Russia in Europe would have been cut off from its Asiatic potential,' he wrote.[17] Hitler was unmoved.

Two days later Guderian was ordered to wheel south from Gomel towards Kiev and away from Moscow. The battle of Kiev, which opened on 25 August and ended on 26 September, was the greatest battle of encirclement of the war. It was aimed at destroying Budenny's Army Group in a huge salient that stretched from near Briansk in the north to Kremenchug in the south, with Kiev in its centre.

Three German Armies, the 2nd, 17th and 6th, were to squeeze the Russians into a semicircle round Kiev from the west. Guderian's tanks were to slice through the Russian rear from the north, linking up with

Kleist's southern Panzer Group 200 kilometres east of Kiev to cut off Budenny's forces in a giant pocket.

The onus of halting Guderian along the Desna river, the main obstacle in his drive south, fell on Lieutenant General Yeremenko. He had elements of four Armies, the 50th, 13th, 3rd and 21st, to do it. Deeply ignorant of armoured warfare, Stalin forbade Yeremenko to husband his forces for a single powerful blow. Russian armour, trying to respond to Stalin's disjointed demands, was squandered in dribs and drabs.

Yeremenko fought at the Desna for a week. On 7 September the Russian 3rd and 21st Armies ripped apart, Guderian broke through. But he was uneasy, his infantry badly mauled, noting that, in 1708, Charles XII of Sweden had headquartered nearby before his armies were destroyed.

Already, 1,100 kilometres to the north, Army Group North had failed in its second assault on Leningrad. Sixty thousand civilians were working round the clock to build the defences of the city, women digging out 675 kilometres of anti-tank ditches. Zhukov was about to fly to Leningrad from Moscow in a bomber to take over command[18] of battle lines that snaked into the suburbs. In the Centre, Timoshenko no longer faced German armour and was claiming to have destroyed eight Wehrmacht divisions in counter-attacks.

The Ukraine was another matter. Budenny was gradually being cut off in Kiev. On 11 September he sent Stalin a signal asking for permission to withdraw. Any delay 'will lead to losses in men and a huge quantity of equipment'.[19] Stalin refused and relieved Budenny of his command.[20] The order was to die in Kiev.

In the late afternoon of 14 September white Very lights, which always heralded German presence, were seen signalling in the Lokhvitsa area more than 160 kilometres east of Kiev. Guderian's tanks had linked up with the southern Panzer Group of Kleist.

The South-western front had been engulfed and the Soviet position in the Ukraine was collapsing in ruins. On 17 September, the day that Stalin finally agreed that there could be a 'withdrawal' from Kiev, the German inner ring began to close in. Some, like General Vlasov, fought their way out but for most there was nowhere to withdraw to. Two days later, in scenes of wild chaos, Kiev was taken. At dawn on 20 September the 1,000-strong command column of General Kirponos, the front commander, was ambushed and surrounded. Kirponos was hit by mine splinters and died.

The trapped Russians fought with extreme courage, battalions with a few rifle rounds per man attacking German artillery that killed them over open sights. Stalin's speeches were played over loudspeakers to the Red army men in key defensive positions, the voice made harsh and metallic by the loudspeakers. The Germans found something diabolical and naive about 'the stubborn, violent gestures of these men who died so terrible a lonely death on this battlefield, amid the deafening roar of the cannon and the ceaseless braying of the loudspeakers'.[21]

It took five days for the first major surrenders to begin. The order for 'Commissars, Communists and Jews' to come forward was given to a group of 10,000 prisoners by 15 SS men in black uniforms with death heads on their caps. Some 300 came forward and were stripped to the waist. The interpreter said that others must be hiding. Anyone who denounced them could have their clothes and belongings. In this way a further hundred were lined up and taken away to be shot.

The booty captured at Kiev was immense. The Germans counted 665,000 prisoners to add to the dun tide that was flowing back to die in German camps and factories, 884 tanks, 3,718 guns and 3,500 motor vehicles. Rifles were flung in piles 9 metres high.

13

THE *TAIFUN* BLOWS OUT

After Kiev, Moscow. Almost three million soldiers fought in the battle for the capital. It seemed to Hitler, and the watching world, that one final lunge would finish it. The OKW[1] estimated that the Soviets had now lost 2,500,000 men, 22,000 guns, 18,000 tanks and 14,000 aircraft, just under half the total strength of the Red army at the onset of *Barbarossa*.

Those at the front were less confident. Though the Germans were driving ever east into the sunrise, each day broke over Red army units that were still fighting. The Germans had proved themselves *Schnell wie die Windhunde, Zäh wie Leder, Hart wie Kruppstahl*. These qualities, swift as greyhounds, tough as leather, hard as the Krupp steel of their armour, had not saved many of their comrades. Groups of German graves, tripods of birch branches topped with helmets, spattered the unchanging immensity.

One of Guderian's Panzer Regiments, the 6th, was reduced to ten tanks during the Kiev battle. Though Kiev had been a great tactical victory, strategic significance would only be secured if the Wehrmacht achieved a decisive result before the autumnal mud.

The German offensive to take Moscow was codenamed *Taifun*, Typhoon. It called for a breakthrough in the Russian Western front on both sides of the Smolensk--Moscow highway. Here Hoth's Panzer Group 3 and Hoeppner's Group 4, whose switch from the Leningrad attack had given the city much needed relief, would sweep forward with pincers to close on the Russians at Viazma. Further south, Guderian's 2nd Panzer

Group would wheel on Bryansk. In this way the bulk of the Russian Western, Reserve and Bryansk Army Groups would be encircled. The way to Moscow would be open.

The Germans had three infantry Armies, the 9th, 4th and 2nd, and the three Panzer groups with 14 armoured and 9 motorized divisions. This was a third of all the German infantry on the Eastern front and two thirds of the armour. Against them, the Red army had 80 rifle divisions, 9 cavalry divisions, 2 motorized infantry and 1 tank divisions, and 13 tank brigades. The Russians had committed around 40 per cent of their available infantry, aircraft, tanks and guns on the sector in front of Moscow. They were concentrated into three Fronts,[2] or Army Groups, South-western, Western and Kalinin.

Guderian opened the battle of Vyazma–Bryansk on 30 September 1941. He achieved total surprise. He had penetrated 135 kilometres on the second day, personally taking prisoner fourteen Russians whom he found hiding in long grass, one of them an officer who was trying to get through to his already captured HQ on a field telephone.

On 2 October the main attack was launched from Smolensk. Its impetus was so great that by the following evening the armour had penetrated 50 kilometres. That day Guderian in the south broke into the major rail and road centre of Orel, his advance so unexpected that the trams were still running as the panzers drove in. The Russians were too late to evacuate its industrial plant to the safety of the Urals. The streets leading to the railway yards were clogged with dismantled machines and crates filled with tools.

The Russians again underestimated German mobility and speed. Before noon on 5 October Soviet fighter pilots reported that a 25-kilometre-long column of German tanks and trucks was advancing on the town of Yukhnov, only 210 kilometres south-west of Moscow and an area thought to be well in the Russian rear.*

In the Centre, Hoeppner's tanks, supported by SS *Das Reich* and the *Gross Deutschland* division, had advanced north-east from Roslavl and was swinging in on Vyazma from the south. The Russian front was split in two. Hoth's Panzer Group was wheeling down on Viazma from the north. On 7 October Hoth and Hoeppner completed the encirclement of Viazma. The next day Guderian and his hard-marching troops surrounded Bryansk, trapping the 3rd, 13th and units of the 50th Soviet Armies.

---

* In 1943 Yukhnov became the only place on the front that Stalin was to visit throughout the war. He spent a few hours in a wooden hut in a grove of trees in the town. In fact, Yukhnov was then almost 110 kilometres behind the front line proper. Nevertheless, a portrait of Stalin at the front that was reproduced on millions of posters and postcards had him looking at Russian troops attacking German positions through fieldglasses.

In less than a week the Red army had seen more than half a million men surrounded, now in front of Moscow. Two huge pockets of men, 663,000 according to the Germans, with 1,242 tanks and 5,412 guns, underwent the grim process of shelling and air strikes that preceded captivity. These were glory days for the Wehrmacht. Napoleon's old battlefield at Borodino was taken. In Berlin, Goebbels told a conference of the foreign press that the war had 'definitely been brought to a close'. Corporal Pabst found marching 'a sheer pleasure. Clean, sweeping country with big houses. People gaze at us reverently.'

On 14 October Hoth's tanks broke into Kalinin, 160 kilometres north of Moscow. They found unusual signs of prosperity as they closed on the capital, asphalt roads, restaurants with fancy names like 'Culinaria' and 'Lucullus'. Hoth's 3rd Panzer moved down the headwaters of the Volga towards the 'Moscow Sea', the great artificial lake that debouched into a canal that ran 110 kilometres south to Moscow.

Moscow was clogging with fear.

The 'Moscow panic', or the *bolshoi drap*, the big scram, reached its height on 16 October. The evacuation of a large number of government offices and the diplomatic corps to the east, mainly to Kuibyshev, was already under way. Stalin's daughter Svetlana was packed off to a Kuibyshev museum, smelling of paint and mice, that had been hurriedly made ready for the Stalin retinue, cooks, waitresses and bodyguards. Her father was expected and air-raid shelters dug and dachas made ready for him on the banks of the Volga.[3]

He was not to go. The State Defence Committee (GKO), the Stavka, a skeleton administration and the main newspapers stayed on in Moscow. But news of the evacuations was published and the official communiqué on the morning of 16 October said that on the previous night the 'position on the Western front became worse. The German-Fascist troops hurled against our troops large quantities of tanks and motorized infantry, and in one sector broke through our defences.'[4]

As Moscow factories turned out anti-tank hedgehogs, to be driven at once to the outer ring roads, crowds jostled to get on trains at the east-facing railway stations. The city's 'Communist Battalions' of pressed volunteers marched sullenly, smoking but not singing, in the opposite direction to the front. The GKO declared a State of Siege in Moscow and the surrounding areas on 19 October.[5] The meeting took place in Stalin's office, Stalin pacing up and down the narrow carpet in the room before dictating the order. Reinforcements of NKVD security troops were brought in to enforce it. A curfew was imposed from midnight to 5 a.m. and all 'persons fomenting disorder are ... to be shot on the spot'.

It is scarcely surprising that there were alarmists. Leningrad was cut off and blockaded. Almost the whole of the Ukraine and the coast of the Sea of Azov had gone, Army Group South taking 100,000 prisoners and 212 tanks in the battle of the latter. Kleist's 1st Panzer in the south occupied Stalino whilst the 11th Army advanced on Sebastopol and Kerch. A German as cautious and pessimistic as Halder was telling his diary: 'With reasonably good direction of battle and moderately good weather, we cannot but succeed in encircling Moscow.'[6]

By 18 October the Germans were in Mozhaisk. It is 105 kilometres from Mozhaisk to Moscow and it had taken Napoleon three days to get there without benefit of the internal combustion engine.

Factors other than German invincibility now came into play.

The Muscovite panic was transitory. The Russians, and the Communists in particular, were historically inured to the loss of vast swathes of territory. The Reds had seen the area of their power in the civil war shrink to Moscow and Leningrad, the apparently stunning spaces of Siberia, the Urals, the North, the Ukraine all lost, then swelling to the outskirts of Warsaw before it contracted as rapidly to Minsk. Space was not given willingly but, even when lost, it remained an invisible asset because the enemy exhausted himself in it.

That same space was a poisoned plus on the meticulous German balance sheet. An area taken was an area won, real estate, even though to hold it and to ship supplies through it sapped strength at the cutting edge. The scale of Russia was remoter to Europeans than that of the United States, and Hitler had visited neither when he launched *Barbarossa*. His generals knew better. It showed in the wear on their tank tracks and engines, the shortage of fuel, the bundles of rope that had to be dropped by air to drag vehicles out of the mire.

The Russians were not *Untermenschen*. On 6 October Guderian's 4th Panzer Division had been mauled by Soviet T-34 tanks. The short-barrelled 75-mm guns of the Panzer IV tanks were only effective if the T-34 was attacked from behind. It required great skill in manoeuvre to get in this firing position and even then a T-34 would only be knocked out if the hit was scored on the grating above the engine. The Russians were now attacking frontally with infantry whilst sending their tanks in mass formation against the German flanks. 'They were learning,' Guderian noted cryptically.[7]

That night the first snow of winter fell.

The same evening Stalin telephoned Zhukov, the Leningrad Front commander. Zhukov was able to tell him that the Germans had ceased attacking in the Leningrad sector and that pilots had seen large columns, including tanks, moving south to join the assault on Moscow.

Stalin ordered him to fly to the Kremlin where, sick with grippe, exhausted, Stalin told Zhukov to go to the Western Front. This had been pushed back close enough to Moscow for there to be no point in flying there. Zhukov was driven, reading situation reports with a weak flashlight in the back of the car, fighting off drowsiness by stopping periodically for a 200-metre run.

Zhukov knew the area well. He had been born there, walking the countryside as a boy, coming back to his village frequently after his parents had sent him at twelve to Moscow to learn the fur trade. His mother and sister still lived in his village. Fearful of what the Germans would do to the close relations of a general who had already done them much harm, he arranged for them to be sent to his apartment in Moscow. On 9 October he was appointed commander of the Western Army Group.

It was a crucial appointment. Zhukov was tough and self-willed, with a flair in strategy that switched from the darting protection of the Soviet jugular in defence to onerously planned battering of the enemy torso in offence. He had a direct and brilliant impact on operations in the field. He could be ruthless and cruel, ordering a divisional commander he thought slow and nervous to be sent to the penal company, ill-mannered, indifferent to casualties. During the battle of Moscow he succeeded in the risky business of dominating Stalin. He spoke in a 'sharp, commanding tone' as if he were the superior officer to his Supreme Commander in Chief who, his face tired and haggard, his voice lacking assurance, 'accepted this as proper'.[8]

Zhukov was developing a unique role that took him to every key sector of the front, in defence and offence – Leningrad, Stalingrad, Voronezh, Berlin. He had no doubt of which was the most critical. 'Whenever I am asked what I remember most of all from the last war,' he wrote later, 'I always answer: *the battle for Moscow*.'[9]

He immediately merged the Western and Reserve Army Groups into a unified command. The defence line at Mozhaisk was untenable. Zhukov had only 45 battalions to hold it instead of the minimum of 150 he thought necessary. A fighting retreat was made. At night, the Germans in Mozhaisk could see the anti-aircraft fire over Moscow.

Zhukov's difficulty was to keep some semblance of a front whilst avoiding encirclement and the temptation to throw in his scant strategic reserves piecemeal. Weakened units had to be reinforced to keep them in combat and at the same time reserves had to be built. He showed a timing and self-restraint that had been lacking in the earlier Soviet profligacy. The Russians had now run out of two of their three traditional saviours. Mass had been swallowed into the German prison cages. Space had gone now that Moscow was at his back. Only winter remained.

He knew that the Germans were approaching exhaustion. He was reduced to a single independent tank force, the 4th Armoured Brigade, but it was equipped with T-34s that savaged Guderian's 4th Panzer Division again on 11 October. The panzer crews were frightened: 'Better machines, that's terrible ... You race the motor, but she responds too slowly. The Russian tanks are so agile, at close range they will climb a slope or cross a piece of swamp faster than you can traverse the turret.'[10]

The weather was closing in. Each evening the Germans saw clouds building above the distant steppe and over the forests, dark masses that 'carried in the stratosphere the rain, the ice and snow of the coming winter'.

The mud, the autumn and spring state that the Russians call *bezdorozhie* or 'roadlessness', often reduced the advance to a horse-drawn crawl. Moscow women dragged sacks of sand through the same mud, Zhukov noted, and along the same impassable roads. The volunteers voted to excuse only breast-feeding girls from this work. They dug over 160 kilometres of anti-tank ditches and built 1,500 mud and timber pillboxes on the outskirts, their selflessness having a 'tremendous effect' on the troops' morale.

Between mid October and the beginning of November the Germans made little progress. Only infantry could advance along sodden forest paths and areas of swampy marsh. Heavy vehicles and tanks were left behind and the bad weather grounded the Luftwaffe. Robbed of its mobile firepower, the *Blitzkrieg* was severely checked for the first time since the beginning of the war. Guderian failed to take Tula, a key position on the way to Moscow, his tank crews kept within the cold and cramped confines of their machines by Russian gunners. He noted that the exhaustion now beginning to affect even his best officers was 'less physical than spiritual'. Corporal Pabst was lucky enough to find an undestroyed house, but it had a 'horrible, living carpet' of bugs and 'the Russians attacked all night. The trees drip in the fog and the crows shake their feathers ... We talk about what is to come of us, of Russia and of Germany.'

Frost was returning mobility to the Wehrmacht when Moscow began to celebrate the 24th Anniversary of the Bolshevik Revolution, short years crammed with ghosts, horrors and achievements.

With a grey snowstorm grounding the Luftwaffe, the traditional parade took place in Red Square on the morning of 7 November.[11] The tanks taking part were armed with combat ammunition, and troops marched straight on from the parade to the front. Stalin spoke to the troops of their 'great ancestors', Alexander Nevsky, who had beaten the Teutonic knights in 1242, Dmitri Donskoi who routed the Tartars in 1380, Suvorov and Kutuzov who had battled Napoleon. The impact of associating the communist regime with the old patriotism of Holy Russia was deepened by the nearness of the panzers.

It helped to build a sense of common purpose and intimacy among the Russians. It was 'as though nothing else existed in the Soviet Union except this gigantic, compelling effort of a vast land and a population of many millions'.[12]

The snowstorm and the icy wind that blew off the grit and sand laid for the parade caused the first severe cases of frostbite among Guderian's Panzer Group. General Winter had arrived.

Temperatures changed with the cloud cover, the pre-dawn reading falling to minus 28 degrees Centigrade in Moscow on 7 December and reviving to 0 degrees Centigrade three days later. On the coldest days a pink dawn slowly turned violet and then grey. The snow would turn grey too and from mid-afternoon to nine the next morning it was dark. With darkness, the temperature fell sharply.

During the blizzards, visibility was reduced to a few yards. In the brilliance of a clear day the horizons were immense and the blue metal of gun barrels reflected the iced indifference of the sky.

At minus 28 degrees Centigrade the cold snapped photographic film and rubber boot soles. Flesh exposed for more than a few seconds was frost-bitten. In the forests the bark of trees burst with sharp cracks under the pressure of the freezing. Oil became first a paste and then a glue which seized up the engines and gearboxes of tanks. The bodies of dead horses and dead men became rigid within an hour or so. Food had to be cut with saws.

The ground froze solid, often to a depth of 1.5 metres. Digging trenches was difficult when feasible and explosives had to be used to blast holes for the stakes to carry telephone wire.* Locomotives could not be fired and far to the west emergency supplies of clothing for the Wehrmacht were snowbound in sidings in Warsaw. Deep into Germany the tracks were clogged by paralysed trains.[13]

The killing machines were blunted. There is an average of thirty centi-metres of snow on the surface of European Russia in winter and the winter of 1941–2 was the hardest for almost a century. Artillery shells were deadened in the snow, the killing range of an 81-mm mortar reduced to no more than a radius of a metre. Rifle aiming was severely affected by the skin temperature of the hand, with a precipitate decline in accuracy registered when the temperature of the hand fell below 8 degrees Centi-grade. Pilots, who can maintain 80 per cent efficiency at minus 2 degrees

---

* It remains a formidable task for the Russian army to dig in even with modern machinery. Artillery tractor-bulldozers first clear the ground of snow from a strip up to 5.5 metres wide. Holes to take explosives are driven into the ground with compressed-air drills. Warsaw Pact fieldbooks allow two men two hours to make four holes 45 centimetres deep. Four charges of 75 grammes each are used to loosen the topsoil before a high-speed trench digger is brought in. Twenty-three charges have to be used to prepare a command bunker. Special shaped charges are used for individual foxholes.

Centigrade, drop to 68 per cent at minus 18 degrees. It could take two hours to start a tank engine and a further hour to half-thaw the gearbox. Telescopic sights were useless without special salve. Infantry weapons and machineguns froze and only grenades and flamethrowers kept their reliability.

The physical conditions were the same for both sides. The Russians, like Canadians or US Midwesterners, were used to them. The Germans were not, no matter how much their officers had read of 1812. 'Winter Fritz', a German soldier rolling across the stage under a slipping pile of blankets, his feet stuffed into bales of straw, became a comic figure in the Russian theatre.

Most Russians had padded jackets, *telogreiki*, fur gloves and mittens, *valenki* felt boots, fur hats with earflaps, and footcloths, squares of material that gave better protection against sores and frost than socks. SS divisions and the Luftwaffe apart, the Germans had only issue denims, overcoats and blankets. Their boots were closefitting. They stripped Russian prisoners and the dead of their jackets and fur hats. Only the national emblem showed that they were Germans. They wound scarves beneath their helmets and slit white sheets for camouflage. An army that had entered Russia with silver lacquered shoulder straps now bound its boots with rags.

Yet the Germans considered themselves obliged to continue. Some argued that it was vital to get into winter quarters before it was too late. Guderian had already written that: 'The unique chance of striking a single great blow is fading more and more.' The chance was still present and the Germans had little option but to take it.

Five days after the parade in Red Square, the decision was taken for a final encirclement of Moscow. The thirty-six divisions of Kluge's 4th Army would make a frontal advance on the capital. To his left, the Panzer Groups of Hoth and Hoeppner would swing round the capital from the north and west. Guderian's panzers would do the same on Kluge's right from the south. The northern flank of the triple attack would be protected by the 9th Army and its southern by the 2nd.[14]

The final stage of the battle of Moscow opened on 16 November. The German armour made heavy gains. Hoth quickly pierced the defence line of the Russian 30th Army and began to threaten the whole of Zhukov's right wing as he moved towards Klin. On 19 November Stalin was rattled enough to ask Zhukov: 'Are you certain we can hold Moscow? I ask you this with pain in my heart.' Zhukov replied that he could, but when Klin fell on 23 November he said: 'It gets worse from hour to hour.'

On the 28th Hoth reached the Moscow–Volga canal at Krasnaya-Poliana, 22 kilometres from Moscow. The towers and domes of the Kremlin can be seen now from the top of its high-rise apartment blocks, but it is not certain that any German infantry or tankman had enough elevation to have seen them in 1941. To Hoth's south, Hoeppner closed on the western outskirts of Moscow and Guderian bypassed Tula and advanced from the south on Kolomna.

Rokossovsky's 16th Army facing Hoth had been reduced to regiments of 150–200 men. The Soviet 17th Cavalry Division had 800 men left. Anti-aircraft guns, their barrels fully depressed, attempted to take on tanks. Most of this sacrifice was anonymous. Only the remnants of the 316th anti-tank unit, 'Panfilov's 28', entered the Soviet Pantheon of heroes as they bloodily succumbed to a tank assault at a vital crossroads.

The Germans were approaching the limits of endurance. Regiments were now led by an *Oberleutnant*, battalions by junior officers. During the whole of the Western campaign in 1940 they had taken 156,000 casualties. In Russia, they had taken 700,000 casualties at the start of the Moscow campaign. By 26 November this had risen to 743,000. Of these nearly 200,000 were dead, seven times the figure for 1940 and including 8,000 officers.[15]

In the centre Zhukov's 5th, 33rd and 43rd Armies were holding. The German armoured wings depended on the advance of Kluge's 4th Army in the centre. Otherwise they would be isolated north and south of Moscow. Field Marshal Bock took over personal command of the battle, convinced that, like the Marne in 1914, the last battalion would decide the issue. The French in 1914 had been helped by the pressure of their Tsarist allies on the Eastern front. Bock had no such allies and despite his frantic energy the right wing of 4th Army was too exhausted to move.

Russian aircraft bombed villages and isolated huts to deny the Germans shelter. They lived in bivouacs of poles pitched like tepees under a roof of pine boughs, urinating into their hands, easing their chilblains and worsening their sores. They burned beams from destroyed houses by their gun pits. Abandoned horses trotted through the snow 'hanging their heads, appearing and disappearing in the solitude'.[16]

Zhukov was building his reserves. Finally banking on continued Japanese neutrality, divisions were transferred from Siberia and the Far East. These were regular troops, fresh and well equipped. A reserve Army, the 10th, 100,000 strong, was flung together in less than a month. Its commander, Lieutenant General Golikov, counted the 328th Rifle Division among his best. Only a quarter of its men had thrown practice grenades. Its platoon and company commanders were unable to hone its combat firing skills since they had no marksmanship training themselves. The army signal regiment had one long-range and two short-range radios and five of its divisions had no radio equipment whatever. It was under orders to move to the front.

The Germans believed that they had assaulted the Red army to its last battalion and that its defence had reached its climax. At 5 a.m. on 1 December, Kluge's 4th Army launched its final and impoverished attack along the Smolensk road to Moscow. By midday it had broken through the Soviet 33rd Army defences to a depth of three kilometres and was threatening to split it from the Soviet 5th Army.

Zhukov ordered every available reserve into the breach, ski troops, a *Katyusha* rocket unit, a rifle brigade, two tank battalions. He had counter-offensive in mind now more than defence. The temperature, minus 8 degrees Centigrade on 1 December, fell to minus 11 degrees Centigrade at 7 a.m. on the 2nd. Where the forests bleed into the western suburbs of Moscow, which one of Kluge's divisions, the 258th Infantry, claims to have reached, the 4th Army was stopped.

On 5 December, when the Moscow temperature dropped to minus 25 degrees Centigrade, the Russian counter-offensive began. Zhukov saw that the enemy had become so exhausted that 'not only could he not continue his offensive but he was also unable to organize a firm defence'.[17]

'We only needed another eight miles to get Moscow within artillery range,' said a German lieutenant. 'We just could not make it.'

14
'I WANT A CHILD, SOON'

The initial impact of Zhukov's seven Armies and two Cavalry Corps was tremendous. Understrength German divisions, riddled with frostbite and dysentery, their automatic weapons jamming in the cold, clumsy in their straw boots, panicked when they were attacked by warmly padded Siberian troops backed by T-34s whose hulls shrugged off German 37-mm anti-tank shells unless hit at the closest range.

On 8 December Japan attacked the United States, confirming the Soviet decision to draw troops from the Far East. Two days later Guderian's Panzer Corps was broken through west of Tula and on the 11th Hitler declared war on the US. The three principal elements of Army Group Centre, Hoeppner and Guderian's armour and Kluge's 4th Army, lost contact with each other.

The Luftwaffe, its aircraft not winterized and its groundcrews taking up to ninety minutes to warm up engines, was less and less visible. Russian pilots, in dog-fur leggings, flew Stormovik ground-attack aircraft equipped with skis, the water and oil pre-heated, antifreeze freeing their guns and bombsights. Russian labour battalions kept runways free from snow for the wheeled bombers, working even at night with January temperatures at minus 40 degrees Centigrade, their mouths and nostrils covered with strips of cloth to keep the moisture from freezing.

The Russians moved west with columns of sledges, the horses' flanks covered with white frost, carrying 122-mm shells, rifle ammunition, blood for transfusions. The sledge drivers walked to restore their circulation and at night, in the dark of the fir forests, warmed themselves at fires of green logs.[1]

A light German tank could not move in more than thirty centimetres of snow, a medium in more than 45 centimetres. Their motorized artillery stuck fast. The Russians had horse-drawn artillery or moved light 45-mm guns by the sweat of nine men. Cavalry attacked the Germans on the southern flanks at night, each squadron of 100 with its own field gun and mortars. They rode small Russian Steppe horses, agile in the snowy, ravine-filled landscape, and could move 110 kilometres across the axis of the Russian advance in a night. They charged with drawn sabres, shouting the Russian battle cry: '*Ourrah!*'

A wounded man would die in ten to fifteen minutes unless stretcher bearers got to him with heavy blankets and a drink of vodka with morphine against the shock. Wounds, exposed to the air, froze.

'Discipline began to crack,' said General Schaal of the 3rd Panzer Group. 'There were more and more soldiers making their own way back to the west, without any weapons, leading a calf or drawing a sledge with potatoes behind them ... Men killed by bombing were no longer buried ... Supply units were in the grip of psychosis probably because in the past they had only been used to headlong advance.'[2]

The Russian refusal to sign the Geneva Convention had a powerful effect on the Germans. The Russians understood it and accepted it.* 'The Germans knew that once they were captured nothing would be heard from them or about them until at least the end of the war,' wrote a British observer.[3] 'Their families would never know. And that at times produced a paralysing fear in their hearts.'

The advancing Soviet 10th Army came across the 'unforgettable sight' of roads blocked with abandoned German equipment. There were tanks, armoured cars, staff cars, buses. The houses had been fired by the retreating Germans. 'All that remained of the villages was stove chimneys and the charred skeletons of houses,' said the writer Konstantin Simonov. 'Twice I saw gallows in liberated villages, and by one of them lay the bodies of peasants hung by the Germans.'[4]

Pabst wrote of the Russians 'roaring like bulls when they attack'. The sun glowed through the smoke of burning villages and the 'night was dark blue like a starless vault over the light landscape ... No more prisoners are

---

* It was not new for the Russians to ignore their own POWs. In 1812 the French General de Segur wrote of Russian prisoners left to 'die of hunger in the enclosures where at night they were confined like brute beasts ... But what could we do? Exchange them? The enemy rejected the proposal.'

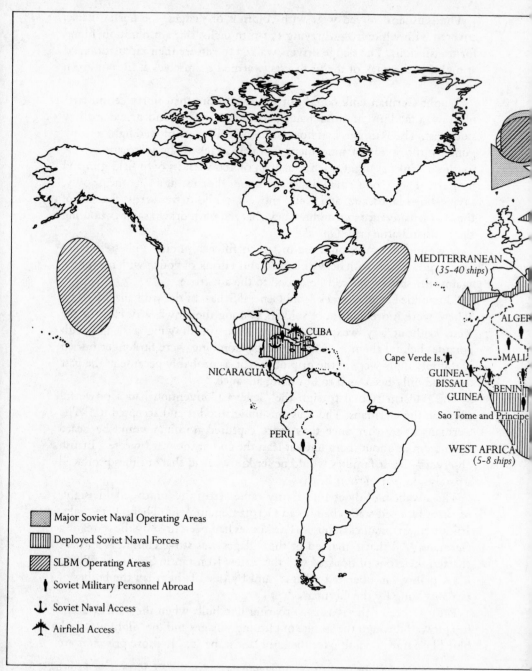

MEDITERRANEAN
(35-40 ships)

CUBA

NICARAGUA

ALGER

Cape Verde Is.

MALI

GUINEA-
BISSAU

BENIN

GUINEA

PERU

Sao Tome and Principe

WEST AFRICA
(5-8 ships)

Major Soviet Naval Operating Areas

Deployed Soviet Naval Forces

SLBM Operating Areas

Soviet Military Personnel Abroad

Soviet Naval Access

Airfield Access

The Soviet Armed Forces operating outside Soviet borders

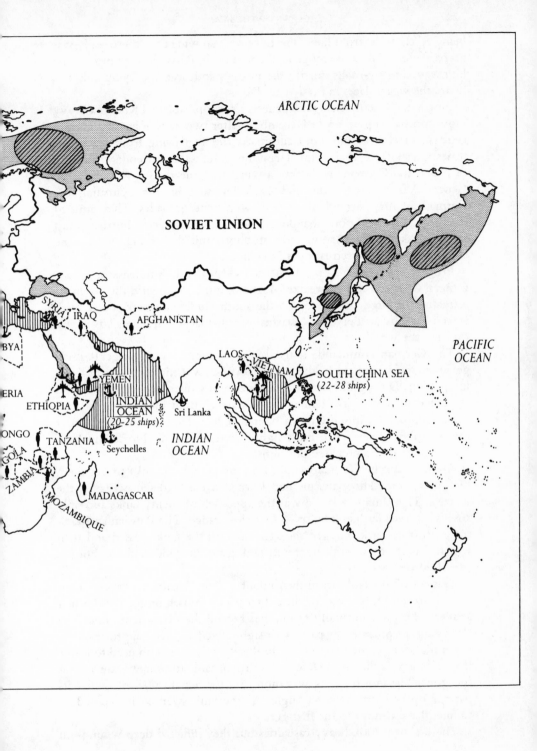

ARCTIC OCEAN

SOVIET UNION

SYRIA IRAQ AFGHANISTAN

BYA

ERIA

ETHIOPIA YEMEN

INDIAN
OCEAN
(20-25 ships)

Sri Lanka

LAOS

VIETNAM

SOUTH CHINA SEA
(22-28 ships)

PACIFIC
OCEAN

ONGO TANZANIA

GOLA

ZAMBIA Seychelles

INDIAN
OCEAN

MADAGASCAR

MOZAMBIQUE

being taken in the front line.' The lines were so wide that 'there really was
no battle line. The best any general could do in Russia was to protect the
highways and by-roads, fortify the villages and organize flying columns
to aid the weak places in his defence.'[5]

North of Moscow General Kuznetsov's troops stormed Klin in a heavy
snowstorm at 11 p.m. on 14 December. After two days of heavy fighting,
German machinegunners and automatic riflemen firing from brick fac-
tories and rooftops, their colonel scrawling a refusal to surrender on a scrap
of paper, the Germans withdrew leaving 3,000 dead. Below Kuznetsov,
General Vlasov routed the 2nd Tank Division, his men pursuing the
German infantry through the woods with hand grenades. They amused
themselves by trying out abandoned German motorcycles. Further south
Rokossovsky's 16th Army, after stubborn initial fighting, forced the
Germans into broad retreat by 8 December.

Progress was slower along the Moscow–Mozhaisk–Smolensk highway.
General Govorov did not retake Mozhaisk until 20 January, the Germans
retreating through Borodino. To the south Guderian's tank forces were
forced back by artillery and 'swarms' of sub-machine gunners advancing
through the woods.

The German command, tested by the younger, post-purge Russian
generals, most of them in their early forties,[6] was showing signs of disintegration. During the retreat Hoeppner and Guderian were sacked and
Bock fell ill. On 18 December Field Marshal Brauchitsch resigned and
Hitler appointed himself Commander-in-Chief. He issued his first order
the next day: 'Every man must fight where he stands. No falling back
where there are no prepared positions.'

Alarmingly, the Germans could no longer rely on tanks to get them
out of trouble. The Russians had learned a costly defence against the
panzers. Their infantry lay low at the approach of enemy tanks and only
rose when the German infantry was at close range. The Russian anti-tank
teams, further back, hugged the ground until the tanks passed and then
rose to engage them with light anti-tank guns, grenades and fuel bottles,
the Molotov cocktails.[7]

This cut off the tanks from their infantry. The German tanks were then
forced either to turn back for their infantry or to dash on for the Russian
artillery. This was normally 550 metres behind the first defence line. The
Russian guns operated in pairs with sights fixed so that trajectories were
never higher than the tank turrets. In this way there was no need to lower
the trajectory as the tanks closed in. German tank armour was thickest at
the front. The gun the tank was motoring for remained silent, whilst its
partner opened fire from an angle. As the tank swerved it exposed its
thinner flank armour to the first gun.[8]

The Russians took heavy casualties but they inflicted deep wounds on the German tankmen. Thirteen of Hitler's twenty-five tank divisions were bleeding badly in the Moscow battle, from the 1st through the 7th, the 10th, 11th, 17th, 18th, 19th and 20th.

Hitler did not panic. He understood instinctively that to retreat west of Smolensk would bring a Napoleonic catastrophe. Short of fuel and vehicles, unsupplied, harried by Cossack divisions on horseback with sledge-born infantry and light artillery and ski troops, Army Group Centre would have been cut to ribbons as it stumbled through the snow swamps. He insisted that the Germans should hold Rzhev, Viazma, Yukhnov, Kaluga, Orel and Bryansk, turning these advanced depots into entrenched camps. The troops falling back on them would have shelter and supplies. Unlike Napoleon, this was not a retreat but a manoeuvre to the rear.[9]

Of these 'hedgehogs', only Kaluga was lost. The Russians were unable to overrun the fortified Rzhev–Gzhatsk–Viazma triangle, less than 160 kilometres west of Moscow. The cost was terrible. Pabst reported that the 427th Regiment came back from Rzhev with 280 men, scarcely the strength of a battalion. 'Only now does one realize, very slowly,' he wrote, 'what this people can endure and of what it is capable.' But, now in shelter and supplied, 'The worst is over.'

The counter-offensive had no real weight behind it. Russian resources were strained to the utmost. Zhukov found himself 'literally wheedling' a handful of anti-tank rifles, 100 sub-machine guns, 10 anti-tank cannon from Stalin. These rifles were 'immediately loaded onto trucks and dispatched to the Armies in greatest need', Zhukov wrote. 'We had to establish a norm of one to two rounds per gun per day. And this, please note, was during the offensive!'[10]

By mid March, the offensive came to a standstill.

'The war is far from being over,' wrote Pabst. ' "I want to have a child," the men say, "soon, on my next leave." '

15

THE FORGE

The German generals memoired their failure on weather, mud and snow, on tensions in the senior command, on Hitler's impossible ambition. They made little mention of enemy fighting ability. Beyond courage, Russian survival depended on the ability to continue to manufacture weapons and to deliver them to the front in a country whose industry had been devastated.

Tsarist Russia, with far more of its territory intact, had been pressed to cope with the simple demands of trench warfare. The Soviet state, twenty-four years old, depended for its existence on engines, turbo-compressors, radiators, carburettors, radios, transmissions, gear boxes, rocket launchers. And this against Germany, able to draw not only on its own industrial brilliance but also on half the labour, forced or otherwise, of Europe.

At the time of the Moscow battles the Soviet Union had lost a quarter of Russia in Europe, the richest slice of the nation where 45 per cent of its population lived and which produced one third of its industrial goods.[1] The labour force had dropped from 31.5 million to 18.5 million. Shortage of men drove the ratio of women in industry up from 38 per cent to 53 per cent.[2] The output of steel had dropped by two thirds. Only a third of the blast furnaces were working. All the coal mines of the Donbas and the Moscow basin had gone, taking with them 55.5 per cent of coal output. The main molybdenum and manganese mines had gone. The plants producing high-grade steels for armour plating in the eastern Ukraine had been overrun. The loss of 303 munitions plants cut the production of shells, air bombs, detonating fuses and hand grenades by 40 per cent. The loss of the Donbas chemical industries slashed the output of explosives. Aircraft production in November 1941 had fallen to 30 per cent of its September figure. Total industrial output had dropped since June by over 50 per cent.

Old Russia, where the Moscow poet Simonov drew strength from 'poor huts where our grandfathers laboured', was equally savaged. Forty-two per cent of the pre-war area under cultivation fell to the Germans. This had produced 38 per cent of the cereals harvest and 84 per cent of sugar. With it went almost half of the country's cattle and horses and 60 per cent of its pigs.*

Centralized planning, the bedrock of the communist system, brought major benefits in the defence industries. Stalin and the GKO supervised *Gosplan*, the State Planning Commission, and the individual *Narkoms*, the People's Commissariats of Aircraft, Tank, Armaments, Iron and Steel and Munitions Production. The dispersal of industry to the east had been planned before the war. Aircraft plants had been sited in Tashkent, Irkutsk and Novosibirsk.[3] But the engine plants were still in the west and the transfers were desultory.

Reaction to *Barbarossa* was immediate. On the second day of the war, overtime was made statutory and annual leave was abolished. The working

---

* Werth, op. cit., pp. 213 et seq. No more than rough equivalents can be given for Western countries. In Britain, the loss of the Midlands, the South Yorkshire and Welsh coalfields and steelworks, with Manchester in a state of siege (like Leningrad) gives some idea of the position. In the US, slice out the great industrial belt from Chicago to Buffalo and as far south as Indianapolis and the West Virginia coalfields, add the Midwest grain states and have Washington under siege and New York threatened.

day was set at eleven hours. By the beginning of July 1941 the head of *Gosplan*, N. A. Voznesensky, was drawing up a detailed plan. An industrial evacuation group was formed and steps were taken for the exploitation of western Siberia, the Urals, Kazakhstan and Central Asia. Huge 'evacuation bases' were planned where plants uprooted from the west would be merged with local factories.[4]

Work began on 2 July. The armour plate mill at Mariupol (now Zhdanov) in the southern Ukraine was to be moved 1,770 kilometres to Magnitogorsk. The tank engine plant at Kharkov was slated to go to Chelyabinsk. The diesel department of the giant Kirov plant in Leningrad and the tractor works in Kharkov were also to be moved east, where the Gorky automobile plant was to switch to tank engines. The foundations of the huge Volga-Urals combine for the mass production of tanks were laid. Both the Stalingrad and Chelyabinsk tractor factories were re-tooled to make tanks. No tractor-making capacity remained in the country.

As the panzers clattered into the Ukraine, the huge Zaporozhie steel mills were loaded on to 8,000 railway trucks and moved to Magnitogorsk. The tube-rolling mill at Dniepropetrovsk was stacked on to nine groups of freight trains starting on 9 August. The final equipment arrived at Pervouralsk, 1,850 kilometres away in the Urals near Sverdlovsk, on 6 September. It was in production again on Christmas Eve. The Taganrog aircraft plant was evacuated under enemy artillery fire. A forty-wagon train left the Yakovlev fighter aircraft plant every eight to ten hours carrying people and machines.[5] Abandoned plants were destroyed where possible, including the Dnieper Dam where the Russians left the turbines unlubricated and then dynamited it for good measure.

The strain on the rail system was enormous. It had to evacuate itself and its own equipment and railwaymen. NKVD men prowled the system looking for evidence of panic. Enormous bottlenecks developed at junctions like Chelyabinsk, 1,450 kilometres east of Moscow. Between July and November 1941, in this vast migration of men and machines, 1,360 large war plants had moved east on the broad-gauge track. The number of people moved in this period was 17 million.[6] They went to the Urals, the Volga area, Kazakhstan and Central Asia, to western and eastern Siberia.[7] The evacuation cargoes, undertaken at the height of the German advance, amounted to 1.5 million railway wagonloads.

Agriculture moved too. More than 675,000 head of cattle and 5,000 tractors, threshing machines and combines were moved east from White Russia (or Belorussia). Women took the place of men. Where 8 per cent of pre-war tractor drivers were women, this rose to 57 per cent.[8]

No buildings awaited workers and machines in the east, but raw sites in winter.

At an evacuated aircraft plant in Kuibyshev, pits were hacked in the ground and wood laid in them. This was drenched with fuel oil and lit, the only warmth. On 18 December there were no windows or roofs, snow covering the shop floor where the workers slept. Machines were carried from the railway cars by hand. The only food was 'something resembling soup' which was served in the open. On 29 December the roar of a motor filled the site. The evacuees searched the sky for an enemy aircraft and then realized: 'They have begun testing!'[9] The thousand workers rebuilding the evacuated Kharkov tractor plant lived in dugouts, setting up the first machines on the earth.

The long nights were lit by arc lamps and electric bulbs suspended from trees. *Voskresniks*, voluntary labour Sundays, meant that many worked seven days a week. Only handicapped men, women and children under fourteen avoided labour mobilization. Millions of boys from fourteen to seventeen, and many girls, worked seven-hour days in munitions plants, housed in barracks. In the Karaganda coalfields of Kazakhstan most of the new miners were women and adolescents. On the farms, women sometimes drew the ploughs.

The effort gradually paid off. The average plant was working within three months of arrival in the East. By June 1942 most re-starts had been completed. A huge new power station was built at Chelyabinsk to supply dozens of armaments plants. Forty-four new coal mines were sunk in the Urals, Kuzbas and Karaganda. Molybdenum mines were developed in the waterless steppe near Lake Balkhash in central Asia.[10] Virgin land was ploughed in the Volga country, the Urals, western Siberia and Kazakhstan.

Aircraft production, a miserable 915 in February 1942, was up to 1,647 in March and by July was 30 per cent greater than in 1941. Where 15,735 planes were built in 1941, 25,436 were made in 1942, 34,900 in 1943 and 40,300 in 1944.[11] Soviet designers developed twenty-five new aircraft types during the war. No longer did Soviet pilots flounder in obsolescence. The YaK-9, with its 37-mm gun, was the match for German fighters. Tu-2 dive bombers and Il-2 *Stormoviks*, both produced in mass, gave the Red army close ground support of a quality utterly lacking in 1941.

Tank production doubled in the year after December 1941 and diesel engine output was up four times. In 1943 16,000 heavy and medium tanks and 4,000 self-propelled (SP) guns were rolled off. Labour input was honed by production engineers. The man hours needed for T-34 dropped from 8,000 to 3,700. Tank turrets were stamped instead of cast. An Il-4 fighter that had needed 20,000 man hours to build in 1941 required 12,500 in 1943.

The Red army infantryman had learnt to fear the German *avtomatchik* and his firepower. In 1942 automatic weapons began to roll in numbers along the rail tracks to the west. Sub-machinegun production increased sixfold.[12] The production of heavy guns was up by a factor of 1.8 and mortars by three. D. F. Ustinov, the armaments minister, a survivor who was defence minister into the 1980s, was able to say: 'A great density of fire for every kilometre of front is now the normal thing.'[13]

On 22 August 1942, whilst a second evacuation was hauling industries from the freshly threatened Stalingrad area and the workers from the first had not had time to draw breath, Pabst found himself 'under drum-fire: rocket salvoes, heavy mortars, tanks. Five fighter attacks. Tanks broke through on our left.'[14] The 'swamp animals', as Hitler called them, were still in the production business.

It was not an entirely internal effort. The first protocol for British and American aid was signed before the US entry into the war. It was celebrated with a banquet in the white marble, glass and gold Catherine the Great Room in the Kremlin on 1 October 1941. Thirty-one toasts were drunk in vodka and champagne and two films were screened in a ceremony that showed that the Russians, though they were seldom to admit it, saw the importance of aid.

From the outset, delivery was grinding and dangerous. The Arctic convoys assembled at Hval Fjord in Iceland or Loch Erne in Scotland and faced U-boats, black torpedo aircraft and dive bombers in polar white paint, ice floes, drifting fog and the heavy Atlantic seas. They had no Soviet naval or air support. Neither were they much welcomed. The third British convoy set sail from Scotland not knowing whether Moscow would have fallen when it arrived. Its sailors crowded the rails as they docked in Archangel. A Scot led a cheer. The faces on the pier were 'blank, disinterested'. After a half minute of silence, the mouth of the Scot hardened and he shouted: 'All right, go to hell then.' The dockers were prison labourers under guard.[15]

The long daylight hours of the arctic summer were the most dangerous, the crews apprehensive as they neared Bear Island, lying in the Arctic Ocean between Spitsbergen and the Luftwaffe bases in northern Norway. One American freighter, the *City of Joliet*, was attacked 8 times by torpedo and 18 times by dive bombers in a day. PQ 17, a convoy of 36 freighters, lost 10 ships to submarines and 13 to bombers, delivering just 164 of the original load of 594 tanks and 87 of 297 aircraft.[16]

Stalin was unimpressed by drowned crewmen. He cabled Churchill that the British arguments for slowing deliveries to the northern harbours were untenable. 'No major task can be carried out in wartime without risks or losses,' he said.[17] RAF squadrons were based at Murmansk but the Russians refused to allow RAF groundcrews to land off their ships. US pilots and mechanics were not allowed into the country to explain how to handle the tricycle undercarriages of newly delivered Aircobras and B25s.

In all, British and American ships carried 4.4 million tons of supplies to
the northern ports. After the convoy losses, the emphasis was transferred
to the Persian Gulf and to the Soviet Far East. The long but safe route to
the Persian Gulf carried 4.6 million tons. There were problems in Iran
with theft and bandits. Most cargo went by rail, but the 450,000 tons that
went by road would have filled a line of US Army $2\frac{1}{2}$-ton cargo trucks
stretching from Baltimore to Chicago.

Almost half the total aid, 9.2 million tons, went from US West Coast
ports to eastern Siberia. Aircraft were ferried on flights that were first epic,
then routine. The Alaska–Siberia route ran from Montana to Moscow,
the South Atlantic route from Miami to Moscow.

There was and there remains little Soviet gratitude.

'The Russian authorities seem to want to cover the fact that they are
receiving outside help,' US Ambassador Standley, an admiral, said bitterly
at a Moscow press conference in 1943. Molotov retorted: 'Every man in
the street knows we are getting Lend-Lease supplies from our Allies.'
'That may be so, Mr Molotov,' said Standley. 'But we have no contact with
the man in the street. The man in the street does not dare talk to us.'[18]

The official Soviet line remains that, despite the outbreak of the Japanese
war, the US and Britain were strong enough to open a second front against
the Germans in Europe by the end of 1941. They did not do so because
they wished to see Germany and the Soviet Union exhaust themselves.
Aid was deliberately slow in order that the Russians should be weakened.
The Second Front, when it came in Normandy in June 1944, was timed to
catch both Germans and Russians in a state of maximum collapse. In 1947
the Soviet deputy premier, Voznesenski, who had been head of *Gosplan*,
claimed that the ratio of Allied deliveries to Soviet wartime production
was 'only about four per cent'. The 4 per cent figure has become a standard.

That is cheap. The Red army was largely clothed, shod, fed and
transported by Western industry. Its dying it did itself.

The Americans sent enough cotton cloth for 34 million summer uniforms and woollen cloth for 20 million, plus $1,598,000 worth of buttons
to do them up. The Red army was supplied with 14,572,000 pairs of US-
made boots. The rapid expansion of US dehydration plants meant that
huge quantities of food could be shipped to Russia. Dehydrating potatoes,
for example, reduced their bulk by nine tenths. *Tushonka* canned pork was
produced from a Russia formula by Midwestern packers. More than a
quarter of a million tons of canned *Tushonka* and 452,084 tons of other
canned meats were shipped, although Red army men before Normandy
considered this a poor substitute for an Allied landing and referred sarcastically to a can of meat as 'Second Front'. Red army cooks used Penick
and Ford corn oil from Cedar Rapids and Pillsbury enriched flour from
Minneapolis.

The total reads like the shopping list of a demented housewife: 517,522 tons of vegetable oil and shortening, 362,421 tons of canned and dried milk, cheese, eggs, dehydrated vegetable and fruit paste, 672,429 tons of sugar, 61,483 tons of vitamins, yeast, tea, coffee, salt, spices and nuts. In all 4.2 million tons of foodstuffs were shipped, much of it dehydrated. This is enough to have supplied 12 million Red army men with half a pound of concentrated food a day.[19]

US trucks and Jeeps were the crucial element in Red army mobility. Two out of three Red army trucks were American built, mainly Dodge and Studebaker with some Macks. There were 409,526 of them, along with 3.1 million tyres to roll on. The ubiquitous Willys Jeeps, known to the Russians as *villises*, numbered 47,238. No longer did fascinated Red army men play with abandoned German motorcycles. They got 32,200 American ones of their own. Massive US truck deliveries enabled the Red army to double the speed of its advances, with mobile units able to average 30 to 35 kilometres a day.

The Russians got almost as much aluminium from the British, Canadians and Americans as they made themselves, 261,000 tons to 285,000. Since the T-34 had an aluminium alloy engine, this was vital for tank production as well as aircraft. Lend-Lease copper, essential for ammunition and weapons, was equivalent to 75 per cent of Soviet production. The Red army signals service got enough field telegraph wire to go round the world 38 times and 245,000 field telephones to hook into it. Allied freighters disgorged enough railway equipment for a new Trans-Siberian. More than 11,000 kilometres of track came with 1,900 locos, 9,920 flat cars, 100,000 tons of wheels and axles and a block signalling system capable of covering 2,900 kilometres of track.

But much Allied equipment was outdated and almost useless. Few of the 11,500 tanks were used, the British Matildas being reckoned as inflammable as match boxes.[20] Though the air ace Alexander Pokryshin used a Lend-Lease Aircobra to shoot down 48 of his 59 kills, other aircraft like Hurricanes and Tomahawks were slow and vulnerable.

Aid was not noticeable until after Stalingrad, when the greatest threat was over. The idea persists that the Allies only supplied it so that Russian boys rather than British or Americans could kill Germans. If they sent medicines, it was so that wounded Russians could be returned to the front. Deep in the Russian psyche, too, is the idea that only they truly suffered and achieved in the war. Life in a warm aircraft assembly plant in Long Beach cannot be compared with frozen toil beyond the Urals. Whatever happened on the Arctic convoys is a bauble compared with the Soviet land battles. The Allies bought the German defeat with Russian blood and paid in Spam.

16

TO THE VOLGA

Slowly, Zhukov's Far Eastern divisions wore themselves out in frontal assaults on German positions. Their bodies lay in piles round Pabst's battery, 'twisted one on top of another, frozen green and brown in their poor nakedness'. As the weather eased, Pabst found that German 'courage and vitality are returning'.

The Wehrmacht slid into the summer campaign of 1942 with greater strength than it had started *Barbarossa*, at least on paper. The number of German divisions was roughly the same, 134 infantry, 24 armoured and 13 motorized. To these were now added 61 satellite divisions,[1] four of them armoured.

But the satellite divisions were poorly equipped and badly led. The strength of the German infantry divisions had been reduced from nine to six battalions. Although six new armoured divisions had been raised, only half of the original nineteen tank divisions had been brought up to full strength because priority had been given to submarine building. The German strategic position had deteriorated immensely. Hitler had failed to destroy the Red army in 1941 when, with the US still neutral and the British contained, he could concentrate German strength against it. In 1942 he faced war on far-flung fronts against a coalition with infinitely more industrial muscle and with increased British pressure and the certainty of a vast American build-up to come.

Before troops returned from Germany on leave, taking the long train ride to the front through country devastated by burning, deportation and mass murder, their families would look at them 'with a certain look in their eyes, that animal curiosity when you gaze on something condemned ... And deep down so many of us believed it ... Some slit-eyed Mongol sniper was waiting for each one of us.'[2] Not that the eye could be seen beneath his inhuman mask. It hung from an elastic band that passed round the leaf-and-twig-covered helmet, a screen of thick cattle hair that reduced the face to an inanimate mass of foliage. When the mask was pushed back over the helmet, it looked like the duck's-arse quiff of a teddy boy.

Casualties were constant. 'Our garden of crosses got bigger and bigger,' a German wrote. 'Now they are already growing grey beneath the hanging irises.'

In terms both of strategy and morale, the Germans had to get done with Russia in 1942. It was that knowledge, running right through the ranks, that gave a desperate edge to the year's campaigning. The Russians felt it as well.

Hitler decided to attack in the south, aiming to cripple the Soviet economy by seizing the Donets industrial belt and the Caucasian oilfields. Their capture would also ease the chronic German shortage of oil. The Red army front between Taganrog and Kursk would be broken. The Caucasus would be occupied as deep as Baku on the Caspian. To cover the operation, a defensive front would be established along the line of the Don from Voronezh to Stalingrad. With Stalingrad captured, the Germans would be able to swing north up the Volga to cut the communications of the Russian armies round Moscow.

This supposed that the Germans were capable of carrying out two widely separated offensives, against Stalingrad and the Caucasus, and that they were capable of defending the 580-kilometre front they would trail behind them as they thrust through to the Don bend at Stalingrad.

Stalingrad itself, the Volga icebound for half the year at this point, was of little strategic significance. At the start of the 1942 summer campaign, the commander of 1st Panzer Army, Ewald von Kleist, recalled that the city was 'no more than a name on the map of my Panzer Army'.[3]

Hitler replaced Army Group South with Army Groups A and B. A was commanded by Field Marshal List, and contained General Kleist's 1st Panzer Army, General Ruoff's 17th Army and the 4th Air Fleet. Its mission was the conquest of the Caucasus. Army Group B, under Field Marshal von Bock, was to cover A's northern flank and seize Stalingrad. It contained 2nd Army, under General von Weichs, 4th Panzer Army under General Hoth, 6th Army under General von Paulus and the Luftwaffe Don Command. Behind these came the 2nd Hungarian, 8th Italian and 3rd Rumanian Armies. Manstein's 11th Army, which included the 4th Rumanian Army, was in the Crimea.

This was the force allotted to Operation *Blau* in the south, 60 German divisions, 10 of them armoured and 6 motorized, and 43 satellite divisions. Hoth's 4th Panzer was to advance towards Voronezh, then wheel with Paulus' 6th Army down the right bank of the Don towards Stalingrad. The 2nd German, 2nd Hungarian, 8th Italian and 3rd Rumanian Armies were to defend the river to its bend west of Stalingrad. The 4th Rumanian Army was later assigned the front south of Stalingrad.[4] Further south, Army Group A would advance towards the lower Don at Rostov. Once 1st Panzer Army had crossed the river, it would be joined by 17th Army. Manstein's 11th Army would join it after the reconquest of the Crimea.

Stalin had plans for his own offensives, marked by a facile optimism and a stubborn refusal to stop squandering men and machines even when it was clear they had failed. The attacks were more scattered than Hitler's. In the North, Stalin hoped to relieve Leningrad by breaking through the

German positions on the Volkhov river with an elite group commanded by one of his most energetic young generals, Andrei Vlasov. Reinhardt Gehlen, the head of German intelligence on the Eastern front and a post-war spymaster of note, had pieced together a remarkably accurate picture of the major Soviet intention in the South. Marshal Timoshenko was to open a violent offensive around Kharkov with a combined force of 640,000 men.[5]

Timoshenko's attack went in against Paulus' 6th Army on the morning of 12 May and bit as deep as twenty-four kilometres before Paulus managed to hold it. Kleist's 1st Panzer Army counter-attacked at first light on 17 May. The panzers had cut sixteen kilometres into the Russian positions by midday and twenty-four hours later they were exploiting a sixty-five kilometre rent in the Soviet front. Against urgent advice, Stalin refused to allow Timoshenko to go over to the defensive and ordered that the Kharkov offensive should continue. It was not called off until 19 May. By then Timoshenko was in a desperate position, with the Germans about to cut off his 6th and 57th Armies in a bloody pocket.

The death agony of these armies lasted a week, as Russian infantry charged gun pits and tanks by day and by the light of flares at night. General Gorodnyansky, the commander of the 6th Army, committed suicide as the ring of tanks and Stuka dive bombers tightened. Besides the dead, Timoshenko lost 240,000 men captured and 1,249 tanks.

There were other grim reminders of 1941. Manstein's 11th Army overwhelmed the Red army in the Crimea when it launched its assault on 8 May. Within two days the Soviet commander, the odious Mekhlis, was ordered to retreat but had already lost control of panicking units in full flight. After a week, Manstein reached Kerch. Mekhlis escaped with his life and a demotion, but 176,000 Red army men and 350 tanks were captured. With the Russians on the Kerch peninsula liquidated, Manstein moved on Sebastopol, blowing apart its great forts in twenty-seven days of continuous bombardment and immolating its defenders in their deep bunkers. When finally even submarines could no longer creep into the shattered port, Sebastopol surrendered with 100,000 men.

Humiliation also stalked the quieter north, where Leningrad, invested by the Germans, had been left to starve to death. Vlasov, a hero of 1941, was trapped with his 2nd Shock Army in the swamps of the Volkhov river at the end of May. He tried to escape for almost a month. Refusing to fly out of the pocket himself, he ordered the remnants of his army to break out in small groups as best they could. He was found in a farmer's shed by the Germans and, his faith in Stalin gone, within six weeks was urging his captors to create an anti-Red Russian army.

The winter nightmare behind them, warm soil and dust under their tank tracks and fresh hordes of prisoners filling the cages, the Germans seemed to have stove in the Red army before the Stalingrad campaign had got under way.

It opened on 28 June 1942, at 10 a.m. on a fine morning, the visibility excellent for the artillery spotters and Stuka pilots. The Germans slammed into four Red Armies. One, the 40th, was smashed apart by the exhilarated tank crews of Hoth's 24th Panzer Division. Losing contact with their divisions, staff officers flew in biplanes to try to locate their formations. Stalin refused to allow the 40th to withdraw. No cold, swamps or forests came to the Russian aid in the flat steppeland and corn country of the south. Tracked by German aircraft in the clear heat of high summer, isolated units of the 40th Army wandered until their fuel or strength ran out and they clustered round an isolated building or a stream-bed to wait for the end.

By 5 July German combat teams were assaulting the western suburbs of Voronezh and panzers had reached the Don on both sides of the city. Four days later, to the south, 1st and 4th Panzer Armies were cutting the Russian communications in the rear of the Rostov region. There was stiff fighting in Voronezh and in the pit towns of the Donets basin, where the slagheaps and mine buildings gave some cover to the Red infantrymen. To the east of these scrappy firefights the *Gross Deutschland* and 24th Panzer Divisions were racing towards the Don almost without check, pulling their dust plumes behind them and finding it eerie 'to plunge into this vast area without finding a trace of the enemy'.[6]

With the South-Western Front peeling apart, and the Southern Front creaking, the Stavka formally set up the Stalingrad Front on 12 July.[7] Into it were hustled by train and by forced marches three reserve Armies, the 62nd, 63rd and 64th. By 20 July they numbered 38 divisions, but 14 of these had been so mauled or dislocated in transit that they mustered less than 1,000 men each.

'The Russian is finished,' Hitler told his Chief of Staff, Halder, on 20 July 1942. 'I must admit, it looks like it,' replied the cautious general. But Hitler, said to be in his best spirits since the fall of France two years before, now contrived to rob his armies of the momentum that was impelling them eastward through the hot landscape of burning crops. He ordered 4th Panzer Army to support 1st Panzer in forcing the crossing of the lower Don and creating a huge encirclement battle east of Rostov, which fell on 23 July, NKVD machinegunners fighting a ferocious fifty-hour battle from houses sealed up as firing points. Paulus and his 6th Army were left to continue their advance on Stalingrad alone, stripped of 4th Panzer.

Hitler failed to snap shut the 'final' pocket east of Rostov before the Russians withdrew. Yet the position remained desperate. Stalin demanded the immediate opening of a second front by the British and Americans in the West.[8] Red army morale was cracking. General Vasily Chuikov, commanding one of the half-formed reserve armies, had a depressing debut at the front. 'I came across two divisional staffs,' he wrote. 'They consisted of a number of officers travelling in some three to five trucks filled to overflowing with cans of fuel. When I asked them where the Germans were, and where they were going, they could not give me a sensible reply ...'

The 6th Army crossed the Don, pontoon bridges following the kapok rafts of the assault troops, Soviet bombers attacking the bridgehead at night by the flares of burning vehicles. At 4.30 a.m. on 23 August the 16th Panzer Division broke out of the bridgehead through the Russian 62nd Army and hurled itself in a concentrated pack across 56 kilometres of bare steppe for the Volga. Stukas wheeled above it to deal with Russian strongpoints whilst heavier bombers set Stalingrad on fire. Shortly before midnight a panzer unit radioed that it had penetrated the northern suburbs of Stalingrad and had reached the river that flows on to the Caspian.

The Germans were on the Volga.

The city, as Tsaritsyn the site of Stalin's civil war struggles against the Whites and against Trotsky, stretched for over forty kilometres in a long and thin industrial clutter on the high western bank of the Volga. Three huge industrial complexes, from the north the Tractor, Barricades and then Red October factories, showpieces of socialism with their surrounding garden cities of schools and apartment blocks, dominated the north of the city and were still producing tanks, guns and armaments. The steeply banked river Tsaritsa runs at right angles to the Volga in the centre of the city, bisecting it near the high ground of the Mamayev Kurgan. This old burial ground, the 'Iron Heights', gives views over the city and the Volga. It marked the rough division of the city between its industrial north and the business and administrative south, with its two railway stations, the big Univermag department store and power stations. The river here is between three and four kilometres wide where islands do not cut its flow into channels. It was the lifeline for small boats and ferries taking supplies to be hoarded in ravines and dugouts for the defenders on the west bank. To cut it, the Germans had to reach the east bank.

There would be no Soviet withdrawal from the city, its wooden suburbs burnt through to their brick chimneys and the streets clogged with debris and the dead from a great air raid on 23 August. Stalin had ordered: 'Ni shagu nazad!' 'Not a step backward!' Further south the Germans were racing through the Caucasus. The day before the panzers reached the Volga, men from Army Group A had unfurled the swastika on the 5,484-

metre summit of Mount Elbrus 640 kilometres south of Stalingrad. Cossack divisions had mutinied and the minorities, Crimean Tartars, Karachais, Chechens, Kalmyks, were welcoming the Germans, presenting them with gifts of white stallions. Stalin sent Beria and strong NKVD forces to deal with the revolts.

The Red army was committed to stand. It now had, at least, young and able commanders. Zhukov was appointed Deputy Supreme Commander to Stalin on 27 August. He was supported by General A. M. Vasilevsky as his Chief of General Staff. A former Tsarist captain, the son of a priest, Vasilevsky had fought in the civil war as a Red deputy regimental commander. He was intelligent and patient in slowly suffusing the army with modern strategy. Vassily Chuikov was waiting for recognition in Stalingrad. The son of a peasant, a nineteen-year-old Red regimental commander in the civil war, he had recently returned from a year as a military attaché to Chiang Kai-shek's Nationalists in China. His optimism and tactical brilliance had been untouched by the humiliations of *Barbarossa*.

The front from Leningrad to the Black Sea, with its immense Stalingrad bulge, now stretched for more than 3,200 kilometres. The German lines of communication were dangerously long and vulnerable to partisans, now well organized enough for leaders to be flown out for regular meetings in the Kremlin. Paulus was dependent on two overstrained railway lines, from Novorossisk and Rostov, the latter constantly cut by partisans.

The Russians in Stalingrad had a fighting chance.

Paulus failed to take the city by storm at the end of August. The Volga and the ferries transfusing supplies to the Russians from the east bank were the key. The course of the river and its islands made it difficult for the Germans to shell the crossings by day. At night, with bombers grounded, small boats could slip over with less danger. The Germans caught larger river boats evacuating non-combatants from the west bank, sinking the steamer *Iosif Stalin*, drowning more than a thousand civilians. Women and children, covered with dust and soot, had 'the one desire of getting away to the other side of the river, away from their wrecked houses, away from a city that had become a hell ... The children, suffering from thirst and hunger, were not crying, but simply whining, and stretching out their arms to the water of the Volga.'[9] To cut the traffic dead, and to force a crossing, the Germans needed as wide a riverbank frontage as possible.

When the assault came, however, it was a brute attempt to smash through the city itself. It broke on the morning of 13 September. Two days before, Chuikov had been appointed commander of 62nd Army, crossing into the burning city by boat whilst shrapnel splashed in the water 'like trout'. The 62nd held the central sector of the city, some of its 10,000-man divisions reduced to a few hundred riflemen and machinegunners, its tank brigades down to a handful of machines dug in for static defence.

Six German divisions smashed into the 62nd Army. Artillery fire pulverized the bunkers of Chuikov's HQ on the Mamayev Kurgan, cutting communications with his units. During the night Chuikov shifted his HQ from the vulnerable heights to a command post sunk into the side of the Tsaritsa riverbank and known as the 'Tsaritsyn bunker'. A counter-attack at dawn on 14 September failed. During the afternoon German infantry of 71st Division and tanks burst into the central sector of the city to chop 62nd Army into reducable pockets. The 62nd Army men, 'snipers, anti-tank gunners, artillerymen, lying in wait in houses, cellars and firing points', watched the Germans hurrying for the Volga. 'The Germans obviously thought that the fate of the town had been settled,' wrote Chuikov. 'We saw drunken Germans jumping down from their lorries, playing mouth organs, shouting like madmen and dancing on the pavements.' They broke through to the Volga at several points, took the crest of the Mamayev Kurgan and closed on the Stalingrad-1 railway station from where they were able to machinegun the main Volga landing stage.

Chuikov, the Germans penetrating to within 180 metres of his new command post, used his last reserve of nineteen tanks to clear the German machinegunners. As night fell he ordered the 13th Guards Infantry Division of General Rodimtsev to cross from the east bank in small groups, leaving their heavy equipment behind them. They were to clear the centre of the city and retake the Mamayev Kurgan. The leading group of Guardsmen splashed from their boats in the shallows and fought their way ashore to establish a small bridgehead just upstream of the central landing stage. More men followed during a night lit by burning barges and buildings, to be savaged by the wheeling Stukas as day broke. They moved straight off to clear German 71st infantrymen from the platforms and halls of Stalingrad-1, the Central Station, to prise away their grip on the landing stage. They fought with tommyguns, rifle butts, flamethrowers, grenades, explosives, lumps of masonry and steel rods. The war diary of 62nd Army on 14 September recorded the struggle: '0800 Station in enemy hands, 0840 Station recaptured. 0940 Station retaken by enemy. 1040 Enemy ... 600 metres from Army command post ... 1320 Station in our hands.'

More 13th Guardsmen were ferried over the Volga the following night. On 16 September they succeeded in clearing the area round the central landing stage and retook the Central Station, the fifteenth time it had changed hands. That dawn, two regiments assaulted the Mamayev Kurgan. A squad of thirty men closed on the summit, clearing the German gunpits in hand-to-hand fighting, taking twenty-four casualties but maintaining a tenuous hold on the summit despite German counter-attacks. The struggle for the great mound continued throughout the battle, shellbursts later melting the snows on its flanks.

Above the city and the river wheeled the Luftwaffe aircraft, their screamer sirens blaring, flying up to 3,000 sorties a day against the Russians' 300. On the ground, Chuikov's men faced twice their number of men and artillery pieces and five times their strength in tanks.

Fighting imploded from blocks to buildings and then to rooms. At the Central Station a battalion of Rodimtsev's Guardsmen dug in behind smashed railway wagons and platforms. Bombed and shelled, 'the station buildings were on fire, the walls burst apart, the iron buckled'. The survivors moved to a nearby ruin where, tormented by thirst, they fired at drainpipes to see if any water would drip out. During the night, German sappers blew up the wall separating the room holding the Russians from the German-held part of the building and threw in grenades. An attack cut the battalion in two and the headquarters staff was trapped inside the Univermag department store where it and the battalion commander were killed in hand-to-hand fighting.

The last forty men of the battalion pulled back to a building on the Volga. They set up a heavy machinegun in the basement and broke down the walls at the top of the building to prepare lumps of stone and wood to hurl at the Germans. They had no water and only a few pounds of scorched grain to eat. After five days, a survivor wrote, 'the basement was full of wounded; only twelve men were still able to fight'. The battalion nurse was dying of a chest wound. The men had 'thin, blackened and strained faces' and the bandages on their wounds were 'dirty and clotted with blood'. A German tank ground forward and a Russian slipped out with the last anti-tank rifle rounds to deal with it. He was captured by German tommygunners. Apparently, he persuaded his captors that the Russians had run out of ammunition, because the Germans 'came impudently out of their shelter, standing up and shouting'. The last belt of machinegun cartridges was fired into them and 'an hour later they led our anti-tank rifleman on to a heap of ruins and shot him in front of our eyes'. More squat German tanks appeared and reduced the building with point-blank fire. At night, six survivors of the battalion freed themselves from the rubble and struggled to the Volga.[10] There they improvised a raft and drifted downstream, to be picked up by a Russian anti-aircraft crew.

Another battalion of Guardsmen defending a concrete grain elevator was down to thirty to thirty-five men when it was reinforced by marine infantry on 17 September. The following day ten attacks by tanks and infantry were beaten off. 'In the elevator the grain was on fire, the water in the machineguns evaporated, the wounded were thirsty,' wrote Andrey Khozynanov, a survivor.[11] 'We sensed and heard the enemy soldiers' breath and footsteps, but we could not see them in the smoke. We fired at sounds.' Breaking out of the elevator on the night of 20 September, Khozynanov was knocked unconscious. He came to in a cellar several days later: 'A door opened and in the bright sunlight I could see a tommygunner in a black uniform. On his left sleeve was a skull. I had fallen into the hands of the enemy.'

The men of the Rodimtsev Division saved Stalingrad for the moment. They did so at the cost of virtual extinction. In their place came the Siberians of the 284th Rifle Division, ferried over the Volga before dawn on 23 September. German tommygunners were within 140 metres of them as they landed in the constant green and yellow flarelight that hung over the city. Though retaking the Central Station was beyond their strength, they reinforced the Mamayev Kurgan and checked the German thrusts in the centre.

Both sides lying exhausted in their cellars and barrows of rubble, the fighting in the city centre gradually eased.

The ante was constantly increased as both sides fed in new troops, Hitler dangerously from the defensive screen of the 320-kilometre front stretching back to the west, Zhukov more happily from the reserves on the east bank. 'They would stand there on the shore, shivering with cold and fear,' said the novelist Viktor Nekrasov of the reinforcements reaching the west bank. 'By the time these newcomers reached the front line, five or ten out of twenty had already been killed by German shells; for with those German flares over the Volga and our front lines, there was never complete darkness. But the peculiar thing about these chaps was that those among them who reached the front line very quickly became wonderfully hardened soldiers. Real *frontoviks*.'[12] The ferries, tugs and barges were augmented by the boats of the Volga fishing fleet.

Chuikov ordered that no-man's land should never be greater than 'the distance of a hand-grenade throw' to nullify German air attacks. Small storm groups of Russians, machinegunners, tommygunners and grenadiers, had learned to close on enemy positions, scurrying on all fours through the craters and ruins. An assault party of half a dozen men led the storm groups, armed with tommyguns, grenades, knives and spades with sharpened edges. A reinforcement squad would move in after the assault group had fired a flare to show that it had broken into a building. This was more heavily equipped with machineguns, mortars, anti-tank rifles, explosives and picks, with snipers to take advantage of the newly won strongpoint.

The Germans supported their attacks by day with aircraft and tanks. A company of infantry would attack with three or four tanks, but the going was hard in the rubble-strewn streets and the crews were fearful to approach buildings where the lightly armoured rear deck could be holed by anti-tank rounds and grenades hurled from above. Armour-piercing shot passed straight through buildings and the limited turret elevation of the panzers meant that high-explosive shells could not reach upper storeys. The grid plan of Stalingrad, with streets running west-east to the Volga, helped the Germans by day since a single tank or firepoint at the western end could control movement. But the Germans found that the enemy swarmed back by night, knocking holes between the attics through which they ran 'like rats in the rafters'.[13]

Paulus launched a further offensive on 27 September, a Sunday, tanks crashing through minefields into the northern industrial zone and Stukas and assault teams throwing the Guards unit off the top of the Mamayev Kurgan. Its remnants dug in on the north-eastern slope. By the evening the Germans had forced their way 2,700 metres into Chuikov's positions, losing 2,000 dead and 50 tanks. Chuikov's western flank was 'nothing but a bloody stump of broken regiments'. Chuikov radioed urgently for air cover and reinforcements. 'One more such day and we would have been thrown into the Volga,' he said.

Men of the 193rd Rifle Division crossed the river into the flarelit and echoing night, moving directly from the mortared bank to the kitchens of the Red October plant where the Germans had seized the bath-houses and school of the factory's garden city. Under the harsh magnesium light of parachute flares, Guardsmen counter-attacked on the raddled slopes of the Mamayev Kurgan.

German bombers were over the city at first light on 28 September. They hit five out of six steamers serving the Red October landing stage. Oil tanks above Chuikov's command post were set ablaze. The staff were 'choking with the heat and smoke', wrote Chuikov. 'Every dive-bomber attack was killing people ... Even Glinka, our cook, who had set up his field kitchen in a bomb crater, was wounded.'

But there was a desperation and lack of cohesion to the German attacks. Men driven beyond exhaustion slid into depression or, fuelled with benzedrine, schnapps and vodka, rallied in half-mad exhilaration. 'Supported by tanks, entire battalions would hurl themselves into the attacks,' said Chuikov. 'This enabled us to concentrate our artillery fire on them.' Russian artillery and *Katyushas* firing from the relative safety of the east bank lashed down. 'I can hardly describe the soldiers' love for them,' wrote the novelist Konstantin Simonov. On the Mamayev Kurgan, its summit a no-man's-land raked by shellfire from both sides, there were 500 German corpses.

By the beginning of October 62nd Army had been reduced to a 20-kilometre slice of the city, with a depth back from the river varying between 230 metres and 2.5 kilometres. The Germans, feeling that a final all-out offensive would finish it, were confident. '*Russ, skoro bul-bul u Volga*,' they shouted from their trenches. 'Russian, you'll soon be blowing bubbles in the Volga.'

In the shrinking Russian bridgeheads, reinforcements had immediate effect. The Siberians of Colonel Gurtiev's division, who crossed on 1 October, 'young and tall and healthy, many in paratroop uniform, with knives and daggers tucked in their belts', were almost instantaneously in action in the northern part of the city. Though the east bank was an 'ant-heap' of Soviet artillery, supply services and reserves, the number who could be physically accommodated on the west was not much more than about forty thousand. Zhukov could coolly feed in a minimum of troops, whilst steadily building his own reserves for the counter-offensive.

Meanwhile the Germans were slowly grinding their divisions to pieces in a desperate attempt to end it before winter came. Already the nights were drawing cooler and cloudbanks were building. General Halder had already noted that a 'gradual exhaustion' had seized Paulus' 6th Army. Companies had been reduced to sixty men. Armour, no longer a moving spearhead but a sullen battering ram, had burnt out in futile street battles. General Kurt Zeitzler, Halder's successor as CoGS, called for the Stalingrad offensive to be aborted, but Hitler was not in the mood to give up 'a single yard'. Paulus' call for a reinforcement of three divisions had been answered with a few sapper battalions flown in from Germany to blunt the Russian edge in house-to-house fighting. Dull, unimaginative, Paulus could come up with nothing better than a further head-on attack on the factory districts.

For it, Chuikov estimated, Paulus had a main force of about 90,000 men, with 2,000 guns and mortars, 300 tanks and 1,000 aircraft. Against it, Chuikov had 55,000 men, 1,450 guns and mortars, 80 tanks and 188 aircraft.[14]

The attack was unleashed by three infantry and two panzer divisions on the 'unforgettable day' of 14 October, a Wednesday. It was sunny and autumnal, but the smoke and soot soon reduced the visibility to 100 metres. The Germans, backed by 3,000 air sorties, attacked on a four-kilometre front towards the Tractor and Barricades factories, where the Russian depth to the Volga was just three kilometres. The Germans crouched in firepoints and trenches as Stukas and artillery shells bounced gouts of masonry and rubble above the Russian positions. When the infantry joined battle in mid morning, they could not distinguish individual shots and explosions above the general cascade of the bombardment.

The Germans slowly closed on the Tractor factory and the Barricades, the Russians hurling grenades and Molotov cocktails at them. By noon, German tommygunners supported by 200 tanks had broken through General Zholudev's 37th Division to the walls of the Tractor factory,

Sailors from the cruiser *Aurora* in Petrograd in October 1917. Then the 'pride and glory of the Revolution' to Trotsky, her sailors were later slaughtered in Trotsky's attack on Kronstadt. (© *David King Collection*)

Below Red Guards outside the Smolny Institute, the former girls' school and focal point of the Revolution during Red October. (© *David King Collection*)

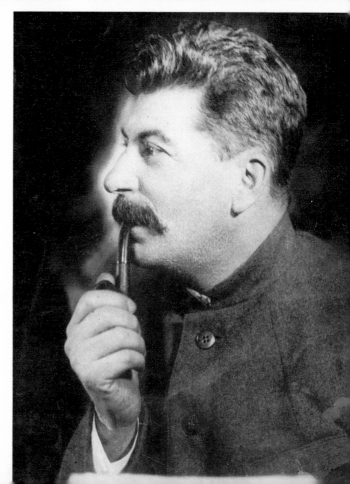

Above Marshal Tukhachevsky, commander of the 7th Army in the attack on Kronstadt in 1921 and the most prominent of thousands of officers shot in the purges. (© *Popperfoto*)

Above right Leon Trotsky, creator of the Red Army, victor of the Civil War and later a victim of Stalin, in a portrait c. 1920. (© *Popperfoto*)

Right Joseph Stalin, 'the Kremlin mountaineer, the murderer', who dominated the Red army for a quarter of a century. (© *Popperfoto*)

The Winter War: a thinly clad Red army man frozen to death during the unsuccessful first assault on Finnish positions at the end of 1939. (© *Popperfoto*)

Below The outbreak of the Great Patriotic War: Red army tanks in the frontier area in June 1941. Although they outnumbered the German panzers by seven to one, virtually all these tanks were lost in the first few weeks of war. (© *Popperfoto*)

Top The Germans a few miles away, troops in Red Square on 7 November 1941 had live ammunition. They marched straight on for the front. (© *Magnum*)

Far left Stalin during the Red Square parade on 7 November 1941.

Left Red army troops break through in December 1942 as they cut off the German 6th army in Stalingrad. (© *Imperial War Museum*)

Above left A German infantryman, in crude straw boots, shuffles into captivity. The Russians ridiculed the German lack of preparation and 'Winter Fritz', stumbling along on straw boots, was a comic figure in theatres.

Above right Soviet troops fighting in the ruins of Stalingrad at the end of 1942.

Red army tank men, the guts of the war effort. (© *Novosti*)

Below The Forge: T-34s on the production line in a plant evacuated beyond the Urals. (© *Novosti*)

Soviet armour attacking in the great tank battle at Kursk in July 1943: 'tragic, unbelievable visions ... tightly riveted machines ripped like the belly of a cow ... the cries of officers and noncoms, trying to shout across the cataclysm'.
(© *Novosti*)

German troops are paraded through Moscow after the collapse of the central front in 1944.
(© *Novosti*)

Red armour rolls into Königsberg in April 1945 – the last German redoubt in East Prussia which, divided between Poland and the Soviet Union, has ceased to exist.
(© *Novosti*)

As Russian assault troops raised the Red flag over the Reichstag in Berlin, Germans were still fighting in the basement. (© *Keystone*)

The end of the Great Patriotic War: Germans surrender with their arms. (© *Novosti*)

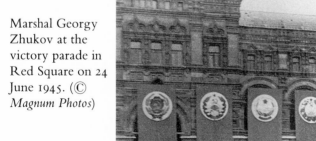

Marshal Georgy Zhukov at the victory parade in Red Square on 24 June 1945. (© *Magnum Photos*)

where they turned into the rear of 112th Division. By late afternoon the 37th and 112th had been surrounded, with General Zholudev dug out alive from the ruins of his command post. Russian units fought until their ammunition ran out. Then their radios would go dead. Without radio communications to provide targets, the bulk of the Russian artillery on the east bank of the Volga was effectively neutered. On the west bank, lorries with *Katyushas* mounted on them were reversed out of their lairs in the cliffs into the river shallows to bring the Germans within range.

By midnight the Germans had surrounded the Tractor factory on three sides and were fighting in small, savage spasms through the machine shops and assembly halls. Reaching the Volga on a front of more than two kilometres, the Germans cut 62nd Army in two. Chuikov's bunker, only 480 metres from the enemy tommygunners, filled with men seeking shelter or orders. That night, as Zholudev's division was torn to pieces squad by squad, a single regiment of riflemen was able to cross the river. After daybreak, German aircraft and six-barrelled mortars interdicted the Tractor factory crossings. Nikita Khrushchev, the political commissar on the east bank, was in contact with Chuikov and agreed that the units trapped round the Tractor factory would have to fend for themselves if the rest of 62nd Army was to survive. By 16 October resistance in the Tractor factory was all but over. Zholudev's 37th Guards had only 200 or so men left alive, one regiment down to 84, another to 30. Before midnight 62nd Army staff confirmed that the plant had fallen and that the enemy were now attempting to seize the Barricades.

During the early hours of 17 October, as another division was flung across the Volga, Chuikov was forced to move his Army HQ again, to a ravine on the open bank of the Volga 900 metres from the Mamayev Kurgan. This was the maximum depth of the bridgehead that remained to the Russians. Cooks, storemen, telephonists and factory workers were impressed into the line as the German attack continued to roll south on to the Barricades and Red October plants. Hundreds of wounded soldiers and civilians huddled by the crossing points or lay untreated on the mid-river islands. Walls were built of rubble and stone to screen the crossing points from enemy machinegun fire. By the evening of 23 October the German 79th Infantry Division supported by tanks and Stukas had cut into a corner of the Red October plant. The following day the Germans penetrated the Barricades factory. Between collapsed roof girders, behind hulks of machinery, from deep burrows of ruined shards, listening for the clink of rubble to warn of enemy movement, the war of knives and tommygun and grenade bursts progressed.

'We have fought during fifteen days for a single house,' wrote a panzer officer, Lieutenant Weiner.[15] 'The front is a corridor between burnt-out rooms; it is the thin ceiling between two floors ... From storey to storey, faces black with sweat, we bombard each other with grenades in the middle of explosions, clouds of dust and smoke, heaps of mortar, floods of blood, fragments of furniture and human beings.' In the 'scorching howling bleeding nights', dogs plunged into the Volga and swam desperately to gain the other bank.

There were some men to whom it was fulfilment, the characters who, as Pabst put it, prowled 'with slung rifles, jackets unbuttoned and caps askew. They have a look in their eyes which makes them different from the rest. You know them immediately. They're the ones who carry on the war. They're indestructible. They drift around, game for anything. Danger attracts them, they love brushing with death. It's rare that such a man is caught. He's too quick, too skilful, too resolute. He masters the game and plays it for a long time. Then he breaks the rules too often or he meets his match . . .'[16]

Such men were often snipers and two of them, the Russian Nikolay Kulikov and a 'Nazi "super-sniper" ' believed to be the head of the German snipers' school at Berlin-Zossen, fought their own slow and patient duel across the rubble. For four days the two lay waiting for a mistake, shielding their telescopic sights from the sun. Across from the Russians were a knocked-out tank and a pillbox. Between them lay a sheet of iron and a small pile of broken bricks. It had been lying there for a long time. The Russians put a mitten on a plank and raised it. It was shot straight through. 'There's our viper!' said Kulikov. He waited until the sun shone on the German's position the next day. 'At the edge of the sheet of metal something was glittering: an odd bit of glass or telescopic sights?' Kulikov began to raise his helmet. The German fired. For a fraction of a second Kulikov rose and screamed. The German half raised his head from the sheet of metal. Kulikov 'took careful aim. The German's head fell back, and the telescopic sights of his rifle lay motionless, glistening in the sun, until night fell . . .'[17]

Most of those fighting on both sides in Stalingrad were conscripts with no abnormal taste for combat. Yet they fought with an equal sense of doom and ferocity, the Germans desperate to break through the 'blood-blossoming' streets to the Volga at any cost before winter and the barbaric but unbreakable sub-humans did for them; the Russians fired by a sense of justice and the comradeship of surviving a foreign-made hell on their own soil. There was no need to resort to the penal battalions at Stalingrad. Both sides were willing.

Early on 27 October battalions of the 45th Division were ferried over the river to take positions between the Red October and Barricades plants. In the concrete and steel hulk of the Barricades the Germans were firing from the foundries at Russians holding the coking ovens. The 62nd Army had no reserve unit left. Chuikov had committed his training battalion.

Though his front was split in places, and only a few hundred metres deep in the centre, he was holding. By 30 October he began to feel that he was winning.

Paulus did try again. At 6.30 a.m. on 11 November the last German assault on the remnants of Stalingrad was opened by Stukas and artillery. The Soviet 138th Division was trapped in a pocket 360 metres by 640, its wounded lying in a downpour of rain and sleet, one of its regiments reduced to thirty-one men. The divisional staff fought hand-to-hand against German tommygunners. Most of the ruined Red October plant was in German hands. In gusts of freezing rain the Germans dragged themselves towards the river. Now covered with ice-floes and navigable only by the smallest boats, it was a hundred metres distant in places where they had not reached it.

Although 'at our last gasp', and failing to cut through the German salient on the Volga with counter-attacks, the Russian bridgeheads survived. They had sucked in German strength from now fragile flanks, luring an invader who depended on grand manoeuvre in open space into a rabbit warren of immobile ruins. Corporal Hitler had despised the German generals who, allowing themselves to be trapped in trench warfare in the First World War, had become 'besotted by an advance of a thousand yards'. In limitless Russia he would not now contemplate a withdrawal of a metre. For Stalin, reverting to type meant the civil war, an affair of extreme fluidity and change of fortune.

At 7.30 a.m. on 19 November after a night of exhausted lull, the Germans heard the distant drum-fire of 3,500 guns and mortars to the far north-west. Such a change of fortune had begun.

17

THE PIT

For once, Gehlen's reading of Russian intentions was faulty. The intelligence chief was confident that the Russians were too weak to attack the flanks of Army Group B. On paper, it possessed seven Armies, one of them 4th Panzer, and the 16th Motorized 'Greyhound' Division.

But four of these armies were satellite forces and the whole was stretched thin on a colossal front. To the south, gaps in German positions were held by poorly equipped Rumanian corps in scattered positions on an extended front. Stalingrad itself was held tightly enough by Paulus' 6th Army. But the Don front stretching away to the north-west from the city was held

first by the 3rd Rumanian Army and then the 8th Italian and 2nd Hungarian Armies. Only the last section from Voronezh to Kursk was held by
Germans, of 2nd Army.

The Rumanians were scantily equipped with plunder captured during
the fall of France. There was only one anti-tank company per division and
most of these had old 37-mm guns, useless against T-34s, rather than the
powerful German 75-mms. They were short of ammunition, mines, food
and winter clothing. The Germans had already noted that General Dumitrescu's 3rd Rumanian Army was more interested in building itself warm
dugouts than proper defensive positions. They had done little to reduce
the bridgeheads which the Russians held south of the Don opposite them.
Some of these were sixteen kilometres deep.

The Russians were well aware of these weaknesses. Attacks at the
beginning of October had shown Rumanian vulnerability, with two
divisions crumbling rapidly under pressure.

Zhukov had succeeded in assembling three Fronts or Army Groups to
fling against the Stalingrad screen.[1] His counter-offensive, planned with
Vassilevsky, called for an attack over the Don from the north together
with an attack from the south of Stalingrad to cut off the Germans in the
city. The northern armies under Generals Rokossovsky, Vatutin and
Gorlikov faced Paulus' left wing and the 3rd Rumanian, 8th Italian and
2nd Hungarian Armies. They were to break through to Kalach. Swinging
up to join them from the south, General Yeremenko's army would face
the 4th Rumanian Army.

The intense husbanding of the troops fed into Stalingrad itself and the
extraordinary efforts made by the arms plants gave him rough equality to
the enemy forces. The three Fronts totalled just over a million men, about
the same as available to the Germans. Though Zhukov's 1,100 aircraft
were marginally inferior to the Germans', he had 894 tanks against 700
and 13,451 guns against 10,000. Virtually all this equipment was brand
new, and had come out of the Urals and Siberian plants during the summer
and early autumn.

Morale was high, helped by the re-establishment of unitary command
on 9 October, which had stripped the military commissars of their controls
and left commanders at last fully responsible for their men. Though the
Rumanians had fought well enough in the Crimea, their morale sagged
as they prepared to spend a winter on the open Don steppes on behalf of
a foreign Fuehrer. The Russians knew this and also sensed the weakness
of the Italians stationed further west on the Don.

The Russians had an overwhelming superiority in the breakthrough
sectors. On an attack frontage of less than 65 kilometres, Zhukov concentrated over half a million men, 230 regiments of field artillery and 115
Katyusha regiments and hundreds of new T-34s. He had a superiority never

before achieved in Russia, with threefold the men and fourfold the artillery and mortars. The build-up had been achieved in the greatest secrecy. All mail had been stopped between the soldiers of the three Fronts and their families for weeks before the offensive. Stalin had said cryptically on 6 November that there would 'soon be a party on our street'. The day before, the British General Montgomery had won the battle of El Alamein and two days later Eisenhower was to invade Morocco and Algeria. But Stalin, who sarcastically referred to the British fighting 'four, yes *four* German divisions', did not have the Allies and North Africa in mind. He was thinking of the guns of November on the Don.

Snowclouds built up after midnight on 19 November, and a sharply dropping temperature brought freezing fog. Rocket salvoes began the bombardment on the twenty-four kilometres of initial breakthrough sector. Then the artillery joined in, the Russian gunners firing blindly at the Rumanian positions through the eddying fog and snow.

The Russian soldiers in Stalingrad, at the most silent hour of their day as the Russian-dominated night bled into the frenzied German day, listened to the far-off ferocity of the guns with 'frantic joy, hope and excitement'.

The Rumanians were overwhelmed as Rokossovsky's T-34s with tommygunners crouching on them clattered through their wire. By mid morning a wind was dispersing the mists and Russian aircraft tossed their bomb-loads on to the still fighting Rumanians. The rout began at noon. A 13-kilometre wide gash was torn in the Rumanian front and armour and infantry poured through it. The tank crews steered by compass across the wastes of the Don steppe south-east for Kalach, the infantry following in their tracks. Infantry divisions dissolved in panic as the 3rd Rumanian Army disintegrated.

As Army Group B headquarters ordered Paulus to break off the attack in Stalingrad and look to his crumbling left flank, the Russians prepared to bash in his right. At 10 a.m. the following day, 20 November, Yeremenko with two armoured corps and nine infantry divisions launched himself against the 4th Rumanian Army on the Ergeni Hills to the south of the city. The Rumanians began to surrender as the T-34s broke into their positions. By evening the Russian Fronts were pouring through the bloody rents in both flanks, driving south-east and north-west over thirty kilometres in Paulus' rear.

Rokossovsky's tanks raced across the icy steppe for the bridge over the Don at Kalach. The bridge was close to a German anti-tank training school, where captured Russian machines were a common sight. Driving through the pre-dawn darkness on 23 November, their lights glowing, the Russian tanks were mistaken for captured machines by the Germans. They raced across the bridge, machinegunning the guards and beating off a German attempt to blow it up. At two that afternoon, green signal rockets identifying each other, the commanders embracing with three kisses, Rokossovsky's and Yeremenko's men linked up.

Paulus was surrounded in an area 55 kilometres wide and 30 kilometres from north to south. With him was his Army, 100 surviving tanks, 2,000 guns, 5 *Generalkommandos*, 20 infantry and armoured divisions, a Croat infantry regiment, assault engineers, meteorologists, medical staff, cryptographers, interpreters, cartographers and vets.

The trap was sprung.

Hitler was in the Berghof, amid the cool and relaxing peaks of the Obersalzberg, when it became clear that 6th Army was in mortal danger. He would have none of it, claiming that his generals were panicking. 'They always overestimate the strength of the Russians,' he sneered.

It was imperative that Paulus' men should break out immediately before the Russian ring set too hard. The troops were keyed up to fight their way through to the south-west to link up with General Hoth's 4th Panzer Army. Some of 51st Panzer Corps, isolated on the bare steppe north of Stalingrad, burned their heavy equipment, blew up their deep winter bunkers and moved south into the city to await the inevitable order for a break-out. That it never came was due mainly to the obese and drug-ridden Luftwaffe overlord, Herman Goering. 'Brisk and beaming like an operetta tenor who is supposed to portray a victorious Reichsmarschall,' as Speer put it,[2] Goering told Hitler: 'I personally guarantee the supply of Stalingrad by air. You can rely on that.' He promised a daily delivery of 500 tons of supplies, although the air fleet responsible had only 298 serviceable aircraft, half of what was needed. Flying conditions were atrocious, with severe winds and pilots making their approaches to rough airstrips through snowstorms.

Hitler's order to stand fast on the Volga was relayed to Stalingrad on 24 November. The perplexed troops, instead of fighting their way out, were now redeployed in defensive positions within the *Kessel*, the cauldron, which, wider across than from north to south, and with a 'nose' jutting out to the north-west, had the grim outline of a compressed skull. The commanders, if not the rest of the quarter million trapped within it, soon had an inkling of what lay in store. On 25 November Luftwaffe transports flying in turbulent snowcloud and harried by Russian fighters brought in less than a third of the needed minimum of supplies. Hitler himself, in the warmth of his Wolf's Lair, expressed himself 'confident about the position of 6th Army' that day.

It was the confidence of the egomaniac. Stalin had already achieved Operation *Uranus*, the cutting off of the enemy on the Stalingrad axis. And *Uranus* was to be followed by *Saturn*, a vast outer sweep aimed at capturing Rostov and sealing off the German Army Group A in the Caucasus. Success would return the coal mines and power plants of the Donbas and the riches of the eastern Ukraine to Russian industry.

It was essential to finish off the Germans in Stalingrad to release enough men for the ultra-ambitious *Saturn* plan. German assault groups, only briefly unnerved by the sound of artillery strikes deep in their rear, were holding the outer line of encirclement with enough vigour to tie down half the available Red army strength.

It is possible that 6th Army saved Army Group A by drawing off Russian strength. That star of *Barbarossa*, General Manstein, was appointed by Hitler to command a new Army Group in the Don bend between Army Groups A and B. This was a weak force, comprising the trapped 6th Army and the battered 4th Panzer and 3rd Rumanian Armies. Despite its grand title, Army Group Don, it had little more strength than a corps. After the war Manstein claimed that had 6th Army broken out 'the entire enemy siege forces would have been released. With that, in all probability, the fate of the whole southern wing of the German forces in the east would have been sealed – including Army Group A.'[3] Zhukov was unwilling to exploit the chaos caused by *Uranus* until the Stalingrad pocket had been cleared.

Manstein nevertheless tried to break through to 6th Army. On the morning of 12 December, a relief force under General Hermann Hoth moved out of the Kotelnikovo area and aimed itself ninety-five kilometres north-east towards 6th Army. One of Hoth's Panzer Divisions, the 6th, had recently been transshipped from France and was in vigorous form. Another, the 23rd, had a battalion of new Tiger 1 tanks, 68-ton monsters with 88-mm guns, in which Hitler placed much hope.

That evening, with 6th Army already starving through his broken promise, a relaxed Goering invited his cronies to a festive performance of Wagner's *Die Meistersinger* to celebrate the reopening of the Berlin State Opera House. They sat in full dress and gala uniform in the Fuehrer's box and laughed away the frivolity of the evening.

Hoth's tank crews pressed across the moonlit steppe, a supply train behind them, with buses for the wounded of Stalingrad, and fuel, ammunition and food hauled in captured trucks and on carts pulled by farm tractors. By 19 December the crews of 6th Panzer could see the flares fired on the Stalingrad perimeter.

They could not continue their isolated advance for long. The Italian 8th Army had been routed on a forty-five-kilometre front and Manstein's front on the Chir river was collapsing. It was essential for 6th Army itself to break out towards the relief column before Hoth was surrounded. The collapse of German position in the Don country was already having an impact far to the south. It was forcing the Germans into a rapid retreat from the vast areas of the Caucasus that had fallen to them during the summer.

Paulus stalled on the question of break-out. He claimed that his tanks had only enough fuel for twenty kilometres, though his tank commanders probably followed tradition by keeping some supplies up their sleeves. 6th Army, the largest single concentration of German arms on the Eastern front, victorious in the Low Countries, Yugoslavia and Greece and unstoppable in Russia three months before, had only forty kilometres of featureless land to struggle through to Hoth's bridgehead across the Myshkova river. The Russians, at least, remain surprised that it did not try.

For four vital days, from 19 to 23 December, Paulus and Manstein vacillated over their teleprinter link. By Christmas Eve it was too late. The Russians had amassed almost 150,000 men and 635 tanks in Hoth's area. That morning General Badanov's 24th Tank Corps, raiding deep in the rear, broke into Tatsinskaya. The village was one of the main Luftwaffe bases for ferrying supplies to Stalingrad. As the Russians poured on to the airfield, a T-34 and a taxiing Ju-52 trying to escape collided in a violent explosion. The air bridge to Stalingrad was flimsier than ever. Badanov heard by radio that he had become the first man to receive the new patriotic decoration, the Order of Suvorov. The Russian breakthrough left the steppe 'a fantastic sight; it was full of dead horses, while some horses were only half-dead, standing on three frozen legs, and shaking the remaining broken one ... The whole steppe was strewn with these dead horses and wrecked gun carriages and tanks and guns – German, French, Czech, even British, no doubt captured at Dunkirk ...'[4]

Manstein was forced to strip Hoth of 6th Panzer to fill the new gaps torn in his front, whilst attention focused on Kleist's desperate and ultimately successful attempts to get Army Group A out of the Caucasus and through Rostov before the ring closed there.

On Christmas Day 1942 Hoth and the last hopes for 6th Army were in full retreat.

The men knew they were doomed. Frostbite was induced as an anaesthetic for the wounded, who might then freeze to death as they waited for a rare transport to touch down at one of the cratered airstrips. The temperature fell to minus 25 degrees Centigrade at the end of December, reviving to minus 5 degrees Centigrade after the New Year before dropping again to as much as minus 40. The men ate their horses, and the skeletons lay in yards covered with the frozen cesspools of their dysentery.

In the ruins, a chaplain celebrated Communion on an altar made from an ammunition box. 'Yesterday the box still held anti-aircraft shells; today my hand spread over it the field-grey tunic of a comrade whose eyes I closed last Friday in this very room,' he wrote. 'I read my boys the

Christmas story according to the gospel of Luke ... The men sat on footstools and looked up to me from large eyes in their starved faces.'

The 6th Army continued to function, if only now by instinct. 'Around me everything is collapsing, a whole army is dying, day and night are on fire,' wrote a meteorologist. 'And four men busy themselves with daily reports on temperature and cloud ceilings.' It maintained its last residue of morale. A pianist, the three middle fingers of his right hand lost through frostbite, noted how a fellow soldier-musician had played the *Appassionata* on a grand piano dragged into the street from a destroyed house. 'Kurt played incredibly well ... If the boy gets home, we will soon hear about him ... A hundred soldiers squatted around in their greatcoats with blankets over their heads. Everywhere there was the sound of explosions, but no one let himself be disturbed. They were listening to Beethoven in Stalingrad ...'

A Russian call for surrender was refused on 8 January 1943. Two days later the Russians opened a concentric tank and infantry assault with a barrage from 7,000 guns. The landscape, white with snow the day before, was 'now grey with soot and smoke and dotted with thousands of black shell-holes'. The Soviet infantry advanced past 'blackened German bodies, wrecked enemy guns and mortars, shattered dugouts and pillboxes'.

The western nose of the cauldron was the first to be sliced off, the Russians paying for it with 26,000 casualties. On 14 January the main German airfield at Pitomnik, twenty-two kilometres west of the city centre, fell as men fought to board the last aircraft. Before the war Pitomnik had been famous for its orchards of apples, pears and cherries. The wounded were now its crop. Hitler ordered that: 'Capitulation is impossible. 6th Army will do its historic duty at Stalingrad until the last man, in order to make possible the reconstruction of the Eastern Front.' In its death throes, it was aiding Kleist's escape from the Caucasus.

It did its duty. 'You can be sure that everything will end decently,' a young officer had written to his father in the last bag of mail to be flown out of the cauldron.[5] 'It is a little early at thirty, I know. No sentiment ... Hand to helmet, Father. First Lieutenant — respectfully gives notice of departure.'

Divisional and corps commanders, where they did not commit suicide, fought with the remnants of their men in the frozen trenches and gunpits. Forced back against Chuikov's 62nd Army on the west bank of the Volga, the 6th inflicted such casualties and gave up so few prisoners, less than 7,000, that the Soviet commanders discussed a pause in the offensive on 17 January. By that time the cauldron had shrunk to fifteen kilometres by eight.[6] Gumrak airfield, the last physical link with the outside world, was overrun on 22 January. That day the Soviet 21st Army made contact at the Red October plant with the survivors of Rodimtsev's Guardsmen of the 62nd Army. The Germans, as Chuikov's men before them, were now split in two. The wounded lay in the moaning dark of cellars whilst above ground, in the seven hours of winter daylight, Russian tanks closed on Paulus' headquarters in the Univermag building.

On 31 January Hitler promoted Paulus to Field Marshal. Later in the day 6th Army radio sent its last message: 'The Russians are before our bunker. We are destroying the station.' Two Russian lieutenants with some tommygunners entered the basement of the Univermag store. They found Paulus lying on an iron bed, unshaven. ' "Well, that finishes it", I remarked to him,' said one of them. 'He gave me a sort of miserable look and nodded.'[7] Paulus, shivering in greatcoat and rabbit-skin cap, came out to surrender. Even then, the German pocket in the north of the city continued to fight. On 1 February they were subjected to a barrage by guns whose concentration reached one every three metres.

On 2 February, at four in the afternoon, the battle of Stalingrad was over. With Paulus, 23 surviving generals, 2,500 other officers and 90,000 other ranks went into captivity.

The Red army was soon pouring out of Stalingrad, in lorries, horse wagons and sleighs drawn by camels which stepped through the snow 'as if it were sand'. Thousands of troops were on the move, in their *valenki* boots and padded jackets and fur caps, with watering eyes and hoarfrost on their lips. They were 'cheerful and strangely happy, and they kept shouting about the job they had done. Westward, westward! ... They were going west. How much better it felt than going east!'[8]

18

TO BERLIN:
CITADEL AT KURSK

The Stalingrad pit had consumed a crack army, mangled the Luftwaffe, broken the morale of the satellite Italians, Rumanians and Hungarians and destroyed any realistic German hopes of knocking out the Red army with a final blow. The German prisoners slunk in 'suffering and idiot-like incomprehension' past the stacked yellow corpses of their comrades. At the summit of the Mamaya Kurgan was a rough wooden obelisk, painted bright blue. Atop it was a Red Star. The Soviet Union, and with it Communism, had survived.* Stalingrad set both towards global power.

* The Soviet Union was the only Communist state in the world and was to remain so until the end of the war.

A surge of confidence ran through the Russians. In the Kremlin itself it flowed into the same overconfidence that had ultimately wrecked the offensives of the winter before. Stalin repeated his error of casting his attacks at the beginning of 1943 too wide. The *Stavka* planned to trap seventy-five German divisions in the Ukraine, one Red army group driving past Kharkov and Kursk, another two liberating the Donbas and eastern Ukraine. The German Army Group Centre was then to be destroyed, with Red armies pushing through Bryansk and Smolensk whilst two other Soviet Army Groups cut down from the north. The Soviet North-western Front was tasked to cut into the rear of the German forces investing Leningrad.

The attacks in the south were initially effective. Rostov fell. By the evening of 15 February the Russians were fighting their way through the outskirts of Kharkov, the country's fourth largest city and the second biggest in the Ukraine. During the night, the SS Panzer Corps pulled out of the city.

The liberation of Kharkov marked a recovery in self-esteem by the party leadership. Shortly after it, Stalin assumed the title of Marshal of the Soviet Union. The Party itself emerged from the closet it had wisely kept in during the defeats of 1942. 'Party organization is the real back-bone of the Army,' *Red Star* crowed three days after Kharkov was re-taken. 'All the magnificent achievements of our Army are due to the fact that the Red army's military doctrine is based on the well-tested principles of the wisest doctrine in the world – that of Marx, Engels and Stalin.'[1]

Kharkov also gave evidence of what had happened to a great city that had suffered for well over a year under the Germans. The population when the Germans had taken it late in 1941 was about 700,000. Only half that number were left in February 1943. Of the missing, some 120,000 had been transported to Germany as slave labour. A further 80,000 had died of starvation, though the Germans had fared well enough, the liberating Red army men living off captured stocks of Hungarian and French wine, Portuguese sardines, Austrian chocolate and Italian pickled lemons. And 30,000, half of them Jews, had been murdered. The Gestapo had thrown people off the balconies of their headquarters with ropes tied to their necks. The Jews had been herded into a brickworks on the outskirts of the city and killed. Whilst the Germans had amused themselves watching Viennese operettas at the theatres and in Armenian-run nightclubs, every secondary school in the city had been closed.

Not that all its survivors had reason for cheer. Almost at once, with the front only a few kilometres away, the NKVD returned. Large letter boxes were set up into which people were encouraged to drop denunciations, and the correspondent Alexander Werth saw civilian prisoners being led away into the burned-out shell of the Gestapo building. The NKVD had already put it to their own use.

The armies which had taken Kharkov, the 69th and 3rd Tank, were exhausted. Two more Soviet armies, the 6th and 1st Guards, were strung out along a vulnerable corridor south of the city. The Russians had advanced for more than 300 kilometres by the end of February, across a destroyed landscape, their tanks as run down as their crews, fighting at the end of increasingly rickety supply lines.

And the Germans were far from finished. Manstein counter-attacked on 20 February, rapidly slicing into the Russian flanks. The *Stavka*, astonished at the resilience of the supposedly routed enemy, was slow to realize the dangers. The *Gross Deutschland* slammed into 69th Army and 3rd Tank, forcing back the Kharkov victors. The 6th Army was partly surrounded. His offensive had already disintegrated into retreat before the Soviet commander, Vatutin, finally went over to the defensive. Though Manstein's pincers closed within a week, many Red army units managed to straggle back to the east over the frozen Donets. By 10 March the Germans were fighting in the northern suburbs of Kharkov. SS Panzer Corps had swung east of the city it had abandoned less than a month before and was threatening the escape route from the city. Units of *Gross Deutschland* were threatening Kursk. Far from the Germans being in danger of sweeping entrapment, it was the Soviet Central Front that was now threatened.

Kharkov was evacuated by the Russians on 13 March.

German tactical brilliance had won a victory that, after the longest lull on the Eastern front, would in turn lull them into a last fatal summer offensive.

When the front stabilized in mid March, it left the Russians holding a large salient west of Kursk. To the north the Germans held Orel and to the south Kharkov. Between them the Kursk salient was about 150 kilometres in width and bulged some 120 kilometres deep into the German line.

The original German plan was to nip through the base of the salient by cutting through its northern and southern flanks, wheeling down on Kursk, and thus throwing the Russian summer offensive off balance. Had they broken through, it was at least conceivable that they could make another attempt to outflank Moscow. But time slipped away as the Germans rested their divisions and built up their tank strength with the new 68-ton Tigers, medium Panthers and Ferdinand self-propelled SP guns.

The Russians were well aware of German intentions. The newly promoted Marshals Zhukov and Vasilevsky were able to persuade Stalin not to launch a premature spoiling attack. From mid April on, Red army strength within the salient grew daily. The major German blow was expected on the north-eastern flank of the salient along the Orel–Kursk axis. Here, General Rokossovsky's Central Front had five Armies, one tank Army and five corps in reserve. His men had sown 40,000 mines.

The German attack on the southern face of the salient would fall on General N. F. Vatutin's Voronezh Front along the Kharkov–Kursk line. Vatutin had four Armies and one tank Army, and a further Army and three corps in reserve. In addition to these Fronts, the *Stavka* also assembled the most powerful strategic reserve of the war. This, General I. S. Koniev's Steppe Front, eventually grew to five rifle, one tank and one air Army. The Germans had finally declared total mobilization after Stalingrad. The armed forces had increased from 8 million in July 1942 to over 10 million at the start of the Kursk campaign. Luxury restaurants in Berlin had been closed and Mercedes Benz had stopped making civilian cars. Weapons production had doubled in a year. But the existence of a whole Front in reserve behind the Kursk salient showed that the Russians were now stronger in both manpower and equipment.

Russian defences had a First World War intensity. Up to 1,500 anti-tank and 1,700 anti-personnel mines were laid per kilometre of front. Behind these were networks of anti-tank resistance points, *PTOP*s, each with anti-tank guns and rifles, sappers and tommygunners, sometimes further beefed up by tanks and SP guns.[2] These were supported by mobile blocking squads, sappers and tommygunners often riding in British and American trucks. Civilians laboured alongside the troops to build anti-tank ditches, bunkers and fire points. The forward defensive zones were up to six kilometres deep, protected by wire, mines, and the *PTOP*s, with positions linked by trenches. Behind these were secondary and tertiary defence zones, extending more than forty kilometres back from the forward edge and merging into the Front zones. As the fine spring weather of May slipped into June without a German move, the Russians continued to train for the coming battle and to fortify the salient. It was finally to have eight defence lines, extending to a depth of 160 kilometres.[3]

Into this was fed the growing production from factories working round the clock. The Kirov tank factory at Chelyabinsk, supplied by a huge new power station fuelled with coal from the new mines in Kazakhstan, was churning out T-34s from sixty-four production lines. New SP guns were appearing in numbers. Russian infantrymen were festooned with *PPSh* machine pistols, anti-tank rifles and grenades. Increasingly, they could ride in US trucks and Jeeps, 183,000 of which had been supplied by mid 1943. Above them, LA-5 fighters flew with boosted engines and the Il-2 ground-attack aircraft revelled in its new cannon.

The German operation, *Zitadelle* or *Citadel*, ceased to be the dynamic proposition it might have been when it was conceived in April. True, its pincers would each have to close only eighty kilometres or so, a mere tremor of the jaw to forces used to biting through far greater lumps of territory. But it was not until 16 June that Hitler decided that *Citadel*, the victory at Kursk that would 'shine like a beacon round the world', would start at the beginning of July. By then, in artillery alone the Russians had amassed 20,000 guns and 920 *Katyushas* in the salient.

The concentrations of armour built up around Kursk have no parallel. In the northern German pincer, Model's 9th Army had three fully equipped Panzer Corps and two infantry Corps. His 1,200 tanks and SP guns gave him a density of 30 to the kilometre, backed by 270,000 men and powerful air support including the new Focke-Wolfe 190A. Hoth's 4th Panzer Army, the southern pincer, comprised 'nine of the finest divisions in the German army, shoulder to shoulder along less than thirty miles of front!'[4] The line ran from 3rd Panzer in the west, through *Gross Deutschland,* 11th Panzer, SS *Leibstandarte, Das Reich* and *Totenkopf* to 6th, 19th and 7th Panzer. Hoth had 280,000 men with almost 1,500 tanks and SP guns and could call on a subordinate shock group, Group Kempf, for operational support.

In all, including reserves, the Germans had amassed seventy divisions, almost a million men, for the Kursk offensive. There were no satellite troops involved in any important area. As they waited on their start-lines, the Germans received a personal message from Hitler: 'This day you are to take part in an offensive of such importance that the whole future of the war may depend on its outcome.'

Into this cauldron, of plain covered by wheatfields and tree stands, cut by streams and valleys, were poured almost seven thousand tanks and SP guns in the primeval struggle between the two competing *isms* of the twentieth century, Fascism and Communism.

The battle was joined on the morning of 5 July 1943.[5] In the south, Hoth's 4th Panzer smashed into the Soviet 6th Guards in an assault wave whose density reached 3,000 men and up to 100 tanks to the kilometre. In the north, Model had concentrated six infantry and one Panzer division into a sixteen-kilometre breakthrough sector. The heavy Tigers and Ferdinand SP guns led the assaults to batter through the defences. Behind them came the lighter Panthers and the Panzer IVs, with the infantry riding on the tanks and in armoured carriers. Above ranged packs of dive bombers, up to a hundred strong, flying a sortie an hour to compensate for the German lack of artillery.

German tactics had not changed. They were repeating the great encirclement battles of the past and simply throwing more ingredients, more armour, more aircraft, into the old mix. The Russians, Guderian noted, 'knew exactly what to expect'. Strategy showed the same lack of fresh imagination. Summer offensives had become a tradition since 1940: France, Moscow, the Caucasus and Stalingrad. Kursk was another but even a victory would have done little more than some line-straightening. 'Why do we want to attack at all in the East this year?' Guderian had asked Hitler in May. As for Kursk, it 'is a matter of profound indifference to the world whether we hold it or not'. Hitler had admitted: 'Whenever I think of this attack my stomach turns over.'[6]

'Leave it alone!' Guderian had cried. The troops themselves had felt a sullen passivity about the attack. The Russians watching them moving up to their start-lines saw the 'dark, stooped figures of weary men ... in a straggling line melting away into the darkness'. The gloom was justified. Many German tanks were disabled by mines within the first half kilometre and their crews, forbidden to abandon them whilst they could still fire, were at the mercy of the Russian *PTOPs* and of roaming anti-tank squads with explosive charges and Molotov cocktails. Where the heavily armoured Tigers and Ferdinands broke into the Soviet positions, they frequently found themselves isolated, with the lighter tanks and infantry well behind them. The huge 100-mm guns on the Ferdinands were devastating against Russian positions, but they had no machineguns as secondary armament. When they closed on the enemy infantry they were, as Guderian put it, compelled 'to go quail-shooting with cannon'. Throughout the afternoon, smoke from burning fields and machines drifting across the brilliant sun, the Germans bled themselves amid the mines and guns of the first defence zones.

That night, as German infantry fought by flare-light to protect the vulnerable armour from the Soviet anti-tank squads, the Russian flanks had been dented by not more than six kilometres. Stalin was kept abreast of the satisfactory position in his regular briefings from the General Staff, in mid morning, early evening and at a night-time session that usually ended at 3 a.m. The Soviet communiqué for the first day of the battle claimed that 586 enemy tanks had been destroyed or crippled. This was a figure 'which captured the country's imagination; there had never been anything like it in one day'.[7]

Both sides threw in more tanks and SP guns on 6 July. The Germans were attacking in armoured flails of a hundred and more machines, hurling themselves against dug-in T-34s and gun pits. To the Russians, the German tanks appeared as a 'huge black rhombus, like a piece of the forest that had broken away from the main mass', advancing across the buckwheat fields. As they closed on their trenches, the Russians could make out the camouflage on an individual tank as 'a map, with dark lowlands, yellow deserts and the brown zigzags of mountain chains, and on those chains the

swastika, its spidery legs reaching down into the valleys ...' As the tanks
crossed their trenches, they 'lay in total darkness, like in a cellar with the
hatch closed' until they passed. Then they could see 'the dark figures of
the sub-machine-gunners in their angular helmets' following behind.

On the north of the salient, Model's 9th Army had mingled with
Rokossovsky in a swirl of combat so intimate that German and Soviet
tanks rammed each other, whilst the Germans hosed their comrades'
armour with machinegun fire to dislodge Soviet infantry who had clambered on their decks to pump flamethrowers through the air intakes. Crews
desperately traversed their turrets against targets a few metres away, whilst
one Russian battery propped up its last anti-tank gun on ammunition
boxes and aimed it by the barrel. Medical staffs were unable to cope with
the wounded, even when they could be extricated from a battlefield
seething with snipers and tommygunners. German casualty stations were
'like slaughterhouses'. Switching his main attack from the Orel–Kursk
road, Model flung two tank corps against the Soviet 307th Division round
the village of Ponyry. Supported by aircraft dive bombing the Russian
gun pits, the Germans put in five tank and infantry attacks on the village
on 7 July. The 307th held, if barely.

The most critical day for Rokossovsky was 8 July. Three hundred tanks,
including Tigers, Panthers and Ferdinands, came close to overwhelming
the Russian anti-tank defences. By midday, two of the three regiments of
the 3rd Anti-Tank Artillery Brigade had been destroyed. They were
reinforced that night and a counter-attack was mounted round Ponyry.
On 10 July Model went on to the defensive. He had lost 50,000 men and
400 tanks to gain about 15 kilometres on a 40-kilometre-wide front.
Ominous signs were building on Model's own left flank where Red army
movements were mounting around the German's own salient at Orel.

The depth of the Russian defences was also blunting Hoth's attack on
the southern flank of the salient. By the night of 6 July up to a hundred
German tanks had broken into the second defence zone. The 7th Guards
Army was being slowly pushed back but it had beaten off twelve attacks.
Vatutin was forced to order up his reserves but was able to report to Stalin
that his Front had destroyed 332 tanks that day. Over the next four days
the T-34s of General Katukov's 1st Tank Army fought the crack crews of
the Wehrmacht and SS panzer divisions, whilst the wreckage of the aerial
battle between the Soviet 2nd Air Army and the German 4th Air Fleet
slammed burning into the stands of wheat. Vatutin and his political officer,
Nikita Khrushchev, moved through clouds of dust and exhaust fumes and
the yellow smoke of TNT explosions to take personal control at 1st Tank's
headquarters. At appalling cost, the Germans managed to drive a fourteen-
kilometre-deep salient into Vatutin's flank. Further east, on the open steppe
beyond Belgorod, Kempf's Battle Group was locked with two Guards

Armies. 'Tragic, unbelievable visions', wrote a soldier with *Gross Deutsch-land*. 'Tightly riveted machines ripped like the belly of a cow that has just been sliced open, flaming and groaning; trees broken into tiny fragments ... the cries of officers and noncoms, trying to shout across the cataclysm to regroup their sections and companies.'[8]

The Germans regrouped for a climactic effort. The weather had deteriorated, with cold winds and rain driving across the sky. The cream of German strength was concentrated in the south to break through to Prokhorovka and achieve a decisive rent in Vatutin's Front. The assault started at dawn on 11 July with the black-uniformed SS men of *Totenkopf, Adolf Hitler* and *Das Reich*, five panzer divisions, *Gross Deutschland* and three infantry divisions. Stalin was given hourly reports of the defence of the Prokhorovka area by Marshals Zhukov and Vasilevsky. They now decided to throw in General Zhadov's 5th Guards Army and General Rotmistrov's 5th Guards Tank Army from the reserves of Koniev's Steppe Front. Rotmistrov made a forced march of 340 kilometres to Prokhorovka.

On 12 July, using the 900 tanks of 5th Guards Tank Army, the Russians counter-attacked. The Germans had rough parity in tanks and the two forces impacted in a cloud of flame and dust. In the main killing ground, an area five kilometres by six near Prokhorovka, the T-34s closed to point-blank range to offset the heavier armour of the Tigers. Gouts of steel and flesh were flung in the air as the tanks, their engines straining, engaged in individual combat, shot clanging on hulls acrid with fumes and exhausted men in the heaviness of a thundery day. The Germans had never experienced 'such an overwhelming impression of Russian strength and numbers as on that day', the T-34s 'streaming like rats'. By midday, after burning machines had rammed each other in the dust of narrow gullies, the Germans had checked Rotmistrov's onrush. Their counter-attack in the afternoon failed. They fought for eighteen hours. When the *Prokhorovka poboishche*, the slaughter of Prokhorovka, ceased, over half 5th Guards Tank had been destroyed. But it was 4th Panzer that withdrew from the darkened battlefield, leaving more than three hundred tanks inert and wrecked.[9]

The Germans claimed that they had destroyed 1,800 tanks and taken 24,000 prisoners on the southern side of the salient alone. They had undoubtedly halved Soviet tank strength in the Prokhorovka area. But the Russians estimated that Kursk had cost the Germans 90,000 dead and 2,952 tanks. Already, the Russians were attacking the Germans' own vulnerable salient to the north at Orel. The Allies had landed in Sicily.

Citadel was ruined. On 13 July Hitler called it off. There was not to be another major German offensive in the East.

PERELOM AND THE GREAT PURSUIT

Stalingrad was the psychological crux of the war, but Kursk was the military *perelom*, the great turning point. Zhukov had held the greatest offensive the Germans could muster. He could now pursue them to the Dnieper with fresh troops.

The Bryansk and Western Fronts had already begun attacking the German bulge round Orel whilst the Kursk tank battles were still swirling. On the morning of 5 August 1943 the Red army broke into Orel, loudspeakers bellowing *The Holy War*, women and children throwing flowers to the troops whilst German tommygunners were blasted out of attics.

At midnight, 120 guns shook Moscow with victory salvoes on Stalin's orders. The Germans had hoped that Kursk had at the least drained the Soviet pool of armour and men. They had themselves lost almost twice as many men in not much more than a week as the Americans were to lose throughout the years of the Vietnam war. But Russian tank strength was by now growing at the rate of 2,000 new machines a month. The manpower pool was increased by its very advance, as men in the liberated territories were impressed into the Red army.

Confidence was breeding a Russian nationalism intense enough for the *New York Times* to refer to 'a return to Tsarism'. The revolutionary aspects of the Red army were being swept away, as Stalin had also scrapped the symbol of world revolution, the Comintern. The political commissars' powers over military commanders had already gone. Guards regiments and divisions, their names recalling Tsardom as much as the new Orders of Suvorov and Kutuzov, had been created and army regulations dating back to Peter the Great were revived. Epaulettes, saluting, officers' clubs and separate messes for senior and junior officers had returned. In December 1942, as Stalingrad had reached its climax, Stalin had promoted no fewer than 360 commanders to the rank of general. He was himself now a Marshal. 'Suvorov schools' were to be set up in the liberated areas. These cadet schools were closely modelled on the Tsarist cadet corps. The young cadets were taught English, fine manners and the waltz and mazurka.[1] Stalin personally ordered Eisenstein's film *Ivan the Terrible*. In September, the Patriarch of Moscow was crowned and the Holy Synod was restored.

It was a Russia in which an *ofitser*, pitchforked on Mogilev station or buried alive at Kronstadt in 1917, could again wear his *pogon* shoulder boards, and where graves could have Christian crosses above them. 'We are under no illusion that they are fighting for us,' Stalin was to tell the

US Ambassador, Averell Harriman. 'They are fighting for Mother Russia.'

Though Leningrad remained under German shellfire, the front from Orel to the Black Sea was driven westward. On 23 August Kharkov was finally recaptured by Koniev's Steppe Front in a combined operation with Vatutin. A few days later the Red army had broken through to the Sea of Azov and was back in Taganrog for the first time since the autumn of 1941. Rokossovsky broke out west of Kursk. The Germans were rapidly retreating from the smashed plants and mines of the Donbas, all of which was liberated by 8 September.

On 22 September the Red army won a bridgehead on the west bank of the Dnieper south-east of Kiev. Three days later Smolensk was retaken in heavy fighting. The days were getting shorter and colder, the sun 'like a reflection of brass', and German morale was sinking with it.

They left utter ruination behind them. The scale of the devastation, to a country that had already suffered the First World War, the civil war, the Polish War and collectivization within a generation, continues to bite deep into the post-war generations.

Few of the wooden villages, Pabst wrote, were left standing two summers after *Barbarossa*. Only the odd fence and posts remained. The bridges had rotted away, the paths were overgrown and wild carrots, lupins and wormwood reigned. 'Now the smoke is going up from the last ruins,' he wrote as his unit retreated. 'Soon there will only be the tracks of the woodmen through the wilderness.'[2] On the railways a trolley would make a last journey down the line to the west, two men sitting on it methodically throwing out explosives. 'Lumps of iron hissed around and the bitter powder smoke blew over our heads ... Every culvert, every defile was mined.'

In the suburbs of Bryansk the sun was red long before evening as the Germans fired the city. 'It hung sick and thirsty above the march of destruction,' wrote Pabst. 'We raced through the white heat of dying streets ... through a forest of chimney stacks which, rigid and angular, revolved before our gaze. Above the black carpet of the conflagration, they had the colour of Brussels lace. They rose in the moonlight like the stiff, lamenting hands of ghosts, and all around them was the foul, repulsive, half-choking smell of cold smoke.'[3]

The human carnage the advancing Russians found was as great. Three million Russians, White Russians (or Belorussians) and especially Ukrainians had been deported to Germany as slave labour. The first glimpse for the Russian public of what horrors lay in store in the liberated areas came at a trial in Krasnodar after the summer offensive had got under way. A handful of Russians were sentenced to death for collaborating with the Gestapo in the massacre of 7,000 Jews and other civilians. They had been chiefly killed by the *dushegubka*, the 'soulkiller' or mobile gas wagon used by the Gestapo. The Krasnodar revelations were minor compared with what was to come, but they were almost the first concrete example of Gestapo behaviour and made a deep impression.[4]

As the partisan movement grew in the aftermath of Stalingrad and Kursk, German terror squads killed the populations of villages and districts. It is impossible today to visit Western Russia, where the modernity of Minsk bears witness enough to physical destruction, without still feeling the sorrow in the villages. Attempts had been made to exterminate the Jews in their entirety. The massacre at Babi Yar, near Kiev, where about one hundred thousand men, women and children were killed, was but the largest of many. The treatment of Russian POWs was little better. 'We were stationed at Rovno [in the Western Ukraine],' a Hungarian tank officer wrote. 'I woke one morning and heard thousands of dogs howling in the distance ... I called my orderly and said: "Sandor, what is all this moaning and howling?" "Not far from here," he said, "there's a huge mass of Russian prisoners in the open air. There must be eighty thousand of them. They're moaning because they are starving." '[5] It is possible that the sum of POWs who died in captivity reached three million. The statistics are so numbing that their repetition can seem almost as inhuman as the savagery that created them. Their effect on the Russian soul, and through it on modern world politics, remains immeasurable.

As the winter cloudbanks swelled and the rains turned roads to mud that glistened and reflected the wet sky like streams, Vatutin closed on Kiev. German units, traumatized by Kursk and their long retreat, fell back to the Dnieper east of the city. They came in endless columns, plodding at five kilometres an hour, their mobility gone through lack of fuel, 'undernourished men, dehydrated men with filthy, suppurating wounds and bodies barely covered by torn, ragged uniforms'. The river was the outer boundary of safety. Thousands of men packed its sandy eastern bank, wrote Guy Sajer of *Gross Deutschland*, 'in a state of indescribable panic, only to find it necessary to trample on the men already there, even drown them, to have any hope of getting onto the wretchedly inadequate vessels, which often foundered before they reached the other side'.[6]

Men stood up to the neck in the water, propping up improvised landing stages. Russian tanks appeared on their way to the Kiev battle. Huddling between clumps of dripping furze, the Germans 'heard the sound of gunfire and explosions coming closer, punctuated by bloodcurdling screams. Men suddenly plunged out of the pale, enveloping cotton, and disappeared like ghosts into the black water.' Waffen SS men and eager volunteers of *Gross Deutschland* who had set out to stamp a New Order on the East had met their first Napoleonic Beresina on the Dnieper.

On 5 November Vatutin's troops broke into the burning suburbs of Kiev. Its demolition squads blasting the historic buildings until the last moment, the German 7th Corps fell back. At 5 a.m. on 6 November Vatutin's 1st Ukrainian Front radioed the *Stavka* in Moscow 'with unbounded joy' that the mother of Russian cities had been cleared of the enemy. This is the heart of old Kievan Rus, the centrepiece of Russian Christianity. Vatutin found only 80,000 people left alive, a fifth of the pre-war figure, in a city that within a quarter of a century had been taken by Austro–German armies, Denikin's Whites, the Poles, the Reds and the Nazis.

The Germans were withdrawing with great skill. Most of Sajer's comrades escaped from their nightmare and few Germans were taken prisoner, only 98,000 since the beginning of the Kursk battle. The Russians were vulnerable to surprise and counter-attack. The Germans were perfecting the art of punctuating a long withdrawal with a sudden counter-punch that sliced through the ponderous and over-calculated Soviet advances. After Kiev had fallen, with Vatutin still in full cry, General Manteuffel broke through the Russian flank with a light armoured force which caused such confusion that the offensive was temporarily halted.

On 6 November Stalin had claimed that 'victory is near'. German tactical brilliance remained deep enough to make that premature, but they could not fend off a strategic disaster made worse by Hitler's continuing refusal to stomach timely retreat.

Stalin could afford to wait. That month, meeting Roosevelt and Churchill in Teheran, he had the measure of the post-war prize waiting for him.

It was the first time the three men had met together, the son of Georgian serfs, oilfield agitator, creator of purges, and, from the West, a descendant of the Duke of Marlborough and the scion of American industrialists. Two of them had first-hand experience of war and that itself underscored the prodigious difference between them, Stalin in a civil war of dizzy fluctuation, atrocity and revolutionary intrigue, Churchill in far-flung imperial campaigns from South Africa to the North West Frontier of India.

The Teheran conference, as Churchill put it, 'probably represented the greatest concentration of worldly power that had ever been seen in the history of mankind'. Stalin began at an immediate advantage. He was close to home. He had flown the last lap to Teheran from his old stamping ground in Baku, Churchill and Roosevelt had had an exhausting trip on from Cairo. Stalin's prestige in the West was at a peak after the dual victories at Stalingrad and Kursk.

Stalin was opposed to any Allied moves that would extend their influence into the Balkans. The earlier the invasion of northern France, *Overlord*, was launched, the more German divisions would immediately be drawn off the Eastern front and the less the Anglo-Americans would be able to meddle in the Soviet sphere of influence. Stalin prised away the unwelcome notion of an Anglo-American presence on his own southern flank. There should be no talk of Italy, Yugoslavia, Rumania, Turkey, the Aegean. Only *Overlord* mattered, and the details of its date, its supreme commander and the place of a supporting landing in southern France should be fixed, at once, in Teheran. He sweetened his insistence with the promise that the Red army would enter the war with Japan once Germany was beaten.

He won the great prize. *Overlord* was set for May 1944. Europe would effectively be divided into two military camps, Soviet and Anglo-American. That was not all that Stalin gained. On the Polish question, it was agreed that the country's western frontier should be moved west to the Oder. As to the eastern frontier, Churchill accepted that the Russians could not be expected to return to the 1939 frontier at Brest. On Germany itself, the talk at Teheran was hazy and inconclusive. Roosevelt talked of dismembering it into five units[7] and Stalin taunted Churchill for his lack of full-blooded support for it.

The antagonism between Churchill and Stalin broke through at a dinner when Stalin said that the 50,000 officers on whom German militarism depended should all be shot. Churchill spat back that the British people would never stand for mass executions. Stalin repeated: 'Fifty thousand must be shot!' Eden, the British foreign secretary, gestured to his premier that it was all in fun. Churchill would have none of it. 'I would rather be taken into the garden here and now and be shot myself than sully my own and my country's honour by such infamy!' Churchill left the dinner table, though Stalin and Molotov, grinning broadly, persuaded him that it was a joke. He returned, later noting that 'Stalin has a very captivating manner when he chooses to use it.'

In truth, the Russians did not shoot captured generals, as the survival of those captured at Stalingrad had already shown. Though there were times when neither side in the front line took prisoners, unlike the Germans the Russians generally restricted summary executions to flamethrower operators and troops wearing the black uniforms of the SS. But Churchill was more aware than any at Teheran that Stalin had purged his own generals.

He also knew what the consequences of Teheran were likely to be.

20

DOSVIDANIA, UKRAINE

The Red army that now pursued the Germans was the largest land force in history. It struck the Germans as a medieval host, an Asian swarm. 'The advance of a Russian army is something that Westerners can't imagine,' said General Manteuffel. 'Behind the tank spearheads rolls on a vast horde, largely mounted on horses. The soldier carries a sack on his back, with dry crusts of bread and raw vegetables collected on the march from the fields and villages ... The Russians are accustomed to carry on for as long as three weeks in this primitive way, when advancing. You can't stop them, like an ordinary army, by cutting their communications, for you rarely find any supply columns to strike.'[1]

The conditions within it were medieval. Most of its men fought without leave, without mail, without contact with their families and without regular pay. They could be inducted off the streets of towns and from village *isbas* as it advanced. Death or severe wounds were the main means of discharge. Due to crude medical facilities, the latter often involved the former. Indiscipline, by officers as well as men, was met by transfer to a penal battalion where tasks included clearing minefields and advancing on positions in winter without white camouflage coveralls in order to draw enemy fire. It had already sustained losses of some five million, in dead, wounded and prisoners, and the heavy toll among ethnic Russians showed in the growing proportion of Asiatics in its ranks.

The horse was still of vast importance to both sides on the Eastern front. Soviet cavalry was deadly against German stragglers. The wounded were often evacuated on horse-drawn *paniye* carts. Horses dragged guns, field-kitchens and supplies and hauled vehicles out of the mud. When desperation came to starving troops and civilians, they ate horseflesh. Both sides scavenged for horses and the Germans fought bitter little engagements with partisans for them. But it was the Germans, the old masters of mechanized warfare, who now had greater need of them. By the end of 1943 Allied trucks had made the Red army relatively mobile and it was well enough fed and shod, often with American Spam and boots. Its high morale and almost all its weapons were Soviet.

The smallest infantry unit was the section of nine men. A platoon was made up of four sections, each with Degtyarev light machineguns. The platoon was commanded by a junior lieutenant, instead of an NCO as in the West, and had its own snipers. Three platoons plus a mortar and medium machinegun section made up a rifle company, commanded by a senior lieutenant or captain. Three companies made a battalion under a major or lieutenant colonel. The battalion also had its own anti-tank platoon, machinegun company and horse-drawn supply and field-kitchen unit.

Three battalions made up a rifle regiment of around 2,500 men under a colonel. Regiments had their own mounted reconnaissance units, engineers for minelaying and clearing, anti-tank companies and a unit of 90 sub-machinegunners used to lead assaults and in street fighting. An NKVD section was responsible for security and censorship and for preventing unauthorized retreats. The regiment also had its communist political staff under the deputy regimental commander for political affairs, usually a major.

Three regiments formed a rifle division commanded by a colonel or major general.[2] Each division had an artillery regiment, an anti-tank battalion, signals, engineers and an anti-aircraft company. Besides its trucks, it could have as many as two thousand horses. A division that distinguished itself could become a Guards division, with a strength of 10,000 men compared with a full strength of 9,000 and a norm of 7,000 for a less glamorous division.

Soviet artillery was the arm most feared by the Germans. By 1943 Marshal of Artillery N. N. Voronov was concentrating it in special divisions rather than parcelling it out among infantry units. Divisional artillery had been reduced to 36 or so guns and howitzers, an equal number of heavy mortars and a handful of *Katyushas*. Guns were now massed into specialist units. The artillery division had 200 guns and howitzers and 100 heavy mortars, with an additional heavy artillery brigade for assault divisions. The intensity of fire which they achieved, Sajer wrote, was such that 'the whole horizon burst into flame, with the sudden, total involvement of the opening bars of a Wagner opera . . . The ground shook in a manner which defied all prediction . . . Torrents of snow and frozen earth poured down on us.'[3]

There were 475 rifle divisions, some 130 of them Guards units, in the Red army by the beginning of 1944. They were grouped with two to four divisions making a corps under a major or lieutenant general, and two to four corps making an army. The bulk of armies were all-arms or Guards. There were sixty all-arms armies on the Eastern front, with eleven powerful Guards armies. The five Shock Armies, *udarniya armiya*, with bolstered firepower and artillery, were used in initial assaults to break through German positions. Casualties were usually so heavy that they were seldom used in pursuit. There were also five Tank Armies with a sixth added in January 1944. The standard armoured formation was a tank brigade of 1,100 men, commanded by a colonel, with 3 tank battalions of 21 machines each, plus a battalion of sub-machinegunners with anti-tank weapons and mortars.

These armies were integrated into a Front, or Army Group, under a marshal or general. A Front could absorb anything from three to fourteen armies, with its own artillery and anti-aircraft divisions and rocket-firing brigades, supported by one or two air armies.

The Red air force benefited enormously from the sharp reduction in Luftwaffe activity over the Eastern front as the Germans were forced to station increasing numbers of aircraft within the Reich itself to counter the growing Anglo-American bomber fleets. By the end of 1943 there were 13 Red air armies on the Eastern front with 12,000 aircraft, including YaK-9 and La-5 fighters, Tu-2 tactical bombers and rocket-firing Il-2s and Il-10s. Anglo-American pressure was also straining the German ground forces. Only 60 per cent of the Wehrmacht strength was facing the full weight of the Red army on the Eastern front.

The Germans were notably inferior in both artillery and air support. Nevertheless, they were a formidable force of 236 divisions and almost 5 million men. They were far from broken yet.

The most static part of the front had been the northern sector round Leningrad. The tight German siege of the starving city had been partially lifted at the beginning of 1943, but the narrow supply corridor along the shore of Lake Ladoga was still ravaged by heavy guns. The Soviet offensive to clear it involved a break-out from the Oranienbaum bridgehead west of the city by the 2nd Shock Army linking up with a drive from the southern suburbs by the 42nd Army. The bridgehead was protected by the Trotsky-haunted guns of Kronstadt. The 2nd Shock had been ferried into the bridgehead from Leningrad on darkened boats and later over the ice.

The 2nd Shock Army attacked on 14 January 1944 after 100,000 rounds, some of them from warships and the Kronstadt forts, had saturated the German trenches and pillboxes round the bridgehead. The following day 42nd Army advanced after a barrage by 3,000 guns. The thunder was such that the city shook and plaster fell from walls. Losses were heavy on both sides, with the two Soviet Fronts totalling 1.2 million men and Field Marshal von Küchler's Army Group Nord almost 750,000.

Gradually the Germans were forced to yield their concrete and steel firing points, some of which were sunk deep in the ground. On the evening of 19 January the forward elements of 2nd Shock and 42nd Army linked up. A week later the Moscow–Leningrad railway line was cleared. The Germans were now streaming west in retreat, avoiding Russian encirclement but falling back to the Estonian border by the end of the month.

On 27 January 1944 a mass of red, white and blue rockets was fired over the city. The siege of Leningrad, which had lasted for 880 days of cholera, dysentery and starvation, had ended.*

As Leningrad was being relieved, 1,100 kilometres to the south Vatutin and Koniev were preparing to slice off the German-held salient at Korsun–Shevchenko on the Dnieper south of Kiev. Manstein's Army Group South was unable to hold a continuous front and holes were being torn by the Russians almost at will. Hitler had ordered the salient to be held as a jumping-off point for a reconquest of the eastern Ukraine, something now utterly beyond German capability.

Koniev's 2nd Ukrainian Front cut deep into the southern side of the salient. This was the former Steppe Front from the Kursk battle, with Rotmistrov's 5th Guards Tank Army as its spearhead. Vatutin's 1st Ukrainian hooked down from the north, sealing off the salient when they met. By the end of January, seven German infantry divisions, an SS Panzer division and the Belgian SS *Wallonia* brigade were trapped in the shrinking Korsun pocket.

Several senior SS officers were flown out but General Stemmermann remained. He refused to surrender. On 8 February Manstein had scraped together four armoured divisons which briefly broke through to the trapped men. The Russians re-sealed the ring after a few hours. On 10 February Koniev reduced the pocket to a bomb- and shell-blasted area nine kilometres by eleven.[4] Four days later Korsun was taken and Stemmermann's men huddled for shelter in the village of Shanderovka. The population were turned out on to the snow- and sleet-driven steppe.

Stemmermann prepared for a desperate break-out on the night of 17 February. His men slaughtered the cattle in the village and ate their last meal with a barrel of pickled cabbage found in a hut. Major Kampov, an officer on Koniev's staff, said that the Germans were in a 'hysterical condition' all evening. Many of them were drunk. Their vehicles useless through lack of fuel, they could not drag their wounded with them on the break-out. They were ordered to kill them to prevent them falling into Russian hands. 'They shot them,' said Kampov, 'as they usually shoot Russians and Jews, through the back of the head.'[5] They then set fire to the ambulance vans, leaving the 'oddest sights of charred skeletons ... with wide bracelets of plaster-of-Paris round their arms or legs. For plaster-of-Paris doesn't burn.'

A blizzard was blowing, but Russian volunteers flying light U-2s located

* The population had fallen to less than 1 million from 2.5 million at the start of the siege. It is possible that 1 million died through hunger and another 300,000 through shelling, in combat and through other causes. During the siege, the city became empty of cats, dogs, birds and even rats. People ate library paste, leather, tooth powder and, very occasionally, each other. Some of the survivors, their wartime heroism insufficient protection, were later purged by Stalin.

Shanderovka and set its wooden cottages afire with incendiaries. The village now illuminated, the Russian guns shelled it from a range of five kilometres. As Koniev himself travelled his dark and snow-racked positions in a tank, the Germans flocked into ravines near the village. The break-out started in the pre-dawn darkness. Two columns of about 14,000 men each stumbled down two parallel ravines to the west, the spearheads and flanks formed by the SS men in pearl-grey uniforms, the interior of the triangles packed with a rabble of exhausted and torn infantrymen.

The ravines led them into two Red Armies, waiting in five lines of infantry, artillery, tanks and Cossack cavalry. The Russians let them pass through the first three lines. By 6 a.m. the Germans had cleared the ravines and were in open country. Thinking they had escaped, they 'burst into frantic jubilant screaming, firing their pistols and tommyguns into the air'. Then the Russian tanks and cavalry attacked, driving directly into the columns. Tanks and horsemen competed to run them down. The tank crews crushed them under their tracks, not using their guns for fear of hitting the Cossacks. 'Hundreds and hundreds of cavalry were hacking at them with their sabres,' said Kampov. They 'massacred the Fritzes as no one has ever been massacred by cavalry before'. Those who escaped the wheeling tanks on the plain were cut down by the Cossacks in the ravines. 'There was no time to take prisoners,' said Kampov. 'It was a kind of slaughter that nothing could stop till it was all over.' Then Cossacks sabred the hands off those who had raised them in surrender.

Some Germans and Belgian SS men struggled through to the banks of the Tikich river. As the T-34s closed on them, they flung themselves into the current and ice-floes, some of them stripping naked. Maddened, they threw away their equipment and emerged on the western bank half frozen and streaming with icy water. The killing lasted for four hours. Kampov had been in Stalingrad but never had he seen 'such concentrated slaughter as in the fields and ravines of that small bit of country'. Twenty thousand of the men who had set out with the columns were dead. The Russians found the body of General Stemmermann, 'a little old man with grey hair' and a duelling scar on his cheek. Over the next few days 8,000 prisoners were rounded up from the ravines and woods where they had hidden.

The Russians considered Korsun of as much psychological as military significance. It reminded the Germans of Stalingrad, just a year before, and it intensified their fear of encirclement. Koniev, veteran of the civil war and a rifleman who had stormed Kronstadt, an austere figure who liked to quote Livy and Pushkin, was elevated a Marshal of the Soviet Union. Rotmistrov became the first Marshal of Armoured Forces.

The day after the Korsun slaughter, Stalin signed the *Stavka* directive for a general offensive. It was aimed at destroying the German forces in southern Russia from the Pripet marshes to the Black Sea. The four Red army Fronts involved had a superiority of two to one in infantry and a slightly greater edge in armour.[6] Whilst preparing for the fresh offensive General Vatutin was ambushed near Rovno by Ukrainian partisans. As in 1918, the Ukraine had become a cauldron of nationalist and Red guerrillas beneath the foreign occupiers. A group of 100 men of the Ukrainian Insurgent Army, who had fought the Germans and now turned their attention to the returning Russians, machinegunned Vatutin's staff car. He was seriously wounded and, although dragged from the ambush site across the snowy fields on a horse-drawn sledge, died six weeks later.

Zhukov took over Vatutin's 1st Ukrainian Front on 1 March 1944. Three days later he launched his Guards Armies in a sea of mud through the northern Ukraine. At the same time Koniev's 2nd Ukrainian Front began to crash through towards the Rumanian border. Further south Malinovsky's 3rd Ukrainian Front was starting its sweep towards Odessa, whilst Tolbukhin's 4th Ukrainian Front began its reconquest of the Crimea.

His tanks and Studebakers slithering through the mud, his infantry often falling far behind, Zhukov was rolling forward at up to fifty kilometres a day. By 7 March his armour had reached the Odessa–Warsaw railway near Tarnopol. He had outflanked the German defensive line along the Bug river before they had time to retreat to occupy it. To the south Malinovsky had struck out from Nikopol and Krivoi Rog. On the left of his sector he took the port of Khersen at the mouth of the Dnieper on 13 March. His right wing swept down towards Nikolayev at the mouth of the Bug, although the Germans desperately defended the city until 28 March.

Protected by the gains of Malinovsky and Zhukov, Koniev surged through General Hube's 8th Army. Conditions were appalling, for the tracks of Rotmistrov's tanks churned the damp, dark brown earth to liquid paste. The 2nd and 5th Guards Tank Armies swept into the large German base at Uman on 10 March. The streets were littered with burned-out German vehicles, files, office records and coloured leaflets extolling the 'German–Ukrainian Alliance'. The dumps were full of supplies. The German rout reached a pitch where fuelled and armed tanks were found intact, mired to their track-guards in the mud. A string of abandoned tanks, guns and lorries stretched from the breakthrough point all the way to Uman.

Koniev spurred on, reaching the Bug a day later and crossing it on an eighty-kilometre front. The width of Russian fronts during their long advance was costly in casualties. It was also less immediately decisive than the narrow, deep penetrations that the Germans had used in the high summer of *Blitzkrieg* in 1941. But, coupled with the overall Russian superiority in men and machines, they were less easily unbalanced and more surely successful.

The spearheads of T-34s and Studebakers, supplied by air drop, pushed on 110 kilometres for the Dniester. Its ice melting in the fast-flowing current, its banks shielded by steep cliffs, the river seemed a major obstacle. The Red army's ability to cross rivers remains a well-honed skill. It constantly surprised the Germans during the war. The Wehrmacht itself would bunch dangerously on nearing a river, before laboriously crossing at a few points. The Russians would fling across companies to form scattered bridgeheads, and the Germans learnt that failure to eliminate these at once would mean that they were soon facing a regiment. The Russians crossed initially by boats and rafts and then speedily threw across pontoons or pile or trestle bridges made from trees felled nearby. The Germans were too weak to crush Koniev's initial bridgeheads and were shocked by the speed with which their pursuers shrugged off the Dniester. Starting to cross in the night of 20 March, an entire mechanized corps had arrived on the western bank shortly after noon the following day. In less than a week, Koniev was on the Rumanian border.

The immensely long front tied down German reserves and robbed them of any initiative beyond local counter-attacks. Striking north of Koniev, Zhukov was closing fast on the Carpathians and the two new Marshals almost trapped 1st Panzer between them. Manstein freed it, almost his last operation before Hitler blindly fired him and Kleist as the old legends of *Blitzkrieg* faded into nightmare. As the Wehrmacht was cleared out of the Ukraine, the retreating Germans sang pidgin ditties:

> *Nema pivo, nema vino*
> *Dosvidania Ukraina.*[7]

No more beer and no more wine. Goodbye, Ukraine. They were saying goodbye further south, where Malinovsky was advancing along the Black Sea coast, liberating the acacia-lined streets of Odessa where the savagery of the Rumanian occupation had been softened by the corruption of the Rumanian army and secret police and their love of high living and gambling dens. The Rumanians were wavering in their support of the Germans and Hitler had already sent German troops into Hungary as his alliances in Eastern Europe creaked under defeat.

Though the whole of the Ukrainian landmass and coast to the north of the Crimea was now controlled by the Red army, Hitler was determined to hold the peninsula. With its vineyards, red bougainvillea and yellow laburnums, its long beaches and cypresses, it held a sweet southern promise for the Germans. Manstein, its conqueror, had been given a palace set among magnolia copses by the 'grateful German nation' in 1942.

The mixed German–Rumanian force holding the Crimea was outnumbered by the Russians by 150,000 to 470,000. The main attack was started by General Tolbukhin on the morning of 8 April. Red infantry and gunners fought through the bitter salt flats of the Sivash lagoon. As the northern gates were battered open the Russians also advanced from their bridgehead at Kerch on the eastern tip of the Crimea. In less than a week the Rumanians had been scattered and the Germans had fallen back on Sebastopol.

The Russians had held Sebastopol for 250 days in 1941–2 and Hitler ordered the Germans to do likewise. They planned to hold the Russians out of artillery range of the port, whilst two divisions dug in on the Sapun Ridge, an exposed forty-five-metre-high crest that dropped into the Valley of Death where the British Light Brigade had charged Russian guns ninety years before in the Crimean War. On 7 May the ridge disappeared in dust and smoke as divebombers dropped their loads on German positions. A Red banner floated from the ridge by mid morning as Russian assault troops overran the German positions.

The way into Sebastopol was now open. On 9 May 1944, as the Russians began to pour into the city, the remnants of the German 17th Army abandoned it. About thirty thousand of them, still hoping for evacuation, fled across bleak moors to the Kherson promontory. This spit of land, with the ruins of a white lighthouse at its tip, was where the last Russian defenders had come to be killed or taken prisoner two years before. Divebombers, *Katyushas* and artillery ranged over a small area, five kilometres by two and a half, where 17th Army waited for rescue ships. A few small ships did come at night, whilst the Germans held off the Russians with anti-aircraft guns firing over open sights. No ships could get near the spit on the night of 11–12 May and in the early hours the Russians attacked. Their nerves stretched by forty-eight hours of continuous bombardment, the Germans fled in panic from their trenches. T-32s pursued them back to the ruined farmhouse where their staff officers huddled in the cellar.

By noon, 25,000 surviving Germans surrendered, many of them wounded. At the very tip of the spit, 750 SS men refused to give up and fought to the death around the lighthouse. Some pushed out to sea on crude rafts, hoping to be picked up by a German or Rumanian ship. Stormovik Il-2s dived on them with their weapons mix of cannon, rockets, HE bombs and anti-personnel cluster bomblets. Dead Germans and shattered rafts bobbed in the brilliant blue sea, whilst helmets, photographs, private letters and a volume of Nietzsche lay scattered on the scorched earth. The fate of the Crimean Tartars was settled with that of the ruined 17th Army, for they had collaborated with the Gestapo, cruelly hunting down disguised Russian soldiers during the occupation. Half a million of them were soon to be transported to the East, not to return.

In the south, with the cream of their marshals and generals operating in open space with fluidity, the Russians had shattered the Germans as much by mind and manoeuvre as materiel. Pulling back over the borders, on foot, in wheezing French trucks and in horse carts, the German infantry distilled the experience of the Eastern front in the bitter song:

Es ist alles vorueber, es ist alles vorbei,
Drei Jahre in Russland und nix ponimai.

For them, it was all over, all gone. Three years in Russia, without comprehension. That had not yet happened in the centre and north of the front, still 3,200 kilometres long. But it would.

21

CENTRE FOLD

The *Stavka* halted operations after the reconquest of the Crimea to aid the build-up of their major strategic campaign of 1944. This was the destruction of the most powerful German force, Army Group Centre. Based on Minsk, it blocked the direct route into Central Europe, the line running from Minsk to Warsaw and on to Berlin.

Army Group Centre had managed to stabilize the 'Panther' line it had retreated to in the autumn of 1943. It held the line on the east bank of the Dnieper between Stari-Bishov and Orsha. It had repulsed repeated attempts by the Russians to seize the strip of land between the Dnieper and the Dvina, holding them in heavy fighting for the supply route at Orsha and in front of Vitebsk. Its salient, bellying east to Vitebsk and Rogachev, was threatened in the south at the Pripet marshes by the retreat of the battered Army Group South.

The fighting was tight and constricted. Despite huge losses, no break-throughs had been attained. A Russian assault coming out of a dawn sun was a terrifying spectacle but the Germans could break it up if their units kept intact. German infantry waited, 'our eyes reduced to slits, dry-mouthed, our guns jammed against our shoulders and our grenades in easy reach'. Then, amid the smell of explosive and burning fuel, the German tanks and artillery would slam into the Russians before they came into machinegun range. The slaughter was made worse by the Russians' 'almost religious belief' in the importance of high ground. They made for any height and fought for it stubbornly regardless of its tactical importance. The Germans read their intentions and would withdraw the night before an expected attack so that the pre-assault barrage often landed on empty forward positions. This was a risky game but the Germans played it well.

Manstein had shown that the Russians were slow to switch the thrust of a ponderously mounted attack and were vulnerable to counter-attack. They found it difficult to cope with surprise and with the capacity of even junior German commanders to seize a local initiative through personal action and leadership. 'Even in the critical years of 1944–45, our soldiers never had the feeling of being inferior to the Russians,' wrote Mellenthin. 'The Germans fought successful actions with a strength ratio of 1:5, as long as the formations were more or less intact and adequately equipped.'

That, at least, was the view of German officers. It was self-seeking, of course. The Russians were praised for minor detail, good camouflage and fire discipline, brilliance in river-crossing and railway repairing, in order to damn them with the greater sins of inflexibility and indifference to casualties. Soviet victories were attributed jointly to Hitler and to an overwhelming Soviet strength in manpower. The Wehrmacht was run over by the Russian steamroller.

This grossly underestimates the Soviet achievement. During the slogging stage of any drawn-out war, the supply of equipment is as vital to the professional soldier as his use of it. Between Stalingrad and the end of the war there was only a marginal increase in the number of men in the Red army but there was a vast increase in the quantity of equipment. Between November 1942 and January 1944 manpower increased by only 11 per cent, whilst the number of tanks was up 33 per cent and the aircraft strength doubled. By January 1945, with only a further 1 per cent increase in the number of men, the tank and aircraft inventories were up respectively 250 per cent and 343 per cent on the Stalingrad figures.[1] Apart from trucks and some aircraft, this equipment was Soviet built. Its production, in an economy that had been half-overrun by the enemy and not simply bombed like the Reich, was an immense professional achievement.

So was its organization and handling after its delivery. If Soviet strategy during the long advance was rarely spectacular, it was highly effective and its consistency and steadiness should not be confused with slavishness. The skill with which the Russians infiltrated German defences, seizing and rapidly building up in key positions, shows that company and battalion commanders could act decisively on accurately gleaned intelligence. They did this with troops who were often illiterate and non-Russian speaking, but whose fieldcraft and ability to sustain an advance with scant resupply and to slither across natural obstacles, marsh, forest and river, exceeded the German.

These qualities were about to be tested against Army Group Centre in Operation *Bagration*,[2] the *Stavka*'s *Barbarossa* in reverse. It was thinly stretched, with the 9th and 4th Armies and 3rd Panzer Army holding a bulging front of 700 kilometres with 32 divisions. The only reserves were a division apiece with 4th Army and 3rd Panzer. Against them, the Russians amassed 166 divisions and better than 4:1 ratios with 4,000 tanks and self-propelled guns and more than 6,000 aircraft. Artillery density in the breakthrough sectors reached 210 guns per kilometre. A fleet of 12,000 trucks had the capacity to ferry 25,000 tons of supplies per journey to the front.

The 1.6 million men were organized in four Fronts. In the north, from the river Dvina to the German strongpoint at Vitebsk, the Armenian General I. K. Bagramyan commanded the 1st Baltic Front, with four Armies, including one in reserve. To his south, between Vitebsk and the Dnieper, General I. D. Cherniakovsky, the Jewish veteran of Moscow and Kursk, commanded the four Armies of the 3rd White Russian Front. The 2nd White Russian was on the Dnieper opposite Mogilev with three Armies under General G. F. Zakharov. The 1st White Russian Front of General Rokossovsky stretched under the German belly from the Dnieper at Rogachev across the Pripet marshes to Kovel, where General Chuikov held his 8th Guards Army. The first two Fronts were under the general command of Marshal Vassilevsky, the other two under Marshal Zhukov.

Russian strength was greatest on the wings. In the north the 1st Baltic and 3rd White Russian Fronts were to cooperate to take the German strongpoint at Vitebsk, driving the Germans out of the strip between the Dvina and Dnieper before the 1st Baltic Front moved westwards on Lepel whilst the 3rd White Russian Front, having engorged the German cornerstone at Orsha, pierced on for Borisov. In the south the 1st White Russian Front was to open the way north of the Pripet marshes by encircling Bobruisk. Once astride the Beresina, the next target of this great offensive was Minsk.

By nightfall on 6 June 1944, 156,000 Allied troops had landed in Normandy and the Anglo-American invasion of Hitler's Fortress Europe had begun. Stalin signalled Churchill that 'the summer offensive of the Soviet troops, to be launched in keeping with the agreement reached at the Teheran Conference, will begin in mid June in one of the vital sectors of the front.' The Germans had been expecting the summer blow to fall in Galicia and had stripped Army Group Centre of a panzer corps on this basis. As elite units began to multiply opposite them, it was slowly realized that they had misread Stalin's 'vital sectors'.

Further evidence came from the upsurge in partisan activity in White Russia, where the partisans were particularly strong. They controlled a huge tract of woods and marsh that extended from the Dnieper almost to Minsk with some 140,000 men. Their war was a vicious affair of ambush and attacks on isolated positions, and German atrocities. Wounded

Germans were found with their heads tied inside the stomachs of dead comrades, or stripped naked with their feet strapped in drinking troughs where the water had frozen solid. During an anti-partisan hunt in the spring, the Germans had ordered the winter crops to be ploughed under and had fired hundreds of wooden villages. The Russian collaborators of the Kaminsky Brigade added their toll of country folk to the million people who were massacred in White Russia during the German occupation. They left swathes of forest yellow as they tried to smoke out the partisans.

That they had failed became clear on the night of 19 June. Thousands of demolition charges destroyed the rail tracks west of Minsk in partisan attacks that had been carefully coordinated with the Red army. The explosions continued for the next two brief nights of luminous darkness.

They were the prelude to Zhukov's great offensive, which started on 22 June 1944, exactly three years after *Barbarossa*. *Bagration* began with the predictable fury of an artillery and rocket barrage, but these were now backed up by strong formations of ground-attack aircraft. The German 6th Air Fleet had only forty serviceable fighters and the Red air force had the run of the sky. It used it to mount low-level attacks on the German artillery positions which, given the shortage of armour and infantry, were the backbone of the defence. This was followed not by the standard tank and tank-borne assault, but by massed infantry attacks. Hand-to-hand fighting cleared the first German trenches. After the infantry had torn chunks out of the German front, the assault battalions were joined by more infantry with artillery support who widened the breaches. These were then exploited by big packs of armour, whilst the fleets of ground-attack aircraft bombed and rocketed the Germans gun pits. Special night-fighting squads were used at nightfall to keep up the bloody pressure and to prevent an ordered withdrawal. In this damp country of streams and woods, engineers worked desperately to keep the momentum of attack rolling.

With 3rd Panzer already reeling from the initial blow, 4th Army was struck by Zakharov on 23 June and 9th Army by Rokossovsky the following day as the four Soviet Fronts were fed into the battle. Though 3rd Panzer was in desperate straits round the strongpoint at Vitebsk, Hitler, worried by the looming defection of Finland from the German side, said that for political reasons 'Vitebsk must be held at all costs.' That day was the last on which Army Group Centre could have been saved. The 9th Army was under heavy attack and 4th Army's line was breached to the east of Mogilev. No order was given to withdraw it from the engulfing disaster.

By the afternoon of 25 June, 3rd Panzer had four divisions trapped in the burning town as Russian machinegunners infiltrated into the suburbs. Hitler said that the garrison must hold until it was relieved. With Russian tanks brigaded into special mobile groups in almost free advance, and fighter-bombers tearing the guts out of the German defence, any hope of relief was unreal. After 20,000 Germans had died in the ruins of the town, the garrison surrendered. A group of 8,000 Germans who succeeded in a brief break-out were trapped by armour and artillery and slaughtered.

A double envelopment of Army Group Centre was an acute danger by 26 June. In the south the armour of 1st White Russian Front was rolling unhindered on the strongpoint at Bobruisk and the rear of 9th Army. Further north the 3rd White Russian Front was driving west of Orsha and slicing into the exposed flank of 4th Army. Forward units of the 2nd White Russian Front crossed the Dnieper and established bridgeheads north of Mogilev, engineers toiling under German fire to throw bridges across the wide river. From Berchtesgaden, Hitler agreed that 9th Army could pull back into Bobruisk whilst the reeling 4th Army retreated to the line of the Beresina. Mogilev and Orsha, supposedly strongpoints but now traps, were to be held.

The three German Armies were losing contact with each other as fast-moving Russian armour cut between them. Orsha fell on 27 June whilst Zakharov's 2nd White Russian Front bore down on the 4th Army at Mogilev, which the Germans abandoned on 27 June. The plight of 9th Army to the south was yet more desperate. Rokossovsky's 1st White Russian Front, lashed on by Zhukov, was driving along both banks of the Beresina to Bobruisk. The bridges and roads leading west were being seized from both north and south as 9th Army was sealed in a ring. The 41st Panzer and 35th Corps were herded in wooded country on the east bank of the river, unable to cross to the town and under shellfire from the other bank. The 20th Panzer Division was badly mauled as it attempted to clear the bridges. In the marshy southern sector the Russians built hasty log roads and laid brushwood along forest trails to keep the tanks and SP guns moving forward.

An attempt by 35th Corps to break out to the north with a spearhead of 150 tanks and SP guns was crushed on the evening of 27 June. 'Not less than two thousand enemy officers and men advanced towards our positions,' said General Teremov of the Soviet 108th Division. 'The guns opened fire against the attackers when they were 700 yards away, machine-guns at a distance of 400 yards. The Nazis continued their advance. Shells burst in their very midst. Machineguns mowed down their ranks. The Nazis stepped over the bodies of their dead ... It was an insane attack. We saw a terrible sight from our observation post.'[3]

The Germans trapped in the Bobruisk cauldron fired their supply dumps and stores. Rokossovsky ordered a raid by over five hundred aircraft, the bombs fuelling the flames in the trap whilst rockets destroyed the last tanks. 'The Nazis ran out of the forests, rushed about in the clearings, many attempted to swim across the Beresina but even this did not save them,' recalled Rokossovsky. 'Soon the bombed area became an enormous cemetery scattered with bodies and equipment destroyed by the bombs.'[4] The following day, as Field Marshal Model replaced Busch as commander of the disintegrating Army Group Centre, Rokossovsky struck into the outskirts of the town. It fell on 29 June.

Within a week the Russians had taken all the German strongpoints and had ripped the front apart over a distance of more than 320 kilometres. Third Panzer was reduced to an infantry corps, 4th Army was pouring back on Minsk and 9th Army had been devastated. The Germans had lost over 130,000 men killed and 66,000 taken prisoner.[5] Although the Russians had also taken fearful casualties, the offensive was far from over. The German 4th Army, as it fell back on the Beresina, found itself outflanked by Russian infantry. The 1st and 3rd White Russian Fronts were driving on Minsk in a double encirclement to take Minsk and trap 4th Army. Beyond the inner pincers fast armoured thrusts on both wings of the Russian offensive front were cutting through towards Slutsk in the south and Lepel in the north. Zhukov was not to be sated by Minsk but was determined to exploit the breakthroughs by getting much further west.

With the 4th Army trapped on the east bank of the Beresina, Model struggled to keep escape routes open rather than hold Minsk. On 3 July the Russians broke into Minsk almost simultaneously from the north and south-east, the city largely ruined and scattered with delayed-action bombs, mines and boobytraps. With the fall of Minsk the 1st and 3rd White Russian Fronts trapped the mass of 4th Army, still trying to fight its way across the Beresina eighty kilometres to the east. There were 105,000 men caught in a cauldron that shifted through the forests east of Minsk as they flailed to escape, their wounded untreated, without food or ammunition, and fuel dwindling. The Luftwaffe flew a final supply drop on 5 July before the airfield at Smilovichi was lost. Like the Russians before them in 1941 the Germans fell back inside the ring until, compacted by artillery and aircraft, the remnants surrendered. The 57,000 survivors, including generals and dozens of officers, some of whom would convert to Communism and lead the new East German army after the war, were marched through the streets of Moscow on 17 July.

The destruction of Army Group Centre in White Russia was the greatest defeat ever suffered by the Germans on the Eastern front. It was a catastrophe beyond the scale of Stalingrad and Kursk. In a fortnight, between 25 and 28 German divisions were destroyed and 350,000 men lost. Virtually the whole of 4th Army and most of the 9th and 3rd Panzer had gone, taking 10 generals killed and 21 captured with them. Eight scattered divisions were left on a front of 320 kilometres to face 116 infantry divisions, 6 cavalry divisions, 16 mechanized infantry brigades and 42 armoured brigades. Unlike 1941, when the Germans had advanced in narrow spearheads, the Red army had rolling and mobile strength behind a flurry of blows on a broad front. Where the Germans had driven through defences with the narrow intensity of a high-pressure jet, the forward edge of the Russian advance was marked by tongues of armour and infantry licking westward in many rivulets across the flood plains of Central Europe. The forward units flowed round the German strongpoints, leaving these to be washed away in their wake.

Even while 4th Army was dying in its trap, the advance continued at up to 25 kilometres a day, sweeping to the East Prussian border and further south to Poland. Cherniakovsky's 3rd White Russian Front took Vilna on 13 July and swept on towards the East Prussian border. With Bagramyan's 1st Baltic Front closing on Dvinsk, the retreat of the German Army Group North from the Baltic states was being blocked by a dual barrier.

Rokossovsky crossed into Poland on 18 July. Chuikov's 8th Guards Army had been assigned to his 1st White Russian Front. The Germans had inflicted heavy losses in this sector, skilfully anticipating a Russian assault, pulling back to well-prepared positions in the rear and launching punishing counter-attacks that caught the Russians off balance. Chuikov, now fighting in wide spaces rather than the Stalingrad pit, determined to disguise the coming breakthrough on Lublin. Units moved up by night and tank and tyre tracks were obliterated. Radio blackout was imposed. The heavy reconnaissance that often alerted the Germans to a coming attack was cancelled and the initial artillery barrage was shortened. The 8th Guards was trained in the laborious arts of movement over marshy and wooded country using brushwood and log roads.

Chuikov's tanks and infantry broke into Lublin on 23 July amid fierce street fighting with German machinegunners firing from stone houses that were slowly reduced by assault guns. Russian tanks destroyed an armoured train with fleeing Germans aboard and a final break-out attempt by the garrison was crushed at noon the next day. In the wake of the Red armies, 8th Guards, 47th and 2nd Tank Armies, would soon come the 'Lublin Poles' of the Soviet-dominated committee set up to run liberated Polish territory. On 26 July several of Rokossovsky's columns reached the Vistula. Two days later Brest-Litovsk, the scene of the humiliating peace of 1918 and the jumping-off point for *Barbarossa*, was abandoned after being outflanked, and the whole of White Russia was cleared of Germans. The same day, the Russians reached Siedlce, sixty-five kilometres east of Warsaw.

The Germans appeared to be in general collapse on 31 July as Rokossovsky cleared Siedlce and the eager inhabitants of Warsaw heard the music of his tank guns firing on German positions in Praga, the suburb on the east bank of the Vistula. In Normandy, Patton's tanks were cascading through the Avranches breach. In Germany itself, Hitler had barely survived the bomb plot of 20 July and a witch hunt for traitors in the Wehrmacht was under way.

To Rokossovsky's south, Marshal Koniev's 1st Ukrainian Front had finally launched the attack the Germans had been anticipating south of the Pripet marshes against Army Group North Ukraine. Though it had been stripped of 6 divisions in a fruitless attempt to save Army Group Centre, it still numbered 38 divisions with some 900 tanks and SP guns. Against it, Koniev disposed 80 divisions with at least 1,600 tanks and SP guns and almost 3,000 aircraft. The defence by the 1st and 4th Panzer Armies was skilful and determined. Koniev threw in his tank reserves in a two-pronged attack. His right wing punched across the Bug to converge with Rokossovsky's drive on Lublin and the Vistula. His left was initially held by Panzer and SS divisions as it attempted to batter its way to Lvov.

Russian weight told. The 1st and 3rd Guards Tank Armies sliced a pocket between Brody and Lvov, trapping 47,000 Germans of whom only 17,000 survived as POWs. It took seventy-two hours of street battles for the Germans to be cleared from Lvov. It fell on 27 July. On that same day, evidence of the vast scale of its effort, the Red army also took Stanislav in the Carpathian foothills, Bialystok in northern Poland, Dvinsk in Latvia and the Siauliai Rai junction between Riga and East Prussia.[6] 4th Panzer Army fell back on the Vistula and 1st Panzer retreated south-west to the Carpathians. Koniev's troops seized a bridgehead on the west bank of the Vistula near Sandomierz on the night of July 29.

But it was in the centre that the Russian advance was the most spectacular. They advanced 725 kilometres in 5 weeks to within earshot of Warsaw. To the men of the Polish Home Army, the underground led from London, it seemed only a matter of hours before Rokossovsky would storm into the city from across the Vistula. On 1 August the Polish commander General Bor-Komorowsky ordered the 200,000 men of the Home Army, by far the largest underground group in Europe, to rise against the Germans in Warsaw.

That same day the Russian tank formations had been ordered to go on to the defensive. Rokossovsky could see the effects of the doomed rising from a forward observation post of 2nd Tank Army. The burning houses and bomb and shell bursts were clearly visible from his eyrie atop a factory chimney.[7] But, whilst Warsaw was martyred for two months, as SS units and packs of released criminals and partisan-hunters immolated the Home Army in cellars and sewers, the Russians stood on the Vistula. They were still there at the end of the year.

General Bor had been confident that German resistance would be slight and that the anti-communist Poles of the Home Army would gain the enormous political prize of taking the city in advance of the Soviet armour. Though the partisans rapidly took half the city, catching the Germans in the streets and in their billets, it was soon clear that the lightly armed rising was in serious trouble. The Soviet high command and Moscow radio remained silent. Having absorbed the initial fury of the attack, the Germans slowly broke out of their strongpoints backed by air strikes, artillery, tanks and SP guns. Stalin was scathing about the Home Army. 'These people do not fight against the Germans, but only hide in the woods,' he said. Darkly, he told the premier of the London government, Stanislaw Miko-lajczyk: 'Hereafter I intend to deal with only one Polish government, not two.'

As he spoke in the Kremlin, the partisans were attacking fixed defences with rifles and machine pistols. The SS men, Russian ex-POWs from the Kaminski brigade and the released criminals of the brutal Dirlewanger brigade, were commanded by SS Obergruppenfuehrer von dem Bach-Zelewski, a gruesome anti-partisan specialist. Himmler ordered in reinforcements, drawing the Hermann Goering division from Italy, the Totenkopf division from Rumania and the Viking division from the Lublin front into the cauldron. The Poles were forced back into three areas of the burning city, maintaining contact by crawling through the sewers.

Churchill signalled Stalin that the RAF, though it would have to fly 1,100 kilometres from Italy, would attempt an air drop of 60 tons of supplies over Warsaw. He added questioningly: 'They appeal for Russian aid which seems very near.' The Red air force was within 160 kilometres. Stalin's reply on 5 August effectively left the Poles to the whirling, smoke-blackened slaughter where the Germans were using screens of Polish women and children for their tank assaults and where Polish men were rounded up and shot when a section of the city was cleared. Stalin told Churchill: 'I think the information given to you by the Poles is greatly exaggerated and misleading . . . The Home Army consists of a few detach-ments, misnamed divisions . . . I cannot imagine detachments like these taking Warsaw.'

The Poles found the inaction of the Red army, its distance from the city pit at 'a dozen kilometres', to be 'incomprehensible, passive and ostentatious'. They rightly felt it had political significance. The head of the pro-Moscow Lublin committee, Boleslaw Beirut, claimed there had been no rising at all. By 13 August Stalin said that the rising was 'a reckless adventure causing useless victims among the inhabitants'. The blame for the charnel house was placed 'exclusively on Polish émigré circles in London'. Polish, RAF and South African units attempted supply drops, but suffered 17 per cent casualties on a long journey over enemy territory where night fighters were plentiful.[8] Stalin refused to allow US aircraft to land at Soviet airfields. On 22 August, he denounced the 'power-seeking criminals' behind the rising. As Churchill noted, the 'men in the Kremlin ... were governed by calculation and not emotion. They did not mean to let the spirit of Poland rise again at Warsaw.'[9]

Using the sewers, the Poles abandoned the Old Town for the centre. The Germans dropped hand grenades and gas bombs down the manholes. Dark battles took place in the sewers between men up to their waists in excrement, fighting with knives or drowning each other in the filth. Above the sewers, the city continued to burn.[10]

On 10 September, with the rising visibly doomed, Russian artillery began shelling the eastern suburbs. Stalin allowed himself some magnanimity. The Americans were allowed one supply drop. The Red air force dropped some canisters which smashed on impact or fell in German positions. Churchill noted that the Russians 'wished to have the non-communist Poles destroyed to the full, but also to keep alive the idea they were going to their rescue'.

After 62 days of continuous combat, with up to 200,000 civilians buried in the rubble or lying wounded and untreated in streets and cellars and 15,000 Home Army men dead, the Poles surrendered.[11]

Stalin's emotional indifference and contempt for the butchered Home Army was entirely in character. But technically, at least, the Russians would have been taking serious risks to help the Poles. The unparalleled speed of Rokossovsky's advance to the Vistula had left his men and machines exhausted. Model had succeeded in re-establishing both morale and some stability in the German centre. The German 9th Army certainly considered that it, rather than any political motive, had halted the Russians at the gates of Warsaw.

Rokossovsky told the Western correspondent Alexander Werth: 'Bor-Komorowsky [is] like the clown in the circus who pops up at the wrong moment and who only gets rolled up in the carpet ... If it were only a piece of clowning it wouldn't matter, but this political stunt is going to cost Poland hundreds of thousands of lives. It is an appalling tragedy, and they are now trying to put the blame on us.'[12] He added that the destiny of Poland lay not with London Poles but with the Red army. '*We* are responsible for the conduct of the war in Poland,' he said. '*We* are the force that will liberate the whole of Poland within the next few months.'

Whilst Warsaw burned, the Germans succeeded in containing Russian attempts to advance from the bridgeheads over the Vistula. By mid August the Vistula front had been stabilized. Further north a Soviet infantryman, Alexander Afanasevich Tretyak, had scrambled over the East Prussian frontier early on 17 August and had raised the first Red battle flag on German soil.[13] But resistance stiffened and the Russian advance on East Prussia was checked. German counter-attacks to the Gulf of Riga were to re-open the line of retreat for Army Group North. German munitions output reached its peak in August, with enough tanks and SP guns produced to re-equip ten panzer divisions. The call-up age in the Reich was reduced from 17 to $16\frac{1}{2}$ as a final attempt was made to replace losses.

In the centre, the Germans won a respite.

22

THE SATELLITES CHANGE SIDES

With the central thrust to Berlin now checked on the Vistula, the Russian impetus switched to the Balkans. The Germans were well outnumbered by two powerful Russian groupings, Malinovsky's 2nd Ukrainian and Tolbukhin's 1st Ukrainian Fronts. These totalled a million men. Malinovsky alone had 1,283 tanks and SP guns and almost 900 aircraft in 6 infantry Armies, 1 tank and 1 air Army.

The German Army Group South Ukraine had some 600,000 men, with 400 tanks and 800 aircraft. But two of its four armies were Rumanian and it had been stripped of its panzer divisions to feed Model in the north. The German 6th Army was dug in along the Dniester. The 8th, which held the northern flank against Malinovsky, had only one armoured division to cope with his plethora of tanks. The resurrected 6th Army had as much reason as its ghostly namesake, destroyed at Stalingrad, to mistrust the Rumanians whose divisions interlaced with its own. Marshal Antonescu, the Rumanian dictator, had visited Hitler on 5 August and had sympathized with him on the July bomb plot. 'Believe me, I can have implicit faith in every one of my generals,' he said. 'The idea of officers taking part in such a *coup d'état* is unthinkable to us!'

The unthinkable took little time to happen. On 20 August the two Russian Fronts attacked. The ferocity of a Russian barrage tested experienced and well-dug-in Germans to the limits. The Rumanians broke under it immediately, and Russian armour poured through the gaps. Within two days the German 6th Army with its sixteen divisions had been trapped. In places Rumanian units were fighting against their former German allies. The 8th Army retreated rapidly west of the Carpathians. The Soviet advance, well directed and so dense that Jeeps and tanks drove with lights on to see through the dust, was unstoppable.

On 23 August, a coup in Bucharest settled the German fate in the Balkans. King Michael of Rumania, told that Soviet armour was pouring through a 100-kilometre-wide rent in the front, ordered the arrest of Antonescu. That evening the King went on the radio to announce an end to all hostilities. The remnants of the two Rumanian armies still fighting with the Germans were instructed to lay down their arms. The Danube and the Carpathians were now open to the Red army, freeing the way through to the Hungarian plains and on to Czechoslovakia and Austria.[1] Bulgaria and Yugoslavia were equally vulnerable. The Red army was on the point of exploiting 'the widest open flank that had ever been known in modern war', its left wing able to wheel through the spaces of south-eastern and Central Europe.[2]

Hitler reacted by ordering Stukas to divebomb the Rumanian capital, concentrating on the royal palace. This merely stiffened anti-German feeling. With his embassy threatened by mobs, the German ambassador Killinger committed suicide. On 25 August, as Paris fell to the Allies, 6th Army was still trying to break out through the Carpathians. Trapped, it was being chopped up into hundreds of small pockets as the process of its disintegration continued. A cross-movement developed as the Red army pressed south-westwards from Bucharest and the oilfields, whilst the Germans tried to cut across the path of the Russians to break out to the west. These small German columns, with five, ten or even fifteen tanks, still dragging the remnants of their artillery, fought with desperate ferocity. 'Whenever they manage to reach a road at a point where no tanks or infantry are moving for a kilometre or so,' wrote the Soviet correspondent Konstantin Simonov, 'but only our supply carts or isolated vehicles, they fall upon them and kill without mercy and break across the road, continuing on their way.'

Russian wireless communications had improved enormously and most of these break-out groups were cornered in the fields of maize and destroyed. A few thousand escaped, drawn irresistibly west 'as the north attracts the needle of a compass', the now familiar wreckage of a once proud army, 'on foot, in rags, their faces livid after so much suffering, dragging along with them nauseatingly wounded men on litters made of branches, like the litters of the Sioux'.[3]

On 31 August 1944, after the great Ploesti oilfields had been taken, Malinovsky's 6th Tank Army entered Bucharest. This was the first time that Soviet troops had entered a major capitalist city. As they clipped through the suburbs the tank crews marvelled at the colour, the canary-yellow water fountains, the brightly painted shop signs for butchers, taverns and barbers and the first yellow Bucharest tramcar that rumbled past them. In the centre they found the houses of the rich, old ones like 'decorated honey cakes' and 'brand new ones like smooth concrete boxes, painted yellow or white and drowned in a sea of greenery'.[4] They were greeted with flowers, wine and huge crowds and by local Communists with banners praising 'Marshal Stalin, the Genius Commander of the Russian Army'.

The tanks had covered 400 kilometres in 12 days. The Russians claimed 98,000 German prisoners and 100,000 killed. By Soviet reckoning, only 25,000 Germans escaped. Amongst them was Guy Sajer, retreating on narrow Carpathian roads near the town of Reghin, with Panzer-grenadiers and other remnants of elite units. Many men had thrown away their heavy helmets, though Sajer and his comrades, machinegun belts encircling their naked chests, their feet bleeding in their crumbling boots, kept theirs as 'a last link with the German army'. They came across the body of a comrade hanging like a sack from a tree. He had looted food from a wrecked truck and a scribbled message was tied to his broken neck – 'I am a thief and a traitor to my country.' A short way off, ten military police in regulation uniform stood by a motorcycle sidecar. 'As we walked by them,' wrote Sajer, 'our eyes met theirs.'

Such ruthless discipline kept Germany in the war, but it could not prevent the desertion of allies. A Rumanian delegation arrived in Moscow early in September, feted and living in luxury at a government guest house whilst the Soviet grip on Rumania tightened as the Red army reached the Yugoslav frontier at Turnu Severin on the Danube. Bulgaria was next. Although at war with the US and Britain, Bulgaria had not declared war on the Soviet Union and had maintained a minister in Moscow (or Kuibyshev) throughout the war. On 26 August the country declared itself neutral. That did not satisfy Stalin. The Russians declared war on Bulgaria on 5 September. Three days later Tolbukhin's troops invaded. There was no resistance and the Russians were met with cheerful peals of church bells chiming 'merrily as one hears at Easter'. Astounded Russian troops found a Bulgarian infantry division neatly lined up on both sides of the road at the frontier, welcoming them with banners and a band. A coup in Sofia set up a pro-Soviet Fatherland Front. On 17 September the Bulgarian army was placed under formal Soviet command and units were integrated into the Red army. Before long, People's Courts were dealing with the bourgeoisie and the army had been purged of its 'Fascist elements'.

Far to the north a Finnish armistice delegation arrived in Moscow on 14 September. An armistice was signed five days later. Reparations were set and the 1940 frontier was restored. No Soviet troops were stationed in Finland, although Russian troops broke through the German positions in Petsamo on their way to liberate northern Norway. The Germans pulled out of northern Norway, after burning the towns, but remained in the rest of Norway until the end of the war.

On 21 September, a Soviet Dakota flew Marshal Tito from the British-controlled island of Vis in the Adriatic to Tolbukhin's Front HQ in Rumania. The Yugoslav partisan leader slipped away without the British realizing it. Decorated with the Order of Suvorov and escorted by Red air force fighters, Tito flew on to Moscow to meet Stalin.[5] Stalin urged

Tito to come to an agreement with King Peter of Yugoslavia, if only temporarily to keep the British quiet, adding cynically that 'then you can slip a knife in his back at a suitable moment'. Tito, already showing signs of independence, argued vehemently against this. Relations between the two deteriorated further when Stalin invited Tito to a drunken supper at his dacha.

Nevertheless, a joint Soviet–Bulgarian–Yugoslav offensive was planned. It was a two-pronged attack, with Malinovsky sweeping west through the northern plains towards Szeged and Hungary, and Tolbukhin struggling more slowly through the rugged country to the south of Belgrade. The Germans, fearful of encirclement, put up a stiff resistance in the Serbian mountains. Split into three milling groups, they fought to keep escape routes open for themselves and for the large German forces still in Greece that now faced isolation. Groups of German anti-tank gunners, with a leavening of Tigers and tommygunners mounted in halftracks, pulverized the T-34s from short range before themselves being destroyed.

The attack on a well-dug-in German force in Belgrade opened on 14 October. The Russians and Yugoslavs took heavy casualties in hand-to-hand street fighting as they worked their way along the broad avenues to the Kalemagdan, the old Turkish fortress. The partisans of the 1st Yugoslav Proletarian Division met up with the Soviet 4th Mechanized Corps on the evening of 20 October, signal rockets streaking out to celebrate their victory. Following the mass burial of Yugoslav and Russian soldiers in communal graves, Tito held a victory parade. The T-34s sweeping past Tito in salute headed straight on for the Danube bridges to join 4th Mechanized's new drive into Hungary.

With Rumania, Bulgaria, Yugoslavia and Finland gone, a rising by the Slovakian partisans under way and Hungary vacillating, the German Eastern front looked to have collapsed beyond repair. Crack units like the *Gross Deutschland* Division were patched up with boys, some carrying school satchels their mothers had packed with extra food and clothes, their eyes 'filled with unease' like children at the start of a new term.

The Hungarian regent, Admiral Horthy, had already told Guderian: 'Look, my friend, in politics you must always have several irons in the fire.' Horthy was Europe's senior head of government. His experience stretched back to the overthrow of Bela Kun's communist regime in 1919. With the collapse of Rumania, the writing was firmly on the Hungarian wall. He attempted to ditch the Germans. A Hungarian armistice delegation arrived in Moscow on 1 October. With Malinovsky closing on Budapest, Horthy agreed to the Soviet terms on 11 October.

The Germans could not afford to let Hungary slide without writing off the last of their divisions in south-eastern Europe and opening the way for the Russians to Vienna. Otto Skorzeny, the rescuer of Mussolini, drew up on Hitler's orders a joint plan to seize Horthy with the *Sicherheitdienst*, the SS security wing. Skorzeny first kidnapped Horthy's son, dragging him off to an aircraft and a flight to a concentration camp. At dawn on 16 October, supported by four tanks, Skorzeny seized the Burgberg, Horthy's citadel in Budapest. A new government was set up under Ferenc Szalasi, the hysterically pro-Nazi leader of the Arrow Cross. With him came anti-Jewish *razzias*, the extermination squads of Adolf Eichmann and the bloody continuation of Hungary as a battlefield.

Stalin was set on winning Hungary for the Soviet bloc that was developing in the wake of the Red army. He had reason for urgency, for the Anglo-Americans were already on German territory and on 2 October the US 1st Army had begun assaulting the Westwall, the German defence line in the West. Churchill had paid a brief visit to Moscow from 9 October. On the surface it had gone well. Churchill had been warmly applauded at a gala performance at the Bolshoi and Stalin had consented to dine at the British embassy, under the Kremlin walls and lit by a display of fireworks celebrating a final victory in Rumania. Churchill roughed out a post-war division of interests in Eastern Europe.

'I wrote out on a half sheet of paper: Romania – Russia 90 per cent, the others 10 per cent; Greece – Great Britain 90 per cent (in accord with the USA), Russia 10 per cent; Yugoslavia 50–50; Hungary 50–50; Bulgaria – Russia 75 per cent, the others 25 per cent,' Churchill noted. 'I pushed this across the table to Stalin ... There was a slight pause. Then he took his blue pencil and made a large tick and passed it back to us. It was all settled in no more time than it takes to set down ...'[6]

But it was far from settled. Stalin had no intention of sharing influence in Bulgaria or Hungary. On 28 October the *Stavka* ordered a frontal attack on Budapest. Malinovsky told Stalin over the telephone that his 46th Army could not seize Budapest off the march. 'You are arguing to no purpose,' Stalin shot back. 'You do not understand the political necessity of mounting an immediate attack on Budapest.' Malinovsky protested: 'I understand all the political importance of taking Budapest and for that very reason I am asking five days.' Stalin rang off after a curt insistence: 'I categorically order you to go over to the offensive for Budapest tomorrow.'

That order doomed Budapest to a long siege. It also aided Austria to escape permanent post-war domination by the Soviet Union since it delayed the Russian advance on Vienna. Malinovsky was right. His precipitate and unsupported advance ran into a German force that included four panzer divisions. His lead tanks reached the southern suburbs of Budapest on 4 November but stalled as they waited for infantry to reach them. German armour held in heavy tank fighting in pouring rain. A second Soviet attempt to take Budapest in November also failed. Even after it was cut off in an encircling attack on Christmas Eve, the city continued to hold out in nightmare conditions. The Germans fought with the careless violence of the doomed. Malinovsky's men had the most savage reputation of any Soviet Front.

Nevertheless, a form of stability had returned to the front running from the Baltic to the Carpathians. A Russian assault against East Prussia petered out against skilful defence in an area chokepointed with marshes and lakes.

Before they were checked the Russians had left in the East Prussian village of Nemmersdorf a terrible warning of what lay in store for German civilians. Red army men went berserk when they broke through on to German soil on 19 October. They took Nemmersdorf on 20 October and the German paratroops who retook the village two days later came upon a horror all too comparable with the conduct of their own side in Russia. In a farmyard they found a cart with four naked women nailed to it through their hands like crucifixes. Moving on, they came to the village inn, the Roter Krug. A barn stood near it and to each of its two doors a naked woman had been crucified. Inside the village houses they found seventy-two women and girls, all dead and all raped.

A German lieutenant who took part in the counter-attack stated: 'I did not find a single German civilian.' On the road into Nemmersdorf he came across a trek of refugees who had been rolled over by Russian tanks so that 'not only the wagons and teams of horses but also a goodly number of civilians, mostly women and children, had been squashed flat by the tanks. At the edge of the road and in the farm yards lay quantities of corpses of civilians who had evidently not all been killed in the course of military operations but rather had been murdered systematically ...'[7]

Only a thin line, with twelve weak divisions in reserve, remained to prevent a repeat of such atrocities. The Russians were flung an immense bonus when Hitler decided to throw the final German assault against the Allies in the Ardennes forests of Belgium, rather than husband what was left of his strength for the climax on the Eastern front. In November and December 1944 only 921 out of 2,229 new German tanks and SP guns went to the East. Twenty-five German divisions from three armies, including 6th Panzer, which had the best-equipped SS units left, attacked a slender American front in the Ardennes on 16 December.

German strength in Poland and East Prussia was stripped. The total number of understrength divisions on the Eastern front, which stretched for 1,930 kilometres from the Baltic to Yugoslavia, was down to 130. Almost thirty of these were invested by the Red army in Memel and Courland on the Baltic and a further twenty-eight were south of the Carpathians.

On the central front the Russians had a superiority that Guderian put at twenty to one in artillery and aircraft, eleven to one in infantry and seven to one in tanks.[8] The end in the East, as the Ardennes offensive ran out of thrust and collapsed in the West, was not far off.

23

THE HOUSE OF CARDS

Two and a quarter million men faced the Germans on the central front along the Vistula. Marshal Zhukov commanded the 1st White Russian Front opposite Warsaw. To his south Marshal Koniev's 1st Ukrainian Front was coiled to spring from its bridgehead across the river at Sandomierz. Between them the two marshals had 163 rifle divisions, over 30,000 guns, 4,772 aircraft and 6,460 tanks, almost half of all the Soviet armour on the Eastern front.[1]

The German forces in the East, already weakened by the Ardennes offensive, were further exposed in the centre by the squandering of precious armour on other sectors. Seven panzer divisions were fighting in Hungary and six were tied up in East Prussia and Courland. Only five were committed to hold the Red armies on the Warsaw–Berlin axis, although General Gehlen's intelligence had accurately predicted that the blow would fall here.[2] Hitler told Guderian just three days before the Soviet assault started that such assessments were the work of a 'lunatic'. Guderian had replied: 'The eastern front is like a house of cards. If the front is broken through at one point all the rest will collapse . . .'

The major Soviet objective was to smash through the centre in two vast drives aimed in tandem at the Oder, 400 kilometres to the west. Zhukov was to break across the Vistula below Warsaw whilst Koniev struck from his bridgehead 110 kilometres downstream, with both Fronts converging towards the Oder at Frankfurt. This was not all. General Cherniakovsky's 3rd White Russian Front would advance on Konigsberg on the Baltic, whilst Rokossovsky's 2nd White Russians cut through to the Baltic around Danzig from their start-lines north-east of Warsaw. These two Fronts poured an additional 1.6 million men, 28,000 guns and 3,300 tanks into this prodigious strategic assault on the Reich.[3] Rokossovsky's task was to pin down the heavy German forces in the north and so to secure Zhukov's long and exposed right flank from counter-attack.

The violent Russian storm was to break on just two German groups, Reinhardt's Army Group Centre in East Prussia, with 580,000 men but only 700 tanks and SP guns and 515 aircraft, and Harpe's Army Group A on the middle reaches of the Vistula with 400,000 men and 1,136 tanks and SP guns and 270 aircraft.[4]

The Germans knew what was afoot. The Russians had been reinforcing the Baranov bridgehead 'in the silence of many nights, without light or noise'. Baranov was 'a pistol aimed at Germany's neck'. The landscape changed abruptly across the grey and still unfrozen Vistula. To the east were expanses of pine forest with patches of ploughland and villages marked by the wooden spires of their churches. To the west, the plains of the left-bank Vistula began and ran unhindered to the Oder and the Reich. Reaches of water meadows were cut by canals and dykes. Oak and beech replaced the pines, and manor houses nestled in the copses. From here, the Soviet war correspondent Boris Polevoi noted, 'the roads lead straight to Germany'.

'Attack imminent,' a German intelligence report warned after prisoners captured south of Warsaw had been interrogated. 'First wave to be composed of punishment units ... Minefields cleared during the night of 8 January.' Prisoners taken on the night of 10 January confirmed that tank crews had moved into their billets.[5] At this stage the Germans would normally have withdrawn most of their troops to safer positions well behind the front line. But Hitler had ordered that this second line should only be 1.5 to 5 kilometres and not twenty behind the front.

The furious artillery storm that Koniev unleashed at 5 a.m. on the grey and misty morning of 12 January 1945 thus raged through the German reserves as well as the first-line trenches. Koniev had amassed up to three hundred guns to the kilometre for the breakthrough from the Naranov bridgehead. The bombardment was followed by the *strafbats*, the penal battalions, driving into the first German trenches.

The more heavily manned second line was then subjected to a hundred minutes of incessant shelling, scything the dead through the living. 'The earth groaned and shook for tens of miles around, and brown powder smoke hung in the air,' said Polevoi. 'The thunder of the shots and the explosions were fused into one solid roar. Above the German defence lines great spouts of earth were flung up into the air, obliterating everything living.' The first prisoners were incoherent and shaking with shock.

Koniev had planned the barrages with great care. The assault troops were not withdrawn from the first German trench line before the secondary bombardment, which was standard Russian drill. Instead, his artillerymen fired over their heads into the second German line, a task which was 'like hitting a mosquito in the eye'. Enemy observation and command posts were accurately singled out for artillery fire and air strikes. Koniev himself was startled by the effect on the German soldier, whom he respected as a man who would, as a 'rule confirmed through the war stay where he was ordered to stay until he was given permission to leave. But that day, 12 January, the fire was so relentless that those who survived it could no longer control themselves.'[6]

At 2 p.m. with 4th Panzer Army's front torn and bleeding, Koniev ordered General Lelyushenko's tanks forward. By evening Lelyushenko's armour was prowling 30 kilometres deep in 4th Panzer's positions. The pursuit did not stop with darkness, but rolled on as the 'red-tailed comets' of *Katyusha* rockets flew westward. After midnight a stiff frost hardened the mud on the roads and in the darkness 'over a vast area could be heard the tramp of the infantry, the clank of tank tracks, the puffing of giant traction engines pulling enormous guns, the creaking of carts and the vibrant ringing of our mobile guns'.

The following day, as heavy Stalin tanks with 122-mm guns fought Tigers and sent oily pyres of smoke above the damp meadowland, the Russians had broken clear through the strongest part of the German line to open country west of Kielce. Koniev had committed thirty-two rifle divisions and eight tank corps in the sector, which the horrified Guderian found 'the greatest concentration of force in the narrowest area that had been since the beginning of the war'.[7]

Early on 14 January Zhukov joined in the offensive from the Magnuszew bridgehead, a small area twenty-five kilometres wide and fifteen deep just south of Warsaw that he had stuffed with near half a million men and over a thousand tanks.[8] His assault battalions burst into the German lines as the preliminary barrage lifted and his tanks were in action at noon. By that evening they had penetrated up to thirty-two kilometres from the breakthrough point. Equal success was won by his Front's left wing which attacked from the Pulawy bridgehead. Ripping through the defensive membrane in two places, Zhukov's tank crews were soon sweeping on the tail of the retreating Germans. Further north Rokossovsky's 2nd White Russian Front had opened its own offensive the same morning, although driving snow and sleet denied it air cover and slowed its advance.

Threatened with encirclement by Zhukov's 1st White Russians, the German garrison began evacuating Warsaw in the night of 17 January. At midday, after final hours of looting and demolition, martyred Warsaw was finally free of German troops. The incoming Russians and the men of the Moscow-raised 1st Polish Army found 'gallows with bodies swinging in the wind, the charred corpses of people burnt alive in their own homes and the emaciated corpses of those who had starved'. Warsaw's freedom, in the dawning age of Soviet domination, would prove as bleak and vulnerable as its own ruins.

By 19 January, the defence lines had been bashed in and the Red armies were pouring westward to the German frontier without opposition. Chuikov took Lodz that day, the tanks of 8th Guards moving in almost without resistance. The 4th Panzer and 9th Armies were pulling back instinctively for the Oder, regiments chopped in pieces, survivors drifting in the mists and darkness, to avoid the strafing Russian aircraft, a tattered mass holding off the cold with Caucasian sheepskin coats and Red army quilted jackets acquired in more successful days, and clinging to a hope of sanctuary beyond the Oder. Crammed atop their tanks, the Russians moving along the road to Poznan were advancing into a near void: 'A flat, snowless expanse, a dead German soldier, bootless, frozen into the earth, fallen horses ... Soldiers' helmets, a steely blue on the battlefield ... Two nuns with huge white, starched headdresses plodding along together. A woman in mourning leading a small boy by the hand.'

They were pouring through an immense and whirling tear in the German lines that stretched 560 kilometres from the Carpathians to the Baltic. The Wehrmacht had nothing with which to plug it. Although they were now attempting to transfer troops from the West, the process took too long on the shattered Reichsbahn and the numbers were pitiful. The results of the Anglo-American slaughter five months before in Normandy, where the Germans had deployed 10 panzer and 19 infantry divisions and lost 15 of them outright, were now felt in full. Hitler had squandered pitiful reserves on Budapest and a futile attempt to hold the small Hungarian oilfields.

In East Prussia the 3rd Guards Cavalry Corps broke into Allenstein as German trains unloaded tanks and artillery in the railway sidings. Samsonov's men had taken Allenstein for Tsar and Empire in August 1914, cheering in their mistaken thought that it was Berlin, five days before Samsonov shot himself after Hindenburg had massacred his men at Tannenberg. No Hindenburg now with Stalin in the ascendant, simply his remains, which the Germans took with them when they abandoned Tannenberg on 21 January. All the elements were now reversed, with Soviet tanks, headlamps blazing, tearing through the shoppers and trams of early evening in Elbing.[9] With that, Rokossovsky reached the Baltic, trapping the 3rd Panzer and the remnants of 4th Army behind him. A furious attempt by 4th Army to break out to the west was repulsed by the 5th Guards Tank Army. East Prussia was now cut off from the Reich.

There was a terrible finality to the invasion of East Prussia. It has ceased to exist, divided between Poland and the Soviet Union, the last German redoubt at Konigsberg now Kaliningrad, the port of Pillau now Baltiysk to which hundreds of thousands of refugees trekked across the ice. As the news from Nemmersdorf and Allenstein spread, civilians fled in mass panic. 'In certain sectors of the Russian zone there were practically no Germans left,' Field Marshal Montgomery was to write. 'They had all fled before the onward march of the barbarians', whose behaviour 'especially in their treatment of women was abhorrent to us'.

In the January sleet and ice, under clouds damp with snow and malice, families stumbled away from the Red army through stands of birch and fir in long columns of horse-drawn carts. Many streamed across twenty-five kilometres of ice on the frozen Frisches Haff to the spit of land in the Baltic at Pillau, hoping to get aboard an evacuation ship. Babies froze and were left by their mothers on the ice whilst Russian aircraft machinegunned the columns and broke up the ice with bombs. Those who escaped to the west then faced the Anglo-American bomber fleets above the cities. Between four and five million people fled from the eastern German territories, East Prussia, Pomerania, Silesia and eastern Brandenburg.

Rape awaited those who did not flee. 'Red soldiers during the first weeks of their occupation raped every woman and girl between the ages of twelve and sixty,' said a British POW whose camp had been in Pomerania. 'That sounds exaggerated but it is the simple truth.' Flushed with victory and the contents of German wine cellars, 'the Reds searched every house for women, cowing them with pistols or tommy guns, and carried them into their tanks or half-tracks'.[10] Alexander Solzhenitsyn wrote of the entry of his regiment into East Prussia: 'All of us knew very well that if the girls were German they could be raped and then shot. This was almost a combat distinction.' The Front Command was eventually forced to intervene to try to restore military discipline.

Further south Zhukov's 1st White Russian Front had driven through to the middle reaches of the Oder and established a bridgehead on the western bank on the last days of January. Two days later Chuikov's 4th Guards Corps crossed the river at Küstrin, just seventy-seven kilometres from Berlin. Koniev had reached the lower Oder, overrunning the death camp at Auschwitz, not allowing himself to see it with his own eyes because 'my duties were so taxing that I did not believe that I had the right to give any time or energy to my personal emotions'. From a hill he watched his 3rd Tank Army crash through the still smoking factory chimneys of the Silesian industrial belt, exhilarated to see for once the movements of masses of troops, usually visible to a commander only on a map. His crews had camouflaged their tanks with lace from a captured warehouse and the infantry riding on the decks above them were relaxed enough to be playing accordions. 'Silesia's smoking chimneys,' he recalled, 'the artillery shelling, the clang of the tank tracks, the curtain lace on the tanks, and the accordion-playing tank-borne infantry, whose melodies did not reach us ...'[11] Koniev's capture of the industries of Silesia ended German hopes of an *Endsiege*, a final stand. With the Ruhr smashed, German military production was ruined. 'The war', Speer realized, 'is lost.'

The strain of the advance, 560 kilometres in 2.5 weeks, destroying 45 divisions, was telling on the Red army. Chuikov's tanks were worn.

Ammunition shortages meant using captured German guns. Flanks were long and exposed. The dim February snow and rainstorms robbed the Russians of close air support. Even so, Chuikov was convinced that his troops could have gone on a further eighty kilometres and 'completed this gigantic operation by taking the German capital from the march'. Stalin would not risk it.

His troops on the Oder, rebuilding their strength for the final push into the heart of the Reich, Stalin took a train to Yalta.

Churchill and Roosevelt had a more arduous journey, flying from Malta in transports and driving for 110 winding kilometres through the Crimea to Nicholas II's Italianate Livadia Palace. They were left in no doubt about the power of the Red army. A soldier was posted every ten metres along the road. The Germans had occupied the Livadia only ten months before. Stalin's armies were now less than eighty kilometres from the *Reichskapital*. The Allies were on the Rhine.

The Russians flattered their guests and fed them sturgeon, sucking pig, vodka and Soviet champagne for breakfast. But the British diplomat Gladwyn Jebb, who was present among the 600-strong Anglo-American delegation, said that the Russians 'were masterful from the first day, in matters great and small'.[12] Roosevelt, 'a dying man ... his neck sunken in', was easy meat for Stalin. 'He had his mind fixed on the idea he wasn't going to annoy Stalin, and he wasn't going to gang up with Churchill,' said General Sir Ian Jacob, the military secretary to the British War Cabinet. 'He really wasn't terribly interested in the internal affairs of Europe.'[13]

The president opened the conference by saying that the Americans would withdraw their forces from Europe within eighteen months of the end of the war. That removed any real check on Soviet domination. Roosevelt compounded the weakness by stating that he would not insist on any Soviet concessions. With the conference limited to six days, and held on Soviet soil, the Allies were at a disadvantage from the start and Roosevelt's generosity made matters worse. He failed to take military advantage, for example, when General Patton arced through southern Germany into Czechoslovakia. Patton reached Pilsen with the road to Prague open, a six-hour tank run. He was ordered not to advance.

'Roosevelt refused ever to give any instructions to General Eisenhower to bring about the kind of result in Europe which would be important from a political point of view,' said Jacob. 'He could not see any point in occupying Berlin, or Prague ... He simply was not interested in that: "Now we have got to win the war and go home." '[14]

There are excuses. Roosevelt was dead within two months, and before then he had accused Stalin of 'vile misrepresentations'. The Americans were fighting on two fronts, against Japan and Germany. Any split with Stalin in the anti-German front would have hurt American troops assaulting the Japanese, who still maintained an ambassador in Moscow. As a power separated from the combat zones by oceans and its own prosperity, the US had a cooler, less self-seeking and sweaty view of war than its allies. 'The American attitude to war is that it is like a game of football,' said Jacob. 'You think out a lot of plays, and you win the match and go home and put your feet up, and have a bath. With that you are not creating a political situation.'

Political situations, war, liquidation were the life skill of Stalin. He made token concessions, on the United Nations and a French occupation zone in Germany. He confirmed that the Soviet Union would declare war on Japan two or three months after the defeat of Germany. His price included the acceptance of Soviet domination in Outer Mongolia, the acquisition of the Kuriles and the recovery of rights lost by Tsar Nicholas II in 1904.

Other than that, Roosevelt and an out-of-form Churchill got nothing beyond a paper Declaration on Liberated Europe. Stalin signed it in the Livadia on the final Sunday morning of the conference. It was a pledge that the Soviet Union would not impose Communism on its neighbours. The Western leaders, unaware of the secret Protocols of the Molotov–Ribbentrop pact, accepted his word.[15] They had little choice. 'We had to reckon with the fact that the Russians would be occupying most of eastern Europe and that it was absolutely inevitable,' said Jebb. In the Declaration, the Big Three agreed to jointly assist the formation of representative governments in liberated countries through the earliest possible holding of free and unfettered elections. Thus was Europe, whose poisons had created the war, to be lanced of its pus.

Noble thoughts, but no more. Within three weeks Stalin had imposed a Communist premier on Rumania. No country held by the Red army in February 1945 has now, half a century later, a government elected by free and unfettered elections. Stalin did not triumph through the weakness of the dying Roosevelt or by his own cunning. Yalta was won for him by the industrialization he had imposed, by his marshals and by his men, massing in the Oder bridgeheads, descendants of Mongols and serfs, *Untermenschen* whose tank assaults, barrages and air strikes had snapped the spine of the Wehrmacht.

'The suggestion that Europe was carved up at Yalta is an illusion,' said Jebb. 'It was carved up by the advance of the Soviet armies.' The Red army had filled Stalin's fist. What the Georgian had, he held and his successors continue to hold.

24

TO THE ZOO STATION

In the western corner of the Kremlin, near the Borovitsky Gate, stands the *Oruzheinaya Palata*, the Kremlin Armoury. It houses, among its robes, jewels, regalia and ancient weapons, the standards of armies defeated by the Tsars. Stalin was on the verge of a victory that would have caused a Tsar to tremble with respect. German, Hungarian, Rumanian, Italian and Finnish armies had crumbled and evaporated. The reports brought to him, in his sparse Kremlin office or his dacha, confirmed the power that the Red army was spawning.

Two days after Yalta, Budapest fell. The broken spans of blown-up bridges above the half-frozen Danube made the city seem like an enormous creature with a smashed spine. Picking their way past craters and the broken canisters of anti-tank rounds, Malinovsky's men stalked with minds fixed on rape and plunder. By 1 April, Hungary had been cleared and the Red army was across the Austrian frontier, preparing to take Vienna. In the West, Patton's tanks had entered Frankfurt-on-Main.

Though the sound of Russian guns was heard in Berlin throughout March, no final assault came. The Germans were surprised that the Russians still concerned themselves with bloody assaults on isolated strongpoints and on the German flanking positions in Courland and East Prussia whose threat was more potential than real. This reluctance to bypass large enemy units, so different from the Germans, had been recognized by Gehlen back in 1942. 'The principal Russian strategic objective is not one of regaining lost territory or pushing the enemy back to the coast,' he wrote. 'Rather the Russian war leadership intends to crush the German army's main striking power. This aim can be realized only if Germany's war-making potential – and that means her military equipment – is destroyed. This is the objective of every Russian operation.'[1]

Germans trapped in their fortresses in Konigsberg, Poznan, Breslau, Danzig and Küstrin, sometimes committed suicide as civilians cowered in cellars or streamed west through a landscape swept by snow and Russian tanks and aircraft. The impact of aircraft rockets would tear 'long, bloody furrows in the dense mass, and for a moment the wind was tinged with the warm smell of disembowelled bodies', wrote Sajer. The children 'stared about them with unseeing eyes – at their swollen hands, which they wished were no longer attached to their bodies; at the people around them, who should no longer exist; and at the frozen grasses trembling in the wind, which they would never again enjoy as part of an innocent game'.[2]

The brilliant Jewish commander of the 3rd White Russian Front, I. D.

Cherniakovsky, who at thirty-eight had become the youngest general in the Red army, was killed by a shell outside Konigsberg and was replaced by Marshal Vassilevsky. The city, now Kaliningrad and part of the Soviet Union, was not battered into submission until 9 April. Chuikov's Guardsmen fought hand-to-hand battles in Poznan before moving on to fight their way across dykes and earthworks into the Küstrin fortress. Breslau held out until 6 May, after which it was incorporated into Poland as Wroclaw and its Opel assembly line was moved in its entirety to the Soviet Union, there to produce 'Soviet' Moskvich passenger cars.

The Russians coped with the appalling casualties endemic in assaulting prepared positions held by a desperate foe. Though they could replenish their ranks with men freed from POW cages, some divisions were reduced to 3,000 or 4,000 whilst clearing the German pockets. The Red army insistence on destroying the enemy forces in being meant that these vicious battles, isolated in the rear, bought time for the German defence on the Oder.

The river, still partly ice covered, reached a flood-swollen width of three kilometres in places. Eager boys with outsize uniforms and *Panzerfaust* anti-tank rockets shared positions with grandfathers and grounded Luftwaffe men, stiffened with SS men and special police squads. Behind them, bodies swung from gallows with scrawled accusations of treason round their necks, warnings that desertion brought a swifter end than battle.

The sound of Russian guns could be heard in Berlin but it was British and American bomber fleets that had reduced its citizens to cellar-dwellers and its streets to rubble-choked gorges that ran through the windowless cliffs of ruined buildings. Dust and smoke from the bombings drifted across the pale winter sun by day and the brilliant white of burning magnesium lit the nights. The *Nebelkrähe*, the black carrion crows whose cawing marks the Berlin winter, had fled. Hitler was under the city in the great Bunker complex by the new Reich Chancellery. There were Russians in Berlin, but they were infinitely less dangerous than the Anglo-Americans above it. They worked as slave labourers in the remaining factories or, bright in their Ukrainian dresses, as maids and servants.

It was the Russians whom the Berliners feared, however, praying that the city would fall to the Americans and British. Revenge was marching with the Red army. 'Not only divisions and armies are advancing on Berlin,' the Soviet propagandist Ilya Ehrenburg put it. 'All the trenches, graves and ravines filled with the corpses of innocents are advancing on Berlin ... The dead are knocking on the doors of the Joachimstalerstrasse, of the Kaiserallee, of the Unter den Linden ... Whirl round in circles, and burn, and howl in your deathly agony. The hour of revenge has struck.'[3]

★

The first Soviet fighter-bombers appeared over the city on 28 March. The following day Marshal Zhukov was summoned back to Moscow, followed later on the 1,680-kilometre flight by Koniev. On 1 April, the two marshals, both former sergeants in the Imperial army, entered the Kremlin through the Spasskaya, the ten-tiered Saviour's Gate built in 1491. Stalin, in simple uniform with the red-ribboned gold star of Hero of the Soviet Union on his left breast, received them in his large conference room, with its long mahogany table and lithographs of Suvorov and Kutuzov.

A telegram was read out by the chief of operations,[4] in which it was stated that the Anglo-Americans were preparing an operation under Field Marshal Montgomery to capture Berlin before the Red Army. This was untrue. Three days before, Stalin had in fact received a cable from Eisenhower which disclosed that the Western Allies would concentrate operations in the northern and southern sectors and that Berlin was no longer considered 'a strategically important objective'. In his reply Stalin had agreed with Eisenhower's plan and added that the main Red army blow would take place in the latter half of May in the Leipzig–Dresden direction. 'Berlin has lost its former strategic importance,' Stalin said. The Soviet High Command would thus allot only secondary forces to it.

Despite this, Stalin turned to Zhukov and Koniev and said: 'The *soyuz-nicki* (the 'little allies') intend to get to Berlin before the Red army. Well, who is going to take Berlin, we or the allies?' Koniev was the first to reply. 'We will, and before the Anglo-Americans,' he said.

There were strong reasons for Stalin's deceit. He had no reason to believe that the Western Allies would continue to ignore Berlin. They were then advancing up to fifty-five kilometres a day from the Rhine against minimal resistance. The German leadership might have no plans to fold in the Western front whilst keeping up stiff resistance in the East, but individual units were acting on that basis. The last available casualty summary of the German Army General staff shows that, between 11 and 20 April, German ground forces had 577 killed and 1,951 wounded in the West. On the Eastern front, these figures were 7,587 and 35,414. The Germans were thus taking between thirteen and eighteen times more casualties in the East. In that apocalyptic period 268,229 Germans went missing on the Western front compared with 25,823 in the East.[5] The vast bulk of the missing were taken prisoner. The figures show the bitterness of the fighting in the East, and the eagerness of the Germans to surrender in the West. Stalin had reason to fear that the Allies would find themselves presented with Berlin.

The city had little strategic importance for Stalin but by this stage of the war political ambitions and the shape of post-war Europe were more important than military considerations. Churchill, aware of the enormous psychological impact its capture would have, shared Stalin's view of its great political importance. The Red army was already on the point of taking Vienna. 'If we deliberately leave Berlin to them,' he wired Eisenhower, 'even if it should be in our grasp, the double event may strengthen their conviction, already apparent, that they have done everything.'

Stalin ordered his marshals to prepare plans for an operation to take Berlin that was to start no later than 16 April and that was to be completed in twelve to fifteen days' fighting.

Zhukov was to attack out of the Küstrin bridgehead with four field and two tank Armies in his 1st White Russian Front. He aimed to have 250 guns to the kilometre for an initial artillery barrage during which he intended to light the breakthrough points with 140 searchlights. He would have 768,100 men. Koniev planned a dawn attack across the Neisse under the cover of a heavy smokescreen. The five field and two tank Armies of his 1st Ukrainian Front totalled 511,700 men. Keeping his tank Armies on his right flank, he would be able to wheel north-west for Berlin once he had broken through.

The two attacks were to start on Monday 16 April. Zhukov was to make for the Elbe after taking Berlin. Koniev, after sweeping through the southern outskirts of Berlin, was to drive on west to meet up with the Americans. Rokossovsky's 314,000 2nd White Russians were not involved in the Berlin operation but would attack later to advance across northern Germany and link up with the British.

Stalin pencilled a demarcation line between Zhukov and Koniev, both men passionately eager for the honour of taking the Reich capital. But he stopped when the line reached Lübben, the old town on the Spree seventy-seven kilometres south-east of Berlin. 'Whoever reaches Berlin first – let him take it,' he said.[6] When the two marshals hurried back to their commands, their aircraft leaving Moscow's Central Airfield within two minutes of each other, Koniev's hopes of being in at the kill in Berlin were still alive.

The preparations were fevered. Zhukov built up a detailed relief map of Berlin from reconnaissance photographs, captured documents and interrogations of prisoners. The 900 square kilometres of the city had been prepared for stubborn defence, using tank turrets sunk in concrete, fire points in buildings with brick walls a metre thick, road blocks made of upturned tramcars filled with rubble. The terrain around Berlin, thick with forests, swamps, rivers and canals, was hard going for armour.

On 11 April, the American 2nd Armoured Division, living up to its reputation as 'Hell on Wheels', reached the Elbe. This brought the Americans as close to Berlin as Koniev. On 12 April, the day that Roosevelt died to be succeeded by Truman, three American battalions crossed the Elbe. Here they halted. Far to the south, Kolbukhin's 3rd Ukrainian Front had broken through the spurs of the Austrian Alps and was fighting its way through the suburbs of Vienna. The burning city fell to the Russians on 13 April.

Ammunition, seven million artillery shells for Zhukov alone, tanks, SP guns, and every type of bridging flowed into the Russian bridgeheads and assault positions by train, Lend-Lease trucks and carts. On 15 April, Koniev went to an observation post in an old pine forest which sloped steeply to the Neisse. Zhukov was in a bunker built in a hillside overlooking the Küstrin bridgehead. Sensing the imminence of the assault, Colonel General Gotthard Heinrici, the German commander and a veteran at such delicate timing, withdrew his troops from the forward defence line. The Russians crammed silently in the bridgeheads were 'almost trembling with excitement – like horses trembling before the hunt'.[7]

Three red flares heralded Zhukov's assault at 5 a.m. on 16 April 1945. The guns opened up, to devour that day the contents of 2,500 railway wagons, 1,236,000 artillery and mortar shells. Then 143 anti-aircraft searchlights shone brilliantly on the German positions facing the Küstrin bridgehead.

The firestorm was so intense that it raised its own wind, kicking up dust and waving boughs in the forests. Chuikov and his 8th Guardsmen found that the searchlight beams 'ran into a solid curtain of gunpowder, smoke and earth ... the most they could penetrate this curtain was 150–200 yards, no more'. Behind the barrage the assault troops moved forward from the bridgehead on the western bank or swam across the Oder grasping petrol cans and lumps of wood. Many units stopped to wait for dawn before tackling the brooks and canals which intersected the Oder valley and which seemed major obstacles in the searchlit and thunderous void.

The infantry cleared the first two lines of German defence on the west bank. But Heinrici had withdrawn the bulk of his men to a main line which ran through the Seelow Heights, a sandy, semicircular plateau that ranged up to 60 metres in height. Though only from 900 metres to five kilometres deep, the defences on the Seelow Heights were well fortified and caught the Russians in well-organized crossfire. Accurate shelling from the Heights pinned down Chuikov's Guardsmen whilst the armour milled in the swampy valley bottom or piled up in great jams waiting for bridges to be laid. His searchlights a failure, his intentions read by Heinrici, his timetable running amok, Zhukov raged at Chuikov.

His own battle plan had stated that his armour would be called on only after the infantry had broken through on the Heights. At noon, in a fury of frustration, Zhukov ordered his tank armies forward. This mass of metal, almost fourteen hundred tanks and SP guns, beat on the 56th Panzer Corps under General Karl Weidling. *Panzerfausts* and 88 mms slammed into the Russian armour at close range whilst machineguns cut down infantry struggling on the sandy slopes. More tanks were sent in at night,

as Stalin taunted Zhukov over the line from Moscow with news of
Koniev's progress, but the breakthrough still eluded him. For all the
weight of artillery and 6,500 sorties by aircraft, Zhukov's troops had
nowhere advanced more than 8 kilometres.

Koniev had chosen to start his assault to the south with smoke, not
searchlights. Without a bridgehead, he planned a complex river assault
involving more than 150 crossing points of the fast-flowing Neisse. To
shield his troops and confuse the enemy, the Red air force laid a smokescreen along the 370 kilometres of his front. This was combined with a
forty-minute artillery barrage. The weather was kind. The wind speed
was less than 1.5 kilometres an hour and the smoke clung to the slate-
grey waters of the river and floated slowly over the German positions,
enveloping the Neisse valley.

His forward battalions began crossing the river under the cover of the
smokescreen at 6.55 a.m. The first echelon scrambled up the steep western
bank and established bridgeheads within an hour. The Russian brilliance
in bridgelaying was immediately on display. It took fifty minutes to lay
light pontoon bridges, two hours for a bridge that would take thirty tons,
four or five hours for a structure that would hold sixty tons, the bridging
teams working up to their necks in the icy water. There were too many
bridgeheads for the Germans, remembering the lessons of the Dnieper and
a score of Russian rivers, to crush before they started inexorably to expand.
The first 85-mm guns had been hauled across on floats and were trained
to fire pointblank at German tanks ten to fifteen minutes after the first
troops had reached the western bank.

By 8.35 a.m. Koniev had secured 133 crossings. At 1 p.m. with sixty-
ton bridges in operation, the lead tanks moved out to the west. By the
evening part of Koniev's 3rd and 5th Guards Armies and the 13th Army
had ripped through the German defences to a depth of almost thirteen
kilometres on a twenty-nine-kilometre front. They were now fighting in
the second defence line where the Germans, unnerved by Koniev's ability
to manoeuvre towards Berlin, had committed operational and even some
High Command reserves.

Zhukov subjected the Seelow Heights to further air and artillery bombardment the next morning. Hundreds of T-34s moved forward again,
Panzerfausts and anti-aircraft guns hitting them from close range as they
closed on the German positions. The ground denying him the space or
surface for manoeuvre, Zhukov relied on brute strength and high casualties
to grind his way through the lines. In places the Germans were outnumbered ten to one and had no need to aim at targets, firing their
machineguns until the barrels were red-hot. A myriad of small battles
broke out in the orchards, gardens and houses of the village of Seelow.

Short of ammunition, fuel and men, trenches collapsing under tank tracks and bombs, without armour for counter-attacks, the Germans slowly gave ground. In Berlin itself the Philharmonic had given its final and grimly appropriate performance, Wagner's *Götterdämmerung*, the twilight of the gods.

To the south, Koniev raced through to the Spree, forded without checking by his tanks. He allowed himself the luxury of pausing at 'the pleasant sight of the rapid and successful crossing'. His tank armies now clear of the German defence lines, Koniev quartered himself in a castle near Cottbus. From here he reported his vigorous progress to Stalin. 'A German battery continued to fire on the castle from somewhere far off,' he said. 'And there I was sitting and talking with Moscow.' Stalin told him that things were hard for Zhukov, still hammering at the Heights. Eagerly, Koniev told him: 'We are in a position to turn both our tank Armies towards Berlin.' This would take him through Zossen, a small town twenty-five kilometres south of Berlin where the German General Staff was headquartered. 'Very good,' said Stalin. 'I agree. Turn your tank Armies on Berlin.'[8] Koniev urged his tankmen to work on through the night.

Frantic lest Koniev steal the prize, Zhukov gave his commanders a tongue lashing and ordered a further barrage and all-out assault on 18 April. The 56th Panzer Corps, which had been exposed to the fury on the Heights for forty-eight hours, began to fissure and split. The 9th Parachute Division broke, its commander left alone on the battlefield as his men fled round him. Encircled time and again, the Germans were forced off the Heights. By the evening of the following day, 19 April, Zhukov finally smashed through the third German defence line.

April 20th was Hitler's 56th birthday. Pale and shaking, he emerged briefly from his Bunker, like 'a submarine commander coming up for air', to inspect boys from the Hitler Youth who had used their *Panzerfausts* on Soviet tanks. Zhukov's troops were now just twenty-five kilometres east of the city.

The next day, with the city under continuous shellfire and the US 8th Air Force flying the last Western bombing raid over it, Zhukov's troops smashed into the north-eastern suburbs. Under Koniev, the 3rd Guards Tank Army of General Rybalko took the High Command headquarters at Zossen. Climbing down a steep spiral staircase, they found a 'whole underground township'. The General Staff had fled in panic, leaving the floors littered with papers, maps and directories. In the CoS's study a dressing gown lay on the writing desk. In the next room a small table stood by a rumpled bed with an unfinished bottle of wine on it. In the dim light, rows of telegraph equipment were intact and the Russians played the tapes of the last conversations held in the nerve centre of the

German command. 'Have you a line to Prague?' asked an urgent voice. 'There are no lines left, you fool, I'm the last one left,' came the answer. 'God, what have we fought outselves to! Germany's *kaput*. Ivan's literally at the door. I'm cutting the wire ...'

Overwhelming firepower enabled the Russians to complete a giant encirclement of the city. Faced by the Teltow canal, where concrete factories formed 'a kind of medieval rampart', Koniev was able to mass almost fifteen hundred guns in one sector. Despite the brilliant advance of the 1st Ukrainian Front, however, the supreme prize eluded him. On 23 April Stalin formally divided the city between Koniev and Zhukov. The Reichstag, the place where the Soviet flag was to be planted, lay just over the division in the 1st White Russian area. By a distance of no more than 140 metres, Zhukov was awarded the race.

On 25 April the outer encirclement of the capital was complete. That day men of the 5th Guards Army met up with units of the US 69th Infantry Division on the Elbe at Strehla and Torgau, respectively 130 and 95 kilometres south of Berlin. This took place, according to the Russians, on 'green sunlit banks amid the sweet aroma of fresh leaves and tuneful birdsong'. The birdsong between the two new superpowers would not last long, but the Reich had been sliced in two.

Berlin was dying, ravaged by Soviet assault squads and the last convulsions of its creed. 'Deserters' were hanged from trees, though Koniev found that the German regulars fought with grim determination and courage whilst the boys and old men of the Volkssturm made a 'hysterical self-sacrifice'. In one district, a one-legged SS man with crutches and a machine pistol scoured the cellars for men, ordering them to the front. If they hesitated, they were shot. Department stores and freight trains were looted. Wounded piled up in abandoned hospitals. Water, gas and power failed. Suicides and desperate orgies multiplied. The Russian shells slammed mainly into existing rubble. There was enough of this, the Reich railways estimated, to make an artificial mountain higher than the 142-metre peak of the Brocken in the Harz Mountains. In the cellar bar of the Adlon Hotel by the Brandenburg Gate, the trapped diplomats accredited to the Third Reich – Japanese, Mussolini Italians, Vichy French – drank themselves into oblivion. With the city airports under artillery fire, an emergency airstrip for light aircraft near the Adlon was the sole way out.

Fighting their way through the streets and apartment blocks, the Russians applied the lessions of Stalingrad. Small groups, company-sized, mixed tommygunners, engineers with demolition charges and flame-thrower operators with a few 76-mm guns and tanks to add punch over a distance. They broke into a building with bursts of automatic fire and grenades, and the dangerous cellars and attics were hosed with flame-throwers. Tanks and artillery smashed strongpoints. As in Stalingrad, tanks were vulnerable in a determined and desperate defence and Chuikov criticized Zhukov's decision to drive his tank armies into the centre of Berlin. 'The enemy organizes his defence in buildings, in attics, in cellars and the tank crews do not see him,' he wrote. 'At the same time tanks are a good target for *Panzerfausts* . . .'

By 26 April almost half a million Russian troops, supported by two air Armies, 21,000 *Katyusha* rocket launchers, 12,700 guns and mortars and 1,500 tanks and SP guns, were hurling themselves towards the centre of the city.[9] Half of Berlin's 248 bridges had been blown up to slow them down, explosives so short that the Germans had to make do with aviation bombs. Taking heavy casualties, the Russians beat and blasted their way forward. Buildings with snipers in them were pounded with tank and artillery fire, whilst below ground the assault squads cut through cellar walls with anti-tank rounds. *Katyushas* spread fires and choking smoke that made it difficult for Russian aircraft to spot targets. Near the zoo, the wounded flooded into a massive flak tower, the height of a thirteen-storey building with reinforced concrete walls more then two and a half metres thick. Beneath the gun platform there was a hospital, an air-raid shelter and a warehouse that protected the finest pieces from Berlin museums – the golden treasures of Priam from Troy, Gobelin tapestries, the sacrificial alter of Eumenes II of the Hellenes. After days within its tomb-like walls, some of the thousands who crammed it slid into madness and others committed suicide. Shellfire drove back those who tried to take out bodies for burial.[10]

The Russian fighting troops behaved with general decency. 'These are good, disciplined and decent soldiers,' a lieutenant said to the mother superior of a convent and maternity home his men had taken. 'But I must tell you. The men who are following us, the ones coming behind, are pigs.'[11] The second echelon, many the dehumanized products of German camps, repeatedly raped the nuns and the pregnant women in the maternity wards. The grunted prelude to rape, '*Frau komm*', rang out in the cellars and air-raid shelters where women had taken refuge and which the second-echelon men sought out as eagerly as the alcohol stocks.* They pillaged

---

* Rape was often fobbed off as a mere repetition of what the Germans had done in Russia. The difference was sharp. As a rule, the Germans did not deign to couple with the women of the *Untermenschen*. In a village outside Stalingrad, during an operation intended to be as final as the assault on Berlin, a woman remembered the insistent call of the Germans as '*Matka, Wasser zu waschen!*' She had the feeling that she was 'no longer a human being. They never stopped rubbing that in. They had no respect for anybody. They'd just undress in front of the women. We were just a lot of slaves.' Werth, op. cit., p. 525. German atrocities were deliberate policy, massive, controlled, debased by their distance from the strains of combat and by the directed slaughter of innocents. The Russian combat soldier might have a rapist on his heels, but the Germans had been followed by an *Einsatzkommando*.

and drank their way through the city. Breaking into a film studio, they danced drunkenly in the costumes from the wardrobe department, Spanish doublets and crinolines, firing their guns in the air.[12] Others liberated canoes and pleasure boats and dragged women with them for bizarre cruises on the lakes.

The assault troops, well versed in the grim ballet of street fighting, taking cover behind a ruin, advancing in a swift line under covering fire, pausing again, drove into the heart of the city. Shortly after midnight on 29 April, the Bunker sour with the fumes of Russian shellbursts, Hitler married his mistress Eva Braun. The bridegroom was hunched, his head sunken into his shoulders like a turtle, his eyes 'like wet pale-blue porcelain, glazed ... his face puckered now like a mask, all yellow and grey'. The bride wore black taffeta. A municipal bureaucrat, Walter Wagner, was taken from his Volkssturm foxhole on the nearby Unter den Linden to perform the ceremony. After it, he ate a liverwurst sandwich and had a glass of champagne before slipping out of the Bunker to regain his post. He was shot dead a few minutes later. The Russians were that close.

Chuikov's Guardsmen broke into the zoo gardens near the flak towers. As the strip of central Berlin held by the Germans shrank, the danger grew that the 1st White Russian and 1st Ukrainian Fronts would smash into each other. Reluctantly, Koniev was forced to sheer off from the centre and its great prize, the Reichstag. As Hitler dictated his political 'testament' a few hours after his marriage, the Russians were firing on the flak towers from the hippopotamus house in the zoo and riflemen were attacking the SS men in the Reichstag. The final conference was held in the Bunker on the evening of 29 April. The Russians had reached the Adlon, about four blocks away. They now held most of the wooded zoo gardens and had penetrated the subway tunnels under the Friedrichstrasse. The end was a few hours away and Hitler prepared to die.

At noon on 30 April, red victory banners were handed out to men of the 3rd Shock Army. An hour later, as Hitler sat down to a final lunch of spaghetti and tossed salad, the assault on the Reichstag began. The building was blasted by tanks and SP guns, *Katyushas* and heavy artillery as small groups of Russians crawled forward and leapt through shattered windows and doors. Firefights broke out across stairwells and offices in a cacophony of exploding grenades and bursts from sub-machine guns. At 2.15 p.m. Sergeants Yegorov and Kantariya of the 150th Division waved a red banner from the second floor.[13]

Three quarters of an hour later Hitler went into his apartment in the Bunker with Eva Braun. Biting into a capsule of potassium cyanide, he shot himself through his right temple. Eva Braun poisoned herself. The bodies were taken up to waste ground at the Bunker exit, doused in petrol and burnt to a cannonade of *Katyushas*. The fighting continued into the dark. When a victory banner at last floated from the summit of the Reichstag at 10.50 p.m., Germans were still fighting in the basement. Shortly before midnight a German lieutenant colonel arranged for General Krebs, chief of OKH, to cross the Russian lines to parley with Chuikov.

Krebs was taken to Chuikov's headquarters in an apartment house in the early hours of 1 May, May Day. He told Chuikov that Hitler had committed suicide the previous day. Chuikov at once passed this on to Zhukov, who in turn contacted Moscow where the late-retiring Stalin had just gone to bed. Zhukov ordered that he be woken and told him of Hitler's death. '*Doigralsya, podlets!*' said Stalin. 'So, that's the end of the bastard.' The original totalitarian had outlived, above all outpowered, the Western upstarts, Mussolini and Hitler.

It was not the end of the fighting. Krebs was unable to accept the Russian demand for an immediate and unconditional surrender of the city. Whilst the May Day parade rolled through Red Square in Moscow, Russian gunners and riflemen began to emerge from their cellars to storm the last islets of resistance. During the evening, with T-34s prowling the Unter den Linden and Russian troops roasting an ox in the Pariserplatz between the ruins of the American and French embassies, Goebbels and his wife committed suicide in the Bunker after killing their children.

That night, as 'shell bursts and burning buildings reflected on a low-lying blackish-yellow cloud of sulphur-like smoke', the last occupants of the Bunker attempted a break-out. A group led by General Mohnke could hear wild screams from a hospital where Russian troops had been drinking ether. They saw 'a terrified, naked woman running along a roof-top, pursued by half a dozen soldiers brandishing bayonets, then leaping five or six storeys to certain death'.

The Russians received a radio message from 56th Panzer Corps shortly after 1 a.m. on 2 May asking for a ceasefire. At dawn the garrison in the basement of the Reichstag surrendered and the streets began to fill with German prisoners. The Russian guns stopped firing at 3 p.m.

Amongst the shattered remnants of the great capital, it was the bizarre that caught the mind as the last skirmishes expired under a rainy sky. At the zoo, noted the correspondent Konstantin Simonov, a hippopotamus lay on a cement terrace, breathing heavily, whilst another floated in the pool with a mortar-shell stabilizer stuck in its side. In the great monkey house, a gorilla and a large chimpanzee lay dead in their cages. By the concrete ledge where the bars started lay two dead SS men. A third, also dead, sat with his back against the raised platform, with a sub-machine gun between his knees. In a bunker room an SS general lay on a bed, his right hand still gripping a parabellum pistol and his left arm round a 'young and beautiful woman, in uniform skirt and white blouse', her eyes closed. The general had a clean shirt on, an open tunic and boots, and an unfinished bottle of champagne was gripped between his legs. In the Reich Chancellery there were rooms chock-a-block with medals, in drawers, boxes and packets, littering the floor, everything from Iron Crosses to fire service medals, so many that it was like 'being in the storehouse of a vast factory where medals were made'. As the search went on among the bodies by the Bunker to identify the former rulers of Europe by their physical defects and teeth fillings, the air was scented with jasmine and hyacinth from Hitler's shattered greenhouse.

The German prisoners being marched out of the city to their captivity in the East saw column after column of Red army support units. A stream of *panye* wagons had soldiers perched atop them on bales of straw, singing and dressed in weird mixtures of looted civilian clothes. When they spotted the Germans, they fired angry volleys into the air. 'There were Circassians, Kalmuks, Uzbeks, Azerbaijani, Mongols,' said the captured General Mohnke. They had with them four-poster beds, toilets, umbrellas, quilts, rugs, bicycles, sinks, ladders and cages with live chickens and ducks. Camp-followers and 'gypsy-like women' mingled with them.

The speechless Germans recognized that what was happening on the streets of Berlin was 'something out of the great vastness of Russia beyond the Urals ... Asia on this day was moving into the middle of Europe.' Behind this exotic calvacade, grimmer Soviet elements were also on the move, men from the NKVD and SMERSH, commissars and handpicked German Communists.

25

VICTORY'S END

The Red army had unfinished business after the fall of Berlin. The drive to the Elbe and along the Baltic coast was completed with the unconditional surrender of Germany, signed on 8 May. Zhukov, Koniev and Rokossovsky paid for their push through Germany since 16 April with 304,887 casualties and the loss of more than 2,000 tanks, proof of the desperate courage of German resistance.

Though Stalin had added Berlin to the long list of capitals overrun by his troops, Prague still eluded him. Koniev's left flank was ordered to march on the city. In a final irony, the turncoat General Vlasov had arrived in Prague in April. Bitter arguments raged between Vlasov and the other Russian collaborators over whether they should now turn on the Germans who had, belatedly and grudgingly, armed and supplied them. Prague, hoping to be liberated by the Americans, rose against the Germans on

4 May. Vlasov units fought their way into the city against SS troops. The refusal by the Czechs to deal with them forced a re-alliance with the SS. Fuelled by a common desire to avoid capture by the Red army, mixed German–Vlasov groups escaped from Prague to seek the temporary sanctuary of the American lines. Later handed over to the Russians, they met their expected fate. Koniev's tanks entered Prague on 7 May.

There remained the Japanese and Stalin's agreement at Yalta to open hostilities against them three months after victory in Europe. By the beginning of August the *Stavka* had collected 1.6 million men for the task. The Soviet declaration of war followed two days in the wake of the nuclear bombing of Hiroshima on 6 August. Russian troops under Vasilevsky crossed the Manchurian border at dawn on 9 August, the day the Americans dropped a second atomic bomb on Nagasaki. From the Mongolian border the Japanese fell back to the Hingan mountains and dug themselves in.

The Japanese had virtually no armour and General Kravchenko's 6th Guards Tank Army had a monopoly of mobile force. The tanks covered up to 110 kilometres a day, supplied by air drop. Spilling on to the Manchurian plain, Malinovsky split 6th Guards Tank to drive south on Mukden and east to Changchun. After initial heavy fighting, Meretskov's troops were moving steadily on Harbin and Kirin. The Pacific fleet landed marines in Korean ports whilst the left wing of Meretskov's 25th Army moved through north-western Korea. Further north, Purkaev's 16th Army was occupying the southern half of Sakhalin.

Although the back of the Japanese Kwantung army had been snapped when Japan surrendered unconditionally on 14 August, the fighting continued. The Russians were moving with verve and precision, easily confident in sweeping great numbers of men over the vast Far Eastern canvas and hungry to take a maximum of territory. On 17 August the commander of the Kwantung army formally offered a ceasefire. Vasilevsky refused. He claimed that Japanese units were still fighting and the Russian position was improving by the hour. 6th Guards Tank were on the approaches to Mukden. Harbin airfield had been taken in an airborne landing. The landing force were not paratroops but, a measure of Soviet confidence, came from a motorized assault engineers brigade.

With Japanese units surrendering piecemeal, the advance went on. Harbin, Kirin and Mukden were occupied on 20 August. In Korea, the 25th Army linked up with the Americans on the 38th Parallel, the bloody symbol of post-war tension that had been accepted by Moscow and Washington as a 'temporary' division of Korea during the Japanese surrender. The Kuriles fell to a mixed force of marines and infantry brought down from the Kamchatka peninsula by the Pacific fleet.

All Japanese forces had surrendered by 27 August, the Russians claiming

609,176 POWs, including 48 generals. The war officially ended for the Soviet Union as the final surrender of Japan was signed aboard the USS *Missouri* on 2 September 1945. In the last easy fighting, against an enemy exhausted by the Americans and the British, Stalin's troops had occupied the whole of Manchuria, north Korea, Sakhalin, the Kuriles and parts of the Chinese provinces of Chahar and Jehol. *Generalissimo* Stalin had more than earned his eighteenth-century title, given him the day after the Moscow victory parade in June.

It is academic to wonder whether Tsarist Russia could also have survived the war. Intriguing, but useless too, to speculate how Trotsky or Tukhachevsky might have performed.

It is certain that the Soviet Union would not have pulled through without the rigorous centralization and industrialization of Stalin's Five Year Plans. To Stalin goes the credit for the enormous, slaving effort of military production in a country that had been largely pre-industrial a generation before. Despite the enormity of the purges, the Red army was not maimed in the same way as the cultural and political life of the nation. The young commanders who emerged after the battle of Moscow were hard and professional, capable of learning quickly, pragmatic and relatively independent. They respected Stalin and admired him with flashes of genuine affection. He handled them well, mixing encouragement and censure and judging performance skilfully.

His application to detail, his work rate and the width of his interests were phenomenal. He married political and military decisions with a tenacity that brought most of Eastern Europe in its train. He spent almost the whole of the war immured in the Kremlin but there was never the slightest doubt who was in supreme command. His troops, at least after Stalingrad, did charge with Stalin and Motherland on their lips.

Vain to think of an alternative to Stalin, then, but tempting to consider the Axis performance. Here are historic 'ifs' in plenty. *If* the Japanese had attacked the Soviet Union instead of Pearl Harbor, the Russians would have gone under. That is certain. *If* the Germans quartered in France, in Greece and the Balkans, those fighting the British in the Middle East and on the North Atlantic had been with Corporal Pabst in his potato field outside Brest in June 1941, *if* the total German strength and imagination had flowed into *Barbarossa*, as the Russians were able to mobilize in their entirety against them, then most probably Russia would have lost. *If* the Germans had concentrated their forces on Moscow, instead of dissipating them through the Russian and Ukrainian vastness, a Soviet loss is likely.

Hitler's own 'if', *if* the Germans had fought harder, had been worthy of him, is beneath contempt. He heaped on them a multiplicity of enemies and battlefronts that no people could have sustained. As to courage, though they often qualify it as the 'courage of despair', the Russians query the bravery of the Germans as seldom as the Germans query their own. In the misery of that war, where the pain of continual movement over vast and freezing distance and the new terror of assault by tank and aircraft added to the familiar and more comradely ghastliness of trench fighting and artillery barrage, the endurance of both sides had nobility.

As to those hardiest of 'ifs' – *if* the Germans had behaved better, *if* they had come to the Ukraine and the Baltic states and the other minorities as liberators, then the Soviet Union would have disintegrated in gratitude – the Germans did not come to improve anyone. It was not on their agenda.

26

PLUS ÇA CHANGE

On 24 June, a day of heavy, warm Moscow rain, the Red army paid its homage to Stalin in Red Square. The rain muffled the echo of the boots and tank tracks on the cobblestones. Stalin, in a sodden greatcoat, stood above the Lenin Mausoleum as troops threw German standards and battle flags to the surface of the square below.

Kutuzov's men had similarly honoured Alexander I with trophies stripped from the Grande Armée, but Stalin's victory was incomparably less constrained than that of the Tsar. The Red army occupied most of Eastern and Central Europe, a shattered and starving landscape where a pig was a mark of wealth, a dog-drawn cart a luxury and where life in the roofless and ruined towns had the mark of a medieval nightmare. The great Central European counterweight to Russia, the Third Reich in its final manifestation, lay prostrate under rubble. Western Europe was more concerned by the threat of internal Communism than with Soviet expansion half a continent away.

Raw power had come to be divided between Russia and the United States, and in Eastern Europe the Russians had the matchless advantage of contiguity and ground troops. Amid the refugee columns, the released slave labourers, the scaffolds for collaborators, Stalin was the power in being. He was sixty-six.

The grim condition of the conquerors gave scant expectations for the conquered. Western Russia was itself in a more desperate condition than much of the occupied territory, large swathes of which had fallen in rapid advances.

The cauldron fighting had taken place largely within Russia. In 1945 there were 25 million homeless in the Soviet Union. Great centres had been destroyed and huge areas of countryside burnt of farms, villages, crops, livestock and people. More than half the buildings in Kiev had been destroyed and three quarters of the people had been killed or deported to Germany. The population was a fifth of the pre-war figure. Eighty per cent of Minsk had been razed and one in five of all White Russians had paid for the war with their lives or with slave labour. Leningrad lost 620,000 people during the siege. Throughout western Russia families lived in caves, drained water tanks and pits covered with tarpaulins. Millions who had been evacuated were still living in earth-floored barracks in the Urals and further east.

Stalin did not repay victory with any relaxation. Work norms in the years immediately after the war were set higher. Rations were frequently less. In felt boots and tattered coats stuffed with rags for warmth, people lived off cabbage and potatoes, the skins made into thin soups. In the growing cities the rations for ten years after the war were half a pound of meat and 110 grammes of fat a week, less than the fillings of two hamburgers and without the grain of the bun, the sugar in the ketchup and the vitamins in the lettuce leaf.

At a time when the US was starting the greatest consumer boom in history, heavy industry and military production remained the absolute priorities in the economy. Grain production in Stalin's *last* four years averaged 80 million tons a year, six million less than in 1913 and 15 million tons less than post-collectivization, mechanized 1939. Women made up a third of the labour force on the primitive construction sites. Stalin suppressed the numbers of those who died in the war, if indeed it was known.★

In February 1946 he introduced the first post-war Five Year Plan with ambitious targets in heavy and arms-related industries. A crash atomic weapon programme, the labour supplied by Beria, was started. A twenty-year naval programme was introduced. The economy responded well to central planning and the targets in coal, oil, steel and machine tools were all achieved ahead of target. War reparations and the labour of about two million prisoners of war helped. The main effort, though, was Russian. By 1952, working ten to twelve hours a day and six days a week, the average worker had reached the 1940 standard of living.[1]

There was no relaxation in subjugation either. The POWs returning from German camps were forcibly transferred to the labour camps of the

★ Into the 1980s, Soviet newspapers continued to carry advertisements from people who had lost contact with their families during the war. The official figure was 7 million, presumably chosen to conceal the extent of the country's industrial and military trauma. Only with the first post-war census in 1959 did the size of the losses, and the consequent dependence on the labour of women, emerge. Of those aged over 18 in 1945, there were 31 million men to 52 million women. Allowing for the longer female lifespan, the extent of wartime deaths is now put at 20 million.

Gulag. Trains with machinegunners and barbed wire sealing the cattle cars moved eastwards through Poland. When one stopped, locals saw that the cars were packed with men. 'Who are you?' they asked. 'Prisoners of war,' came the answer. 'Where do you go?' 'To Siberia.'[2] Suspected of treason and infestation with foreign ideas, men who had survived German captivity since 1941 moved seamlessly into Soviet captivity throughout the spring and summer of 1945 without glimpse of their families. The Allies were harried to return collaborators, Cossacks and Ukrainians who had fought with the Germans and men of General Vlasov's army. British ships returned some of them to Odessa in May 1945. Prisoners were marched or dragged into a warehouse and shot or taken behind sheds on the quayside for execution.[3]

Censorship was more severe after the war than before it. Newspapers were now censored twice, before printing and before being distributed. The marshals and leading generals ceased to be household names within a few months of the Moscow victory parade. Public references to them dried up. Zhukov had slid from sight by 1946. In 1948 *Pravda* was able to commemorate the capture of Berlin without mentioning his name.

The influence of the *zampolits* and informers remained unabated. The links with the old army, which had already seen Tsarist decorations, ranks and Guards units restored, continued with uniforms. Grey-blue trousers with the red *lampa* stripe, close to the old style, had already been revived. The traditional Tsarist bluish-grey officers' greatcoat returned, embroidered in red for general officers. Wartime khaki greatcoats for the men, often made from British material, were replaced by the traditional brownish-grey of the First World War.[4] Though the army had been reduced to 2.8 million men in 1948, it was back up to nearly 6 million by the time of Stalin's death. It differed little from the wartime force and continued to rely on the T-34. Despite the nuclear age, Stalin continued to think in terms of *Blitzkrieg*[5] and armoured and motorized divisions. Strategy atrophied until his death.

The post-war conservatism ran into politics. The politburo of 1948 changed little from 1939. Beria, his NKVD briefly rechristened MVD in 1946, was among the fresh recruits.[6]

The political killings resumed, their dark outline breaking surface most notably in the 'Leningrad affair' of 1949, a purge in which those shot were largely but not exclusively drawn from the Leningrad party apparatus. Its main victim was Nikolai Voznesensky, who had become head of *Gosplan* in 1938 at the age of thirty-five. He was one of the most brilliant of Stalin's young generation. In March 1949, a few months after winning the Stalin Prize, he was abruptly dismissed. With him fell Aleksei Kuznetsov, who had been the party number two in Leningrad throughout the horrors of the siege. It was probably Beria, 'plump, greenish and pale, with soft damp hands ... and bulging eyes behind his pince-nez',[7] who instigated the arrests. They were sentenced to death by a military court for treason.

Stalin had now, his daughter says, 'reached the point of being pathological, of persecution mania ... He saw enemies everywhere.'[8] He was himself a prisoner of a system in which he was 'stifling from loneliness, emptiness and lack of human companionship'. When he travelled by his special train from the Crimea in 1948 he would stroll with Svetlana on the station platforms. No passengers were allowed on to the platforms and the dictator walked alone with his daughter, a 'sinister, sad, depressing sight'. He travelled by curtained car on emptied roads, in a cortege of five black limousines, the drivers frequently changing their route and overtaking each other. Beria had built a marble pavilion over the hut where he had been born and the guides who showed Svetlana round were 'trembling with reverence'.

After the autumn of 1951 he never left Moscow. A light burnt in a Kremlin window all night, so that anyone walking on Red Square could look up and know that, as the slogan had it, 'He lives, thinks and works for us.' In fact, he spent most of the time in his Kuntsevo dacha. Here he let his salary pile up in packets on his desk. He thought of money in pre-revolutionary terms, since he 'never spent any money. He had no place to spend it and nothing to spend it on.'[9] Sometimes he would rage at the commanders of his bodyguards: 'You parasites! ... Don't think I don't know how much money is running through your fingers.' He was 'impotent in the face of the frightful system that had grown up around him like a huge honeycomb and he was helpless either to destroy it or bring it under control'. There were two walls round the dacha, Khrushchev recalled, with watchdogs between them. His private rooms were protected by armour-plated doors with automatic sliding panels through which trays of food were passed when he signalled for them. He spent rambling evenings, eating and drinking, with Beria, Malenkov, Bulganin and Mikoyan. Khrushchev was a rising star and also came. Stalin would not touch 'a single dish or hors d'oeuvre or bottle' until one of the others had tasted it. He liked to watch them getting drunk and dancing with each other. Khrushchev was forced to dance the Gopak, a Ukrainian folkdance, squatting on his haunches in front of top party officials. 'When Stalin says dance, a wise man dances,' he said. When that palled, Stalin would watch an old film, Charlie Chaplin or his purge-time favourite, *Volga-Volga*.

If the system was finally destroying him, he still used it to destroy others. The 1952 Congress was followed by what looked to be the start of a new purge. His dinner companions, Molotov, Malenkov and Mikoyan, seem to have been among the intended victims. In January 1953 The 'Doctor's Plot' was unveiled. It was said that nine doctors, seven of them Jews, had murdered the censor Zhdanov and others while treating them as patients.

They had done this for an American Jewish organization. Confessions were obtained, two of the doctors dying under interrogation.

Death at Kuntsevo saved the others. Stalin spent the evening of 12 February 1953, a Saturday, with his usual companions, Malenkov, Beria, Bulganin, Khrushchev. They heard nothing from him the next day. Late on Sunday night, the duty officer of the bodyguard rang to say that Stalin had not asked for his dinner. The bodyguards were too frightened to enter the room but a maid said that he was lying on the floor. When the four Politburo men finally plucked up enough courage to enter, they found Stalin in a coma. He had had a cerebral haemorrhage.

It took him four days to die, slowly suffocating. His face became dark, his lips black, his features unrecognizable. At the last moment he opened his eyes and cast 'a terrible glance, insane or perhaps angry and full of fear of death'.[10] He raised his left arm as though, his daughter thought, he was bringing down a curse. With that final gesture, 'full of menace', he died. Within a few years, he was to become a non-person like Trotsky, the other architect of the Red army. His coffin was taken from the Lenin Mausoleum at night:

> Silent the marble.
> Silent the glass scintillates.
> Silent stand the sentries
> in the bronze like coffins poured.
> And the coffin smoulders slightly.
> Though its chinks breath percolates.
> As they carry him through the mausoleum doors,
> Slowly floats the coffin,
> grazing bayonets with its edges.[11]

A deep pit was dug not far from the Mausoleum and the coffin was covered with concrete.

Beria was the first to speed from the deathbed. His face 'twisted by his passions, by ambition, cruelty, cunning and a lust for power', Beria drove off to plot his succession. Of the dinner guests at Kuntsevo, however, it was Khrushchev, the adventurous, hectoring, energetic ex-miner and commissar, who would eventually inherit one eighth of the earth. With that came fresh problems and new enemies in the West. Stalin had kept Russia itself tied to the 1930s, to purge and Plan, during the eight post-war years.

But outside the Soviet Union, there had been drastic changes as shooting war had given way to Cold War.

Curtain Fall

———◆———

A LUNCH AT THE LUBIANKA

The Red army had advanced into a moral vacuum. The old order, the compromised kings, politicians, churchmen and aristocrats, had gone. Russian tanks and infantry were the sole authority in the rubble-choked streets and sacked villages of Central Europe. Matyas Rákosi, later the communist premier of Hungary, put it with brutal simplicity: 'Under the conditions in our country, where the troops of the liberating Soviet Union were staying in our Fatherland, an open armed revolt was impossible.'

Any influence the Americans and British might have brought to bear evaporated in the Cold War. The warning flags were soon snapping, first in Iran. British troops pulled out of Iran six months after the end of the war, as agreed in the Teheran conference. The Red army remained. 'Now Russia stirs up rebellion and keeps troops on the soil of Iran,' Roosevelt's successor, President Truman, wrote furiously in January 1946. 'Unless Russia is faced with an iron fist and strong language, war is in the making. Only one language do they understand – "How many divisions have you?"' When the British moved a brigade to Basra in Iraq[1] the Red army withdrew from northern Iran. In March 1946, speaking at Fulton, Missouri, Churchill noted the 'growing challenge and peril to civilization' from communist fifth columns which could bring about 'a return to the Dark Ages, to the Stone Age'. An 'Iron Curtain' was falling across Europe. Five months later, Truman countered Soviet military pressure on Turkey in the Dardanelles by sending a carrier task force.

The formal onset of the Cold War followed in March 1947, when Truman outlined the shift to permanent US involvement against communist aggression that was later called the Truman Doctrine. The American decision to support foreign countries, by military means if necessary, in peacetime was historic.[2] Washington made itself responsible to counter any communist movement threatening the stability of any country and held the Soviets responsible for inciting such threats. In July 1947 the National Security Act was passed, creating the Central Intelligence Agency, the CIA. A year later, the CIA was authorized by directive NSC 10/2 to run 'covert operations against the Soviet Union, including sabotage ... subversion against hostile states, including assistance to underground resistance groups, and support of indigenous anti-communist elements in threatened countries of the free world'.

Whether the two superpowers could have got at each other at this stage is doubtful. Ninety per cent of Soviet strength was in the army, where it had undoubtedly broken the Werhrmacht, inflicting on it nine out of

Territory annexed by Russia 1939-40,
and re-incorporated in Russia in 1945

Former German and Czechoslovak
territory annexed by Russia in 1945

States liberated by the Soviet army
and in which Communist regimes came
to power between 1945 and 1948

Russian occupation zones (evacuated 1950)

British, French and American occupation zones

The 'Iron Curtain' in 1948

0   500 km

0   300 mls

FINLAND

Vyborg

Leningrad

Reval

ESTONIA

Pskov

Riga

LATVIA

SOVIET
UNION

Baltic Sea

North Sea

Memal

LITHUANIA

Kovno

Königsberg

EAST
PRUSSIA

Vilna

Minsk

Bremen

Stettin

Posnan

POLAND

Bialystok

Pinsk

Berlin

Warsaw

GERMANY

Breslau

SILESIA

Cracow

Bonn

Dresden

Prague

CZECHOSLOVAKIA

GALICIA

Lvov

Nuremburg

Chernovtsy

Kishinev

Munich

Vienna

Jassy

BESSARABIA

FRANCE

SWITZ.

AUSTRIA

HUNGARY

Budapest

RUMANIA

Trieste

Bucharest

Black Sea

Belgrade

YUGOSLAVIA

Sofia

BULGARIA

ITALY

Adriatic Sea

ALBANIA

Tirana

GREECE

Aegean
Sea

TURKEY

Europe 1945-48

The Iron Curtain: Europe 1945–48

ten of its casualties in the three years to the Normandy landings. Only 50 per cent of US strength was on land, the remaining half being at sea and in the air. These extraordinary variations in the nature of strength would have made it difficult for the adversaries to grapple. In one area, at least, the US had an overwhelming edge.

The US foreign secretary, General Marshall, launched a vast programme of US economic aid in 1947. The Marshall Plan restored confidence and underpinned the growth of half a shattered continent. In all $13.5 billion flowed to Western nations as, under US pressure, the French and Italian Communist parties lost their positions in post-war coalitions. Though Plan aid was on offer to socialist countries, Stalin rejected it. The prospect of exposure to the American Dream and the booming US economy held little attraction. The Soviets signed a series of trade agreements with their satellites in August 1947 and the economic division of Europe was completed.

Stalin vigorously re-expanded the Red army. When Truman declared his doctrine, the wartime strength of over 11 million men had been slashed to less than 3 million. He began a fresh build-up from 1948 that brought it, at great strain to Soviet resources, up to 5.5 million in five years. The Communist International, disbanded to lull Allied sensibilities in 1943, was up and running as the renamed Cominform from September 1947.

The US had money, resources and the A-bomb. Stalin had the brute strength of the Red army to serve as the curtain behind which he could break resistance to communist will.

The *bastinado*: Hungary

The communist takeover in Hungary was outlined in its simplicity by a skilled practitioner. The Hungarian prime minister, Matyas Rákosi, a commissar during the brief Bolshevik regime in Budapest in 1919, a veteran of sixteen years in Hungarian prisons before returning from wartime exile in Moscow with the Red army in the autumn of 1944, described the process with pride to members of an indoctrination course of the Hungarian Workers' Party on 29 February 1952.

First, the existence of the Red army was essential as underpinning. 'It was the Red army which made it *ab ovo* impossible for the forces of reaction in Hungary to make armed attempts upon us like those of Denikin, Kolchak and other White Guard generals during the Russian revolution,' he said. Next, a 'temporary alliance' with other parties aided communist entry into government. Here, Rákosi said, the basic rule was to keep the opposition split up, nervous, 'perplexed and hesitating. Join with non-communists and a coalition and then proceed, by various methods, to take over.' How? 'Salami tactics. Demanding a little more each day, like cutting up a salami, thin slice after thin slice.'

Make sure that Communists control the police. 'There was a single position, the control of which was claimed by our party from the first minute,' Rákosi explained, 'where it was not inclined to consider any distribution of posts or any appointments according to the proportionate strength of parties in the coalition. This was the State Security Authority [the political police].' To do this, 'it was essential to have control of the Interior Ministry'. How was this achieved, given that the Communists were a minority? Through Soviet troops and the threat by General Voroshilov, the chairman of the Allied Control Commission, to bring more Red army units to Hungary if a Communist was not named interior minister. Rákosi's chief ideologue, Joseph Revai, admitted in early 1949, after the communist success was safely in the bag, that 'the force of the party and the working class was multiplied by the fact that the Soviet Union and the Soviet army were always on hand to come to our aid'.[3] Revai wrote of the importance of gaining 'defensive control over the police force'.

This pattern was repeated throughout that great swathe of land, 1,019,165 square kilometres with a population of 92 million, the guts of Central Europe where the Red army was quartered in old POW camps, Werhrmacht barracks, half-bombed railway stations and disused factories.*

An appearance of legality was maintained, for the model was not Russian revolution and civil war, but the part peaceful, part legitimate method used by Hitler and Mussolini. It was 'a policy of learning from the success of fascism'.[4] Since local communist parties were too small to gain power through the ballot box, rivals in the new 'Democratic Front' coalition were absorbed by accusing their leaders of treason. The economy became reliant on the state and the unions were placed under communist control. Education, the press and radio, youth movements and the information ministry were the next targets. Terror was freely used by the secret police, with their uniform of bulky suits and felt hats, imitation leather briefcases, spool tape recorders and dark green issue spotlamps for interrogations. At length the country, like a rotten plum, would fall.

As a former enemy state, Hungary was immediately malleable. Its army had been ruined by its German alliance, Admiral Horthy claiming that the Stalingrad disaster alone had cost it 80,000 officers and men. The Red army, which has never left Hungary, deported 110,000 'enemy sympathizers' from Budapest after its fall and a further 500,000 from the rest

---

* In addition were the 466,200 square kilometres of the Baltic states, and parts of Finland, Poland, Germany, Czechoslovakia and Rumania, which Stalin had added to the pre-war Soviet Union. Here, 24 million new Soviet subjects were swallowed whole.

of the country. The Russians had already selected a provisional government under General Bela Miklos, who had defected to the Red army.[5] The monarchy, which had survived since St Stephen in 1001, was abolished. Marshal Voroshilov, the chairman of the Allied Control Commission in Hungary, brought immediate pressure for land reform. A country of large estates, owned by landowners and the Church, was to have a maximum unit of 180 hectares. Red army officers arrested Hungarians with 'reactionary' tendencies and sent them to internment camps.

Relatively free elections were held in October 1945. The moderate Smallholders' Party emerged with a majority, holding 245 seats out of 409. The Communists won only 70 seats, one ahead of the Social Democrats. A coalition government was formed with Zoltan Tildy, a Calvinist pastor and a Smallholder, as president and Ferenc Nagy, another Smallholder who had been arrested by the Germans in 1944, as prime minister. The Cabinet was divided evenly between moderates and leftists. The Smallholders wanted to appoint Bela Kovacs, a tough, hard peasant, who was an under-secretary, as interior minister. The Communists said they would quit the government unless their nominee, Imre Nagy, got the job. 'Look around you in south-east Europe,' said Rákosi. 'See if you can find a country where the ministry of the interior isn't in the hands of the Communist Party.' Voroshilov backed this with a threat to transfer further Russian troops to Hungary.

'We had no choice but to surrender,' said Ferenc Nagy, who had no illusions as to how the Communists exercised control. 'One can truthfully say that the Communist Party conquered the country with the Red army,' he wrote after he had been deposed.[6] Allegations against rivals began. General Vadim Sviridov, Soviet deputy chairman of the Allied Control Commission, acting in its name but without consulting his British and American colleagues, delivered a sharp note to the government on 28 June 1946. It stated that 'fascist terrorist organizations' had murdered a number of Red army soldiers and recommended that they be dissolved. The Russian list included the Smallholders' youth movement, the Catholic Youth of Hungary and the Boy Scouts.

Many Smallholders were arrested at the beginning of 1947. 'There was no court in Hungary that would have convicted Bela Kovacs,' admits Zoltan Vas, a former colonel in the Red army and then communist Mayor of Budapest. 'So we turned to the Soviet army, requesting that they should arrest him. They snatched him from Hungary.'[7] Kovacs, accused of spying for the West, was imprisoned for ten years in Russia.

In May, Ferenc Nagy, still prime minister, left for Switzerland on a holiday. Rákosi claimed that Nagy was implicated in a 'confession' of treason made by Bela Kovacs. The British and American representatives on the Allied Control Commission were refused sight of the confession.

Nagy agreed to resign on condition that his younger son, still in Hungary, should be allowed to join him in Switzerland.

The army, which had been controlled by the Smallholder Eugene Tombor, was held to 12,000 men instead of the 70,000 allowed by the peace treaty. Russian-trained 'orientation officers' and 'D' officers, or security police, were posted to units to hunt down 'war criminals' who had fought against the Red army. The commander of the 'D' officers, Lieutenant General George Pálffy, executed many officers or handed them to the Russians. Tombor died in 1946. His successor as defence minister, General Albert Bartha, fled into exile in September 1947. His replacement, Peter Veres, was a fellow traveller.

The growing communist influence showed in the acceptance of Soviet 'suggestions' not to attend the Marshall Plan conference in Paris in July 1947. In elections the following month the Communists, after opposition complaints of fraud and disenfranchising, increased their vote from 17 per cent to 22 per cent. Political opponents fled in numbers to the US Zone in Germany.

Vas explained how the increase was won. 'In the election regulations there was a paragraph according to which anyone who was not staying at his permanent address at the time of the election could go to the Election Committee and ask for a document to enable him to vote in another constituency. The document was printed on a blue card,' he said. 'What we did was to forge blue cards and give them to Communists, thus creating about 80,000 fake ballot papers ... Each voter had to appear before a committee to prove he had never been a fascist ... On this basis a lot of people were disqualified from voting.'[8]

The police force was refined with the creation of the AVO, the state security police, in 1947. It was run by Gábor Péter, amply backed by former NKVD officers as advisers. Péter was under the direct control of an NKVD major general, Theodore Belkin.[9] AVO was rechristened AVH, which would become the most emotive name in the 1956 rising, at the end of the year. It had its own minister separate from interior, and attached counter-intelligence officers, Elháritók, to each Army battalion.

The Russians supervised arrests. When Bela Szasz, whose communist odyssey had taken him to Argentina to edit an anti-Fascist paper during the war, was arrested three years after his return to Budapest in 1946, he recalled that: 'I was brought to the chief of the Russian Secret Police ... That was Major General Belkin. He was Chief in Eastern Europe of the Russian Secret Police ... He wore a tunic made from a fabric which normally women would wear, a silver grey, shiny tunic.' Szasz was left in no doubt of the importance of this 'rather small, fat man with a big nose' who smoked American cigarettes. The Russian colonel who interrogated him told him that Belkin was a 'much, much greater man than your governor Horthy was! Because he is not only Governor of Hungary, like Horthy was, but he is Governor of Austria, and of Romania, and of Yugoslavia and of Czechoslovakia and of Albania. Because you know Comrade Belkin is the Chief of the Secret Police for Eastern Europe.'

As for Gábor Péter, Szasz met him too for an interrogation of dreamlike sadism. Péter's first question was: 'Who is Wagner?' Szasz first thought of the composer but then opted for a foreign office consul with the same name. A senior foreign service official was brought into the room. Péter asked him: 'Did Szasz give you a message from Wagner?' He said: 'Yes.' Péter did not have a consul in mind as Wagner. 'Wagner' was the codename for Allen Dulles, the head of the CIA. Szasz denied any such exotic connection so Péter said: 'Well, *bastinado* to him.' 'You have to lie on your stomach,' said Szasz. 'Two or three people sit on you, and your feet are naked. They hold your feet and they get rubber truncheons ... they hit your feet, the soles of your feet ... About twenty-five times each. I got twenty-five each thirty-six times ... It was like beefsteak, my feet. And I had to stand on these feet for nine days and nine nights.'

If Wagner was not a musician, not a consul, but could weirdly become Allen Dulles, the pain would stop. More than that. 'When I make my confession they will take me away, in a few months' time, and I will have a beautiful time in the Crimea,' Szasz recalls of his temptation by an NKVD-trained Hungarian colonel. 'Then I will come back and they will let me do whatever I want, and so on and so on. But first you have to confess. You have to help the party.'[10]

Rákosi's work came to fruition in 1948. Much of industry was nationalized in March. The Communists 'fused' with the Social Democrats on 12 June. On 16 June independent and church schools were abolished. On 30 July Zoltan Tildy, marked for retribution as a pastor and for his reputation against the Nazis, resigned as president following the arrest of his son-in-law. A hard-line Communist, Michael Farkas, became defence minister in September 1948. A military academy with Soviet instructors was introduced. The orientation officers became 'political officers' on classic commissar lines. Trained at the Petöfi academy in Budapest, they countersigned all orders and could overrule the regular commanders of units. The force became a 'People's Army'. 'The officers were recruited from workers and peasants,' Rákosi said with pride. 'And as they visited their former factories or native villages, they demonstrated by their mere presence the shift in the balance of power between the classes.' A former tram driver, Stephen Bata, became chief of staff, with an agitator and an ex-labourer as lieutenant generals.

On 21 November Cardinal Mindszenty issued a pastoral letter on the persecution of Catholics. He was shortly arrested. In February 1949 the Catholic Prince Primate was sentenced to life imprisonment by a People's

Court for 'treason, espionage, attempting to overthrow the Republic and illegal currency transactions'. The evidence against him was based on forged letters to the US envoy in Budapest, Selden Chapin, who was expelled from the country.

Mindszenty, and Hungary, were to enjoy only the briefest future liberty.

Lunch in the Lubianka: Poland

Poland went as easily because many of those who might have resisted were dead, deported and killed by the Russians after the Soviet invasion in the aftermath of the Molotov–Ribbentrop pact, or killed by the Germans during the Warsaw Rising. No country suffered more than Poland in the war. One in five Poles died, a rate double that of mere decimation, reaching 6 million, 3.2 million of them Jews.

The first moves in the subjugation of Poland came with the 1939 invasion. By the time of *Barbarossa* some 1.5 million Poles had been deported from the 180,000 square kilometres of Soviet-occupied Poland. About 250,000 Polish officers and men were transported into the Russian interior as POWs. Fifteen thousand officers were separated from their men and taken to three camps at Kozielsk, Starobielsk and Ostashkov. They were guarded by the NKVD. A Polish government in exile had been established in London under General Wladyslaw Sikorski. With *Barbarossa* under way, the Poles signed a military agreement in Moscow. It provided for a Polish army to be raised in Russia under General Anders. Polish POWs were to be 'amnestied',[11] although the Soviets refused to accept a return to the pre-1939 frontiers.

Anders was at once concerned at the lack of Polish officers coming out of the Russian camps. Their fate remains a subject that the Soviet Union cannot bring itself to discuss, *glasnost* or not.[12] The evidence of Soviet guilt is overwhelming.

The Polish ambassador in Moscow, Stanislaw Kot, raised the question with Stalin on 14 November 1941. 'Are there still Poles who have not been liberated?' Stalin asked. Kot replied that he was concerned with the fate of about 15,000 officers. Only between 350 and 400 had reported to General Anders. Stalin picked up a telephone and made a personal inquiry. He listened on the telephone for some time. He then hung up and refused to speak about the officers for the remainder of the audience.[13] In an interview with Sikorski in December 1941 Stalin claimed simply: 'Your officers were liberated.'

On the evening of 13 April 1943 Berlin Radio announced that 'a great pit' had been found by German troops in the forests of Katyn, near Smolensk. It was '28 metres long and 16 metres wide, filled with 12 layers of bodies of Polish officers, numbering about three thousand'. The bodies were in military uniform, 'many of them had their hands tied, all of them had wounds in the back of their necks caused by pistol shots'. New layers were unearthed. The German estimate ran to 'about 10,000, which would more or less correspond to the entire number of Polish officers taken as prisoners of war by the Bolsheviks'. Moscow Radio said this was 'a foul lie'.

The missing Poles were murdered, probably on Stalin's direct orders, in the spring of 1940. The last man to see some five thousand of his fellow officers alive was Professor Stanislaw Swaniewicz, who recalled his experience in an interview with the BBC commentator, Michael Charlton.[14] Swaniewicz's units had surrendered to Russian cavalry in September 1939 and he was sent to a POW camp at Kozielsk. There were over four thousand officers in the camp, together with civilians, mainly judges and doctors, who brought the total close to five thousand.

At the end of March 1940 their guards told them that an important decision had been made over their future. 'The worst we expected was that we would be handed over to the Germans,' said Swaniewicz. 'No one expected to be executed.' The first group was taken from the camp in prison railway wagons at the beginning of April. Other groups followed every few days. 'It was Spring. Beautiful sun. The general feeling was of a certain excitement . . . We just said goodbye.'

Swaniewicz's turn came on 29 April. He was loaded on to a wagon with 300 others. The train passed through Smolensk travelling west. The Poles assumed that they were to be handed over to the Germans. Shortly after Smolensk, the train stopped. Swaniewicz's name was called out by an NKVD colonel and he was separated from the rest. He watched as his comrades were transferred in groups on to a bus and driven away. Armed guards with fixed bayonets surrounded the train. 'There were trees and a big forest, so I did not see directly where the bus was going,' he said. 'But the question that interested me was why – this place was obviously very near – they did not simply ask us to go on foot, and yet there was a convoy. The day was really beautiful . . . There was still a bit of snow on the fields.'

Swaniewicz was spared because the Russians wished to interrogate him about an economic study of Germany he had written. His brother officers were shot in the nape of the neck in the forest of Katyn. The instructions came directly to the Kozielsk camp from Moscow. 'We knew it very simply because, when there was transport they gave the orders from Moscow who to take, personally,' he said. 'People who worked in the office of the camp heard it . . . because it was a beautiful Spring day and the window was open. This was a very complicated operation, the giving of so many foreign names over the telephone from Moscow.'

The motive appears to have been to liquidate any natural leadership in

Poland. Like the *kulaks*, the Polish officer class was killed for its potential independence of mind. The Soviet government used Katyn as a pretext to break off relations with the pro-Western Poles in London, accusing them of 'cooperating with the Hitlerite hangmen'. A Polish National Council was formed in Moscow, under the Communist Boleslaw Beirut. Troops of the Soviet-controlled Polish army advanced into Poland with the Red army in 1944. As the strength of the Home Army and the London Poles was shattered in the Warsaw Rising, a pro-Soviet administration was established on Polish soil at Lublin.

The victory banners in ruined Warsaw had not had time to fray after the liberation before the Russians gave notice of their intentions. Polish underground leaders, including Jan Jankowski, the vice-premier of the London government, were invited to a meeting on 6 March 1945 by a Red army officer, Colonel Pimonov. They were asked to meet Colonel General Ivanov, commander of the 1st White Russian Army in Pruszkow, near Warsaw. Pimonov gave in writing his 'word of honour that, from the moment of your arrival among us, I shall be responsible for everything that happens to you, and that your personal safety is completely assured'. It was explained that Marshal Zhukov, then C-in-C of Soviet forces in Poland, wished to have talks with the underground leaders to maintain calm in the rear of the Red army during the final phase of the assault on Germany. Pimonov said that the Russians were prepared to release those underground leaders already arrested as a gesture of goodwill. They would also provide a Soviet bomber to fly eight underground leaders to Britain for talks with the Polish government in London.

There was one condition. Before the flight to London, the main civilian and military leadership of the underground must meet a Soviet representative. Pimonov said that this would be Zhukov, who had been given authority by Stalin. The Soviet colonel insisted that General Niedzwiadek-Okulicki, C-in-C of the underground Home Army, be present.

The Poles arrived in Pruszkow for lunch with Zhukov at noon on 28 March. Jankowski and Okulicki had gone to the Soviet HQ the night before to make arrangements for the talks. They had not returned. Zhukov was also absent. He was, the Russians explained, otherwise engaged in his final offensive. The Poles were driven to Wlochy, near Warsaw, for the promised lunch. Two NKVD officers were talking by telephone to Moscow. Pimonov explained that Zhukov was still detained. Food arrived from the officers' mess. No talks were started and the Poles were sent in groups of four to different rooms, with Soviet escorts, to rest in the late evening.

A Soviet general explained the next morning that Zhukov was still detained at his field HQ, but was so anxious to see them that he was placing his private aircraft at their disposal. The Poles accepted. They were taken to the large Warsaw airfield at Okecie. Their spirits rose when they saw that Alexander Zwierzynski, the chairman of the national defence committee who had been arrested by the Russians, was already on board the aircraft.

The senior Soviet officers saw the Poles off, leaving a captain as the ranking officer on board. The converted bomber flew east, not west. The captain explained that Zhukov had been called to Moscow, where Jankowski and Niedzwiadek-Okulicki were awaiting them. They were indeed, but in prison. The Poles were landed west of Moscow and transferred by train and car to a large building in the centre.

Lunch meant the Lubianka.

With the Polish underground leaders safely crammed in their basement cells in Moscow, Beirut signed a treaty of friendship and mutual cooperation with Stalin. This required the Poles not to enter any alliance or coalition directed against the Soviet Union. In San Francisco on United Nations business in May 1945, Molotov casually admitted that the Poles had been arrested for 'diversionary activities' in the rear of the Red army.*

Twelve of the Poles were sentenced, Okulicki to ten years, Jankowski and the speaker of the underground Parliament, Kazimierz Puzak, to eighteen months.[15] A provisional government was formed in Moscow and the Powers 'took note [of it] with pleasure' at the Potsdam conference. Less pleasured, General Anders warned his Polish troops in Italy that they would be sent to Siberia if they returned home.

The Communists held only five ministries, but these included the crucial interior ministry and they had control of the army. Mikolajczyk, a vice-premier with the communist Gomulka in the new coalition government, was confident that his independent Polish Peasant Party could win the elections required by Allied agreements. The peasants, Catholic and anti-

* There runs in the history of the trumped-up charge in the Soviet Union a flair for outrage so confident and so vacuumed of decency that it nears a brilliant black comedy. Note it here. The Poles were accused of 'diversionary activities' in the rear of the Red army. And they had, of course, indulged in diversionary activity in the largest single partisan action of the Second World or any war. Molotov could not have had his little joke without the Warsaw Rising. The diversion did not take place in the rear of the Red army, of course, but of the German. The Russians, having done nothing to assist the Rising, then tricked some of its leaders into the Lubianka, on the pretext of luncheon with Zhukov, tortured them, forced them to sign 'confessions' and then tried and sentenced them. Who can say that beneath the clichés and Sovspeak on the charge sheets there lurked no sense of humour? Try another Polish joke. Having deported over a million Poles to the Soviet Union after 1939, Moscow decided in 1943 to regard them as Soviet citizens since they lived on Soviet territory. Some were then imprisoned because they had no valid entry permits and were thus illegal immigrants! The Lubianka is quite a joke in itself, on display in a major square in bright brick, located opposite the main children's store of the Soviet Union, its windows full of cuddly bears and babushka dolls.

communist, were in a majority. Mikolajczyk did not allow for the influence of the Red army. Under its protection, the Communists broadened their control of the economy and the media whilst the police preyed on the parties temporarily allied with them. NKVD men were posted as advisers to the rapidly growing secret police, the 'UB'. Before even the first Christmas of the liberation'2 the UB showed its mettle by breaking up a protest against political prisoners in Grogel and taking demonstrators, including members of the Peasant Party, to be shot in a forest.

An election was held in January 1947, the choice of the coldest month calculated to cut the rural Catholic vote. As many as 100,000 members of the Peasant Party were arrested. Candidates were illegally struck from ballot papers. Mikolajczyk claimed that 104 out of 700 of his candidates were arrested and a further 300 disbarred by an electoral law which disenfranchised those suspected of collaborating with terrorists. Telegrams were sent to country districts with the false news of Mikolajczyk's death in a plane crash. Votes were cast by picking pieces of paper numbered from 1 to 6 according to the party. The Communists were 3 throughout Poland, a fact well advertised on radio. The Peasant Party number varied between regions.

Outside observers put the Peasant Party vote at 60 per cent. Officially it was 8 per cent. The British and US governments refused to be represented at the opening of the new parliament, saying that the election had not been 'free and unfettered'. The US ambassador resigned his post. The socialist–Communist coalition confirmed Beirut as president, whilst a campaign was opened to suppress the Peasant Party. The editor of the party paper was sentenced for 'collaborating with underground organizations'. Mikolajczyk was warned that he would be arrested, and fled the country for Britain. Right-wing socialists were arrested on charges of 'subversive activity among the working masses'. A 'union' of Communists and social-ists was achieved by the end of 1948.

Marshal Rokossovsky was appointed a Marshal of Poland, minister of national defence and C-in-C of Polish armed forces in November 1949. Though born Polish, his career in the Red army and his retention of Soviet citizenship made his appointment clear notice of Poland's satellite status.

'Until you meet St Peter': Bulgaria

The external affairs of Bulgaria were complex, since the country had contrived at one stage, in September 1944, to be simultaneously at war with Germany, Russia, Britain and the US. Internally, the familiar and simple pattern was followed. The local Rákosi figure was Georgi Dimitrov. A founder of the Bulgarian Communist Party, a former type-setter, he had fled the country in 1921. Acquitted of complicity in the

Reichstag fire in 1933, he served as secretary general of Comintern in Moscow for nine years before returning to Sofia with the Red army.

A coalition government was thrown together in September 1944. The ministers of Justice and the Interior were Communists and made rapid use of the police and courts. It was officially stated that, by March 1945, 10,897 people had been found guilty in 131 trials and that 2,138 had been executed. The three regents who had ruled on behalf of the boy King, Simeon of Saxe-Gotha, were among those shot.

As in Poland, the rural peasants were both anti-communist and a majority. The fate of their Agrarian Party and its leader, Dr G. M. Dimitrov, mirrors that of Mikolajczyk and the Peasant Party. Dimitrov, who had spent much of the war as an adviser to the British in Cairo, was accused of being a British agent. He was replaced by the more malleable Nicolai Petrov after a show of hands in which four voted for Petrov and forty-eight, mute through fear of the secret police, abstained. Dimitrov took refuge in the Sofia house of the US representative on the Allied Control Commission. Fleeing to the US, he was sentenced *in absentia* to twenty years for 'subversion'. Elections were held in November 1945. The opposition decided to boycott them, 'not wishing to expose Bulgarian voters to the terror perpetrated by the government in order to win the election at all costs...' President Truman's personal representative complained at 'the threats of coercion and later reprisals'. The communist-dominated coalition claimed 75 per cent of the poll.★

The country still had, at least in theory, an eight-year-old king. Colonel General S. S. Biryusov, the Soviet deputy chairman of the Allied Control Commission and himself a survivor of Stalin's camps, was anxious to remove the anomaly. The opposition continued to refuse to merge with the government. Despite heavy pressure from Red army units, the opposition insisted on fresh elections, a free press and a commission to decide on the release of political prisoners. Experience also persuaded it to press for a justice minister and an undersecretary at the interior ministry. A referendum was held on the monarchy in September 1946. The Saxe-Gothas had brought Bulgaria into both world wars on the losing side and this dynastic bungling was rewarded. As a child, Simeon was excused the sins – mainly avarice – of his unlamented father and left peacefully for Egypt with a generous £5 million in compensation for his lost estates.

Bulgaria was declared a People's Republic on 15 September 1946. Vassil Kolarov, who had been exiled in Russia since 1923, became its first president. Political commissars appeared in the army and officers were purged. The minister of war, the anti-communist General Velchev, left

★ The list of the parties that were disappearing in Eastern Europe – Agrarians, National Peasants, Liberals, Ploughmen, Smallholders, Farmers, Social Democrats, Independent Catholics, Labour, New Liberation – is the rollcall of a forgotten *Gulag*.

Bulgaria for Switzerland. Georgi Dimitrov, who had become a Soviet citizen during his lengthy stay in Moscow, was confirmed as premier after an election that London said took place in 'an atmosphere of terror'.

A series of political trials culminated in that of Nicolai Petrov. The Agrarian leader had become less malleable. A bitter exchange in the Sofia parliament was sparked when Dimitrov accused him of harbouring foreign agents. 'I will not allow you to go on talking like that,' said Petkov. 'Let me remind you that I have never been a citizen of a foreign country, nor have I ever been in foreign service . . .' Dimitrov replied: 'I was a citizen of the great Soviet Republic . . . This is an honour and a privilege.' Petkov: 'You became a Bulgarian subject two days before the elections. This was officially announced from Moscow.' Dimitrov spat back: 'I'll teach you a lesson soon.'

Stripped of his parliamentary immunity, Petkov was accused of plotting to seize power through a group of officers called the 'Military League'. His co-accused gave evidence against him at the reward of their lives. Petkov said that his trial was 'the sad fate of a Bulgarian who defends democracy today'. The former coalition partner of the Communists was found guilty in August 1947 and was hanged a week later. A British Note to Sofia called it 'judicial murder'. The Agrarian Party survived him by three days. 'They ran their heads against the wall. Their leader is under the ground,' Dimitrov warned his people. 'You must think whether you want to share their fate . . . If you have not been wise in the past and do not try to gain wisdom you will receive a lesson from the nation you will remember until you meet St Peter.'

The lesson-giver's own Petrine rendezvous followed eighteen months later, when he died of illness in Moscow. By then, the Social Democrat Kosta Lulchev, leader of the sole surviving independent party, had been arrested and his party 'fused' with the Communists into the Workers' Party.

The joy of the confessional: Rumania

There was also a king, Michael, to be got rid of in Rumania. A national democratic front, the FND, was formed of Communists and Social Democrats. The prime minister, however, was the Chief of the Rumanian General Staff, the anti-communist General Niculae Radescu. A large anti-Radescu demonstration was held in Bucharest on 24 February 1945. Eight demonstrators were killed. The Communists held government troops and Radescu responsible. Radescu said that the bullets were of a calibre not issued to the Rumanian army and claimed that a lorryload of Communists had deliberately opened fire on the demonstration. The communist press demanded Radescu's execution as a criminal.

Two days later Andrei Vyshinsky flew to Bucharest. Now Soviet deputy foreign minister, Vyshinsky had been prosecutor during the purge trials, famous for the line with which he invariably closed his case against the accused: 'Shoot the mad dogs!' The Soviet High Command moved into the Rumanian general staff headquarters and other government buildings and ordered all Rumanian troops in the capital to be disarmed. Vyshinsky, in an audience with the king, said that Radescu was plotting against the Red army. Radescu gained sanctuary with the British political representative, eventually fleeing by air to Cyprus.

Vyshinsky, demanding that the FND come to power, slammed the door on leaving an audience with the king with such violent anger that he cracked the plaster surrounding it. An FND-dominated government was duly appointed, with a fellow traveller, Dr Petre Groza, as premier. The interior ministry went predictably to a Communist, Teohari Georgescu, a house painter. In August 1945 he announced the discovery of 'terrorist organizations' involving followers of Radescu. *Izvestia* in Moscow accused King Michael of bowing to British and American pressure. A loyalist demonstration outside the Royal Palace was broken up by Communists, armed with staves, who arrived in state-owned trucks.

Intimidation spread. With naked contempt, Dr Groza told oil workers on 11 February 1945: 'We shall be victorious in the elections. If the reaction succeeds, do you think we shall let it live twenty-four hours? We shall seize what we can and strike.' General Susaikov, head of the Soviet section of the Allied Control Commission, pressured the king to purge the military of non-communists. In August 1946 the king signed a bill transferring some 10,000 officers and warrant officers from the Rumanian army, navy and air force to the Reserve List. Those retired were chosen on a political basis by the Communist-controlled Cultural and Propaganda section of the army. With them went the king's last hope of armed resistance to Russian pressure.

Elections were set for November 1946. Communist railwaymen were issued with metal coshes. Official British and US protests were ignored. The result was duly announced as a government victory. Arrests accelerated during 1947. On the night of 14 July a group of National Peasant Party Leaders were arrested as they tried to flee to Turkey. The party was dissolved on 29 July. The police then turned on the National Liberals.

By the onset of winter the Communists held every important ministry except defence. Anna Pauker, a veteran Communist who had been a propaganda specialist in the Soviet Union during the war, and who took a 'particular pleasure' in staring down the king, had been appointed foreign minister. On 24 December the final pawn slipped into place when Emil Bodnaras, latterly the head of the secret police, became defence minister.

There remained the king, still popular but without military support in a country that still had a strong Red army presence. Michael had attended the Westminster Abbey wedding of Princess Elizabeth to Prince Philip in November, the high colour of drab 1947 in London. He met Princess Anne of Bourbon-Parma at the celebrations. Their engagement was announced early in December. Anna Pauker scoffed at the engagement, saying that the marriage would be too expensive for Rumania, it was reactionary. She herself lived in the fashionable Bucharest house where ex-King Carol had kept his mistress Mme Lupescu before he married her.* King Michael spent Christmas on his country estate at Sinaia. He was telephoned by Groza on 29 December, the premier asking him to return to Bucharest urgently.

He went back to his capital on the morning of 30 December. His palace was surrounded by troops of the Communist-officered Tudor Vladimirescu division. Groza was awaiting his monarch with an abdication decree ready for signature. King Michael signed it at 2 p.m. He left for Switzerland on 3 January. The final act, the fusion of the Social Democrats and Communists into the new Rumanian Workers' Party, took place in February 1948.

A fall from a window: Czechoslovakia

Two factors make Czechoslovakia unique to the Rákosi pattern. It was the only country to have had a significant Communist Party before the war, which won 10 per cent of the vote in 1935. President Beneš considered Soviet friendship to be essential for Czech security. He felt that 'real world catastrophe could only be prevented by devoted work for a firm and permanent agreement between the Anglo-Saxons and the Soviet Union'.

Beneš is a key figure in Soviet expansion into Eastern Europe. He did not believe that Soviet Russia was a menace to his or other countries and he spread this view with energy, to President Roosevelt among others. Given the Soviet record, it was a risky philosophy but Beneš had signed a treaty of friendship, mutual assistance and post-war cooperation with Moscow in December 1943. He told Stalin, who acted as 'an old uncle of sorts', joking and patting Beneš on the shoulder, that Czechoslovakia would always act in a way agreeable to the Soviet Union. Beneš 'promised to the Russians things that were far beyond anything that the Russians themselves were asking for.'[16]

Some Czechs saw it as a second Munich, another disastrous exercise in

---

* The remarkable Anna Pauker, herself a widow whose husband had been shot as a Trotskyite conspirator during their stay in Russia, was to be disgraced herself in 1952 for 'left and right deviation', 'tolerance of kulaks' and 'living on a slope of aristocracy'. She confessed to the charges, having once told a Western diplomat that the confessional was a 'joy that only a true comrade could know'. *How Did the Satellites Happen?* p. 203.

trusting dictatorships. Not Beneš. He wrote from Moscow to Jan Masaryk, the son of Thomas Masaryk, the first president of democratic Czechoslovakia, with enthusiasm of the 'great, genuine and final' development to liberty in the Soviet Union. In truth, with the help of the ambitious and nominally Social Democrat Czech ambassador in Moscow, Zdenek Fierlinger, those Czech Communists who had fled to Moscow had already begun the long process of grasping power. Their leader was Klement Gottwald, a short, lively former carpenter, who had gone to Moscow before Munich.

By January 1945, with parts of Czechoslovakia liberated by the Red army, the Soviets invited Beneš and his Czech government in exile to move from London to the liberated zone. A new provisional government was announced on 4 April at Kosice, the capital of east Slovakia. The key ministries went to Communists. Vaclav Nosek, Moscow-trained, a former miner, became interior minister with control over the police. Education and information, with their influence on the young and control over broadcasting and the press, were assigned to hardline Stalinists. General Ludvik Svoboda, who had commanded the Czech brigade in Russia, became defence minister. Though the independent, tragic Jan Masaryk was foreign minister, foreign service personnel were controlled by his deputy, the Slovak Communist Vladimir Clementis. Gottwald was a vice-premier. Fierlinger was named premier at communist insistence. A fellow-travelling prime minister made their domination less overt.

It was a regime without an opposition. The only legal parties, Communist, Social Democrat and Populist, were united in a National Front. They had no licit opposition. Catholics were excluded on grounds of collaboration with the Nazis. So, at communist bidding, were the Agrarians who had been the largest pre-war party.

Those whom the Communists found awkward disappeared. 'There were quick trials,' said Professor Edward Taborsky, private secretary to Beneš. 'There was no *habeas corpus* or anything. If you opposed them, and they wanted to get rid of you, they would either denounce you to the Soviet NKVD who would deport you, or they would put you in jail.

'They would say, "We saw you with the Gestapo." So there was simply a lawlessness, and that's how they flourished.'[17]

The Communists got 38 per cent of the vote in elections a year after liberation. That remains the highest communist poll ever recorded in a free election. Gottwald became premier and the Communists added internal trade and finance to their portfolios. On 10 July 1947 the government reversed its approval of Marshall Aid under Soviet pressure and refused to attend the Marshall Plan conference in Paris.*

* The US-supported UNRRA had already sent more than $1 billion in aid to Eastern Europe, including $270 million to Czechoslovakia and $491 million to Poland.

Their popularity soon on the wane, the Communists packed men into the police in anticipation of new elections due in the summer of 1948. This provoked open crisis. Nosek, the interior minister, had steadily transformed the SNB, the Czech police, into a private army. Non-communists were sacked, sent to dull postings or cajoled into joining the Party. In February 1948 Nosek retired or transferred eight non-communist regional police commanders. Beneš did nothing. His private secretary, Taborsky, describes his behaviour as 'unbelievable ... The Communists began to fill the vacancies with their people, especially in the Police and so on, and he did nothing about it ... Several times, I mentioned to him ... "Mr President, this is not right legally. You should not sign it." And he said, "No I won't sign it." But when Gottwald came to see him, he did sign it...'[18]

The pace quickened. On 19 February 1948 Valerian Zorin, once the Soviet ambassador in Prague and now the deputy Soviet foreign minister, flew unexpectedly to Prague from Moscow. Zorin explained that he had come 'to supervise the delivery of Soviet wheat'. That day the Communists ordered supporters 'to action stations'. Crowds gathered outside party headquarters and the offices of the communist paper *Rude Pravo*, where loudspeakers blared out Soviet songs. Communists in blue overalls with weapons in their belts marched the streets. A manifesto was distributed accusing the non-communists of plotting to break up the government, though they were in a majority in the Cabinet over the police issue.

Two days later twelve non-communist ministers, seeing the ominous outline of a *putsch*, handed their resignations to Beneš in protest at Gott-wald's refusal to order Nosek to stop hounding non-communists out of the police. *Svonodne Slavo*, the Czech socialist newspaper, accused the police of using methods 'at least as bad as those of Himmler and the Tsarist Okhrana (the old Russian secret police)'. The official spokesman at the Communist-controlled Information Ministry said that the ministers who had resigned were 'agents of the German General Staff'.[19]

The police on the streets of Prague were issued with rifles and tommyguns on 23 February. They raided the offices of rival political parties and arrested leading opponents. Rumours were spread that the Red army was massing on the border ready to intervene. Cold, short of coal and food, in scrappy clothes and peeling apartment blocks the Czechs entered a state of anticipated violence.

A week after his arrival, his mission of preparing a coup apparently completed, the enigmatic Zorin flew back to Moscow. By 25 February fourteen newspapers had been closed and the free press dissolved. The rector of Prague university, doctors, industrial managers lukewarm to the Party had been dismissed. President Beneš, given the choice of yielding to the coup or risking civil war, appointed a new Gottwald government. A purge of officers began immediately. More than 1,000 senior officers were dismissed, including 124 members of the Czech air force command and most of those who had fought in the West.

On 10 March the body of Jan Masaryk was found on the pavement of the courtyard of the Czernin Palace, the foreign ministry, below his official apartments. Some feel that his fall from the bathroom window of his rooms was suicide induced by the fresh loss of Czech liberty. Nosek, whose policemen were swiftly at the scene, blamed 'Depression increased by recriminations from the West'. Others claim that he was murdered by the Soviet NKVD. His underclothes were soiled, suggesting that he was in fear of his life. The bathroom window was awkward to climb out of. The doorman of the Czernin Palace had seen people coming in and unaccountable cigarette stubs were found in his room.

Thus died a man who had said in London during the war: 'My aim is simple. I want to go home. And I want to be able at any time I like to ride in a tramcar down the Wenceslas Square in Prague and say "I don't think much of our present government."' With a brief interlude in 1968, to criticize the Czech government on a tramcar has risked a ride further than Wenceslas Square.

Beneš resigned on 7 June. Ill and broken, he had rarely been seen in public since the February coup. On 3 September 1948 he was dead.

The xenophobes: Albania

Albania took care of its own eccentric fate. It had been invaded by Italy on Good Friday 1939, Mussolini's troops meeting little resistance. King Zog fled from his tiny and impoverished kingdom over the border to Greece. The resistance movement was led by Enver Hoxha, a rare, educated Albanian who had lost his job as a teacher at the French lycée in Korca after refusing to join the Albanian Fascists. He then kept a tobacco kiosk, the early centre of the resistance. Sentenced to death *in absentia* by the Italians, he organized a resistance army, the Levizija Nacional Clirimtare.

A small British Military Mission was parachuted into Greece and crossed into Albania in April 1943 to contact 'influential feudal troops' to help against the Axis. To its astonishment, it found an organized national liberation movement directed from Moscow.

Hoxha was elected prime minister and C-in-C of resistance forces in May 1944. Tirana was cleared of Germans on 17 November 1944, and the last German troops quit Albania at the beginning of December. Elections with a single list of candidates were held later in the month. Non-communists fled to Egypt and Italy and the largely illiterate Albanians were cowed by heavily armed security police commanded by Major General Mehmet Shehu, a former officer cadet under Zog, cashiered for

revolutionary activities that took him to fight for the Republicans during
the Spanish civil war. A People's Republic was declared at the beginning
of 1946 with a constitution modelled on Tito's Yugoslavia.

Hoxha became his own foreign and defence minister that March. His
interior minister was Lieutenant General Koci Xoxe, once a tinsmith and
now his chief and much-feared assistant. Torture and execution were used
on the remnants of opposition, with particular effect on the Christian
clergy, both Catholic and Orthodox. Albanian xenophobia, which still
runs strong, was in immediate evidence against the British. Two Royal
Navy cruisers, *Orion* and *Superb*, were shelled by Albanian shore batteries
whilst in the Corfu channel on 2 May 1946. In October two British
destroyers, *Saumarez* and *Volage*, were mined in the channel, killing forty-
four crewmen.

The Yugoslavs were the next to suffer from the Albanians' pathological
mistrust of foreigners. For four years after the German withdrawal, Albania
was closely merged with Yugoslavia. Belgrade provided half the annual
budget, currency was interchangeable and there was a customs union. The
economy, such as it was, relied on Yugoslav technicians. This dependency
rankled. When Tito broke with Cominform in June 1948 the Albanians
sided with Stalin. Yugoslavs were expelled en masse, the customs union
was scrapped and work stopped on the Scutari to Titograd rail link.
Stalin sent in Soviet technicians and 2,700 Red army officers.

Hoxha questioned the loyalty of Xoxe, an admirer of Tito. The threat
of a coup or defection by the interior minister had to be liquidated. The
trial began in May 1949 in Tirana of a 'Trotskyite group of the enemies
of the people headed by the chief bandit, Koci Xoxe'. Xoxe was sentenced
to death on 11 June 1949 and shot two days later. Anti-communist émigrés
who landed on the Albanian coast that year, parachuted in from the British
base at Malta, were betrayed by the British spy Kim Philby, rounded up
and executed.

Hoxha was later to split with the Soviets over de-Stalinization and for
a period the Russian place was taken by Maoist China. Albania then
resorted to friendlessness, its countryside dotted with grey bunkers like
tumuli to guard against any manner of foreign assault, the beaches opposite
Corfu empty except for endless patrols that opened fire on any windsurfer
foolhardy enough to stray too close across the Corfu channel.

The one that got away: Yugoslavia

The Rákosi pattern also failed in Yugoslavia, at least in terms of Soviet
influence. The communist achievement in the partisan movement was
remarkable enough to breed an independence from Moscow. The Communists had little support in Yugoslavia before the German invasion,

probably less than 1 per cent. A small group of Yugoslav Communists had fled to Russia in the early 1930s, where most of them were murdered during the 1936–7 purges.[20] The war and their resistance made them, with the Albanians, the only people whose progression to Communism was internal.

Yugoslavia had been dismembered after the German invasion in April 1941. Resistance ran deep and by the end of 1943 the partisans were holding down thirty-four Axis divisions. King Peter's government in London mistrusted the partisans and appointed Draza Mihailovic, the Cetnik leader, as 'commander in the homeland'.

The communist partisans were led by 'Tito', the assumed name of Josip Broz. Conscripted into the Austro-Hungarian army, he had gone over to the Russians in 1915 and gained his first experience of guerrilla war fighting for the Reds in the Russian civil war. He joined the party in 1920, returning to Croatia as a metal worker active in trade unions. He became leader of an underground labour movement, visiting the Soviet Union several times and becoming secretary general of the Yugoslav Communist Party in 1937. The Germans failed to include him in their haul of Communists and he organized the first rising against them in Serbia in June 1941.

The British government backed Tito's partisans as a far more effective fighting force than Mihailovic's. A British military mission was parachuted in and made contacts with the partisan command in May 1943. The Red army mission did not arrive for a further nine months, in February 1944. A national liberation committee had been elected by the various partisan forces, who numbered 700,000 by the end of the war. Tito was named its president, a Marshal of Yugoslavia and C-in-C. Despite the arrival of the Red army in the autumn of 1944, Yugoslavia was, like Albania, largely liberated by its own partisans. The aid from the Red army had been limited and a mixed blessing. 'Men and parties of men in the Red army committed so many serious assaults on citizens and on members of the Yugoslav army that a political problem arose,' wrote Djilas.[21] 'The Red army commanders were deaf to complaints.'

Tito arrived in Moscow on 5 April 1945 at the head of a Yugoslav delegation. He signed a treaty of friendship and mutual assistance, on the lines of those already signed by the Poles and Czechs, with Stalin on 11 April. His popular front government won a substantial majority in elections in November. He was confirmed as prime minister and minister of defence, and other Communists became ministers of interior, finance and industry. The monarchy was abolished in November 1945. The remaining Cetnik bands were eliminated and Mihailovic was executed. The only serious challenge to Tito came from the Catholic Church, and the government was confident enough to take it on at the end of 1946. The Primate of Yugoslavia, Monsignor Stepinac, Archbishop of Zagreb, was sentenced to sixteen years for collaboration during the conspiracy after the war.

The fledgling Yugoslav Communist Party had, in six years, reached a stature second only to the Russian Party. Belgrade was chosen as the site for the Cominform headquarters in September 1947. Such Stalinist honours did not last for long.

Tensions had already been created by Red army behaviour. The Yugoslavs had logged 121 cases of Red army rape, 111 of them involving rape and murder, and 1,204 cases of looting with assault. The figures, Tito's Agitprop chief Milovan Djilas noted, 'are hardly insignificant if it is borne in mind that the Red army crossed only the north-east corner of Yugoslavia'. Stalin, receiving a Red army delegation, spoke of Djilas's 'insults' to a Red army that had not spared its blood. 'Can't he understand it if a soldier who has crossed thousands of kilometres through blood and fire and death has fun with a woman or takes some trifle?' he asked.

Djilas complained that the Russians were organizing intelligence services within the Yugoslav Party and they were deliberately overplaying their own limited role in the liberation. 'We had created our *own* State and our *own* police apparatus,' he said.[22] A puritan streak ran in the Yugoslavs that was outraged by Red army habits. 'The drinking parties of the Soviet representatives,' Djilas wrote, 'were becoming more and more like real bacchanalia.' To make matters worse, 'they were trying to entice the Yugoslav leaders'. Nor were the Yugoslavs overawed, in the manner of a Dimitrov, by Stalin in their visits to Moscow. 'He knew that he was one of the cruellest, most despotic figures in human history,' Djilas wrote. 'But this did not worry him a bit, for he was convinced that he was carrying out the will of history.'

On 18 March 1948, as Russian power in Czechoslovakia was finalizing, Yugoslavia was expelled from Cominform. Stalin withdrew all Soviet specialists and advisers on the grounds that they had been 'surrounded with hostility' and, insult of insults, had been 'controlled and supervised by Yugoslav security organs'. Russian complaints to Belgrade spoke of Yugoslav 'brutal, dogmatic, unreasoning, almost insane arrogance and ignorance'.

Tito was summoned to the Kremlin but refused to go. The Yugoslav Politburo member Edward Kardelj who went in his stead recalled that when he arrived in Moscow, Molotov threw a paper in front of him and said, 'Sign this!' 'I picked it up and read that our two countries, the Soviet Union and Yugoslavia, would be obliged to consult each other on all matters of foreign policy,' Kardelj recalled. 'My blood boiled, and I felt that, not only was I being insulted and humiliated, but also the whole of Yugoslavia.'

Stalin may have planned to invade Yugoslavia. The Hungarian general Bela Kiraly claims that he was designated commander of a Hungarian army that was supposed to create a bridgehead on the Danube. Belgrade itself, the 'heretic capital', was reserved for the Red army. 'Everything was prepared,' said Kiraly. 'What saved Tito against the military invasion was the Korean War. America stood up. Consequently, (the Russians) assumed that if they invaded Yugoslavia, America would stand up again.'[23]

Tito wrote to Moscow that however much 'each of us loves the land of Socialism, the USSR, he can in no case love his own country less'. That earned a sharp Russian rejoinder, 'On the Arrogance of the Yugoslav leaders and their Incorrect Attitudes towards Their Mistakes'. Tito's letter was described as 'devoid of honest intent, childish and merely laughable'.

But he had escaped, even if 'those few in the West who took the trouble to reflect on the matter' thought the chief distinction of his regime in Eastern Europe to be that 'it was more ruthless'.*

* Hugh Thomas. *Armed Truce*, London 1988, p. 433.

The Mouth of the Cannon

Khrushchev and the Bomb

28

ARMAGEDDON: THE BOMB

The Russians were slow into the nuclear field. They had made little headway in nuclear physics before the war and *Barbarossa* stopped most research. There was some native base, besides the treason of physicists in the West, to build on when Stalin ordered an all-out effort for a nuclear bomb following Hiroshima and Nagasaki.

Igor Kurchatov, the leading force in this drive, was directing four nuclear physics laboratories at the Leningrad Physicotechnical Institute by 1934.[1] Abram Ioffe had established a laboratory to study the nucleus at the end of 1932. The Radium Institute was directed by V. G. Khlopin, a radiochemist who later developed the industrial processes for producing plutonium.[2] The director of the Leningrad Institute of Physical Chemistry was N. N. Semenov, later to win a Nobel Prize for his work on chain reactions. A keen eye was kept on research abroad, notably at the Cavendish Laboratory in Cambridge.

Soviet research was remarkably open, a sign that the leadership had little idea of its importance. Papers were published on the separation of isotopes and the production of heavy water in the spring of 1940. Two physicists working under Kurchatov discovered the spontaneous fission of uranium. A Uranium Commission was established in June 1940. Plans were made for the production of heavy water, the construction of cyclotrons, studies of isotope separation and for exploration of scarce uranium deposits. But funding was modest. A proposal by Kurchatov for an experimental reactor was turned down by the Uranium Commission in November 1940.[3]

Progress was largely halted by *Barbarossa*. Kurchatov found himself by the Black Sea working on counter-measures to German naval mines. The efficient Russian spy network reported in 1942 that the British, Americans and Germans were working on a nuclear bomb. An observant former student of Kurchatov, a young air force lieutenant, noticed that US scientific magazines were no longer publishing anything of interest on nuclear fission and that the names of the leading Western physicists had vanished from print. He concluded that the Americans were working on a bomb in secret. He wrote to Stalin, who was irritated that such important intelligence had come from a mere lieutenant rather than the Academy of Sciences.

Stalin was assured that the development of a uranium bomb would take between ten and twenty years and that its cost would be astronomic. The Russians lacked the vast resources in science and cash necessary to get ahead with real development whilst still fighting a war. However, Kurchatov was brought back to Moscow as director of a small nuclear centre in February or March 1943.[4] He set himself three main research goals: to achieve a chain reaction in an experimental reactor using natural uranium, to develop methods of isotope separation and to study the design of both the U-235 and the plutonium bombs. By the end of 1944 he had a hundred-strong team, tiny compared with the US effort. Kurchatov began to build a uranium pile to produce fissionable material early in 1945, as the first US atomic device neared readiness in New Mexico.

The Anglo-Americans were opposed to passing any of their secrets to the Soviets. Churchill and Roosevelt signed an aide memoire in September 1944 that stated: 'The suggestion that the world should be informed re Tube Alloys [the then codename for the bomb project] with a view to an international agreement regarding its control and use is not accepted. The matter should continue to be regarded as a matter of the utmost secrecy.' Several scientists thought that the Russians should be told of the bomb project in order to prevent any post-war feeling of betrayal. Niels Bohr, the physicist smuggled out of German-occupied Denmark to Britain during the war, was among them. Churchill thought that Bohr 'ought to be confined or at any rate made to see that he is very near the edge of mortal crimes'.[5]

Secrecy was maintained after the victory in Europe and Trinity, the code name for the first explosion of an atom bomb.

At 5.30 a.m. on 16 July 1945, at Alamogordo in New Mexico, an eyewitness noted in his diary,[6] there came 'a great blinding light that lit up the sky and earth as if God Himself had appeared among us'. The new era, brilliant in its intellect and primeval in its military significance, dawned across the desert 'golden, purple, violet, grey and blue'.[7] 'I am become death, the shatterer of worlds' was the line that ran through the mind of the senior American scientist, Robert Oppenheimer. War was transmuted. A 220-ton test cylinder set in concrete was shattered 800 metres away from the explosion point. Closer, steel and concrete structures disappeared.

The Potsdam conference on the occupation of Germany began outside Berlin on 17 July, the morning after Trinity. The British and Americans knew that the Alamogordo test had been a success. Churchill 'was already seeing himself capable of eliminating all the Russian centres of industry and population'.[8] Vague reference to the bomb was made to the Russians for the first time. President Truman wrote: 'I casually mentioned to Stalin that we had a new weapon of special destructive force.' Stalin 'showed no unusual interest. All he said was that he was glad to hear it and hoped that we would make "good use of it against the Japs".'

Stalin may have appeared incurious but Soviet intelligence in Canada and the US had already indicated the scale of Western nuclear progress.

The exploit of the single US bomber *Enola Gay* over Hiroshima on 6 August confirmed the power of the West's new weapon. Its one bomb outshone the morning sun 300 metres above the city, killing 70,000. The power of simple numbers, Stalin's 300 divisions, had been humbled.

The US then had the ability, the philosopher and mathematician Betrand Russell wrote, to 'establish a world empire by means of the atomic bomb'. It chose not to. To US politicians, the bomb was simply a last-resort weapon, comforting to possess but of little everyday use. It also induced Western guilt feelings which, extended to scientists working on the nuclear programme, gave the Soviets a rich crop of traitors. It was clear that the nuclear monopoly would not be eternal.

Well before Potsdam, the Russians had been at pains to scoop up all German high technology and scientists who fell to them and to deny the West access. Hitler had not grasped the destructive potential of nuclear fission. Speer says that 'the idea quite obviously strained his intellectual capacity. He was also unable to grasp the revolutionary nature of nuclear physics ... We scuttled the project to build an atom bomb by the autumn of 1942.'[9] Delivery systems were another matter. The Germans had made vast strides in rocketry from which the Russians as well as the Americans were about to profit. The V1 and V2 rockets which fell on London showed the potential for delivery systems far more sophisticated than manned bombers. When a British and American team returned in September 1944 from a visit to the German missile centre at Blizna in Poland, which had been overrun by the Red army, they discovered that the Russians had filled their crates not with rocket parts but rusting aircraft equipment.[10] The Peenemünde rocket research centre had also fallen to the Red army.*

The Soviet Zone contained much more advanced industry, precision engineering, aircraft, engine and machine-tool plants, than the Western zones with the brute steelmaking and mining of the Ruhr. The Russians actively recruited German scientists to work either in their zone or in the Soviet Union itself. By September 1945 the Americans were noting with alarm the 'growing swell of German scientists moving into the Russian sector'.[11] Among those flown to Moscow were three leading nuclear physicists, Dr G. Hertz, Dr N. Riehl and Baron Manfred von Ardenne.

Where enticement with high wages and comfortable villas failed, the Russians kidnapped.[12] Colonel General I. A. Serov, the Russian com-

---

* Although much of its equipment and senior figures, including Wernher von Braun, had already gone. The Americans also transferred men and equipment from the underground Nordhausen rocket plant, which fell to US troops, before it was merged into the Soviet Zone of Germany. Taken to the US, von Braun and other German rocket scientists became a vital part of the US missile and space programmes.

mandant in Berlin, ordered his senior scientific adviser Serge Tokaev to acquire German experts. If they refused to sign contracts, they would be kidnapped. 'Nobody will interfere with you,' Serov told Tokaev. 'But remember, Comrade Stalin relies on you to produce results.'[13] In Operation *Osvakim*, which began on 22 October 1945, Red army troops sealed off areas of East Berlin. Arrest squads seized about 15,000 scientists and technicians and took them to railway stations on trucks. The first trains left from Berlin for Russia the next morning. The scientists had been given the choice of accepting contracts promising high wages and comfortable conditions in Soviet research centres and plants, or of signing a declaration that read: 'The undersigned herewith declares his unwillingness to assist in the reconstruction of the Soviet Union.' This being a virtual passport to prison, most accepted.[14]

German scientists were more use in delivery systems than in the nuclear field. The Soviet drive for the bomb itself started shortly after the Potsdam conference. One version has Stalin ordering Kurchatov and armaments commissar B. L. Vannikov to 'provide us with atomic weapons in the shortest possible time' at a Kremlin meeting in August 1945. 'You know that Hiroshima has shaken the whole world,' Stalin said. 'The balance has been destroyed. Provide the bomb – it will remove a great danger from us.'

A cipher clerk from the office of the Soviet military attaché in Ottawa defected the following month, revealing that a strong espionage effort was already underway to get Western nuclear secrets. The Russians were aided by Western traitors and by other security lapses, such as the open publication of the 1945 Smythe report which traced the development of the American nuclear programme in all too frank detail. By the end of the year, the US embassy in Moscow was warning Washington that: 'The USSR is out to get the atomic bomb.'[15]

Scientific-Technical Councils had been set up for atomic bomb and rocket development. Vannikov was in charge of the atomic council, with Pervukhin and Kurchatov as his deputies. The NKGB had a department for atomic energy. Overall control of the project was vested in the 'man with the vulture face', the secret police chief Lavrenti Beria. Half of the research for nuclear weapons development took place in prison institutes. The Gulag extended into construction and mining for the project, most of which was done by prison labour.[16] The rocket programme was headed by the armaments overlord and future defence minister, Dimitri Ustinov.

Soviet lack of uranium was a major problem. Shipments of uranium ore from mines in Czechoslovakia and East Germany became a top priority and forced labour extracted it from mines in the Altay and Turkestan regions of Soviet Central Asia. The nuclear project, codenamed *Borodino*, was working as a super-ministry in a 'gigantic conglomeration of mines, plants, proving grounds, airfields, towns and depots, spread over hundreds of square kilometres and kept under special wartime security'.

Stalin gave the impression that the importance of the bomb had been exaggerated. 'Atom bombs are designed to scare those with weak nerves,' he said. 'But they cannot decide wars because there are not enough of them.' He warned that, in any event, 'the monopoly of the bomb will not last'. As relations between the West and the USSR deteriorated over Europe, the US air force drew up plans for *Half Moon,* an operation to bomb twenty Soviet cities.

Lack of intelligence made it difficult to measure Soviet atomic progress. Hindsight shows it to have been badly underestimated. In October 1946 General Leslie Groves, the head of the *Manhattan* project, predicted that it would take the Russians from ten to twenty years to build the bomb 'by normal effort'. He was ignorant of the efforts of slave labour, toiling to build some thirty-two large mining complexes, and the major spying efforts by the NKGB and GRU in Canada, the US and Britain. The information passed on by Klaus Fuchs and other atom spies may have hastened development by a year or two.

The Americans did not know when the Russians would be ready to test. To be certain that the test would be recognized when it came, from 1947 American aircraft flew wearying, constant patrols off the Soviet borders taking air samples for analysis.

The blockade of West Berlin by the Russians, which started on 18 June 1948, was the only full-blown crisis in which the West still enjoyed the nuclear monopoly. With road, rail and river links cut, the city faced starvation. Stalin eventually bowed to the Anglo-American airlift to the city and lifted the blockade on May 1949. Had the blockade degenerated into fighting, the deficit in conventional strength in the face of the Red army would have rapidly forced the West to resort to nuclear weapons. General Lucius Clay, who was responsible for the airlift, said that he 'would not hesitate to use the atomic bomb'. For good measure, he added that he would 'hit Moscow and Leningrad first'.[17]

But time was rapidly running out for the monopoly. As Stalin called off the blockade, the Russians had produced enough plutonium for their first bomb. It was called *Twyka,* or Pumpkin. In September 1949 a US aircraft over the north Pacific sucked in a radioactive air sample. The cloud containing traces of fall-out was tracked to Europe where its radioactivity was confirmed by the RAF.

The Russians had the bomb. Neither Truman, Groves nor the US defense secretary, Louis Johnson, at first believed it. They put the air samples down to an accident in a nuclear laboratory. President Truman simply announced on 23 September that an 'atomic explosion' had taken place in Russia.* The following day Mao Tse-tung proclaimed the People's Republic of China. The Russians themselves first publicly referred to a bomb on 25 September. It had been detonated in Kazakhstan at 4 a.m. on 29 August.

The test was codenamed *Pervaya Molniya,* First Lightning, by the Russians, *Joe-1,* for Stalin, by the West. The US reaction to the loss of monopoly was vigorous. It was decided to press ahead with the hydrogen bomb, which used fusion rather than fission, with a fission bomb triggering the fusion device. Funding was helped by the anger that followed the arrest of Klaus Fuchs in February 1950. A German-born Briton, Fuchs had passed the Russians a mass of information on Western nuclear research. Within a month of his arrest, the Special Committee of the National Security Council had recommended that research on thermonuclear weapons should be given absolute priority.

The cost was prodigious even for the US. The Savannah River plant for producing essential tritium cost $1.5 billion alone, or three quarters of the budget for the whole *Manhattan* A-bomb project.[18]

It was ruinously expensive for the Russians to attempt to close the gap but the system was experienced in coping with the massive distortions of military spending. Andrei Sakharov, the dissident physicist who was the father of the Soviet H-bomb, recalled that after 1950 'for the next eighteen years I found myself caught up in the rotation of a special world of military designers and inventors, special institutes, committees and learned councils, pilot plants and proving grounds. Every day I saw the huge material, intellectual and nervous resources of thousands of people being poured into the means of total destruction, a force potentially capable of annihilating all human civilization.'[19]

The Americans maintained their lead. In November 1952 they succeeded in achieving an explosion equivalent to 10 million tons of TNT, though its liquid deuterium fuel had to be cooled to minus 250 degrees Centigrade. The refrigerating equipment brought the weight of the device up to 65 tons. This was not a practicable weapon, though it vaporized the islet of Elugelab in the US Marshall Islands and left a crater fifty-three metres deep and one and a half kilometres wide in the bed of the Pacific. The same month the US tested a deliverable A-bomb with a power of 500,000 tons of TNT, about twenty-five times greater than Trinity.

The Russians were not far behind. On 8 August 1953 Georgy Malen-

* The decision was controversial. As late as October 1949 the General Advisory Committee of the Atomic Energy Commission, chaired by Robert Oppenheimer, had come out against an all-out effort on the grounds of 'the extreme dangers to mankind inherent in the proposal'.

kov[20] told the Supreme Soviet: 'The USA has long since lost its monopoly in the production of atomic bombs. The government deems it necessary to report to the Supreme Soviet that the USA has no monopoly in the production of the hydrogen bomb either.' Four days later patrolling US aircraft took air samples whose radioactivity showed that the Russians had exploded a thermonuclear device. The Russians still claim that they developed the thermonuclear bomb before the US. This is an exaggeration. The US device tested in 1952, though not a deliverable weapon, had a yield of ten megatons compared with a Soviet yield in the *Joe-4* explosion in August 1953 of only 400 kilotons.[21] Nevertheless, as the British scientific adviser Lord Cherwell wrote: 'People do not seem yet to realize that the whole situation has changed now that the Russians appear to know pretty well as much as anyone if not more.'

The US was first with a provenly transportable H-bomb. It was set off at Bikini atoll on 1 March 1954. The yield was almost twice what had been expected. A single aircraft could now carry the equivalent of fifteen million tons of TNT. The Soviet response followed the next year, though its 'superbomb' was considerably less powerful with a yield of 1.6 megatons.[22]

The superpowers now had their superbombs. Brute strength, the destroyer of worlds, had been achieved. Grossness in nuclear weapons has since given way to refinement, in power to weight ratios, in miniaturization, in specialties and above all in the delivery systems. Since the mid 1950s, funding, resources and espionage have swung more to the design, manufacture and control systems of the missiles and their air, sea and land launchers than to the content of their warheads.

Nikita Khrushchev was the prime mover in Soviet missilry.

29

NIKITA: THE ROCKET MAN

Nikita Khrushchev was a squat, earthy, first-generation product of the Revolution. Born to a peasant family in 1894, a shepherd and cowherd until he was fifteen, he was educated in the coal pits of the Donbas: 'a working man's Cambridge, the university of the dispossessed of Russia', he said. Visiting Hollywood in 1959, he said proudly at a reception at 20th Century-Fox: 'I worked in a factory owned by Germans, in coal mines owned by Frenchmen and in chemical plants owned by Belgians – and now I am leader of the great Soviet state.' A strike leader in the coalfields, he joined the Red Guards in the Donets in October 1917. He was an able political commissar with the Red army during the civil war, fighting at Tsaritsyn, present at Denikin's surrender in 1920. He returned to the Donbas in 1922, finding 'famine in the mines ... and even isolated cases of cannibalism'. His first wife died of typhus. Energetic and self-confident, Khrushchev was made political leader of sixteen pits. It was an immense task for semi-illiterates to restart the mines and rebuild a broken community. It was a goal, Khrushchev admitted, 'sometimes requiring sacrificing moral principles as well as material comfort'.[1] The Donbas recovered to pre-war production levels. Khrushchev's reward was a place at the new Industrial Academy in Moscow in 1929. Nadezhda Alliluyeva, Stalin's wife, was a fellow student and became a friend. Khrushchev met Stalin frequently at family dinners. He called this 'the lottery ticket that I drew – the lucky lottery ticket. And this was why I stayed alive when most of my contemporaries ... lost their lives because they were regarded as enemies of the people.'

He became a member of the Central Committee in 1934 when he was thirty-nine. He was soon a senior figure in the Moscow party, working on the crash building of the Moscow Metro. The purges were a second lottery ticket. He survived 1937 Moscow, referring to the victims as 'despicable traitors'. The slaughter in the Ukraine that year was so great, with more than 150,000 party members arrested, that Stalin had to rebuild its leadership. Early in 1938, now a candidate member of the Politburo, Khrushchev was sent to the Ukraine as the new party boss, safely removed from Moscow and proximity to Stalin. Though a political figure, he was frequently at or near the front during the Soviet collapse in the Ukraine and the recovery at Stalingrad and Kursk. He entered Kiev in November 1943 as it was still burning, remaining to oversee the reconstruction of the Ukraine until the end of 1949. He was marked by the suffering he saw in the Ukraine, knowing that it had been inflicted by the Party as well as the Germans. He kept his impulsive side under careful check when he returned to Moscow, moving subtly and with assurance to take the leadership after Stalin's death.

Beria was executed within four months of his master's death, arrested by Marshal Zhukov and General Moskalenko as tanks squatted at key road junctions in Moscow. But the survivors had no desire for changes in the hierarchy to be marked by death or imprisonment. They have succeeded in this, at least at the top level.[2] Khrushchev eased out Malenkov as premier in 1955, without having recourse to a Lubianka-induced confession and trial. When he took over the premiership himself in 1957 his opponents found themselves in minor posts, but alive, Molotov as ambassador to Mongolia, Malenkov as director of a Siberian power station.

A major rising in the Gulag had been recorded under Stalin. A group of Red army officers, all graduates of the Frunze academy who had fought against the Germans, killed their guards in a camp near Vorkuta in the Arctic in 1948. Paratroops and dive bombers were used to halt their march on the town. The deaths of Stalin and Beria gave the *zeks* some hope and led to waves of revolt in camps in the Arctic, northern Siberia and Kazakhstan. Armoured troop carriers were needed to suppress a rebellion at the Kapitalnaya mine in Siberia and several hundred *zeks* were killed. Tanks were called in to a coal-mining camp outside Vokuta in July 1953. Women prisoners from the Ukraine linked hands and walked towards them. 'The tanks only accelerated,' claimed the eyewitness report. 'They drove straight over the live bodies. There were no cries. All we heard was a horrible sound of bodies being crushed and cracking bones. Meanwhile soldiers went round the barracks shooting down everything they came across.'[3]

It was feared that the *zeks*, many of them former Red army men and partisans, might succeed in taking over a complex of camps. There was a gradual relaxation of terror. By the end of 1955 about ten thousand *zeks* had been freed and some of the dead were rehabilitated. The security police were downgraded, separated from the MVD and renamed the KGB, for the Committee of State Security. A special commission was set up under a Central Committee secretary, Pospelov, to look into Stalinist illegalities.

Khrushchev read his speech on Stalinism, titled 'On the Cult of Personality and its Consequences', to a closed session of the 20th Party Congress in Moscow on the morning of 25 February 1956. It is known as the 'secret speech' and remains unpublished under Gorbachev. Its dramatic content was, however, known virtually at once in both the West and the Soviet bloc. In Stalin's homeland of Georgia, indeed, pro-Stalin riots were put down by troops.[4] Khrushchev savaged every stage of Stalin's career. He spoke of Lenin's belated mistrust of Stalin. He hinted that Stalin had been involved in the murder of Kirov – 'it is an unusually suspicious circumstance that when the Chekist assigned to protect Kirov was being brought for an interrogation ... he was killed in a "car accident" in which no other occupants of the car were harmed.' He detailed the killings and arrests of senior party figures. Stalin was blamed for the early disasters of *Barbarossa*, which 'followed Stalin's annihilation of many military commanders and political workers ... because of his suspiciousness and through slanderous accusations'. Khrushchev said that it was only Stalin's death that had prevented a fresh series of purges. The speech was partly self-interested. The party hierarchy, which Stalin had devastated, had yet more reason than the common citizen to end terror. Though Khrushchev's own claim to be 'amazed' at the Pospelov revelations was exaggerated, he was less intimately involved with Stalinism than rivals like Molotov and Malenkov, and stood to gain from the revulsion created by his speech. But he was also an emotional man, with a streak of idealism, and the closing of camps and the release of millions of *zeks* was an act of fundamental humanity.

It was met by an outpouring of poetry and literature within Russia, some of which was later banned and remains so under *glasnost*, and by revolt in Eastern Europe. As seen immediately in Budapest, liberalizing a communist regime is an intensely risky enterprise.

Khrushchev tampered compulsively with the Soviet economy. His failures put back serious efforts at reform to Gorbachev. Agriculture was the most spectacular disaster. In 1957 Khrushchev announced that the Soviet Union would overtake the US in the production of meat, milk and butter within four years. By then production from the 'Virgin Lands', the previously untilled steppelands of Kazakhstan and western Siberia, had already peaked. The natural fertility of the soil was exhausted. Once ploughed, it was subject to dust storms which ruined four million hectares of land in Kazakhstan. Khrushchev was unable to rid himself of the ingrained Stalinist habit of setting absurd production targets. The local party secretary in Ryazan, A. N. Larionov, vowed that he would triple meat production in two years. He did so by slaughtering dairy cattle and buying in meat from other districts. In 1959 Larionov was made a Hero of Socialist Labour. The following year, meatless, he shot himself.

The drawbacks of central planning were also obvious in Khrushchev's passion for maize, which brought him the nickname *kukuruznik*, the maize freak. He developed a passion for the Iowa maize fields on his US tour in 1959. Within three years, thirty-seven million hectares of maize had been planted on his orders. Only seven million could be harvested ripe. Hay yields dropped, setting off a chain reaction so serious that meat and dairy prices had to be increased by a third in 1962. Troops had to be called in to put down the resulting food riots in Novocherkassk, where angry workers tore up the Moscow–Rostov railway line and yelled: 'Cut up Khrushchev for Sausages!' A combination of a dry summer and the maize and Virgin Lands fiascos forced Khrushchev into a humiliating purchase of grain on the international market in 1963.

In industry, Khrushchev spoke frequently of switching emphasis to consumer-oriented light industry from the heavy and defence industries, which he said 'have now developed an appetite for giving the country as much metal as possible'. In fact, the increased funding was slight. Troop numbers were cut back hard from 1955. This had little connection with any favours done to light industry. Throughout the demobilizations,

Khrushchev was pushing through an ambitious missile and modernization programme that produced an actual increase in the defence budget. The troop cuts, which anyway reflected a drop in the wartime birthrate, were a way of reducing manpower costs and so freeing funds for nuclear weapons development.

A report on the economy in 1965, after Khrushchev's fall, remains depressingly familiar for Gorbachev. Abel Aganbegyan, the director of the Novosibirsk institute, found that the growth rate was declining, and agriculture, housing and services were backward. The economy suffered from 'extreme centralization and lack of democracy'. The lack of information and data-processing equipment was chronic. The statistical office 'does not have a single computer and is not planning to acquire one'. Secrecy was rife. 'We obtain many figures from American journals sooner than they are released by the Central Statistical Office,' he complained.

The root cause was seen in the huge commitment to defence, which was thought to employ between 30 and 40 million people out of a working population of 100 million. Khrushchev had an absolute belief in missiles. The military did not like the cuts in conventional forces, nor the pride of place given to rocket forces. In December 1963, the month that Khrushchev called for further troop reductions, Marshal Chuikov claimed that Nato was building up new ground forces. The C-in-C of Soviet Ground Forces said that Western military leaders had abandoned 'one-sided theories' and saw that 'in a future war they will not be able to get along without mass missiles'.[5] Chuikov got his comeuppance in September 1964, when his post was abolished and ground forces were directly subordinated to the ministry of defence.

By then, Khrushchev was himself in deep trouble. He was brought back from a holiday in the Crimea on 14 October 1964 to a plenum of the Central Committee. He was accused of indulging a personality cult, of imprudent foreign policy and of trying to be a specialist in every sphere. Friendless, his good wartime relations with the army spent, he was voted out on grounds of 'advanced age and poor health'. Within a few months Rotmistrov, the veteran of Stalingrad and Marshal of Tank Forces, was openly ridiculing 'one-variant war' and the new defence minister Marshal Grechko was holding large-scale manoeuvres to test the Red army's non-nuclear capability. Apart from a brief mention of his death in 1971, Khrushchev became a non-person under his successor Leonid Brezhnev and was not heard of publicly again until the Gorbachev era.[6]

His efforts and failures remain a key to modern Russia. He made the last full pre-Gorbachev effort to reform the economy. It foundered, as Gorbachev is faltering, on the immovability of the beast and the burden it bears from defence expenditure. He invented missile diplomacy, a game now played with infinitely more sophistication than he brought to Cuba.

In doing so, he provoked a new nuclear arms race which extended through Brezhnev's long and sleepy tenure. The Chinese split first appeared in the communist monolith, and in Hungary he had need of that older weapon, the tank, to suppress the first yawning crack in the moral edifice of the Soviet bloc.

Instinctively, he was a rocket man.

The Russians were early convinced of the importance of rockets. The Reaction Research Institute had been established by Tukhachevsky in 1933, although it suffered badly after his death in the purge. The solid-fuel *Katyushas* had proved their worth in the war. The Americans remained devoted to the manned bomber. Dr Vannevar Bush, Roosevelt's scientific adviser, described ballistic missiles as impractical, inaccurate and expensive in an influential book published in 1949. The US had cut back on its ballistic missile programme.

Intelligence reports of a German-based rocket being fired on a Kazakh-stan test range were received as early as October 1947. This was the R-1, a development of the German V-2. A Council of Chief Designers was created to manage the Russian rocket effort that year. It was chaired by S. P. Korolev, later to design the first Soviet ICBM.[7] Other major figures were V. P. Glushko, whose design bureau developed liquid-propellant rocket engines for most of the strategic missiles, A. M. Isaev, the chief designer of a rocket engine bureau and A. N. Pilyugin, a control systems specialist.[8] By 1955 the Americans were receiving consistent reports of major advances in Russian missile programmes. In December of that year a second Soviet H-bomb was exploded at great height and physicists and mathematicians, including Sakharov, I. Tamm and B. Khariton, were honoured by election to the Academy of Sciences. In the summer of 1957 there were frequent reports in the Soviet press of the testing of A- and H-bombs and of ICBMs. The first Soviet cyclotron was completed the same year and the first nuclear-powered ship, the icebreaker *Lenin*, was launched.

On 4 October 1957 the world's first satellite was launched and the word *Sputnik* coined. The sophistication of Soviet missiles was proven.[9] A month later, to rub in this lead, a satellite with an animal aboard was launched. Test launches of ICBMs accelerated, expanding the Soviet threat beyond Europe and projecting it to the continental US. The Americans were unable to respond with a satellite launch until 1 February 1958. The first American ICBM, the 25,750-k.p.h., 8,000-kilometre-range Atlas, was launched in December 1957.

A series of papers, known as the Special Collection,[10] was produced in 1958 on the impact of nuclear-tipped rockets on military science. The chilling conclusion was that 'a future war will begin with a sudden nuclear strike against the enemy. There will be no declaration of war.'

The Strategic Rocket Forces, SRF,[11] the cream of the cream, outranking all the other services, were formed to use the new weaponry in 1959. An artilleryman, Chief Marshal of Artillery M. I. Nedelin, became the first C-in-C of the SRF. The first men came from Guards *Katyusha* units. Nedelin took precedence over the commanders of the other four services. The SRF remain 'the youngest and most formidable of our Armed Forces and compose the basis of the defensive might of our Motherland and are troops of instant combat readiness'.

Nedelin was killed the following year when a new booster exploded on launch at the Tura Tam missile range. Up to 300 officers and scientists died with him in what was officially described as an 'aircraft accident'. This secrecy extends down to uniforms. SRF officers and men wear the same gorget and arms patches as army artillerymen or the SAM crews of air defence. The satellite launches sent the prestige of the SRF soaring. In 1959 *Lunik II* succeeded in landing on the moon. *Lunik III*, launched shortly after, took the first pictures of the dark side of the moon.

Khrushchev was characteristically blunt when he outlined the new military philosophy in 1960.[12] A deep rocket strike would replace land invasion as the first act in war and 'not a single capital, no large industrial or administrative centre and no strategic area will remain unattacked in the very first minutes, let alone days, of the war'. If the Soviet Union was attacked, he boasted, it 'will wipe the country or countries attacking us off the face of the earth'.

This was not good news for the Red army, for Khrushchev concluded that nuclear weapons made huge infantry and tank armies redundant. It no longer mattered 'how many people are wearing soldiers' greatcoats'. The size of the army would be slashed.[13] In fact, the horrors of the war and its crippling effect on the birth rate had worked its way through to the pool of military-age males. Where the Soviet Union had 6.9 million males aged between 18 and 21 in 1959, this fell to a low of 3.1 million in 1964, slowly recovering to 4.6 million by 1967. Even so, the depth of Khrushchev's cuts shocked the army. Between 1955 and 1964 armed forces strength was slashed from 5.7 million to 2.6 million. More than a quarter of a million officers were returned to civilian life, most before they had completed the twenty-five years service needed for an adequate pension. In his enthusiasm for rocketry, Khrushchev also cut army pay and privileges. 'The number of troops and rifles is no longer decisive,' he wrote.[14] 'Now the important thing is the quality and quantity of our nuclear missile arsenal ... Our potential enemy – our principal, our most powerful, our most dangerous enemy – was so far away from us that we couldn't have reached him with our air force. Only by building up a nuclear missile force could we keep the enemy from unleashing war against us.'

His enthusiasm was understandable. The peasant state had stolen a clear lead on the American industrial titan. In May 1960 a Soviet spacecraft weighing 4.5 tonnes had orbited the earth. Three months later another spacecraft with two dogs aboard showed that safe return from orbit was possible. The head of the space research and development bureau, S. P. Korolev, told Khrushchev that manned spaceflight was feasible. On 12 April 1961 Yuri Gagarin[15] was strapped into a spacecraft atop a missile rocket. 'The command was given: "Blast off!" – and we heard the voice of our comrade shouting, "We're away!",' wrote Gagarin's understudy for the launch, Herman Titov. 'It was seven minutes past nine, Moscow time. Into the sky roared the first piloted spaceship, *Vostok*, with the first Soviet cosmonaut on board.' There was another new word to add to the universal vocabulary, *cosmonaut*.

On 14 April Gagarin returned from Central Asia to a Moscow triumph. Khrushchev met him at the airport and drove back with him to Red Square in an open car. There were some omissions from those who oversaw the parade from the tribune of the Lenin Mausoleum. None of the men who had designed and built the rocket and its spacecraft was present. The obsessive Soviet secrecy was maintained in the hour of triumph.[16]

The triumph was shortlived, however. Khrushchev gave priority to SS-4 medium range and SS-5 intermediate-range missiles. Almost 750 of these were deployed between 1959 and 1965. Effective enough in Europe, they did not have the legs to get to the US unless launched from Cuba. Only four of the intercontinental SS-6s were in service. The deployment of the next generation of ICBMs, the SS-7 and SS-8, was scarcely under way. The Americans had developed a major lead in long-range strategic weapons. The first nuclear-powered submarine, the USS *Nautilus*, had begun trials in 1954. The first test of a Polaris missile fired from a submerged submarine, the USS *George Washington*, followed in July 1960. The first Polaris could attack any target in the Soviet Union with the exception of a central area round Omsk. Polaris A2 had a range of 1,700 nautical miles. Nowhere on the planet is further from the sea than that. By the mid 1960s Polaris A3 with a 2,500-nautical-mile range was operational together with new Minutemen ICBMs. In 1964 the US had 1,880 strategic delivery units compared with 472 on the Russian side.[17]

The 1960s were the period of maximum danger of nuclear war, with the Cuba crisis the apex. The Russians were convinced that any war would be nuclear from the outset and that they would win it. 'It will lead to the deaths of hundreds of millions of people and whole countries will be turned into lifeless deserts,' said the defence minister, Marshal Malinovsky.[18] 'The Socialist camp will win and capitalism will be destroyed forever.' Khrushchev said that: 'We're satisfied to be able to wipe out the United States the first time around.'[19] The danger lay in the fact that that was all he was able to do. Weakness of logistics, of ships and transport aircraft, so humiliatingly revealed during the Cuba crisis, meant that Soviet global reach was restricted to nuclear missiles.

The failure to deploy the medium-range SS-4 in Cuba led Brezhnev to a major effort to catch up with US intercontinental forces. Between 1966 and 1969 the Russian ICBM force grew by about 300 new silo launchers a year, mainly the heavy SS-9 with a 20-megaton warhead and the SS-11 with a 2-megaton strike power. By 1969 the Russians had achieved a slight lead in ICBMs. An overall lead in total numbers followed in 1972 and by 1974 the Russians had reached parity in submarine-launched SLBMs to add to their ICBM lead. This made it clear that the Russians were not content with a MAD philosophy of 'mutually assured destruction' with the US but were striving for parity at the least.[20]

Khrushchev's departure in 1964 had little immediate impact on a situation which heeded only out-and-out missile conflict. Future war was treated almost with relish by military publications. 'It will be the decisive clash of two opposing sociopolitical systems,' said one in 1966.[21] 'The basic contradiction of the modern world will be decided in it, the contradiction between socialism and imperialism . . .'

At the end of the decade the first grudging admission was made that conventional weapons might be used 'in individual instances'. Nato's fresh policy of 'flexible response' had shown that the West was thinking in terms of conflict control. 'The main and decisive means of waging the conflict will be the nuclear rocket weapon,' the new Defence Minister Marshal A. A. Grechko wrote in 1970. 'In it, the "classical" types of armaments will also find use. In certain circumstances, the possibility is admitted of conducting combat actions with conventional weapons.'[22]

This post-Khrushchev switch was not the result of conciliation or détente. Under Stalin, the huge Russian edge in conventional force in Europe had been offset by the US nuclear lead. The rocketry and nuclear advances of the 1960s gave parity in the outright destruction business. The expansion of Soviet air and sea lift capacity under Brezhnev was now providing a new attraction to conventional capacity. It was no longer limited to Europe. Not that the rocket men have been downgraded. Like their predecessors in the Tsarist artillery, they remain the elite of Gorbachev's Russia. Their 'rocket academy', the Dzerzhinsky Military Academy,[23] is close to Red Square in Moscow. This arcane temple of MIRVs and throw-weights enjoys the closest physical proximity to the Kremlin of any force.

It was in Cuba that they made their deepest impression.

IN UNCLE SAM'S BACKYARD:
CRISIS IN CUBA

On 17 April 1961, Khrushchev's sixty-seventh birthday, American-backed Cuban exiles landed at Bahia de Cochinos, the Bay of Pigs, on the southern side of the island near the port of Cienfuegos. They were poorly armed, lacking proper air support and anti-tank weapons. Only 1,500 strong, without reinforcements, they needed to move swiftly from their beachhead but were forced into the swamps of the Zapata peninsula. There they were killed or captured.

It was a disaster for President Kennedy. Khrushchev's attempt to exploit it, however, was equally misjudged and hugely more dangerous. It brought the world to the edge of thermonuclear war.

The Bay of Pigs reinforced Khrushchev's view that the Americans were 'too liberal to fight'. Instead of using their strength to crush Cuba, the Americans had merely connived at the dispatch of a doomed group of émigrés. When the Russian position in Hungary had been threatened eight years before, Khrushchev had ordered in tanks. Meddling in Cuba without being determined enough to finish Castro off seemed an invitation to blackmail. US missiles in Turkey, which General Maxwell Taylor, chairman of the Joint Chiefs of Staff, later called a 'pistol pointed at the head' of the Soviet Union, suggested a means.

Khrushchev sent Kennedy two notes after the abortive invasion. The first warned that Cuba could count on Soviet support in 'beating back' any armed attack. The other suggested that bygones would soon be bygones: 'Our government does not seek any advantages or privileges in Cuba. We do not have any bases in Cuba and we do not intend to establish any.' The Soviets had been cautious of the new Castro regime. Raúl Castro, Fidel's brother, was considered a 'good Communist' along with Che Guevara and 'some of the others'. They were not sure of Castro himself.

Limited arms deliveries were made and Khrushchev noted that Castro was 'beginning to behave like a full-fledged Communist even though he didn't call himself one'. Moscow began shipping oil to Cuba to compensate for the US embargo. The Russians, still with a small merchant fleet, had to order tankers from Italian yards. Krushchev noted with glee that 'if a capitalist country sees a chance to make some extra money from trade with a Communist country, it couldn't care less about economic solidarity'.

The Bay of Pigs encouraged the relationship. 'After Castro's crushing victory over the counter-revolutionaries, we intensified our military aid to Cuba,' Khrushchev noted.[1] 'We gave them as many arms as the Cuban army could absorb.' At first, these were conventional: tanks, artillery and some fighters. More than a year after the émigré invasion, Castro's brother Raúl, the Cuban defence minister, made an unexplained visit to Moscow. The same month, July 1962, US navy reconnaissance aircraft tracked Russian merchantmen steaming for Cuba in significant numbers. They docked at Mariel,[2] a port on the north coast of Pinar del Rio province. CIA intelligence showed that Russians were unloading the cargoes and guarding the docks. A State Department briefing on 24 August 1962 claimed that 20 Soviet-bloc ships had arrived in Cuba in the past month, together with between 3,000 and 5,000 military technicians. These were thought to be surface-to-air missile specialists, a view apparently confirmed when a U-2 spy aircraft photographed SAM sites.

No Soviet comment was made until 2 September. Che Guevara, the Argentine-born symbol of revolutionary chic who was later killed on a guerrilla mission in Bolivia, was in Moscow. It was explained that he had come to ask for armaments and 'specialists for training Cuban servicemen'. Kennedy was concerned, although the U-2s had turned up nothing more than SAMs whose forty-kilometres slant range could propel them less than a quarter of the distance to Key West, let alone Florida proper. He asked for and got congressional permission to call up 150,000 reservists.

On 14 October a U-2 returned from a mission[3] with worrying evidence. Flying over the San Cristóbal region of Cuba, the U-2 took photographs that corresponded in detail to medium-range missile sites in the Soviet Union. No missiles were in place, but the Americans had already noted that two of the Russian freighters, the Japanese-built *Poltava* and the *Omsk*, were lumber-trade ships with wide hatches. They rode oddly high in the water for ships that had supposedly carried bulk cargo across the Atlantic. Missiles, eighteen metres long, relatively light and capable of being stowed below deck, were one explanation. A nuclear crisis was developing at a gallop.

The Americans were still in shock from the humiliating failure of the invasion. Defense Secretary Robert McNamara said: 'We were hysterical about Castro at the time of the Bay of Pigs and thereafter.' A senior Kennedy aide, Chester Bowles, thought that a decision to bomb or land troops in Cuba would have been supported by 90 per cent of Americans. Weird plots were discussed. Thallium salts would be used to make Castro's beard fall out. His cigars would be soaked with hallucinatory drugs. His mistress would be given poison capsules. His wetsuit would be impregnated with skin fungus and a tuberculous bacillus. Explosive would be planted in a seashell where he swam.[4]

Khrushchev's ambitions were more pragmatic though a wildness also lurked in the cheapness of his intent. Despite the Sputnik and space programme, the Soviet Union had become increasingly vulnerable to US strategic forces. The Americans had overwhelming superiority in ICBMs, submarine-launched missiles and long-range bombers. The Russian strength in intermediate and medium-range missiles could not be brought to bear on the US from sites in the Soviet Union or Eastern Europe. Freight these missiles to Cuba, leapfrog Nato defences in Europe, and Soviet strikepower against the US would be doubled at minimal cost. It was an irresistible scenario if Kennedy's weakness proved real enough and the US became frozen by fear of the two-minute warning time involved in Cuban-based missiles.

Kennedy established an Executive Committee, the Excom, to deal with the situation. He had his confirmation of Russian intent by 17 October. Missiles were going into Cuba, 1,600-kilometres-range mobiles and fixed-position 3,200-kilometre weapons that could range as far as Montana. Unprotected by silos, they were first-strike weapons. With the American lead in warheads and systems, Khrushchev was running an enormous risk.

As Khrushchev half admitted, he fell for the temptation to teach the Americans a lesson, to give them 'a little of their own medicine'. He wrote that the US had surrounded the Soviet Union with military bases and nuclear weapons. 'It was high time America learned what it feels like to have her own land and her own people threatened.' This desire may be petty but it is strong and constant. The Americans are felt to be shallow and insolent because they have not suffered enough. Go to the Soviet Union and it is a theme that cannot be shaken off. It is a potentially lethal mix of self-pity, pride and moral superiority: 'We know what suffering is. Everything we have, we have died for. Doesn't the world understand that?[5] The Americans got their place in the world on the cheap. We are still paying for ours. What you pay for, you get. That's one capitalist lesson we'll be delighted to teach them.' Khrushchev poured this bitter cocktail into Cuba.

'We Russians have suffered three wars over the last half century,' he wrote. 'World War I, the Civil War and World War II. America has never had to fight a war on her soil, at least not in the past fifty years. She's sent troops abroad to fight in the two World Wars – and made a fortune as a result.' He thought that lack of suffering in the American soul would translate into military softness. 'I knew that the United States could knock out some of our installations,' he went on. 'But not all of them. If a quarter or even a tenth of our missiles survived – even if only one or two big ones were left – we could still hit New York, and there wouldn't be much of New York left.'

Apart from that, he thought he wouldn't be found out until it was too late. 'My thinking went like this. If we installed the missiles secretly and then if the United States discovered the missiles were there after they were already poised and ready to strike, the Americans would think twice before trying to liquidate our installations by military means.' Andrei Gromyko, the Soviet foreign minister, was still banking on US ignorance when Kennedy saw him in Washington on 18 October. The Russian assured the president that only defensive weapons and short-range SAMs* had been shipped to Cuba. In fact, 42 missiles with a 1,600-kilometre-plus range and 24 with a range of 3,200 kilometres had been sent or were on freighters heading for Cuba. The Americans knew they had been lied to.†

Kennedy left Washington to campaign for congressional elections in Illinois. He held his tongue until 22 October when he revealed the offensive build-up in Cuba on television. He warned that the US would 'regard any nuclear missile launched from Cuba against any nation in the Western hemisphere as an attack by the Soviet Union on the United States requiring a full retaliatory response upon the Soviet Union'. He announced a naval blockade of the island. This he referred to as a 'quarantine'. That under-played the virulence of the virus loose in the Caribbean. Dean Rusk briefed non-aligned ambassadors: 'I would not be candid ... if I did not say that we are in as grave a crisis as mankind has been in.'[6]

The Defense Secretary, Robert McNamara, was wholly specific at a briefing he gave to Pentagon correspondents on 22 October. Russian skippers who stopped when challenged would be boarded. Ships without offensive weapons aboard could sail on, those with could go anywhere other than a port of Cuba. 'If the captain refuses to change his course,' said McNamara, 'we will use force.'

During the day, women and children were evacuated by air from the US base at Guantánamo in Cuba. B-47 bombers were diverted to civilian airports and fifty-five B-52s were readied for immediate takeoff from their dispersal positions. A further ninety B-52s were airborne over the Atlantic with nuclear payloads. Nuclear warheads were readied on 103 Atlas and 54 Titan rockets. All forces were at Defcon-2, a Red Alert one step below war itself,[7] and 156 ICBMs were readied for launch. The Americans were prepared to go to war. They had successes in the propaganda battle. The

---

* Surface to air missiles. SS are surface to surface missiles. SLBMs are submarine-launched ballistic missiles. IRBMs and MRBMs are intermediate and medium range missiles.

† In his 1988 Memoirs, Gromyko denies that he misled Kennedy. 'In spite of several allegations circulating in the West,' he claims, 'not once in the whole conversation did Kennedy raise the question of the presence of Soviet missiles in Cuba. Consequently, I did not have to answer whether or not there were such weapons in Cuba.' If they did not discuss missiles, it is difficult to see what Kennedy and the notoriously short-spoken Gromyko did talk about. The price of cigars perhaps.

Organization of American States voted nineteen to nil in favour of the blockade.[8] In Western Europe, Nato remained solid. In Cuba, Russian technicians continued work on the missile sites by the light of flares.

Dean Rusk sensed a 'considerable victory' on 23 October because he was 'still alive'. Soviet ships were still heading for Cuba, a fact welcomed by one officer at the Soviet embassy in Washington. 'I have fought in three wars already and I am looking forward to fighting in the next,' he said. 'Our ships will sail through. And if it is decreed that those men must die, then they will obey their orders and stay on course or be sunk.'[9] It was not decreed. There were no Soviet counter-moves against Berlin or the US Jupiter missile bases in Turkey, though the Defense Department in Washington was now claiming that the Russians were building eight to ten bases with thirty missiles at sites round four Cuban towns.

Task Force 136, nineteen ships of the US 2nd Fleet, imposed the blockade at 10 a.m. on 24 October. It extended in an arc 800 kilometres from Cape Maisi on the eastern tip of Cuba, beyond the range of Cuban MiGs. The Soviet tanker *Bucharest* was allowed to steam through the blockade at 8 a.m. on 25 October after her skipper declared that she was carrying oil. The East German *Völkerfreund* with a passenger manifest of students followed her thirty-five minutes later.

Russian communications were poor.[10] Ignorance preyed on crisis nerves. Khrushchev admitted to 'intense anxiety' and suggested to other government members that they should go to the Bolshoi theatre. He felt that this would calm 'our own people as well as foreign eyes'. In fact, Muscovites consider a mass descent of a Kremlin posse to the Bolshoi as proof of a crisis. Beria went there the night before his theatre companions had him arrested and shot.[11]

By now, the Russians wanted a settlement. In a bizarre attempt to get the British involved as peacemakers, the Russian naval attaché Captain Ivanov contacted his friend Stephen Ward, an osteopath who subsequently committed suicide after being convicted of living off the immoral earnings of a girl who had received favours from both Ivanov and John Profumo, the British war minister. Through Ward, Ivanov appealed to a Conservative MP for the British government to arrange a summit in London to defuse the situation. The British turned him down.

At 7 a.m. on 26 October 290 kilometres north-east of Nassau, the US destroyer *Joseph P. Kennedy* hailed the freighter *Marucla*. The destroyer ran up an Oscar November flag, signalling: 'You should heave to. Stop at once.' On a Soviet charter from the Baltic port of Riga, the Panamanian-registered, Lebanese-owned ship complied. Kennedy ordered overflights of the missile sites to be made at 200 metres every two hours. An impression was being made on Khrushchev. On 25 October he accused Kennedy of piracy and of 'recklessly playing with nuclear fire'. On the 26th this gave way to an offer to trade the Soviet missiles against a US pledge not to invade Cuba.

The next day, a Saturday, was the most dangerous. 'I can recall leaving the White House that night,' McNamara said,[12] 'walking through the gardens of the White House to my car to drive back to the Pentagon and wondering if I'd ever see another Saturday night.'

At 10.05 that morning, Major Rudolf Anderson Jr, who had brought back the first pictures of the missile sites, was shot down in his U-2 on another sortie over Cuba. The SAMs were operational, increasing the danger of keeping surveillance on the missiles and of destroying them. Radio Moscow broadcast that the Americans would have to remove their Jupiter missiles from Turkey if they wanted the Russians to follow suit in Cuba: 'You say Cuba worries you because it is a distance of 90 miles by sea from the coast and America. But Turkey is next to us. Our sentries walk up and down and look at each other.'

President Kennedy approved plans for air strikes on the SAM and missile sites to take place on Monday. 'We were ready to go in forty-eight hours,' said McNamara. 'If pressed we could have done it in thirty.'

The Joint Chiefs of Staff warned that at least one of the twenty missiles already operational on the island would survive the strike to retaliate on the US east coast. Casualties from a single missile were estimated at one to two million. McNamara told a meeting of Excom that 'invasion had become almost inevitable. If we leave US missiles in Turkey, the Soviets might attack Turkey. If the Soviets do attack the Turks, we must respond in the Nato area.' Under the Nato treaty, the executive director of the National Security Council said, an attack on Turkey would have led to 'general war'.[13] The Russians were made aware that 144 Polaris, 103 Atlas, 105 Thor and Jupiter, and 54 Titan missiles, plus 600 IRBMs, 250 MRBMs, 1,600 long-range bombers and 37 aircraft carriers were 'ready to convert the USSR into a radioactive heap of rubbish within thirty minutes'.[14]

Krushchev had miscalculated and his bluff was called. 'Cuba was 11,000 kilometres from the Soviet Union,' he admitted. 'Our sea and air communications were so precarious that an attack against the United States was unthinkable.' The long letter he sent to Kennedy, which had arrived the evening before by telex from the US embassy in Moscow, showed signs of alarm and a desire to be let off the hook. He would accept the removal of the missiles in return for an American pledge not to invade Cuba. A second message proposed that the Americans should remove their Jupiters from Turkey.

Kennedy responded by ordering that the fifteen Jupiters in Turkey, which could penetrate 2,400 kilometres inside the Soviet Union, should be disarmed immediately. There was to be no retaliation for the shot-down U-2. He also authorized his brother Robert to assure the Russians, through their Washington ambassador, that the Jupiters would go from Turkey if the Cuban missiles were withdrawn. The removal of the Jupiters, which in any event were obsolescent, was to be kept secret. A decision had to be made the next day.

At 9 a.m. on Sunday 28 October Radio Moscow broadcast Khrushchev's reply: 'Orders for the dismantling of the weapons you describe as "offensive", their crating and return to the Soviet Union' had been given 'in order to liquidate with greater speed the dangerous conflict . . . and to calm the people of America.' At midday the Voice of America broadcast Kennedy's acceptance. 'We looked into the mouth of the cannon,' Dean Rusk commented. 'The Russians flinched.' When Castro, who had not been consulted, got the news, he swore in his anger and smashed a mirror. He should perhaps have been grateful that Khrushchev had not abandoned him. The Kremlin was on the rack and another turn of the screw might have achieved a neutral and disarmed island.

Khrushchev claimed that it was Kennedy who had 'given in'. Though he admitted that some thought he 'had turned coward and backed down', he said that it was a 'great victory for us that we had been able to extract from Kennedy a promise that neither America nor any of her allies would invade Cuba'. The Politburo appears not to have agreed. When he was toppled in October 1964, the Soviet Presidium spoke of his 'harebrained schemes, hasty conclusions, rash decisions and actions based on wishful thinking'.[15]

If the Soviets backed down in the backyard of the *glavni vrag*, the 'main enemy', there has never been question of them doing so in their own.

Invasions

The Four Seasons

———◆———

HUNGARIAN AUTUMN

Repression, backed where necessary by invasion, has remained the touchstone of Soviet policy in the *glacis* countries of East and Central Europe. The first revolt, in Hungary, haunts the Gorbachev Kremlin. It was a 'flash that illuminated reality', as Lenin said of Kronstadt. Budapest remains a warning that a greater storm may be lurking out in history, feeding on Russophobia and anti-communism, waiting for the right meteorological conditions to build afresh.

After his triumph in 1948 Rákosi followed Stalin as a role model with particular intensity. As Yagoda and Yezhov had been purged, so Rákosi took care to break the craftsman of his own police state, the interior minister Laszlo Rajk. Rajk, who was replaced by Janos Kadar, was executed on 15 October 1949. Rákosi's idolatry of Stalin was thoroughgoing. A bronzed booted statue of the Soviet leader dominated Budapest. The army was Russified. The first Soviet advisers had arrived in November 1948 and by 1951 Hungarians were dressed in Red army uniforms and were subject to Soviet drill and regulations.

There was a brief thaw after Stalin's death in 1953. Rákosi was replaced in June 1953 by Imre Nagy, a man with impeccable communist credentials but with little Stalinism in his soul. He had been taken prisoner by the Russians in the First World War in his late teens and, remaining in Russia until 1921, had joined the Russian Communist Party in 1918. Jovial and cheerful, he was a rarity, a minister who could be seen in Budapest coffee houses discussing politics and the brilliant Hungarian football team. Nagy was a tolerant enough Communist to let his daughter marry a practising Protestant minister, and he announced a more liberal New Course in July 1953. By the spring of 1955, Rákosi was back in power and the relaxation was over.

The *Allamvedelmi Hatósag*, the AVH secret police, were considered a more reliable and efficient means of repression than the still suspect army. Between 1952 and 1955, despite the thaw, 516,708 Hungarians had been sentenced to prison terms, mainly on AHV testimony.[1] Most, Nagy complained, 'are industrial workers'. Active resentment of Communism was working-class. Living standards, under a Worker's Party, were grim. The average space per inhabitant was less than a railway compartment.

Into this volatile mix of repression and deprivation was tossed Khrushchev's speech to the 20th Party Congress. Rákosi was in Moscow on 16 February 1956 to hear it, and was said 'to have listened in a daze'. He had reason. Stalin, Khrushchev said, had 'abandoned the method of ideological struggle for that of administrative violence, mass repression and terror'. Whoever had opposed Stalin was 'doomed to moral and physical annihilation' including 'many honest Communists'. Change Stalin to Rákosi, and the Hungarian was listening to his own biography.

Rákosi was considered Stalin's apprentice and the disgrace of his master was noted in Budapest. Tension was fanned by the country's traditional Russophobia and by hatred of the *funkcionariusoks*, the party functionaries. 'We thought of the funkies as Quislings,' says a refugee, Imre Peter. 'They lived in villas, where we slummed in a room off a dark stairwell. We were sallow from turnip soup and they looked rosy even in the winter. We froze in greasy jackets and they had leather overcoats. And the Russians owned them, and through them and their files and their prisons, us.'

The Yugoslav ambassador was reporting back to Belgrade by April 1956 that there could be a revolution if Rákosi did not go. Memories of less bitter days under Nagy were strong. The Russian reaction appeared conciliatory. Khrushchev was looking for better relations with the West and reconciliation with Tito. Rákosi was flown from a military airfield to Moscow in July for treatment for 'high blood pressure'. Ernö Gerö, once the NKVD chief in Barcelona,[2] replaced him as general secretary. Gerö, humourless, working an eighteen-hour day, the 'communist Savanarola', was loved little more than Rákosi.

The disgraced Nagy was rehabilitated and reinstated as a Budapest university professor. Such gentilesse came too late for Rajk, but he was exhumed from a prison ditch and given a macabre funeral. Nine generals hanged after his trial were also dug up and reburied. The ceremony was broadcast live on Hungarian radio on 6 October. The first unofficial demonstration in communist Hungary took place that day. Students began openly to demand the withdrawal of Soviet troops. Three Red army divisions were stationed in Hungary under the Warsaw Pact.

On 18 October Soviet garrison troops and the AVH were put on alert. The following day a Kremlin delegation of the highest level – Khrushchev, Molotov, Kaganovich, Mikoyan and thirteen Soviet generals – flew to Warsaw. Unrest in Poland was also causing grave concern to the Russians. The fact that Ladislas Gomulka, the new, soft-line Polish leader, survived this visit made a considerable and cheerful impression in Hungary. The Kremlin appeared to be losing its nerve.

On the most sensitive ground, demonstrators demanded a public trial of Mihaly Farkas, the hard-liner who had introduced political commissars as the first defence minister of the People's Army, plus the Russian recognition of Hungarian independence and the withdrawal of Soviet troops. All three were gut blows at Moscow. The denigration of the Party was implicit in any bringing to book of Farkas. Formal recognition of Hungarian independence would have instant repercussions on the credibility of the Warsaw Pact. The removal of the Red army would liquidate the only real force that could prevent the first two.

Face was not important. The Soviets have an acute instinct for the realities of power and do not hesitate to scrap its trappings. They were prepared to see, and to be seen to be urging, the removal of local *funkies*. The reinstatement of Nagy was acceptable. Had not Rajk been dug up from his grave and made respectable again? In reverse manner, Khrushchev would later dig up Stalin from his place of honour in Red Square and re-inter him in unconsecrated ground. Liberalizing a failing economy was acceptable. So was penal reform, when *zeks* by the tens of thousands were being rehabilitated in the Soviet Union itself.

The sticking point was the Party. Reform could not flow from outside the Party. It must not lose its moral ascendancy. To lose the leadership of history, in Hungary or elsewhere, is to lose all. The Party can accept that it has made mistakes so long as these are isolated and self-contained, a flaw but not a basic design error in the Marxist-Leninist framework of history. But the Hungarians were beginning to compare their 60-hour week with the 45 hours worked in neighbouring Austria for 230 per cent more wages, claiming that the sharp material rise in Austria resulted from the year-old withdrawal of the Red army. This was intolerable.

'The West is seeking to revise the results of the Second World War,' Khrushchev told the Yugoslav ambassador, Veljko Micunovic.[3] 'They have started in Hungary, and they will go on to crush each Socialist state in Europe one by one. But the West has miscalculated.'

The rising started on 23 October 1956, a Tuesday.

Students marched on a clear, early autumn day to the statue of the poet Petöfi. They were joined by hundreds of officer cadets from the Petöfi Military Academy and a big contingent of Communist Youth, clear signs to the regime and the Russians that something was cracking. Many wore the red-white-green cockade of the national colours. Petöfi's emotional poem, 'Arise, Hungarians!' was read. Soldiers peered out from windows in a barracks overlooking the statue. The crowd yelled to them: 'Long Live the Hungarian Army! Soldiers, join us, come with us!' The windows opened and the troops began to tear the Soviet stars from their caps and throw them into the crowd.

As evening fell the crowd went to Parliament Square. All the lights in the building and the square were switched off, leaving the crowd in darkness. 'This was probably meant to be a signal, if not a command, to go home,' wrote George Mikes, a Hungarian expatriate who had returned for the BBC.[4] 'But it seemed the command of frightened people. The crowd did not go home. They stood there, in silence and darkness, watching the huge, dark building ... Someone had an idea and lit a newspaper. The example was followed. In a minute or two about 100,000 newspapers were lit and Parliament Square flared in a sea of yellow, menacing flames.'

Gerö gave a clumsy and provocative speech on radio, saying that the students were slandering the Soviet Union. Rumours of the speech reached the angry crowd. Some marched from Parliament Square to the Radio Building in Sandor Street to demand air time. Another segment tore down the vast statue of Stalin in the city park. They dragged it, cheering, to the front of the National Theatre where it was broken up into souvenir-sized bits. Only Stalin's boots remained on his plinth. The slogans grew bolder: 'Ruszkik Haza', 'Russians, go home', 'Death to Gerö!' 'Death to AVH!' A delegation went into the Radio Building. When it failed to reappear, before midnight on Tuesday, a Hungarian tank officer started kicking at the door of the building, demanding that the delegation be released. A shot was fired from inside the building. The officer fell dead, probably the first casualty of the uprising.[5]

Machineguns opened up as people surged forward. They did not flee at first, thinking the AVH men were firing in the air. Up to a hundred were killed. AVH men in trucks attempted to seize people from the crowd but were stopped and beaten up. By 1 a.m. on Wednesday 24 October, with a huge crowd in Parliament Square shouting for Nagy, the uprising was well under way.

Before dawn the Radio Building fell to the rebels. At first light they began to open fire on the few Red army tanks in the capital. Startled Russian officers grasped the scale of what faced them in the exposed streets. 'Grazhdanskaya voyna, civil war,' they muttered. Fighting licked into flames throughout the day. Armouries and weapon plants were stripped of arms and ammunition. Mobs attacked party buildings. Younger officers and cadets, from the Kossuth Officers' School and the Rákóczy Military Academy, drifted over to the rebels.

The Russian tank crews, confused, often fraternized with the crowd, letting Hungarian flags be draped on their tanks. With the Kremlin reluctant to crush the rising, there was a bizarre edge to the fighting. Angry radio messages from officers cut into the fraternizations. The crews then 'handed the flags back to their newly-acquired Hungarian friends, shook hands with them, closed their turrets, moved on to the next corner and opened fire'.[6]

Western reaction was muffled. The British and French were deeply embroiled in the Middle East crisis that had followed Nasser's nationalization of the Suez Canal and the war alert between Israel and Egypt. President Eisenhower was in New York, caught up in his own re-election campaign. On the evening of 24 October, John Foster Dulles, the secretary

cavity connected to an adjacent boiler by a steam tube. Cells, foul and small, were thrown open 'to let out the terrible stench of many years'.[10] There was a large room, rigged 'like a telephone exchange', with equipment to record forty phone calls simultaneously. Rows of tapes sat on shelves, each with an AVH card attached to it, with Name of Caller, Name of Called, Duration of Conversation, Subject of Conversation and Remarks – 'interesting', 'suspicious', 'to be followed up'. The short-wave radio found in the building became the uprising's Free Radio Györ. At Sopron students ransacking the AVH building discovered that the secret police had their own Five Year Plan, with each AVH man required to enlist six new police informers every three months. There were details of how informers were recruited, often through the blackmail that their family belonged to the 'former classes'.

In Magyaróvár, AVH men were captured after firing into a crowd with machineguns. Their execution was almost casual. 'We are going to hang you,' a freedom fighter, as the rebels were now known in the West, said to a wounded secret policeman. 'Anything you want?' 'Give me a cigarette.' He was given one and it was lit for him. 'I was only doing my duty,' he said. 'Sorry for what you have done?' he was asked. 'No, I am not.' The man finished his cigarette, was hanged head down from a tree and beaten to death.

Exhilaration mounted throughout Thursday 25 October. Shortly after midday it was announced that Gerö, who had appointed Nagy Prime Minister two days before, had been dismissed.[11]

The following day 'Red Csepel', supposedly the pride of the Budapest proletariat, fell to rebel workers. The stream of newspapers, pamphlets and broadcasts showed that the revolt retained a leftist, socialist core but the movement for Russian withdrawal was hardening. Though Red army tanks shelled Maleter in the Kilian barracks on 27 October, Russian forces were in general in a low profile. Shortly after 11 a.m. that day it was announced that Imre Nagy had formed a government in which four cabinet members were non-communists. The Soviet ambassador in Budapest, Yuri Andropov, tried to persuade Nagy to sign an appeal for the intervention of Soviet troops, similar in format to those used later in Czechoslovakia and Afghanistan. He refused.

On 28 October, a Sunday of fervent Masses, Nagy announced a ceasefire. 'The Hungarian government has come to an agreement with the Soviet government whereby Soviet troops shall immediately begin their withdrawal from Budapest,' he said on radio. Talks had begun 'on the question of the withdrawal of Soviet troops stationed in Hungary'. That evening, Gerö, the defence minister General Bata and Ladislas Piros, the interior minister, were flown to Moscow from the Soviet military headquarters at Tököl outside Budapest. They were taken to the dachas of the Soviet

of state, gloomily told the US ambassador to the United Nations, L
that: 'People are going to accuse us that here is one of history's
moments, with these Hungarian fellows ready to stand up and die
we have been caught napping and doing nothing.'

By the next day the rising had spread to the provinces. Side-swit
of a nature deeply worrying to the Russians was becoming comm
Magyarovar, where the AVH had massacred fifty-nine demonstrat
revolutionary council was set up. It was headed by a former party me
and included AVH men themselves.[7]

With large areas of Budapest in rebel control, General Stephen Bat
defence minister, ordered Hungarian troops to 'liquidate all cou
revolutionary elements still in the capital' by noon. Colonel Pal Ma
a tall, charismatic Hungarian tank officer, was briefed to take five
against rebels at the Kilian barracks. He reversed his T-34 into the
gates of the barracks. He then spoke to rebels who had been taken pris
'When I arrived at the scene of the battle, I convinced myself tha
freedom fighters were the loyal sons of the Hungarian people,' he
later.[8] 'I informed the Minister that I had gone over.' In Parliament Sq
Russian tanks faced crowds and rebel Hungarian troops. A *New*
Times report put the death toll at 170.

Tactics were worked out against the Red army troop carriers and ta
Cobblestones and masonry were heaped on to streets that were made
and treacherous with soap and oil. Rebels filled bottles with petrol
cotton wicks ripped from shirts, Molotov cocktails, named ironically
the hardest of hard-line Soviet politicians who was lobbying in Mos
for Red army action. They threw them into tank engine slats and
intakes. It was relatively safe to throw a charge at a single tank if
rebel could get close enough. The Russians soon learned to send tank
patrol in pairs, where their machineguns offered mutual protection.
rebels threw up barricades to force the tanks on to the pavements
into side streets where Molotov cocktails could be dropped from
rooftops.

The Russians were reluctant to shoot. The commander of the So
forces that moved into Hungary, General Pavel Ivanovich Batov,
later: 'For the first five days we did not even return the fire ... I remem
clearly there are two Soviet cities, Uzhgorod and Mukachevo – two So
cities in the Carpathians. And we set up something like eighteen f
hospitals in them to treat the soldiers injured by the coun
revolutionaries. Only later did we return fire. And the moment we
our casualty rate dropped significantly ... We were very patient.'[9]

Hatred focused on the AVH, particularly those wearing the blue co
markings of the political section. In the important provincial town
Györ a search of the AVH centre revealed a torture chamber, a br

Central Committee on their arrival. The Budapest police chief, Alexander Kopacsi, had gone over to the Nagy government. With the defence, interior and police props knocked away, the rising seemed to have succeeded. The scrappy fighting against confused and isolated Red army units was dying away. Nagy's broadcast held the promise that they would soon be rolling back to Russia on their tracks, trucks and railway flatcars.

So it seemed to the rebels, in their motley of uniforms and cordite-pungent civilian jackets, army caps and dyed armbands. They celebrated the traditional joy of all revolutions, the break-in to the ex-dictator's lair. Rákosi's villa was on Lorant Street in Budapest's best quarter, the 12th arrondissement. The crowd revelled in the discovery of its unproletarian luxury, its cinema, liqueurs, American piano, West German television set, blue bathroom, and its rows of unread Russian books.

But they lacked real strength themselves and real support abroad, and the Bear was finally stirring. Three Soviet armies, totalling twenty-seven divisions, were converging on Hungary from Rumania, Czechoslovakia and the Ukraine. Despite Nagy's upbeat broadcast, the Red army continued to hold three mechanized divisions in key positions in Budapest. On Monday 29 October the Soviet foreign minister Dmitri Shepilov announced that 'no Soviet units have arrived in Hungary during the last 24 hours, in fact during the last 64 hours'.[12] This was untrue. Columns of armour and trucks of the Soviet 3rd Army were crossing the border into north-eastern Hungary. Soviet activity at the Bud, Budaörs and Tököl airfields was intense. Hungarian air force officers met on Monday 29 October to discuss bombing raids on the Russian supply routes. Potential targets included the frontier bridge at Zahony, the roads across the Tisza river and the Tököl airfield. There was also a plan to drop Hungarian paratroops at Komarom to block the bridge leading from Czecho-slovakia.[13]

Soviet policy on the rising was not yet clear. Zhukov, the defence minister, wanted the 'capitalist and imperialist mutiny' crushed. So did Peking. Liu Shao-chi, the Chinese deputy head of state, flew to Moscow to urge action. Khrushchev was indecisive. He was not in full control in Moscow. He faced real opposition within a Central Committee that was eager to take advantage of any weakness or failure. Within the Presidium his secret speech to the 20th Congress was criticized for unleashing counter-revolution in Hungary and Poland and undermining Soviet leadership of the communist bloc.

The Presidium was meeting in the Kremlin almost daily. It was swaying, ordering the immediate withdrawal of Soviet troops from Budapest whilst also sending fresh reinforcements into other areas of Hungary. 'I don't know how many times we changed our minds back and forth,' Khrushchev wrote.[14] Anxious to have Chinese support, he sat through a night with Liu Shao-chi in one of Stalin's old dachas, discussing a problem that had become 'like a nail in my head'.

At 1.28 p.m. on 29 October Nagy abolished the one-party system by broadening his government to include non-communist Smallholders. The 'People's Army' was restored to its old title of the 'Honvéd Army', named for the soldiers of the 1848 uprising against the Russians and a designation it had kept under Horthy. The same day a Hungarian officer, Captain Palinkas, freed the detained Catholic Primate Cardinal Mindszenty from arrest and drove him to Budapest.

The Politburo went into session in the Kremlin at 2 p.m. It seems likely that the decision to invade was taken then. The hard-liners, Molotov and Kaganovich, had always favoured it. There were few military problems. Marshal Koniev, the Warsaw Pact commander, was asked how long it would take to 'crush the counter-revolutionary forces in Hungary'. Khrushchev recalled that the marshal thought only for a moment before replying: 'Three days, no longer.' Bulganin and Malenkov, who had originally backed Khrushchev's conciliatory policy, now found, like Khrushchev himself, that Hungarian 'liberalism' had gone too far. The 'Honvéd Army' was a direct challenge to the Warsaw Pact. The abolition of one-party rule, set off by the release of the 'reactionary' cardinal, threatened the communist system in its entirety with its promise of free elections.

Fighting had by now broken out between Israeli and Egyptian troops. World attention slipped from Hungary.

The following day, Wednesday 31 October, the Hungarian air force command radio called for ambassador Andropov to guarantee the immediate withdrawal of Soviet forces. Failing that, the air force would be forced to take action. There were demands that Hungary should quit the Warsaw Pact and that pro-Soviet officers should be dismissed. The Kremlin could not ignore these provocations. Nevertheless, Russian army officers and diplomats lined up on the embankments to leave on Danube riverboats. At noon, with Anglo-French air forces now bombing Egypt, the last Red army tanks round the defence ministry withdrew.

Far from quitting, Khrushchev rallied support for an invasion. Reports of Russian troop movements flooded into Budapest throughout Thursday 1 November, from the provinces. Sensing the scale of the coming doublecross, Nagy demanded an explanation from Andropov. None was forthcoming.

Just before 7 p.m. Nagy cemented his fate. He went on the radio to declare that: 'Our heroic struggle has made possible the enforcement, in the international relations of our people, of their fundamental national interest: neutrality.' Though by now well aware of the huge Russian tank formations that were approaching central Hungary, Nagy received

Andropov. He informed him of the decision on neutrality and terminated Hungarian membership of the Warsaw Pact. Nagy sent Voroshilov, the chairman of the Presidium of the USSR, a formal telegram of confirmation. Soviet tanks surrounded Hungarian airfields, under the pretext that Russian civilians and wounded troops were being airlifted out.

On Friday 2 November two Soviet armoured trains rolled across the frontier at Zahony and troops occupied the railway station. Troops reinforced the tanks round the airfields. By about 7 p.m. Budapest had been sealed off in a pincer movement cutting off the western frontier with Austria. A diplomatic convoy to Budapest from Vienna was stopped fifteen kilometres inside the border at 11.30 p.m. That evening the US ambassador to Moscow, Charles 'Chip' Bohlen, was at a reception and noticed that Zhukov left early with an 'air of satisfaction and triumph'.

Late on the Friday evening Khrushchev, with Malenkov, took off for Brioni, Tito's private island in the Adriatic. Khrushchev had placed great importance on the improvement of relations with Yugoslavia in 1955, and during Tito's subsequent visit to Russia he had accompanied him throughout his tour. He wanted the Yugoslavs on board for the attack on Budapest. 'We climbed into a motor launch,' Khrushchev wrote.[15] 'Malenkov was as pale as a corpse. He gets car-sick on a good road. We had just landed after the roughest flight imaginable, and now we were heading out into a choppy sea in a small launch.' Khrushchev and Tito embraced and kissed at the pier. Khrushchev told him that it had been decided to send troops into Budapest and that General Malinin had been appointed by Zhukov to command the invasion. Tito said that 'we were absolutely right and that we should send our soldiers into action as quickly as possible'. He advised the Russians to appoint János Kádár, who had suffered in Rákosi's prisons, as premier. His past experience as interior minister and his expertise in interrogation and 'purification' would be invaluable. Kádár, with the former NKVD agent Ferenc Münnich, had flown from the Tököl air base to Uzhgorod in the Ukraine and on to Moscow on 1 November. He had already begun talks with his Soviet hosts on crushing the rising.

It was becoming clear that the Russians would have a free hand. In Washington, President Eisenhower announced a gift of £20 million worth of surplus food and medical supplies for Hungary. This was the total given to Hungary and none of it arrived. Dulles, sickening with the cancer that would kill him, complained: 'We don't have any hard information as to what is going on in Hungary. But about Egypt there is no doubt!' The United Nations was in uproar over Suez, not Hungary. In the Security Council Arkady A. Sobolev said that reports of Soviet troops pouring into Hungary were 'utterly unfounded'. Apart from the now worried Poles, the Hungarians had no friends in the Eastern bloc. The Czech president, Zapotocky, went on Czech radio to claim that a counter-revolution had brought 'fascist white terror among the workers'.[16] In the saying of the Eastern bloc, 'The Hungarians behaved like Poles, the Poles behaved like Czechs, and the Czechs behaved like pigs.'

In Budapest, almost clear of Russian troops, the Nagy government still hoped to survive. Trains were running normally. Glaziers were working overtime to replace blasted windows. Big green collection boxes sat on street corners for the families of those killed. Autumn chestnuts were on sale in paper cones.[17] Nagy, who had formed a third government which had only three Communists in the Cabinet, including himself and Maleter, met a Soviet delegation for military discussions. The Soviet delegation was led by General Malinin. Maleter was confident that the Russians were interested only in saving face, in a farewell parade and the rebuilding of wrecked Soviet war memorials. At 2.18 p.m. Budapest radio announced: 'The Soviet delegation promised that no further trains carrying Soviet troops will cross the Hungarian frontier.'

Later in the afternoon the American Legation cabled Washington that the Russians had one army and two corps in Hungary, with about 4,500 tanks 'and more coming'.[18] Ferihegy airport was jammed with Russian armour and troops were arriving at Tököl airfield on a shuttle of military flights. Maleter agreed to drive to the Tököl base for further talks in the evening. He was saluted by the Russians on his arrival, with his Chief of Staff General Kovacs, at 9 p.m. The Soviet negotiators from the morning's session were present and General Malinin was pleasant and sympathetic. The Hungarians were sitting in conference when armed and uniformed Russians burst into the room. They were led by General Ivan Serov, the chief of the Soviet security police. 'You are prisoners of the Soviet army,' said Serov. The Hungarians were led out into a courtyard.

Soviet armour moved into Budapest at 3 a.m. on Sunday 4 November. Nagy was told that the Russians were back in the capital at 4 a.m. Soviet tanks opened fire twenty-five minutes later at a barracks in a Budapest suburb. The Hungarian defence ministry realized that Maleter – now a general – and his delegation had failed to return from their Tököl rendezvous. They were in the hands of Russian counter-espionage men in a cellar in Gorky Avenue.

The Red army deployed some 15 armoured divisions with 6,000 tanks in Hungary, about 1,000 of them in the capital. By 7.20 a.m. they were in Parliament Square, seizing key points, particularly bridges and road intersections. Nagy gave a final statement on Budapest radio. 'Today at daybreak Soviet troops attacked our capital with the obvious intention of overthrowing the legal Hungarian democratic government,' he said. 'Our troops are in combat. The government is at its post. I hereby inform the people of our country and the entire world of this fact.'

Bitter telexes chattered out to Vienna. 'Please tell the world of the treacherous attack against our struggle for liberty,' a reporter on *Szabad Nép*, who had enjoyed just three days of freedom from censorship, telexed Associated Press in Vienna. 'Help ... SOS ... SOS. We have almost no weapons. People are running up to the tanks, throwing in hand grenades and closing the drivers' slits ...

'It is only a pity that we cannot last long ... What is the UN doing? ... Don't mind my style. I am excited ... The tanks are coming in, masses of them. The noise of the tanks is so loud we cannot hear each other speaking.' Still some hope remained: 'We have just heard a rumour that American troops will get here in an hour or two ... Our love to you all.'[19]

The Red army was fast and efficient. Its street-fighting experience from the war was not forgotten. Indeed, some troops brought in from the Soviet Union apparently believed they were fighting in Berlin, not Budapest, against German fascists, not Hungarian workers.[20] Tanks squatted on each main intersection in the city. Bridges were seized before the Hungarians could react. Soviet tankmen used surviving AVH officers as guides. They were heard talking to each other on the 70-metre radio waveband. The earlier attitude had gone. The Russians opened fire on bread queues, used phosphorus to shell the university hospital and looted with abandon. The stock of the Divatcsarnok, the big store in Rakoczi Street, was taken off in tanks and trucks. In Rakoczi Square, Russian firing squads shot those who arrived to hand in their arms responding to an appeal that promised them immunity.

Cardinal Mindszenty fled to the American Legation at 7.58 a.m. He was to remain there for fifteen years. Nagy and forty-one supporters raced to the Yugoslav Legation. The telex line from the parliament building was cut at 8.24 a.m. after a final message to the offices of United Press International in Vienna: 'Goodbye, friends; goodbye, friends; goodbye, friends. Save our souls. The Russians are too near.'

A new government had already been announced and the disappearance of Kádár and Münnich explained. They were still in Russia, but speeches they had made were re-transmitted from Szolnok, the Russian garrison 105 kilometres south-east of Budapest. A new 'revolutionary' government, with Kádár as premier and Münnich as minister of the armed and security forces, had asked for Soviet help against 'fascism and reaction and its murderous bands'.

Heavy fighting continued in both the twin cities that make up Budapest. In Buda, Russian tank crews supported by infantry and artillery were trying to clear the areas round the main railway stations and Marx Square. In Pest, there was heavy combat in Moscow Square. The Kilian barracks, burning from Russian tank and mortar fire, held out for thirteen hours.

By early afternoon on 4 November the Russians had taken the Eastern station and were shelling Csepel island.

Firing was still intense on Monday morning, 5 November. As Mindszenty said his first Mass in the US Legation, the windows rattled and shattered from Soviet tank fire. A Yugoslav diplomat was killed in his legation, where Nagy was seeking asylum. The Polish Embassy was also shelled. Zhukov seemed determined that Communists as well as capitalists should be reminded of Red army strength. The US Legation messaged Washington: 'Soviets have been systematically cleaning up city; slaughter has been continuous over last 3 days of men, women and children with hospitals and clinics included among targets . . .'

The Kádár government was sworn in on 7 November. Outside the capital, where Csepel continued to resist, the Russians used tanks and aircraft against steelworkers holding out in Dunapentele. Long lines of refugees continued down the wet roads, slippery with autumn beech and birch leaves, to the Austrian and Yugoslav borders. The fighting was all but over. More than 200,000 Hungarians fled to the West, leaving behind them some 5,000 killed and 20,000 wounded.

Young Hungarians were deported by rail to the Soviet Union as hostages. The first cattle trucks were loaded on 13 November. Rebels halted some of these sealed trains and freed their occupants. The Russians then trucked deportees into Czechoslovakia for onward dispatch to the Soviet Union. Vérmezö, a large open square in Budapest, was the assembly point for the deportees, whose numbers UN Ambassador Lodge estimated at 16,000 by 19 November.

A final kidnap was planned. Kádár urged the Nagy group to leave the Yugoslav Embassy, promising that they would not face any charges. A bus was sent by Münnich's security ministry at 6.30 a.m. on 22 November to collect them and take them to their homes. There were Russian NKVD men on the bus. Nagy sensed this and insisted that they get off. The Yugoslav ambassador warned Nagy not to go, that a trick was about to be played out. He put two of his own staff on the bus. Nagy, trusting Kádár as a close ex-colleague and a fellow Communist, stepped on the bus and other asylum-seekers followed. As soon as it moved off, the bus was blocked by armoured cars. A Soviet colonel boarded and ordered the two Yugoslavs off. The bus then took the Hungarians, not on a drop-off tour of their homes and apartments, but to the Soviet command headquarters on Gorky Avenue. Nagy and his partners were flown to Rumania on 27 November and handed to the Rumanian secret police.

Kádár was scarce freer himself. He refused to allow UN observers into Hungary but Nehru's special ambassador, Krishna Menon, arrived in Budapest and saw him on 5 December. He reported that Kádár was virtually a prisoner, 'surrounded by Soviet tanks and with Soviet sentries inside the [parliament] building'.[21]

Nagy was returned from Rumania to Hungary when the world fuss over his kidnap had died down. His first trial, in January 1958, was abandoned when he refused to 'confess'. He was tried again, with Maleter, in prison from 9 to 15 June 1958. Both he and Maleter were hanged, to the particular fury of the Yugoslavs but to little other reaction, immediately after the verdict on the final day.

In all, about 280 people were hanged over a period of three years for their part in the rising. Most are buried in an overgrown and obscure corner of the Pest Lorinc cemetery in Budapest. Nagy is thought to be in this Section 301 of the cemetery, a wilderness of grass and wild poppies. Its existence is known only because the mother of a student who was sentenced for his part in the Budapest street battles learned that her son was to be hanged with three other students on a day in February 1957. She followed their coffins from Gyuto jail to Section 301.

Within a few years the Hungarian students were 'tired, disillusioned, hedonistic ... interested in pop-music, in the Beatles, in Carnaby Street fashions'.[22] Section 301 has an epitaph, by Francois Mauriac: 'I fear that with Imre Nagy the liberty of the small peoples of Europe was killed without hope of resurrection because the atomic age forbids all intervention.'

32

BERLIN SUMMER

For sixteen years East Germans had a privilege unique in their bloc. By buying a ticket on a bus or a metro train, they could leave.

The post-war pattern in East Germany was typical of the Soviet bloc except where it ran up against the existence of Berlin, with its joint US, British, French and Soviet control. Communists, returning from exile in Moscow with the rear echelons of the Red army, fused with the democratic left in the familiar way. The result was the SED, the Socialist Unity Party, a front supposedly broad enough to include the new Social Democratic Party. The merger went ahead in April 1946 despite the fact that 82 per cent of Social Democrats voted against it. The SED was controlled by a communist caucus responsible to the Russian military authorities.

It failed to make progress in Berlin. Elections were held throughout the city at the end of 1946. The Red army provided SED candidates with food and coal, but non-communist parties took 80 per cent of the vote.

'To the man in the street, we were known as the "Russian" party,' said a prominent SED man who later fled to the West.[1] 'Our leading officials lived in large country houses hermetically sealed from the rest of the population and guarded by soldiers of the Red army.'

Nowhere else but Berlin were the Western Allies present to prevent Stalinization. The military authorities were able to deal handily enough with the lack of enthusiasm for the SED in the rest of the Soviet zone. Student council elections at Leipzig university in 1947 show the use made of the Red army. The Russians had two divisions in and around Leipzig. In the Western Zone, the British made do with a single battalion in much larger Hamburg. Students were warned that a non-communist vote could lead to dismissal. Liberals and Christian Democrats polled 1,240 votes to the SED's 600.

The communist humiliation was swiftly reversed. The university president was obliged to accept that the 'sons of workers and farmers' should be granted 60 per cent of student places. SED students carried out a constant and violent campaign against 'reactionary' professors, boycotting or interrupting their lectures. The Liberal students' committee was dissolved on the orders of the Russian military. Student arrests followed in Leipzig, Dresden, Halle, Rostock and East Berlin. They were taken at night to prisons under Soviet military control, and accused by Soviet military tribunals of giving information to unspecified 'enemy agents'. Some disappeared on freight trains to Siberia. Others went to the old Nazi concentration camps at Sachsenhausen, Bautzen and Buchenwald. The Evangelical Bishops of East and West Germany sent a letter to the four Allied Military Governors in 1947 claiming that 2,000 young people had been arbitrarily arrested and imprisoned by the Russians in the past year. Within two years an estimated 15,000 political prisoners were in Sachsenhausen and 18,000 were thought to have died in Bautzen since the Russian occupation.

The existence of West Berlin, with its resurgent economy, was a threat to Soviet hegemony. Three years after Sergeant Yegorov had raised the Red banner on the Reichstag, GIs were still firmly implanted in the city. Stalin determined to drive them out. On 20 March 1948 the Soviet Military governor, Marshal Sokolovsky, walked out of the Allied Control Council, which combined the military governors of the four occupation zones and which was the supreme authority in Germany. A fortnight later, the traffic links between West Germany and West Berlin were harassed. Red army men attempted to board American military trains and General Lucius Clay, the American Military Govenor in Germany, posted armed guards to keep them off. Soviet fighters buzzed airliners on the air corridors. Clay warned Washington: 'If we mean to hold Europe against Communism, we must not budge.' The Russians quit the Allied Kommandatura, the four-power body responsible for Berlin. On 18 June the Western Allies brought in the new Deutschmark to replace the inflation-ridden Reichsmark in their zones. Any pretence of the four-power government of Germany and Berlin had gone.

On 24 June 1948 the Russians severed all rail, road and canal links to West Berlin to leave it isolated 160 kilometres deep in Red army territory without its own resources of fuel and food. Stalin's invitation to abandon the city was not considered. 'There is no discussion on that point,' Truman said. 'We stay in Berlin – period.' The idea of running military convoys along the autobahns was dropped since, although the Americans still had a nuclear monopoly, the Red army could bring overwhelming conventional forces to bear against the 6,000-man Western garrison in the city.

Stalin underrated the Western airlift capacity. His advisers seem not to have realized that the British and Americans were rich enough in transport aircraft simply to fly above the land blockade. Operation 'Plain Fare' to aircrews, *Luftbrücke* to Berliners, the airlift was under way in forty-eight hours. The backbone was the American C54 Skymaster, carrying 9 tons of cargo, and the British York with 7.5 tons. Aircraft were brought in from Hawaii, Panama and Alaska. Former RAF and USAAF bomber pilots, once tasked to destroy the city with high explosive and incendiaries, flew in coal, fuel oil and food. Charter companies, often operating a single war-surplus aircraft, boomed on twenty-four-hour-a-day contracts.[2] Crews flew at least two round trips a day and some managed four. They bounced in the low-altitude turbulence along three corridors across the Russian zone, each 30 kilometres wide and from 300 to 3,000 metres in height.[3]

As winter set in the Russians could observe that the blockade was biting. The electricity supply in West Berlin was cut to four hours a day. There was no public transport and no light after 6 p.m. Coal dust was compressed into briquettes as valuable as cigarettes. Flying conditions deteriorated. Freighters that could not land in poor visibility could find marginal conditions when they returned, still laden, to West German airfields.[4] But by the end of the winter 6,000 tons of supplies were arriving each day for 2,108,000 West Berliners. A counter-blockade was imposed banning supplies going from the Western zones to the East. This prevented the East Germans from getting essential coking coal and steel. As the Marshall Plan began to boost the *Wirtschaftswunder* in the Western zones, the East German economy rotted.

Stalin had miscalculated grievously. A block system ensured proper spacing in the time of arrival over Berlin and rigorous control of altitude and speed. Sophisticated ground handling enabled German labourers to turn round a four-engined aircraft in thirty minutes. These new techniques were to nourish the infant civil airline industry in the West. 'The flying control organization has proved itself capable of carrying the severe and continuous burden with great efficiency,' the delighted British noted at the height of the airlift.[5] 'A major strategic reorientation may be brought about to the immense advantage of the Western Allies.' It was not until the 1970s that the Russians developed a similar airlift capability.

The Russians threw in the towel after eleven months in May 1949. Autobahns, canals and rail lines reopened. The incessant drone of aero engines over Berlin, from 276,926 flights that had brought in 2,300,000 tons of supplies, was stilled. Serious damage had been done to Soviet interests. US leadership of the West was confirmed. There was no longer talk of bringing the GIs out of Europe. US defence budgets, which had been falling, now increased. Moral revulsion against the Germans in the West was replaced by a steady if suspicious acceptance that they were on the same side, at least when it came to the Soviet bloc.

The airlift also speeded the creation of two separate German states. On 12 May 1949 the Allied Control Commission, in Sokolovsky's absence, approved the Basic Law of the new Federal Republic of (West) Germany.[6] On 23 May West Germany came into being. On 17 September 1949 Konrad Adenauer became chancellor, the first freely elected German leader since 1933. Bonn, a 'small town in Germany', a leafy riverbank of the Rhine, with an ochre-washed university and some memories of Beethoven, became a capital.

On 7 October the German Democratic Republic was proclaimed in the Soviet Zone. Its leader was Walter Ulbricht, the goatee-bearded SED first secretary. Fleeing the Nazis for Russia before the war, he had survived the purges of foreign Communists, so many of whom were taken in evening raids by the NKVD on their quarters in the Hotel Lux in Moscow.[7] He returned to Berlin with the Red army in 1945. Though he was able to seal off his new state behind minefields and barbed wire, which soon stretched from the Baltic to the Frankenwald, he could not seal Berlin.

Three months after Stalin's death the Soviet Zone of Berlin rose in the first major unrest in a country occupied by the Red army. On 17 June 1953, led by workers building the vast blocks of the Stalinallee in the centre, crowds ranged through the zone protesting against increases in work norms. They demanded free elections, the return of German POWs still held in Russian work camps and the dismissal of Ulbricht. The communist flag was torn from the top of the Brandenburg Gate on the border between the Soviet and British zones.

Strikes spread to other cities. Some *Volkspolizei* collaborated with the strikers. Though the regime had armed police, quartered in barracks and trained to use infantry weapons, and *Kampfgruppen* or 'battle groups' of factory workers, it could not cope. Red army tanks had to be called in to patrol the streets in East Berlin, opening fire on the shirtsleeved youths who hurled bricks and cobblestones at them. The rising was crushed by the end of the month, with 246 East Berliners and several hundred others in the rest of East Germany killed. Some survivors were sentenced to death by Soviet military courts. The loss of population accelerated as East Germans took the *U-bahn* or the elevated *S-bahn*, or simply walked, to West Berlin. There were 118,000 refugees in 1952, 306,000 in 1953.[8] By 1957 Ulbricht was forced to create a new criminal offence, *Republikflucht*, fleeing the Republic.

The Republic was being laid to waste. More than half the refugees were under twenty-five, and three quarters were under forty-five. They included doctors, the entire law faculty at Leipzig university, scientists, engineers and so many skilled workers that special 'shock brigades' of women workers had to be formed to replace them. 'As many as a third of all graduates departed for the Federal Republic as soon as they had completed their studies,' the Soviet historian Roy Medvedev noted.[9] In 1960, 4,000 SED members fled and the blonde who won the Miss Universe contest at Miami Beach in 1961 was an East German refugee.

Each Germany melded into its own bloc. West German entry to Nato in May 1955 was immediately followed by the Soviet creation of the Warsaw Pact, which East Germany joined the following January.

Berlin remained, as a Soviet Note to the Western powers put it, a 'smouldering fuse connected to a powder keg'. Khrushchev suggested that it should become a 'free' city and that any routes to it should be negotiated with East Germany. Ulbricht pleaded with the Kremlin to get the West out of Berlin and Khrushchev was under pressure from the Politburo to achieve a settlement. A summit meeting in Paris was arranged for 16 May 1960 at which Khrushchev hoped to get an agreement on Berlin.

On Sunday 1 May 1960 Gary Powers was woken two hours after midnight at the air base in Peshawar in the North West Frontier Province of west Pakistan. Powers was a CIA pilot and his U-2 was being fuelled for a flight 6,000 kilometres north from Peshawar to Bodö in Norway. The aircraft was to photograph installations with its powerful cameras as it crossed the Soviet landmass. The U-2 could fly for 10 hours at 21,000 metres, gliding in the stratosphere for periods to save fuel weight.

Powers was equipped with a poison pin with shellfish toxin. Should he wish to take his chances if he came down, his seat pack contained 7,500 roubles, 14 gold Napoleons and a silk banner that read, in 14 languages: 'I am an American ... I need food, shelter, assistance ... If you help me, you will be rewarded.' In fact, the CIA thought that there was one chance

in a million that the pilot would survive a mishap'.[10] Neither the aircraft
nor Powers' silver flight suit had identification marks. Against orders,
however, Powers was carrying his US social security card, his driver's
licence and a photograph of himself and his wife in a nightclub. He did
not wish to be nameless if something happened.

He took off at 6.26 a.m. After an hour he had crossed the tumbling
whiteness of the Hindu Kush. Taval'dara lay just to his east as he entered
Soviet airspace at 19,750 metres. He penetrated the heartland of Soviet
Central Asia above Tadzhikistan, the ancient caravan city of Samarkand
to his west. The matt-black aircraft passed close to the Tyuratam cosmo-
drome, the satellite-launching base at Leninsk east of the Aral Sea. The
Soviet air defences knew he was there. Soviet interceptors were scrambled
when U-2s came calling, but dropped back well below the intense blue of
the stratosphere. None could get within 4,250 metres of the American
aircraft.[11]

Powers was nearing the eastern edge of the Urals and Sverdlovsk,
deathplace of Tsar Nicholas, 2,300 kilometres deep into the Soviet Union,
when he heard a muted explosion. The aircraft went out of control and
its slender wings sheared off. As it spun down tail-first, Powers loosed the
cockpit canopy and clambered out of the aircraft. He did not arm the
switches that would have destroyed the telltale electronic and camera
equipment in seventy seconds. His parachute filled and he landed heavily
in a ploughed field. He decided not to use his poison pill.[12] The Russians
had developed a surface to air missile.

May Day passed without announcement. On 4 May Khrushchev said
that a spy plane had been shot down in Soviet airspace. He did not say
what had happened to the aircraft or the pilot. The Americans, assuming
that Powers was dead and the aircraft destroyed, said that a U-2 had been
lost on a meteorological flight over Turkey and Iran at high altitude. On
7 May Khrushchev said that the Russians had both the pilot and the spy
equipment and that the U-2 had been brought down in Sverdlovsk, well
over 1,600 kilometres from either Turkey or Iran.

The Paris Summit failed and Khrushchev left Paris for East Berlin. The
chance of an agreement on the city evaporated. Khrushchev continued to
find the situation intolerable. 'The GDR (East Germany) had to cope
with an enemy who was economically very powerful and therefore very
appealing to the GDR's own citizens,' he wrote.[13] The 'drain of workers
was creating a simply disastrous situation in the GDR ... If things had
continued like this much longer, I don't know what would have happened.'

West Berlin flaunted its prosperity. Wasteland and ruins were cleared.
The Ku'damm stretched for three neon-lit kilometres of cafés, nightclubs
and luxury shops, overseen by Kempinski's hotel, its plump patrons
gorging their *Schlagsahne*. East Berliners, their marks worth a fifth of the

Westmark, window-shopped or crowded into Western Zone cinemas for a glimpse of Hollywood. The Russian sector was drab, grey, red slogans the only colour in the apartment blocks that ran on to the empty streets like waves breaking on a winter coast. It sounded of metal brakes on railway sidings and had the smell of brown coal. Its few street lights were dull against the bright glow from the West. Apart from Soviet patrols and a few two-strokes, the traffic had West Berlin plates, people over to watch the brilliant *Komische Oper* or to visit whatever friends had not fled.

The replacement of Eisenhower by President Kennedy offered Khrushchev a new target, particularly after the humiliating outcome of the Bay of Pigs landing in April 1961. The two men met at a Summit in Vienna on 3 June 1961. Khrushchev delivered an ultimatum. Unless the West came to an agreement on Berlin by the end of the year, the Russians would sign a separate peace treaty with East Germany which would, by 'normalizing' the situation in Berlin, leave no reason for Allied garrisons to remain. 'It is necessary to establish deadlines,' he added ominously. 'The Soviet government regards a period not exceeding six months as adequate.'

Khrushchev did not bluff. In the first six months of 1961, 103,000 people fled from East Germany to the West. Ulbricht could not long survive such a haemorrhage. Since 1949, when the GDR was established, 2,800,000 of its citizens had abandoned it for the West. That was one in six, a total greater than the remaining populations of the dozen largest East German cities.[14] The situation worsened in the early summer as *Torschlusspanik*, the fear of being left behind when the door slammed, began to bite.

On 8 July Khrushchev announced that Western attitudes had obliged him to increase the Soviet military budget by a third. Kennedy responded on 25 July, asking Congress to boost the US defence budget and to call up reservists. 'West Berlin has now become, as never before, the great testing place of Western courage and will,' he said. 'It is as secure as the rest of us, for we cannot separate its safety from our own. I hear it said that West Berlin is militarily untenable. And so was Bastogne.[15] And so, in fact, was Stalingrad.'

The weekend after the speech 3,895 refugees arrived at Marienfelde despite the *Vopos*, the East German police, hauling others off the Metro trains. Volunteers from Communist Youth groups denounced potential refugees to the police. On 7 August Khrushchev went on Soviet television to warn that the situation was so dangerous that the Soviet Union might call up reservists and increase the number of troops stationed on her western borders.[16] In the US the biggest manoeuvres since the war were under way at Fort Bragg, North Carolina. The small Western garrison in Berlin was outnumbered by something like 7:1 by the 67,500 East German and Red army troops, backed by 1,200 tanks, who were stationed within 50 kilometres of the city. Any attempt by Khrushchev forcibly to change the status of Berlin would thus invite a nuclear response from the US. Robert McNamara, the defence secretary, had warned Kennedy that any military challenge would have to be swiftly raised to nuclear level because of the weakness in conventional forces.

'We decided to accept the challenge which Kennedy had issued,' Khrushchev wrote.[17] 'We appointed Marshal Koniev commander of our troops in Berlin. We had picked up the gauntlet and were ready for the duel.'

At midnight, as the new belltower at the Kaiser Wilhelm Memorial Church tolled in a Sunday, 13 August 1961, East German troops and border guards were roused in their barracks by sirens. West Berlin taxi drivers radioed their dispatchers not to accept trips that involved driving into the Russian Zone.[18] Truck convoys began to clog the streets east of the border, unloading concrete posts and rolls of barbed wire. By 3.30 a.m. barbed-wire fences were going up across all the streets used as the main crossing points to the West. As dawn broke, East Berliners who worked in the West, kitchen workers and cleaners, walked to underground and S-bahn stations to catch their trains. The gates had been padlocked. Trains still ran but they no longer stopped in the Soviet sector where *Vopos* patrolled the platforms. At the Friedrichstrasse station by the Spree river, would-be refugees wept as they realized they had left their escape a day too late. Berlin, where settlements on both banks of the Spree had joined in one city in 1432, had been torn in two.

Four days later cheap concrete breezeblocks started to replace the wire and the outline of the Wall was imprinted on Berlin. Four crossing points remained, the most famous of them Checkpoint Charlie on the Friedrichstrasse.

The Wall caught the West unawares. It was probed. US tanks in battle order ranged up to it and sighted their guns down the Friedrichstrasse. Khrushchev claimed that the Americans were 'preparing bulldozers to break down our border installations.[19] The bulldozers would be followed by tanks and wave after wave of Jeeps with infantrymen . . .'[20] In fact there were no incidents and Khrushchev claimed a 'great victory'. Though the Allies remained in the city, the Wall stemmed the refugee flow.

The process is still being refined. The Wall now runs to 250 observation towers, 135 bunkers, 260 dog runs, 100 kilometres of vehicle ditch, 130 kilometres of alarm fencing, 5,445 mercury vapour lights, which, since they cast no shadow, make it easier to shoot at night, and 14,000 men. It runs through open fields, apartment blocks, a church. On the Western side, houses run up to it. A Dog Salon – 'everything for the pet in your life, wash, trim 'n cut' – is built to it. No such frivolity on the other side. It has become an industry. A man sets off to work in East Berlin. In one hand he carries a briefcase and a packet of sandwiches. In the other, a chain with a muzzled Alsatian at the end of it.

The Wall was a summer phenomenon. By the autumn of 1961 'East and West settled back into their customary state of polite distrust and wary *bonhomie*'.[21]

33
PRAGUE SPRING

The next crisis in the *glacis* was in Czechoslovakia. Like Hungary, it followed a change of leadership and a shift away from repression. The critical factor was again the Soviet fear that the Party was losing its monopoly of power. Once that was established, the Kremlin sent for the Red army.

In January 1968, a grey month of damp cold that conceived the Prague Spring, Alexander Dubček replaced the old Stalinist Antonin Novotny as first secretary of the Party.[1] There seemed no cause for Soviet alarm. Dubček was welcomed when he went to Moscow at the end of the month. 'Sacha' Dubček was a party product, a slightly built, rather shy *funky*, largely Russian educated. Born in a West Slovakian village in 1921, his communist father took him to Russia when he was four and he stayed there, in Gorki and Frunze, until 1938. He joined the underground Slovak Communist Party at eighteen. His brother was killed fighting with a partisan brigade in Slovakia in January 1945 and young Sacha was twice wounded. He became a full-time party official in 1949, returning to the Soviet Union for three years from 1955 to attend an advanced party school attached to the Soviet Central Committee in Moscow. He rose fast when he returned home, joining the party Presidium in 1963, and became first secretary of the Slovak Party the following year.

What was seen as a palace revolution, a reshuffle within the Party, changed on 30 January when a group of 175 party members called on Dubček to create a 'climate of mutual trust in which every Communist will be able to freely express his views'. On 4 March preventive censorship, the advance vetting of the press, radio and TV, was abolished.

Such liberalism was unknown in any mature communist state. The Russians were also alarmed by new Czech tolerance of voluntary non-communist organizations which they thought would develop into a political opposition. 'Club 231', the name referring to the paragraph number of the penal code under which political prisoners were sentenced, was set up on 31 March as an interest group for the victims of political injustice.[2]

In March, General Ludvik Svoboda, the former defence minister, replaced Novotny as president. Both he and Oldrich Cernik, the new prime minister elected in April, supported Dubček. The liberals were rapidly consolidating their power. On 5 April the Czech Central Committee approved an 'Action Programme' laid down by the Dubček group. This declared that the Party was not a 'universal caretaker' of society. It said that party members had 'not only the right but the duty to act according to conscience'. The rights to travel abroad, to freedom of speech and to a free press were guaranteed. It said that the Party should 'lead, not command' and that the *nomenklatura*, the system of appointing middle and senior bureaucrats only from party ranks, should be abolished.

A date, 9 September 1968, was set for the 14th Party Congress. That forced a time span on the Russians. Any effective reversal of the reforms would have to be made before then.

Dubček never hinted at going the whole Hungarian hog, or quitting the Warsaw Pact or declaring neutrality like the dead Nagy. The Action Programme took care to stress that the Czechs would 'fight the forces of imperialist reaction'. The East Germans were not satisfied. An East Berlin paper ran a report that West German and American army units, supported by tanks, were operating on Czech territory. These turned out to be film extras, using grey-painted 'armour', who were shooting a film on the wartime Battle of Remagen in western Bohemia.[3] When Czech border guards began to remove the barbed-wire fences along the Bavarian border in the spring, the East Germans complained that Czechoslovakia would become a halfway house for refugees fleeing to the West.

The May Day crowds in Prague were ecstatic despite a thin drizzle. 'For the first time, of our own free will' read the calico banner of one group of marchers. 'No more repression for the opposition' said another, noted no doubt by observers from the Soviet Embassy, reflecting Dubček's 'socialism with a human face'. Former political prisoners and ex-servicemen who had fought with the British and French, non-people for two decades, paraded. So did Boy Scouts.[4]

Dubček flew to Moscow on 4 May but failed to mollify the new Soviet leader, Leonid Brezhnev.[5] A Soviet Military Mission arrived in Czechoslovakia to arrange Warsaw Pact manoeuvres. Soviet armoured units in Poland were moved from Cracow to the Czech border. On 15 May the Polish frontier with Czechoslovakia was closed and a joint Soviet–Polish exercise was held near the border under the eyes of Marshal Grechko, the C-in-C of the Warsaw Pact.

Purges in the interior ministry and the Czech army increased Soviet fears. The defence minister, General Lomsky, and the Chief of Staff, General Rytyr, were sacked and the Red army nominees were losing control in the Czech forces. The new defence minister, General Dzur, transferred or pensioned off officers known to be Russian informants. The system of appointing senior officers by decree was scrapped, making it easier for non-party officers to get promotion.

The Czech military had been trusted. It was the only country in the northern tier of the Warsaw Pact that had no Russian troops. After the communist takeover in 1948, all career officers whose political loyalty was not certain had been purged. Younger officers, brighter and better trained, were beginning to come through by 1968. They resented constant party control. The party Central Committee abolished its military department, the '8th department', a Stalinist bastion that had maintained the party grip over the military. There was talk of a trade union for officers and other ranks and a new organization to defend the rights of non-party members. Non-party clubs were allowed to operate in military units. Officers were at the cutting edge of the Prague Spring.

Unease at new Russian ideas of nuclear war, which left Czechoslovakia vulnerable, began to surface in public. Sokolovsky's *Military Strategy*, published in Moscow in 1963, had studied the possibility of limited nuclear war in Central Europe. That would have involved the sacrifice of the Czech army in the first few days. Warsaw Pact operational plans estimated that losses on the Czech front would run between 60 and 70 per cent. Officers said that the lack of a proper Czech military doctrine was the 'source of paralysis in the army'.[6] Defence minister Dzur complained that Czechs merely followed Soviet orders.

For the Russians, one of the most notorious documents to be published under Dubček was the Memorandum of the Klement Gottwald Military-Political Academy. It was issued in May. It said that Czech military development since the communist takeover had been 'deformed' and was based on 'primitive logic'. The subordination of Czech national interests to Russia was criticized. In a bitter reference to the Novotny regime, it said that military policy before 1968 was 'exclusively' in Soviet interests 'regardless of one's own sovereign interests'. The Russians read this as an attack on the Warsaw Pact.

In May, Soviet officers and units moved into western Bohemia for the general staff manoeuvres. Ten Antonov transports arrived at night at the Milovice airfield from East Germany without the Czech defence ministry being informed. Two marshals, Grechko and Yepichev, joined the senior Russian officers in Czechoslovakia. A third, Marshal Yakubovsky, said that the Russians would remain in Czechoslovakia 'at least until September 20', after the closing day of the planned party Congress. Another visitor, General Ivan Pavlovsky, was the Russian the Czechs had most reason to fear, though they were ignorant of his mission. He was to prepare the invasion, experience that would stand him in good stead when he flew into Kabul twelve years later.

Dubček was given only a few hours' warning of the visit of the Russian Politburo member Alexei Kosygin to the Czech health resort of Karlovy Vary. Kosygin came supposedly for a cure, in fact for informal talks with Czech Communists. Kosygin agreed that the 14th Congress could be held, and economic reforms go ahead, provided that the Czech Party kept its monopoly of power. His warnings were ignored. On 27 June, the day after the National Assembly had formally confirmed the earlier abolition of censorship, seventy figures in Czech intellectual and cultural life signed a 'Manifesto of 2000 Words'. It 'regretted' the monopoly power of the Communist Party in the state. No action was taken against the signatories.

Dubček was now in a critical position. It took considerable Czech pressure to get the Russians to withdraw the troops who took part in the June Warsaw Pact manoeuvres in Czechoslovakia, 'Exercise Sumava'. On 11 July a *Pravda* editorial compared the Czech situation with Hungary in 1956. The writing was on the wall. Soviet invasion forces were being readied. In the Ukraine, motor rifle divisions assembled in the forests, protected from US satellite surveillance.

The Czech leadership was invited to Warsaw to meet with the five fraternal parties on 14 and 15 July. The Czechs declined and the conference went ahead without them. A Letter was sent by the five from Warsaw as an open threat to Prague. It said that the internal affairs of one socialist country were the legitimate concern of all socialist countries if they jeopardized the 'achievements of socialism' or the 'interests of the international proletarian movement'. In what was to become the basis of the 'Brezhnev doctrine', the Warsaw Pact warned the Czechs that 'a decisive rebuff to the forces of anti-communism' was 'not only your task but ours too'. The Letter also offered 'all possible help to ... block the way to reaction'. Few doubted that this help would include Red army units.

Before the official reply was made General Prchlik, head of the Czech Central Committee military department, gave a remarkable press conference. He denounced the total domination of the Warsaw Pact and its joint command by Russian officers. He said that the East Europeans 'held no responsibilities nor had a hand in making decisions'. Prchlik claimed that Czech demands for greater influence had been ignored. He said that preparations to work out a Czech military doctrine had been made. The sharp nationalism now evident in the officer corps gave the Russians the unpleasant vision of a neutral Czechoslovakia. Dubček argued that, far from losing power, there was a 'growth of the authority of the new democratic policy of the Party in the eyes of the broad working masses'.[7] This was logical. It was also heretical and a heresy, with its roots in a communist party, was all the more dangerous for being an enemy within. Soviet military pressure increased. On 23 July the Kremlin made a formal proposal to Prague that, in view of the 'imminent danger from the West', permanent Russian garrisons should be set up along the western frontier of Czechoslovakia.

The Czechs met with virtually the whole Soviet Politburo at the border railway station of Cierna on 29 July. Four days of talks were held, in the carriages of a Soviet official train on Czech territory. The train had a radio link to Moscow, the windows had armoured glass and the whole was protected by a division of Soviet troops. The Politburo had taken a long spoon to sup with the Czech devils.

Brezhnev started the talks with a four-hour harangue on the lack of censorship and the liberalism of the Czech press. The Czechs were adamant that it should be recognized that Czech forces were able to defend their western frontier. They also insisted that there had been no changes in Czech foreign affairs and policy towards the Warsaw Pact and the Soviet Union. Little progress was made. The train shunted the Russians 300 metres back on to Soviet territory at 10.30 p.m. Unable to sleep, worried that the Russians were bugging his confidential phone line to Prague, Dubček stayed up chatting to local railwaymen until 3.30 a.m. The talks on 30 July were soured by further Soviet harangues. 'You'll get used to it, Alexander,' Svoboda told Dubček. 'Marshal Koniev treated me as an underling all through the war.'[8] A close associate of Dubček, the young Czech party secretary Zdenek Mlynar, says that Dubček would have signed 'anything affirming the hegemony of Moscow and the membership of Czechoslovakia in the Soviet bloc' in order to buy off military intervention.[9]

Invasion rumours were growing in Prague, where the interior ministry was reporting the arrival of large numbers of Soviet 'tourists' in stout boots. Tank and aircraft movements were reported from Cinovec on the East German border. There was no Suez crisis to divert world attention, but the Russians noted that President Johnson left Washington for his ranch in Texas on Friday 2 August. He told reporters that he expected to be on holiday for a month. Johnson, at least, was not in a state of alert.

The brief final communiqué from Cierna referred to a 'broad comradely exchange of opinions'. That meant failure, repeated at further meetings in Bratislava. It was only after the conclusion of talks in Bratislava on 8 August that Soviet troops were withdrawn. They were soon to be back.

It is possible that the hawks in Moscow were preparing a coup against Brezhnev, using Czechoslovakia as an excuse. Zdenek Mlynar thinks that they were ready to move after most of the Politburo left Moscow on summer holiday on 10 August. General Shchemenko, a hard-liner, was abruptly named C-in-C of the Warsaw Pact. The highest-ranking marshals began shuttling between the Ukraine, Poland and East Germany. On 15 August, presumably sensing what was afoot, the Politburo members interrupted their vacations to hurry back to Moscow. Mlynar considers it 'highly probable' that Brezhnev and the moderates forestalled a Kremlin putsch by taking the initiative and joining with the hawks in favour of invasion. This defused the anti-Brezhnev group.[10]

On 17 August Dubček met Janos Kadar. The Hungarian first secretary, an expert on the subject, warned the Czech that military action was imminent. Responsibility for an invasion had been transferred from the Warsaw Pact, under Marshal Yakubovsky, to General Pavlovsky, the C-in-C of Soviet Ground Forces.

The formal decision to invade was taken at an extraordinary session of the Central Committee on 19 August. Brezhnev was later to claim that he had been assured by the US that Washington 'fully recognized the results of Yalta and Potsdam'. With the US apparently on the sidelines, the danger of invasion spreading into general war was reduced. The Czechs had no possibility of effective resistance. The General Staff told Dubček that, since it had planned only for a Nato invasion from West Germany, the frontiers with East Germany, Poland, Russia and Hungary were defenceless. A plan for resistance had been drafted by General Prchlik in July but it was not a real option in the face of Soviet armour.

The pre-pattern of the invasion, the same template to be used in Afghanistan with its emphasis on radio stations, airport control towers and false pleas for intervention, went into effect on the morning of 20 August, a Tuesday. It was well planned. 'For four whole months, the battalion had worked at its task with maps and models,' wrote an officer in a Russian motor-rifle division who took part in the invasion, Viktor Suvorov.[11] 'The battalion chief of staff had a complete set of photographs of all the crossroads along the route ... Staff commander exercises had been held during which all the twenty officers of the battalion had visited Prague and travelled by bus along their future routes.'

Positions were taken for the coming propaganda war. The head of the Czech Press Agency, suspended for his hard-line views, reappeared in his office that morning. Sacked secret policemen met at the interior ministry. The three pro-Soviet members of the Presidium voted to ask the Russians to cleanse the Czech crisis.

Electronic screens blocked Western surveillance of the troop build-up and radio traffic was kept to a minimum. Long-range US and Nato radar did show up a heavy concentration of flights over Poland, active refuelling of military transport aircraft in Leningrad and the alert of the Soviet Strategic Rocket Forces. There were no direct links with Czechoslovakia. A note had been sent to President Johnson agreeing to a summit meeting in Leningrad on 30 September. The Russians were careful to stress that 'the current events should not harm Soviet–American relations'. Though Johnson cancelled the Leningrad summit, damage control by Soviet diplomats was to prove effective.

Shortly after 10 p.m. on 20 August the control tower of Prague airport was taken over by Soviet commandos who landed in an Aeroflot civilian airliner. The Russians knew the landing procedures at the airport and slipped in without resistance. Aeroflot aircraft in six other flights were used to seize communications centres before the military airlift began.[12]

It was a hot, sticky Tuesday night. Many Czechs were abroad, for passports were easier to get that summer than for twenty years. Though Prague was nervous, the heat and the withdrawal of Russian troops had induced a listlessness. If the Russians came, there was nothing to be done.

The first reports to the Czech government came from the border regions. Tanks and armoured personnel carriers had lanced through the wire and red and white poles at frontier posts, pulling long convoys in their wake. They came from the Ukraine, Poland, East Germany and Hungary in four armoured prongs. An invasion over the 2,625 kilometres of the four frontiers was more effective than mounting it over the mere 98 kilometres of Soviet border. The distance from East Germany to Prague as the tank rolls is 105 kilometres, where a column entering from the Ukraine had to motor for 750 kilometres.

At 11.40 p.m. Cernik told the Presidium meeting: 'The troops of five countries have crossed the frontier of our Republic and are occupying us.'[13] By midnight the first tanks, their exhausts glowing and their searchlights playing on the cobblestones, were moving into Bratislava. The city, the Slovakian capital, paid for its nearness to the Hungarian border. Kosice fell next.

The first public warning, to those lulling away the early hours with a radio, did not come until 1.58 a.m. on Wednesday. Radio Prague announced: 'Yesterday, on August 20 1968, at about 2300 hours ...' It then went dead. Through open windows in Prague came the dull sound of Soviet aero engines. Antonov transports were landing one a minute at Prague airport.

The V-12 tank diesels, turning over at 2,000 RPM, were heard in Karlovy Vary, near the East German border, at 3 a.m. Many Czechs slept through it. A tank column, shepherded by a black Volga car from the Soviet embassy, ground its way to the Central Committee building in Prague shortly after 4 a.m. Mlynar watched soldiers in 'paratroop uniforms with wine coloured berets and sailors' jerseys under their shirts' jump out of armoured cars carrying automatic weapons.[14] The building was blocked off with tanks and a platoon of troops ran inside. Mlynar was watching with Dubček from Dubček's office. He felt he was watching a film. He had to tell himself that these troops, whom he had welcomed in 1945 and with whom he had drunk vodka as a student in Moscow, were not 'shadows of the silver screen' pointing their guns at 'Tsarist cadets in the Winter Palace or at the surviving Germans in the gutted Reichstag'. The sub-machine guns were pointing at 'me, personally'. Other tanks went to prime minister Cernik's office, where he was arrested.

It was breakfast and a misty sun was up when the squat hemispherical turrets, a regulation 100 metres apart, moved in convoy into Plzen and Brno. The Soviet delegation at the United Nations in New York was now claiming that the troops had gone in 'upon the demand of Czech and Slovak patriots and communists'.

Dubček swore 'on my honour as a Communist' that he was innocent of any foreknowledge of Russian intentions. 'I, who have devoted my whole life to collaboration with the Soviet Union, now they do this to me! This is the tragedy of my life!' During the morning the doors of his office were flung open and eight soldiers and junior officers rushed in, aiming their sub-machine guns at the back of the first secretary's neck. They were followed by a short, much-medalled colonel with the 'arrogant authoritarian bearing of a sergeant major'.[15] The telephone lines to the room were cut and the troops closed the windows so that the crowd, which had gathered beyond a cordon of paratroops, could not be heard singing the national anthem and chanting Dubček's name.

Mlynar found that the troops assigned to guard the Central Committee building, from the famous Taman 'court' division used in Kremlin displays, were rather special. The lieutenant guarding him was a literature graduate and one of the troopers spoke French. The Russians had had no food since the night before. Dubček's chauffeur brought in salami, bread and beer in the afternoon. The Red army men ate the left-overs.

Mlynar reckoned that he could convince his lieutenant of the absurdity of the invasion given enough time. Five days later he told Marshal Grechko as much in the Kremlin, saying that he thought the Russian army in Czechoslovakia was ideologically disintegrating. 'Perhaps,' replied Grechko. 'But it doesn't matter. If they fall apart, we'll replace them. I can replace them ten times over.' Not very idealistic, perhaps, but realistic. The Czechs, too, were as realistic about what faced them as they had been in 1938. A broadcast Appeal by the Czech Presidium called for all to 'maintain calm and not to resist the invaders, as the defence of our frontiers is now impossible ...' The armed forces were ordered to remain in barracks. Many units were disarmed by the Russians and at first locked into their barracks. They were later evicted by the five Russian divisions that have remained permanently in Czechoslovakia since the invasion.

'Throughout the entire night, in an endless stream, the troops were marching past our armoured personnel carriers and tanks,' Suvorov wrote. Tanks, APCs and troops from every Warsaw Pact country except Rumania were flooding across the borders. If standard distance had been kept between vehicles, each division would have sprawled for 150 kilometres. The constant order was 'Close up!' Broken-down tanks, artillery tractors and APCs were pushed off the road. The dense columns would have been a perfect target for Czech fighter bombers, but none came. The Red Star markings on the Soviet armour were stuck over with newspaper. The invading tanks and guns had white stripes painted on them to distinguish them from Czech machines, quickly covered with layers of dust. Helicopters clattered over the columns.

The invaders had come in strength. They numbered 250,000 combat troops in 29 divisions, 1,000 aircraft and 7,500 tanks.[16] There were a further 250,000 support troops, giving a two to one superiority over Czech forces.

General Pavlovsky, the invasion commander, had twice the force that had been available to his predecessor in Hungary fourteen years before and twice as many tanks as the Germans had at the start of *Barbarossa*.

The Czechs were rolled under 270,000 tons of armour, moving along the roads at up to 50 k.p.h. Each tank crew, cramped, suffering the violent vibrations, heat and carbon-monoxide build-up that marked the Russian machines, had available a 100- or 115-mm gun which would penetrate up to 380 mm of toughened steel at 900 metres and reduce a building to rubble at 2.5 kilometres. For smaller prey, they had coaxial 7.62-mm machineguns. Each machine, T-54 or T-62, had a road range of over 480 kilometres and carried 40 shells.

During the occupation of key points, Soviet officers were recognized from the Warsaw Pact summer manoeuvres. Poles made up the bulk of the non-Soviet troops, perhaps 50,000 strong, with 40,000 Hungarians and East Germans and 10,000 Bulgarians 'to make up the furniture', as the Russians put it.

The Russians feared a clash with NATO, with many of their men coming 'from mountainous kishlaks and distant reindeer-breeding farms', with little grasp of Soviet and none of Central European geography. Skilful and bold planning stopped the invaders from spilling over into West Germany and Austria. The tinder of a third world war was not tempted by sparks. General Pavlovsky deployed five Soviet divisions along the main highways and feeder roads about five kilometres back from the West German border.[17]

As the tanks chewed up the thin tarmac on the Czech roads, crowds pelted them with stones and rotten fruit. In Prague youths forced crews under their hatches with stones and then set fire to the spare fuel drums on the tank decks. Some Soviet units mistakenly opened fire on each other. Two Czech collaborators were blocked in a Soviet armoured car following a collision with a tram. They preferred to remain inside, sweating in the August heat, than run the risk of being spotted by the onlookers drawn by the accident. President Svoboda, surrounded by Russian troops in

Hradcany Castle in Prague, refused to appoint a new government. Students sat in front of tanks and replaced road signs. Czech officers refused any cooperation with the invasion force. Police cars, klaxons blaring, swept past Russian checkpoints on Prague bridges with messages detailing passive resistance.

Passive it was. Not more than eighty were killed[18] in an operation which, if it showed that Warsaw Pact logistics were imperfect, in terms of tank breakdowns and shoddy communications, was textbook in the political use of force. The repression was all but bloodless. It continues to subdue the Czechs a generation later.

It took the Soviets until the next March to mop up.

After being held in his office, Dubček was arrested by KGB officers and their Czech collaborators late on 21 August.[19] He was taken first to the staff headquarters of the Warsaw Pact in Poland and transferred to a KGB prison on Soviet soil in the Transcarpathian Ukraine. He was treated as a traitor and kept under close guard.

The Russians were unable to impose a hard-line government in Prague with the ease they expected. They had a core of anti-reformists, who appealed for cooperation with the Soviet authorities and attempted to legalize the invasion. These were a minority, unable to raise enough support to create an anti-Dubček government. An attempt to set up a puppet regime was made at a meeting in the Praha hotel in Prague on 22 August which was attended by Soviet officers and Czech hard-liners. President Svoboda refused to back this group. Czech opposition was cemented by huge demonstrations in Prague and other cities. The same day, the 14th Congress of the Czech Party was brought forward and held, despite roaming Soviet tanks and patrols, at a factory in the Vysocany district of Prague. About a thousand delegates were there. Only one voted against an affirmation of complete support for Dubček.[20]

Radio appeals were specific and effective. On 23 August news was given of a Russian train entering Czechoslovakia with radio-jamming equipment. The train was held up in a station, then stopped on a main line because the electricity was cut off and finally blocked by abandoned locomotives on a branch line.[21] Other broadcasts gave the car registration numbers of Russian agents in the interior ministry.

The resistance was the more effective because it was legitimate. The Russians had failed to impose a new government and their claims that the invasion forces had been invited in by 'party and government leaders' had no conviction. There was blanket condemnation, though no action, from the West and from the Chinese, Rumanian, Yugoslav and Albanian communist parties. The Chinese voted against the Russians in the UN Security Council.

The Russians were forced to negotiate with Svoboda and Dubček, who was released from his handcuffs and brought to Moscow on the evening of 23 August. Far from the 'traitors' being delivered to a 'revolutionary tribunal', as the Russians had planned a few days earlier, they remained for the time being in power. Mlynar arrived two days later and was taken by Chaika limousine to a government villa in the Lenin Hills. 'I was no longer in the Moscow of my youth,' he wrote. 'I was in the capital city of an occupying power.' He had been a post-war student in the Lomonosov State University in the Lenin Hills at the same time as Mikhail Gorbachev.

Taken to the Kremlin, he found Svoboda and Cernik, the prime minister. Dubček was in a small room, lying in a bed, naked to the waist, limp and 'obviously under sedation'. A sticking plaster on his forehead covered a small wound where he had slipped and hurt himself. In a state of 'utter nervous collapse', Dubček took no part in the first day's negotiations.[22]

The Czechs were split into pro-reform and pro-Soviet camps but there was never much doubt that they would sign an agreement acceptable to the Russians. Svoboda shouted at them: 'There you go, talk, talk, talking again! You've already talked and talked until your country's occupied.'

When Mlynar returned to his villa in the Lenin Hills at 3 a.m. on 26 August, after an exhausting session in the Kremlin, he found tables laden with vodka, cognac, caviar and sturgeon and a girl in a negligee waiting for him. 'Is there anything more you would like, comrade?' she asked. Inducements were not necessary. Mlynar realized that the Czechs were being 'blackmailed by gangsters', who told them brutally: 'If you won't sign it today, you will in a week.'

The Czechs met the full Soviet Politburo in the Kremlin on the afternoon of 26 August. Brezhnev opened the meeting, saying reproachfully to the drugged Dubček: 'Our Sasha is a good comrade, I said. And you disappointed us terribly.' He said that the Czechs had not sought approval from Moscow for changes which had incited 'antisocialist tendencies' and 'counterrevolutionary organizations'. The suffering of Soviet troops to liberate Czechoslovakia during the war had linked the two countries 'forever'.

'For us the results of the war are inviolable and we will defend them even at the cost of risking a new war,' Brezhnev said. Not that there had been such a risk, he went on. He had asked President Johnson whether the US government still recognized the results of Yalta and Potsdam. 'On 18 August I received the reply,' he said. 'As far as Czechoslovakia and Rumania are concerned, it recognizes them without reservation.'[23] Brezhnev was unsentimental. 'We have already got the better of other little nations, so why not yours too?' he said. Nothing would help the Czechs.

'War will not break out. Comrades Tito and Ceauşescu [the Yugoslav and Rumanian leaders] will give speeches, also Comrade Berlinguer [the Italian Communist]. And what? You rely on the communist movement in Western Europe, but it already lost its meaning fifty years ago!'[24] When Dubček tried to argue with him, Brezhnev walked out with the rest of the Politburo following him 'like a line of geese'. Dubček, close to collapse, said: 'Let them do what they want, I won't sign it.' He allowed himself to have another tranquillizing injection and finally gave way.

The Moscow Protocol was signed at midnight on 26 August. The 'temporary' stationing of the invasion forces was accepted. Censorship, or 'ideological supervision', was to be restored together with the traditional repressive role of the interior ministry. The 14th Party Congress was declared 'invalid'. At the moment of signature, the door of the conference room flew open and a posse of photographers came in as the Soviets, Brezhnev, Grechko, Gromyko and all, leant forward on cue to embrace the humiliated Czechs.

It was not yet capitulation. The invasion was not justified and the policies of Dubček and the 'right-wing opportunists' were defended.

The Czechs were back in Prague before dawn, but re-Stalinization was a pace behind them. There was an immediate crackdown on the Czech forces. General Prchlik was dismissed. General Otakar Rytir, responsible for liaison with the Red army, began a long purge of suspect officers. In all, 11,000 officers and 38,000 NCOs were purged or resigned from the Czech forces and the shortage of men became so acute that entire Czech divisions had to be disbanded. Not that this worried the Russians. They made up the shortfall by stationing 80,000 of their own troops permanently in Czechoslovakia. Two tank divisions, the 31st and 51st, were established with equipment left behind by units returning to East Germany. Three motor rifle divisions which had invaded from White Russia stayed on Czech soil and were simply reassigned from the USSR to Czechoslovakia.

The final reckoning between the Czechs and re-Stalinization, or 'normalization' as the Russians put it, reached its climax at an ice hockey match. On 28 March 1969 the Czech ice hockey team scored a second victory over the Soviet team at the world championships in Stockholm.

Most Czechs were watching the match live on TV. The result was an explosive triumph for a small people over the Bear. 'The Soviet team,' the paper *Lidova Demokracia* wrote, 'this non-professional group of players who are on the ice 11 months of the year, obviously forgot that the brain is sometimes more powerful than muscle.' Dubček and Cernik sent telegrams to the team. Thousands of car horns blared in Prague. 'Improvised fireworks, bonfires and firecrackers suddenly lit up the night,' reported *Rude Pravo* the next day. 'In about 30 minutes, a hundred thousand people were celebrating the victory and others were still arriving. St

Wenceslas' statue was covered with flowers.' The Aeroflot office in the centre of Prague was burned out during the celebrations. Soviet Ambassador Chervonenko complained that police had stood idly by. Russian troop commanders said that their men were being 'ridiculed' by crowds. No Czech forces intervened when they were asked to act against demonstrators.

It was the excuse the Russians were looking for. On the afternoon of 31 March the Soviet defence minister Andrei Grechko landed unannounced with a group of General Staff officers at Milovice, the Soviet HQ in Czechoslovakia. The deputy foreign minister, Konstantin Semyonov, arrived at Prague airport. Both senior Russians denounced the acts of 'counter-revolution' following the ice hockey victory. They claimed that Czech soldiers had taken part in the 'provocations' which had been coordinated from abroad. They said that serious breaches of the Moscow Protocol were continuing.

Grechko, who had been met at Milovice by a group of pro-Soviet Czech officers, told them that the failure of the Czech military to come to the aid of their Soviet colleagues amounted to counter-revolution. He criticized the 'lack of military, moral and political preparedness' and announced that a further 35,000 Red army troops were being moved into the country.[25]

Grechko had still to deal with the Czech commander-in-chief, President Svoboda, and General Dzur, the defence minister. He met both of them on 1 April at Hradcany castle, together with Dubček and Cernik. The meetings were icy and tense, with Svoboda angry at the Russian marshal's unannounced visit. Grechko, for his part, told them that 'part of the [Czech] army has disintegrated' and that the situation was worse than it had been in August.

The Kremlin threw its weight behind Gustav Husak. It was a shrewd move since Husak, though a hard-liner, was not then known as a Soviet stooge. Like so many of the East European Communists, Husak had himself suffered under the faith. In 1951 he had been taken by security police to Kolodeje castle near Prague. Before his interrogations, he had undergone disorientation sessions. He was taken from a freezing room to a sweat chamber kept at 40 degrees Centigrade, without doors or points of reference, the whole padded in material so that the victim lost his sense of space and came to think he was being crushed before his interrogators, in shorts and light cotton shirts, joined him through a hidden door. Husak served six years in prison without his faith in either the Party or the Soviets being diminished. He had seen the invasion as his chance for power from the start. 'I shall lead the nation out of this catastrophe,' he is said to have shouted as the roar of tank engines flooded over Bratislava on the first dawn of the intervention.[26]

On 17 April 1969 Husak replaced Dubček as first secretary.

The Prague Spring was over, bar the detail. That was taken care of in 1970. On 9 May the 'temporary' stay of the Red army became permanent. On 25 June Dubček was expelled from the Communist Party and the 'slight figure with the human face' became a forester. In the only Russophile nation in Europe, a Czech noted, the Russians had succeeded in creating enemies out of friends. Husak, though his regime became an embarrassment to Gorbachev, was to survive for two decades.

34

POLISH WINTER

Poland lives on the edge of Russian invasion. The Kremlin has put armoured units on the alert for 'fraternal intervention' at least three times. Part of the invasion force was installed in 1980 and 1981. It was bought off with neat cynicism by having the Polish military itself do the repression. This proud and profoundly Catholic country, despite its reputation for romantic folly, has managed to stop short of provoking an incursion of Soviet tanks.

It has consistently produced a core of pro-Soviet ultras. General Jaruzelski is no exception. Jakub Berman, now disgraced, in 1956 the most powerful member of the Polish Politburo, nostalgically remembers dining with Stalin during the dictator's late gluttony period. Stalin would put on a record to amuse his guests, and the guests would dance. 'Once, I danced with Molotov,' said Berman. Surely he meant Mrs Molotov, Comrade Zhemshuzhina, a Jewess and a prominent supporter of the Yiddish theatre in Russia? 'No, she'd been sent to a labour camp,' Berman says. 'I danced with Molotov. It must have been a waltz, or at any rate something simple because I didn't have a clue about how to dance. I just moved my feet to the rhythm.' Molotov led. 'He wasn't a bad dancer, actually.' Thus Berman, himself a Jew, danced to amuse Stalin at a time when the Georgian was in a fit of anti-Semitism. Berman accepted his later dismissal and humiliation. 'When you're cast out, you don't exist,' he said philosophically. 'When I was in power, they even included me in the Soviet encyclopaedia. Later they deleted all that.'[1]

Poland also has a profound sense of danger and of Russian power. Catherine the Great sent 40,000 men marching on Warsaw in 1772, saying: 'The future will show whether anybody but me can give Poland a King.' By 1795 the country had ceased to exist. Neither the 80,000 Polish volunteers who joined Napoleon's Grande Armée in 1812, nor revolts in

1830, 1846 and 1853, were successful in restoring it. Catherine's descendant Tsar Alexander II warned the Poles on his accession in 1855: 'Pas de rêveries, Messieurs.' No dreams.

Pilsudski, the nationalist leader of the Poland reconstituted after the First World War, was born under Alexander and banished to Siberia. He was aware that Polish independence relied on divine coincidence. It was only possible, he said in 1914, if 'Russia is beaten by Germany and Germany is beaten by France'. Now, of course, Russia has beaten Germany and maintains a large army *west* of Poland, and French concern for Poland is largely of sentimental value, like a Fabergé egg.

Poles realize that, like Catherine, Gorbachev remains their king-maker. The risk of invasion and loss of nationhood is a constant. All sides agree on that. 'My dear lady, we simply couldn't refuse to have them,' Berman sniffed at an interviewer goading him over the post-war Russian presence. The Solidarity leader Lech Walesa said[2] that Poland would have been dragged into the Russian orbit, Yalta or not, and that 'perhaps it was better to get it over with quickly'. Grudgingly, Poles accept that the country is tied by politics and geography to socialism and to the Soviet Union. It is this that has kept the Warsaw Pact tanks at bay.

It has been a fine-run thing.

Worker unrest and living standards were at the heart of the first unrest, in 1956, as they still are. Poles lived 1.7 to a room in shanty blocks in which less than one in three had piped water, one in five a lavatory and one in seven a bath. Peasants had been herded into collectives, the Catholic Primate, Cardinal Wyszynski, into a monastery. 'People were caught in the streets and released after seven days of interrogation, unfit to live,' a leading Communist admitted.[3] 'These people had to be taken to lunatic asylums. Others sought refuge in lunatic asylums to avoid the security police ...' A Soviet marshal, Rokossovsky, was defence minister and C-in-C.

Workers took to the streets in Poznan in June. Regular army units refused to obey orders to open fire on strikers. An elite unit of the internal security corps, the KBW, was drafted to Poznan from Warsaw to restore order. At least fifty-three were killed.

The Party was split between pro-Berman Stalinists and progressives, encouraged by Khrushchev's secret speech, their hopes pinned on Ladislas Gomulka. The Gomulka faction made progress. In May, Berman had gone. In August, a crowd of a million made the pilgrimage to Częstochowa to celebrate the anniversary of the Virgin Mary being declared the 'Queen of Poland'. If they could not have a king, the Poles had a queen. Alarmed, the Kremlin threatened to hold Red army manoeuvres in Poland and on 19 October Khrushchev flew to Warsaw.

On his unannounced arrival, Soviet divisions moved out of their bar-racks towards the capital. Some key unit commanders, including the head of coastal units, Admiral Jan Wisniewski and General Jan Frey-Bielecki of the air force, prepared to resist the Russians. The KBW, under the reformist General Wraclaw Komar, took up defensive positions round Warsaw. Warned by Rokossovsky that the half-million-strong army might side with Gomulka, Khrushchev accepted him. Gomulka, for his part of the bargain, gave a speech on 24 October in front of the Palace of Culture, Stalin's monumentally hideous gift to the luckless people of Warsaw. Red army units would return to their bases, Gomulka said. Relations with the Soviet Union were 'normal'. 'If there is anyone who thinks that it is possible to kindle anti-Soviet moods in Poland,' he warned, 'he is deeply mistaken.' Economic changes were possible. Changes in relations with Russia would be national suicide.

Gomulka exploited the Hungarian autumn. Rokossovsky and other Soviet officers were recalled. Polish uniforms and traditional marching songs were reintroduced. Polish sovereignty was confirmed and Red army units stationed in Poland required Polish consent to move. The collective farms were largely junked. Within 6 months, only 1,700 out of 10,500 were left.

Cardinal Wyszynski was released from his monastery-prison. On 5 November, the day after Budapest had been attacked, he preached a sermon to the packed Church of the Holy Cross in Warsaw. 'A man dies once and is quickly covered with glory,' he said. 'But if he lives for long years in difficulty, in hardship, pain and suffering, that is greater heroism. Just that greater heroism is called for ... on this day so pregnant with events and so full of anxiety on all sides.'[4] The message was clear on both sides. The Russians had had a sharp reminder of Polish sensibilities. The Poles, Church and state, accepted that Bear-baiting was a dangerous business that could not be allowed to get out of hand.

The Russians had won back much ground by 1968. Wisniewski and Frey-Bielecki had been dismissed, a young general, Wojciech Jaruzelski, criticizing the 'excessive nationalism' of the officer corps. The entire leadership of the air force defence command was sacked, accused of a 'pro-Israel stance masked by nationalism', after officers had sneered at the performance of Soviet aircraft in the June war of 1967. Polish units took part in the invasion of Czechoslovakia, if sandwiched between Red army groups.

Major changes were needed again in 1971, following riots in Gdansk and Szczecin in December 1970. These were sparked by a rise in food prices. The leaders were elite workers who had tasted the West on training courses with Zulzer in Switzerland and Baumeistr in Denmark.[5] Gomulka attempted to use the regular army to suppress them. The military refused

INTERMEDIATE RANGE
BALLISTIC MISSILE BASE IN CUBA

PROB NUCLEAR STORAGE BUNKER

BATCH PLANTS

PRE-FAB CONSTRUCTION MATERIAL

LAUNCH PAD

CONTROL BUILDING

OTECTED
POSITION

LAUNCH PAD

Top left Nikita Khrushchev demands a humiliating public apology from Eisenhower after the U-2 incident. (© *Popperfoto*)

Above The approach to Armageddon in the Cuban crisis of 1962. A Soviet freighter is bound for the port of Mariel in Cuba. It carries equipment for a missile base, photographed by U.S. reconnaissance pilots in October. (© *Popperfoto*)

Left A flagged map of the Cuban missile bases. (© *Keystone*)

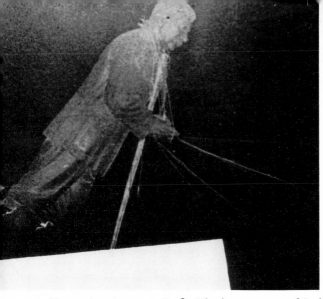

Hungarian Autumn: **Left**: The huge statue of Stalin is toppled in Budapest at the start of the 1956 uprising. (© *Popperfoto*)

Right The charismatic Pal Maleter, the tank colonel who joined the rebels and was later executed. Despite Moscow's promise to withdraw, Soviet tanks swarm back into Budapest on 4 November.

Below Defiant insurgents swarm onto tanks as Hungarian armoured units come out in support. (© *Keystone*) Most of the 'counter-revolutionaries' were, to Soviet alarm, embittered factory workers.

Prague Spring: **Left** Top: Soviet armour enters the Czech capital in August
1968. Infantrymen are met by silent and contemptuous Czech youths. (© *Keystone*)

Right Alexander Dubcek, who said of the invasion: 'I who have devoted my
whole life to collaboration with the Soviet Union, now they do this to me!
This is the tragedy of my life!' (© *Popperfoto*)

Berlin Summer: **Below**: US troops enter East Berlin as the Wall goes up in
1961. (© *Keystone*)

Above A Soviet tank in the centre of Prague. (© *Keystone*)

Right Polish Winter: Lech Walesa, leader of the disbanded Solidarity union, leaves the Gdansk shipyard. (© *Popperfoto*)

The Bear Trap: Kabul airport on 31 December 1979, at the start of the Soviet invasion.

Pinned down and frustrated by lightly armed mujaheddin, happy Soviet troops give peace signs as they prepare to pull out a decade later. (*Top* © *Gamma/Frank Spooner. Bottom* © *Popperfoto*)

Above left A prominent Gorbachev victim, Admiral Gorshkov, the creator of the modern Soviet navy, rated a one-paragraph mention when he was replaced by a Gorbachev man, Admiral Chernavin. (© *Novosti*)

The Old Guard. **Above**: Wartime armaments chief and beneficiary of the Brezhnev build-up, defence minister Dmitri Ustinov reviews troops in Moscow before being replaced. (© *Popperfoto*)

Left Gorbachev meets Reagan at the Geneva Summit in 1985. (© *Novosti*)

OPPOSITE PAGE

Top left and right Mathias Rust, the teenage pilot who flew his little Cessna to Red Square, gave Gorbachev a providential chance to purge the Old Guard. Out went the defence minister Marshal Sokolev and the air defence chief, Marshal of Aviation Koldunov. In heady promotion, General Yazov (right) became defence minister. (*Both photos* © *Popperfoto*)

Middle Left: A T-80 main battle tank, the mainstay of elite armoured divisions. Despite the Gorbachev cuts in armour, 260 tanks are still being produced a month.

Middle right Though most nuclear weapons are carried atop missiles, the Soviets are building Blackjack bombers. Its inspection by US officials marked a new level of trust between the superpowers.

Bottom The Mi-8 Hip attack helicopter carries combat troops and supports them with rocket fire. The Red army has three times as many Hips as the combined British forces have helicopters.

Top The might of the new Soviet navy. A 'boomer', a Hotel-class ballistic submarine whose missiles could be used in city-busting attacks on the West.

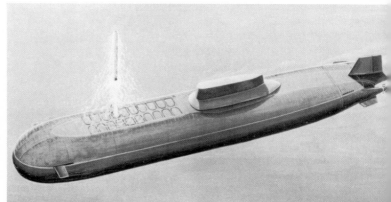

Middle The world's largest submarine, the 25,000-ton *Typhoon*. Each carries 20 missiles with up to nine warheads apiece, and can seriously damage a continent.

Bottom Generations: decorated veterans of the Great Patriotic and the Afghan wars meet at a gathering in Moscow's Gorky Park.
(© *Popperfoto*)

to act on orders to use immediate and overwhelming force to crush the demonstrations. Regular units of the Gdansk garrison did inflict some casualties, their officers complaining that 'the coastal events were painful for the entire country and probably most painful for ourselves'. Walesa described how workers pushed forward 'to see if the boys in Polish uniforms were really Poles or Russians in disguise'. They were Poles and they did open fire. Most of the dirty work, 45 dead and 1,165 injured by official count, had to be left to the militia.[6]

Jaruzelski, now defence minister, said that 'difficult morale problems have arisen ... Public opinion has turned against the military.' The army was not prepared to support Gomulka and he was replaced by Edward Gierek. Gierek bought off trouble with a price freeze, increased welfare and more meat. Army pay was boosted so that a lieutenant got three times the money of a civilian with similar qualifications, plus an apartment in a country with a ten-year waiting list.[7]

The economy, in Western-financed expansion, had overheated by 1976 with a hard currency debt of $8 billion. Price increases, 69 per cent for meat, 100 per cent for sugar, again led to crisis. Gierek was forced to cancel them within twenty-four hours. Jaruzelski is said to have warned him that 'Polish soldiers will not fire on Polish workers.' Enough Polish workers had been arrested by the police, however, for a Committee of Workers' Defence, KOR, to be set up in September 1976. Poland was on course for the Solidarity crisis.

Moscow is poorer than Warsaw but it is not as drab. In Warsaw, the buildings of the Old Town are post-war reconstructions and Stalin's Palace of Culture broods over them. The queues shuffle in line, not in deference to their own guns coming before butter, but as tribute to far-off Soviet submarines and rockets. The empty shops echo with alien power. Without the consolations of national authority, Poles need meat more than Russians.

As fresh Western funding dried up, the economy stagnated. The growth rate, 11 per cent in 1973, was minus two by 1980. The hard currency debt was up to $20 billion. Into this, Gierek tossed a demand in February 1980 for a 'spirit of perseverance and sacrifice'. In July, meat price increases were announced. The Lenin Shipyard in Gdansk went on strike on 14 August. Long a thorn for the regime, the government was to announce the closure of the Lenin shipyards in Gdansk in November 1988. The yards were held to be no longer economically viable – an admission that a symbol of Lenin is not for ever immune to market forces. Two days later delegations from 388 plants met to form an Inter-Factory Strike Committee, MKS.

MKS put forward a list of twenty-one demands that went beyond wages and meat into the dangerous ground of free unions, the right to strike, freedom of speech, the abolition of privileges for the police and secret services. On 22 August the government sent vice-premier Mieczyslaw Jagielski to Gdansk to negotiate. The following day, the ninth of the Gdansk strike, he went to the shipyards with a government commission in a bus. A crowd of workers halted it, beat on the windows and shouted: 'Get down! Continue on foot! On your knees in front of the workers!'[8] Jagielski got out of the bus and walked to meet Lech Walesa, the young electrician who was emerging as the shipyard leader.

At a meeting on 24 August the government, shaken, discussed a counterattack. Colonel Ryszard Kuklinski, a senior officer on the Polish General Staff, trained at the Soviet Armed Forces Academy and present at meetings of the Warsaw Pact military council, noted an ominous development in the information he was sending to the Americans and Solidarity contacts.[9] The introduction *in extremis* of a State of War, the closest approximation to martial law allowed under the Polish constitution, was being mentioned.

On 30 August, though plans were already under way to abrogate them, Jagielski signed the Gdansk accords. Free unions were allowed. Solidarnosc, the Solidarity union, was created. The Party hoped that the taste of power would corrupt the new union leaders. Walesa obtained a tape of a speech given to party hard-liners by the first secretary of the Katowice area. 'We must give them offices and equip them as lavishly as possible,' said this cynic.[10] 'I have always said it and I say it again. I do not know a man who has not been weakened by power. It is only a question of time and degree. You can already see it happening to them. The ready money, the taxi rides to Gdansk, telephones, easy access to Jagielski. They travel, they go through their money. Everything has started off right.'

Concessions continued. At a late-night meeting of the Central Committee on 5 September Gierek was replaced by Stanislas Kania. Polish workers had again brought down the party leader.

The agreements reached with the workers at Gdansk and Szczecin were published. The PEWEX hard-currency stores, the equivalent of the Soviet *Beriozkas* where party bigwigs did their shopping, were instructed not to sell Polish goods unavailable to the public. The government insisted on two riders to forestall the Soviet gut reaction that had led to the Czech and Hungarian invasions. The free unions would have to recognize 'the leading role of the PZPR [the Polish Communist Party] in the State' and 'not oppose the existing system of international alliances'. No messing round with the Warsaw Pact and no bad-mouthing the Kremlin.

By December 1980 membership of Solidarity had reached 7.5 million. This included up to a third of party members. The Russians were not mollified by vague statements about Party supremacy and adherence to the Warsaw Pact. Invasion plans were drawn up under cover of the 'Soyuz 81' exercises. These entailed joint manoeuvres in Poland by fifteen Soviet divisions, together with one East German and two Czech divisions. According to Kuklinski, Moscow was unmoved by Jaruzelski's plea to drop the East German contingent.

Jaruzelski emerged in a 'state of shock' from the Russian 'intransigence and brutality'.[11] The Polish General Staff was 'paralysed' with fear of invasion. 'Everybody waited for a miracle,' says Kuklinski. On 5 December, after President Carter had warned the Russians to 'let the Poles solve their own problems', Jaruzelski proposed the 'national solution' of a Polish military takeover. The invasion, which had shown up planning weaknesses in Soviet mobilization procedures,[12] was postponed. To remind the Poles of their obligations, Red army units remained concentrated on the frontier.

After another wave of strikes, Jaruzelski was appointed prime minister on 9 February 1981. Twelve days later he accepted the authoritative plan for the State of War, which had been prepared by forty-five senior officers and two members of the Central Committee. He told the Russians that he would send his detailed proposals to the 26th Congress of the Soviet Party. They were angry at Polish stalling. 'Soyuz 81' was resurrected. Marshal Viktor Kulikov, the Warsaw Pact C-in-C, brought eighteen Soviet generals to Warsaw, supposedly to check on preparations for the exercises. The nature of the manoeuvres was not in doubt. The Soviet General Chtcheglov asked the commander of a regiment stationed near Warsaw: 'How would you deal with removing strikers from a factory?'

From 14 February Soviet reconnaissance units began arriving in Poland. They checked out Warsaw airport, the radio and TV centre and major buildings and plants. They wanted no repetition of Prague, with tank crews asking civilians for street directions. Buildings were selected for barracks and headquarters.

'Soyuz 81' started on 16 March involving 150,000 troops. On 19 March three Solidarity supporters were killed in militia beatings in Bydgoszcz. A general strike was called in protest. Kulikov installed his officers in the Polish air defence centre at Pyry, near Warsaw, thus confirming Soviet control of Polish airspace. On 27 March a Soviet government jet arrived at Warsaw airport with thirty KGB and Red army officers aboard. Two days later the Soviet news agency Tass spoke of 'Polish terrorist crimes'.

On 30 March Walesa announced an agreement with the government and called off the strike. It cost him savage criticism inside Solidarity. Together with the Hinckley murder attempt on President Reagan that day, which switched American attention away from Poland, it helped to defuse the invasion.

The Soviets remained particularly worried that the Polish Party had lost its monopoly on information. Forty per cent of journalists and 60 per cent of TV crews had joined Solidarity, which started its own legal weekly,

Tygodnik Solidarnosc. It reached an immediate 500,000 circulation. The 'Soyuz 81' exercises were prolonged. Asked why, the Warsaw Pact CoS, General Gribkov, said: 'Because they have not achieved their objectives.' Kulikov was blunter: 'Because of the counter-revolution in Poland.'

On the night of 3 April Jaruzelski and Kania flew to Moscow. The Russians started a war of nerves. Without informing Polish air traffic control, they transferred thirty-two Mi-6 attack helicopters from Czechoslovakia to Poland and landed ten An-12 freighters at Brzeg with non-specified military equipment.

Brezhnev ended the 'Soyuz 81' manoeuvres on 8 April. Polish forces had been placed on combat readiness status in October 1980, and were kept at it throughout 1981. Soldiers who had finished their tour of duty were not discharged.[13] Soviet harassment continued. Thirty-seven new flights were made by heavy transports to Brzeg, in the south-west near Wroclaw. A group of officers arrived in Warsaw to study the State of War plans. These were approved and the flights stopped. However, Jaruzelski did not fix a precise date. Kulikov refused to disband the Soviet command structure set up for 'Soyuz 81' and forty-seven senior Soviet staff officers remained throughout the year. The Soviet handling of the crisis was much more a military than a political affair, with Kulikov playing the major role.

Walesa was well aware of the Soviet danger. To the irritation of his own hard-liners, he stressed that he would help the Polish Party if it started to collapse. 'There are no other realities here,' he warned. 'We cannot overthrow the Party. We cannot take the power away from it. We have to preserve it. At the same time, tame it and let it eat with us, so that it will relish what we create.'[14] The Party was, however, getting ready to eat him.

Solidarity was seen to have overdrawn its account with strike calls. Walesa, too moderate for some, too extreme for others, was finding it difficult to control the movement. The sense of national pride and cohesion, boosted by the election of the Polish Cardinal Wojtyla as Pope John Paul in 1978, was wavering. Towards the end of 1981 46 per cent of the population supported an outright ban on strikes. Although Solidarity was still respected, the number of those 'decisively' supporting it had dropped from 58 per cent to 31 per cent in a year.[15]

On 18 October 1981 Jaruzelski, already premier and defence minister, replaced Kania as first secretary of the Party. No other Communist has ever held this galaxy of posts. Kania went at Soviet urging. Marshal Kulikov held him in personal contempt after Kania had turned up at his residence drunk. Though Jaruzelski was talking of martial law in concrete terms, Kania was unable to reconcile himself to force.

It is beyond doubt that what happened was planned jointly with

Moscow. The Russians have access to Polish military communications traffic. Soviet liaison officers are attached to Polish units. Jaruzelski is a graduate of Soviet infantry and General Staff schools and started his military career in the Soviet Union. Five days after his appointment as first secretary, Jaruzelski signed a decree forming Military Task Groups, TGOs. Each group had units of three or four men, led by career officers and manned by career NCOs and warrant officers. They were dispersed through villages, city precincts and factories. Their task was to prevent local waste, abuse and mismanagement and to improve food distribution. In itself, that was a condemnation of thirty-five years of civilian party rule. It also set up a network for the military control of the country.

A strike called by Solidarity at the end of October got only 40 per cent support. 'This was the best news Marshal Kulikov had heard in months,' says Kuklinski. Kulikov came to Warsaw to talk with Jaruzelski on 24 November. On 2 December special units of ZOMO riot police attacked striking cadets in the Firefighters School in Warsaw in a slick operation that smacked of dress rehearsal. On 7 December Kulikov was back in Warsaw. On 10 December Tass spoke of 'counter-revolution in Poland'.

The coup came at midnight on 12 December 1981. Jaruzelski imposed a State of War, *Stan Wojenny*. He did this not as first secretary of the Party, but as the head of a new Military Council of National Salvation, WRON. The Soviet headquarters was only 100 metres away from the Council of State, where nervous party members asked each other at a meeting held an hour later: 'Have they intervened yet?' Only one man, the deputy Ryszard Reiff, spoke out against martial law: 'The people will lose the enjoyment of its rights because the governors are no longer on its side but are ranged against the governed. A minority in this country claims the recourse to force, but this minority is armed and sustained by the overwhelming power of its foreign allies ...'[16]

Before the general himself appeared on television at six a.m. on 13 December, the arrest of Solidarity leaders was under way. Telephone and telex communications were cut. Transport was halted. Factories were militarized and strikes became a military offence punishable by court martial. The TGO officers took over local administration. Television announcers were put in uniform.

Care was taken to make sure that ZOMO riot police rather than troops were used to impose martial law. Jaruzelski was wary of army sensitivities.[17] Walesa, in fact, was 'convinced above all that we must not touch the twin pillars of the regime, the army and the militia. If we did, even if some of them came over to us, there'd have been applause. But it's at that moment that we would have risked drowning in tragedy.'[18] Kuklinski says that, if the takeover had failed, a Soviet invasion would have followed with 'an incredibly bloody massacre of the population'.

A certain care was taken with famous prisoners. Walesa found himself stuffed with liver, fish, first French and then Hungarian champagne, white and rosé, like the Czechs in Moscow in 1968, but without the women. A certain freedom survived, certainly more than in the Soviet Union, Czechoslovakia or East Germany. On the day he was re-arrested, in May 1983, Walesa spoke with fifteen Western news groups and with the US embassy.[19]

Officially, as vice-premier Rakowski put it: 'This isn't a military government. In 1981, the army was the only intact force. That's why Jaruzelski called on it. There are a few generals in the government. That's all. Haig was Secretary of State in the American government and he's a general.' It appears, indeed, to be more of a police government. It is the ZOMOs and the secret police who continue to display the relaxed confidence shown in the murder of Father Popieluszko in October 1984. The murderers, led by the security officer Captain Piotrowski, used their own official car to kidnap the charismatic priest. They let his chauffeur escape and did not pursue him. They sailed through three police checkpoints with Popieluszko in the boot. They drew into a hotel car park where the priest got out of the boot and shouted for help before they stuffed him back in again. They stopped at a garage for oil whilst he banged on the boot lid. After beating, binding and then drowning him, they left their car without cleaning the boot or disguising it.

The army does not have that absolute habit of impunity. It has not prevented itself from hijacking Poland either.

35

AFGHANISTAN: THE BEAR TRAP

The first outright invasion beyond the Stalinist frontiers also took place in Asia, a much lower risk area than Europe or Latin America, far from the US, an apparently secure place in which to capitalize on the steady expansion in military power under Brezhnev.* In fact, Afghanistan

---

* Distant from its troublesome European satellites, the Soviet Union is a great Asian power. It is an area where the Russians have twice equipped armies fighting the Americans, in Korea and Vietnam.

In the Korean War, which broke out in 1950, Stalin restricted the Soviet effort to weapons and to providing a limited number of advisers and Russian MiG-15 pilots who confined their flights to North-Korean-controlled airspace. Red army units were also placed in Manchuria as a deterrent to American attack whilst Chinese troops were freed to fight in Korea. It was not until near the end of the war that up to 20,000

degenerated into a stalemate that marks the first major defeat for the Red army since 1942. As the US found in Vietnam, stalemate for a superpower is defeat.

It began much like Prague. The first wave of Russians, paratroopers of the 105th Airborne Division, landed at Kabul airport after dark on Christmas Eve 1979. A round-the-clock airlift followed for two days, with 400 military and Aeroflot transports dumping their loads of troops and armoured cars once every three minutes and flying off for more without stopping their engines.

By the morning of 27 December there were around five thousand heavily equipped Red army men in the Afghan capital. Soviet advisers told the Afghan units they were attached to that they had come on manoeuvres. As in Czechoslovakia, they ordered the Afghans to turn in live ammunition and to resupply with training ammunition. Tank engine batteries were removed for 'winterization'. At 7 p.m. the Kabul telephone system was knocked out by an explosion. A few minutes later Russian

---

Soviet troops were placed in Korea, not to fight the Americans but to inhibit them from a second attempt to drive north.

However, the conflict thoroughly stirred up the Americans, and the US defence budget quintupled. Vietnam was a happier experience for Moscow, whose equipment was essential to the North Vietnamese throughout the war, in trucks, tanks, artillery, radio, aircraft, anti-tank and anti-aircraft missiles.

It was a cheap victory for the Russians. Their military aid was never more than one thirtieth the annual amount of US spending, which totalled more than $110 billion, but largely offset it. The US lost 56,226 men, 8,000 aircraft and an indefinable amount of prestige. Congress shackled the president's war-making powers and public hostility to the military did not exhaust itself until the end of the decade. A few Russians were killed in the strikes on the North.

With China, tensions developed after Mao Tse-tung won the long civil war in 1949. Khrushchev disliked Mao intensely, finding him full of 'Asiatic cunning ..., cajolery, treachery, savage vengeance and deceit'. Mao found that: 'We must not blindly follow the Soviet Union ... Every fart has some kind of smell, and we cannot say that all Soviet farts smell sweet.'

Khrushchev withdrew Soviet advisers from China in 1960. Pro-Chinese parties splintered the communist movement. The Chinese began to refer to the 'unequal treaties' by which Tsarist Russia had annexed an area more than twice the size of Texas, and compared the Kremlin leaders to Hitler and the Ku Klux Klan.

The border dispute degenerated into fighting on 2 March 1969 on Damansky island in the Ussuri river north of Vladivostok. Thirty-one members of the KGB border guard were killed in a machinegun ambush on the frozen island. Two weeks later a battalion-size Russian force with tanks and artillery avenged the attack on the same mid-river island. Sino–Soviet relations have rollercoastered since, though never reaching the depths of 1969. American détente with China has imposed a triangle in which Moscow is forced to make permanent military allowance both for potential Chinese hostility and for the state of relations between Washington and Peking. The Chinese would not strain the defensive strength of the Red army in a war. But their presence cuts back on Soviet aggressive strength elsewhere.

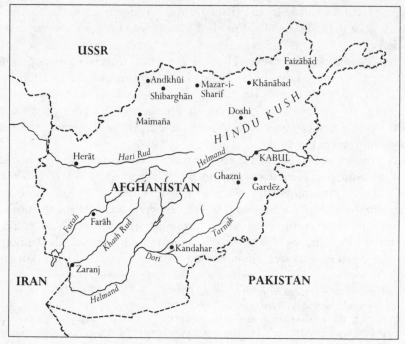

Afghanistan

paratroops attacked the interior ministry building, police headquarters and the Darulaman palace complex where the Afghan president Hafizullah Amin was living.

The Russians had tried to murder Amin before Christmas in his Kabul residence, the House of the People. A KGB officer working in the kitchens at the Darulaman poisoned the presidential food. Amin had much personal experience of murder. During his brief reign, executions at Pul-i-Charki, the large prison on the eastern outskirts of Kabul, had run at fifty a night. Aware of the hatreds he had stirred, Amin constantly refused and switched the food and drink set before him. The KGB kitchen hand was out of luck. A further attempt to kill Amin was made on 17 December. Guards opened fire, giving him a superficial leg wound but injuring his nephew Asadullah Amin seriously enough for him to be mede-vaced to the Soviet Union for treatment. Asadullah was the head of the intelligence service.

With his nephew gone, Amin no longer had intelligence on what was closing in on him. The signs were ominous. Within Afghanistan, troops from the Soviet 105th Guards Division were moving to the Bagram air base north of Kabul. A Soviet armoured unit had secured the highway through the Salang Pass tunnel north of Kabul. Within the Soviet Union, transport aircraft were massing in the Moscow and Central Asian regions.

US military attachés in Moscow were refused permission to travel to the USSR's Central Asian republics to check on rumours of major troop concentrations. Fighter-bombers flew to bases in Uzbekistan close to the Afghan border. Two elite airborne divisions, the 103rd in White Russia and the 104th at Kirovabad between the Black Sea and the Caspian, were on alert.

Exposed in the House of the People in Kabul, Amin moved to the Darulaman complex eleven kilometres out of the city on 17 December. He settled into the stoutly built Tajbeg palace building within its walls with a force of his most trusted guards, eight tanks and some armoured personnel carriers. On 26 December he ordered the 4th Tank Brigade to join his defences. Its commander stalled under Russian prompting.

In the final assault the next day, KGB officers in Afghan uniforms directed the Soviet paratroops attacking the Tajbeg palace under the command of Colonel Bayerenov. At 8.45 p.m. a powerful radio at Termez in Soviet Uzbekistan drowned out Kabul Radio. It transmitted a taped speech by Babrak Karmal, an Afghan exile, a long-time KGB agent and the Soviet choice to replace Amin.

Fighting in the Tajbeg palace lasted into the early hours. The paratroops and KGB officers fought their way through it room by room, finally cornering Amin and his mistress in the bar on the top floor. At 3.15 a.m. on 28 December Kabul Radio, now in Russian hands, announced that: 'The revolutionary tribunal has sentenced Hafizullah Amin to death for crimes against the noble people of Afghanistan ... The sentence has been carried out.'[1] Bayerenov also died, victim of his own orders that no witness in the Tajbeg should be allowed to live. He was wearing Afghan uniform and a Soviet paratrooper, mistaking him for a member of Amin's guard, killed him.[2]

Later that day two Soviet motorized rifle divisions began crossing pontoon bridges on the Amu Darya, the river which marks the Soviet–Afghan border. Two more were preparing to cross the border further to the west. Each division was at full strength with 266 tanks and 400 APCs apiece. They had modern Kamaz trucks, replacements for the Ural truck, built with American equipment at the new Kama River plant. Nixon had not embargoed it on the basis that it would only be used for civilian vehicles.

The 350th and 201st Divisions crossed at Termez, the Soviet border town where Marshal Sergei L. Sokolov had set up a special headquarters to command the invasion. They headed for Kabul. The 66th and 357th Divisions moved through Kushka to the west and swung down on Herat and Kandahar. The 15th Tank Division followed the advance on the Herat road.[3]

Babrak Karmal was brought from Russia to Kabul on New Year's Day,

1980. The only real resistance outside Kabul came from the Afghan army 26th Paratroop Regiment which refused orders to disarm and was annihilated by the Russians at Bala Zhar.[4] In less than a month 90,000 Russian troops had been airlifted and trucked into Afghanistan, supported by 1,850 tanks and squadrons of MiG-21s and 22s and SU-17 fighter-bombers.

They set up a command headquarters in the Tajbeg palace.

Thus far, it was a textbook operation and Brezhnev had initial reason for pleasure. But he was ill advised on the scale of the country and the nature of its people. Afghanistan is the size of Texas, 400,000 square kilometres. It is a place too wild and poor for a railway to have been built through its escarpments, deep valleys and mountain tangles. A line toils up on the Pakistani side, through old British-built switchbacks and tunnels, until it emerges in the thin blue air of an Afghan plateau and stops, exhausted. Landlocked, the country runs into the scrub Baluchi desert in the south 320 kilometres from the waters of the Arabian Sea. It has few exploitable riches, beyond natural gas. Wool and hashish are its cash crops.

The population at the time of the invasion was 15.2 million, almost all Moslem and 90 per cent illiterate. The people are tribal, speaking more than twenty languages, xenophobic, suspicious, riddled with feuds and obsessed with weapons.* They are skilled in the arts of ambush and assassination. The fissures and ill blood that divide in normal times heal in the face of the foreigner. They fought the British army at its imperial height to a draw in two Afghan Wars. In the first, hacking in defiles and snowfields, they reduced a British force of 4,500 troops retreating from Kabul in January 1842 to a single man, Dr Bryden, and his pony.

It was likely that the Soviet invasion would provoke long and savage resistance.

Brezhnev ignored Tsarist precedents, for the Russians have traditionally been leery of getting too involved in Afghanistan. After the Tsars set up a protectorate over Bukhara in 1869, Russian power reached to the Amu Darya and the outer perimeter of Afghanistan. Despite the 'Great Game' played between the British and the Russians for influence in Afghanistan, the Russians were generally content for Kabul to remain an isolated buffer. After 1900 Russian interest passed on to the Far East. Lenin greeted Afghanistan in 1919 as 'the only independent Muslim country in the world'

---

* The author was once invited to take tea with a tribesman on the Afghan–Pakistan border. The tea was served off a low table made from the gravestone of an officer of the Oxfordshire and Buckinghamshire Light Infantry, taken from a nearby British military cemetery. For casual wear about the house my host wore two cartridge bandoliers, two daggers, a pistol and a pair of fieldglasses.

destined for the 'historic task of uniting around itself all the enslaved Moslem peoples and leading them on the road to freedom and independence'.[5] Afghanistan declared itself neutral in the last war, expelling German and Italian nationals at Russian prompting.

After the break-up of British India in 1947 the Soviets considered US aid to Pakistan to be a threat to Afghanistan and its buffer position. 'It was clear that the Americans were penetrating Afghanistan with the obvious purpose of setting up a military base,' Khrushchev wrote.[6] He had the US-built Kandahar International Airport in mind, which may have been a potential USAF recovery base for American bombers to land after attacking Russian targets in Siberia and Central Asia that were out of return range from Nato airfields in western Europe.[7] A new Great Game was under way between America and Russia. The Soviets provided more than $1 billion worth of aid, including the Salang Pass tunnel bored at 3,000 metres through the Hindu Kush that was to prove useful in the invasion, and MiG-21s and the Mazar-i-Sharif and Bagram air bases to fly them from. Relations between Moscow and Kabul became more intimate. Afghan air force pilots trained in Russia, though the civilian crews of the Ariana national airline flew Boeings.

Afghanistan remained a monarchy, shambolic, malnourished, impervious to Communism and most things else, until 1973. Mohammed Daoud, a former prime minister, overthrew King Zahir Shah whilst the monarch was absent wallowing in the medicinal mud baths of Ischia in Italy. In the Afghan manner, Daoud was both the first cousin and brother-in-law of the man he deposed. He installed himself as president, premier, and foreign and defence minister at the modest coup cost of four dead policemen. He created his own party and, a traditionalist, set about torturing his opponents.

These included members of the tiny Marxist Party, the PDPA. Its leaders were young, half timid and half brutal, contemptuous, eager in the pursuit of the power that the collapse of colonialism and *ancien régimes* have put on bargain offer so often this century. Nur Mohammed Taraki had worked as a translator in the Afghan embassy in Washington, a writer of charm and inspiration, shy and insecure. Hafizullah Amin had also been in the US, at Columbia University where he was remembered as 'a very decent guy'.[8] Babrak Karmal – the name was said to be an abbreviation of Karl Marx Lenin – was a leftist from a leading family, the son of a lieutenant general, self-confident and hard.

Radicals seemed to matter little until Daoud fell out with the world power across the Amu Darya. Daoud visited Moscow in 1977 and had a 'flaming row' with Brezhnev, slamming his fist on the conference table in the Kremlin and railing that Afghans were masters in their own house. A senior Afghan official with long experience of dealing with the Russians is said to have whispered to a colleague, after seeing the anger on Brezhnev's face, that Daoud had just written his death warrant.[9] It was executed the next year. A group of young Marxist officers, commanding just 600 men, 60 tanks and 20 aircraft, attacked the walled royal Arg palace in central Kabul where Daoud had his office and housed his presidential guard.

For a revolutionary coup that was to lead to invasion, mass terror, civil war, the whole range of horrors suffered on a broader canvas by the Russians themselves, it was oddly lethargic.

It did not get under way until 9 a.m. on 27 April 1978, a late hour for a coup. It started at an odd location, Kabul International Airport, a stopping place for hippies and other cosmopolitan vagrants. The airport was taken by a few tanks. The Arg palace was not attacked until noon and the 1,800-strong presidential guard had little difficulty in holding off the small rebel tank force. Daoud had sensed trouble in the air and had ordered the arrest of PDPA leaders. Despite the airport being taken, rebel pilots did not appear over the city until 4 p.m. They then strafed and rocketed the palace with MiG-21s and Su-7s. By early evening, rebel tanks and infantry had taken Kabul Radio, next to the US embassy. A rebel broadcast claimed success for the 'revolution' at 7 p.m. No crowds on the streets, no hoarse agitators greeted the news. It was not until four the next morning that the palace was taken and Daoud and his family killed.

The Soviet embassy appeared to have been taken by surprise. The ambassador, Alexander M. Puzanov, a seventy-two-year-old with a weakness for the bottle and fly fishing, was away casting for trout in the Hindu Kush.[10] In Kabul, the Russians were hooked. Afghanistan was no longer an eccentric throwback, a place where Soviet diplomats certainly kept the Americans out, but which could hang itself as long as it kept itself hulldown to the world. On 30 April Taraki formed a government with Amin as foreign minister. When Amin flew to Moscow two weeks later, foreign minister Andrei Gromyko greeted him with kisses on both cheeks. Afghanistan had become a Marxist state. Soviet prestige and socialist ideals were committed.

A resistance movement started within a month of the coup. It was backed by most of the country's 320,000 mullahs. Troops slipped out of their barracks and joined the guerrillas, ubiquitous in the hills, as desertions multiplied. The worried Soviets got deeper involved. In December 1978 Taraki signed a treaty of friendship and cooperation with Brezhnev in Moscow. It was later used to justify the invasion. Mounting arrests created bizarre complications. In February 1979 four Afghans kidnapped the American ambassador, 'Spike' Dubs, and held him hostage in a room in the Kabul Hotel in the city centre. They hoped to force the release of friends from prison. Police surrounded the room in the modern hotel block. Four Russian advisers were seen to post snipers round the building and to load weapons. The Russians ignored pleas from American diplomats not to open fire. Afghan police burst into the room under covering fire. The kidnappers were killed. So was Ambassador Dubs.

The big western town of Herat rose in March. Mobs ranged through the narrow warrens of mean streets and bazaars, slaughtering government officials and every Russian – man, woman or child – they could set daggers on. Corpses were disfigured for good measure. Twenty Russians were in the official death toll. The real figure may have reached 100.[11] In the aftermath of Herat, Amin became prime minister and Russian women and children were repatriated.

In the opposite direction, heavy with foreboding, came General Alexei A. Yepishev, the chief of the Main Political Administration, the ideological head of the Red army. He arrived in Kabul in April with a group of 'political workers', who included six generals, and stayed for about a week. He cannot have been much pleased at what he found in the Afghan army. It was falling apart under the pressure of guerrillas and Amin's terror. Fresh light tanks, APCs and Mi-24 helicopter gunships, equipped with rockets and heavy machineguns, were flown in from Soviet stocks. Soviet advisers went down to company level. Soviet pilots, paratroops and artillery officers were used in combat.[12] On 11 June 1979 Brezhnev confirmed the Soviet commitment by promising that 'we shall not leave our friends, the Afghan people, in need'.

Another Prague Spring veteran, General Ivan G. Pavlovsky, now C-in-C of ground forces, came calling with a large staff shortly after. Bloody melodrama infected the heights of the regime as well as the demoralized soldiery at its base. Taraki flew to Moscow in September for talks with Brezhnev. Amin went to see him on his return, Ambassador Puzanov giving him a personal assurance that it was safe to go. Amin and his escort were shot at on a staircase on their arrival. Escaping, Amin returned with a force of bodyguards and took Taraki prisoner. At 11.30 p.m. on 8 October three secret policemen went to the second-floor room in the palace where Taraki was held. Realizing he was done for, he gave them a bag of jewellery and money for his wife. He did not know that Amin had already had her arrested. He was taken to another room, tied to a bed and suffocated with a cushion. The process took a quarter of an hour.[13]

Moscow's distaste for Amin's Borgia-like excesses was heightened by the fact that he was losing the war in the countryside. Amin's writ, fitfully exercised in city centres and prison cells, scarcely ran in his own army. He had purged almost half the officers and NCOs. Their place had been taken by 3,500 to 4,000 Russians.

General Pavlovsky completed his study of the Afghan situation. He presented it to the Politburo and defence minister Ustinov in Moscow. Amin's fate was probably decided at a Politburo meeting on 19 December.

The unreliability of the Afghan army, the heavy losses of Soviet equipment and the atrocities against Russians were stressed. The failure of the West, particularly the US, to respond to the Marxist seizure of power in 1978 gave the Politburo reason to believe that Afghanistan would be accepted for practical purposes as part of the Soviet sphere.[14] The Politburo, like the White House over Vietnam in 1965, was interested mainly in stabilizing the situation. Like the Americans, it hoped to complete this and withdraw its troops within five or six years. The invasion was on.

The situation facing the Russians and the returning Karmal after the invasion remained critical. As much as 90 per cent of the countryside was in rebel hands. The Red army units occupied major cities and the rectangle made by the roads connecting Kabul, Mazar-i-Sharif, Herat and Kandahar. Soviet pilots flew strafing and missile attacks in MiG-21s and 23s and Su-17s. Ground combat was initially an Afghan army affair, although Soviet forward controllers integrated this with overall direction from the main command centre at Termez in Soviet Turkestan. But the Afghans remained demoralized and barrack-bound and the Soviet divisions, equipped to fight Nato, were too road-bound for effective use against guerrillas in rock and crag country.

In February a general strike paralysed Kabul and spread to the bazaars and government offices. It was started by 'midnight mail', with strike instructions and anti-Russian tracts pushed under the doors of houses by night. A night curfew was imposed but insurgents climbed to the roofs of the flat-topped buildings to snipe at Soviet patrols. They responded with mortar flares and heavy machinegun fire. The rebels used coloured kites to show the movements of Russian patrols through the streets. When they realized what was happening, the Russians used kites to lure the Afghans into ambush. The packs of stray dogs in the city were shot as their barking alerted the rebels to Soviet night patrols.[15] Psy-war helicopters dropped leaflets and used loudspeakers to order shopkeepers to reopen.

It was soon clear that, even on Pavlovsky's gloomy analysis, the usefulness of the Afghan army had been overestimated. It was evaporating through desertion, its numbers down to 35,000 from 80,000. The combat onus was falling on the Red army, which evolved a four-stage plan to contain the *mujaheddin*.

Operations began on 1 March 1980. The *mujaheddin*, investing the towns from gullies and crag tops, were attacked by rocket and napalm from fighter-bombers. Mi-24 helicopter gunships closed in with machinegun and rocket fire. Then troop-carrying Mi-6 helicopters dropped their loads of assault infantry, seventy-five men at a time. The sieges were lifted.[16] A month later an attempt was made to drive the *mujaheddin* out of the fertile valley bottoms, with their precious roads, and into the wildness and flaking rock of the mountains. Airstrikes were followed by tanks and lines of infantry. A further stage was the creation of a desolated free-fire zone along the Pakistan border in the Khyber Pass area. Weapons, food and medicine were flowing through this supply route. The *mujaheddin* were then to be slowly divided and reduced in the last resistance centres in the barren brown massifs above 2,500 metres.

That happened no more to the Afghans than to the Viet Cong in 1965. The vital first impetus of invasion failed the Russians.

This was, marginally, a question of troops and tactics. The Russians had not been trained in counter-insurgency or mountain warfare. Their armour tied them to the roads and to valley fields. Initially, they had no counter-ambush drills and they dealt poorly with convoy ambushes. Instead of counter-attacking from the road, convoy tanks would abandon trucks hit by the *mujaheddin* and shepherd the convoy survivors to safety. Machine-guns, primitive weapons in air defence, were enough to persuade the pilots of Hind gunships to keep at altitude and fly evasive patterns, degrading the effect of their rocket and strafing runs.

Essentially, though, it was the nature of Afghanistan that blunted the Soviet assault. A wild, subsistence country is different meat from an East European capital. A single tank in a street in Prague can control the shops where the people get food and the offices and factories where they go to work. Their crops burnt, Afghan villagers found an apricot tree and a mule from another valley carrying rice. The workplace of the shepherd stretches into the brown haze. Low living standards bring low vulnerability. To win the xenophobic hearts and Moslem minds of these thin, tattered people was the precondition of quick success. Neither the ideologue Karmal nor the Red army came close to it.

By the time Gorbachev first indicated that he wanted to call it a day, in 1987, the Russians were mired in ponderous search and destroy missions. Airpower was overwhelming during a sortie and then gone, able to bludgeon but not to finish off.* The scale and the terrain are different, but the comparisons are compulsive enough for the defector Vladimir

---

* The ferocity of an airstrike, with its rockets, napalm and cluster bombs, is mocked in guerrilla warfare by its brevity. In Vietnam, a target was a treeline, a green strip and a grey canal. 'That's ours,' the pilot said. On each run, we descended on to it with the intimacy of a shrike over a harvest field, the whole, a boat moored to the canal bank, the softer green of a stand of bamboo, a lopsided clearing with a thatched lean-to, open as a target. Afterwards we climbed back to height, power over the landscape spinning away with the altimeter until the outlines of ponds, paddies and paths became a mixture of colour, the surface of a giant minestrone with the treeline a scrap of green

Kuzichkin to have been told by a weary KGB general: 'Afghanistan is our Vietnam ... We are bogged down in a war we cannot win and cannot abandon.'[17]

The Red army could, of course, have sustained its effort in Afghanistan indefinitely.

Combat experience is welcome to the officer corps. It speeds promotions and it sharpens tactics. Radio communication, a traditional Red army weakness, improved greatly. The helicopter forces came of age in Afghanistan and military journals 'almost bubbled with articles' on the new tactics they permitted. Ground-air cooperation in fire support and evacuation was tested and 'the art of the helicopter ambush learned from the enemy'. Armoured bellies were redesigned and new exhaust systems cut down missile-attracting heat emissions.[18] Hind Mil-24 helicopters, flying in pairs, emerged as excellent gunships although both fixed-wing and helicopter pilots were reluctant to fly at low level. The elite Spetsnaz special forces, easily recognized in their striped jerseys, won a formidable reputation in special operations and assassinations.

It was a miserable war for the ground troops, the men with the traditional 'We're tired' tattooed on their toes, quartered in tents. 'There were 30 men to a tent,' says Oleg Khlan, a Soviet sergeant who served in Afghanistan.* 'In summer, dust and grit blew in everywhere. In winter, you boiled if you were in the centre by the stove and you froze further out. In the autumn, the duckboards sank under the mud.' Sloppy hygiene led to epidemics of hepatitis and intestinal diseases. Hepatitis was common, followed by typhoid fever, dysentery and pneumonia. A deserter, Sergeant Alexei Peresleni, says that normally half the six-man crews in his battery were incapacitated.[19]

Officers could afford vodka, smuggled in by truck drivers resupplying from Soviet Uzbekistan to the north. When they could not get it, at a cost of up to £50 a bottle, they brewed their own *samogon* liquor. Hashish, *plan*, a cheaper hemp derivative, cocaine and opium were widely used among the men. 'It helped you to forget where you were,' says Yuri Povanitsyn, a sergeant captured by the *mujaheddin*. 'Men exchanged drugs for bullets ... There was one case when three soldiers were sentenced for selling bullets.'[20] Others bought drugs with money plundered from civilian

---

pasta. 'It's theirs again,' said the pilot. Airpower can be decisive when used against massed forces or an enemy's fixed assets, airfields, dockyards, factory plant and so on. The *mujaheddin*'s main assets, themselves, are mobile. There was little else to hit except Afghanistan itself, puffs of smoke and contrail in a massif.

* Taken by the *mujaheddin*, an interest was shown in him in the West and he eventually got to Britain via Pakistan. Homesick, he contacted the Soviet embassy and was repatriated to the Soviet Union. After his return he was quoted in Soviet newspapers alleging that his time in Britain was a 'nightmare' and that he had been taken

homes during patrols or by bartering diesel oil, soap, rain capes, belts and boots.

The Kremlin did not acknowledge that a state of war existed in Afghanistan, for all Gorbachev's reference to it as 'a bloody wound', and the *mujaheddin* rarely showed much interest in prisoner exchange. Russians taken prisoner expected a rapid trial under Islamic law, with no interpreter provided, and execution. Asked what would become of him, a captured Russian sergeant interviewed by Western journalists said: 'Of course, they'll slit my throat.' A National Islamic Front resistance official admitted: 'They are normally executed.'[21]

Off-duty, the Russians stuck to groups of half a dozen, weapons slung on their shoulders as they sat in cafés. Frustrations could, as in Vietnam, spill over into looting and killings on field operations. There are stories of Afghan prisoners being blown to pieces by armoured-car shells, and villagers being shot out of hand during sweeps. Individual brutality, however, was not a hallmark. Systematic ill treatment was at a higher level, in KHAD secret police interrogations, the probable use of phosphorus and toxin weapons, and widespread scorched-earth tactics, using the foot soldiers to cordon off villages and strafing and bombing them into rubble.

The war produced few Soviet deserters. There were scant signs of the serious erosion in army morale and the collapse in public opinion the Americans suffered in Vietnam. The flow of zinc-covered military coffins back to the Soviet Union caused some unrest, notably in the Ukraine and the Baltic states.

It was mute, however. Disease harvested more casualties than combat. An institution the size of the Red army can cope with an Afghan level of attrition, and with localized morale and drug problems, without much effort.

Not that the achievements were high.

The murderous in-fighting within the regime was not stilled by the invasion. A cabinet meeting degenerated into a gunbattle between ministers. Car bombings in Kabul were not the preserve of the *mujaheddin*. Factions fought their own dirty war with explosives crammed into the boots of Toyotas.

Karmal served his purpose in giving some credibility to the post-invasion government. Tired and ill, he failed to ease the internal strife or win

---

there 'against his will'. *The Times*, 3 December 1984. When the author met him shortly before his return, Khlan was literally living the life of lord. He was lodged in the house of Lord Philimore in softly rolling hills near Henley-on-Thames, absorbing large quantities of vodka, rock music and summer sun and showing every sign of being in daydream rather than nightmare.

international recognition. Russian combat troops outnumbered the sagging Afghan army in the field by three to one. Afghan officers, including two generals in January 1986, were arrested for passing operational plans to the *mujaheddin*, and pilots flew to Pakistan to seek asylum. In May 1986 Karmal was ousted by Major General Mohammed Najibullah, known simply as Comrade Najib.

Najib was the director for six years of the KHAD secret police, the acronym for *Khedamat-e Etela'at-e Dawlati,* the State Security Bureau. KGB officers frequently directed its interrogation sessions, in which 'widespread and systematic torture' were commonplace.[22] The KHAD was active in Pakistan, its agents setting bombs in restaurants and camps used by refugees over the border in Peshawar and sowing landmines on refugee trails in Pakistan.

Ruthless, with a secret policeman's twin instincts to coerce on essentials and to concede elsewhere, Najib gave Gorbachev enough confidence to announce at least token troop reductions. The ground was already prepared. On the sixth anniversary of the invasion, *Pravda* had admitted that 'errors' had been made in the first phase of the revolution by 'the enforcement of social reforms without regard for the actual situation as well as the social and national characteristics of the country'.[23]

Najib announced a unilateral Soviet and Afghan ceasefire in a speech in Kabul at the start of 1987. Within a few days the resistance leaders had rejected it and the heads of the Afghan National Reconciliation Commission in Kumdiz and Nangahar had been murdered. Almost a decade into the war, Soviet pilots taking off from Kabul airport were still climbing their Antonovs in tight circles over the city, seeking to stay over friendly territory. They let drop magnesium flares with a dull thump which fell in white smoke trails over the houses of the capital. The 3,000-degree Centigrade heat of the burning magnesium served to deflect *mujaheddin* missiles. The aerial arteries were vital since it was not safe to travel more than fifteen or twenty kilometres by car from the centre of towns, Kabul included.

In cash terms, some estimates of the Kremlin debit ran as high as $12 million a day. In addition to military spending, the Russians had to fund most of the Afghan civil budget. The Soviet death rate was low, however, probably 15,000 by the end of 1988 and nowhere near the rate suffered by the Americans in Vietnam.

Only the small part of the middle class not to have fled abroad seemed, with delicate irony, resigned to be led by the yet smaller group of party believers. 'We don't like the Communists or the Russians,' said an educated woman, no longer forced to wear the veil. 'The alternative is a lot worse. Victory by the *mujaheddin* would mean being bossed by Muslim integrists. That would be the end of the few freedoms we have left.'[24]

The Russians were more tactful than the Americans in Saigon. There were no visible brothels for Russian troops, no girlie bars, no happy hours and no giggling girls riding on tank transporters as red dust flushed their faces and smeared to the purple of their slit *ao dais*. Afghan society is puritan and the Russians were discreet, keeping in Kabul to the new section of Microrayon.

Yet Afghanistan dragged on as Vietnam before it. The Russian writer Artiom Borovik saw an attempt to encircle a band of *mujaheddin* in 1987. The Russians were, as ever, road-bound. The road, not yet quite dry, shone like a strip of aluminium foil. 'But you only need to go a few yards to see that the surface is covered with wounds from shells and mines like all Afghan roads,' he noted. 'The armoured cars rock like boats in a gale.'[25]

The Russians had become so familiar that the donkeys 'trot with total indifference at the side of the road. Neither a wing of jet fighters flying above them at sixty feet nor the explosion of a mine disturbs their tranquillity.' There were wrecks of Kamaz trucks and Afghan buses at the roadside. Borovik watched puffs of smoke hanging in the air from artillery strikes through the slit of his armoured car, feeling 'like a tortoise that's crawled out of its shell' when he climbed out.

They were trying to capture a local *mujaheddin* leader called Gaiour, who ran through caravans of arms, ammunition and medicine from Pakistan. 'He's a difficult one,' said the Soviet colonel in charge of the operation. 'He knows our tactics well. He even studied in the Soviet Union. Then he went over to the *dukhs*.' Gaiour escaped the sweep. He had been tipped off.

A mullah was taken prisoner. He was led in for Borovik to inspect. He pulled his sleeves up to show delicate hands and arms. 'He shows off his hands to prove he never killed anyone,' said an Afghan colonel. 'But don't believe it. They are covered with blood. He was a judge in the villages here. After his verdicts, they killed, shot, cut off the ears of sympathizers with the revolution.' The mullahs 'always have a medallion of Lenin or a Red flag under their caftans'. This one swore his fidelity to the ideals of the revolution. Cold and wet that night, quartered in his armoured car, Borovik was lent a quilted jacket with captain's epaulettes. 'In the pockets, I find English tablets for purifying water. And American cigarettes. You can find them in all the Afghan bazaars.' He wondered what happened to the captain. Then he slept.

After almost a decade of such futility, Gorbachev finally set a timetable for withdrawal.

tradition of the post – not a tank man, not a war veteran and not a Marshal. Persistent rumour had it that Yazov himself was soon to be replaced, and by a *shpak*, a civilian, at that.

The West continues to press for further reductions. Gorbachev must do the same if he is to survive the stagnant economy, too much of it eaten by Yazov's men. The Soviet economist Alexander Zaychenko says that the Russians now eat worse than they did in 1913, the last year of peace under the Tsars. As to consumer goods, 'towels, toothpaste, toilet paper, lotions and light bulbs have disappeared from the shelves,' *Izvestia* complained in 1989. 'What will it be tomorrow?'

The general knows how rich are his assets, compared with the society that produces them, and how privileged are his officers.

Both they, and he, are part of the *nomenklatura*, the 'new class' of Communism, the Soviet establishment. It has an aura of power that cloys in the air after it has passed. Black cars drum their wheels on the Kremlin cobbles, a bulky man in the back, in grey overcoat and hat or olive tunic with slashes of red at the shoulders. A convoy of limousines sweeps down the centre of streets, traffic parting nervously from its path, policemen hurriedly wiping their boot toes on greatcoats as it nears. Aides and army baggage carriers fuss round their masters before the night train from Minsk to Moscow pulls out, tut-tutting civilians out of the corridor as they tidy their way to the mahogany warmth of the sleeping compartments in First.

The Party has always looked after its own. 'A worker-agitator who is at all gifted and promising *must not be left* to work 11 hours a day in a factory,' Lenin emphasized. 'We must arrange that he is maintained by the party.' It has no doubt of its own pre-eminence. But the political class must rely on others for the brute strength and cunning necessary to keep both the masses and foreign powers, Nazi Germany or Nato, at arm's length. Police terror and military strength are vital to the Party. It needs secret policemen, pilots, tank army commanders. So senior officers are included among the three million or so members of the *nomenklatura*.[1]

Pay, status, perks and conditions, so low for the 4.50-rouble-a-month recruit, are warm and coddling in the upper reaches of the Red army.[2] A marshal gets 2,500 roubles a month, two and a half times Gorbachev's official salary and double that of a top ballet dancer or the president of the USSR, a position Gorbachev also enjoys. Colonel generals and full generals also outpull the first secretary in pay, with 1,200 and 1,500 roubles a month respectively. As a whole, officers get at least one third more pay than civilians with equivalent qualifications.[3]

Not that a senior officer has much need of crude cash.

He gets a special issue of luxury foods and goods. A shop in the basement of Voyentorg, the army-navy store on Kalinin Prospekt in Moscow, keeps him supplied with export-quality vodka, French cognac and Armenian

The View from the Frunskaya Embankment

Present Strength

36

RED ELITE

These are strange times for General Dmitry Yazov, as he tabulates his assets and gazes from the Frunskaya Embankment.

The three comfortable certainties that he and his officers have lived with are being undermined. For more than forty years, the *glavni vrag* has been the US. Whatever window dressing is given the civilian economy, the military challenge to the West has been maintained regardless of cost. Soviet military philosophy has been offensive. Hit first, hit hard.

Whilst Yazov was scrubbing intermediate large missiles from his nuclear strength in 1988, enough of a revolution in itself, his Chief of Staff was visting the US and peering into the cockpit of a B-1 bomber. The American defense secretary inspected its counterpart, the Blackjack. In 1989, the head of the KGB, General Vladimir Kryuchkov, who has spent much of his career extracting intelligence from the US, reversed the process by briefing the US Ambassador to Moscow.

So much for the *glavni vrag*. In that lesser but still important enemy, Britain, MiG-29s flew at the Farnborough Air Show and Soviet officers were taken on a tour of cruise missile bases.

No more escalating budgets, either. Gorbachev has ordered Yazov to make do with 'defensive sufficiency'. Spending that may reach 17 per cent of the Soviet gross national product crosses Yazov's desk each year, bloated beyond mere 'sufficiency'. As proof that he is in earnest, Gorbachev announced, and in New York, cuts of 500,000 men, 10,000 tanks, 8,000 artillery systems and 800 combat aircraft.

Troops who spend more than 80 per cent of their training on offensive exercises have been ordered into a more defensive role. The detail makes it look that Gorbachev, at least, is serious. The withdrawal of six armoured divisions and river-crossing equipment from forward positions in Eastern Europe cuts directly into offensive muscle.

The pull-out from Afghanistan is another bitter pill. Casualties may become more likely in controlling nationalist riots in Azerbaijan than in foreign combat.

It was too much for Yazov's CoS, Marshal Sergei Akhromeyev. The official reason given for his resignation at the end of 1988 was high blood pressure. Few doubt that this was the result of Gorbachev's cuts, made unilaterally without any Western *quid pro quo*, and on the advice of a new breed of civilian defence analyst the Red army has not had to bother about before.

His replacement, General Mikhail Moiseyev, rates a negative in every tradition of the post – not a tank man, not a war veteran and not a Marshal. Persistent rumour had it that Yazov himself was soon to be replaced, and by a *shpak*, a civilian, at that.

The West continues to press for further reductions. Gorbachev must do the same if he is to survive the stagnant economy, too much of it eaten by Yazov's men. The Soviet economist Alexander Zaychenko says that the Russians now eat worse than they did in 1913, the last year of peace under the Tsars. As to consumer goods, 'towels, toothpaste, toilet paper, lotions and light bulbs have disappeared from the shelves,' *Izvestia* complained in 1989. 'What will it be tomorrow?'

The general knows how rich are his assets, compared with the society that produces them, and how privileged are his officers.

Both they, and he, are part of the *nomenklatura*, the 'new class' of Communism, the Soviet establishment. It has an aura of power that cloys in the air after it has passed. Black cars drum their wheels on the Kremlin cobbles, a bulky man in the back, in grey overcoat and hat or olive tunic with slashes of red at the shoulders. A convoy of limousines sweeps down the centre of streets, traffic parting nervously from its path, policemen hurriedly wiping their boot toes on greatcoats as it nears. Aides and army baggage carriers fuss round their masters before the night train from Minsk to Moscow pulls out, tut-tutting civilians out of the corridor as they tidy their way to the mahogany warmth of the sleeping compartments in First.

The Party has always looked after its own. 'A worker-agitator who is at all gifted and promising *must not be left* to work 11 hours a day in a factory,' Lenin emphasized. 'We must arrange that he is maintained by the party.' It has no doubt of its own pre-eminence. But the political class must rely on others for the brute strength and cunning necessary to keep both the masses and foreign powers, Nazi Germany or Nato, at arm's length. Police terror and military strength are vital to the Party. It needs secret policemen, pilots, tank army commanders. So senior officers are included among the three million or so members of the *nomenklatura*.[1]

Pay, status, perks and conditions, so low for the 4.50-rouble-a-month recruit, are warm and coddling in the upper reaches of the Red army.[2] A marshal gets 2,500 roubles a month, two and a half times Gorbachev's official salary and double that of a top ballet dancer or the president of the USSR, a position Gorbachev also enjoys. Colonel generals and full generals also outpull the first secretary in pay, with 1,200 and 1,500 roubles a month respectively. As a whole, officers get at least one third more pay than civilians with equivalent qualifications.[3]

Not that a senior officer has much need of crude cash.

He gets a special issue of luxury foods and goods. A shop in the basement of Voyentorg, the army-navy store on Kalinin Prospekt in Moscow, keeps him supplied with export-quality vodka, French cognac and Armenian brandy, caviar, sturgeon and salmon. He can eat at a special canteen, perhaps the one at 2 Grankovsky Street if he is attached to the Kremlin, with its spreads of salmon, cucumber, beef soups, cream cakes and *kumys* made from mare's milk from the eastern steppes. He can use the *Beriozka* hard-currency shops, where he gets Japanese cameras and hi-fi equipment, American film, Danish tinned meats, English woollens, cartons of Marlboros and boxes of Havanas. A fourth-floor cinema is reserved in the Goskino building where he can see foreign films that are not on general release.

He is not subject to the Soviet average of twelve square metres of living space. He will have a large apartment, four rooms or more, in the smart Kutuzovsky Prospekt or Kuntsevo district of Moscow. It will have Finnish furniture, Swedish machines in the kitchen. In the country, he qualifies for a state dacha on a residential estate with a good grocery store, a canteen, a cinema, a library and a sports ground.

The dacha country is in the rolling hills west and south-west of Moscow, like the village of Zhukovska, on a bluff above the slow-flowing Moscow River.[4] If he wants to build his own dacha, the traditional wooden country cottage, comfortable with wood stoves and summer verandahs, he will be given a plot of a hectare instead of the 0.08-hectare area allowed to less privileged people. More luxurious, stone-built villa country is found at Oreanda and Pitsunda on the Black Sea coast. The 'Country House of the High Command of the Warsaw Treaty Army', modestly concealed in pine forests on the outskirts of Kiev, has footpaths of grey granite, Chinese bridges and marble summerhouses.[5]

As a junior officer he may have got his children into a Suvorov or Nakhimov school, founded in 1943 for war orphans, popular for their high standards. Later, he can use his *blat,* his influence, to send them to an elite university, like Moscow State, MIMO, the Moscow Institute of International Relations, or the Foreign Languages' Institution. He qualifies for the best health treatment, perhaps at the Fili hospital on the Moscow–Minsk road used by Stalin, or at a clinic on the Baltic or Black Sea coast. Unlike the leaveless recruit, he takes a month's holiday a year, forty-five days if he is a pilot or submariner, hunting for deer or bear or sunning in the southern heat. His room at a Black Sea hotel reflects his status in its sea view and the size of the TV set and the refrigerator.

The son-in-law of a general, Edward Lozansky, went on a family holiday to a small resort for the military elite near Yalta. The largest room, with refrigerator, colour TV and telephone, was assigned to the daughter of the commander of the Kiev military district. Lozansky was given a room with a black and white TV set, a small fridge and a phone that did not work. He came back from the beach one day to find that he had been moved to the luxury room. The manager explained that the Kiev district chief had been removed and that it was thought that Lozansky's father-in-law would get the post.[6]

Like his Tsarist predecessors, when 'a Russian officer will never undertake a journey on horseback but only in a carriage', he likes to travel well. As one of the *Vlasti,* the powers that be, he can bump people off perpetually overbooked Aeroflot flights and jump taxi queues. Special military ticket windows and waiting rooms ease his railway journeys. Batmen have made a comeback since the idealistic days of the 1920s, and they carry his bags to his compartment. He will, however, never travel abroad on holiday, not even to fraternal countries. It is easier for a Hungarian to get to the West than it is for a Russian to get to Hungary.

He will have an officer assigned as his car driver, speeding him down the central lane of main streets reserved for VIPs, known as the Chaika lane for the black limousines that use it. The car will be serviced in special military garages and be fuelled at military petrol stations.

Care is lavished on him by his juniors. Colonel General Viktor Kulikov, then head of the Group of Soviet Forces in East Germany, attended manoeuvres by the 20th Guards Army at the Magdeburg firing range. To save him from dirtying his uniform, two engineer battalions laid a new asphalt road for him to walk on. In the event, Kulikov crossed the asphalt once and left by helicopter.[7] To make sure that all goes well on important manoeuvres, junior officers sometimes play the part of the 'men'. The Red army has nine 'court' divisions which specialize in parades and demonstrations. The Moscow military district, with its frequent visits by foreign dignitaries, has two, the 2nd Guards Taman Motorized Infantry Division and the Kantemirov Tank Division.[8]

When he retires he becomes part of the Defence Ministry's 'paradise group'. He retains all his privileges, the Chaika and driver, the official four-room apartment, the aide de camp, the free rations and the finely woven uniforms. His pension rises from half pay after twenty-five years' service to 75 per cent of salary at thirty-five. The civilian ceiling of 120 roubles a month does not apply to him. He will, however, continue to treat such largesse with discretion, keeping it masked, *maskirovannoye.* And when he dies, the state will bury him with full military honours, slow marching guardsmen, bands and imposing wreaths of red flowers and ribbons. A general may rest in the cemetery of the Novodevichy monastery, where Khrushchev lies, reopened to the public in 1987 after a flood of pilgrims to Khrushchev's grave had made a nervous Kremlin close it. If he is a marshal, he may qualify for the ultimate honour in Soviet death, a place in the Kremlin wall.

★

Western generals are well paid, too, though the differentials between ranks are far smaller. In 1987, a British field marshal was entitled to £77,400 a year and the lowliest private to £6,250. They have their perks, and special tarmac roads and their equivalents are built for them. It is in their position as members of the *nomenklatura* that senior Soviet officers are profoundly apart as military men.

The privileges showered on them are designed to buy off any envy they may have of their political masters. There is an unwritten rule that the army *nomenklatura* must have no interest in politics. The way to get stars on one's tunic is to keep a clean political nose, obey the *shpak,* the civilians, no matter how much one despises them, and to intrigue against rival brass.[9]

The military have seldom meddled directly in Russian politics. In 1762 Guards officers, angered by the weakness of Tsar Peter III, ousted him and brought his wife Catherine, that well-known admirer of Guardsmen, to the throne. The unsuccessful Decembrist revolt in 1820 was led by younger officers who had served in France and been exposed to Western freedoms. The Tsarist army remained loyal to the throne until its disintegration. Only the navy has a flimsy tradition of revolt.

The officer can pride himself on the number of telephones in his office, the shine on his Chaika, the number of places in which he controls troops, tanks or aircraft. If he begins to get political ambitions, he should remember the cautionary tale of Georgy Zhukov who was twice disgraced for making a *shpak* nervous.

In July 1946, after heading both the occupation administration in East Germany and the Soviet ground forces there, Zhukov was abruptly demoted to command the obscure Odessa military district and was turfed off the Central Committee. Stalin was jealous of his fame and worried lest Zhukov, like Trotsky, develop signs of Bonapartism. Zhukov's reputation was kicked so far into the gutter that by 1948 a foreign visitor was told that he had been sacked for looting jewellery in Berlin.[10] Stalin's death revived him. Within a few days of that final, dark death rattle, Zhukov was back in Moscow as first deputy defence minister. Two years later, he replaced Nikolai Bulganin as defence minister.[11] He took the place of the dead Beria, whom he had arrested, on the Central Committee. In June 1957 he became a full member of the Politburo, the only career officer to do so before Marshal Grechko in 1973. No sooner there, the cup was dashed from his lips. In October 1957 he was summoned back to Moscow from a trip to Albania, sacked as defence minister and stripped of his party posts.

Both Stalin and Khrushchev broke him because they were leery of his political ambition. 'We were heading for a military coup d'état,' Khrushchev claimed. 'We couldn't let Zhukov stage a Latin American style military takeover in our country.' The medal-heavy hero was accused of 'plotting the actual overthrow' of the regime, sponsoring a cult of his own personality and running the army in a 'non-party way'. In fact, he did not retire until the following year. A plotter would hardly have been kept on the active list. He was then pensioned off to the same Moscow apartment building where Khrushchev himself was sent after his fall six years later. With Khrushchev gone, the Georgy in Kremlinland saga took a new turn. Zhukov reappeared at May Day parades in full uniform atop Lenin's tomb. His memoirs were issued with a 600,000 pre-publication print run, and sold out. Amongst the hands that helped place his ashes in the Kremlin wall after his death were those of Brezhnev and Mikhail Suslov, members of the Politburo that had sacked him.

The senior officer will remember the more recent dismissal of Marshal Nikolai Ogarkov from his post as CoGS of Soviet forces in 1984 or of Marshal Sergei Sokolov as defence minister in 1987. Such sackings are rare, perhaps, but that has more to do with the political subservience of the officers than any diminution in the self-esteem of the party bosses. The officer remains subject to 'the organs', the secret police. He retains his fear of the Lubianka, that place where a 'mere urchin in a cap gave himself the airs of a Genghis Khan' when confronting a general.

The KGB keeps a constant check on the officer corps. It mans the army's 'first department' covering all units at home and on foreign postings. Its presence is ubiquitous, expected, part of the normal landscape of military life. 'There is always a KGB officer around,' says V. Shaligin, who served with engineer troops. 'Even if he is an alcoholic and a loafer, nobody can question him. He is under the command of his own kind.' A defecting Mig-25 pilot, Lieutenant Belenko, recalled that a fellow pilot was warned by the KGB that he would be thrown out of the service if he continued playing 'subversive' songs on his guitar. Officers are held responsible for the conduct of their men. Thus Belenko was rapped when the KGB discovered that one of his mechanics had written a letter home complaining about the food and an extortion racket organized by second-year soldiers. This results in a reluctance by officers to report their men for indiscipline.

KGB officers enforce a fog of secrecy that blinds as well as protects. The slogan, printed on military calendars and diaries, 'Don't tell your best friend what your brother shouldn't know,' is taken to absurdity.[12] A navy captain visiting a Soviet merchant ship came across a Canadian magazine with an article on British, American and Russian naval strength. He began flicking through it. 'Suddenly, as he noticed the pictures and silhouettes of warships alongside columns of facts and figures, he turned white as a sheet,' said the skipper of the merchantman.[13] '"Do you realize what this is? ... How is it possible? ... There are things I only know from hearsay ... My own officers don't have the first inkling about most of this. They are not even allowed to know it!"'

Many Soviet officers could thus go to war blind both to their own capability and to enemy strength. *V Izvestiakh nyet Pravdi, i v Pravda nyet Izvestii* runs the sour pun on the sources of information. In the News (the title of the newspaper *Izvestia*) there is no truth (*Pravda*), and in the Truth there is no news.

The news agency Tass does issue daily news reports to members of the *nomenklatura* that go further than the stilted newspapers. In ascending order of detail, there is Green, White and Red Tass. Even Red Tass contains little that the reader of a quality paper in the West would not take for granted.[14] Military books, manuals and magazines from the West are translated and are available, numbered and signed for individually. The Lenin Library has its special stacks of books, the *spetskhrany*, hidden away from the public shelves and catalogues.

The degree of ignorance remains deep. Marshal Ogarkov, negotiating arms control with the US, was 'outraged' by the American disclosure of figures of Soviet strategic weapons to Soviet civilian negotiators.[15] The US negotiators were startled to find that Vladimir Semenov, the deputy foreign minister and nominal head of the Soviet delegation, knew virtually nothing about the Soviet strategic arsenal. The Russian military had not told him, so the Americans did.

Information is issued grudgingly and only when clearly essential. In a country where only 50,000 phone books are printed for Moscow's 8 million population, and street plans are a rarity, the military suffer from an acute shortage of material as basic as detailed maps.

Details of military accidents and deaths are rarely given. Thus the death of Colonel General Semen Romanov, a Hero of the Soviet Union, a potential C-in-C of the Warsaw Pact and the man the South Koreans held responsible for giving the order to shoot down the KAL 747 in August 1983, was announced in May 1984 simply as 'died suddenly in the performance of his official duties'. That formula could mean death in a plane crash, in Afghanistan or, given this date, in a huge explosion in a missile store at Severomorsk near Murmansk. When Sadat threw the Russians out of Egypt in 1973, and the military advisers were sent home, the only official announcement was a small item in *Pravda* that Sadat had thanked the advisers for 'completing their mission'.

As a further check, the military has no monopoly on force. There are divisions of internal and frontier troops, outside their influence and control, commanded by the KGB and the MVD, the Interior Ministry. These units are fully equipped and manned, quite capable of 'putting down a revolt by any army unit'.[16] The Politburo's drivers and bodyguards come from the KGB's Section 9, not from the military. The *zampolits* are another sign

Major Offensive Operations of the Soviet Armed Forces, 1941–45

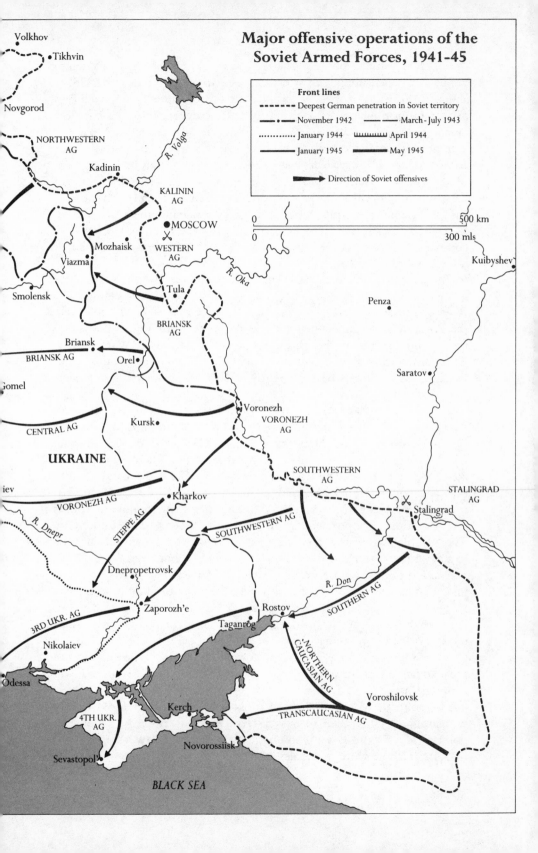

Major offensive operations of the Soviet Armed Forces, 1941-45

Front lines

- – – – Deepest German penetration in Soviet territory
- –·– November 1942
- – – March - July 1943
- ········ January 1944
- ⊔⊔⊔⊔⊔ April 1944
- ──── January 1945
- ▬▬▬ May 1945

➤ Direction of Soviet offensives

| 0 | | 500 km |
| 0 | | 300 mls |

Volkhov

Tikhvin

Novgorod

NORTHWESTERN AG

R. Volga

Kadinin

KALININ AG

MOSCOW

WESTERN AG

Mozhaisk

Viazma

Kuibyshev

Smolensk

Tula

R. Oka

Penza

BRIANSK AG

Briansk

BRIANSK AG

Orel

Saratov

Gomel

CENTRAL AG

Kursk

Voronezh

VORONEZH AG

UKRAINE

SOUTHWESTERN AG

STALINGRAD AG

iev

VORONEZH AG

Kharkov

STEPPE AG

Stalingrad

R. Dnepr

SOUTHWESTERN AG

Dnepropetrovsk

R. Don

3RD UKR. AG

Zaporozh'e

Rostov

SOUTHERN AG

Taganrog

Nikolaiev

NORTHERN CAUCASIAN AG

Odessa

4TH UKR. AG

Kerch

Voroshilovsk

TRANSCAUCASIAN AG

Sevastopol

Novorossiisk

BLACK SEA

of mistrust, grinding political zeal into officers as well as men. The senior *zampolit,* General Epishev, is said to have read out a speech to the USSR Young Officers' Congress in duplicate, repeating himself every second page without noticing.[17] But it is a sign of the dependence of the system on the military that a modern *zampolit* never outranks his commander. It is now unusual for him to hold the same rank. The commander is acknowledged as the *glavnaia figura,* the main figure in his unit.

Abroad, the Kremlin puts on a show of strength. Its statistics claim that only 19 per cent of the world's population lives in capitalist countries, compared with socialism's 35 per cent and 45 per cent in the Third World. It says that socialists rule 26 per cent of the land surface of the planet, compared with 23 per cent for capitalists. And, of course, it claims that history is on its side.

The fear of encirclement runs deep, to Yazor's great profit. 'My country is ringed by over 400 big and about 2,000 smaller bases in 30 countries,' a Russian wrote to the London *Times.* The Kremlin is more adept than the Pentagon, itself no slouch when it comes to justifying its budget, at reeling off details of the threat to its existence. The Warsaw Pact has more territory to defend than the US, Europe and China combined. It faces Chinese, British and French nuclear weapons as well as US missiles.

Abroad, be it a capitalist country or a socialist neighbour, is dangerous. Every Soviet frontier – and how many there are, with Finland, Norway, Poland, Czechoslovakia, Hungary, Rumania, Turkey, Iran, Afghanistan, China, Mongolia and North Korea – has three zones. There is the frontier zone, where every resident has a permit and a special stamp in his identity card and where the unauthorized are arrested. Then a fortified zone 100 metres deep, with barbed wire, searchlights, earth strips to show footprints and wire loops, like poacher's snares, hidden in the grass and brushwood. There is finally a 'neutral zone', a no-man's-land, hardly neutral since the frontier guards who patrol it are under orders to shoot.

These chronic anxieties strengthen the military. Party leaders boost the image of its wartime successes with huge memorials, like the Mamayev Kurgan in Stalingrad [now Volgograd] where choral music bays through loudspeakers and a statue of Mother Russia soars eighty-five metres into the air with a sword in her hand. The epitaph is everywhere: 'No one has been forgotten, nothing will be forgotten!' So vivid is the war, to the great advantage of the officer corps, that after thirty years *Pravda* was still blaming a poor harvest on 'war damage to Soviet farms'.

The politicians have often tried to associate themselves more closely with military glory than their war records allow. Brezhnev, though a political officer who saw no combat, had a mania for awarding himself medals which he wore on resplendent uniforms. It was suggested that he should be buried in the Tomb of the Unknown Soldier on the grounds that it was unknown if he was a soldier. During Chernenko's brief reign a documentary film startled Muscovites on its release. It gave an account of life in an obscure frontier post in remote Kazakhstan in the early 1930s. The reason for the quaint location was soon clear. The hero of *Outpost of Youth* was the young frontier guard Konstantin Chernenko, performing feats of courage and resource on horseback against assorted counter-revolutionary bands. Chernenko was not in the Red army during the war but did party work in Moscow.

Gorbachev is the first leader to be too young to have been involved in the war, but the Party itself shows no sign of losing the traditional military anxieties. It has 'no capacity to accept the idea of a world that would not be hostile', said Milovan Djilas.[18] Through the system it has created, it has 'condemned itself to thinking conspiratorial thoughts and to living in fear for its existence'. Party 'bosses are aware of their system's organic and above all economic lack of efficiency', Djilas continued. 'They cannot eliminate this in any other way than by military dominance or ... by exploitation, through military power, of developed areas.' Hence Gorbachev's efforts to improve both the system and the economy. Until it happens, and it will be immensely difficult, Gorbachev remains in hock to senior officers.

This shows in a modest political influence. The Kremlin coup against Khrushchev in October 1964, for example, was supported by the military. His cuts caused a slump in service morale. In 1960 a navy captain described to the high-ranking defector Arkady Shevchenko[19] how officers wept as they watched nearly completed cruisers and destroyers at the docks being cut up for scrap on Khrushchev's orders. Khrushchev tried to take the bitterness out of the demobbed officers by giving them admission to universities, without entrance exams, retraining grants, supplements to civilian incomes and easy housing allocations. Nevertheless, revenge was sweet when it came. Charges of corruption, common enough against politicians in the fall-out of a change at the top, are rarely levelled against the military.[20]

It is in economic and industrial clout where senior officers score most. 'The Soviet system produces good quality only in weapons and war material,' Djilas said baldly. 'Weak and insufficient weaponry could threaten the power and thus the supremacy of the ruling caste.' The armaments industry is part of the military *nomenklatura*.

True cost is an arcane subject in the Soviet Union, but there is no doubt that the military are the only consumers who are taken seriously. The defence ministry has its own huge complex of 'closed' factories which work only to its orders. Where it shares a plant with a civilian production line, its products are made to a different standard and under rigorous quality control. Military quality is better than export quality. The domestic consumer gets the *brak,* the junk.

There are plenty of faults in Soviet equipment – tanks whose turrets cannot be operated until two minutes after the power has been turned on and whose machinegun cannot be fired at the same time as the main cannon, armoured personnel carriers whose thin steel gives little protection from artillery. Fighters lack manoeuvrability and endurance. Shortcomings in Nato equipment are also endless, from the Sergeant York anti-aircraft system to the Nimrod AWACS package. The point is that the military have great economic independence.

Officers are told that their Nato counterparts are skilful and brave. To write them off as incompetent, doomed capitalists would reduce the combat awareness and respect for a powerful enemy that the *zampolits* stress constantly.

To explain how such moral degenerates remain dangerous opponents, the *zampolits* explain that they are semi-mercenaries who serve capitalism 'for money'. This applies to Western officers. From childhood, from the clips of Fifth Avenue and Miami that are served up on Soviet television, the Russian is aware that there is plenty of money in the West. This is rationalized as gross plenty for the few, misery for the masses. It is possible for a Western pilot to join the few in return for cash. That can hardly apply to the foot soldiers of Nato, and Nato is said to produce 'soldier robots' who 'fulfil orders mechanically'.

This shows a deep ignorance of the motivation of Western forces. It may well be true that the Russians are right to claim that the 'military heads of imperialist states' cannot rely on their 'military masses' to fight 'in the name of capitalist interests'. Few would fight consciously for capitalism. But they will fight for an extraordinary range of other reasons: for Queen and country, for Mom and apple pie, for their buddies and their unit, for family traditions, because they like uniforms, because it is a job, because they can't think of anything else to do.

The Red army is not itself averse to rewards.

Incentive awards, engraved watches and other gifts, are given to junior officers on a casual basis. Senior inspecting officers make their tours with a stock of watches engraved 'For a high level of flying skills, from an Aviation Commander', and so on. Even the defence minister does this. Pistols, cameras, samovars and harmonicas are other gifts. Cash awards and extra leave are handed out. Those who win 'Service to the Homeland' orders are rewarded with priority housing, free local and rail travel and a 15 per cent pension increase. Pilots who fly successful training missions are sometimes given flowers on their return.

The *prestizh* of the officer corps is maintained by rigorous smartness, at least in cities. Two thirds of the officers stopped by military police patrols in Moscow are hauled up for uniform offences, a further 18 per cent for failing to salute. They should use the impersonal *vy*, you. The once revolutionary army has dropped the comradely *ty*, thou, because it could 'later lead to other familiarities'. Junior officers are expected to give up their seats on public transport to their seniors as well as to women.

'Officer comrade courts of honour' deal with minor offences seen as unworthy of an officer. These informal courts can issue public warnings or impose a reduction in rank of one grade. Even here, the Party likes to keep a grip. Misdemeanours by regimental commanders and ship's captains are dealt with by party commissions and bureaus rather than by military tribunals. Lest anyone forget it, this is to affirm that 'a commander or political officer who commits a misdemeanour is responsible first to the Party and only secondarily to his own commander, that is, to the armed forces'.

Junior officers do well enough, particularly pilots and those in the Strategic Rocket Forces. As a lieutenant, fighter pilot Belenko earned 300 roubles a month at a time when the average teacher earned 100 and a doctor 120. They are fed far better than the men. Belenko recalls breakfast in the 513th Fighter Regiment – goulash, rice, fruit compote, white bread, buttermilk and tea. After morning flights the pilots had a second breakfast of sausage, boiled eggs, white bread, butter, tea and a chunk of chocolate. There was always meat and fruit for lunch. Accommodation is better than the civilian norm, though that may not be saying much. Belenko[21] was given a brand new apartment when he was working as a flying instructor in Salsk, a city in the southern steppelands. The floor had been built with green lumber and was already warped. Plaster peeled off the walls, the bath leaked, the toilet did not flush and none of the power points worked.

Drink is a problem, despite the Gorbachev clampdown. Pilots, for example, widely ignore orders not to drink for five days before flying. Alcohol stored for aircraft braking and coolant systems is used. Belenko cites a colonel who, though haranguing officers to curb alcoholism, supervised the wholesale theft of aircraft alcohol and used military trucks to take it to the nearest town to sell. Records were forged to increase flight time to account for the use of alcohol and aviation fuel was sold off or dumped to correspond. 'This regiment is not combat ready,' Belenko's commandant complained. 'Our planes often cannot fly because everyone is so drunk or people have run away.' The MiG-25 is known as the 'flying restaurant' because of the amount of alcohol it needs. Too much hard drinking or philandering can bring a charge of *amoralka*, misconduct or amorality. It is usually covered up and seldom leads to an officer being cashiered or having to resign.

Officers dread remote rural postings, particularly to the Far East. They long for a semi-permanent posting to Moscow or Leningrad. Belenko was sent to a village 200 kilometres north-east of Vladivostok. The streets were unlit and unpaved, with worms and flies everywhere. There was no cinema and no restaurant (apart from the MiG-25s). Isolation is a problem in the *kadrirovannye* or skeleton divisions, which exist with a few regulars who are fleshed out by reservists on mobilization. Some tank battalions have just twelve men, the commander, a captain and ten tank drivers. On mobilization, all the phantom soldiers, gunners, loaders, tank commanders and even the company sergeant major come from the reservists.[22]

Officers often marry very young to offset the loneliness and boredom of a dull posting. Three quarters of all army lieutenants are married, though not necessarily for long. Divorce rates are high. Efforts are made to keep younger officers and their wives happy by making consumer goods available for them, important in a society where products are generally in shorter supply than the cash to buy them. The increase in the supply of refrigerators, cars, washing machines, motorcycles and furniture to officers has been four times greater than for civilians.

There are military self-service stores, mail-order and book-by-post schemes. But the PX system is wildly erratic. *Red Star* has reported that the military in one district were getting early vegetables by air where another was out of matches. Military items like shoulder boards and insignia are often unavailable in the desolate Transbaykal, Ural and Central Asian districts. Housing privileges and children's allowances are highly prized. Uniforms are smart, considered 'fine, severe, elegant'. The semi-dress uniform is used to cut a dash at the theatre, receptions, on holiday. The air force is particularly noted for the sharpness and style of its dress.

The officer corps is young.

Two thirds of regimental officers are under thirty. Company and battery commanders are generally under twenty-five, battalion commanders twenty-eight to thirty. Some units promote every second or third officer to company or battery commander at twenty-five or under as a matter of policy.[23]

They are overwhelmingly from the cities and big towns. Increasingly, they are well educated. By 1983 more than half had had higher education, up from 10 per cent in 1953. The rate reaches 100 per cent in missile submarines and 75 per cent in the Strategic Rocket Forces but is down to 20 per cent in some infantry outfits. Eighty-five per cent are listed, coyly, as the children of 'manual and office workers' and 15 per cent as sons of 'agricultural workers'. That shows a huge swing away from the peasant sons of Stalin's day, and the 'worker' tag is there largely for form's sake. One in five is promoted through the ranks.

The officer corps is almost entirely Slav and predominantly Russian. A Rand Corporation study in 1980 found few people who had seen a single minority officer of Central Asian or Caucasian origin and only the odd Balt or Jewish officer.[24] Nobody had seen a minority officer above the rank of major. Large numbers of non-Slav officers were weeded out during Khrushchev's manpower cuts, and the corps is becoming more rather than less Russian. A former professor at the signals corps academy in Leningrad said that he could only remember a handful of non-Slav officer cadets, though thousands had passed through the academy and many foreign students had been there. The Russian share of officers is now over 80 per cent, with 10 to 15 per cent Ukranians and White Russians and a smattering of others. Yet Jews, Balts and Soviet Germans are among the best-educated people in the Soviet Union. The few Jewish and Balt officers are mainly technical specialists, though some Jews have been noted as *zampolits*.

Family traditions are growing. The press praises the 'continuity of generations' and there is talk of second and third generations of 'military dynasties'. The first man to follow his father on to the Central Committee was a general and the son of a general, Vladimir Govorov. About a third of officer cadets come from families with a military tradition, who may have sent them to Suvorov or Nakhimov schools from the age of eight.

Flying has the highest prestige and attracts most competition. A Soviet study shows that physicists are rated highest in status by the public with a point score of 6.6. Pilots are in the next ranking at 5.3, slightly above writers and artists. Career officers in the army rate 4.3, below university teachers but above party ideologists and other teachers.[25]

The men in Yazov's forces are far distant from his officer elite.

37

THE THREE MILLION

The Russian soldier, a primeval force in European and Asian history, is now a bedrock of the modern world. He, rather than trade or industry, is the glue of the Soviet bloc. His old qualities of endurance and stoicism have been leavened by first-rate equipment and training, and the subjugation of a vast economy to his needs. Modernization has been added to mass.

Conscription is a rite of passage in Russian life. The conscript makes up three quarters of the armed forces as junior NCOs and privates.[1] He is a truly imperial soldier even if he has a 'home' posting. Twelve of the fifteen

Federated Republics of the Soviet Union were acquired by conquest or colonization. It is the conscript who stitches the landmass together.

Each year 1.3 million eighteen-year-olds are inducted in two great sweeps, one in May and June, the next in November and December. They will serve for two years, or three in the navy or border guards.*

Plenty of preparatory work in introducing children to the military has already been done. Each year, about sixteen million Young Pioneers, aged from ten to fifteen, take part in *Zarnitsa* or Summer Lightning war games. They take place under the command of a Soviet marshal. At a typical exercise in the Vladivostok area, 6,500 Young Pioneers passed before an admiral in a formal review after practising assault landings. In Moscow's Lenin Hills, children with blue patches scatter amongst the trees like partisans whilst those with green badges search to take them prisoner.[2]

Conferences on military-patriotic education are held in Moscow's Pioneer and Schoolchildren's Palace, the aim being to form 'a juvenile deep conviction of the historic justice of the ideas of communism and the indisputable advantages of the Socialist system over the capitalist system'.[3] Children are encouraged to help with the gardens in war graves and to build monuments to heroes. In a bitter wind in the fortress at Brest, with snow flurries scudding in from the east, Young Pioneers in red scarves stood guard at the memorial.

All youths undergo basic military training, *nachal'naia voennaia pod-gotovka*, a 2-year, 140-hour programme which covers drill, the use of light weapons and a technical speciality such as truck driving. In border areas children are taught to be alert and to operate as the 'combat friends' of the border troops. 'All an unidentified person has to do is to appear in the border area and the border guards learn of him from their "combat friends",' boasts *Red Star*.[4] Children are taken to 'combat glory museums', to 'hero cities' and to battle sites.

From fourteen, a child can join DOSAAF, the vast All-Union Voluntary Society for Assistance to the Army, Air Force and Navy. Its entrance fee is a nominal 10 kopeks, the annual dues the same. At least 75 million are said to be members of it, making it by far the largest organization in the world. The million drivers it teaches each year make it the world's largest driving school. It has 315,000 branches encouraging training in collective farms, factories and schools. Every town has a standard, three-storey DOSAAF block with garages, lecture rooms and a rifle range. The sharpest children fly, parachute jump or aqualung. L-29 jet trainers are used and every second-year member of a DOSAAF aviation club will have got in

---

* The draft means that, unlike the US, women are a rarity in the Soviet forces. About 10,000 serve as nurses and radio and telegraph operators. During the war, about 800,000 women served as snipers, bomber and air defence pilots and machinegunners as well as making up 40 per cent of doctors and surgeons.

ten hours' flying time. There are 100,000 uniformed instructors, most of them reserve officers.

Training is topped up by the summer camps that about 80 per cent of Soviet children attend. The camps, with the children divided up into battalions, platoons and squads, normally last a week or a fortnight. Children from isolated areas, in Siberia or the Far East, do a month or more. A DOSAAF naval school in Khabarovsk gives a two-month naval course for pre-draft children from remote farms and timber-cutting settlements.

If many children enjoy their summer games and camps, however, the call-up itself for those eighteen-year-olds selected for service is a grimmer event. With its titanic disdain for reality, the Soviet defence ministry describes a moment of 'happiness and joy' as young men are 'escorted by their parents' and strewn with 'flowers from local Pioneers'[5] on their way to join their units. That is a far cry from the frightened youths and their desperate late-night drinking in the 1982 hit film *Rodina*.

'I chucked up my job as a truck driver when I got my papers telling me when to turn up,' said Igor Rykov, a former paratroop sergeant. 'I just had a good time. We had a big party the night before I had to go to the induction centre. I got plastered and then I put on some filthy rags, because I knew that anything good would be nicked, and turned up at the centre in Sochi.

'They shaved my head and gave me a bath and got rid of my clothes. We all hung around for three days waiting for the *pokupateli*, the buyers. This officer turned up and they put 700 of us on a troop train and rattled us off for two days to a training division.'

These midsummer and late autumn troop trains always head for the far side of the country. It is policy that troops should not be stationed in their home areas. 'They took us for a six-day ride from Volgograd to a place called Termez,' recalls one recruit, Vladislav Naumov. 'There was plenty of vodka on the train. We could buy it from the train staff for fifteen roubles a bottle.'

Some conscripts go by air, but the drinking remains. Thus, in the final induction of 1988, 176 of them flew from Tbilisi in Georgia to start their service 7,200 kilometres away in Khabarovsk. En route the Il-76 began 'rocking from side to side as if it was caught in air pockets'. But this was 'no air turbulence – it was a fight in the passenger cabin'. The pilot radioed Barnaul, three thousand kilometres out from Tbilisi, for an emergency landing as he feared he would crash. The conscripts were subdued by local army units, who found dozens of bottles of moonshine aboard.

The *pokupateli* are officers who select recruits for various units. In theory, this is based on gradings already made that take into account political reliability, the criminal record of the recruit and his family, his attendance at rallies, his height, physique and IQ. Categories run from 0 to 10.

The obsession with political reliability means that both conventional and political IQ are taken into account. 'Political IQ' is judged by giving the recruit proverbs printed on a card, where he scores high if he rejects bourgeois claptrap such as 'Art is the solace of the community' and accepts 'Without a collective, life is unhappy'.*

When he joins his unit a recruit's morale is judged by a questionnaire designed to assess the 'Soviet soldier's relationship to Imperialism'. He is asked: 'What machinations and plots do you know about that have been directed against the Soviet Motherland? What consequences, as a soldier of the Soviet army, do you draw from the acts committed by the USA aggressors?'

In practice the huge throughput in the armed forces, which turn over almost a quarter of their strength every six months, make such fine tuning impossible. Race, parental influence and luck are as decisive.

Draft-dodging was blatant under Brezhnev, with the children of the powerful slipping off into Institutes and the rich paying a few thousand roubles to a military commissar to have their son classified as unfit. Georgians, skilled in the arts of the black market, were renowned for the finesse with which they avoided military service.

The gilded youth of few countries gets drafted into leaky tents in obscure encampments in distant campaigns at a time of general peace, however, and Vietnam was no exception. 'My mother has connections. She got it so that my Pioneer camp as a boy was on the Black Sea coast. For Afghanistan, it wasn't enough,' said Oleg Khlan, who deserted in Afghanistan with Rykov.[6] Gorbachev had cut corruption even before the Afghan withdrawals made draft-dodging less attractive.

Pacifism, religious or otherwise, is no excuse. The *Soviet Military Encyclopaedia* describes it as 'as unscientific now as it was at the time of its inception in the 1830s'. The Red army is atheist. The tolerance of religion forced on Stalin during the war dissolved under Khrushchev, in the early 1960s. The Party fears that the Russians may still follow Solzhenitsyn in seeing Marxism as a 'dark, un-Russian whirlwind that descended on us from the West'. The *zampolit* and the Lenin Rooms in each unit are there to ensure that only so much of the army's switch from Christianity to Communism remains unquestionable.

Baptists are often openly defiant, however, refusing to take the military oath or to carry arms. Most are West Ukrainians, anti-Russian and anti-Soviet, proselytising for their faith and sometimes sent to Siberia for it.

---

* *War on the Mind*, Peter Watson, London, 1980. In a motorized infantry division, the category 0 cream goes to the intelligence staff and category 1 to the rocket sections. Category 2 recruits are numerate enough for fire control batteries and the anti-aircraft rocket regiments. Tank crews come in at category 6 and infantrymen slot in below that.

Like Orthodox Christians, Muslem Central Asians and Caucasians are more discreet, preferring to keep their religion to themselves whilst in the military.

Racial factors are becoming steadily more important as the Russians lose their predominance in the Soviet Union. This is sensitive, and the full results of the last census in 1979 have never been published.[7] It is clear that the Russians will no longer be a majority in the 270 million population by the end of the 1990s. The Russian birth rate is growing at less than 0.7 per cent a year, with an even bleaker picture in other Slav republics like the Ukraine and White Russia. This is blamed on the high divorce rate among the young and crowded living conditions which make abortion attractive.

The Muslim birth rate is five times higher than the European. Within two decades Muslims are likely to grow from 45 to 100 million. Uzbekistan, with a population of 17 million, has the highest birth rate in the world. The population in Kazakhstan, where anti-Russian racial rioting broke out late in 1986, has gone up by more than half in the past twenty-five years. An increasing number of conscripts come from Soviet Central Asia, Kazakhstan and the Caucasus, with Muslim backgrounds and little interest in an army career. Where up to 90 per cent of Russian youths join DOSAAF, the figure in Kirghiz is 31 per cent, in the Kazakh Republic only 20 per cent.

Where 74 per cent of the 1970 draft pool was Slav, and 13 per cent Muslim, the Slav proportion had already fallen to 63 per cent by 1985, with Muslims up to 24 per cent. There is no evidence that this will harm combat efficiency. Asians were over-represented after the loss of the western Slav lands in the war and fought well. A third of those at Stalingrad came from minorities and a survey of 100 infantry divisions in July 1944 showed 48 per cent of the troops to be non-Slavs.

In theory, all nationalities are mixed. An ideal is an 'isolated air defence unit with Russians and Ukrainians, Georgians and Armenians, Tartars and Kazakhs, Jews and Uzbeks, in all 17 nationalities'.[8] In fact, it is as well that unit is isolated since it is unlikely that it would stand much scrutiny. Few Central Asians are used in combat units, where they make up just 20 per cent of current strength, normally as hewers of trenches and carriers of ammunition. Fewer still are commissioned or serve in units as technical as air defence.

The *stroibats*, the construction battalions that are the slum postings for recruits, are as much as 80 per cent non-Slav. Russians consider them a punishment posting. Unarmed, virtually untrained, toiling at barrack and road and rail building, they draw more than half their men from Central Asia, with the balance from those suspected of anti-Soviet dreaming, Balts, Caucasians, Jews and West Ukrainians.[9] Central Asians, reckoned to have little sympathy with the largely Slav inmates, are extensively used as MVD prison camp guards.

Russians dominate among border troops. Ukrainians and White Russians are also used, though never on their own borders. Troops for Eastern European postings are largely selected from Russian villages in the Kalinin, Yaroslavl and Tula areas, 'real Mother Russia boys' who are 'reasonably civilized but not too much'.

Despite the integration of units, nationalities stick together. This is partly a matter of language. Russian is the language of command as well as the 'language of international intercourse voluntarily chosen by all the USSR peoples'. All orders are written in it. Officer cadets take exams in Russian language and literature. Even in the *stroibats*, all regulations, training manuals and documents are in Russian and soldiers are expected to speak it off duty. In practice, only East Ukrainians, a group who often re-enlist to become career NCOs, scorned by others as *makaroniks* for their love of stripes, stick to Russian. Others use their own language and many have only a basic grasp of Russian. Uzbek becomes a common language for Kazakhs, Kirghiz, Turkmen, Tartars, Azerbaijanis and Bashkirs, as well as Uzbeks.

Latvians, Lithuanians and Estonians are intensely insular. 'They say we Balts are arrogant but that's only because we've got higher living standards than the Russians,' says an Estonian who deserted from East Germany. 'The Russians always say we're fascists. They say, "If we hadn't liberated you, you'd still be capitalists." ' Balts use the Latvian word *cuke*, meaning 'swine', when referring to Russians. 'Russians respected the Balts because they are strong and very European, although the Balts absolutely hate the Russians,' said one conscript.[10] 'The Russians I served with felt a sort of inferiority complex towards them.' That Russian modesty does not extend to other groups, as the rich vocabulary of service slang shows. *Churka, Chernozhopy, Kosoglazyi, Zheltoe gavno, Evreichik*, woodchip, black arse, slant-eyes, yellow shit, little Jew are the common descriptions for those who are collectively and witheringly called *Nerusskie*, non-Russian.

All armies are cliquish, however, most deal in stereotypes and elites, and there is little evidence to show that Soviet forces are dangerously riven by racial and national tensions.[11] There was some minority unrest over Afghanistan. Kazakhs in Alma-Ata demanded proper Muslem funerals for soldiers killed in Afghanistan. Many Muslem conscripts were withdrawn from Afghanistan and replaced by Slavs, though this was at least partly because the original units drawn from close to the Afghan border had a high proportion of Muslems. Balt dissenters compared the military occupation of Afghanistan with the Russian takeover of Lithuania, Latvia and Estonia in 1940. Such protests were relatively rare.

Nor does language seem to have much effect on performance. It seems as though it should. Over half non-Russians, themselves almost half the population, do not have fluent Russian.★ But the young speak better Russian than their parents and the need for good conversational Russian in a *stroibat* or a tank hull is not great. Any army is a closed world dealing in its own military language, which a recruit learns readily enough and whose basics he will already have grasped at school.

'The Uzbekhs, the Azerbaijanis, even some Ukrainians didn't speak Russian, or very little,' said Khlan of his paratroop section of the 75th Guards Armoured Division in Afghanistan. 'Sometimes you'd tell them to go to the left and they'd go to the right. But in conditions like ours, they learn fast.

'Anyway, if you smack them a couple of times, they learn faster. That's the best way to teach Russian. Use the fist first.'

Political training is continual, frequently running into the brief two hours a day of free time allowed to troops. 'You had classes all the time. They told you all these nonsenses, that you're fighting Chinese and Americans in Afghanistan when you could see that you're not,' said Rykov. 'But you can't ask questions. You do, and they say, "What's up, you want a pale face?"'

Propaganda is an unceasing stream, verbal, visual or on cheap paper. Each recruit is issued with a Soldier's Calendar with a daily note. On 11 April he should think of Alexander who 'smashed the German dog-knights on this day in 1294'. On 7 August he is reminded of the fighter pilot V. V. Talalikhin who rammed a German aircraft this day in 1941, the 'first of 500 Soviet pilots to do so'.[12] There is, of course, no let-up at Christmas. In December the recruit is reminded that 'Soviet soldiers are made of metal', that 'faith in the Party is our strength' and that 'from discipline to heroism is one step'.[13]

Submariners are said to 'demand spiritual "fuel"'. They get enough to power them through the longest patrol off the US seaboard or under the icecap. A day in the life of a submarine political officer starts with a political information session. The theme is 'Sailor, protect and add to the heroic traditions of the Baltic submarines'. Next comes a radio newscast with 'Talks by advanced production workers in the socialist competition'. The *zampolit* now holds a seminar with warrant officers on 'Helping subordinates to fulfil Socialist pledges'. A radio meeting then covers the 'Roll call of outstanding combat posts'. As evening draws on beneath the

★ The last full census gave 53 per cent Russians, and 17 per cent Ukrainians. With between 3.8 and 1.3 per cent, in descending order, came White Russians, Uzbeks, Tartars, Kazakhs, Azerbaijanis, Armenians and Georgians. The remaining 28 nationalities made up 12.6 per cent. Muslems had increased their numbers by almost a half since 1959.

waves, another meeting inspires '*Unabashed hatred* for the enemies of the Socialist Motherland' which, with Miami a few minutes' missile time away, should not be allowed to get out of hand. Before the exhausted political officer can hit his bunk, he must present 'At Evening's End' with verses and songs on the Motherland.[14]

The *zampolit* has some of the duties given to chaplains in Western armies. He is the keeper of the 'Lenin room', the communist shrine with its propaganda and posters in each unit. He comforts soldiers at times of distress. He tries to soften racial friction. He is meant to deal with drinking problems. His main task is to keep the men's Red zeal up to scratch with sermonizing. There are complaints that he often reads lectures written by others and delivered with 'all the energy of melting ice'. Trotsky's leather-jacketed commissar, with a gun in one hand and a fiery tract in the other, has been replaced by a 'man like a train conductor'.[15]

There are, of course, survival tricks that a nation with a sharp sense of humour uses to endure such assaults. The ability to switch off is highly developed in most military men. Propaganda is ignored. Checking on a warehouse in Lithuania, DOSAAF found that only six in a hundred of its books had been so much as distributed. There are complaints that even officers 'at times show an incomprehensible preference for foreign films' to home-grown socialist epics. The department of Marxist-Leninism at the Kharkov Guards Higher Tank School concedes that it is forced to give its students 'a three instead of a failure or a five instead of a three'.[16]

Although regulars get a month's leave a year, the draftee is officially allowed ten days in his two years but in practice usually gets none. That is, unless he is good at sports or has unusual initiative. Sport is important in the Red army. Every base has its athletic field and its volleyball, football, hockey and boxing teams. If a unit team is doing well, its members get local leave passes and the pick of duty positions, the drivers' pool in a motor rifle battalion, headquarters' clerks in an armoured division.

The ingenious can also get leave. A mechanic can trade ten days' leave by fixing an officer's car. Others arrange for friends at home to send a fake telegram claiming that a mother or close relative is ill. *Red Star* reported that one regiment was famous for the souvenirs it gave to top-ranking visitors, wooden bears playing the balalaika, model deer, all hand carved. These were being crafted by two conscripts whose reward for spending their military service making curios was to have two home leaves a year.[17]

If sons cannot get home, some parents manage to visit their sons. This is also frowned on. A regimental commander, Colonel V. Archipov, wrote to *Red Star*[18] to complain that too many parents were wangling permission to visit their conscript offspring. He said that this was bad for discipline, since parents taught their children to drink and made them selfish. The colonel claimed that parents gave their soldier-children 'hot-water bottles full of vodka, stewed plums in brandy, bottles of home-brewed spirits in jars of jam'. Archipov quoted a case in his own regiment. Ivan Stepanovich arrived in the garrison town and asked if his son could spend a night in an apartment he had hired in town. Permission granted, father and son went off on a binge. The father passed out and the son, carousing in the streets, was arrested.

Passes out of barracks are only issued to trained soldiers at the discretion of their sergeant. There are not more than three a month, for use on Saturdays and Sundays until 11 p.m.

Conscripts on foreign postings are sometimes not paid for months. 'We were meant to get 25 East marks a month,' says a recruit who deserted from an air defence battalion in East Germany in 1987.[19] 'But it was often late and sometimes we didn't get any. The NCOs hold back your pay because they say you've broken something.' A conscript NCO is better off with fifteen roubles a month. Those in elite units and with higher education qualifications can earn up to 200 roubles as senior NCOs at the end of their service. Regular career soldiers, who sign on after completing their draft service, start at 100 roubles a month.

Red army units outside the Soviet Union are sealed off from the population. Garrisons in Eastern Europe live totally self-contained lives, as if still in Russia.

Rail carriages with soldiers going to East Germany, swilling beer and eating processed peas from aluminium plates as if there were no tomorrow, are dropped off at sidings outside the cities. There are 380,000 Soviet troops in East Germany. Their officers can be seen shuttling in staff cars or shopping in East Berlin. But the men are a ghost army, its shadows glimpsed in wire compounds and wooden huts on the edges of forests, tank parks by the rail line near Magdeburg, high-wheeled Jeeps on the autobahn and an occasional and correct small group of conscripts photographing each other in front of a war memorial. Outside the garrisons, in smaller and more intimate units like radar installations, rapid rotation ensures that the men do not become familiar with local life.

Two recruits who deserted to the West from East Germany in 1987 described conditions.[20] Tauno, from Tallinn, was serving in an air defence battalion and Peter, from Tartur, was in the medical unit of the 20th Guards Motorized Infantry Division near Leipzig.

After call-up, they were first kept in a camp in Tallinn, sleeping on bare boards without sleeping bags or blankets. They were then put on a train which was kept in a siding for two days. 'Nobody told us where we were going. We hoped it wasn't Afghanistan,' said Tauno. 'But we didn't know what was waiting for us in East Germany.' They had little idea of where they were stationed. When they deserted, they thought they were close to the West German border when they were in fact 250 kilometres away. They navigated from a map they found in the glove compartment of the civilian Lada car they stole.

'Contact with East German civilians was absolutely forbidden,' said Tauno. 'German girls were taboo. Anyone who was caught going out of the barracks, over the wall, got bread and water in the guardhouse.'

This was not simply because of the fear that troops could become infected with whatever dissidence might lurk in East Germany.[21] It is also because the satellites are richer and have a notably higher standard of living than the Soviet Union itself. In the Soviet empire, in a curious role reversal, the subject peoples are wealthier than their masters.

The conscript has 90 minutes to himself in the evenings, to write letters, to play dominoes and chess, watch TV or read in the regimental library, stocked with *Pravda*, *Izvestia*, military and patriotic magazines and thrillers, often starring CIA villains, and the Russian classics. The political officer supervises the regimental choir, folk dancing and music. At the weekends there are patriotic films, which the conscripts call '*hurrahs*'. At postings in the Soviet Union there are dances at the regimental club at the weekends, though local girls tend to avoid the penniless conscripts. There are lectures on venereal disease and all conscripts have blood tests on finishing their service but there are no issue contraceptives.

The barracks, the *kazarma*, are poor and overcrowded, the recruits sleeping in bunks with only a small locker of their own. Lavatories are often a hole in the ground or a shed in the barracks. Apart from a weekly session in a *banya*, a steam bath, washing is a cold and bleak affair that soldiers try to avoid despite the white strip sewn into their collars as a check on their hygiene. 'It is bath day,' the military joke runs. 'A change of underwear is announced. "Hut 2 to change underwear with Hut 6 ..."'

Troops in East Germany are quartered in old, wooden Wehrmacht barracks. 'We were with twenty-three others in a room four metres square,' says Peter. 'We had showers of cold water. One of us asked where we could dry and an NCO shouted at him: "You're not at home now. Get dressed and get out. That'll dry you quickly enough."' This was in a medical unit, where there was warm water only on Saturdays and the doctor visited once a week. Men sleep 100 and more to a room in other barracks. Privacy means little – indeed there is no Russian word for it.

The patriotism of Russian recruits remains intense, though that of the minorities may sometimes have a more dubious edge to it. It is sometimes called *kvas* patriotism, after the peasant drink, earthy and collective. There is a deep feeling that *nasha luchshe*, 'ours is best', and everything else is *chuzhoi*, other, alien, Western, Chinese. The Second World War, aptly named the Great Patriotic War by the Russians, keeps a tangible hold. Children grow up amid eternal flames, ceremonies and coach trips to Hero Cities or to the lonely sites of German atrocities, like the butchered village of Katyn in White Russia, where only the stone fireplaces survived the German torch and where bells toll the quarter hours from the chimneys.[22]

The desire to pick at the scab of the wound of war, to probe and worry at it, remains urgent. Monuments are still being built, eighty in one recent five-year period, although there were already 675 military monuments and memorials in the Ural Military District alone – an area in which no land battles were fought during the war. War films are a freshly minted staple. 'Every weekend we had to watch one,' says Peter of barrack life in East Germany.

Most recruits now come from the cities, more sophisticated, resentful of the austerity of *kazarma* barrack life, depressed by distant rural postings and the enforced absence of their civilian status symbols, their *jeansi* and Western rock cassettes, and irritated by the constant regulation.

The easiest oblivion lies in alcohol. Drunkenness is technically a serious offence, the more so since Gorbachev's anti-drinking drive. Soldiers on a pass are only allowed to drink beer. They should be checked for slurred speech and gait when they return.[23] Drunks who have to be brought back to barracks are held for the cost of the military transport and drunken military drivers are liable to pay the full amount of the damage they cause. It is common to all ranks,* although technically alcohol is forbidden in barracks.

Vladimir Rybakov, who commanded a howitzer crew on the Chinese border, recalled how his men 'swigged eau de cologne and smoked pot until the black rock of sleep rolled over them'.[24] Posted to Siberia, an 'effective defence against the cold and army bullshit was for up to twenty men to inhale alcohol fumes under a groundsheet'. Some sniffed burning plastic. Rybakov sold dog carcases to prisoners in exchange for dope.

'Drinking is a problem in the army, as it is everywhere else in Russia,' said Vanya Sharigin, who served as a conscript with a radar unit. 'We would exchange kerosene with local villages for *samogon* home-brew. The

---

* And all armies, not just the Soviet one. Drug-taking, outside Afghanistan, is much rarer than in the US army. The claim that the Red army is permanently drunk is as exaggerated as the one that the US army is on a permanent drug high. The prospect of smashed Red army tankmen advancing through West Germany's Fulda gap towards stoned American anti-tank crews is intriguing. Perhaps it would lead to World War III being called off on the ground that nobody was fit to fight. It is, regrettably, not a very likely battle scenario.

officers would pretend not to notice. They wouldn't notice, either, if some radio equipment went missing. Everyone is stealing or exchanging something that belongs to the army for vodka.'

To get money, soldiers sell off petrol to private motorists. It has been estimated that at least 150 million gallons of petrol are stolen from the military each year and *Izvestia* has claimed that over a third of private motorists drive on state-owned fuel. Military drivers operate *na levo*, on the left or under the counter, as unofficial taxicabs for cash. When the daily British military train to West Berlin stops at the East German border, Soviet conscripts on the platform stare longingly at the dining car, and, with sign language, plead for liquor from the tables.

Food is dull and monotonous and meal strikes are fairly common, the only form of protest tacitly permitted in the Red army. On the morning that he flew his MiG-25 from an air base near Vladivostok to Japan, Lieutenant Belenko was told by his squadron commander Yevgeny Pankovsky that the airmen on the base had refused to eat their breakfast. 'They threw their food at the cooks and one of them hit a cook,' said Pankovsky. Belenko said that if they took a pig to the mess hall, it would faint. He asked if Pankovsky would eat there. 'No,' replied the squadron commander.[25]

Breakfast is a bowl of *kasha* porridge, two pieces of black bread, one of white and three sugar lumps for an unlimited quantity of milkless tea. Lunch is a bowl of potato and vegetable soup, a small piece of meat, salt pork, with macaroni or more *kasha* and bread. Eggs are seldom served, and cheese, ham, sausage and milk never. Potatoes, cabbage and sauerkraut provide bulk. Fridays are meatless. For supper, there is mashed potato or macaroni with tea and bread and dried fish. 'Sometimes there was stew at weekends,' says Tauno. 'That was rare. The meat used to get sold off on the black market.'

Units eat together in cramped mess halls. Most halls operate in shifts, so the time for a meal is often limited to thirty minutes. Special meals are served on holidays like May Day with white bread instead of black, a tin of jam between two or three soldiers and a slice of meat in the morning *kasha*. Most mess halls have a buffet for luxuries like milk, white bread, butter, cigarettes and extra sugar. Besides their pay, many conscripts get a few roubles a month from home.

The military are encouraged to grow their own food and raise chickens and pigs on special military farms and in garrison towns. *Red Star* carried long reports on the gardening achievements of army and navy units from the hot Black Sea coast to the polar north and the Urals, where onions, radishes, dill and lettuce 'thrive under ultraviolet light in the hothouses of remote garrisons'.[26]

The chief of logistics and supply, General Semen K. Kurkotkin, says that the army's own food programme is curing the diet deficiencies that cause sores, bad teeth, eye infections and other indications of lack of vitamins among the conscripts. Political officers are quick to jump on any idea that Western soldiers are better fed without having to tend their own vegetable plots. Seven million Americans are starving, according to Lieutenant Colonel N. Karasev, and twenty million US families 'live permanently on the brink of hunger'.

The raw recruit has a miserable entry into the army, bullied and abused by his seniors for the first six months of his service, before in turn imposing brutality on others. 'Recruits are called "novices",' says Devlet Tabolov, who served in the navy at Kronstadt. 'All the dirtiest and worst jobs are carried out by novices. The experienced men treat the novices badly. You could say with cruelty.'

'It's very bad for the new arrivals,' said Igor Rykov. 'They have to work twice as hard so that the longer-serving men, the bosses, can skive. They get the thick end of everything. In Afghanistan, we lived twenty-five to a tent. In the winter, you put the new guys in the cots on the edge of the tent where they freeze. In May, you turf them out into the middle because it's beginning to bake with heat.'

Every scrap of private property is taken from him by his seniors on arrival at his unit, the reason why recruits traditionally wear rags and leave watches, family photographs and other items of real or sentimental value at home. Food parcels and pay are stolen from juniors. 'Everyone tries to hide their things,' wrote Kirill Podrabinek, who served in a barracks in Turkmenistan.[27] 'Some even bury them in the ground.' At meals, 'more senior soldiers take all they want and the rest, if there is any, is for the "slaves".'

Recruits could not look to officers, who they call 'jackals' or 'dogs', for protection. In extreme cases of fazing, some recruits try to desert or commit suicide. 'The only real form of protest known in the Soviet army is suicide by shooting,' says Devlet Tabolov. 'It is done when young men realize how little value their life has in something so colossal and indifferent. The huge gap between officers and men doesn't help, though it is getting better with the inflow of younger officers.'

Zakharov claimed that three soldiers shot an officer because of severe beatings by sergeants. These were almost routine in his camp in Afghanistan. 'They did it to make us submit to everything. The sergeants told us, "We were beaten, so now we beat you." Sometimes it got so bad that soldiers would try to defend themselves with their guns.' Tauno found the career NCOs stupid and brutal: 'They slap you in the face if you don't jump to every command.' Some level of recruit bullying exists in every

army, however, and there is no evidence that it seriously affects the Red
army.

Desertion has a long tradition in Russia. In 1707, desertion left the 23
dragoon regiments on the Vistula with 8,000 men out of a supposed
strength of 23,000. Divisions quietly dissolved during the civil war.[28]
Cheka repression eventually slowed desertion and the treatment handed
out by Stalin to returning POWs in 1945, sending them to labour camps
as 'deserters', made it clear that the definition of desertion is deliberately
broad. Present-day controls, frequently examined papers and internal
passports, have all but ended it.

It lives on in the folk memory and in the occasional desertion in
Afghanistan or doomed spree in Eastern Europe. Belenko was told that,
at a nearby army base in the Soviet Far East, 'two soldiers had killed two
other soldiers and an officer, confiscated machineguns and provisions and
struck out through the forest towards the coast, intending to steal a boat
and sail it to Japan. They dodged and fought pursuing patrols several days
until they were killed.' Harsh sentences give desertion a desperate edge
and there have been a few cases in East Germany where young soldiers
who have got drunk and stolen a vehicle, more AWOL than deserters, are
thought to have been killed in shoot-outs with military police. After two
soldiers deserted to the *mujaheddin* in Afghanistan, Zakharov says that:
'Our commanding officer ordered us on parade and said: "Two have run
away, but where can you run to? You don't know yourselves."'

The navy had a tradition of mutiny, from the *Potemkin* to Kronstadt,
but this too has all but passed. The last recorded incident started in
the pre-dawn darkness of 8 November 1975 when the missile destroyer
Storozhevoy slipped to sea from the Baltic port of Riga.

The 3,800-ton, three-year-old vessel had a Captain Valery Sablin as
political officer, a *zampolit* with a rare reputation for listening to complaints
from the crew. He had been criticized in *Red Star* the year before for not
running his political education meetings properly. He gave his last lecture
on the afternoon of 7 November, when many officers and men were on
leave in Riga commemorating the October revolution. That night, Sablin,
another officer called Markov and about a dozen petty officers locked the
captain in his cabin, tied up some other officers and ordered a skeleton
crew of unwary conscripts to take the destroyer to sea. As the ship moved
out, a sailor jumped overboard and swam ashore. It took him two hours
to reach the naval HQ in Riga and convince senior naval staff that
something was amiss.

An officer on board the *Storozhevoy* freed himself and broadcast an
emergency message as the ship headed for the Swedish island of Gotland,
a 320-kilometre voyage that would normally take seven hours. Astonished
Swedish radio operators heard radio traffic between the mutineers and

Soviet bombers sent to stop the ship. The *Storozhevoy* refused to heave to
and the Soviet aircraft opened fire on it. During the attacks, a pursuing
ship was more seriously damaged than the *Storozhevoy*.

The aircraft succeeded in slowing the destroyer and the ship was captured
by other surface vessels at 8 a.m. on 8 November only 50 kilometres from
the Swedish coast. Sablin had a three-day trial in front of the military
division of the Soviet Supreme Court and was executed together with a
number of enlisted crewmen.[29]

Intense use of informers makes dissent almost as rare as desertion or mutiny.
Recruits are used to it from their schooldays, where *zvenovois*, form leaders
who report to teachers on the behaviour of their fellow children, are the
first introduction to the trained informers who dog adult life. Pavel
Morozov, a fourteen-year-old who reported his own father for grain
hoarding in 1932,[30] is held up as a hero for young Pioneers.

Conscripts call the KGB informers in their units 'goats', or *Stukachi*.
Viktor Suvorov described how, after a briefing for the invasion of Czechoslovakia in 1968, everyone ran back 'to reach the column before the *Stukachi*
and to see them all together in a group before they dissolved into the grey-
green mass of the other soldiers ... Oh, hell, that dark fellow! I would
never have thought he was an informer. As far as I remembered, he
couldn't even speak Russian.'[31]

'There's a whole chain of informers saying what we got up to,' said
Igor Rykov of his service in Afghanistan. 'Right down to a private. He
was the main spy on us sergeants. I could have ordered him to do this or
that. But I knew who he was, so it was better not to.

'He was a Tartar. All Tartars are informers. We could have shot him in
the back except that he was never sent on combat operations. We never
got the chance. Anyway, every unit has a *stukach*. It's better that you know
who they are.'

As the Red army retained and multiplied the Tsarist informers, so it has
returned to *prinuzhdeniya*, coercion and strict discipline. The revolutionary
concept of a people's army, in which the soldier was 'educated' to his
duties, did not last long in practice and in 1940 it went in theory. A new
disciplinary code, the *Distsiplinarnyi Ustav*, was introduced which was
clearly punitive. The number of punishable offences for the rank and file
was increased. Soviet discipline was to be marked by 'severer and harsher
requirements than discipline in other armies based upon class subjugation'.[32]

So it has remained for the modern recruit. Total obedience is expected
and discipline is severe although its enforcement is often sloppy. Drunkenness should, for example, result in an immediate ten days in the guardhouse. This will, however, show up on a unit record and officers are loath

to impose it. There are two types of arrest. In 'simple' arrest, a prisoner is put in a cell, his belt and shoulder straps removed, and works at hard labour whilst eating normal rations. In 'severe' arrest, for fighting, theft, drug abuse, the soldier serves his time in solitary confinement with hot food one day and bread and water the next. Serious cases, such as desertion, are tried by courts martial and prisoners are sentenced to disciplinary battalions.

Initiative is a high-risk virtue in the Soviet Union, the more so in the army. Soviet combat experience since the war is limited.[33] The Afghan guerrillas found the Russian soldier as predictable as the Germans did. An Israeli tank lieutenant, who had previously been conscripted into the Soviet army, found on the Golan Heights in 1972 that: 'There was no mistaking who had trained the Syrian tank crews. They fought just as we had been trained to on manoeuvres in Kiev. They did everything by the book.'*

Size, however, is a comfort to any soldier and Yazov's audit sheet shows that, despite Gorbachev's cuts, they have that in plenty.

38

ARMY AUDIT

For all the insecurity, the continuing sense of inferiority to the Americans, the men on the Frunskaya Embankment can read one famous historical analysis with pride and a smile.

'Russia was ceaselessly beaten for her backwardness,' Stalin said in 1931. 'She was beaten by the Mongol Khans, she was beaten by the Turkish Beys, she was beaten by the Swedish feudal lords, she was beaten by Japanese barons, she was beaten by all.' Russia was not beaten by the Germans. The capitalists do not talk of beating her now. They talk only of *deterrence*, of not being beaten themselves. The Americans do not talk in terms of Soviet *parity* any more. They talk of Soviet *superiority*. The beating is on the other foot.

In public, of course, the Kremlin claims that Soviet superiority is just

---

* That is traditional. During eighteenth-century naval battles against the Swedes, several Guards officers were thrown in to the water. An order rang out to save the officers of the Guards. 'One of these unfortunates stretched his hand from the water and called for help. A soldier, before he would consent to haul him out, asked him "Do you belong to the Guards?" Incapable of making a reply the officer sank beneath the surface and drowned.' C. F. Masson, *Memoires secrets sur la Russie pendant les Regnes de Catherine II et de Paul Ier*, Paris, 1859, qu. Duffy, op. cit., p. 136.

Yankee propaganda. In private, Yazov's simplest audit shows how lavishly he is supplied.

The guts of the *Sukhoputnyye Voyska*, the ground forces, are the 142 divisions of motorized infantry.[1] A front-line, category-one division is a formidable unit with 13,000 men, 266 tanks and 500 armoured personnel carriers and armoured fighting vehicles.[2] It has its own tank regiment of ninety-five machines. Each of its three motor rifle regiments has three motor rifle battalions and a forty-strong tank battalion. The infantry ride in BTRs, amphibious armoured personnel carriers which can make 80 kph on land and 10 kph in water, or in the BMP infantry combat vehicle. This has a crew of three and carries eight troops who have multiple periscopes and can fire from the nuclear and chemical-warfare protected hull on the move. It has a 73-mm anti-tank gun and an anti-tank launcher. Reflecting the importance of rivers to the Russians, it is also amphibious, with a sharp bow.

Each regiment of the *Motostrelkoyve Voyska* has powerful support units. It has an anti-tank company with wire-guided missiles and an anti-aircraft battery, plus towed or self-propelled artillery. The reconnaissance company is equipped with heavy armoured vehicles, light helicopters, radar and radio direction finders. The rivers of Central Europe and the likelihood of Nato nuclear assault are reflected in river-crossing and decontamination units.

At divisional level, a powerful reconnaissance battalion has battlefield radar and maintains a parachute company for deep penetration. A tank battalion of fifty-one machines is held in reserve. Besides the regimental guns, the division holds its own artillery assets. A battalion of missiles and twenty-four towed AA guns provide air cover. The divisional anti-tank battalion holds eighteen 100-mm guns. Three battalions of field artillery provide support for fifty-four 122-mm or 155-mm guns. Four surface-to-surface missile launchers, Frogs with a 60-kilometre range, or Scuds with 240 kilometres or more, give the division nuclear capability.[3]

The emphasis in the Red army is on mobility, firepower, armour, deep manoeuvre, all the elements that combine into shock. Divisional logistics are much slimmer than in the West. The technical support battalion provides a patch-up rather than a repair service. The same holds for the medical battalion's field hospital. It has only sixty beds, small in view of the casualties expected from any clash in Central Europe, and eager to evacuate serious cases swiftly.

These divisions are supported by a powerful army aviation with 4,400 helicopters. A huge increase in helicopters over the last decade has given the infantryman great mobility with only a minimum of training needed to convert him to heliborne assault. The Mil Mi-26 Halo helicopter is the world's largest and will carry 100 combat-loaded troops at over 320 kph

with a 200-kilometre range. Alternatively, it will take two airborne infantry combat vehicles. The earlier Mi-6 Hook carries 68 combat-equipped
troops and tactical missiles. The skill of Mikhail Mil's design bureau in the
Ukrainian city of Zaporozhye in rotors and shafting was matched by the
development of its three-and-a-half-ton gearbox, which weighs more than
its two engines.

The Red army has 470 Hooks, more than the combined British forces
have helicopters. It is stronger still in attack helicopters, disposing 1,200
Mi-24 Hinds and over 1,500 Mi-8 Hips. The workhorse Hip carries 26
combat troops and provides them with fire support from its 8 pods of 57-
mm rockets. The Hind, although it will carry a dozen troops, is an attack
specialist as the Afghan resistance bears witness. It has a multi-barrel 12.7-
mm gun in a nose turret. Its stub wings have rails for four anti-tank missiles
and space for four other stores, bombs, missiles, rockets or gun pods. Its
bulbous insect shape, the engine air intakes squatting above the perspex
and metal nose like inanimate eyes, gives it a top speed of 309 kph.

Six Hinds are included in divisional helicopter squadrons, together with
transports.

The gut strength of such divisions is stark beyond this air power. Just *four*
of these *motor rifle* divisions have *more tanks* than the entire British army.
The proportion of tanks to infantry is the highest ever reached anywhere.
The machines in three specialist tank divisions outnumber the British, one
the Belgians, sixteen the US tank force in Europe. Yazov has forty-seven
of them. In all, the Soviet Union has 53,000 tanks.[4]

Each tank division of the *Tankovye Voyska* has 325 tanks and 350 other
armoured vehicles. Smaller than a motor rifle division, with 10,500 men,
it cannot hold ground easily and is at a disadvantage in difficult country,
in forests or marshes.[5] The tank divisions used in Budapest in 1956 were
vulnerable in street fighting without infantrymen to inhibit the petrol
bombers and rooftop snipers.

It is fast, easy to handle and command, with the impetus to break
through, pursue and envelop the enemy in the open spaces of West
Germany. Category 1 divisions are equipped with T-64, 72 and 80 tanks.
The T-64 and T-72 have strong 'combined' armour where the thickness
of the actual armour is enhanced by the slope of the design. Both have
automatic loaders and laser rangefinders and can equal Nato tanks in
accuracy, range and rate of fire.[6] Both have smooth-bore 125-mm guns
which can fire HEAT and Sabot ammunition.[7]

New T-80s have been introduced from the mid-1980s. It is a sensitive
machine; a US major, Arthur Nicholson, was shot dead by a Soviet guard
when attempting to photograph one in an East German tank park in 1985.

Its 125-mm smooth-bore-gun has a digital fire-control computer. The forty-two-ton machine has a hydro-pneumatic lifting suspension that allows it to increase its clearance of obstacles and to lower its silhouette for firing. Its low profile cramps its three-man crew and means that its gun can be depressed less than on Western tanks.

It has 'reactive' armour, which uses boxes of chemically ignited explosives bolted on to tank hulls and turrets. When hit by a HEAT round, its reactive armour explodes against the incoming round, distorting it and making it less effective. It is thought that up to 90 per cent of Nato infantry anti-tank weapons would be ineffective against it. In addition, 75 per cent of US tanks, and 50 per cent of British, are equipped with 105-mm guns which will not penetrate a T-80 head-on. A new Soviet tank, the FST-1, is turretless and has heavy laminated armour that will protect it from most NATO tanks and ant-tank missiles.

However, the older Soviet tanks are vulnerable. More than 55 per cent were designed before 1965, compared with 20 per cent for Nato.

Artillery battalions have recently been added to tank regiments to make them more rounded, combined arms forces. This reflects a general artillery build-up which gives Yazov up to a third more tube artillery, rocket launchers and heavy mortars than the dead Ustinov. Nuclear-capable heavy artillery brigades are being equipped with mobile 240-mm self-propelled mortars and 203-mm self-propelled guns. A 220-mm multiple-rocket launcher has been deployed with sixteen tubes capable of firing chemicals as well as high explosives.

The Red army has considerable chemical capability, though an offer was made to start phasing it out at the Paris chemical warfare conference in 1989. The 122-mm BM-21 launcher, operating in battalion groups of eighteen, can land 720 rockets on a square kilometre within 15 seconds. It can use non-persistent agents like HCN, which kills anyone within a target area without a respirator within a few minutes of inhaling the vapour. However, this evaporates so quickly that Russian assault troops could move through the rocketed area shortly after. Major targets such as airfields can be attacked by persistent agents, mustard or nerve gas, to cause maximum and prolonged disruption. The *Katyusha* has travelled far. Chemicals can also be delivered by Frog missiles, aircraft spray tanks and conventional artillery.

Traditionally the finest of Russian arms, the artillery shows no slackening of ambition. At army level, artillery regiments are being expanded to brigades. The holdings of artillery pieces, 29,000 of them with 4,580 self-propelled, are backed up by 1,570 nuclear-capable missile launchers. SS-1 Scuds, 635 of them, are designed to strike at enemy marshalling areas, storage dumps and airfields up to 240 kilometres away. The smaller SS-21 Frogs have a range of about 60 kilometres, whilst the SS-12 Scaleboard threatens Western Europe with its 800-kilometre range and one-megaton warhead. All these missiles are designed for 'shoot and scoot' operation, firing from trailers which are then driven off into distant cover.

Anti-tank missiles range from the simple, wire-guided Sagger to the laser-guided Spiral. The Sagger made its operational debut in the Yom Kippur war in 1973. Egyptian troops crossing the Suez canal banks were seen to be carrying canvas-covered 'suitcases' strapped to their shoulders or in their hands. These opened into a launch platform. On firing, a finned rocket flew like a fast model aircraft paying out fine electrical wires that were attached to a joystick controller. The soldier tracked it visually by its bright tail light on to its target with his joystick. One Egyptian Sagger unit knocked out eight Israeli tanks in ten minutes.[8] The more sophisticated Spandrel wire-guided missile is mounted, five in a row, on armoured cars.

The army is equally equipped against aircraft, with some 21,000 anti-aircraft guns and 4,300 mobile missile systems. The Grail is an infantry weapon, widely held at small unit level, normally lethal only against helicopters and small aircraft. Half the Israeli aircraft hit during the Yom Kippur war returned safely. It is being replaced by the hand-held Gremlin.

Gainful is held at divisional level. It tormented Israeli pilots. They could escape the attentions of older missiles with radar guidance and control by releasing chaff, a shower of metal strips that produce multiple radar reflections, or by using their electronic counter-measure pods to transmit signals at radar frequencies that jammed the missile guidance channels. Gainful's targeting radar calculates the launch instructions for the missile. Another ground radar tracks the missile in mid-flight and guides it towards the target. In the terminal phase, the missile guides itself by seeking the infra-red radiation from the enemy's jet exhaust. The missile is considered a work of beauty. Its length is restricted to 19 feet, compared with the 35 feet of the cruder Guideline, by using ram/rocket propulsion. A solid boost motor accelerates the missile to Mach 1.5 and then burns out. The casing of the booster rocket is then used as the combustion chamber for the ram-jet second stage, taking its speed up to Mach 2.8. No electronic response is possible by the intended victim during the heat-seeking homing phase. Decoy flares can be used to confuse the infra-red sensing, although filters can be fitted to distinguish between the flares and the jet exhaust. Pilots used violent evasive manoeuvres, turning the 'cold' side of the aircraft towards the missile and sharpening its turning angle. The 'split-S' defence involved two aircraft. The lead aircraft dived sharply into and across the missile's approach, while the second aircraft passed through the first aircraft's track to increase its turning angle.[9]

At army level, the powerful Ganef with a range of almost eighty kilometres will be replaced by the SS-X-12.

If he can project missiles into the sky, Yazov can also bring seven airborne divisions down from it. The *Vozdushno-Desantnye Voyska* are an elite, used to spearhead the invasions of Czechoslovakia and Afghanistan. Airborne units cream off the pick of the conscripts, many of whom will have gone on DOSAAF youth parachute courses before being called up. The *zampolits* are particularly active among airborne units. Their primary task is to destroy Nato nuclear capacity. They would be dropped at the very start of war to destroy missile launch pads and nuclear stockpiles. Small teams would also be dropped deep for reconnaissance and sabotage missions.

It is unlikely that they would be used in much more than battalion size because of the dangers of counter-strike. A battalion group nevertheless has a heavy punch. Portable anti-tank and anti-aircraft launchers, recoilless anti-tank guns and 82-mm mortars are standard equipment. Infantry combat vehicles, 120-mm mortars and anti-aircraft cannon can be air-dropped to them.

Other paratroops are members of the *Spetsnaz* special forces. These are controlled directly by the GRU, the military intelligence wing of the General Staff. They are trained to operate in small groups deep behind enemy lines, rough equivalents to the US Green Berets and the British SAS. There are many more of them, however, in sixteen brigades and three regiments. Each brigade is expected to field a hundred or so small *Spetsnaz* teams in war. They attract the fittest and strongest conscripts, with an emphasis on sportsmen, skiers, long-distance runners, gymnasts. In Afghanistan they were used for the assassination of enemy leaders, ambushes of supply lines, sudden raids on strongpoints, and deep reconnaissance. Their striped jerseys became a commonplace after the original wave of paratroops and infantry failed to subdue the guerrillas.

In Western Europe their missions would include attacks on missile sites and arms dumps, attempts to confuse and swamp communications with multiple raids deep in unexpected places and the orchestration of civilian panic to cause traffic chaos on roads and at junctions vital to Nato convoys. They would operate in teams of up to twelve men in the enemy rear.

Reverse panic, in the Soviet Union, will not figure large in Yazov's fears. His civil defence programme goes down to rural and factory level. The civil defence troops, who come under his ministry, have a permanent staff of 150,000 including 50,000 military personnel and can mobilize up to 16 million helpers. They have some 75 command posts and 1,5000 hardened deep shelters within 120 kilometres of Moscow, enough to protect at least 175,000 officials. Every city has hardened shelters for the essential workforce and some of the general population. Important defence plants and their workers are protected. Mass evacuation schemes for the cities have been prepared.[10]

Only a proportion of Red army divisions are maintained at full strength. To do so for all of them would implode the economy. Only category 1 divisions are maintained at near peak, with complete equipment, supplies for at least four days sustained combat and 100 per cent manning within 24 hours. Divisions on category 2 of combat readiness have between half and three quarters of their full strength. They have a full scale of fighting vehicles and other weapons, though not necessarily the most up-to-date models. They can be fully manned with reservists in three days and should be fully operational within a month. Category 3 divisions are manned between 20 and 50 per cent, holding up to 75 per cent of their equipment, with the rest mothballed. They should be fully manned with reservists within eight or nine weeks of mobilization.

Manning the category 2 and 3 divisions involves the call-up of 2.1 million men.[11] Since 1.7 million conscripts are discharged into the reserves each year, the understrength divisions can be fleshed out quickly with reservists whose military experience is still fresh. The system of military districts, which divides the Soviet Union into sixteen administrative units, simplifies mobilization and training in this vast land.

Both deployment and category show Yazov's priorities. All Soviet divisions in Eastern Europe, thirty tank and motor rifle and one artillery division, are category 1. The Soviet forces in East Germany have twenty category 1 divisions, divided between tank and motor rifle and forming five Armies.[12] The two tank divisions in Poland, two tank and three motor rifle divisions in Czechoslovakia and the two tank and two motor rifle divisions in Hungary are all category 1, as is the artillery division.

All the airborne divisions, four out of seven of them held in western Russia for immediate use in Europe, are category 1. So are fifteen of the sixty-five divisions in western Russia.[13] The majority of the remaining 148 divisions, 83 of them in the Soviet Far East and the south and centre of the country, are category 3. All the divisions in the centre of the country, in the Urals and Volga districts, are category 3. To the east, in the Central Asia, Siberian, Transbaikal and Far Eastern districts, there are two airborne divisions, with the remaining seven tank and thirty-five motor rifle divisions divided equally between categories.

Yazov had 112,000 troops in Afghanistan at the height of the Soviet involvement, and 17,000 divided between Vietnam and Cuba, where there is a Soviet brigade. A further 13,700 troops and advisers are stationed abroad, notably in Syria, Libya, Angola, Ethiopia, Algeria and North Yemen.

It is in the European strategic theatre that the Russians concentrate their offensive power, both in quality and quantity. The force levels facing China are enough to cope with a Chinese invasion of Soviet Asia but are quite inadequate to mount a successful invasion. Force levels in western Russia and in Eastern Europe are much higher than those needed to beat off a NATO attack. They are strong enough for an invasion of Western Europe.

The planners on the Frunskaya Embankment foresee three major Strategic Theatres in war, the western, southern and Far Eastern. It is the western theatre that concentrates force and chills NATO. It has 94 divisions and disposes of 3,640 aircraft for frontal aviation. It can also call on the sixteen divisions of the Strategic Reserve held centrally around Moscow. The southern theatre, which borders Turkey, Iran and Afghanistan and which includes Syria, Iraq and the Gulf within its sphere, holds 29 divisions with 845 tactical aircraft. The Far East theatre, encompassing China, Japan, Korea and South-East Asia, is made up of 52 divisions which can call on 1,715 aircraft.

The mighty western theatre, responsible for all Europe, is subdivided into three regional theatres. The ground forces of the north-western theatre, headquartered in Leningrad, dispose of 2,000 main battle tanks, 2,100 heavy artillery pieces and 100 SS surface-to-surface missile launchers. It could produce a Front and two all-arms Armies on mobilization. The western theatre, with its ground-force headquarters at Legnica, could field five Fronts and fourteen Soviet Armies as well as Polish, East German and Czech units. Purely Soviet holdings include 19,500 tanks, 14,000 artillery pieces, 595 SS launchers, 2,500 SAM surface-to-air missile launchers and some 1,220 helicopters. The south-western theatre, headquartered at Vinnitsa, holds up to 7,000 Soviet tanks, 4,800 artillery pieces, more than 200 SS launchers, 900 SAMs and 335 helicopters.[14]

Equipment is always upgraded first in the western theatre. It is here that T-80s are replacing T-64s. Frog, Scud and Scaleboard nuclear-capable missiles are being replaced by more accurate and longer-range SS-21, 23 and 12s. Add in the 39 nuclear bombardment submarines of the northern fleet, the ballistic-missile fields, the 1,680 combat aircraft available for tactical support in the western region alone, and the absolute emphasis placed on this theatre is clear.

Two powerful bodies of ground troops, set apart in uniform only by the colour of their shoulder boards and caps, are outside the direct control of the Frunskaya Embankment, The 230,000 border troops come under the KGB and 340,00 internal troops answer to the MVD, the interior ministry. This total of 570,000 men, carefully selected as 'Soviet patriots, the most reliable, the healthiest', are seldom directly included in Soviet war strength.

They are referred to as 'para-militaries', or 'police' or 'internal security forces'.

Nevertheless, the strength of the KGB and MVD armies is not greatly inferior to the combined numbers of the West German and British armies. They are full-time troops drawing on the pool of conscripts, and their equipment runs to tanks, heavy machineguns, artillery and aircraft. They have legal status as part of the armed forces, albeit that they escape the overlordship of the defence ministry. They are used in combat. They bore the brunt of most of the fighting along the Chinese border in the late 1960s. They are distinct from other forces and kept so with their own system of hospitals, rest homes and health resorts in the Crimea and the Caucasus. The KGB and MVD are themselves divided, the better to ensure the party writ, and have their own cross-jealousies and hatreds which saw the KGB boss Andropov sack his MVD counterpart Shchelekov on his rise to power.

Their major peacetime preoccupation is security but they constitute a formidable combat force.

No love is lost between the Red army and these parallel forces. They exist to make sure that the army does not get ideas above its station, guarding arms dumps, checking radio traffic for any evidence of a nascent coup.[15] They are a permanent and armed reminder of the subservience of the military to the Party.

It is KGB special troops in royal blue flashings who guard Lenin's tomb, a KGB general who is the Kremlin commandant, KGB officers and enlisted men who are stationed in the corridors when Gorbachev receives guests. They guard all nuclear plants and Strategic Rocket Forces sites. They are responsible for handling nuclear warheads. The honour of defending the 60,000 kilometres of the Soviet frontiers falls to KGB border troops in green shoulder boards and green caps. It is KGB signal troops, not the army, who are trusted with government communications and the security of nuclear warheads. MVD men, in rust-red shoulder boards and blue-top caps, guard other sensitive installations.

It is they who arrest military men on serious charges, and who are responsible for sealing off the rear areas of combat zones. The KGB has a counter-intelligence cell in every military formation, now called the *Osobyi Otdel* or Special Section, *Smersh* during the war, to monitor loyalty.

The MVD finds its normal forces, the Militia civil police and the GAI State transport police, inadequate for internal security. Its separate MVD troops are responsible for maintaining local order and for guarding bridges, rail junctions, power stations, defence plants and other potential targets for saboteurs. They are at hand to deal with large-scale rioting, such as the nationalist outbursts in Kaunas, Dnepropetrovsk and Dneprodzerzhinsk. Special Designation Troops, OSNAZ, are maintained in units up to divisional size to intervene in internal trouble spots if a situation cannot be controlled by local forces. OSNAZ weapons include tanks, artillery and anti-aircraft guns. MVD manning and equipment, and the military rather than riot-control training given to officers at MVD officer schools in Novosibirsk, Ordzhonikidze and Saratov, makes sense only in terms of mutinous army units.

The combat potential of these two large groups of trained men has already been seen. Though not used so prodigally as their German counter-parts, the Waffen SS, they fought as shock units at Moscow, Kiev, Odessa, Pskov and on the Karelian Isthmus. They made up three armies: The 29th, 30th and 31st,[16] and three divisions of border troops attached to the 70th Army fought from Kursk to the Elbe. They were, and remain, expert snipers and more than 20,000 were assigned as snipers along the fronts. Each Army had an NKVD regiment in its rear, both to stiffen it, to seal the battle area and to act as a blocking screen of executioners during the early panic and retreats of the invasion. It was their convoy troops, sometimes wearing the white coats of medical orderlies to dissipate the grimness of their mission, who forcibly transported the undesirables of the Soviet Union and eastern Europe. At the end of the war, they were used in the assault against the Japanese along the Soviet border.

Such duties, along with anti-paratroop defence, the herding of POWs and other rear security roles, await them in a future war.

39

RED NAVY: BLUE-WATER BUILD UP

It is not new for the Russians to have a major fleet. The traditions of the service go back more than 250 years to Peter the Great.* Founding St Petersburg in 1703, he built a dockyard and began laying down seagoing ships. He fortified Kotlin island, creating the naval base at Kronstadt. The Russian fleet was the strongest in the Baltic by the time of Peter's death in 1725. Three years later, Vitus Bering discovered the Bering Strait, so that Russian seamen were active on both edges of their landmass.

* Rivers, of course, have always been important in Russian expansion. The move towards Siberia and the Pacific started with fur trappers and traders crossing the Urals by the Pechora, Ural and Ob portages in the thirteenth century. Trappers discovered the Lena in 1630 and two years later founded Yakutsk, later the Russian centre in eastern Siberia. In the 1640s a small expedition reached the mouth of the Amur river. Another sailed down the now Gulag-cursed Kolyma river, rounded the tip of western Siberia opposite the Seward Peninsula of Alaska and reached the Anadyr river, thus proving the separation of Asia and America.

Geography was and remains a severe handicap for naval forces in a country whose borders are washed by the Arctic and Pacific Oceans and by eleven seas, most of them icebound. It took seven months for the Baltic fleet to arrive in the eastern Mediterranean to fight the Turks under Catherine the Great, although its annihilation of the Turkish fleet at Chesma in 1770 is the greatest of Russian or Soviet naval successes.

Its nineteenth-century development was fitful. The first Russian ship did not cross the equator until 1803. Though the Tsarist empire soon slopped over the Bering Strait to Alaska and down to Fort Ross, north of San Francisco Bay in California, there was little attempt to consolidate the American holdings with sea power. The Fort Ross settlement was sold in 1841 and Alaska followed in 1867. Relations with the US were particularly close. Ships of the Baltic fleet docked in New York in 1863, and Lincoln went aboard the frigate *Osliabia*. The same year, the new Pacific Squadron visited San Francisco. There was considerable interest in US naval design and the build-up of the Imperial navy roughly parallels that of the 'new navy' in the US. By the end of the century, now possessing a warm-water base at Port Arthur, close to Japan, the Imperial navy was comfortably the third largest in the world.

Its history this century has been humiliating. It took the Russian navy until Stalin's last days to recover from Tsushima. During the war, the Red navy failed to sink a single major Axis warship, whilst losing a battleship, two cruisers and as many as fifty destroyers. The Russians began the war with the largest submarine fleet in the world, numbering about 250, but its ratio of submarine losses to gains was the worst in submarine history.

Stalin revived pre-war plans for a large fleet after 1945. He had been deeply impressed by the British and American ability to shift troops across the Pacific and Atlantic in large numbers and to mount and support huge seaborne invasions. The navy was glamorized in films and the *Aurora* became a national monument. Fourteen Sverdlov-class cruisers with 6-inch guns were built. A crop of 220 Whiskey-class submarines appeared in the mid-1950s, slow and short-range 1,000-tonners, based partly on the German Type XXI U-boat.[1] The Z-class ocean-going submarine was developed. When converted to carry missiles, these diesel electrics could carry three missiles with an 800-kilometre range. Roughly three quarters of the US population and industry lie within 800 kilometres of the sea. The Z boats were intended for a 'city-busting' attack on the US, with the whole north-east target system from Boston through Washington within easy range.*

---

* Major coastal or near coastal cities include Boston, New York, Philadelphia, Baltimore, Washington, Miami, New Orleans, Houston, San Diego, Los Angeles and San Francisco. The Z boats could also strike as far inland as Pittsburgh, Cleveland,

Khrushchev cut back savagely on the surface fleet. He reckoned that cruisers were good only 'to show off to foreigners' and for state visits,[2] and four being built on slipways in Leningrad were scrapped. He gave up Soviet rights to bases at Porkkala in Finland and to Port Arthur, now Lü-Shun, in Manchuria. In 1957 he cut the navy to under half a million men and 375 surface ships were mothballed. Admiral Kuznetsov, the naval C-in-C, had objected to the cuts and was fired in 1956. In mid-1960 a special session of the Supreme Soviet sanctioned further naval cuts.[3]

The expansion of the submarine fleet, however, continued under Khrushchev. Hotel-class missile submarines were built from 1958, cruising off the coasts of North America with three missiles mounted vertically in the fin. Khrushchev's appointment of Admiral Sergei Gorshkov as Kuznetsov's successor was crucial. Gorshkov had a very clear idea of sea power and the patience at the age of forty-five to achieve it. He presided over the Soviet navy for almost thirty years, transforming it from a small and largely Baltic-bound affair into a blue-water force with global reach.

Gorshkov joined the navy at seventeen and was a purge-speeded admiral at thirty-one. As commander of the wartime Danube Flotilla, which played an important part in the capture of Vienna and which ended the war at Linz, he had impressed both Khrushchev and Brezhnev. Gorshkov benefited greatly from the Cuban fiasco of 1962, which showed that US command of the sea was near absolute. The Red surface fleet would not have survived an all-out engagement, and the six Soviet submarines sent to Cuban waters were easily tracked.[4]

The post-Cuba desire for a strong navy coincided with the strain of the Vietnam war on the US and a new philosophy under the defense secretary Robert McNamara. The cost of the US effort in Vietnam escalated enormously after the first combat troops landed there in 1965. At the same time McNamara emphasized quality in weapons above quantity. The huge US lead in naval power was whittled down as much by American decision as by Soviet expansion.

By 1966 Gorshkov was claiming the end of 'the complete domination of the sea by the traditional naval powers'. The following year he warned the Americans: 'Sooner or later, they will have to understand that they have no mastery whatsoever of the seas.' The sinking of the Israeli destroyer *Elath* by a Soviet Styx missile fired by the Egyptians during the June War of 1967 showed that Soviet naval weapons were increasingly sophisticated.

The Russians learnt as much as they could from their British and American rivals. Their warships and electronic intelligence trawlers, masts

---

Buffalo, San Antonio and Dallas. Though the Soviet landmass is not so vulnerable, the American Polaris could hit it launching from off Iceland, the Irish Sea, the Bay of Biscay, North African waters, the Arabian Sea and the north Pacific. Mitchell, op. cit.

bristling with eavesdropping equipment, dogged Western warships and maintained a permanent watch off Cape Kennedy, the nuclear submarine base at Holy Loch in Scotland, Rota in Spain, Puget Sound, Norfolk and Pearl Harbor.[5] A large oceanography programme, much of it designed to help submarines retain their invisibility by using water layers and the topography of the ocean floor, was supported by a fleet of 200 ships that included the 45,000-ton *Yuri Gagarin*.

Russian skippers were encouraged to play chicken with Western captains, steaming directly into NATO formations and cutting across the bows of US and Royal Navy warships.[6] Soviet aircraft approached Western carrier fleets, hoping to draw a Combat Air Patrol in response and thus study techniques and capability. The Americans also buzzed Soviet ships and maintained complex plots of their positions. In theory, an agreement signed by Gorshkov and John Warner, the US navy secretary,[7] in 1972, banned steaming into rival formations, provocations such as shining searchlights on the bridge of another warship or simulating attacks by arming guns and torpedo tubes. In practice they remain.

Submarines play the roughest games. Russian attack submarines try to follow US nuclear bombardment submarines, or 'boomers', as they slip out on their sixty-day patrols from Rota, Guam or Holy Loch. When an American boomer is picked up by a Russian, an American attack sub will cut in behind it to create sonar interference and to provide a decoy. By moving in and out of the wake of the electronic sub, the attack submarine confuses the Russians by distorting the electronic signature left by the boomer. Boomers will sometimes swing a tight circle to verify if they are being followed. The pursuing attack sub immediately kills its reactor power to reduce its sound profile, trusting that its momentum will not hurl it into its circling quarry. It is dangerous sport. One American attack sub needed two months' repair work at Rota after a violent submerged collision.

The introduction of the Yankee-class nuclear bombardment submarine in 1968 was a great advance for Gorshkov over the Hotel and Zulu boats with their inventories of three short-range missiles. Each Yankee carried 16 missiles with a range of 2,800 kilometres. The pressurized-water reactor gave a high submerged speed of 30 knots, although the Yankee is very noisy. When first deployed, the Yankees had to keep in close to the US coast to get missile coverage and there was a band between the Rockies and the Mississippi that could not be reached. This was rectified when the Yankees were modified to carry the SS-N-8 missile with a range of 5,600 kilometres.

Yankees were produced in volume, largely at the Severodvinsk yard near Archangel in the Arctic. The yard was doubled in size in the late 1960s to give a capacity of eight to nine subs a year. In 1972 the Russians laid down their forty-second Yankee, thus outnumbering the US Polaris boomers. The US reacted by MIRVing, fitting multiple warheads to Minutemen and Polaris warheads. The first converted Polaris boat, the *James Madison*, put to sea in April 1972. The new Poseidon missile carried ten warheads.

Charlie-class nuclear-powered boats, which could fire anti-ship missiles whilst submerged, came into service from 1968. The Charlie, with a fat spindle-shaped hull, is a threat to US carriers and other high-value surface assets. Victor-class attack boats were introduced at the same time, with a fat but streamlined hull capable of 33 knots submerged, equipped with powerful torpedoes for surface ships and SS-N-15 missiles for sub killing.

A large force of attack submarines accompanies the bombardment boats. The Alphas are the fastest in the world, capable of 40 knots, though, like the Charlie cruise-missile boats, they are noisy. The new Oscar cruise missile boats are thought able to launch up to 24 anti-ship cruise missiles with a 450-kilometre range whilst submerged. Two new attack classes were introduced in the mid-1980s, the big, 110-metre-long Mikes and Sierras, deep diving with their titanium pressure hulls. In all, the Russians have eight classes of attack boat to the American one, the Los Angeles 688 class.

Gorshkov was, however, by training and affection a surface-fleet man and it shows in the surface build-up. The Kashin-class destroyer, carrying surface-to-air missiles, was the world's first all-gas turbine major warship when it appeared in 1962. New Kresta-class cruisers were produced from 1967, Karas from 1973 and in 1977, the *Kirov*, a nuclear-powered 32,000-ton battle cruiser, appeared. The *Kirov* is the largest warship apart from carriers built since the war. It is armed with twenty anti-ship cruise missiles, twin anti-aircraft and anti-submarine missile launchers and twelve vertically launched anti-aircraft missile systems based on the SA-10 used in strategic air defence.

The first helicopter carrier, the 17,000-ton *Moskva*, appeared in 1967. Her forward part crowded with anti-submarine rocket launchers and missiles, her stern an operating platform for over a dozen helicopters, she is an anti-submarine specialist. With her sister ship, the *Leningrad*, she operates in the Atlantic, Mediterranean and the Red and Barents seas.

Five years later Gorshkov confirmed his entry into the major league with the first of the 38,000-ton Kiev-class aircraft carriers. The *Kiev* completed fitting out in the Black Sea at Nikolayev in the autumn of 1972 and a sister ship was at once laid down. She was a strange hybrid, the bow part a missile cruiser stacked with surface-to-surface and surface-to-air missiles and anti-submarine weapons, her stern a 200-metre flight deck for

Yak-36 jump jets. Gorshkov justified the new carriers by saying that a naval air capability was needed with the extension of Soviet interests into underdeveloped areas. At the same time, the head of naval flying was made a Marshal of Aviation. The naval air force is larger than the British RAF. It has some 1,400 aircraft, including swing-wing Backfire bombers armed with anti-ship missiles capable of flying 280 kilometres at Mach 3, the Su-17 Fitter anti-ship strike aircraft, Tu Bear and Badger bombers and reconnaisance aircraft and shipboard helicopters for missile targeting and anti-submarine work.

The first big conventional carrier with a full-length flight-deck, a nuclear-powered 75,000-tonner, is under construction at Nikolayev on the Black Sea and is expected to go into service in the early 1990s. The new Udaloy and Sovremenny-class guided-missile destroyers, 8,000-tonners as big as previous cruisers, can be used in carrier task forces.

Amphibious assault ships, like the 13,000-ton *Ivan Rogov,* give the Russians a considerable capability of projecting their power into the Third World. The Ivan Rogovs have two helicopter decks and a rear hangar, and can carry three air cushion landing craft in a docking bay. They take 550-man units of naval infantry, with 40 battle tanks and armoured personnel carriers. An 8,000-man division of naval infantry is based near Vladivostok for deployment in the Pacific area. Gorshkov's passion for innovation shows in the hovercraft carried by the Ivan Rogovs. The Russians have developed 220-ton machines, originally a British idea, for use in rapid, 70-knot coastal assaults.

The Red navy has more intelligence-gathering ships than the rest of the world put together, with a known total of more than seventy. Some are based on ocean-going trawler hulls. Others are custom built, like the Primorye-class, 5,000-tonners with secure links to Soviet military satellites and to Moscow.

There is little conservative about the fleet that Gorshkov has built, apart from the aim of creating a 'balanced navy'. That ambition is classic and highly expensive.

It has drawn the Russians into naval diplomacy. The Cienfuegos base on Cuba abuts the Gulf of Mexico and Panama. The ending of British sea power in the Red Sea and the Indian Ocean immediately attracted Soviet interest in the Suez and Red Sea bottlenecks. The attempt to gain a hold over Egypt, and hence Suez, collapsed with the expulsion of Soviet personnel by Sadat in 1972. The Russians have had greater success in the Red Sea, with a base at Aden and a major ally in Ethiopia. The Dahlak Archipelago in the southern Red Sea is used as a base.

The wooing of Indonesia failed to insert Russian naval power in the

Malacca Straits but they inherited the Cam Ranh Bay base in Vietnam from the Americans after the fall of Saigon in 1975. The Pacific fleet, based at Vladivostock, is the fastest growing. It has two out of four aircraft carriers. Its 31 nuclear-missile submarines include 15 Deltas, 140 metres long, each with up to 16 missiles in vertical expulsion tubes 15 metres high, capable of being fired at US targets without leaving friendly air cover in the Sea of Okhotsk. Its 544 combat ships in the Pacific well outnumber, though they do not outclass, the 180 of the US navy. Cam Ranh has been expanded to include missile storage depots, and up to thirty warships, including attack submarines, range from it out through the South China Sea. Tu-95 Bears, long-range reconnaissance aircraft, monitor the shipping lanes through the Malacca Straits from their base at Cam Ranh and are only two hours' flying time from the troubled Philippines.

On the face of it there is little reason for the Russians to maintain so vast a navy. The size of the Soviet Union and its self-sufficiency in oil and raw materials make it all but immune to blockade. Much of its coastline is protected by ice. Its history has been more affected by rivers than by seaborne invasion. Its geography obliges it to maintain four fleets, the Northern, Baltic, Black Sea and Pacific, with choke points making transfers between fleets dangerous in wartime. Its weakness in long-range aviation leaves the surface fleet vulnerable when it steams beyond the cover of shore-based aircraft. The lack of big carriers severely affects its survivability in mid ocean. The Russians would have to build fourteen large carriers to match the Americans, at huge cost.

The fleet build-up has failed lamentably to have any effect on the Americans in the one area where the Russians have tried hardest to be rid of them, the Mediterranean. 'There is no justification whatever for the constant pressure of the US fleet in waters washing the shores of southern Europe,' Brezhnev said shortly before the June War in 1967. 'The time has come to demand the complete withdrawal of the US 6th Fleet from the Mediterranean.' The Israelis duly defeated the Arabs, regardless of attempted Soviet naval pressure. Twenty years later, the 6th Fleet continued to dominate the Mediterranean with two large carriers with 100 aircraft apiece.

Soviet submarines have a dangerous transit to make from their complex of granite-protected bases round Murmansk to their bombardment stations off Miami and the US east coast. They have to enter two choke points to break into the North Atlantic. Attack submarines await them at the western extremity of the Barents Sea between Norway and the arctic ice. There are further patrols and aerial reconnaissance between Scotland and Iceland and in the Denmark Strait between Iceland and Greenland. LAMPS helicopters, DIFAR sonobuoys and the SOUSOS system attempt to pick them up further in. Yet the Northern fleet, headquartered at Severomorsk near Murmansk, is the most important because it is only through the Barents Sea that the Red navy can slip into a major ocean without a high risk of detection. The Baltic fleet must creep through the Danish Sounds, the Kattegat and the Skagerrak, to get to the North Sea before reaching the Atlantic through the equally dangerous English Channel or Norwegian Sea. The Black Sea fleet has to run the Bosporus to enter the Mediterranean before exiting to the Atlantic through the Gibraltar Straits. The Pacific fleet is hemmed in by Japan.

The Cuban base at Cienfuegos offsets the long passage and is close to major targets, the Panama Canal, the Norfolk, Virginia carrier base and the Charleston submarine base. It is highly vulnerable to a US strike, however. In the Pacific, both Cam Ranh Bay and the attack submarine base at Petropavlovsk could be mined. Warships from Vladivostock must run through the Sakhalinsky Zaliv, La Perouse or Korea Straits to reach the North Pacific and the base itself is vulnerable to American air strikes from Japan and South Korea.

Missile bombardment apart, the main task for the navy in war would be to disrupt Western sea communications. 'We must consider that up to three quarters of all the material and personnel of the probable enemy are located across the ocean,' a Soviet strategist writes of the Americans.[8] 'In the event of war, 80 to 100 large transports should arrive daily in European ports, and 1,500 to 2,000 ships, not counting security vessels, will be en route simultaneously.' That is in the North Atlantic. In the Pacific, the navy would try to cut the sea lanes between the US west coast and Japan, South Korea and Taiwan. Although the Soviets now have a large merchant fleet, with a considerable sealift capability, its protection would be secondary to denying sea lanes to the West.

The submarine and anti-submarine elements are justified easily enough as crucial elements in nuclear strategy. The rest is attractive emotionally, a challenge to the US, a means to project Soviet strength along the oceanic shores, and consolidate superpower status. It makes less sense economically and operationally. Apart from the inbuilt geographic flaws, it is a fragile animal that seems to have outgrown its strength. It is so plagued with breakdowns that it has been estimated that only 30 per cent of it is operational, with another 30 per cent undergoing repairs and the rest obsolete. The carrier *Minsk* is thought to have spent more of its life in dry dock than at sea.[9] Soviet ships spend on average 85 per cent of their time in port, compared with 66 per cent for the US navy. Radiation leaks are a danger on submarines, which have also suffered from propulsion breakdowns and sinkings.[10] The Forger vertical-take-off aircraft carried aboard the Kiev-class carriers are grossly inferior to their Western equivalent, the Harriers.

Under Gorbachev, Gorshkov lost the argument over the unsatisfactory cost effectiveness of the surface fleet. In December 1985 he was replaced virtually without comment. His successor is a submariner, Vladimir Chernavin. Gorbachev, who is more interested in performance than prestige, is concentrating on submarines.

The fact that the surface fleet played only a minimal role in the Persian Gulf during the Iran–Iraq war, despite the US presence, shows that Gorbachev is reluctant to see it as much more than a cripplingly expensive exercise in flag-waving.

The submarines that Chernavin has inherited are a different matter. The Russians now have a much larger strategic attack submarine force than the US. It numbers 62 submarines with 944 nuclear missiles compared with 36 American boats with 640 missiles.[11] A new submarine-launched ballistic missile, the SS-N-23, was introduced in 1985. Liquid-fuelled with an 8,300-kilometre range that opens up all the North American landmass, it can deliver 10 MIRV warheads with a 200-kiloton yield to within 800 metres of targets. Two-thirds of the missile boats are fitted with long-range rockets so that they can patrol in safe waters close to Soviet shores. They could, indeed, fire missiles from their own bases.

The big Deltas and older Yankees make up the bulk of the boomers, or ballistic missile subs. They are stationed off the Pacific and Atlantic coasts of the US, in two large belts in the Barents and Greenland Seas, in the Sea of Japan, in the Okhotsk Sea between Sakhalin and Kamchatka, and in the Pacific east of Kamchatka.

The Typhoon, the world's largest submarine, is more than 150 metres long and over 23 metres in the beam. Its 25,000-ton displacement is a third greater than the US Trident. Typhoons, which started coming into service in 1984, can operate from beneath the ice of the Arctic. Each boat carries 20 SS-N-20 solid-fuel rockets with an 8,300-kilometre range, enabling it to fix on targets throughout the US, Canada and Asia from the safety of the Barents and White Sea bases. The missiles are 14 metres high and carry up to 9 warheads apiece, compared with the 9-metre height of the 8-warhead Trident missile. It is thought that the Russians will have eight or more Typhoons, each with the capability seriously to damage a continent, in service by the early 1990s.

AIR: FLOGGERS, FLANKERS AND THE WILD RED YONDER

Until the beginning of the 1970s the Russians saw air power mainly in terms of army support. This stemmed from the war, when ground-attack aircraft like the Il-2 *Stormovik* so harassed the Wehrmacht. Soviet factories were turning out over 40,000 aircraft a year by 1945, but they had no jets, no radar early warning and no four-engined bombers. The air force was subservient to the army.

The sale of Rolls-Royce Nene and Derwent engines to the Russians by the British government in 1947 helped them to move into the jet age. The Soviet version of the Nene, the RD-45, was installed in the MiG-15s flown in the Korean war.[1] American nuclear bombers obliged Stalin to emphasize interceptors and a separate air defence force was set up in 1948. American Boeing B-29 bombers that had force-landed in the Soviet Far East towards the end of the war were copied by Andrei Tupolev and manufactured in quantity as the Tu-4.

The Russians nevertheless remained short of heavy transport aircraft and bombers. Though they could outnumber NATO in numbers of fighters and tactical aircraft, these machines were sharply inferior in quality. They handled badly and had poor range. NATO was satisfied that it could maintain air superiority whilst checking any advance of superior Soviet ground forces by striking hard and accurately at Russian columns whilst they were concentrated and at their most vulnerable. NATO tactical aircraft and weapons systems fed off Western superiority in high technology, in engines, electronics and airframe design.

Russian second-generation jets originating from the late 1950s and early 1960s suffered from poor range, bad cockpit visibility, inferior load-carrying capacity and crude avionics. Though the MiG-21 had become the most widely used combat aircraft in the world by the 1970s, this was due more to its low cost than its military effectiveness. Israeli pilots achieved kill ratios of 20 to 1 against Egyptian and Syrian pilots. No American pilot reported seeing a MiG-21 more than 160 kilometres from its base during the Vietnam war. Thirty pre-production aircraft had to be built before service delivery started and, though reckoned a sweet-handling aircraft apart from its high landing speed, it suffered from serious limitations in range, endurance and armament.

The Su-7 was built in large numbers although it was inadequate in its original role as an air superiority fighter. It had poor weapons load and range and needed a long runway, a severe disadvantage in its new life in ground attack. These aircraft were fast, indeed the Su-7's 1,055 mph maximum was ridiculously fast for a ground-attack specialist, but they could not fly far, carry much or drop it accurately. The Americans were little troubled by MiG-21s in the Vietnam war and the same aircraft plus the Su-7 caused equally little inconvenience to Israeli pilots during the Yom Kippur War of 1973.

The appearance of the first prototype MiG-25 Foxbats at the end of the 1960s showed that Russian third-generation jets would have to be treated with new respect. The prototypes knocked off a string of world records including closed-circuit speed, payload-to-height and rate of climb records. It outclassed all other combat aircraft. By 1971 Foxbats were overflying Israel with the same impunity once enjoyed by U-2s. The US air force was obliged to seek a new fighter, eventually the F-15 Eagle, to counter it. Western radar has tracked Foxbats on reconnaissance missions at Mach 2.8 and its estimated maximum speed is Mach 3.2.

It has its problems, however. The defector Viktor Belenko who flew an interceptor model to Japan confirmed that pilots are not able to use its full performance, to avoid heat fatigue to the airframe. He was also almost out of fuel after a 400-mile flight. The life of Soviet engines is limited by the use of inferior metals and machining. Airframes are heavier for the same reason and this restricts the weight of fuel that can be uplifted.

At the same time, the swing-wing MiG-23 Flogger was introduced. Its radar, doppler navigator and electronics were a considerable improvement on earlier Soviet equipment. It has problems, too, of basic design. The Syrians contrived to crash thirteen of the first fifty ground-attack models supplied to them. Libyan MiG-23s, 'surprisingly fast and surprisingly blind', fell easy prey to US fighters in 1989. At least in performance, Russian aircraft were becoming roughly comparable with Western types. The twin-seat Su-24 Fencer fighter-bomber, a more recent swing-wing design, is capable of all-weather, low-altitude penetration, able to carry out the type of deep strike that had previously been a Nato preserve. Comparisons with the American F-14 Tomcat have been made although, of course, it is in the interests of both the Pentagon and US manufacturers to gild the Russian lily.

Swing wings dominated new Soviet aircraft in the 1970s. The Americans had gone for the idea with the F-111 in the 1960s with remarkable lack of success. The intention is to get the best of both worlds. Extended, the wing gives low landing speeds and economical high-altitude cruising. Swept back, the wing creates less drag and enables the aircraft to fly much faster. In practice, the mechanism to swing the wings on the F-111 proved so heavy that it is short on range, bomb load and manoeuvrability.

The Russians did not appreciate this in time and persisted with swing-wing designs at great expense. 'The best thing that ever came out of the

F-111 programme,' a US air force official has said, 'is that the damnfool Russians went out and copied it.'[2] Like the Americans before them, they have now reverted to fixed-wing fighters.

The Su-27 Flanker and MiG-29 Fulcrum are new fighters that started to be widely deployed in the late 1980s. They are twin-engine jets, considerably advanced in the old weak areas of range, thrust-to-weight ratios and manoeuvrability. Supersonic, all-weather fighters, they have look down/shoot down weapon systems and beyond-visual-range air-to-air missiles. How effective this is remains an open question. Classic radar, though it will pick up a target flying above it against the pure background of sky, suffers from background clutter when it is beamed down and responds to the ground surface as well as the target. With modern doppler processing, radar should be able to isolate a target through the changes in its frequencies as it moves. It can be done. A specialist American AWACS plane tracked both the Iraqi fighter below it and the Exocet missiles it fired at the USS destroyer *Stark* in the Persian Gulf in 1987.[3] The miniaturized systems carried on fighters are much more difficult to perfect and the Soviet avionics industry has traditionally lagged well behind the American.

The new aircraft are designed to give the edge in air superiority the Russians have thus far lacked. The big Komsomolsk-built Flanker is about the same size as NATO's F-15 Eagle. It is thought that the Fulcrum, a single-seat fighter similar to the US F-16 Falcon, will have a secondary ground-attack role. Improved versions of the high performance Fitters and Floggers have been joined by the slower Su-25 Frogfoot in ground attack. Frogfoot, used in Afghanistan and built in Stalin's old stamping ground of Tblisi in Georgia, is a specialist in close air support for ground forces and may prove more effective than its sophisticated, swing-wing partners. Engines, however, continue to burn out quickly, the electronics are crude.

To match the ambition of air superiority, the Russians are emphasizing new tactics. These include the subtleties of manoeuvring air combat, independent search missions for targets and multi-role sorties involving, for example, fighter-bomber escort and ground support. Greater demands are now being made on pilot initiative and the individual sortie. However, NATO pilots are reckoned to be better trained than the Russians, with US air crews getting in twice as much flying time.

The Far Eastern theatre has about 1,800 aircraft, more than 90 per cent of them third generation, in position for operations against China and Japan. But the Western theatre has the lion's share, with the core at its centre where the western region alone has 2,850 aircraft. It is along the West German border that both the targets and NATO aircraft are thickest. Added to its cornucopia of helicopters, the Red army now has richness of quality as well as quantity in its air support. Its own tank hordes will be less vulnerable to strike aircraft and attack helicopters if the Flankers and Fulcrums can undermine NATO's air superiority over the battlefields. And NATO armour will be at risk if Hinds and Frogfoots can roam beneath the fighter protection.

The air force has never shared the US bomber-fleet outlook. Elderly Bears and a few Bisons remain the backbone of its strategic bombing capability. No Bears, with their huge swept swings, monster Kuznetsov turboprop engines and eight-bladed, 6-metre contraprops, have been made since 1962. One hundred and forty of them survive as bombers, together with twenty ageing, four-turbojet Bisons. Though they have plenty of range, and are found on probing missions over the Arctic, Atlantic and Pacific, they are 1950s aircraft as obsolescent as their medium-range contemporary, the Tu-16 Badger. A new variant of the Bear has been produced to carry long-range cruise missiles. The venerable aircraft is also capable of dropping free-fall nuclear bombs on most US targets on a two-way mission, although the odds of it getting into, let alone out of American airspace are not high.

Manned bombers are not on the edge of extinction. The Backfire, a twin jet with variable geometry on its outer wings, was introduced in the mid-1970s. It will cruise reasonably economically at high altitude with its wings spread. It can fly supersonically at low level with its wings swept, which improves its survival prospects. Refuelled, it could fly high-altitude missions against the US. Brezhnev claimed that it did not have intercontinental range and that inflight refuelling would not be used, despite the fact that refuelling probes had already been fitted.[4] Most Backfires are based in western Russian and the Far East, for use in low-level attacks in Europe and Asia. It has not been a happy design. Its bomb load is poor, only a sixth of the US B-1, its low-level range is only 900 miles and its landing gear was originally carried in protruding boxes.

A large new swing-wing bomber, Blackjack, is expected to upgrade bombing potential in the 1990s. It is bigger and faster than the American B-1, although its combat radius is expected to be less and it is unlikely to match the B-1 in low-level attack. A new air-launched cruise missile, with a range of 1,800 miles, will improve Blackjack's capabilities and give the old Bears some protection in standoff attacks.

The across-the-board expansion in the 450,000-man air force is shown in this determination to keep up even in manned bombers, minor league stuff for the missile-minded Russians. The expensive desire for balanced, all-round forces is as strong in the air as in Admiral Gorshkov's navy, and has yet to attract Gorbachev's unwelcome attention. Though Gorshkov's seaborne power projection has been more noticed in the West, the build-up in military air transport has been impressive.

VTA, *Voyenno-Transportnaya Aviatsiya*, has grown apace since the old An-12 Cub turboprop first gave the Russians the ability to project 20 tons of cargo or 65 paratroops 2,200 miles from their bases. That was in 1959, and it marked the first expansion beyond that of a continental power. The An-22 Cock upped the payload to 80 tons, then the biggest in the world, and the range to 4,800 kilometres in the 1960s. The Cock, however, showed itself unable to deliver tanks because of aerodynamic problems and thus signed its death warrant. Production stopped in 1974. By then the Il-76 Candid with its four turbofans was filling the gap. The Americans claim that the successful Candid, used in the Ethiopian and Afghan airlifts, was copied from a US Starlifter heavy jet exhibited at the Paris Air Show. The Russians photographed the Starlifter, measured it and took metal samples. By 1987 the Americans were refusing Russians access to their Paris exhibits. The new giant Condor transport has improved VTA's heavy lift capability. It has a maximum payload of 125 tons.

The VTA can call on more than a thousand medium- and long-haul aircraft of Aeroflot. The state airline is the world's biggest. It is directed by an air force marshal and the civil aviation minister is an active-duty general. Most Aeroflot pilots are reserve officers.

The Russians are also making great efforts to reduce their old vulnerability to low-flying aircraft and cruise missiles. The Air Defence Troops, *Protivovozdushnaya oborona* or PVO, who number 371,000 and who outrank the air force in seniority, are divided into three. The *Aviatsiya PVO* is responsible for aviation, maintaining and flying 1,200 interceptors in the interior military districts and defending its airfields with SAMs.[5] The Zenith Rocket troops man some 9,300 launchers at 1,200 SAM sites. Radiotechnical troops maintain a radar density unequalled anywhere except perhaps tiny Israel.

Soviet air defence is capable at medium and high altitudes but its performance tails off closer to the ground. Hence NATO's developed skills in low flying and the hi-lo-hi profile of attack where an aircraft flies high on the approach to enemy territory, to gain speed and save fuel, puts in its attack at treetop level and returns to high altitude once clear of defences.

Improvement is a hugely expensive task, involving the upgrading of early warning and data transmission systems, AWACS, new SAMs and air-to-air missiles and new fighters. The new MiG-31 Foxhound, capable of 1,375 knots and carrying eight air-to-air missiles for a radius of 1,450 kilometres, is the first true look down/shoot down air defence interceptor the Russians have had. It is equipped with a new air-to-air missile, the AA-9, for use against low-flying aircraft. Foxhounds, Fulcrums and Flankers will operate with the new Il-76 Mainstay AWACS,[6] which can detect aircraft and cruise missiles flying at low altitude.

The air defence effort is tremendous. The Gorki-built Foxhounds, for example, are simply the latest addition to a force of 1,200 interceptors and almost 10,000 SAM launchers at 900 sites devoted purely to strategic territorial air defence. An additional 2,000 tactical interceptors and 1,800 SAMs are also deployed from Soviet territory and could be called upon. The Vietnam war showed that the early SAMs, though a SAM-2 scored a world first on Powers' U2, were already virtually useless. Towards the end, only one SAM in two hundred was scoring a hit on US fighter-bombers, which could outmanoeuvre the missiles, although they did marginally better against the big and cumbersome B-52 bombers. Hanging on to outdated equipment is a very Russian trait. It is also expensive.

The Russians have the world's most extensive early warning system for both ballistic missile and air defence. Early warning against missile attack includes a launch detection satellite network, over-the-horizon radars and phased array radars on the borders. They enjoy about thirty minutes' warning of US ICBM and SLBM launches from nine satellites. Two over-the-horizon radars, near Minsk and at Nikolayev in the Caucasus, are targeted on the US and the Polar regions. Another on the Amur is targeted on China. These also give a thirty-minute warning of ICBM launch, which can then be confirmed by tracking radars that will show the size of an attack. Phased-array radars for missile warning and tracking form an arc of cover from the submarine-rich Kola peninsula in the north-west, around Siberia to the Caucasus. The final gap to the west is closed by Hen-House tracking radars with a 5,800 kilometre range. There are more than 7,000 radars for air surveillance at 1,200 sites, giving almost complete coverage against high and medium-altitude attack. Coverage of low-altitude attack, by cruise missile or bomber, is concentrated in western Russia.

These efforts, that have led to the development of one new aircraft type and a new missile every year over the past two decades, become yet more extraordinary in view of the poverty of the country that is making them.

Gorbachev must set them against the backdrop of the Russia of queues, the 'by-chance bags' filled with Hungarian shoes that can then be bartered for Ukrainian light bulbs, toilet paper so rough that tender-arsed foreigners import their supplies from Finland, half lit window displays of canned mackerel, restaurants with long menus that serve one dish.

Multiple altitude SAM-10s are deployed in black earth fields so badly farmed that Argentine and American grain must be imported. Flanker pilots navigate by radar over cities through which they could not drive for lack of available road maps. Digital information races through phased-array radars whose operators cannot find local telephone numbers because the directories ran out a year ago. Il-76 crews plot distant targets and worry whether their irreplaceable windscreen wipers have been stolen from the base car park.

SENIOR SERVICE: NUCLEAR ATTACK FORCES

The nuclear rocket is the proof of the astonishing advance from peasant state to superpower, the cult object of Red Square parades that gives evidence that the economic sacrifice has been worthwhile. It is the only means of projecting the power of the Red forces into the heartland of the *glavni vrag*, the main enemy, the United States.

The White House is five minutes' flying time from depressed-trajectory Russian SLBMs aboard submarines off the US east coast. The Americans have estimated that 100 million Russians would be killed in a retaliatory US strike against unevacuated Soviet industrial and military targets. This could fall to 35 million if civil defence measures had been taken, though it would rise again to 70 to 85 million if the US targeted the evacuation sites. The Russians are less precise with their estimates, preferring to speak of 'hundreds of millions' caught in 'a maelstrom' with 'the future of all mankind at stake'.[1]

The ICBM is the backbone of Soviet strategic power. In its first stage, the modern Soviet ICBM accelerates to 4,420 kph reaching a height of 29 kilometres after 30 seconds. A minute into its flight, the rate of acceleration drops from 10g to 1g, 32 feet per second. The first-stage engine falls away with its attachment ring and the second stage ignites.

At zero plus 90 seconds, as the missile reaches 91,000 metres, 91 kilometres high, the second stage falls away exhausted. The third stage ignites out of the atmosphere, 965 kilometres above the planet.

At zero plus 100 seconds, small rocks blow off the nose fairing, designed to protect the warheads and guidance system from friction heat in the atmosphere. At zero plus 110 seconds, the third-stage rocket separates from the 'bus' which carries the warheads and decoys. The computer controlling the two-metre-high bus verifies by stellar navigation that its course and speed are correct. The bus is manoeuvred by gas thrusters so that the re-entry vehicles, the weapons load and the decoys, can be fired on finely calculated tracks at 27,000 kph towards the targets on Earth.

At zero plus 112 seconds the first warhead fires from the bus to hurtle back into the atmosphere and on to its target. The accuracy with which the small, sharply pointed bomb hits its target should be within 120 metres over the 7,200 kilometres it has travelled. The explosive power of a single small warhead will be around that of 100,000 tons of TNT.

The Soviet Union has no master in the efficiency of its rockets and warheads and no equal in their number.

★

The Strategic Rocket Forces are the senior Soviet service, the height of Yazov's pecking order. This does not prevent the Party from mistrusting them. The physical control of their warheads is vested in the KGB. Russian silos have two Rocket Forces men to launch the missile and two KGB troops to arm the warhead. Yazov may not like it, but this KGB control extends to all nuclear warheads, for artillery shells, bombers and short-range army launchers as well as missiles.

The 298,000 Rocket troops, backed by 112,000 men from the navy and air force, are responsible for all missiles with a range of more than a thousand kilometres.

The lion's share of these are land-based. The operational ICBM force is made up of 1,398 silo launchers. Of these, 818 are new-version SS-17, 18 and 19, deployed during the 1980s. The SS-17 and 19 are medium missiles which can carry respectively four and six independently targeted warheads. The SS-18 is a heavy giant, 30 metres tall, and can fling up to 10 warheads of 600 kilotons apiece on to targets 10,000 kilometres away. The SS-19 is 'hot' launched, firing directly out of its silo and damaging it in the process. The other two are 'cold' launched from re-usable silos on compressed gases before the engine ignites. The silos are hardened against nuclear attack.

These fourth-generation ICBMs are at least as accurate as the US Minuteman III equivalent, or so the Americans claim. These estimates of accuracy are based on intercepting Soviet telemetry as the missiles are tested on flights from the Tyuratam base in stony Kazakhstan to Kamchatka or out into the northern Pacific. American monitoring stations, along the southern Soviet borders, pick up the stream of signals from the rocket and analysis of the number of corrections given by the guidance system are a guide to accuracy. The US estimates are flattering. It is claimed that the 308 SS-18s that the Russians deploy could destroy more than 80 per cent of the thousand American ICBM silo launchers. Each warhead on an SS-18 has twenty times the destructive power of the Hiroshima bomb, and each SS-18 has ten of them aboard. The 360 SS-19s have a similar capability and could be used against targets in Europe, China and Japan.

The remaining 580 ICBMs are SS-11s and 13s, first deployed in the 1960s, housed in less-survivable silos, less accurate and less capable against hardened targets but effective enough if used against European or American cities. The SS-11 was the main ICBM of the 1970s, with 960 in position by 1973, enough to threaten every Western capital and industrial area, deployed in a broad belt 400 kilometres wide and 4,800 long, beginning east of Moscow and ending at Chita to the east of Lake Baikal. Neither it nor the SS-13, a solid-fuel rocket with such problems that only sixty were built, are notably accurate.

As well as these ICBMs, the Strategic Rocket Forces had around 700 medium-range weapons, capable of destroying much of Western Europe or China if deployed. The most notable medium-range rocket is the SS-20, which carries three 500-kiloton warheads and which can be fired from a mobile launcher, but whose use has been severely limited by the INF treaty.

The fact that the bulk of Russian missiles are land-based underlines the problems that they have had with solid-fuelled rockets rather than any prejudice against the sea. A submarine is more difficult to trace than a silo, but liquid-fuelled rockets are so dangerous aboard a ship that the US navy forbids their use. The Russians have found it difficult to produce reliable solid fuel and were forced until recently to have liquid-fuel rockets in their submarines. The problem persists and the SS-NX-23, a new long-range SLBM expected to enter service in the 1990s, is liquid fuelled.

Missile accuracy is academic to civilians. It matters little whether a city-busting missile has a CEP, the 'circular area of probability' in nukespeak, of 0.7 nautical miles like a venerable SS-11 or 0.25 like an SS-19. It fascinates the military because absolute accuracy opens the possibility of absolute success in first or counter strike. Some Russian silos have been hardened to withstand over-pressures of more than 3,000 pounds per square inch. It requires virtually a direct hit to destroy them. The nuclear dream is a counter-force strike in which all enemy silos are destroyed. A CEP of 0.25, which is 462 metres, or better could achieve this.

In theory, at least. In practice it remains unlikely that Russian submarine-launched missiles could get anything like that accuracy on a consistent basis. Land-based ICBMs are more accurate but there are plenty of uncertainties. The Americans test their missiles from their Vandenberg base to Kwajalein Lagoon in the south-west Pacific, from east to west. The Russians test from Tyuratam to Kamchatka, from west to east. In a war, both sides would fire their missiles in a different direction, to the north over the Arctic and the Pole. This brings fresh anomalies in the earth's gravitational field into play, different densities in the upper atmosphere and untested winds that can make the warhead drift off course. Minutely. It has been calculated that an error of one six-hundredth of a degree in computing the direction of gravity in the boost phase will cause an impact error of 90 metres. A 48 kph wind speed can cause a warhead to drift 400 metres outside its lethal radius from the target.[2]

Not much, over 8,000 kilometres. But it is quite enough to ensure that, despite the efforts the Russians and Americans have put into missilry, perfect counter-force remains a dream. In addition, a nuclear exchange is no longer limited to weapons launched from an observable silo or a theoretically trackable submarine. The cruise missile can be produced relatively cheaply and be transported on a simple truck trailer.

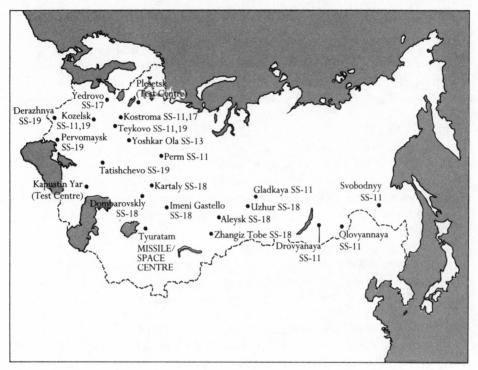

Rocket Sites

Cruise is a particular and lethal mini-weapon. It looks like a drone, a pilotless aircraft no more than 5.5 metres long, with a miniaturized turbojet engine and a radar cross-section one-thousandth that of a B-52 bomber. It hugs the terrain, its guidance system fed by computer and satellite, checking the ground ahead with pre-programmed navigational instructions. It can carry either a nuclear, a chemical or a conventional warhead. It can be launched from a mobile truck-trailer that will make 110 kph on a motorway. Navies can carry it aboard ships or on submarines. Air forces sling them under the wings of bombers as a 'stand-off' weapon that enables a bomber crew to attack a target without getting within an ocean's breadth of it.[3]

Early cruise missiles were slow, flying about the same speed as commercial jetliners though at a much lower altitude. The original designs are being polished. 'Stealth' technology will reduce their already tiny radar profile with new non-reflective materials and rounder profiles. A high-performance engine should allow the second generation to fly at over Mach 3, better than a human-piloted interceptor even if its radar picks it up. Cruise will then have come of nuclear age. It will become a potential first-strike weapon that will be a nightmare for verification in arms

negotiations. A fixed silo can be photographed. A bombardment submarine can be tracked. An SS-20, which can be transported as easily as
any other fifteen-metre load on the back of a truck, is near impossible to
keep tabs on. A 5.5-metre cruise is more so and, whereas an SS-20 plant
can be checked to ensure its production line is halted, a cruise assembly
line is smaller and more difficult to verify.

A missile is vulnerable. It has three phases. For the first few minutes of its
life, it is accelerating up from the ground. It is detectable through the hot,
bright trail of fire from the thrusters, called the exhaust plume. At the end
of this *boost phase*, it will have travelled 160 kilometres and will be in free
flight above the atmosphere. It now releases its independent warheads,
which travel in an expanding swarm through the lengthy *mid-course phase*,
until they re-enter the earth's atmosphere and head for their targets, heating
up through air friction in the *terminal phase*.

The mid-course phase is the most difficult to attack. Since the MIRVs
have been released, there are several separate targets to hit. An American
interceptor fired from the Kwajelein archipelago atop a Minuteman
booster destroyed the dummy warhead from a Minuteman ICBM over
the Pacific in 1984. The target had been fired 7,200 kilometres away from
Vandenberg Air Force Base in California thirty minutes earlier and the
interceptor homed in on it with infra-red sensors. A bottle of champagne
was cracked and a toast to discomfiture in the Kremlin was made as the
4.5-metre aluminium ribs on the interceptor unfurled and the incoming
warhead was destroyed at a closing speed of 29,000 kph. But this was a
single target and there were no decoys. The largest hydrogen-fusion bomb
can now be packed into a 40-gallon oil drum. An SS-18 carries ten
warheads. Destruction in mid-course is a cripplingly expensive affair.

The US Strategic Defense Initiative or Star Wars programme aims at
boost-phase kills, destroying missiles shortly after launch. A single hit on
the missile should destroy all the warheads, still riding in their 'bus'. The
light and heat poured out of the booster is easy to detect from geostationary
satellites 35,887 kilometres above the equator. There are a number of ways
of destroying the missile. Laser travels at the speed of light, giving zero
time to target and disintegrating the missile by burning or melting the
metal skin. The neutral particle beam fires a stream of hydrogen atoms at
96,500 kilometres a second, which pass through the missile skin and disrupt
its guidance system. The aluminium ribs over the Pacific were a relatively
crude kinetic weapon that destroys through impact.

The sensors that pick up the climbing rocket cannot see around the
curve of the earth. Lasers and neutral particle beams also need to have a
clear line of sight on the target. They must therefore be in space, which
involves having a fleet of satellites at the ready over the Soviet missile

fields. There is not much time to identify and destroy missiles at this stage. Soviet ICBMs are now in boost-phase for about five minutes. Fast-burn booster technology may cut this fighting window of time to less than fifty seconds. Weapons must not be tempted by the huge plume of heat and gas given off during boost, but must identify and attack the hard body, the actual missile.

Mid-course gives twenty minutes for attack. Here simple pellets known as smart rocks can destroy a target by the kinetic energy of their motion. But a major attack would involve decoys and reflective metal scraps, forming a threat cloud to the defence of up to a million objects. Warheads can be picked out by interactive sensors, highly accelerated neutral particle beams. Gamma rays are emitted when the beams hit a massive object like a warhead, distinguishing them from decoys, which have little mass.

The terminal phase lasts only two minutes as the warheads sweep the 200 kilometres to their target. They can be picked up on radar and can be destroyed by ABM missiles with nuclear tips or smart rocks. However, radar can be blinded by nuclear air bursts, known as precursor bursts, that create a background of nuclear emissions, magnetic pulses and heat that fools sensors.

The Russians have invested heavily in anti-missile missiles in ABM defence. The world's only operational Anti-Ballistic Missile system is established around Moscow. This uses the Galosh ABM, launched from silos and with three propulsion stages giving a range of at least 320 kilometres. It is designed to kill incoming missiles with a three-megaton nuclear warhead. A new ABM radar at Pushkino, a few kilometres north-east of Moscow, is designed to control this war of the missiles. Its phased-array radars are protected by a hangar-like structure 35 metres high and 150 metres long. The Soviets have also developed the SH-8, a silo-stored interceptor missile that can be quickly reloaded. In mid-1983, it was discovered that a large radar station was being built at Abalakova in central Siberia that could only be part of an ABM system. It showed that the basis for 'a rapidly deployable anti-ballistic missile defence system' was under way.[4]

This involves the rejection of MAD, the principle of Mutually Assured Destruction in which it is assumed that some ICBMs will always get through and that it is thus insane to begin a nuclear exchange. It is very doubtful, however, whether the system could cope with the MIRVed warheads that would be used in a missile attack on Moscow. The radars are vulnerable to decoys and can be saturated with targets. Nor is it clear what the effect would be of exploding a Galosh warhead at a height even of 150 kilometres. The creation of electrically charged particles in the explosion might swamp the radar system and leave Moscow blind to further attacks.

This is not a problem with laser weapons, where Soviet investment is reckoned to be three to five times that of the American. There are twelve major research centres, a plant for laser systems at Troitsk and a huge land-based laser installation at Saryshagen that has an optical beam redirection system that could be used against US satellites. The artificial crystals grown in the Soyuz space stations could reduce the gap in microelectronics. Major research effort is going into systems to produce high-energy radio frequency waves and particle-beam weapons.

Three types of laser weapons are being studied for air defence. These are intended to protect important strategic targets within Russia, such as command centres and ships at sea, and for theatre-forces defence. High-energy lasers can do structural damage to strike aircraft at close range and cause serious eye injury to strafing pilots at greater distances. Satellites have become major targets in a war because of the high value of the information they gather for the enemy. The edge in the opening stage of a war will go to the country that is most effective in satellite-killing, by chemical laser, charged particle-beam or by simple pellets. The Russians were first into the field, succeeding in intercepting one of their own satellites, Cosmos 248, in October 1968. Eight years later, an interceptor satellite made a fast fly-past of a target and re-entered the atmosphere over the Pacific in less than one orbit.

Ground-based lasers, under development at the Sary Shagan proving ground on the remote shores of the Balkhash Ozero lake in Kazakhstan, may eventually be used as satellite-killers. The Tyuratum space base, east of the Aral Sea in stony Kazakhstan, has an anti-satellite interceptor that can reach targets orbiting at 5,800 kilometres. It uses a radar sensor and a blast of pellets, like a giant shotgun, to destroy its victims.

Given the number of ICBM warheads, an ABM or SDI system would have to be at least 95 per cent effective to reduce destruction to anywhere near acceptable limits.[5] Missile-killers cost about three times as much as missiles. It has been estimated that the cost of housing the satellite platforms and the production of missile-killers themselves, that is the laser beams and high-energy particle beams, will be about $73 million per missile-killer.[6] A Soviet SS-18 is reckoned to cost about $25 million.

In any arms race the economic strain is on the country that invests in missile defence, not in missile production. Nothing is as cost-effective as a nuclear missile. The CIA estimates that the annual cost of the entire Soviet ICBM construction programme during the 1970s rarely exceeded $6 billion, or one thirtieth of the overall defence budget.[7] Nothing matches the destructive capacity of a single nuclear bombardment submarine. Each warhead creates an instantaneous fireball that burns people at 20 kilometres from the epicentre and sets all buildings afire at 4 kilometres. It is followed by a blast wave that levels buildings within 3 kilometres, topples many of them up to 6 kilometres and creates a giant firestorm with 550-kph winds. Fires, a general conflagration up to 8 kilometres, persist up to 16. A single Soviet Typhoon submarine carries 20 missiles with up to 180 such warheads.

Because they are so cheap – a new US MX warhead costs only $million to deliver to target – nuclear weapons have also proliferated to the point where they become disposable. The investments that are written off are relatively small. They are high profile in public opinion and the military downside is slight. Reassigning a few SRF crews does not have the same effect as laying off a clutch of armoured divisions. Neither does it much upset the balance of power. The Soviets now have rather more reason to favour nuclear cuts than the Americans. It places moral pressure on the US to drop the SDI programme, which is both too expensive for the Soviets to follow and too great an investment for the Americans to negotiate on should it appear to be becoming viable. It also blurs the decisive Soviet superiority in conventional forces. All this at the negligible cost of a 3 to 4 per cent reduction in nuclear capacity.

It is, nevertheless, a painfully slow and complex business. The Strategic Arms Limitation Talks, SALT, between the US and the Soviet Union produced an interim agreement in 1972. This placed a five-year freeze on ICBMs, SLBMs and ABMs. ICBMs were frozen at 1,618 Soviet missiles to 1,054 American, and submarine-launched missiles at 950 Soviet in 62 submarines to 710 US in 44 submarines. Anti-ballistic missiles were restricted to 100 apiece. The following year, it was agreed to reduce the ABM ceiling.

The West Europeans were worried at the prospect of a reduction in the level of US troops stationed in West Germany. The Mansfield Resolution, calling for this, was defeated in Congress but the pressure remains and has been increased by the US trade deficit and the weak dollar. The Europeans pressed for Mutual and Balanced Force Reductions, MBFR, in which any US and NATO force reductions would be matched by the Soviets in Eastern Europe. The Russians, for their part, favoured a European Security Conference, CSCE, that would lead to a system of multilateral guarantees in Europe. This was largely a paper exercise to the West but it offered the Russians the chance of getting formal Western acceptance of post-war frontiers. Legality, of borders at least, weighs heavy on the Soviet soul.

Full-scale talks began on both in 1973, MBFR in Vienna and CSCE in Helsinki. The CSCE talks finally produced the Helsinki Agreement in August 1975, signed by thirty-three European countries and the US and Canada. True to form, Albania was the one stop-out. In return for a paper commitment to respect human rights, the Russians obtained recognition

of the frontiers of Eastern Europe and implicitly legitimized their pre-
dominant role within them.

The MBFR, in which the West had a real interest, dragged on without
conclusion. So did SALT 2, with the added disadvantage to the West that
the Russians were rapidly closing the technology gap opened up in MIRVs,
ALBMs, Trident submarines, and cheap cruise missiles under Johnson and
Nixon. By 1976 the Russians had tested a missile with Multiple Independent Re-entry Vehicles, MIRVs in nukespeak. The new Backfire
bomber had flown and they had launched their first carrier, the *Kiev*. The
American qualitative edge over the Russians was eroding under *détente*,
whilst providing the Russians with US technology, finance and food.

Jimmy Carter, who entered the White House in January 1977, linked
détente to the Soviet human rights record. He also confused the Kremlin, as
well as his NATO allies, with some curious decision-making. He cancelled
the B-1 bomber programme and the deployment of the neutron bomb.
This Enhanced Radiation Weapon, with its low blast but high short-range
neutron radiation, was well suited to counter mass tank thrusts in Europe.
It would kill tank crews whilst inflicting minimum damage on dense
industrial belts. The Russians were able to portray it as the ultimate
capitalist weapon which destroyed people but not property. At the same
time, Carter called for NATO to raise defence expenditure by 3 per cent.

Congress refused to ratify the eventual SALT 2 accords, which restricted
each side to 2,250 launchers apiece and placed a ceiling of 1,320 on all
types of MIRVed missiles as well as 300 on heavy missiles such as the
Soviet SS-18. In December 1979 the NATO Council decided on a response
to the Soviet deployment of Backfire bombers and over 150 of the
medium-range SS-20 missiles. It was recommended that Pershing II rockets
and Tomahawk cruise missiles should be sited in West Germany, Britain,
Italy and Belgium to upgrade NATO's theatre weapons. The Soviet
intermediate-range or INF forces were targeted on Western Europe and
Britain, mainly from sites just east of the Urals, and the US missiles were
targeted on the western USSR.

This was based on a perception of a 'window of opportunity' that had
been opened by Brezhnev's high defence spending. Soviet conventional
forces and shorter-range nuclear weapons had considerable superiority in
Europe and the traditional US long-range superiority had been whittled
down.

The Russians launched a major propaganda campaign within Western
Europe, particularly in West Germany, against cruise and Pershing deployment. The effects of this were countered by the invasion of Afghanistan.
Carter increased the 1981 defence budget by 5 per cent, embargoed
excess grain deliveries, limited Russian purchases of high-tech equipment,
boycotted the Moscow Olympics and withdrew SALT 2 from con-

gressional consideration. He also decided to create a 100,000-strong Rapid Deployment Force for use in the Persian Gulf area. *Détente* had run its course.

Arms talks survived. Intermediate Nuclear Force talks, INF, began in 1981 and Strategic Arms Reduction Talks, START, in 1982. Neither made much progress until the arrival of Gorbachev. START was the Reagan administration's attempt to improve on SALT, covering the long-range missiles that the superpowers would fire directly at each other's territory in war. The Americans want deep cuts in the number of Soviet heavy ICBMs. The 'double build-down' is an American idea for each side to destroy two or more missiles for each new one it deploys. The Soviets, whose main strength is in heavy SS-18s, claim this is weighted against them. They want ceilings on all strategic 'launchers', including submarine missile tubes and intercontinental bombers as well as missile silos, at a lower level than SALT 2. The Americans fear that this would leave the Russians with a big lead in land-based heavy missiles that could be used in first strike.

INF bogged down over SS-20 and the linkage of the British and French nuclear deterrents to the US total. Gorbachev broke the INF impasse. He proposed a 'zero option', where the US would withdraw its Tomahawk cruise and Pershing II missiles and the Soviet Union its SS-20s, and then a 'double zero option' which would include short – as well as intermediate-range weapons. A successful agreement on the scrapping of INF has been achieved. Welcome as that is, the SRF crews and their KGB minders can reflect in their isolated sites that all Soviet conventional strength and 97 per cent of nuclear strength remains intact.

Reductions in conventional forces are far more complex than simple trade-offs in nuclear weapons, where both superpowers retain overkill. The Russians have huge advantages in conventional arms, both in outright numbers and in geography. It is easier for them to get men and armour to central Europe than it is for the Americans, and they have more of both. Reductions will have to be deeply asymmetrical, of the order of 4:1, to be attractive to NATO. The Russians can afford to look generous with minor cuts, for these will make little difference. For NATO to be able to hold a conventional Warsaw Pact attack for 30 days within 25 miles of its start-line, for example, it is reckoned that the Soviet bloc would need to disband no fewer than 25 to 30 divisions.[8]

The planned Gorbachev cut of 500,000 men was partly forced by the same drop in the birth-rate that is reducing the conscript pool in every NATO country except Turkey. In any event, crude manpower is becoming less important on the new high-tech battlefield.

Soviet acceptances early in 1989 that talks on conventional forces should set agreed ceilings, rather than argue about what each side has to start with, shows that the political leadership is beginning to acquire a defensive philosophy. So does the decision to withdraw six armoured divisions from East Germany, Czechoslovakia and Hungary.

The military are happy enough to go along with modernization. The Reagan build-up gave the US a clear lead in 'smart' weapons, controlled by microchips, sensors and state-of-the-art computers. The Russians must modernise to counter CS, the 'competitive strategies' by which the West uses its huge superiority, in intelligent, target-evaluating hardware to stun Soviet forces with swift, intricately coordinated attacks in great depth.

In CS, the West is to fight 'smart, not rich'. Given the Soviet lag in smart weapons, the temptation to remain 'rich', with offensive capability, remains strong for Yazov.

42
THE SPIES: RUN SILENT

No need for trenchcoats and languid blondes in the search which most excites and profits Yazov. He has his own intelligence service, the GRU, and access to KGB material. The cheque book is the most effective way of getting at Western high technology.[1] A computer-controlled machine tool that mills marine propellers seems humble enough. One delivery from Japan to the Baltic Shipyard in Leningrad, however, is estimated to have done the US Navy at least $1 billion worth of damage. The cost to Allied shipping and seamen would need a war to calculate.

The Russians were aware at least as early as 1979 that their submarines were easily detected by NATO ships and aircraft through propeller noise.[2] Propeller cavitation makes submarines noisy. As the propeller spins through the water it produces a vacuum cavity on the surface of the blade. This cavity sheet is swept behind the boat in its wake where its bubbles are collapsed by water pressure. The result of these continuous cavity collapses is a roar that can be picked up on sonar. The interaction of the propeller slicing the turbulence created by the submarine's superstructure and fins produces a sonar pattern characteristic of its class. The finishing of individual propellers gives a boat its own detectable 'signature' within its class.

Soviet designers minimized noise by increasing the diameter of propellers so that they spin less quickly. Propellers have become so large that the blades stick out above the waterline when the submarine runs on the surface. Multi-bladed propellers heighten the pitch of the propeller sound and reduce the distance it travels. Swept blades slice into the wake at sharp and quieter angles, and setting them at an angle on the propeller shaft reduces the amount of wake they encounter. Submarine commanders reduce noise by diving deep when on transit to a bombardment station and by moving at minimum speed when they have arrived there.

This knowledge was held in common. But the Russians lacked state-of-the-art machinery in the physical production of propellers, which can measure 6 metres in diameter and weigh 10 tons. The slightest flaw or irregularity in the surface of a blade brings on cavitation by separating the blade surface from the water. A precise amount of metal must be ground out of a blade to create a perfect profile.[3]

The answer lay in less than $20 million worth of propeller milling machines and numerical controllers from Japan and Norway. The critical factor in milling propellers is the number of independently controlled axes that can be used in shaping them. The more axes, the more delicate and silent the propeller. Under the regulations of the Coordinating Committee for Multilateral Export Controls, COCOM, no machine tool with more than three independent axes can be shipped to the Soviet Union or its allies.

The KGB worked skilfully and patiently to break the embargo. The Soviet machine-tool import agency Tekmashimport contacted a small Japanese trading firm with offices in Moscow. The trading firm, Wako Koeki, approached Toshiba Machine in Japan. Toshiba manufacture the MBP-110 milling machine which turns and sculpts propellers on nine independent axes. Tekmashimport signed a contract in Moscow in 1981 for four of the machines, together with a service and spares agreement.

In its application for an export licence, Toshiba referred to its TDP 70-110 machine. It said the machine was limited to two axes, comfortably within the COCOM rules, and was to be used to improve the civilian power utility in Leningrad. Toshiba engineers arrived at the Baltic Ship-yard early in 1983 to begin assembling the two-storey-high machines.

The numerical control computer to guide the Toshiba milling tools was ordered in Norway. The Russians ordered an NC-200, capable of controlling work on nine axes, from the marketing subsidiary of Kongsberg Vaapenfabrikk. The company was in financial difficulties. It specified on export documents that it was shipping a relatively crude controller suitable for two-axes work. Kongsberg technicians worked with Toshiba men to marry their systems in the Baltic Shipyard. The MPD-110s from Toshiba cost a mere $4 to $5 million each. The Kongsberg controller cost a little over $2 million.

For this modest outlay the Russians have been able to correct a major flaw in their multi-billion-rouble submarine fleet.

★

This particular operation was controlled by the KGB. The military has its own intelligence service, the GRU or the Main Intelligence Directorate of the Soviet General Staff, centred at the old Khodinka airfield in Moscow. Several thousand GRU officers work abroad, either as military attachés or else under civilian cover as embassy drivers, Aeroflot airline staff, merchant navy men and officials in trade missions. Though there is inter-service rivalry between KGB and GRU men, the two combine in an efficient industry for stripping technological secrets from the West.

An extraordinary document was leaked to the French newspaper *Le Monde* in 1985. It was signed by Leonid Smirnov, the head of the VPK, *Voienno-Promychlennaia Komissia*, the Moscow clearing house that channels intelligence from field agents to defence industries, design bureaux and ministries. It detailed the information passed on to the aerospace industry through 'special channels' abroad. Bureaucratic and assured in style, the document estimates the savings realized through espionage on Western technology.

In one year, the VPK passed on 156 items of equipment and 3,896 technical documents to the aerospace industry ministry. Of these, '140 samples of equipment and 3,543 technical documents were judged useful by this industry'.[4] 'The use of foreign experience has assisted our country to increase technical levels in a rapid manner,' Smirnov continued. It 'has also permitted several advanced technology processes to enter manufacture'. The 'borrowing of foreign technological methods' had resulted in savings 'in research and pilot schemes of 48.6 million roubles, an increase of 18.8 million roubles on the year before'.[5]

Two concrete examples are given. One refers to documents obtained by the GRU and used by the Sukhoi and Mikoyan aircraft plants for Su-27 and Mig-29 fighters. They concern onboard computers, independent fuel tanks, integrated command systems and fire controls. Savings of 8 million roubles are quoted. Other documents used by the Sukhoi plant covered studies and tests on supercritical wing design. These were used in the design of the leading edge of wings on the Su-25 fighter-bomber. Soviet engineers were able to resolve stubborn design problems with the high-performance wing of the Su-25 with the stolen technology. Three years after a GRU agent had sent back Western documents to Moscow, Su-25s were flying ground-attack missions in Afghanistan.

Smirnov also boasted that Russian agents had helped to neutralize the US-made TOW anti-tank missile. 'On the basis of studies of the installation of ground controls on the anti-tank guided missile system TOW,' he wrote, 'we can determine the amount of jamming necessary to counteract this weapon.'

The nine ministers of the major defence industries are represented in the VPK. Besides sifting stolen material, the VPK coordinates espionage efforts through the five 'acquisitions departments' which carry out the spying abroad. The First Department is run by the KGB's T division, the T standing for technology. The Second is managed by the GRU, the Third by an external department of the State Committee for Science and Technology, the Fourth by the external service of the Academy of Sciences and the Fifth by the Ministry of Foreign Trade.

The KGB and the GRU share responsibility for three quarters of technology espionage. The Americans have to contend with 2,500 Soviet bloc officials in the US, of whom up to 40 per cent are known or suspected spies. So acute are the problems of tailing such a number that in 1985 foreign diplomats were required to display new car registration plates indicating their country, such as SX for the Soviet Union and DC for Cuba.

Cover given to members of the acquisitions departments is broad, as seen in the expulsion of forty-seven Soviet officials from France in 1983. These included embassy personnel from every section: military, cultural, scientific and commercial, UNESCO advisers, Tass correspondents, trade representatives and the consul in Marseilles.*

Western intelligence services estimate that the Russians and their allies, most notably the Czechs and East Germans, have 20,000 trained agents ferreting out technology secrets in the West. Not all their targets are purely military. Gorbachev's insistence on closing the technology gap has led to emphasis on dual-use products and processes, including new metals and ceramics, lasers, fibre-optics and computers.[6] Richard Perle, US assistant defense secretary, put the savings to the Soviet bloc in weapons research and development costs as high as $50 billion. He claimed that virtually all the equipment in Zelenograd, the Soviet Union's Silicon Valley, comes from the West. A West German and a Swede are thought to have sent more than $30 million worth of Western technology, including an entire semiconductor manufacturing plant. The West German, Richard Müller, was alleged to have tried to ship 100 tons of illegally diverted electronics equipment through the Swedish free port of Helsingborg.[7] This included a Digital Equipment Corporation VAX 11/782 computer, a huge advance on the Russian military's own Minsk and Ryad machines.

Competition between Western companies for lucrative Russian contracts is a problem. Russian trade with the US dropped by 50 per cent in the aftermath of the Afghan invasion in 1980. The shortfall was made up by a 58 per cent increase with France, 32 per cent with Italy and 11 per cent with West Germany. As Khrushchev mocked when ordering tankers

* The British had expelled 105 Soviet officials in 1971, which gives an idea of the size of KGB and GRU staffs abroad. So sweeping were those expulsions that when the author's newspaper, the *Sunday Times*, telephoned the embassy the following year to arrange the annual football match between them, an embassy spokesman said: 'We have only the goalkeeper left!'

from Italian yards to supply Cuba with oil in 1961, capitalists seem prepared to do anything for money.

IBM 360 and 370 computers, illegally diverted to the Soviet Union through dummy companies and false customs declarations in 1972, still provide the basis for the command system of the Soviet air defence system. US grinding machines are used to produce guidance systems for the SS-18 missile and West German Gildemeister machine tools help manufacture high-quality artillery tubes. Microprocessors for missiles and laser mirrors for satellite killers travel from California via European middlemen. The major Swedish firm Datasaab was fined $1 million by the US government in 1984 for evading American export controls. The company had re-exported high-performance US-made semiconductors for air traffic control systems in Moscow, Kiev and Mineralnyve Vody.[8]

The items banned by COCOM, often resented by non-American companies who feel that the US is not above hindering competing nations' exports, include many dual-use items. Floating dry-docks were included after the Soviet Pacific Fleet started using a supposedly civilian 80,000-ton floating dock to service Kiev-class aircraft carriers. The US defense department claims that the Russians have acquired turbine-blade coating technology, a complete Western high-bypass turbofan engine, image intensifiers, frequency analysers, production plants for integrated circuits, wire memory and bubble memory technology, radar-absorbing coatings, and electronic-grade silicon for ballistic missiles.

They have also obtained secret reports on advanced Western weapons systems. This includes the French Mirage 2000 fighter and the Ariane rocket engine, the radar systems of the F-15 and the B-1, Phoenix air-to-air missiles, Patriot surface-to-air missiles and NATO air defence systems. It was revealed in 1989 that empty vodka bottles and a Soviet sailor's cap found on a beach on Kwajalein atoll suggested that a Russian submarine had landed a party to steal a flight recorder which had gone missing after a Minuteman missile had been test-fired from California.

The lists are endless and the effort enormous.

The GRU has a familiar history of purge and horror, set against the KGB in the grim Soviet waltz that traps Army, KGB and Party ever together and ever in changing relationships of romance and spite.

When Stalin began in 1935 purging the overseas elements of the KGB, then the NKVD, he looked to the GRU. The GRU chief Yan Berzin travelled to the Far East and to Spain liquidating the NKVD men. Then came the turn of the army. NKVD men now hunted down the GRU in the Soviet Union and abroad. Berzin was arrested on his return from Spain and shot on 29 July 1938.[9] The GRU had a good war.[10] Though Stalin ignored the *Barbarossa* warnings of its brilliant agent in Japan, Richard Sorge, its 'Red orchestra' penetrated the German High Command. After Beria's death, GRU men again tortured their rivals in their cellars on Gogol Boulevard.[11]

Care has been taken since to prevent the absolute control of the army over the GRU by appointing ex-KGB generals to run it. Gorbachev is not a GRU ideal. As Andropov's protégé, he has close KGB links, though his sacking of Viktor Chebrikov as head of the KGB in October 1988 pleased the GRU.

Affections change and anyway the GRU has plenty to keep it busy. It has, according to the pseudonymous GRU defector Viktor Suvorov,[12] more than five thousand senior officers and generals with specialist academic qualifications in intelligence on its payroll. Its brief is the external threat to the Soviet Union and thus broad. It interests itself with the military, technological and economic capability of foreign powers. It wishes to know the functioning and strategic and tactical philosophies of opposing forces, their weaponry, the industrial and scientific potential of the countries they belong to, their strength and vulnerability.

Such a remit is enormous. It sweeps from the highest grade of cipher cracking, obtained in the crudest way, by providing women for the Marine guards at the US embassy in Moscow. It targets the electronic profile of counter-countermeasures and the downtime on an engine change on a tank. It is restless. It is not content with knowing the movements of Western submarines. It must know what the enemy knows about the movements of Soviet submarines. Thus the value of the Walker spy ring in the US navy[13] lay in information about the American ability to monitor Russian submarines.

Each of its four area directorates has 300 high-ranking officers in the Moscow centre, according to Suvorov,[14] and a similar number abroad.[15] Further directorates cover specialized electronic and 'cosmic' intelligence. For cosmic, read space. The GRU is the prime mover in satellite espionage, a field where it has a clear advantage over its KGB rivals. It is responsible for military and intelligence-gathering satellites, which account for up to a third of Soviet launches. It maintains its own launch pads and can coopt space specialists at will.

Abroad, the GRU 'resident' is normally a senior officer in an embassy, with a staff of operational officers who deal with agents, cipher officers for encoding and technicians who monitor communications in the country. The increasing use of cordless and car telephones in the West has greatly increased the opportunities for commercial and technological espionage. Aeroflot, the Soviet civil airline, is an exclusive GRU preserve and so much use is made of it that eight countries have officially complained at its activities. Among them are the Swiss, who sent two fighters to escort

an Aeroflot Ilyushin airliner to Zürich airport.[16] It had been overflying the
Saint-Gotthard massif where the Swiss army was on manoeuvres. Leonid
Barabanov, Aeroflot's man in Switzerland, left for Moscow shortly after.

The GRU takes the highest-quality officers. The defector and former
Soviet diplomat Vladimir Sakharov studied at the most prestigious school
in the country, the Moscow Institute of International Relations. All students had obligatory training in military intelligence. After languages and
area studies, it occupied third place in a busy schedule. The military
department of the school was in a restricted area where the walls were
'covered by all sorts of diagrams and classifications of American, English,
French and German tanks, rockets, airplanes and military maps'.[17] Sakharov learned how to handle most Soviet and some Western light weapons.
He had to pass an exam in reassembling them with his eyes shut, an odd
test for a potential diplomat. When Sakharov had graduated from the
Institute he was automatically commissioned as a lieutenant in the Red
army and became an officer in the GRU.

Agents may be Soviet professionals, like Rudolph Abel, trained in
Moscow and inserted into position after complex journeys via third countries to acquire a bland and unsuspicious identity. They are given saturation
courses in the social mores and habits of the West. Some are slotted easily
into place by marrying a foreigner. As many as 100 Frenchmen married
Russians whilst their companies built the Cosmos Hotel for the Moscow
Olympics. 'A lot of these marriages did not last,' said a French expert.[18]
'Once they had French nationality, the wives got divorced. Often they
then remarried, changing their name and becoming very difficult to track.'

Local agents are sometimes recruited through the Soviet friendship
societies in their countries.[19] The GRU will wait patiently whilst a local
agent works his way to a humble but profitable job, like the French
Zolotarenko affair where the agent worked a photocopying machine in
Neuilly-sur-Seine that spewed copies of aerospace information. Or it will
monitor the progress of a minor civil servant, like the Briton, Geoffrey
Prime, as he established himself at the top-security GCHQ communications centre in Cheltenham. An ideal cover for an illegal can come
with a humdrum job like a garage owner, who is free to hire and fire staff,
to travel and to launder money easily through a second-hand car business.
Such was Bernard Sourisseau, the *garagiste* who dealt in French naval
secrets before his arrest in 1985.

With technology espionage, small businessmen are particularly at risk.
GRU staffers, officially military attachés, Aeroflot managers or trade
representatives, can offer an inflated sum for a legitimate service or item
of equipment as bait for the hook of treason.

In addition to its agents, satellites and electronic eavesdroppers, the
GRU also commands the *Spetsnaz* special forces. Some *Spetsnaz* troops

are used directly in potential battlefield reconnaissance in Western Europe. They come as members of sports teams or, more frequently, as truck drivers. According to a West German report,[20] 350,000 Soviet-bloc trucks circulate in Western Europe each year. *Spetsnaz* officers, in civilian clothes, act as drivers to get first-hand knowledge of the lie of the land in predicted battle areas. The strength of bridges and the depth of canals and rivers are calculated for use in planning tank offensives. Neutral countries are not exempted from their attention. The Austrians arrested a number of East-bloc truck drivers in 1981 and the Swiss General Herbert Wanner complained that: 'It is clear that our country is also included in the sphere of Eastern espionage activity.'

They come not singly, GRU spies, but in Ilyushins and Mercedes trucks.

43

WARSAW PACT:
THE UNEASY ALLIANCE

The Warsaw Pact is an essential element in Yazov's deployment in Eastern Europe. It legitimizes the presence of the 550,000-odd Soviet troops in the satellites. It gives the Russians forward deployment beyond their borders. It also robs the satellites of independent military strength through Soviet-dominated 'socialist integration'. Its loyalty is, however, questionable.

The Pact was established, a year after West Germany was invited to join NATO, in 1954. Its non-Soviet members[1] provide 1,168,000 men. In war, the satellite divisions would be integrated into Soviet Armies, as happens in peacetime manoeuvres. No satellite has the right to establish its own Armies or Fronts. The major decisions are taken at the Red army headquarters on Gogol Boulevard, Moscow.[2]

The satellites are without nuclear weapons or independent anti-aircraft defence. All major equipment is Russian-made, although economies are strained by having to supply large amounts of less sophisticated weaponry. The East Germans gave up their small military aircraft industry in 1961 and the Poles renounced the development of advanced combat aircraft in 1969. Satellite armies are restricted in exercising on their own soil and are too short of locally produced equipment and stockpiles to be able to act for long on their own. Only a third of exercises are held on national territory and most are under 'allied', or Russian, command. The Military Council, which organizes exercises, is headed by the Soviet C-in-C of the Pact. The Armaments Committee, responsible for weapons research and procurement, and even the Sports Committee, are Soviet led.

Some sops to satellite feeling are made. A Political Consultative Committee, supposedly a watchdog composed of party leaders, meets fitfully. Rumania is permitted its own deviation, refusing to allow Soviet troops to transit or Pact manoeuvres to be held on its soil. Rumania, however, is not of great strategic value to the Russians.[3]

To stiffen the satellites, the Russians provide 60 per cent of the troops in the front line facing NATO.[4] In all, the Pact gets 75 per cent of its manpower and 80 per cent of its funding from the Soviet Union. Since the US provides only 42 per cent of NATO troops and 60 per cent of costs, the Soviets have frequently offered to dissolve the Pact if NATO did the same. Because Moscow would be able to maintain its thirty-one divisions in Eastern Europe, Pact or no Pact, whereas NATO is a transatlantic affair, this is no bargain offer.

Satellite territory, particularly East Germany, Poland and Czechoslovakia, is of deep emotional importance to the Russians. It is their *glacis*, the 'open slope in front of a fortified place' where the battles and destruction involved in a NATO offensive would be contained and halted before they could spill into the Soviet Union. The Pact is also a vital military component. More than half the initial offensive force in a European war would consist of East Europeans of different degrees of reliability. Russian strategy assumes an unreinforced offensive against NATO forces with 'prompt, substantial and reliable participation by non-Soviet northern tier Pact forces'.[5] The Soviet philosophy of a rapid, all-out offensive strike against NATO minimizes the risk of defections. The shorter the preparation time, the less the consultations, the quicker the battlefield success, the more effective the satellite armies will be.

The armies are conscript-based. Young Poles and Czechs have little respect for Soviet values. It is unlikely that they would willingly die for Soviet interests in a long war of attrition. They might fight hard initially, as the Hungarians and Rumanians did for Hitler, but any reverses would see morale in danger. NATO has thus changed its perception from a massive Pact attack with prior reinforcement and good warning time to an unreinforced, forces-in-being attack with very little warning.

An unreinforced attack would place major responsibility on the satellites. Of the 58 Pact divisions that are in-place, 31 are non-Soviet. These include 15 Polish, 10 Czech and 6 East German divisions.[6] The area to the south is less important. Hungary can field 1 tank and 5 motorized infantry divisions. No Soviet troops are deployed in the South-West Front, where the Bulgarians and Rumanians can run to 2 all-arms Armies, each with 4 tank and 16 motorized infantry divisions.

★

Czechoslovakia showed in 1968 how rapidly a satellite officer corps, apparently well-purged and pro-Soviet, can turn nationalist. The Czech army is still not trusted. It remains more directly supervised and controlled than any other Pact member. The Czech army would still be used on the South-West Front. Ten Czech divisions would fight on the Pilsen–Karlsruhe axis attempting to break through to the Rhine at Karlsruhe. But there is no longer any question of Czech troops fighting alone in the first echelon. Soviet units are also included in the battle order and the Czechs would come under direct Russian command.

The low level of Soviet confidence is shown by the decline in the size of the Czech military and in its budget, at a time when Polish and East German forces have been increased. Gorbachev may have considered the regime of Gustav Husak to be too hard-line for safety, to have snubbed him by breaking off early from a visit in April 1987, and to play with force reductions. That does not mean he places much faith in the Czech armed forces.

These total 201,000 men. The army makes up the bulk, with 5 motorized infantry divisions and 5 tank divisions with 3,500 machines. Whether it would fight with any determination in a war in which it would have no interest is doubtful. Czech officers in 1968, worried at the prospect of being used as Russian cannon fodder, slammed Pact policy as 'exclusively in the interest of the coalition regardless of one's own sovereign interests'.

If that was true then, it remains so.

Poland is the largest Pact country, with the biggest population[7] and armed forces, of 402,000. It is the best equipped. Its whole operational army, with 15 divisions and 3,800 tanks, is slated for a rapid offensive against NATO. It is as large as the French army.

Two out of the three Polish Armies would advance across the north German plain towards the Netherlands. The third would attack and occupy Denmark. The Russians appear reasonably confident that the Poles would be reliable as long as they were advancing and fighting, if possible, West Germans on West German soil. Two Polish divisions are unique to the satellite armies, elite and special purpose, a sea-landing and an airborne-assault division. The army is 'programmed for massive and rapid offensive operations on to NATO territory in a nuclear environment'.[8]

This is a country whose loathing of Russians has sometimes seemed as profound as its attachment to its Catholicism and its Polish Pope, which knows who was responsible for the slaughter in the Katyn forest, a country with blood links to the United States.

The Soviets bank on three factors. One is geography, the eternal tragedy of Poland. It has suffered continuously and terribly as the cockpit for big neighbours, Russians, Prussians, Austrians, Germans. The Poles have an interest in fighting well to the West rather than at home. If they can combat one slice of one traditional enemy, West Germans, so much the better. The second reason is the 40,000-strong group of Soviet forces based at Legnica in Silesia, with their 2 armoured divisions and 350 combat aircraft and their ability to call on reinforcements from the western districts of the Soviet Union and from East Germany.

The third is General Jaruzelski, himself a graduate of the Ryazan infantry school south-east of Moscow. He represents a stable military leadership which is professionally close to the Russians, which served as young officers in the Polish army raised in Russia during the war, and which has learnt that the Polish people cannot be pushed too far.

Conscripts and reservists share the national sullenness to the system. Recruits are negative to the Warsaw Pact and to the Soviet Union and are hostile when the Red army's 'liberating mission' is mentioned. They feel no sense of loyalty to 'fraternal armies' and no desire to do any 'internationalist duty'. Reservists, many of whom are ex-Solidarity members, are if anything less politically reliable than the raw recruits.[9]

This is not as serious for the Soviets as it sounds. There is no possibility of the Polish army turning unannounced on its fraternal ally. The Russians have access to all Polish communications systems. Combat-ready Soviet divisions are also stationed in the west of the country.

And recruits are less important than regulars. Professionals make up almost half the Polish armed forces, more than two thirds of the air force and three quarters of the navy. In units with high combat capability, career soldiers outnumber draftees by two or three to one. These regulars are well insulated from civilian Poland. They have separate housing, shops, sports grounds and holiday homes. About half are said to be 'pragmatic', more interested in promotion than politics. Though a proportion of the rest are patriotic and resentful of Soviet domination, a majority assessed at 80 per cent are reckoned to be politically reliable.[10]

NATO reckons that elite units would fight 'even with distinction' in any external war. But in a purely internal confrontation with their own people, it is said that the armed forces would become a 'slate hammer' that would crumble in Jaruzelski's hand.

As long as the Russians ensure that the Polish army is handled with care, 'deployed quickly and against the Germans', it may be much more effective than the history and Russophobia of the Poles give it any reason to be.

★

The East German army was the last satellite army to be created, in 1956, and is the most reliable.* Its 6 divisions, with 2,400 tanks, would be used with large Soviet forces to attack in central and northern West Germany.

There is little evidence that it would blanch at fighting fellow Germans. 'I believe the hate cultivated (against NATO and the West German Bundeswehr) will bring results,' said a defecting officer. 'There will be shooting. Nobody in the NPA (the East German army) will say, "Those people are Germans." They will fight ... I would like to warn anyone who says, "Well, it's not going to be so bad, the NPA will think it over and won't shoot at its brothers and sisters." '[11]

The military shows absolute loyalty to the ruling Socialist Unity Party, which has recently encouraged the development of a national feeling and a sense of Prussian and German history. The goosestep is not the only part of the Prussian *Gloria* which is on display. Frederick the Great is back on his pedestal on the Unter den Linden in East Berlin.

That does not prevent the NPA from being more integrated with Soviet forces than other satellite armies.[12] The East German leadership fully backs the Soviet strategy of an offensive strike against NATO, though it announced a ten per cent cut in the defence budget, and reductions of 10,000 men and 600 tanks in 1989. Worried at its legitimacy in a divided country, it is hostile to any scenario that could see the Russians make a separate peace with the West at its expense.

Its own interests dictate that any war should be fought from the outset on West German territory. The NPA has been designated, with the Group of Soviet Forces in Germany (GSFG), as the Pact's 'first strategic echelon' since 1965. The level of subordination to the Russians is high, understandably in view of the war. East Germany has not even the technical right to control the numbers, stationing and movement of Russian troops on its soil. The supreme commander of GSFG can declare a state of emergency in the country. About eighty Soviet staff officers are present in the East German defence ministry. A Red army general is normally present at high-level NPA meetings.

Most senior officers have been on courses in Russia, normally to the Frunze Academy or the General Staff Academy. Although the NPA would fight as national units up to divisional level, the divisions would be included in a Soviet Army and efforts are being made to achieve Russian good enough to cope with combat stresses. The NPA navy is closely integrated with the Soviet Baltic fleet.

NPA officers enjoy the highest status in the satellites. Educational stan-

---

* Yazov trusts it enough to use East Germans, referred to sarcastically as the 'second Afrika Korps', as proxy troops in Africa. The Cubans are also thought of highly enough to be used as convenient surrogates in Angola, Ethiopia and Yemen and to have attempted the 1983 takeover of Grenada.

dards, pay and perks are good. Ninety-seven per cent are party members. To prevent disaffection, officers and men of 'Administration 2000' of the ministry for state security are assigned throughout the NPA. They operate a network of informers. One defector has claimed a ratio as high as one informer to each eight to ten soldiers.

Prussian military spirit thrives in East Germany. For each 10,000 citizens, 433 are members of regular or paramilitary units. In the Soviet Union itself that figure is 185. They are likely to prove loyal enough. The problem for the Russians is isolating their own men from their far more prosperous and relatively freer allies.

'If one sees how the Russian soldier lives compared to the NPA, we had it much better,' says a defecting NPA officer. 'We saw how 127 Soviet soldiers slept in one room ... Doubts and conflict have developed in the Soviet soldier's consciousness after he has seen how the NPA soldier lives in his barracks, what rights he has as a person in the army...'[13]

44

THE METAL EATERS: DEFENCE INDUSTRY

Defence rests on economic power and the Soviet system is failing. In population terms, NATO enjoys a 155:100 advantage over the Warsaw Pact. In gross national product, in terms of industrial power, that gap widens to 284:100 to NATO's advantage. Add in Australia, New Zealand, Japan, Taiwan and South Korea as likely Western allies, and give the Russians Cuba, Mongolia, Vietnam, Kampuchea and Laos. The Western population ratio improves marginally to 172:100. In industrial production, it soars to 347:100.[1]

The Russian position is deteriorating sharply in terms of industrial skills. Although they have reached strategic nuclear parity or better, the revolution in computerized 'smart' weapons is leaving Russian conventional forces at a growing technological disadvantage.

The military can argue that this means more rather than less should be spent on defence. It is defence that offsets GNP. The Japanese may have a GNP that is 85 per cent higher than the Soviet with half the population. But ultimately higher Japanese living standards and production are meaningless. They rest on imported raw materials and export markets that the Russians can cut and the Japanese cannot defend. Western Europe and the US are as dominant in world trade as Japan. From their bases on the Kola peninsula, permanently on station from Iceland to Shetland and the Faroes, Russian submarines can cut the Atlantic trade lifeline. As long as they have strategic parity or superiority, Russia remains a superpower whatever the Western industrial lead.

Light and consumer industry staggers on in an atmosphere of *skoro budet*, it'll be here soon. Slovenly manufacture worsens shoddy products. Factories start the month with ten days of *spyachka*, languid hibernation. They then accelerate into *goryachka*, a hot period before ending with a burst of *likhoradka*, a fever to fulfil production quotas.[2] It is a world of crash programmes and wild work rhythms producing refrigerators with handles that fall off, boots with laces that wear out, TV sets that slowly distintegrate as enraged viewers thump them to get them to work.

Defence industries are an absolute priority. Every Five Year Plan since the first in 1928 has placed more emphasis, if not lip service, on defence and heavy industry than on consumer goods. It is one sector of the economy that has performed brilliantly. It outperformed the Germans during the war. It has since rivalled and often outpaced the US, despite the much greater size and sophistication of the American industrial and technological base. It is a painful process, this 'Upper Volta with rockets', where a country whose output per capita is no better than thirtieth in the world competes with the US.

The cost of defence is not known. It supposedly amounts to 4.7 per cent of total spending. The CIA puts it at 13 to 16 per cent of gross national product compared with 5.5 per cent in the US. At that it is running somewhere near US levels of $250 billion a year, though taken from a far smaller economy.

Gorbachev has nevertheless made an improvement in the general economy a priority. Throughout the Khrushchev years, the Soviet growth rate was sharply higher than that of the US. War damage and a lower starting point are major factors, but the USSR managed an average 6 per cent growth a year between 1956 and 1960, compared with 2.3 per cent in the US. The first decade of the Brezhnev era, from 1965 to 1975, saw an average growth rate of nearly six per cent. The strains of defence expenditure and the lack of a vigorous consumer market then took a heavy toll. By the second half of the 1970s the Soviet economy's rate had dropped below that of the US.[3] The Brezhnev regime fell into an idle corruption, the leader himself collecting hunting trophies and Western cars, a Rolls-Royce, a Cadillac, a Citroën-Maserati.

Total consumption growth in Russia is now steadily falling. Gorbachev inherited an economy that had recorded a growth rate of 2 per cent or less for the past seven years. Compared even with the relatively sluggish American performance, the USSR invests twice as much capital in the production of each unit of GNP and uses 2.75 times as much labour.[4]

Economic growth has depended on new input, on new labour coming off the farms, the creation of new industries, new cities and new regions.

The opportunities are being exhausted. Investment is down from the traditional increase of 50 per cent in each new Five Year Plan to 32 per cent in 1976–80 and 10 per cent in 1981–5. The birth rate in the heavily industrialized western part of the country has been declining steadily.

As for existing manpower, it is dying earlier. In 1897 Tsarist Russia offered its people a life expectancy of about thirty years.[5] By the late 1950s this had improved to 68.7 years, longer than Americans who had started the century with a seventeen-year lead. Infant mortality, the highest in Europe in the 1920s, was lower than in Austria and Italy and almost the same as West Germany. Yet the life expectancy of Soviet men dropped from 67 in 1964 to 62 in 1980, the only drop ever registered in an industrial society in time of peace. Measured by the health of its people, the Soviet Union is no longer a developed nation. It is on a par with Jamaica, Mexico, Malaysia and Costa Rica. Life expectancy is now six years lower and the infant mortality rate three times higher than in Western Europe.[6] The *babushka* outlives her man by an extraordinary average of eleven years.

Oil production has been declining since 1984 for the first time since the war. Resources of raw materials are dwindling in the western part of the country and must increasingly be wrested at high expense from Siberia. The Siberian share of oil production has tripled in a decade. Siberia and the Far East now account for 88 per cent of all raw material and energy reserves.[7] Modernization of old plant is slow. The Russians are as reluctant to junk worn-out plant as they are to scrap old tanks, which, compulsively, they mothball or dig in along the Chinese border. The result is that much-needed skilled labour is soaked up in keeping obsolete machinery going.[8]

The Russians should now be an economic as well as a military super-power. Demonstrably, they are not. As the younger generation of officers realize, this will threaten the country's military status in the long run.

The problem is partly human. Take the alcohol crackdown, last attempted by Nicholas II in 1914. If the Soviet worker is really so hard-working and upright, why has Gorbachev gone to such lengths to stop him getting drunk and stealing state property? Sales of sugar were up by 11 per cent in the first year of the crackdown, a sign of the home distilling of *samogon* moonshine. Russian per capita intake of hard liquor is double the American, and city-living families spend nearly the same proportion of their income on alcohol as Americans spend on food.[9]

As to the system itself, it may work well enough on a flow chart. In practice, it is riddled with weakness. Resources are squandered in order to meet output targets for goods people do not want. Prices are rigid and only the black market reflects supply and demand. It is an old joke that, in the coming triumph of socialism, one capitalist country will have to be left. Otherwise, how could prices be fixed?

The vastness of industrial empires leads to bottlenecks in individual parts and transport. The *tolkachi*, the fixer, is a vital figure in a factory as he negotiates and makes exchanges for materials. *Blat*, influence, and the black market are as important in industrial life as in private. So is skimping on materials and creaming off the surplus. Managers and workers in an agricultural machinery plant in Cheboksary, 640 kilometres east of Moscow, set up a sauna-equipped brothel complex with stolen materials and entered it on their books as a workers' convalescent home. The railways ministry has complained that three quarters of its wagons 'are now occupied by goods and have virtually been transformed into warehouses on wheels'. Truck shortages mean that vehicles hauling vegetables in the Russian Republic had to be drafted in from the Caspian. Managers and workers are obsessed with the quantity targets on which their pay depends.

Time spent on quality and service reduces output and wages. Up to a third of the trucks coming off the assembly line at the showpiece Kama river plant are rejected and returned before leaving the factory. Cars are so poorly made that the roads are peppered with *smotrovois*, 'looking places', concrete ramps which drivers use for their own repairs. Packaging, design and market research are condemned as frivolity. With the best designers and production engineers serving the military, a country capable of producing space systems and 25,000-ton nuclear submarines is obliged to get Italian and American help in the manufacture of saloon cars and trucks.

The technology lag with the West includes new materials, robots, automated manufacture and biotechnology. The gap in computers and telecommunications is enormous. The US has 80 phone lines per 100 of population, the Soviet Union perhaps 10, and the quality of the lines is so poor that data transmission is often impossible. There are more than 25 million home computers in the US. The Poles, with perhaps half a million privately owned Ataris, Commodores and Sinclairs, are better off than the Russians. With large and mainframe computers, the Russians have at most one tenth of the US capacity. Their mainframes are mainly copies of the US technology of the early 1970s, IBM 370s and Digital Equipment PDP 11s. It was not until 1973 that the Soviet-made Minsk machines had disc units and could support multi-programming and remote processing. Minsk M-20 and M-222 machines, the backbone of military computer servicing, are being replaced by Ryad ES-1020 machines, comparable with the IBM 360/30. The Soviets are dependent on East German and Czech developments of the Ryad. Having a home market where consumers are grateful to grab what they can means that there is little incentive to make products that tempt sophisticated export customers. The huge photographic industry produces over three million cameras a year for a world market that does not want them.

Reform of the system upsets the millions who have snuggled deep into its featherbedded and uncompetitive heart. And the system may prove itself to be unreformable. How can initiative and enterprise be rewarded without diminishing political control? Independence of mind is both vital and a threat.

Gorbachev is obliged to try. If the Soviet Union fails to make contact with high-technology mass production, it will drift further into an industrial limbo where ever-higher military demands are placed on a weakening economy. What is the use of being the world's largest maker of titanium if, because of the backwardness of civilian industry, its sole destination is submarine hulls?

Resentment at defence cuts goes further than the military. The defence industry has up to seven million direct employees. There are 134 major final assembly plants and shipyards turning out missiles, aircraft, armour, ships, weapons and ammunition and a similar number producing combat support equipment such as radar, trucks and communications gear. These are supported in turn by 3,500 or so component manufacturers.

The main plants are run by ministries on the same lines as Stalin's original Commissariat of Heavy Industry. New ministries have been added to keep up with technological change but there are still some weirdly broad briefs. The General Machine Building Ministry is responsible for strategic missiles and space rockets – as well as refrigerators and combine harvesters. The so-called Medium Machine Building Ministry makes nuclear warheads. The Radio Industry Ministry turns out TV sets and electronic counter-measure pods. The Aviation Ministry manufactures Raketa vacuum cleaners and children's prams.

Managers and workers are used to continual expansion and job security. Major weapons plants have nearly doubled in size since 1970. The Severodvinsk shipyard near Archangel, the world's largest submarine yard, has increased in size by 80 per cent in the past two decades and is only one of five similar yards. A large and brand-new aircraft plant has been completed at Ulyanovsk, south-east of Gorki. The main tank plant at Nizhniy Tagil, which can produce twice the total of 940 main battle tanks in the British army in a year, is supported by other works in Kharkov, Omsk and Chelyabinsk. Artillery production provides thousands of jobs in Sverdlovsk and Perm, helicopters fuel the wages in Kazan, Ulan Ude, Arsenyev and Rostov. Missile systems are produced in Moscow, Leningrad, Sverdlovsk, Kirov and Kovrov, the new Blackjack bomber at Kazan, fighters in Gorki, Tbilisi and Komsomolsk.[10]

The development of new weapons involves a further 550,000 or more of the 900,000 Russian scientists and engineers employed in research and development. Pay is higher than in civilian work and housing is better, though it may be in a place as bleak and remote as Novaya Zemlya in the Barents Sea. Assured growth has become a habit. The major research, design and test facilities employed in designing new military aircraft, missile and space systems have grown by at least 30 per cent in the past ten years.[11] The Tupolev Design Bureau, responsible for the Blackjack bomber, has doubled in size in the last decade.

Featherbedding is endemic. Under Stalin, designers who failed to produce acceptable aircraft risked being shot and their bureaux closed. The design bureaux, powerful and semi-autonomous baronies, are now comfortably protected against competition and cutbacks. A precedent was set in 1955, when a Sukhoi interceptor which was clearly inferior to the MiG-21 was converted to a ground-attack role instead of being junked.[12] The bureaux and the aircraft plants have thrived as a result. They produce no less than eight air defence interceptors, the MiG-25 Foxbat, the Su-15 Flagon, the Su-27 Flanker, the Tu-128 Fiddler, the YaK-28 Firebar, the MiG-23 Flogger, the MiG-29 Fulcrum and the MiG-31 Foxhound. The US makes do with three.[13]

The great aircraft bureaux have become family enterprises in their maturity. Alexander Yakolev's son Sergei is now responsible for his late father's YaK trademark. Andrei Tupolev's son runs the Tu Bureau. Although no direct descendant of Mikoyan or Gurevich has inherited the MiG Bureau, it passed to the veteran house engineer R. A. Belyakov.[14]

The same comfortable traditions have been nourished by the missile design bureaux. An easy *modus vivendi* has grown up between the two major 'competitors', the Yangel and Chelomei Bureaux. M. K. Yangel was given his own bureau after working as a deputy of S. P. Korolev, the first post-war rocket designer. V. N. Chelomei was originally a naval missile designer.[15] The SS-19, an 11,000-kilometre-range missile with six MIRVed warheads, was developed successfully by the Chelomei Bureax and went into series production in 1974. Yangel's competing SS-17 has a slightly smaller range and carries only four MIRVed warheads. It also went into production although its inferiority is marked enough for its numbers to be less than half those of the SS-19.

As with interceptors, so there is grotesque duplication in ICBMs. The Americans have three types, the Minuteman II and III and the MX. The Russians have seven, the SS-11, 13, 17, 18, and 19 and the new SS-X-24 and 25. One of these, the solid-fuelled SS-13 of the V. N. Nadiradize Bureau, created such problems that only sixty are deployed. Most Soviet ICBMs have had liquid fuel motors developed by V. P. Glushko's Bureau. The Americans have two submarine-launched ballistic missiles, Poseidon and Trident. The Russians have six. The Americans make do with four surface-to-air missiles to the Russians' twelve.

The defence industry is protected from competitive and civilian pressure.

There are few civilian defence analysts, though Gorbachev has introduced
some, no public incensed by cost overruns. It has to compete with the
West from a much lower technological base and that comes expensive.*

Secrecy is obsessive and squanders resources through duplication and
lack of cross-fertility. Engineer-Admiral Berg, the prime mover in Russian
radar, complained that: 'We are stuck fast in secrecy like a fly in treacle.'
The KGB has a 'First Department' in all defence plants and research and
design bureaux. Its control is not as complete as it was in the bureau-
prisons run by Beria but it remains pervasive. The KGB checks on all
employees and its distrust of Jews means that this highly educated group
are rarely trusted to work directly in defence. It controls access to all
classified information.[16] Twin typing pools, with separate staffs and filing
for secret and non-secret work, twin libraries where the most readily
available Western scientific magazines are restricted to those with the right
grade of security clearance, KGB control over the most basic swapping of
information between different researchers, seriously impede the R and D
effort.

Secrecy is, of course, very convenient for the industry and the Party.
Khrushchev was well aware of this. 'Because the production of defence
industry enterprises is secret, shortcomings [are] closed to criticism,' he
said.[17]

Gorbachev has redeployed some top defence industry personnel to draw
on their skills. Prime Minister Nikolai Ryzkhov and the planning director
Nikolai Talyzin started their careers in the defence industry. Ryzkhov has
filled the council of ministers' staff with defence industry managers from
Sverdlovsk, a hub of the industrial-military complex. The intent is to
duplicate the efficiency and high growth of military industry in the civilian
sector.

Gorbachev may find it as difficult as Khrushchev to succeed. Both the
military and its suppliers are wedded to the old concept of pre-emptive,
offensive warfare. It is doubtful that Gorbachev has any objections to the
offensive doctrine in principle. It is simply that this comes expensive in
men and machines. With strategic nuclear parity achieved by Brezhnev,
it is also unnecessary.

It would be entirely sensible and practical for him to concentrate minds

* The Russians have been reckoned superior in technology to the US in surface-to-
air missiles, ballistic missile defence, infantry combat vehicles, and chemical and mine
warfare. The US has a lead in submarine-launched and cruise missiles, bombers,
fighters, air-to-air missiles, 'Smart' bombs, naval air power, amphibious assault, anti-
submarine warfare, surveillance and early warning. There is reckoned to be parity in
ICBMs, nuclear submarines, tanks, artillery, anti-tank missiles, attack helicopters,
theatre ballistic missiles, surface ships, communications, command and control and
electronic countermeasures. US Department of Defense assessment, qu. Holloway, op.
cit., pp. 138–9.

on reforming the system, and resources on improving industrial efficiency, at the expense of reducing the present wasteful edge in offensive capability. This assumes, of course, that the Russians do not intend using that edge over the powerful industrial nations of the West. They could cut levels considerably and still be in a comfortable position to apply overwhelming force in the areas where they have used it since the war, against their fraternal socialists in Eastern Europe and against ill-equipped anti-communists in the Third World. A shift to a more defensive position would allow Gorbachev to cut regular troop strengths and weapons levels. A hint of this came in 1987, when the CoGS, Marshal Sergei Akhromeyev, said that 'the defensive nature of the Soviet military doctrine' entails 'the reduction of military potentials to limits that are adequate and necessary for defence'.[18]

No such defensive doctrine has yet emerged. 'There has been a lot of talk about it,' General Hans Henning von Standrart, chief of Allied Forces in Central Europe, said three and a half years after Gorbachev came to power.* 'What interests us is capability and there has been no change in numbers, in structures and training.' He noted that the clearest improvement had been in the 'capability for deep thrusts', for more attack, not less.

When the Kremlin does insist on defensive strategy, it is likely to get a rough ride. Both the defence industry and their military customers are sensitive to their status. Though Gorbachev has placed his own Lev Zaikov as overseer of the defence industry, and Yazov as defence minister, he still faces formidable resistance to cuts. The prospect of major arms initiatives, such as dismantling rocketry in Europe, may make grudging sense to the military mind but not to its heart. It will argue that US development in 'smart' weapons and the Star Wars initiative prove the case for more spending, not less. Streamlining and reform involve unpopular cuts in manning and perks.

Marshal Viktor Kulikov, the Warsaw Pact C-in-C, admitted that the military has dragged its boots in response to Gorbachev's call for modernization. His own reluctance was expected to be a reason for his replacement. 'The process of restructuring is taking place slowly,' he said. 'The forces of inertia are making themselves felt.' The inertia that a body as vast as the Red armed forces can drum up is mighty indeed.

* *Le Monde*, 24 November 1988.

45

THE RIVAL GENERAL: SECRETARY GORBACHEV

The Kremlin is close to the Frunskaya Embankment, a few minutes in an official limousine or, as the passengers in the Zils know too well, a few seconds in a Cessna 172. The physical fear of the Kremlin that was rampant under Stalin, and the economic fear of cutbacks that surfaced under Khrushchev, were lulled by the benign and high-spending torpor of Brezhnev. They were already reviving by the time Mathias Rust, a nineteen-year-old West German computer operator, landed his Cessna by the Kremlin Wall on a May evening in 1987. Rust had flown the single-engined aircraft through 650 kilometres of Soviet airspace from Helsinki.

It was a prank to the West. To Gorbachev and the Politburo, it was a 'major dereliction of duty in the guidance of forces by the Ministry of Defence'. The Frunskaya Embankment had exposed itself to the wrath and discipline of the first general secretary not to have taken part in the war.[1] The party secretary, as Yazov well knows, outranks any marshal.

Young Rust navigated the hierarchy into trouble with maximum aplomb. His flight path from the Baltic took him across the two most heavily protected of the ten PVO Strany air defence districts in the country. His timing was wicked. For a decade, the military had been demanding air defence systems to counter low-altitude intruders. By 1987, at vast expense, they had got them. Su-27 Flanker and Mig-29 Fulcrum interceptors with look down/shoot down capabilities were operational to deal with low-flying targets. Two new air-to-air missiles, the AA-9 carried by Foxhound interceptors and the AA-10 for Fulcrum and Flanker, also waited for Rust.

He flew low enough to see the famous green caps of the KGB border guards. Indeed, he chose Border Guard Day to make his flight, but the first KGB troops he met were wearing the royal blue flashes of the special Kremlin Guard and were stationed in Red Square. The square itself made a handy landing ground for the young German. It is large, though not completely flat, falling away to the south-east towards the river. The one-ton red stars atop the Kremlin towers are useful landing aids. Mounted on ball-bearing mechanisms, they move into the wind like windsocks.

The flight was a ghastly embarrassment to the Soviet military and a providential excuse for Gorbachev. What if a US army private had stolen a helicopter in 1974 and landed it on the South Lawn of the White House? Rust had parked his Cessna with its nose towards the holy of holies, the western wall of the Kremlin with urns with the ashes of Soviet statesmen and the black and dark red marble of the Lenin Mausoleum. To get there, his $75,000 plane had cocked a snook at perhaps 20 billion roubles' worth of low-altitude hardware. It had circled over the training college of the Strategic Rocket Forces, one of the most sensitive academies in the world, near the bulk of the Rossiya Hotel before making its final approach over the British embassy.

Gorbachev took immediate advantage of Rust to impose his own man on the Frunskaya Embankment and to deal a blow to the Brezhnev generation. He fired the defence minister, Marshal Sergei Sokolov. Marshal of Aviation Alexander Koldunov, the head of PVO Strany and a survivor of the shooting down of a Korean Jumbo jet in 1983, also went. The seventy-five-year-old Sokolov was replaced by General Dmitry Yazov, one of the most junior four-star generals in the Red army and a man who had finished the war as a humble deputy company commander. General Ivan Tretyak took over air defence.

It was bad luck that Koldunov should go, for he bore no close responsibility. His sacking showed clearly that the military have a formidable and wilful contender in Gorbachev.

Mikhail Sergeevich Gorbachev was born, an ethnic Russian in an area where Catherine the Great first established a Governorship in 1785, on 2 March 1931 in the village of Privolnoye in the Caucasus.[2] He was fourteen when the Red flag was raised on the Reichstag and he was still a student when Stalin died. He is the first Soviet leader whose baggage train is free of wartime service and guilt over the purge.[3]

His Soviet bloodline is highly respectable. Both his grandfather Andrei and father Sergei were peasants and party members. Andrei was involved in setting up the local collective farm. Collectivization was notably brutal in the north Caucasus, with the NKVD commander, General Frinovsky, reporting in 1930 that the rivers were carrying thousands of bodies to the sea. Resistance was strong enough for Stalin to appoint a special commission to crush it. The Germans briefly overran the Stavropol area in the 1942 Caucasus campaign. The boy first worked on a combine harvester, like his father, in the grain and sunflower fields round his village. He distinguished himself at school and in the Komsomol youth movement. At 19, he was one of the rare country boys to be awarded a place at Lomonosov State University in Moscow, the first Soviet leader to have gone to University since Lenin.

The train ride a thousand miles to the north made a deep impression on him. 'I travelled through Stalingrad, which had been destroyed, through Voronezh, which had been destroyed. Rostov was destroyed ... I saw it all. The whole country was in ruins,' he said later.[4] He read law, a subject that took most of his fellow students into the KGB or the State prosecuting administration, a service debased by Vyshinsky's tenure as prosecutor general. Gorbachev appears as unaffected by this as by the dark miseries of collectivisation, which he described in 1987 as 'basically correct'.

His fellow student at Moscow, the Czech Zdenek Mlynar,[5] recalled the young Gorbachev as highly intelligent, honest, pragmatic and assured but not arrogant. Dealing with hostile questioning he remains confident and fluent. When tackled on human rights abuses, however, an edge of anger can match the red birthmark on his brow. Seated at a conference, he is a formidable and sophisticated figure, hands expressive and forceful. Put him in the bureaucrat's street clothes, the overcoat and the grey felt hat, and he looks shorter and bulkier and more recognizably the traditional party boss.

He joined the Party in 1952. Two years later, he married Raisa Titorenko, a pert and auburn-haired philosophy student. They spent their wedding night in his room in the crowded Stromynka student hostel, which his room-mates temporarily vacated. He graduated with distinction in 1955.

Returning to the Caucasus, he became secretary of the Komsomol Communist Youth movement in Stavropol in 1956, the year of the Secret Speech and the Hungarian Autumn. He switched to the Party proper in 1962 in the management of agriculture in the Stavropol Region. In 1966 he became first secretary for the city of Stavropol and in 1971 provincial party chief. His green-painted house was opposite the local KGB head-quarters in Dzerzhinsky Street in Stavropol. There were several health resorts in his region. The mountain spa at Kislovodsk was visited by Kosygin and Andropov and other senior figures who sped his career.

In 1978 he returned to Moscow after twenty-three years to become Central Committee secretary for agriculture. By 1980, in an extraordinarily rapid rise, he became a full Politburo member before his fiftieth birthday. At the time, the average age of Politburo members was seventy. The promotions had little to do with his performance at agriculture. Though he inherited a record harvest of 230 million tons of grain in 1978, that fell to 179 million tons the following year and was so disastrous in 1981 that the figure was classified secret. US estimates put it at 155 million tons.

Gorbachev consolidated his position under Andropov, acting as a liaison man between the ailing leader in his Kuntsevo hospital rooms and the Kremlin. Andropov was Gorbachev's sponsor and the military have no reason to remember the former KGB chief with any affection. As the KGB rose in influence, the privileged days enjoyed under Brezhnev began to darken. Andropov's anti-corruption drive caught up the military. Two generals were found by police in a Turkish bath during duty hours. General Nikolai Shcholokov, Brezhnev's interior minister, was sacked for corruption and later stripped of his military ranks.[6] No general rose in the political hierarchy.

The shooting down of the Korean jumbo jet on its evocatively numbered Flight 007 in the seas off Sakhalin on 31 August 1983 was a humiliation. The CoGS, Marshal Nikolai Ogarkov, was forced to explain the action at the first press conference given by anyone in that position since Tukhachevsky. It showed up weaknesses in air defence and in crisis management. The sick Andropov, returning to Moscow from a spa in the Caucasus, gave the military grudging cover and Koldunov kept his job as C-in-C of PVO Strany. Andropov used the incident to keep them under tighter control.*

Marshal Ogarkov was fired a year later, partly to ensure that so inde-

---

* The Korean pilot strayed north of his track on a flight from Anchorage to Seoul. This took him into highly sensitive Soviet airspace. He overflew the tip of the Kamchatka peninsula, which has a nuclear submarine base at Petrapavlovsk, a long-range air base and two missile sites, all presumed targets for US pre-emptive nuclear strikes. He then continued over the Sea of Okhotsk to Sakhalin with its Korsakov naval base and five military airfields. The airliner was in this dangerous airspace, apparently unwittingly, for over two hours. The decision to shoot it down involved a chain running from the local air defence commander and the head of the Far East regional command in Chita, General Vladimir Govorov, to Air Marshal Koldunov, as the commander of air defence, in Moscow. The ultimate sanction to use missiles was probably taken by the C-in-C of the air force, Marshal Pavel Kutakhov. At sixty-nine, age may have been a factor in Kutakhov's apparent bungling of a snap decision involving supersonic fighter aircraft and the fast-moving Korean jumbo jet. The airliner was not forced to land but shot down, with the loss of 269 lives, shortly before it would have left Soviet airspace.

The dialogue of the Russian interceptor pilot (flying an Su-15 in some reports, a MiG-23 in others) shows no hesitation. At 18.21 and 24 seconds GMT he told his ground controller on Sakhalin: 'I'm approaching the target, I'm going in closer.' It was at night and he reported ten seconds later: 'The target's light is blinking. I have already approached the target to a distance of about two kilometres.' A minute later, he complained: 'How can I chase it? I'm already abeam of the target.' At 18.23 plus 37 seconds his flight profile had improved: 'I'm dropping back, now I will try a rocket...' He had it picked up at 18.24 plus 22: 'Roger. I am in lock-on.' He came in for the kill at 18.26 plus 11: 'I am closing on the target, am in lock-on. Distance to target is eight [kilometres].' He had armed his missiles by 18.25 plus 18: 'I have already switched on.' At 18.25 plus 46 he reported: 'ZG.' His missile warheads were locked on to the big Boeing. At 18.26 plus 20 the fire buttons were punched: 'I have executed the launch.' Two seconds later, at 18.26 plus 22 he reported: 'The target is destroyed.' Five seconds later he broke off the attack.

This was more complex than the brutal and efficient destruction of an innocent stray. It is still uncertain whether the Korean airliner was ever identified as such, or whether it was confused with a US Air Force RC-135 reconnaissance aircraft which had been on a routine intelligence mission (or spy flight, depending on one's loyalties) in the area from its base in the Aleutians. Neither is it known why the Korean pilot, Captain Chung Byong-in, was so far off course, nor whether the Soviet decision to fire was

pendent a military man should not succeed the ageing Dmitri Ustinov as defence minister. Ogarkov had also complained publicly at modest cutbacks in military budgets and had called for increased spending on conventional weapons. His dismissal was the most dramatic humbling of a senior military figure since Khruschev sacked Zhukov, and Gorbachev was widely felt to be behind it.[7]

Gorbachev narrowly missed out on the supreme prize when Andropov died in February 1984. The ageing conservative Chernenko, already half dead with emphysema, became general secretary of the Party. He represented a return to calm and corruption against the reforms and rigorous morality of Andropov and his crown prince Gorbachev.

Chernenko died on 10 March 1985. Gorbachev started with a gesture designed to show his independence of the forces' Old Guard. He gave the address at Chernenko's funeral, his first public speech as general secretary, without having the traditional senior officer at his side. After Ustinov died at seventy-six in December 1984, Gorbachev ensured that the grey and uninfluential Marshal Sergei Sokolov should succeed him as defence minister.

He showed rapidly that he could deal with rivals. Within months of his accession, Grigori Romanov, his main contestant for the leadership, had been pensioned off. Romanov had been secretary for the defence industry, a hawk, a high arms expenditure man and a friend of the military. Shortly after Romanov had been retired 'for health reasons' in July 1985 Gorbachev started weeding out the elderly and more resentful figures of the Brezhnev era. The Supreme Commander of the GSFG, General Mikhail Zaitsev, and his senior political officer were ordered back to Moscow from East Germany. General Lizichev, a man of Gorbachev's own generation and the former political commissar with GSFG, replaced seventy-seven-year-old General Yepishev as the Red army's political overseer at the Main Political Directorate.[8] Yepishev had held the post since 1962. Gorbachev also changed the heads of the two most important missile commands.

Marshal of Artillery Vladimir Tolubko, a seventy-one-year-old, was replaced as head of the Strategic Rocket Forces by a protégé of Andropov and Gorbachev, Yuri Maximov.[9] At the end of the year, without expla-

---

bungled somewhere in the system between Sakhalin and Moscow. The Korean crew should certainly have been aware of the danger of straying into Soviet airspace. A Korean Boeing 707 airliner on a flight from Paris to Seoul wandered 1,600 kilometres off course in 1978. It overflew important naval installations around Murmansk before a Russian interceptor fired on it, forcing it to crash land on a frozen lake.

It is easy to see the frustration felt by the Russians over both the KAL and the Rust flights. 'You criticize us for shooting down a plane, and now you criticize us for not shooting down a plane,' said the foreign ministry spokesman Gennady Gerasimov after the Cessna had landed.

nation, a brief paragraph in *Red Star* reported that the C-in-C of the Soviet Navy, Admiral V. N. Chernavin, had left on a visit to Tunisia. The previous C-in-C, Admiral Sergei Gorshkov, the creator of modern Russian naval power with its huge new surface fleet and 150 nuclear submarines, had been sacked without a line of praise or thanks.[10] The emergence of the Soviet Union as an oceanic power has been one of the most important strategic events since the war, and Gorshkov had presided over it for twenty-nine years.

Gorbachev's protégé, Vladimir Chernavin, was at fifty-seven almost twenty years younger than his predecessor. He typifies the younger breed of officer Gorbachev is trying to promote.[11] A driving and respected man, Chernavin is an experienced submariner. He was given command of one of the first Russian nuclear submarines and in 1962 became the first commander to launch a missile whilst submerged. A pioneer of navigation under ice, he was awarded the Order of Lenin for his part as a staff officer in the first submerged circumnavigation of the globe by a detachment of Soviet submarines. He is politically sound. He joined the Party in 1949 and was later a deputy to the Supreme Soviet.

Yazov was a virtual unknown when he was appointed as defence minister in June 1987, a snub by Gorbachev to the whole Brezhnev generation of military leaders. Yazov is a former infantryman and commander of the Far Eastern military district, where previous army high-fliers have been tank men like Sokolov with experience in Eastern Europe. He caught Gorbachev's eye on a visit to Khabarovsk. Gorbachev asked him about discipline in his command. Instead of the normal cover-up, Yazov said that it had not improved and in some cases had got worse.

This *glasnost* frankness impressed Gorbachev, who brought Yazov to Moscow as deputy minister for personnel. *Red Star* suggested that Yazov's commitment to Gorbachev's modernization and *perestroika*, restructuring, was also a motive. Gorbachev is impatient with military resistance to change. It is natural that a new leader should wish to be done with the old. Yet he inherited from Brezhnev nuclear parity with the US, conventional superiority, global logistics reach and a new source of power in the blue-water navy. Gorbachev's easy confidence in world affairs rests on the Brezhnev build-up of strength. His lack of gratitude is worrying to the military.

So is the way in which he has lived up elsewhere to his reputation as a 'man with a nice smile and iron teeth'. That description comes from Andrei Gromyko, the veteran foreign minister whom Gorbachev kicked upstairs as head of state. In October 1988, Gorbachev strengthened his position by downgrading Gromyko and two other key figures leery of liberalism, the KGB chief Viktor Chebrikov and the party ideologist, Yegor Ligachev. Chebrikov's replacement by General Vladimir Kryuchkov, a former KGB station head in New York, meant that Gorbachev had succeeded in imposing his own man on both the military and the KGB.

Gorbachev is young and the military remains dominated by old men. Yazov himself is sixty-three. An officer can be a major before he is thirty and a lieutenant colonel at forty. After this initial burst of fast motoring, he hits a tailback. All marshals and generals of the army are exempt from age limits for retirement. Where the Zhukovs and Rokossovskys were marshals in their forties, most are now in their seventies. Any general or colonel can remain in the service for ten years beyond retirement age if his superiors recommend it.[12]

These veterans, who had settled down so comfortably under Brezhnev to enjoy their dachas and Black Sea vacations, and who believe as an article of faith that only a continuing and massive defence effort will prevent a second *Barbarossa*, are suspicious and wary of their rival general, the secretary. They had been used to dealing with old men to whom progress was a new submarine or missile and who stumped up funds at a hint of US superiority. Gorbachev has committed himself to cut the defence budget by 14.2 per cent, and the production of arms and military technology by 20 per cent, from 1990.

The struggle between consumer industry and arms spending continues. There is a limit to the number of officers Gorbachev can place in key posts. Cuts in defence spending are not welcome to veteran marshals such as Vassily Petrov, the deputy defence minister. During celebrations of the fortieth anniversary of VE Day, Gorbachev was at pains to stress that the younger generation did not believe that war was 'fatally inevitable'. He told assembled wartime veterans rather pointedly that it was up to them to pass on their experience to 'the new generation'. The people wanted: 'Order at home and peace abroad'. Peace not at the forefront of his mind, Petrov remarked grumpily that American imperialists were wrong if they hoped that Star Wars would give them world hegemony. The last imperialists to try that, the Nazis, had been defeated by socialism. The war had 'proved the superiority of the Soviet system'.[13] It is unlikely that Petrov and his group consider that anything has subsequently gone wrong with the system that some more defence spending will not fix.

Gorbachev has built a powerful position in the National Defence Council. Of its military members, Chernavin and Maximov owe him their support. The prime minister, Nikolai Ryzkhov, is a former director of the Uralmash heavy industry complex which is central to the defence industry.[14] He is the second youngest member of the Politburo, after Gorbachev himself, though he has close links with the military. The deputy prime ministers appointed to help him in economic reform all have backgrounds in the defence industry. It shows the premium put on defence efficiency penetrating the civilian economy.

He also has support to mine from younger officers. Blocked for promotion whilst in their professional prime, they have no reason to feel sentimental about Brezhnev. They have much to hope for from Gorbachev and his protégés like Moiseyev, only fifty when appointed, and General Vladimir Lobov, who was given the sensitive task of convincing officers that they would suffer 'neither materially nor spiritually' from the cuts. Not all were convinced. 'It must be said openly: It is difficult to adjust psychologically to such a reduction,' warned a Guards lieutenant in a letter to *Red Star*.

In peace, Gorbachev is at risk mainly to the elite, to the many, senior officers included, who feel that *glasnost* and accommodation with the West threaten the system. Nevertheless the self-fear shown by the KGB appears to justify Western hopes that the Soviet Union, splitting into its constituent nationalities under the strain of war, would only command the full-blooded loyalty of ethnic Russians. In theory, the empire is vulnerable. To the west are Latvians, Estonians and Lithuanians, who still bitterly resent their forced inclusion into the Soviet Union after the Ribbentrop–Molotov pact. Anti-Russian demonstrations were held in all three Baltic republics in 1987 and 1988. Along the underbelly with Turkey and Iran, racial clashes between Christians and Moslems broke out early in 1988 in Armenia and Azerbaijan, two of the Caucasus republics which enjoyed a brief independence during the civil war. The Moslem population in Central Asia, above Afghanistan, is growing rapidly and may take religious heart from the Soviet defeat to the south. Crimean Tartars exiled under Stalin demanded the right to return to their homeland in demonstrations in Moscow in 1987 and again in Uzbekistan, the site of their exile, the following year.

Both *perestroika* and *glasnost* are appealing to minorities who want to weaken Moscow's central grip. Gorbachev, no expert on minorities, is highly vulnerable to accusations that he is unleashing a whirlwind. There are nationalities whose sense of *Rodina*, the motherland, does not embrace the Soviet Union. Gorbachev has pointedly hailed 'Soviet patriotism' and slammed 'nationalism', 'chauvinism' and 'attempts at self-isolation'.

Many Jews are openly disaffected and seek to emigrate. Gorbachev has whittled away at Brezhnev's corrupt and easygoing system of running distant republics as satraps, where local party figures could dole out patronage and get prestigious jobs in Moscow. Those with their snouts deepest in the trough have been fired and replaced by Gorbachev's men, most of them ethnic Russians. No Asian now sits on the Politburo.

Huge demonstrations have been held in Yerevan, the capital of Armenia, to demand the return of an Armenian-dominated slice of the Azerbaijan republic to Armenia. Vicious riots in Sumgait, a town forty kilometres north of the Azerbaijan capital of Baku, left thirty-one Armenians dead and showed that old and pre-revolution hatreds between Christians and Moslems are no longer dormant. Moscow blamed them on 'a group of hooligan elements ... wavering, immature people who fell under the influence of false rumours'. They go deeper than that. But they did not involve specific anti-Russian feeling, and Muslim fundamentalism has shown no real sign of crossing the border from Iran, much of which is anyway sanitized by the waters of the Caspian.

The Balts have little love for the Russians. The ghosts of their independence live on in the present republics. In 1938 thirty consuls-general were accredited on the Riga diplomatic list.[15] Though today half the population of Latvia is ethnic Russian, Soviet hegemony is now being questioned on the Baltic, the most European and vulnerable edge of the empire.

Another area of potentially critical doubt is the Ukraine. It is one of the richest parts of the country. It has 50 million people. One in every five Red army men is a Ukrainian and Ukrainians are the biggest power factor in the Soviet Union after ethnic Russians. It had a brief independence during the chaos of the revolution and the Polish war. Ukrainian independence was proclaimed in Lvov immediately after *Barbarossa* and a provisional Ukrainian government was formed under Yaraslav Stetsko. The Red army had to put down nationalist revolts after the end of the war by force. It has been relatively docile since then, but it is a place on which the most hawkish eye is kept.

Violent disaffection with the system and its symbols is rare. There may have been an attempt to assassinate Khrushchev in Minsk in 1962.[16] An attempt was certainly made on Brezhnev by Anatoly Iline, a twenty-two-year-old lieutenant in a Leningrad regiment, on 22 January 1969. Brezhnev was returning on a bitterly cold morning from greeting the cosmonauts of Soyuz 4 and 5, who had returned from the first space link-up. As the cortege of official cars entered the Kremlin through the Borovitskaya Gate, Iline opened fire with an automatic weapon. He killed a driver but Brezhnev was untouched. Iline was sent to a psychiatric hospital in Kazan, where he may still be held. Another attempt may have been made on Brezhnev in Tashkent in 1982.

Some terrorism against the *nomenklatura* has been reported on the fringes of empire, amid the black markets and corruption of Georgia and in the wastes of Kirghistan on the Chinese border. General Arif Gueidarov, the head of the KGB and interior minister in Azerbaijan, was murdered along with his vice-minister in Baku in 1978. The gunman, a prison administrator, then committed suicide. Sultan Ibragimov, president of the council of ministers in Kirghistan, was assassinated in 1980.

About twenty-five hijacks are known to have been attempted. In one, eleven Jews were betrayed to the KGB before they could take over an aircraft to fly to Sweden.[17] At least five Georgians have succeeded in hijacking Aeroflot aircraft to Turkey. A further nine, six boys and three girls, were not so fortunate when they tried to commandeer a Tu-134 airliner on a flight from Tbilisi to Batum in November 1983. The co-pilot and a hostess were killed in a gunbattle, but the aircraft returned to Tbilisi and was stormed by a KGB assault squad. Four of the surviving hijackers were executed, including a former priest, two young doctors and the son of a famous Georgian film director. Other hijackers more recently returned from Israel.

In one reported terrorist attack, a bomb placed in a Moscow metro carriage in 1977 caused a fire which killed seven people. Tass eventually announced that three dissident Armenians had been shot for the bombing. A crude car bomb exploded outside the Lubianka in 1981, though not with enough force to do the KGB headquarters staff any harm. Home-made devices have been set outside Lenin's Mausoleum and in the huge Rossiya hotel. A dissident protesting against the country's 'military psychosis' set a small charge outside a recruiting centre in Kubyshev before a court found that it was he who was suffering from psychosis and ordered his detention in a lunatic asylum.

The Gulags themselves have sometimes been restless. Revolts behind the wire took place in camps at Solikamsk in the Urals, Erevan in Armenia and at Praveniskis in Lithuania in 1981.

Most cases are not reported, so this may be the tip of an iceberg of terrorism and dissent. It is, nevertheless, an extremely small tip of what is by any standards a very small iceberg. No major Western country, suffering the attentions of the IRA, Action Directe, the Red Brigades, assorted Palestinians, the murders and attempted murders of presidents and prime ministers, violent confrontations between police and demonstrators, has got off so lightly.

In his flat outside Moscow, a dissident asked me to guess how many like him there were in the Soviet Union. About as many as there are Poles who support the regime, I replied. 'Nonsense, nonsense!' he cried. 'There could be six, seven per cent of Poles who support it. Here, it is *one per cent* who are against. You may find *little concentrations* that are higher. Like the camps, like *certain people* in *Leningrad* who feel themselves *superior*, or some *Christians*, and more *Jews*, like me, who feel themselves *different*. But I am a mathematician. I know how to *average out. One per cent*, I tell you.'

He had been waiting for seven years for an exit visa and depression may have clouded his calculation. But to claim that the Soviet Union has serious fault lines that could crack it, that the nationalities are as ripe for exploitation now as they could have been for the Germans in 1941, is still to play with straws. War would only add to the sense of cohesion.

The wellspring of his dissidence is Judaism. Religion is perhaps the deepest threat to the Soviet state. Communism is confident that it can deal with capitalism, at least on the ideological basis. That is simple system against system. If the Soviet system is in trouble, it is always possible to whistle up a New Economic Policy or some restructuring.

Religion is persistent despite the onslaught against it. Research by experts in 'scientific atheism' in Kiev admits that at least 20 per cent of the population are believers. About half the children born in the countryside are baptized. Of 222 graves dug in the southern cemetery of Leningrad in one period, 132 are marked with a cross, 73 have no marking and just 17 have a Red Star.

The Orthodox Church has proved malleable enough to the new Tsars in the Kremlin. Other Churches are more vigorous in their opposition. The Ukrainian Catholic Church, its members known as Uniates, was outlawed in 1946 and forcibly incorporated into the Orthodox Church. The ban was justified by the alleged collaboration of priests with the Nazis. There are some five million Uniates and the KGB cracks down on them hard. The leading dissident Oleksy Tykhy died in labour camp in 1984 and another, Valery Marchenko, died after a gruelling political trial. Uniates often refuse to serve in the Red army. A clandestine *samizdat*, the Chronicles of the Catholic Church in the Ukraine, reports that one labour camp has 300 Uniates and 90 others from smaller sects such as Jehovah's Witnesses and Baptists serving hard labour for refusing the draft. In 1984 a group of 920 Christians in the western Ukraine renounced their citizenship by burning their identification papers.

Islam is similarly feared. Seven years' hard labour has become the norm for the illegal publication of Islamic books. In one case in 1985 hard labour was given to a group who had published religious tracts using the print workshop of the Azerbaijan Ministry of Oil Machinery.

There is a real fear of religion by the Party. But it is a long-term worry for Gorbachev. A loyal people can, for the moment at least, be fed into any scenario for war he may have, or that may be forced upon him.

Future War

46

VOYNA

Voyna is a sad and keening word. *War* is half horror and half martial glory. It needs definition, civil war, Vietnam war, Falklands war, to decide its bias. *Krieg* is a shellburst, an absolute that can be won. The victory *Sieg* goes with *Krieg*. *Voyna* contains an infinity of suffering. A man cannot have a good *Voyna*, as he can have a 'good war'.

Perhaps that is why the Russians treat the idea of their causing a war with such incredulous and genuine contempt. They have too much to lose. Their desire for peace shows in their very vocabulary. Only a German could relish a war. Only an English-speaker could take it, pragmatically, as it comes. If war was words, the Russians would never start one.

As matters and more particularly armies stand, however, it is the Russians who have an offensive doctrine for conventional war and the means to see it through. The NATO posture is of necessity defensive. Soviet military philosophy is offensive. The concept of deterrence has 'never held much appeal'.[1] Deterrence does not lead to victory and victory is the only political objective of war. Victory is the survival of Russia, the occupation of Western Europe and the dominance of Soviet socialism in the world. It is achieved through pre-emptive strikes, to minimize damage to the Soviet Union, and through 'inflicting total defeat on the enemy'. The offensive is all.

This does not mean, of course, that the Russians intend unleashing a future war. The Bear may become satisfied with rough parity.

But both sides are prepared. It is easy enough to ridicule the military, to mock the incompetence that allowed Mathias Rust into Red Square and the Iraqi missile into the USS *Stark*, the inability of the musclebound Goliaths to deal with Afghans in turbans and Vietnamese in rubber flip-flops, the cost overruns on aircraft that don't work, the multibillions of dollars and roubles spent on forces who have not fired a shot at each other since the dim civil war skirmishes seventy years ago. Yet sides they remain, divided by minefields of the mind, separate and real.

If 'twere done, 'twere better it were done quickly. Old advice that the Russians have compelling reason to follow in any attack on NATO.

They believe deeply in the power of the sudden mass offensive. It is embedded in the expansiveness and sense of moral superiority in their political philosophy. Only Khrushchev has been an adventurer. Other leaders have been externally cautious and slow to act. But once a decision has been taken, the execution, in Budapest, Prague or Kabul, has had precise qualities of surprise and mass.

The belief in the offensive is reinforced by the Russian view of themselves as always victims, of Stalin's Mongol Khans, Turkish Beys and Swedish feudal lords, of the Germans, now of American plots. Ultimately either Communism or imperialism must conquer, Lenin wrote in 1919, and 'until this end occurs, a number of terrible clashes between the Soviet Republic and bourgeois states is inevitable'. There may be respites, but when an aggressive world looks likely to go out of control, it is best to choose the time and place for the first blow.

It has been a constant in Soviet military thought since Trotsky and Tukhachevsky. Stalin preached but did not practise it. Hitler did both and no Russian, of the Gorbachev generation or younger, will forget the lesson. The war memorials and the battlefields spread too far east for that. No more retreats to Moscow.

Time is on NATO's side. Give NATO forty-eight hours, and it will be fully deployed in Western Europe. Give it a fortnight, and the first convoys of ships will be transfusing American military strength into Europe. The first cracks may be appearing among the Warsaw Pact allies. How long will Czechs die for a Red army that neutered their nationhood? Best not to find out. Will the French fight on the forward line in West Germany? Will the Spanish fight at all? What will those other potential enemies, Chinese, Japanese, Australians, make of it? Will they be tempted on to an anti-Soviet bandwagon? Get rid of NATO quickly enough, and nobody need ever know.

A surprise assault should also bring out the worst in the West Europeans and the Americans, soft people without the backbone that suffering has given the Soviets, certain to panic as they see the threat to their over-indulgent and corrupt lifestyles. Peace movements will paralyse the nuclear bases. Refugee traffic will clog roads their armies should deploy along. Soviet strategists also feel that US forces are highly vulnerable to surprise attack, which leads to 'a drastic decline in morale and sometimes even panic'.[2] Most vital of all, it will throw NATO into confusion over whether or not to respond immediately with tactical nuclear weapons. The stockpiled warheads in the special nuclear ammunition stores, near Gütersloh, outside Frankfurt, help balance out NATO's conventional weakness.

A surprise offensive will not allow the Red army to use its full strength. Heavy reinforcements drawn from western Russia to the Central European sector would give NATO advance warning. So would mobilization of reserves to flesh out understrength divisions. It would also be ineffective in a short campaign, for the reservists would take weeks to retrain and would be vulnerable in combat with their outdated equipment. Adequate forces would also have to be left in the Far East and along the Chinese border.

Invasion will have to use the unreinforced forces in being in the Central European area. This involves a limited number of highly concentrated armoured assaults into West Germany, the most important of them in the central region.

Here the Fulda Gap is critical, at the point where East Germany butts furthest into West Germany, reducing its width to less than 160 kilometres. Open tank country runs from the border 15 kilometres to Fulda. The outer suburbs of Frankfurt are 88 kilometres to the west. The Rhine at Mainz is less than 140 kilometres from the border. The Russians already have a good idea of how the US divisions in the area will react. Detailed divisional battle plans were handed to them by the spy Clyde Lee Conrad, a former sergeant in the US 8th Infantry Division, who was arrested in 1988.

The staging areas for the Soviet assault troops are in the green farmland and wooded hills near Eisenach, Gotha and Erfurt. This was a German heartland before the rupture of 1945. Its villages were untouched by the war, the American armour rolling in with little opposition in the final days of the Reich. Later the Americans withdrew under the zoning arrangements and the Red army moved in. Window-boxes of bright roses and geraniums cascade against beamed walls below steep gothic gables. As they move west the Russians can look back at the high skyline of the Wartburg above Eisenach, its castle and its memories of Martin Luther.

Their armour will growl past the Herleshausen checkpoint on the Frankfurt–Berlin autobahn. The first Western civilians to know what is afoot will be startled drivers being checked by East German border officials in the inspection sheds. The paraphernalia of the border, the guard huts, warning signs, dog runs and the first wire, is set well back from the small numbered stones that mark the actual demarcation line. Russian troops, if they are of a mind to read such small things, will know they have passed out of the border zone into the West proper when they see the first freshly painted farmhouses and villages. In East Germany, effort is not wasted on such frivolity. Border guards will have cleared the minefields at the points along the frontier where the attack is going in.

The first troops to meet them will be the American tankmen of the 11th Armoured Cavalry Regiment based at Fulda. Tactics demand that defenders should not join serious battle close to the enemy start line. Politics, however, and NATO's policy of forward defence makes this impossible. A quarter of the West German population live within fifty kilometres of the border, and they cannot be abandoned in the first hours.

The Americans will see a mass of squat shapes moving on both sides of the autobahn, tanks and APCs, lapping round their hilltop positions in an armoured flood. Heavy artillery barrages precede them, firing at the American GDPs, the general defence positions of the forward screening troops. The map coordinates of the GDPs have been obtained in advance by *Spetsnaz* troops. The Soviet gunners are aiming for *porazhenie*, annihilation, and 150 rounds will fall on each acre during the barrage. Further west, waves of Soviet fighter-bombers have already attacked NATO airfields, radar sites and nuclear depots. The early weight of air attack is well back from the front, hitting air bases and control systems and attempting to prevent NATO troops from moving up to their defensive positions. Later, it will switch to give maximum support to Red army breakthroughs at the front. High above the globe, US communications and intelligence satellites have been attacked.

The Soviet 8th Guards Army is attacking in this sector, with 3rd Shock Army engaging the British and West Germans to the north, and 1st Guards Tank Army to its south. A superiority of three or four to one is necessary for the odds in modern war to swing in favour of the attacker. On the crucial Central European front, the Russians can only achieve something near this if they draw on forces in western Russia, and then only in tanks. Here, the Warsaw Pact has an advantage over NATO in combat divisions of 72 to 53, in combat aircraft of 2,997 to 1,834. The ratio is much better in main battle tanks, 24,200 to 8,799. But with the Warsaw Pact attacking only with forces held in Central Europe, the advantages disappear. The tank superiority slides to 12,650 to NATO's 8,799 and in men there is actual inferiority, 805,000 to 823,000.*

The Russians do not have enough strength for a broad thrust to force NATO back right along the front. Not in theory, at least, though the Germans threw the rule book away when they pushed back a *superior* defending force the length of the colossal front at the onset of *Barbarossa*.

---

* Not that there is agreement even on NATO figures, a factor which will make any agreement on conventional arms reductions a laborious and drawn-out affair. For example, an official British government statement in 1987 put the total number of NATO troops on the Central front at 790,000 compared with 960,000 for the Warsaw Pact. This 1:1.2 ratio in favour of the Pact increases to 1:1.3 with soldiers in fighting units, where NATO is said to field 580,000 to the Pact's 725,000. The ratio in main battle tanks is more alarming at 1:2.1, with NATO holding a tank park of 7,800 against the Pact's 16,700. The same ratio is said to hold true of fixed-wing tactical aircraft, where a NATO force of 1,250 face 2,650 Pact machines. Things deteriorate further with artillery, where NATO is outgunned by 1:3.1, with 3,000 big guns facing 9,200. HMG statement on the Defence Estimates, 1987. Cm. 101–1.

By adding together forces in France and the Benelux as well as West Germany, the magazine *The Economist* comes up with a very different estimate. The ratio in troops slides to NATO's favour by 1.1:1, with just over a million NATO men facing 975,000 Reds. Tanks improve to 1:1.4 with 9,700 NATO machines against a Pact holding of 14,000. In artillery, NATO acquires 400 105-mm guns and the Pact loses 2,300 to give a 1:2 ratio. Overall air strength, including air defence fighters as well as ground-attack fighters, improves to 1:1.5 with 2,180 NATO aircraft pitted against 3,190 Pact aircraft. *The Economist*, Vol. 300, No. 7461.

They must therefore aim for encirclement battles, panzer-style where NATO forces are caught in pockets to be reduced by air and artillery, and encounter battles where, having cut through to the rear of the enemy defences, NATO reserves are destroyed as they move up and the Russians expand their attack sideways against the NATO flanks. Both these require an initial breakthrough. Hence the mass of armour expected in the Fulda Gap, with the Russians striving for a local superiority of at least seven or eight to one.

War is ever noise and fire but technology has fed both into a swelling cacophony where the individual soldier is caught in a gigantic, exploding sound system. The quick clatter of tank tracks gives a light syncopation to the piercing clamour of their shells. The jet hiss of wire-guided missiles is drowned by fighter bombers, dragging a rake of engine noise behind them and projecting gouts of flame from their weapons pods. Black clouds of smoke are slicked across the battlefield on the wind, bringing the acrid smell of explosives and the sweeter, cloying scent of kerosene and burning oil.

The battlefield extends deeper than ever before, subject to tactical missile launchers 150 kilometres distant. The airspace above it has layers of speed and height, attack helicopters straining their gearboxes to achieve 190 knots whilst strike aircraft howl in at high subsonic speed, and high above air superiority combat dances to a supersonic choreography.

Separate disciplines are woven in the fighting like multicoloured cloth. Tank crews are like submariners in the oily dark of their machines, subject to the turbulence and violent motion of the earth's tidal stream as they hustle across fields and lanes, reading the ground like waves, manoeuvring to keep hull-down beneath the crests. Infantry lie watching the glowing light on the back of a missile, the thin scream of the outgoing control wire half heard, willing it to hit fast before the tank spots it and lumbers its turret on to them. Regimental commanders swivel the periscopes in the cupolas of their armoured command vehicles, trying to make sense of the battle, cursing when jamming pours white noise through their earphones.

Old aerial disciplines – trusting instrumentation rather than gut instinct, coordinating a stream of information, plotting on radar, conceiving of the battlefield in terms of the air and missile space above it as well as simple topography – are part of the ground war now. The air is an extension. A helicopter pilot hides his hovering machine behind a stand of trees or a ridgeline, rising, observing and firing at a target and descending out of line of sight. The terrain unfolds in front of a ground-attack pilot with the swift implacability of an arcade game, filling his windscreen as he shoves the nose down to keep below a hundred feet as he comes off an escarpment on to the plain, relying on speed to leave the rapid-fire AA shells and SAMs behind him until his ordnance leaves in a flash of rocket exhaust towards a tank column, the aircraft flinging him against his straps under the recoil. The fighter pilot, the battlefield lost beneath his altitude, fights in a world of G-forces, instruments and missile lock-on.

Few of the men will have any experience of war. Vietnam is almost a generation away, the veterans of Tet now past forty, and the Russians have not rotated men from Afghanistan to Central Europe. Their officers will know better what to expect and their units will have a collective memory of war. The 3rd Shock Army fought in the winter offensives of 1941–2 round Kharkov, destroyed the Wehrmacht in front of Berlin in the Oder–Vistula operation and seized the Reichstag. The title of 8th Guards gives other links back to the Tsarist armies. 11th Cavalry, the Black Horse regiment, fought in the Philippines, Mexico, in Europe and Vietnam.

In any event, they will quickly learn. The urgency of breakthrough means that the baptism of fire will involve total immersion. The lead Russian forces immediately engage the American Abrams tanks, Sheridan light tanks and Bradley armoured fighting vehicles. They call in heavy air and artillery strikes on enemy strongpoints. Concentrations reach 87 guns to a kilometre of front, or one gun to every fourteen metres of a barrage. Behind them the main forces advance at speed to overwhelm defences and to break through into the American flanks and rear. Breakthrough sectors are narrow, perhaps a couple of kilometres wide, though there will be several of them, fingers worrying at the defences with the mass of clout behind them. But the attacking divisions will be strung out over a long distance behind the breakthrough to avoid making a rich target for a NATO airstrike or nuclear artillery attack. The distance between the forward and rear regiments of a division will be up to fifty kilometres. A regiment itself will tail back for perhaps fifteen kilometres, and a battalion for three.

The first machines to reach the American positions outside Fulda are T-80s and T-72s of the leading tank regiments of the armoured divisions. A few hundred metres behind them come the motor-rifle companies in their BMP armoured combat vehicles, the infantrymen firing from the gun ports as they move, their task to knock out the American anti-tank defences. Next in the first echelon come the motor-rifle divisions, capitalizing on the armoured breakthrough by sweeping off the assault axis and assaulting the Americans throughout the depths of the defence. And behind them the second echelon waits on its start-lines, to sweep later through the torn and smoking gaps to drive fresh movement into the assault.

To shock and unhinge the enemy, and to disrupt NATO's C³I, command, control, communications and intelligence, the Russians stress the deep operation, *glubokaya operatsiya*, and the deep battle.[3] Deep means not only distance into enemy territory, but also the distance that the lead troops advance ahead of the main forces. The *glubokaya operatsiya* destroys the enemy defence with several deep penetrations that fragment the forward defence and enable the enemy rear and flanks to be attacked. The enemy is thus under strain not only at his front, but through the whole depth of his deployment.

The Soviets have recognized the intensity that breakthrough operations on the central front will involve. Though the concept of *Blitzkrieg* has not greatly changed, has indeed been reverted to since the Khrushchev days when the ground forces fell out of fashion to the nuclear strike, both tanks and the means of their destruction have developed enormously. The Soviet tank is incomparably advanced on the T-34. The T-72 and T-80 are both built for battlefield nuclear war, with radiation liners of lead and plastic to shield against gases and neutrons, automatic sealing against blast effects and sophisticated ventilation systems. It is deployed in huge numbers. A motor-rifle division has 16 times as many tanks and 37 times as many armoured personnel carriers as its wartime predecessors. Where wartime tanks needed to fire an average of thirteen rounds to hit a stationary target, a T-80 will hit a sitting duck first time.

The T-80, however, is meeting much rougher opposition than the T-34 dreamed of. Both the American M-1 Abrams and West German Leopard 2s can make 70 kph, outrunning the T-80. NATO HOT and TOW anti-tank missiles fly at 950 kph with ranges of around 5 kilometres. Cobra helicopters can make 300 kph carrying 8 TOW missiles and the bigger Hughes Ah-64 carries 16 anti-tank missiles or 76 rockets. A-10 ground support aircraft can deliver fifteen times the weight of ordnance that a Stormovik carried, and the ordnance itself is several times more destructive.

The 11th Armoured Cavalry, besides its own formidable tank-busting capacity, will be able to call on helicopter and fighter-bomber support. No reliance is placed on tank numbers alone. The Russian tank divisions field powerful artillery and infantry forces, together with tactical command vehicles, engineering support and a wealth of tank transporters and fuel trucks to increase their mobility.

Speed is essential, not only for its own sake in momentum, but to force an issue before NATO is reinforced on the battlefield. Troops have to move to their positions within West Germany, to be ferried in from Britain and flown in from the US. The French, who are not part of the integrated NATO command structure, have political decisions to take. Convoys of heavy equipment have to be loaded and escorted across the North Atlantic. It will take time for the West's greater industrial muscle to be felt. The Russians must pre-empt that by speed.

One scenario by NATO's Supreme Headquarters has it that the lead Red army units could advance to the line running from Hamburg through

Frankfurt to Munich within seventy-two hours if NATO were not allowed early use of nuclear battlefield weapons.[4] This gives them Hamburg and Hanover in 12 hours, Bremen in 26, Kassel in 60, Munich 5 hours later and Frankfurt in 72.

Hamburg lies only sixty-five kilometres from the Pact start-lines and is rapidly bypassed by the East German 5th and the Soviet 2nd Guards Tank armies. The Russians do not wish to get involved in street fighting, which heavily favours the defenders. Wherever possible, they have run down NATO units in open country, keeping them out of towns and cities.

3rd Shock slams into the 1st British Corps east of Hanover. It is tasked to destroy the British, attacking the weak point where the British and the 1st West German Corps meet, and to move rapidly west towards Osna-brück and Münster. It is fielding nearly 60,000 troops and 1,240 battle tanks. Add in its 1,100 armoured infantry vehicles, its 18 surface-to-surface missile launchers, over 400 guns and almost 6,000 trucks, attacking on fronts only a few kilometres wide,[5] and its impetus past Hanover is irresistible. The 1st British Corps has almost the same number of men, but has only half the number of main battle tanks and artillery. The 3rd Shock averaged advances of 20 to 22 kilometres a day during the Vistula–Oder assault in 1945. Much more is expected of it now. Its three spearhead tank divisions, 10th, 12th and 47th Guards, should cover up to 50 kilometres a day in conventional conditions and 100 if the conflict turns nuclear.[6]

Further south towards Kassel, the Red army meets the Leopard tanks of the Belgians and 3rd West German Corps before the Americans come into the line between Fulda and Nuremberg. Below that are the German 2nd Corps, deployed east of Stuttgart and Munich, and, if they so decide, the French.

As the Russians learnt so bitterly during *Barbarossa*, it is difficult to counter-attack a rapidly moving mass of armour. NATO, needing to move units swiftly to counter the developing Russian thrusts, finds the roads clogged with refugees. That is less of a problem for the Red army, where combat engineer tractors move with the lead tanks to clear wrecked cars.

Fast penetration ahead of the main attacking forces is provided by raiding formations of at least divisional strength. These Operational Manoeuvre Groups, OMGs,[7] are committed to the destruction of nuclear and other high-value targets deep inside enemy territory. They attempt to seize nuclear warheads in special ammunition sites, bridges and airfields and to attack enemy flanks and rear. They have heavy air support from MiG-27 Floggers and Su-25 Frogfoot.[8] Smaller raids are mounted by heliborne infantry, paratroops and *Spetsnaz*.

Within seventy-two hours, half Germany and all Denmark and Holland have gone. NATO, in its last act, sues for peace.

★

This sketch is plausible, as far as *voyna* games go. It could go much further. A longer war in Central Europe would involve essential convoys of reinforcements and supplies crossing the Atlantic. This, in turn, would involve an attack by the Soviet Arctic Front on northern Norway. Seizing the Norwegian coastline and airbases flanking the Northern fleet's entrance from its bases on the Kola Peninsula to the North Atlantic would be a vital task. The Northern Front includes the Soviet 6th Army. One of its motor rifle divisions, the 45th, is only ten kilometres from the Norwegian border at Pechenga. Another division is in Murmansk and the 27th Army Corps is at Archangel. The terrain from the border at Pechenga to the vital strategic area of Norway around Tromso is rugged and difficult. It is likely that the Russians would take the easier invasion route across northern Finland and drive along the Norwegian Skibotn valley to the coast of the Arctic Ocean.

This would be necessary to protect the submarines and surface ships of the Northern fleet as they passed off the northern Norwegian coast en route to attack Allied convoys in mid-Atlantic. For their first two days at sea the convoys are within range of land-based Canadian and US aircraft. RAF aircraft from Cornwall cover them for the last two days. Soviet attacks would be fiercest during the two mid-Atlantic days. The attacking cruise-missile submarines, and the Backfire bombers from the sixteen military airbases on the Kola peninsula, would be vulnerable to Norwegian-based fighters and anti-submarine aircraft.

The longer the war, the greater the chance both of a general nuclear exchange and of an eventual Soviet defeat. The Russians incessantly complain that they are surrounded by potentially hostile states. As long as the *glacis* of the Eastern European countries is ignored, and the interesting question of why they should excite so little affection is glossed over, they are quite right. The NATO belt extends from Norway to the Turkish–Iranian border. What would happen in Iran and Afghanistan in a Third World War is anyone's guess. Pakistan is unlikely to be friendly to the Soviet Union, although concern over India is a priority. Next, a China with little respect for Soviet-style Communism and major territorial claims. North Korea is a better bet, but not the South which has US forces in place. Then Japan, the world's most dynamic capitalist state, also with a territorial claim. Finally, the US itself in Alaska. Given the polar flight path of missiles, the Russians can also note that these will overfly NATO Canada and Greenland.

The oceans are unfriendly, too. The US maintains the 3rd and 7th Fleets in the Pacific, the 2nd in the Atlantic, the 6th in the Mediterranean and a Task Force in the Indian Ocean. These are powerful forces. The 2nd Fleet has 6 aircraft carriers, 720 combat aircraft, 41 nuclear submarines and 103 escort ships. The US has more than half a million men stationed at 1,500 bases in 32 countries abroad.

Industrial capacity will be equally telling in a long war. The huge firepower of the Americans in the last war meant that in some of the island campaigns in the Pacific they were losing men at a rate better than 1:200 against the Japanese. Soviet industrial strength is completely outclassed by its potential opponents.

There is no evidence that the Soviets believe that they have a reliable first-strike nuclear capability. Although their global capability has grown enormously, they still have every reason to fear a world war that would be sprawling and lengthy. Their best option remains a violent and rapid strike into central Europe, a bigger and more concentrated *Barbarossa*.

It has been played out many times on both sides of the border. But it has far too many imponderables for anyone to take it at face value. The use of battlefield nuclear weapons by NATO from the outset would swing the balance away from the Warsaw Pact.

Apart from that, it presupposes that the Floggers, Fulcrums and Foxhounds are at least a match for their NATO rivals. If the Russians do not achieve superiority over the breakthrough points, at the very least, the invasion is likely to fail. If NATO communications survive, and the less sophisticated Soviet systems are heavily jammed, Soviet divisions and their air support will flounder. If NATO concentrate air strikes on the second echelons successfully, the lead elements will find themselves isolated and without support in a lonely and very hostile environment.

A meatgrinder they will win. But the West should ensure that this is not on the agenda. It takes great skill and flair to mix air, missiles, tanks, artillery, heliborne and APC-riding infantry in modern mobile warfare. The great unknown is whether Yazov's men possess the flexibility and initiative that go with it. Or whether its sombre history has ripped from the Red army these most elusive and vital twins of war.

Its position at home is already paid for. It outfought, and outbuilt, the Germans. It has stopped satellites from spinning out of a system that otherwise has failed. It has earned its own parity with the US. It is master of one slice of Soviet life that manifestly works.

The Red army, not the Party, is the superpower.

NOTES

INTRODUCTION

[1] The Red army was redesignated the Soviet army in 1945. Changes in nomenclature are common in the Soviet Union. The secret police, the KGB, are now on their fifth name and the city of Volgograd on its third. The Red army has a continuity which enables the classic name to be used throughout here.

[2] It was expected to take several years before Soviet-published street plans of Moscow reached the accuracy of those produced in the US by the CIA.

CHAPTER 1 RED OCTOBER

[1] *Ten Days that Shook the World,* John Reed, first pub. US 1919, London, 1977 edn., p. 37.

[2] Trotsky, op. cit., p. 666.

[3] 26 October in the old Russian calendar. Hence the revolution still being called Red October in Russia.

[4] Reed, op. cit., p. 96.

CHAPTER 2 FLAWED TITAN

[1] *Nicholas and Alexandra,* Robert K. Massie, New York, 1985, p. 283.

[2] *Russia's Military Way to the West,* Christopher Duffy, London, p. 90.

[3] Duffy, op. cit., p. 154.

[4] *The Eastern Front,* Norman Stone, London, 1985 edn., p. 21.

[5] *A History of Russian and Soviet Sea Power,* Donald W. Mitchell, London, 1974, p. 236.

[6] *The Economic Development of the USSR,* Roger Munting, London, 1982, p. 32.

[7] Treaties which Mao Tse-tung, who came of age in 1914, was to declare unequal.

[8] Stone, op. cit., p. 49.

[9] Massie, op. cit., p. 312.

[10] Massie, op. cit., p. 313.

[11] Stone, op. cit., 170.

[12] Stone, op. cit., p. 169.

[13] Massie, op. cit., p. 310.

CHAPTER 3 1917

[1] Goldston, op. cit., p. 104.

[2] Massie, op. cit., p. 398.

[3] Goldston, op. cit., p. 105.

[4] 27 February by the old Russian calendar.

[5] Meriel Buchanan, qu. Massie, op. cit., p. 401.

[6] Massie, op. cit., p. 412.

[7] April by the old calendar, May by the new.

[8] Goldston, op. cit., p. 134.

[9] *The Russian Soldier in 1917*, Marc Ferro, Slavic Review No. 3, Sept. 1971, p. 500.

[10] *The Soviet High Command*, John Erickson, London, 1962, p. 7.

[11] *US Military Intelligence*. Vol. II. New York, 1978. p. 32.

[12] Trotsky, op. cit., p. 551.

[13] The German High Command had indeed helped fund the Bolsheviks, as it had arranged and paid for Lenin's chartered train.

[14] One of the greatest Bolshevik demagogues, whose ability to 'conquer, convince, bewitch, opponents of the party', attested to by Trotsky, would not prevent the party from liquidating him, as the pretty phrase has it, in the 1930s.

[15] Ferro, op. cit., p. 502.

[16] *And Quiet Flows the Don*, Mikhail Sholokhov, London, 1967, p. 316.

[17] *Soldatskie pia 'ma* 9 Aug. 1917, qu. Ferro, op. cit., p. 504.

[18] *US Military Intelligence*, op. cit., pp. 10–11.

[19] Trotsky, op. cit., p. 745.

[20] Trotsky, op cit., p. 745.

CHAPTER 4 TROTSKY

[1] He had rebelled as a unit commander in 1905. Condemned to death, he had escaped to Paris. In Red October, Antonov-Ovseenko led the Red Guards in the assault on the Winter Palace.

[2] For founding an illegal union! Someone should run that one past Lech Walesa and Solidarity.

[3] In Russian translation. This example of *sang froid* is shared by the former British Prime Minister, Harold Macmillan, a man of somewhat different political outlook. Macmillan read Petrarch while lying wounded in no-man's-land during the First World War. He did so, however, in the original.

[4] *Khrushchev Remembers*, London, 1971, p. 20. The memoirs of the former Soviet leader, generally accepted as genuine.

[5] *Dr Zhivago*. Boris Pasternak, London, 1969 edn., p. 409.

[6] *The White Generals*, Richard Luckett, New York, 1971, p. 242.

[7] Sholokhov, op. cit., p. 507.

[8] Pasternak, op. cit., p. 197.

[9] Luckett, op. cit., p. 263.

[10] Qu. Luckett, op. cit., p. 295.

[11] Luckett, op. cit., p. 275.

[12] Luckett, op. cit., pp. 351–2.

CHAPTER 5 KRONSTADT

[1] The Whites, many of them in Paris where they would provide a generation of taxi drivers and legionnaires, played the revolt for all it was worth. They raised money to help, selling jewels and paintings, but there was no conduit to send the funds. A detailed contingency plan for a revolt in Kronstadt had been drawn up by the 'National Centre' in Paris, a coalition of moderate émigrés. Some ex-Tsarist officers serving on Kronstadt as *voenspets*, including the former Major General Alexander Kozlovsky who commanded the fortress artillery, gave advice to the mutineers. But, like a sound suggestion to shell the ice round the island, it was largely ignored.

[2] As it would in Spain, where the Communists meted them out similar punishment.

[3] It was the last time, a fact hardly appreciated in Kronstadt, that the black flags of anarchy would be seen on Moscow streets.

[4] *The Prophet Armed*, Isaac Deutscher, London, 1970, p. 512. Few of the original veterans had survived and the sailors whom Trotsky would deal with were largely freshly recruited Ukrainian peasants.

[5] *The Bolshevik Myth*, Alexander Berkman, New York, 1925.

CHAPTER 6 THE STEEL MONSTER

[1] *Twenty Letters to a Friend*, Svetlana Alliluyeva, London, 1967, p. 212.

[2] *Stalin*, Isaac Deutscher, London, 1966.

[3] He took the name, which means 'implacable', from a short story. He was called Koba by Old Bolsheviks well into the 1930s, one of them threatening: 'I'll cut your ears off, Koba.' Cf. *High Treason*, Vitaly Rappoport and Yuri Alexeev, Duke University, 1985.

[4] The others were Lenin, Trotsky, Zinoviev, Kamenev, Sokolinikov and Bubnov. The anonymous, self-effacing Georgian had established himself on the most important of the new Bolshevik institutions.

[5] Now the focal point of a global belief, containing the mummified relic of the Red saviour, with an attendant line of humbly shuffling pilgrims, in fur caps from Siberia, headdresses from Central Asia, felt hats from White Russia, snaking round and submissively dominating the square. The Lenin ikons are as far flung as those of Christ, and in more temporal places, the wardrooms of nuclear submarines, the shop floors of East German industrial plants,the repair depots of Cuban sugar plantations. The site of the cult is controlled by KGB guardsmen, their Kalashnikovs more worldly weapons than the Swiss pikestaffs of Rome.

[6] For all its obsession with politics and disdain for religion, the Stalin Oath attempts to combine both. It is Caesar and Christ, Tsar and Patriarch. As Christ, it offers eventual heaven on earth and nobility of soul that can redeem South Vietnamese soldiers and Cuban bar-owners as surely as it will redeem, with similar 're-education', Wall Street brokers. As Caesar, it provides a complete dictatorship.

CHAPTER 7 STALINISM

[1] The Cheka changed to OGPU, one of the several titles it has had on its journey to becoming the KGB.

[2] *The Red Army*, Erich Wollenberg, 1st edn 1938, London, 1978 edn, p. 182.

[3] Trotsky later claimed that Frunze had been 'medically murdered'. He said that Frunze had been advised not to undergo an operation since his weak heart would be placed at risk. Stalin, worried by Frunze's independence and support of Zinoviev, hand-picked doctors who recommended operating.

[4] *The Soviet Union since 1917*, Martin McCauley, London, 1981, p. 61.

[5] This was the first of many stopping places that took him, via Turkey and Norway, to the outskirts of Mexico City where he was murdered by a Stalinist agent as he sat at his desk working on his rival's biography in August 1940.

[6] Deutscher, *Stalin*, op. cit., p. 332.

[7] Wollenberg, op. cit., p. 206.

[8] Deutscher, *Stalin*, op. cit., p. 325.

[9] *The Gulag Archipelago*, Alexander Solzhenitsyn, London, 1974, Vol. I, p. 56.

[10] As, of course, it pre-dates the Holocaust, the Cultural Revolution in China, the killing fields of Cambodia.

[11] Lieutenant General A. I. Todorsky, qu. Rappoport and Alexeev, op. cit., p. 182.

[12] Liddell Hart Archives – Section II. Notes on Talk with Martel, 6 October 1936.

[13] Colonel Philip R. Faymonville, Report 520 on 'Relationship of Red Army to Soviet Government', 4 March 1936, R.G. 165, M.I.D., 2037–1854/29.

[14] It has continued to do so ever since, and the world has continued to be surprised. Unaccountably so, since the track record dates back so far.

[15] Khrushchev later suggested Stalin was responsible. A few days before the murder, Kirov's bodyguards had been withdrawn on the orders of the NKVD head, Yagoda. His personal bodyguard, Borisov, was called away to the phone when Kirov was shot in an ornate corridor of the Smolny. After the murder, Borisov was taken to the Smolny in a truck which was smashed into a wall by its NKVD driver. Two other NKVD men beat Borisov's head in with iron bars. His death was put down to a traffic accident. Robert Conquest, *Power and Policy in the USSR*, Macmillan.

[16] The 1929–30 purge expelled 11.5 per cent of party membership as a whole, but only 4.7 per cent of members in the army. Though 6.7 per cent of the military membership of the party was excluded or demoted in 1933–4, this was only a quarter of the average. It had been announced then that the army organizations were the 'party's healthiest'.

CHAPTER 8 THE GREAT TERROR

[1] Rappoport and Alexeev, op. cit., p. 10 et seq.

[2] A. I. Kork, superintendent of the Frunze Academy, Corps Commander V. M. Primakov, deputy commander of the Leningrad military district, Army Commander First Class I. P. Uboverich, commander of the White Russian military district, Corps Commander B. M. Feldman, chief of the central administration, Corps Commander R. P. Eideman, chairman of *Osoaviakhim*, Army Commander First Class I. E. Yakir, commander of the Kiev military district. Tukhachevsky had been, before his transfer as head of the Volga military district a month before, senior deputy defence commissar and chief of Combat Readiness of the Red army. Rappoport and Alexeev, op. cit., p. 10 et seq.

[3] Personal trains were an early mark of superiority in Soviet Russia, a fashion set, ironically enough, by the arch-traitor Trotsky. All the crew of the armoured train from which he had fought the Whites were purged in due course. The author met a *zek*, or prisoner, a Don Cossack who had shared a bunk in a lumber camp with the train's engineer. The engineer perished, though the Cossack survived to sing Orthodox chants in the church off Emperor's Gate, London.

[4] Rappoport and Alexeev, op. cit., p. 242.

[5] Rappoport and Alexeev, op. cit., p. 11.

[6] A 'red folder' is said to have contained evidence against Tukhachevsky and the others, concocted in Germany and deliberately slipped into Stalin's hands. Tukhachevsky, who had visited Germany six times since his wartime imprisonment, was on close terms with several members of the German General Staff. The Gestapo and the NKVD, faking evidence of Tukhachevsky's treachery, leaked it to Stalin via the Czech President Beneš. This was done through General Nikolai Skoblin, a White Russian émigré in Paris who had links to both the Gestapo and the NKVD. Skoblin subsequently disappeared from Paris in September 1937. Rappoport and Alexeev, op. cit., p. 258 et seq.

[7] The description by Ossip Mandelshtam, the Soviet poet who himself disappeared into the camps and died, probably in 1938. Another, modern poet has remembered the murdered generals and the millions of other victims in a plea for a memorial. Yevgeny Yevtushenko wrote 'Monuments Not Yet Erected' in 1987:

> Monuments not yet erected stride over the mossy tundras
> Flattening Siberian snow down to its base of blood ...
>
> The bloody tears of Blucher, hero of the Revolution
> once devoured, will be re-cast as tears of bronze!
> Marshal Yakir will extend his granite arm to the nation ...
>
> Monuments, your time has come – the time for decent marble!
> The dirt comes streaming off the slandered victims!
> And Marshal Tukhachevsky's violin, smashed during his arrest,
> Splinter by varnished splinter, melts into wholeness and is turned to marble!

Glasnost or not, the time for monuments is not close. Yevtushenko was bitterly attacked in *Izvestia*.

[8] Colonel General A. T. Stuchenko, quo. *Stalin and his Generals*, ed. Seweryn Bialer. Columbia University, London edn, 1970, p. 80.

[9] Solzhenitsyn, op. cit., Vol. I.

[10] Solzhenitsyn, op. cit., Vol. I, p. 10.

[11] Rappoport and Alexeev, op. cit., pp. 243–4.

[12] Rappoport and Alexeev, op. cit., p. 244.

[13] Nakanune, Moscow *Voenizdat* 1969, qu. *Commissars, Commanders and Civilian Authority*, Timothy J. Colton, Harvard, 1979.

[14] Alliluyeva, op. cit., p. 86 et seq.

[15] Colton, op. cit., pp. 146–7.

[16] Or so he told *Komsomols'kaia Pravda* during the Khrushchev era. But then he would have done. In a world without truth, the two-tongued man is king.

[17] In fact, Budenny was one of the charmed circle who had served with Stalin on the South-west front during the civil war. Those who survived for the same reason included the defence commissar, Marshal Voroshilov, and others who later gave a poor account of themselves against the Germans.

[18] Alliluyeva, op. cit., p. 156.

[19] Solzhenitsyn. op. cit., p. 132.

[20] This Cossack leader broke down and wept when he was reprieved, finding it easier to 'part with life than to return to it'. Summoned to Moscow after his apparent escape, he travelled in style with a rail car for himself, his wife, his two orderlies and a cook, with another heated car for his Cossack horses. The distinguished traveller was taken to the Butyrka prison and shot in the head. *High Treason*, op. cit., p. 66.

[21] He survived to become the most powerful member of the Polish Politburo in the late 1940s. *Granta 17*, p. 50 et seq.

[22] Rappoport and Alexeev, op. cit., pp. 282–3.

[23] Not a profound saying, indeed. As for eggs, Ivan the Terrible may have killed from ten to twenty a day. Under Stalin, on some days 1,000 are believed to have been shot. Between 1936 and 1938, at least 500,000 and possibly 1 million Russians were executed. A further 8 million were imprisoned.

From 1936 to 1950, perhaps 12 million died in the Gulags, a figure to graft on to the 7 million who had died before 1936 in the collectivization famine and deportations.

These were Western estimates. An added obscenity in these figures is that the victims were taken in the name of a numerate, humanitarian New Order that laid down production quotas to the nearest ton but that has neither accounted for, nor been able to account for, the deaths it has imposed.

[24] Solzhenitsyn, op. cit., p. 62.

[25] Solzhenitsyn, op. cit., p. 125.

[26] Qu. Solzhenitsyn, op. cit., Vol. II, p. 91.

[27] Qu. *Kolyma*, Robert Conquest, London, 1979, pp. 21–2. Gorbatov was one of the few survivors, military and otherwise, of this particular Calvary. His legs swollen, teeth loose in his gums, he lived because he made a grater from a piece of tin to eat raw potatoes. His teeth were too far gone to be able to gnaw. He wrote his memoirs during the brief Khrushchev window into the purges, in 1964.

[28] Qu. Conquest, *Kolyma*, op. cit., p. 133.

[29] Conquest, *Kolyma*, op. cit.

[30] *The Road to Stalingrad*, John Erickson, London, 1983, p. 18 et seq.

[31] Khrushchev, op. cit., p. 103. Khrushchev noted that before his arrest, Meretskov had been a 'strapping young general, very strong and impressive-looking. After his release he was just a shadow of his former self. He'd lost so much weight he could hardly squeak.' To confront Beria one day, and Hitler's legions the next, is the stuff of moral horror.

CHAPTER 9 THE BENEFICIARIES

[1] Rappoport and Alexeev, op. cit., pp. 276–7.

[2] Respectively Admirals Koshchenov, Dushkanov and Zivkov.

[3] Mitchell, op. cit., p. 373.

[4] Bailer, op. cit., p. 63.

[5] Not that the newly promoted were safe from Stalin. Rychagov was arrested in June 1941 and shot shortly thereafter. Some battalion commanders at the start of 1938 were divisional commanders by the end of the year and dead a few months later.

[6] 'Pered vonoi, Oktiabr', 1965, qu. Bialer, op. cit., p. 90 et seq.

[7] In an equally extraordinary promotion in 1987, Gen. Dmitry Yazov exchanged a minor posting at army Far East HQ in Khabarovsk to become defence minister within a few months.

[8] Bialer, op. cit., p. 98 et seq.

[9] In 1939 he designed the 'Yak' fighter which accounted for more than half the Russian fighters produced during the war, 37,000 of them.

CHAPTER 10 THE WINTER WAR

[1] *The Triumph of Tyranny*, Stephen Barsody, London, 1960, p. 70.

[2] Lithuania, Estonia and Latvia.

[3] An NCO in the Tsarist army, he became an officer in the Red army, took part in the Polish and Finnish campaigns and rose to colonel in the tank arm before breaking with the Soviets.

[4] Bailer, op. cit., p. 132.

[5] 'Beating the Russians in the Snow', Allen F. Chew, *Military Review*, June 1980. p. 39 et seq.

[6] *The Road to Stalingrad*, John Erickson, London, 1983, p. 14. This, together with its

sister work *The Road to Berlin*, is the classic work on the Red army and the Second World War.

[7] *The Memoirs of Marshal Mannerheim*, New York, 1954, p. 261, qu. Bialer, op. cit., p. 574n.

[8] Perhaps as well since it would have involved France and Britain in war with the Soviet Union as well as Germany.

[9] Bialer, op. cit., p. 137.

CHAPTER 11 'CAN WE OPEN FIRE?'

[1] It still runs to the same schedule.

[2] Bialer, op. cit., pp. 241–2.

[3] *The Outermost Frontier*, Helmut Pabst, London, 1986, p. 11.

[4] Erickson, op. cit., p. 98. There were soon 154 German divisions and 29 divisions and 16 brigades of Hitler's allies.

[5] *Barbarossa*, Alan Clark, London, 1965.

[6] A. Clark, op. cit., p. 36.

[7] *Russia at War*, Alexander Werth, London, 1964, p. 151.

[8] Bialer, op. cit., p. 225.

[9] Bialer, op. cit., p. 197.

[10] Werth, op. cit., pp. 152–3.

[11] He had said much the same thing about the British Empire, a 'great estate in bankruptcy'. His soldiers fought their way as far as the named city of the Eastern emperor, Stalingrad. They never set foot on the soil of the British Empire, save the Channel Islands. The Russian colossus, half-smothered, recovered to add immeasurably to its strength. The British Empire, inviolate but exhausted, has all but gone. Such are the curious effects of war.

[12] The largest army ever then assembled, half a million men, had invaded almost to the German timetable, the first troops crossing on to Russian soil on 23 June 1812. Napoleon entered the Kremlin on 15 September, sleeping in the Granovitaya palace whose stone facings look east now to the Presidium of the Supreme Soviet. The city was set afire the same night, Napoleon commenting bitterly on Russian courage: 'What a people! They are Scythians! What resoluteness! The barbarians!' The retreat from Moscow started before dawn on 19 October. 'I beat them every time,' Napoleon complained, 'but cannot reach the end.' The Grande Armée disintegrated on the retreat, dressed 'in the rags of their summer uniforms, or in motley clothes gathered from Moscow's palaces and boutiques, sometimes merchants' winter clothes if they were lucky...' *Napoleon 1812*, Nigel Nicolson, London, 1985, p. 127. Of the half million who had crossed the Niemen river in June, 5,000 returned over it in organized units and 25,000 as stragglers. The Imperial Guard, which had set off in plumed splendour 47,000 strong, counted 1,500.

[13] *The Decisive Battles of the Western World*, Vol II, J. F. C. Fuller, London, 1970, p. 549.

[14] It was named for the twelfth-century German king and Holy Roman Emperor, the red-bearded Frederick Barbarossa.

[15] Nevertheless, in the first three days of the invasion, they destroyed almost their own number in Soviet aircraft.

[16] At the end of January 1941, qu. Cecil, op. cit., pp. 117–18.

[17] Cecil, op. cit., p. 162.

[18] *Panzer Leader*, Gen. Heinz Guderian, London, 1974, p. 151.

CHAPTER 12 DIE IN KIEV

[1] A. Clark, op. cit., p. 41.

[2] Qu. *War on the Eastern Front*, James Lucas, New York, 1982, p. 33.

[3] It took Napoleon a month longer to get to Smolensk. He reached it on 16 August 1812 and was in Moscow itself on 14 September.

[4] Qu. A. Clark, op. cit., p. 74.

[5] Erickson, *The Road to Stalingrad*, op. cit., p. 83.

[6] Erickson, *The Road to Stalingrad*, op. cit., p. 49.

[7] Erickson, *The Road to Stalingrad*, op. cit., p. 160.

[8] Starinov, qu. Bialer, op. cit., p. 237.

[9] N. Popel, *V tiazhkuiu poru*, Moscow 1959, qu. Bialer, op. cit., pp. 686–7.

[10] Liddell Hart, op. cit., p. 169.

[11] Bernd von Kleist, qu. A. Clark, op. cit., p. 47.

[12] Werth, op. cit., p. 194.

[13] Guderian, op. cit., pp. 193–4.

[14] Werth, op. cit., p. 196.

[15] *The Siege of Leningrad*, Harrison E. Salisbury, London, 1971, p. 82.

[16] Konstantin Simonov's description in his novel *The Living and the Dead*.

[17] Kesselring, *Memoirs*, p. 98, qu. *The Decisive Battles of the Western World, Vol II*, J. F. C. Fuller, London, 1970, p. 471.

[18] From Voroshilov. Zhukov arrived late in the morning of 13 September and had an immediate, electric effect on his new command.

[19] Erickson, *Road to Stalingrad*, op. cit., pp. 207–8.

[20] As an old Tsaritsyn crony of Stalin, Budenny was not shot. He was flown out of the cauldron and survived to a ripe old age.

[21] C. Malaparte, qu. A. Clark, op. cit., p. 125.

CHAPTER 13 THE *TAIFUN* BLOWS OUT

[1] The German Armed Forces High Command.

[2] The Soviets refer to 'Fronts' and thus Zhukov's command was the Western Front. The Western equivalent of these semi-autonomous Fronts is an Army Group and this term is used. Where 'front' is used this refers in the normal way to the front line.

[3] Alliluyeva, op. cit., pp. 178–82.

[4] Werth, op. cit., p. 235.

[5] Zhukov, *Bitva za Moskvu*, Moscow, 1966, qu. Bialer, op. cit., p. 286.

[6] Halder Diaries, 9 October 1941, qu. Fuller, op. cit., p. 479.

[7] Guderian, op. cit., pp. 234–5.

[8] Colonel General P. A. Belov, *Za nami Moskva*, Moscow, 1963. qu. Bialer, op. cit., p. 296.

[9] G. K. Zhukov, *Vospominanlia komanduiushchego fromtom. Bitva za Moskvu*, Moscow, 1966.

[10] A. Clark, op. cit., pp. 144–5.

[11] It was scarcely surprising that the Red air force was unable to cope with the Luftwaffe and that the parade was forced to rely on the weather for protection. V. P. Balandin, the commissar in charge of aircraft engine production, had been arrested. The brilliant aircraft designer A. S. Yakovlev asked Stalin about the arrest of this key figure. Stalin admitted: 'Yes, he has already been in prison for about forty days but has acknowledged nothing whatever. Perhaps he isn't guilty of anything. It is very possible. It can happen that way.' The next day Balandin, with 'hollow cheeks and

shaven head', was back in his office and working as though nothing had happened. Qu. Bialer, op. cit., p. 301.

[12] *Conversations with Stalin*, Milovan Djilas, London, p. 48.

[13] Speer, op. cit., p. 222.

[14] Fuller, op. cit., p. 480.

[15] Werth, op. cit., p. 260.

[16] Pabst, op. cit., p. 39.

[17] Zhukov, *Bitva za Moskvu*, 1966, qu. Bialer, op. cit., p. 323.

CHAPTER 14 'I WANT A CHILD, SOON'

[1] *The Russian Army, Walter Kerr, London, 1944, p. 9.*

[2] *The Art of Blitzkrieg*, Charles Messenger, London, 1976, qu. p. 178.

[3] Kerr, op. cit.

[4] When they retook the village of Petrishchevo, the Russians were told of the hanging of 'Tanya', an eighteen-year-old partisan girl who had been caught by the Germans a month earlier trying to set fire to some stables. She had been tortured and hanged. Her story was published in *Pravda* in January 1942. Her real name was Zoya Kosmodemyanskaya and she still personifies millions of victims to the Russians. They have their heroes killed in combat, of course, Panfilov's twenty-eight anti-tank men, the pilot Captain Gastello who had crashed his burning aircraft into a German tank column in the first week of the war, the defenders of Hero Fortress Brest. 'Tanya' represents the other, more shocking deaths.

[5] Kerr, op. cit., p. 45.

[6] Zhukov himself was forty-eight, Rokossovsky forty-six, Nikolai Voronov, the artillery chief, thirty-six, General Lelyushenko thirty-eight.

[7] Molotov's own taste ran to champagne and vodka.

[8] Kerr, op. cit.

[9] Fuller, op. cit., p. 484.

[10] Zhukov, *Bitva za Moskvu*, Moscow, 1966, qu. Bialer, op. cit., p. 334.

CHAPTER 15 THE FORGE

[1] *Glavnyi geroi voiny*, V. A. Muradian, ed., Erivan, 1975.

[2] *Sovetskii tyl v velikoi otechestvennoi voine Izdatel 'stvo Misl'*, P. N. Pospeloved, Moscow, 1974, 2 Vols, Vol. I, p. 22.

[3] In the spring of 1941 the Russians had made a point of showing a group of Germans these eastern factories. Nobody in Berlin heeded their warnings or believed that the Russians had any real industrial muscle east of the Urals. Erickson, *The Road to Stalingrad*, op. cit., p. 65.

[4] Erickson, *The Road to Stalingrad*, op. cit., pp. 232–3.

[5] *Rasskazi avia-konstruktera*, A. S. Yakovlev, Moscow, 1959, p. 130.

[6] *Esheloni idut na vostok*, V. P. Butt, Moscow, 1966, p. 13. The total of those evacuated from the front-line areas in the war reached 25 million.

[7] *Sibirskii tyl v velikoi otechestyennoi vione*, G. A. Dokuchaev, Novosibirsk, 1968, p. 54.

[8] Muradian, op. cit., pp. 18 and 137.

[9] Pospelov, op. cit., ii, pp. 88–9.

[10] Werth, op. cit., p. 221.

[11] A. S. Iakovlev, *Isel' zhizni*, Moscow, 1968, p. 352.

[12] Muradian, op. cit., p. 124.

[13] Werth, op. cit., p. 633.

[14] Pabst, op. cit., pp. 93–4.

[15] Kerr, op. cit., p. 128.

[16] *The Roads to Russia*, Robert H. Jones, Oklahoma, 1969, p. 106.

[17] Jones, op. cit., pp. 108–9.

[18] Jones, op. cit., p. 234.

[19] Jones, op. cit., p. 219.

[20] Werth, op. cit., p. 623.

CHAPTER 16 TO THE VOLGA

[1] 22 Rumanian, 17 Finnish, 10 Italian, 10 Hungarian and 1 Spanish and 1 Slovak.

[2] Qu. A. Clark, op. cit., p. 170.

[3] Qu. A. Clark, op. cit., p. 169.

[4] Fuller, op. cit., p. 508.

[5] Erickson, *The Road to Stalingrad*, op. cit., p. 344.

[6] Qu. A. Clark, op. cit., p. 184.

[7] Erickson, *The Road to Stalingrad*, op. cit., p. 360.

[8] This resulted in the abortive Anglo-Canadian raid on Dieppe in August. It suffered grievous casualties and was easily contained, though it did rattle Hitler enough to transfer two crack divisions to the West.

[9] *Memoirs*, V. I. Chuikov, Moscow, 1959.

[10] Anton Kuznick, qu. Chuikov, *The Beginning of The Road*, London, 1963, pp. 123 et seq.

[11] Qu. Chuikov, op. cit., pp. 99 et seq.

[12] Werth, op. cit., p. 456. Nekrasov served as an infantry lieutenant in the Mamayev Kurgan sector through most of the battle. After the war his novel *In the Trenches of Stalingrad* won the 1947 Stalin prize for literature on the personal intervention of Stalin. Nekrasov fell out with the Khrushchev regime for his approving accounts of his travels in the West. He criticized the Soviet invasion of Czechoslovakia in 1968 and supported Solzhenitsyn. He emigrated to the West in 1974 and died in Paris in September 1987.

[13] A. Clark, op. cit., p. 199.

[14] Erickson, *The Road to Stalingrad*, op. cit., p. 421.

[15] Qu. A. Clark, op. cit., p. 210.

[16] Pabst, op. cit., p. 80.

[17] Qu. Chuikov, op. cit., pp. 142–3.

CHAPTER 17 THE PIT

[1] The South-west Front under Vatutin, the Don Front of Rokossovsky and the Stalingrad Front under Yeremenko.

[2] Speer, op. cit., p. 248.

[3] A. Clark, op. cit., p. 225.

[4] Henry Shapiro, qu. Werth, op. cit., pp. 499–500.

[5] None of these letters, which the men knew would be their last, reached home. They were impounded by the German High Command and their content analysed. Apart from the fact that they were overwhelmingly considered to be 'negative' to the German leadership, many were ridden with guilt over the war.

[6] *The Road to Berlin*, John Erickson, London, 1983, p. 37.
[7] Werth, op. cit., p. 541.
[8] Werth, op. cit., p. 553.

CHAPTER 18 TO BERLIN

[1] Qu. Werth, op. cit., p. 598.
[2] Erickson, *The Road to Berlin*, op. cit., p. 72.
[3] Erickson, *The Road to Berlin*, op. cit., p. 72.
[4] A. Clark, op. cit., p. 292.
[5] A Yugoslav conscripted into the Wehrmacht had deserted to the Red army the day before and given the hour of the attack. During the night, Russian patrols had surprised German engineers clearing the minefields. Kursk was one of the best-advertised battles of the war.
[6] Guderian, op. cit., pp. 308–9.
[7] Werth, op. cit., p. 683.
[8] *The Forgotten Soldier*, Guy Sajer, London, 1977, p. 228.
[9] Erickson, *The Road to Berlin*, op. cit., pp. 110 et seq.

CHAPTER 19 *PERELOM* AND THE GREAT PURSUIT

[1] Werth, op. cit., pp. 739–40.
[2] Pabst, op. cit., p. 189.
[3] Helmut Pabst, falling back through 'dark overgrown rivers of silent streets, hostile-hunched houses', was killed shortly after.
[4] Werth, op. cit., p. 731.
[5] Qu. Werth, op. cit., p. 704.
[6] Sajer, op. cit., pp. 312 et seq.
[7] Prussia; Hanover and the north-west; Saxony and Leipzig; Hesse-Darmstadt, Hesse-Cassel and the section south of the Rhine; Bavaria, Baden and Württemberg.

CHAPTER 20 *DOSVIDANIA*, UKRAINE

[1] Manteuffel to Liddell Hart, qu. Fuller, op. cit., p. 507.
[2] The Red army had no rank between the two and the major general corresponded roughly to a US or British brigadier general.
[3] Sajer, op. cit., pp. 392 et seq.
[4] Erickson, *The Road to Berlin*, op. cit., p. 177.
[5] Werth, op. cit., pp. 782 et seq.
[6] Erickson, *The Road to Berlin*, op. cit., p. 181.
[7] Werth, op. cit., p. 811.

CHAPTER 21 CENTRE FOLD

[1] Werth, op. cit., p. 858.
[2] Bagration was one of Suvorov's commanders, later mortally wounded during the 1812 invasion.

[3] *Password Victory*, compiled Vladimir Sevruk, Moscow, 1985, Vol. II, p. 233.

[4] Ibid, p. 233.

[5] Erickson, *The Road to Berlin*, op. cit., p. 224.

[6] Liddell Hart, *History of the Second World War*, London, 1970, 1973 edn p. 608.

[7] Erickson, *The Road to Berlin*, op. cit., p. 273.

[8] *Royal Air Force 1939–1945*, Denis Richards, Hilary St George Saunders, London, 1974, Vol. III, p. 240.

[9] Winston S. Churchill, *The Second World War*, Vol. VI, p. 124.

[10] Churchill, op. cit., p. 122.

[11] German casualties were some 10,000 killed, 7,000 missing and 9,000 wounded. The fact that the dead outnumbered the wounded is witness to the ferocity and close quarters of the fighting.

[12] Werth, op. cit., p. 878.

[13] Erickson, *The Road to Berlin*, op. cit., p. 308.

CHAPTER 22 THE SATELLITES CHANGE SIDES

[1] Erickson, *The Road to Berlin*, op. cit., p. 360.

[2] Liddell Hart, op.cit., p. 613.

[3] Sajer, op. cit., p. 461.

[4] *Liberation*, Boris Polevoi, Konstantin Simonov, Michael Trachmann, Moscow, 1985.

[5] He had last visited the Soviet Union in 1940, using a forged passport and an alias. At that time, he had been an insignificant Comintern agent from an obscure Communist party that seemed to have little prospect of success. The war was changing the entire Who's Who of Eastern Europe along with its political shaping. Erickson, *The Road to Berlin*, op. cit., p. 381.

[6] Churchill, op. cit., Vol. VI, p. 181.

[7] Lieutenant Heinrich Amberger later gave evidence for the defence at the Nuremberg Trials. Qu. *Nemesis at Potsdam*, Alfred M. de Zayes, London, 1977, pp. 62–3.

[8] Guderian, op. cit., p. 382.

CHAPTER 23 THE HOUSE OF CARDS

[1] Bialer (ed.), op. cit., p. 467.

[2] Official Soviet sources put the Red army superiority over the Germans at 5.5:1 in manpower, 7.8:1 in artillery, 5.7:1 in armour and 17.6:1 in aircraft. On the main assault axis, the ratio reached 9:1 in men and 10:1 in armour. Ibid., p. 467.

[3] Erickson, *The Road to Berlin*, op. cit., pp. 448 et seq.

[4] Erickson, *The Road to Berlin*, op. cit., p. 449.

[5] Guderian, op. cit., p. 389.

[6] Marshal I. S. Koniev, qu. Bialer (ed.), op. cit., p. 484.

[7] Guderian, op. cit., p. 390.

[8] Erickson, *The Road to Berlin*, op. cit., p. 458.

[9] Erickson, *The Road to Berlin*, op. cit., p. 467.

[10] De Zayas, op. cit., pp. 67–8.

[11] Koniev, qu. Bialer (ed.), op. cit., p. 490.

[12] *The Eagle and the Small Birds*, Michael Charlton, London, 1984, qu. p. 12.

[13] Charlton, op. cit., p. 44.

[14] Charlton, op. cit., p. 49.

[15] The Protocols did not become known until 1949, when the Americans published captured German archives.

CHAPTER 24 TO THE ZOO STATION

[1] General Reinhard Gehlen, *The Service*, New York, 1972, p. 62, qu. *Military Review*, March 1980.

[2] Sajer, op. cit., p. 532.

[3] Qu. Werth, op. cit., p. 965.

[4] Colonel General S. M. Shtemenko. He claimed after the war that: 'There remained no doubt whatsoever that the Allies intended to capture Berlin before us, even though, according to the Yalta Agreements, the city fell within the zone designated for occupation by Soviet troops.'

[5] Bialer (ed.), op. cit., p. 621.

[6] Colonel General S. M. Shtemenko, qu. Bialer (ed.), op. cit., p. 500.

[7] Captain Sergei Golbov, qu. *The Last Battle*, Cornelius Ryan, London, 1980, p. 243.

[8] Marshal I. S. Koniev, *Sorok piatyi*, Moscow, 1966, qu. Bialer (ed.), op. cit., p. 527.

[9] Erickson, *The Road to Berlin*, op. cit., p. 595.

[10] Ryan, op. cit., pp. 118 and 358.

[11] Ryan, op. cit., p. 343 et seq.

[12] Ryan, op. cit., p. 367.

[13] Erickson, *The Road to Berlin*, op. cit., p. 605.

CHAPTER 25 VICTORY'S END

None.

CHAPTER 26 PLUS ÇA CHANGE

[1] *Endurance and Endeavour*, J. N. Westwood, Oxford, 1981, pp. 360–61.

[2] *Victims of Yalta*, Nikolai Tolstoy, London, 1979.

[3] Ibid., p. 174.

[4] *The Soviet Army*, Albert and Joan Seaton, London, 1986, pp. 162–3.

[5] Though this expression was never used by the Russians, nor for that matter by the Germans.

[6] Stalin, Mikoyan, Molotov, Voroshilov, Khrushchev, Andreyev and Kaganovich served in both. Of the other 1939 members, Kalinin had died in 1946, Zhdanov died in 1948, after setting new standards in the crudity of censorship and triggering the coming Leningrad affair with an anti-Semitic and anti-intellectual campaign. Beria, Malenkov, Voznesensky and Bulganin were new members. Voznesensky did not live long to enjoy his new eminence.

[7] In Djilas's description.

[8] Alliluyeva, op. cit., p. 207.

[9] Alliluyeva, op. cit., p. 219.

[10] Alliluyeva, op. cit., p. 18.

[11] 'The Heirs of Stalin', Yevgeny Yevtushenko, qu. *Khrushchev*, Roy Medvedev, Oxford, 1983, p. 210.

CHAPTER 27 A LUNCH AT THE LUBIANKA

[1] Later a key centre in the Iran–Iraq war. *Sic transit* Pax Britannica.

[2] 'At the present moment in world history, nearly every nation must choose alternative ways of life.' said Truman. 'The choice is too often not a free one. One way of life is based upon the will of the majority and is distinguished by free institutions, representative governments, grants of individual liberty, freedom of speech and religion, and freedom from political oppression. The second way of life is based upon the will of a minority forcibly imposed upon the majority. It relies upon terror and oppression, a controlled press and radio, fixed selections and the suppression of individual freedoms. I believe that it must be the policy of the United States to support free peoples who are resisting attempted subjugation by armed minorities or by outside pressures. I believe that we must assist free peoples to work out their own destinies in their own way.' Not quite the Gettysburg address, perhaps, but a direct descendant.

[3] *Uprising!*, David Irving, London, 1981, p. 38.

[4] H. R. Trevor-Roper, 'The Politburo Tries a New Tack', *New York Times Magazine*, 19 October 1947, p. 67.

[5] The coalition Cabinet, true to Rákosi's dictum, had three Communists, three Smallholders, three Social Democrats, one National Peasant and three non-party members.

[6] Ferenc Nagy, *The Struggle Behind the Iron Curtain*, New York, 1948, qu. *How did the Satellites Happen?* A Student of Affairs, London, 1952, p. 142.

[7] Charlton, op. cit., p. 64.

[8] Charlton, op. cit., pp. 64–5.

[9] Later a victim of Stalin's anti-Semitic purges in the early 1950s.

[10] Charlton, op. cit., pp. 54–5 and 80–81.

[11] These men, who had found the Red army clawing at their backs as the undivided weight of the Germans compelled their retreat in 1939, were not 'liberated' from the Gulag when the Germans turned on their captors, but *amnestied*. Sweet amnesty!

[12] It is easy enough to see why Soviet victims of Stalinism are allowed to break surface from time to time, but Polish officers never. If Moscow did take advantage of the cheap days of the Nazi pact to do some murdering of Poles on its own account, it wipes out much of the moral credit that accrued to the Soviet people during the war proper.

[13] *How Did the Satellites Happen?* London, 1952.

[14] Charlton, op. cit., p. 20 et seq.

[15] This light sentence was a mere plaything for Puzak. He was duly released in 1946 and returned to Poland. He was re-arrested the following year, tried once more in Moscow and died in a Soviet prison in May 1950.

[16] Edward Taborsky, private secretary to Benes who attended the Kremlin meeting, qu. Charlton, op. cit., p. 70.

[17] Charlton, op. cit., p. 63.

[18] Charlton, op. cit., pp. 69–70.

[19] An imaginative touch. The German General Staff had ceased to exist almost three years before.

[20] Djilas, op. cit., p. 27.

[21] Djilas, op. cit., p. 70.

[22] Charlton, op. cit., pp. 94–5.

[23] Charlton, op. cit., pp. 77–8.

CHAPTER 28 ARMAGEDDON

[1] *The Greatest Power on Earth*, Ronald W. Clark, London, 1980.
[2] *The Soviet Union and the Arms Race*, David Holloway, London, 1983, p. 16.
[3] Holloway, op. cit., p. 17.
[4] Holloway, op. cit., p. 18.
[5] R. W. Clark, op. cit., p. 177.
[6] The scientist James Chadwick.
[7] Brigadier General Thomas Farrel, qu. R. W. Clark, op. cit., p. 199.
[8] Sir Alan Brooke, qu. R. W. Clark, op. cit., p. 205.
[9] Speer, op. cit., p. 227.
[10] *The Paperclip Conspiracy*, Tom Bower, London, 1987, pp. 64–5.
[11] Bower, op. cit., p. 138.
[12] Bower, op. cit., p. 226.
[13] Bower, op. cit., pp. 227–8. The US, Britain and France also recruited German experts. Although, as Bower shows, they were slower off the mark, they were equally indifferent to the Nazi sympathies or atrocities of their new immigrants.
[14] A. Lavrent'yeva, qu. Holloway, op.cit., p. 20.
[15] Thomas Whitney, attaché at the embassy, qu. R. W. Clark, op. cit., p. 208.
[16] Tad Szulc, *The Times*, 29 August 1984.
[17] In Britain, the socialist Prime Minister, Clement Attlee, thought that there was no split in public opinion over using the bomb. This view was backed by an editorial in the relatively doveish *Observer*. 'It is we who hold the overwhelming trump cards.' the paper wrote shortly after the start of the crisis. 'It is our side, and not Russia, which holds atomic and post-atomic weapons and could, if sufficiently provoked, literally wipe Russia's power and threat to the world's peace from the face of the earth.'
[18] R. W. Clark, op. cit., p. 267.
[19] Andrei Sakharov, *New York Review of Books*, 21 March 1974, qu. R. W. Clark, op. cit., pp. 267–8.
[20] Then chairman of the Council of Ministers.
[21] A megaton is equivalent to a million tons of TNT, a kiloton to 1,000 tons. The US device thus outblasted the Russians by 10 million:400,000.
[22] Britain became an H-power at Christmas Island in May 1957, the Chinese in 1967 and the French in 1968.

CHAPTER 29 NIKITA

[1] Khrushchev, op. cit., p. 17.
[2] The record at a lower level is patchy. Gorbachev has been careful to let senior Brezhnev figures float into retirement. But Yuri Churbanov, Brezhnev's son-in-law, was arrested and charged in 1987 with taking 650,000 roubles in bribes as a first deputy interior minister. Gennady Vrovin, Brezhnev's private secretary, was sentenced to thirteen years for bribe-taking in 1987.
[3] *A History of the Soviet Union*, Geoffrey Hosking, London, 1985, p. 331, qu. from an underground Ukraine source.
[4] Medvedev, op. cit., p. 92.
[5] Holloway, op. cit., p. 41.
[6] In 1988 workmen chiselled the name Brezhnev off the walls of a Moscow square, and left the Cyrillic letters lying in a heap in the snow. The square and its suburb will revert to its old name, Cheryomushki. At the same time, the name of Khrushchev was

being restored in Soviet histories. It was a late recognition that the Khrushchev decade, for all its economic failure and its erratic and volatile relations with the West, was a watershed. Gorbachev is now trying to thaw out some of the ideas and experiments brandished by Khrushchev, that were lazily frozen during Brezhnev's big sleep.

[7] Intercontinental ballistic missile.

[8] Holloway, op. cit., p. 23.

[9] The work of groups led by the Academicians S. P. Korolev, M. Keldysh, V. P. Glushko, V. P. Barmin and M. K. Yangel.

[10] Sent to the West by the British-directed spy within the GRU, Colonel Oleg Penkovsky, later discovered and shot.

[11] *Raketnye Voyska Strategicheskovo Naznacheniya.*

[12] In a speech to the 4th Session of the Supreme Soviet on 14 January 1960.

[13] *Armed Forces of the USSR*, Harriet F. and William F. Scott, London, 1984, pp. 42–3.

[14] Khrushchev, op. cit., p. 516.

[15] He was killed in a flying accident in 1968.

[16] The names of most of the men who created the Russian space programme remain unpublished in the Soviet Union. The contribution of S. P. Korolev, the chief rocket designer, was learned only after his death. Medvedev, op. cit., p. 175.

[17] The US had 834 ICBMs to the Russians' 190, 416 SLBMs to 107 and 630 bombers to 175.

[18] At the 22nd Congress in October 1961, qu. Scotts, op. cit., pp. 44–5.

[19] Khrushchev, op. cit., p. 517.

[20] Holloway, op. cit., pp. 43–4.

[21] *The History of Military Art*, Officers' Library Series, Moscow, 1966.

[22] Qu. Scotts, op. cit., p. 54.

[23] Let ordinary military men have their Frunze, Kirov and Voroshilov schools. [Lest they be in any doubt of their subservience, body, soul and potential cell, to the Party,] The rocket men's school is named for the First Chekhist.

CHAPTER 30 IN UNCLE SAM'S BACKYARD

[1] Khrushchev, op. cit., p. 492.

[2] The same port from which Castro was later to speed large numbers of criminals and a small leavening of dissidents to Florida in the Mariel 'boatlift'.

[3] Direct confrontation between Americans and Russians in uniform has been rare enough for the USAF crew, Majors Rudolf Anderson Jr of Spartanburg, S. Carolina and Richard S. Heysler of Battle Creek, Michigan, to deserve a footnote for this sortie. Anderson was killed on another mission over Cuba two weeks later.

[4] Johnson, op. cit., pp. 624–5.

[5] Khrushchev, op. cit., p. 494.

[6] Qu. *The Missiles of October*, Elie Abel, London, 1966, p. 117.

[7] So were Soviet nuclear forces, the only time that this has been announced. In contrast, this was the sixteenth time that US forces had been put on alert status since 1945.

[8] Uruguay abstained.

[9] Lieutenant General Vladimir Dubovik, qu. Abel, op. cit., p. 125.

[10] They remain so. Secure-graded links to Moscow failed when command staff in the Soviet Far East sought instructions over the Korean Air Lines 747 flying in Soviet airspace in September 1983. They were reduced to using a non-scrambled line.

[11] Khrushchev, op. cit., p. 497.

[12] Qu. Walter Pincus, *International Herald Tribune*, 26 July 1986.

[13] Bromley Smith, qu. Pincus, op. cit.

[14] Qu. *Cold War to Détente*, Colin Bown and Peter J. Mooney, London, 1981, p. 86.

[15] Johnson, op. cit., p. 626.

CHAPTER 31 HUNGARIAN AUTUMN

[1] Irving, op. cit., p. 160.

[2] Gerö, a Comintern leader who had worked in Paris, was Stalin's agent responsible for the purge in Catalonia during the Spanish civil war. It is ironic that he should now serve Stalin's debunker, Khrushchev.

[3] Irving, op. cit., p. 290.

[4] Mikes, op. cit., p. 79.

[5] Irving, op. cit., p. 272.

[6] Mikes, op. cit., p. 89.

[7] Irving, op. cit., pp. 325–6.

[8] Irving, op. cit., p. 311.

[9] Op. cit., p. 341.

[10] Mikes, op. cit., p. 115.

[11] He avoided a certain lynching by escaping to Moscow, returning to Hungary in 1960 and dying in poverty, forgotten, in Budapest in 1980.

[12] Irving, op. cit., p. 390.

[13] Irving, op. cit., pp. 392–3.

[14] Khrushchev, op. cit., p. 418 et seq.

[15] Khrushchev, op. cit., p. 420.

[16] Irving, op. cit., p. 504.

[17] *Thirteen Days that Shook the Kremlin*, Tibor Meray, London, 1959.

[18] Irving, op. cit., p. 498.

[19] Mikes, op. cit., pp. 150–51.

[20] The Italian Legation noted on 8 November: 'From two separate sources it is learned that Soviet troops have been told by their commandant that they are suppressing a Nazi movement in Germany.' Irving, op. cit., p. 531.

[21] Irving, op. cit., p. 641.

[22] George Mikes, *The Independent*, 13 October 1986.

CHAPTER 32 BERLIN SUMMER

[1] *The Berlin Wall*, Norman Gelb, London, 1986, p. 26.

[2] Many went under when the airlift ended. Sir Freddie Laker and British Caledonian Airways both originated in commercial flying during the airlift.

[3] Airliners to West Berlin still take these corridors and abide by the same height restrictions. And the route remains the monopoly of US, British and French airlines.

[4] Thirty-nine British and thirty-one American aircrew were killed.

[5] Royal United Services Institution, *RUSI Journal*, February 1949, p. 86.

[6] The Basic Law remains the effective constitution of West Germany.

[7] Four members of the Politburo of the German Communist Party and ten members of the Central Committee disappeared, together with the head of the Party's military

wing. Others were handed over to the Gestapo during the years of the Nazi–Soviet Pact.

[8] Gelb, op. cit., p. 39.

[9] Medvedev, op. cit., p. 181.

[10] *Mayday*, Michael R. Beschloss, London, 1986.

[11] Medvedev, op. cit., p. 151.

[12] He was later exchanged in a spy swap. He was killed when flying a helicopter for a California radio station monitoring morning traffic jams.

[13] Khrushchev, op. cit., p. 454.

[14] Gelb, op. cit., p. 57.

[15] Held by the Americans against the final German offensive in the Ardennes at the end of 1944.

[16] Medvedev, op. cit., p. 183.

[17] Khrushchev, op. cit., p. 458. It was, of course, Khrushchev who had issued the challenge by demanding a change in the status quo.

[18] Gelb, op. cit., p. 146.

[19] In Soviet terminology, the Wall is simply an 'installation'.

[20] Khrushchev, op. cit., pp. 459–60.

[21] Medvedev, op. cit., p. 184.

CHAPTER 33 PRAGUE SPRING

[1] Novotny had planned a coup against his young rival in December 1967. A tank brigade was to move on Prague and the police were to arrest 1,032 people, including Dubček. Open-dated arrest warrants had been made out and Novotny had got the support of two hard-line generals, Mamula and Janko. The plot was scotched by General Prchlik, a reformer. Janko committed suicide and Mamula was arrested.

[2] In June the *Kan-Klub angazovanych nestraniku* or club of Politically Engaged Non-Partisans, was established. It was a powerful discussion group covering wide opinions, rather than an opposition political party. But the 'Soviet White Book' published by Moscow after the invasion particularly stressed the dangers of this and Club 231.

[3] *Why Dubček Fell*, Pavel Tigrid, London, 1971, p. 57.

[4] A year later, speaking in Moscow, the new Czech leader Gustav Husak dubbed all this: 'Naivete and political romanticism'.

[5] Leonid Brezhnev had emerged in leadership with Aleksei Kosygin and Nikolai Podgorny after the overthrow of Khrushchev. Brezhnev had become party general secretary in March 1966. The vigorous action taken against the Czechs, and the later invasion of Afghanistan, are both out of character with the lazy, out of sight, out of mind attitude he took towards the Soviet Union itself.

Until his death in 1982 Brezhnev allowed Soviet domestic politics and the economy to bury its head deep in consensus and stagnation. His benign neglect saw large parts of industry slowly rust up. He fitted a mood well enough, for the country needed a breathing space after the Stalinist terrors and the alarums and excursions of Khrushchev. Eighteen years without major reform or fresh imagination, however, left a heap of problems for Gorbachev to deal with.

Where large slices of Stalinist Russia had been run by men in their thirties and forties, the country became a gerontocracy in which virtually every member of the Politburo was over sixty. Signs of rising nationalism, small enough but significant in a multi-ethnic state in which Russians were beginning to lose their demographic dominance, in the Ukraine, the Baltic states, Georgia, Armenia and central Asia, were ignored.

Despite the windfalls of soaring oil and gold prices, industrial growth was sluggish well before his death and the agricultural record continued to be appalling. Waste, low productivity and giganticism combined to atrophy industry to such an extent that arms sales were the only major finished products in an export list dominated by raw materials.

The military, however, were not neglected. Brezhnev was fond of things martial. He had risen to major general during the war, albeit as a commissar, and had taken part in the great victory parade in Red Square in June 1945. He remained attached to rank, promoting himself first general and then marshal in 1976, and awarding himself several chestfuls of medals. Under him the Soviet Union built up its sea power and its influence in the Third World. It also attained nuclear parity with the US, an equality that made détente possible.

[6] *Eastern European Military Establishments: The Warsaw Pact Northern Tier*, Rand Corp., 1980, p. 139.

[7] Tigrid, op. cit., p. 70.

[8] Tigrid, op. cit., p. 84.

[9] Zdenek Mlynar, *Night Frost in Prague*, London, 1980.

[10] Mlynar, op. cit., p. 169.

[11] The pseudonym taken by the officer when he defected to the West. *The Liberators*, Viktor Suvorov, London, 1981.

[12] *Soviet Blitzkrieg Theory*, Peter Vigor, London, 1983.

[13] Tigrid, op. cit., p. 105.

[14] Mlyner, op. cit., p. 177. The striped jerseys show that they were Spetsnaz special forces troops.

[15] Mlynar, op. cit., p. 179.

[16] The figures given by Central Committee member Frybet on 31 August 1968, qu. Tigrid, op. cit. At least this number of troops would have been available but, in view of the lack of Czech resistance, such forces were not required to cross the frontiers.

[17] In Europe, the West claims its own territory in fullness. Not the Eastern bloc. For the length of the Iron Curtain, the Eastern wire, watchtowers and minefields are almost invariably well back from the actual frontier, sometimes by three or four kilometres. Only reconnaissance troops, in pairs, selected, patrol to the geographic limit of the bloc. What looks like no-man's-land is thus communist and whatever killing takes place there is, should Western lawyers or politicians become involved, beyond their right.

[18] On 13 September a member of the Czech Presidium said on television that 'up to today there were killed ... more than 70 of our citizens'. Qu. in *Czechoslovakia 1968*, Adam Roberts and Phillip Windsor, London, 1969, p. 123.

[19] An editorial in *Pravda* on 22 August accused Dubček of being the head of a 'minority group' with 'right-wing opportunist positions' who, though paying 'lip service to their desire to protect socialism', were plotting 'counter-revolution'. These charges, which amounted to treason, were similar to those levelled against Nagy.

[20] Roberts and Windsor, op. cit., pp. 126–8.

[21] The jamming equipment was finally flown in on a Red army helicopter. Roberts and Windsor, op. cit., p. 120.

[22] Mlynar, op. cit., pp. 210–11.

[23] In the case of Yugoslavia, Brezhnev said the Americans had indicated that it would 'have to be discussed'.

[24] Jiri Volenta, *Soviet Intervention in Czechoslovakia, 1969*, Baltimore, 1979, p. 151.

[25] *Zealots and Rebels*, Z. L. Suda, Hoover Institution, 1980.

[26] Mlynar, op. cit., p. 224.

CHAPTER 34 POLISH WINTER

[1] *Oni*, Teresa Toranska, *Granta* No. 17.

[2] *Chemin d'Espoir*, Lech Walesa, Paris, 1987.

[3] Leon Wudzki, in a speech to the Polish Central Committee on 20 October 1956. qu. *Poland*, Konrad Syrop, London, 1968, p. 153.

[4] Syrop, op. cit.

[5] Walesa, op. cit.

[6] *East European Military Establishments*, Rand Corp., p. 61.

[7] *Warsaw Pact: The Question of Cohesion*, Ottawa, 1984, Vol. II, p. 81.

[8] Walesa, op. cit.

[9] *Kulture*, Paris, 1987.

[10] Walesa, op. cit.

[11] *Kulture*, op. cit.

[12] *Problems of Communism*, March–April 1982, pp. 22 et seq.

[13] *Warsaw Pact*, op. cit., p. 144.

[14] *Public Opinion and Political Change in Poland*, David S. Mason, Cambridge, 1985, p. 159.

[15] Mason, op. cit., p. 127.

[16] Walesa, op. cit.

[17] Post-coup events give him surprisingly little reason. An army unit near Cracow and one in Radom are said to have mutinied, tanks in Gdansk to have been decorated with Solidarity signs and carnations, soldiers to have been arrested for refusing to obey orders in Cracow and Warsaw. That is all.

[18] Walesa, op. cit.

[19] CBS, NBC, ABC, AP, UPI, the *Washington Post* and the *Los Angeles Times*, the BBC, ITN and the *Financial Times*, AFP, DPA, ZDF, Kyodo and the Spanish Information Agency.

CHAPTER 35 AFGHANISTAN

[1] *Afghanistan and the Soviet Union*, Henry S. Bradsher, Durham, N.C., 1983, p. 182.

[2] Vladimir Kuzichkin, who was in the KGB department responsible for Soviet 'illegal' agents abroad, defected to Britain in 1982 with details of the Afghan operation. Christopher Andrew, *Daily Telegraph*, 29 December 1986.

[3] *The Grand Strategy of the Soviet Union*, Edward N. Luttwak, London, 1983, p. 57.

[4] Colonel James T. Haggerty, *The Army Quarterly and Defence Journal*, Vol. 110, No. 2, April 1980, p. 147.

[5] Did any paratrooper stumble across these words in his unit Lenin Room before leaving for the invasion?

[6] Khrushchev, op. cit., pp. 560–62.

[7] Bradsher, op. cit., pp. 29–30.

[8] Bradsher, op. cit., p. 41.

[9] Bradsher, op. cit., p. 66.

[10] Bradsher, op. cit., p. 83.

[11] Bradsher, op. cit., p. 101.

[12] 'The Russian Military and Afghanistan', Ronald R. Rader, *Soviet Armed Forces Review*, annual vol. iv, 1980, Gulf Breeze, Fla.

[13] Bradsher, op. cit., p. 116.

[14] Rader, op. cit. In fact, the Western and Moslem response to the invasion was tart

and costly. The US embargoed technology exports and important grain sales, many nations pulled out of the summer Olympics in Moscow in 1980 and détente all but gave up the ghost.

[15] Edgar O'Ballance, 'Soviet Tactics in Afghanistan', *Military Review*, August 1980, p. 48.

[16] O'Ballance, op. cit., p. 49.

[17] Christopher Andrew, *Daily Telegraph*, 29 December 1986.

[18] Martin Walker, *The Guardian*, 26 June 1986.

[19] *International Herald Tribune*, 3 August 1984.

[20] *Soviet Analyst*, Vol. 9, No. 12.

[21] *Soviet Analyst*, op. cit.

[22] Amnesty International report, *The Times*, 19 November 1986.

[23] For which read the failure of Marxism, midnight interrogations and the murder of mullahs to win friends or influence Afghans. The sterility of Sovspeak, the absence of everyday language and expression, is a terrible handicap to any attempt by the Kremlin to explain itself. *Pravda* went on to urge the creation of 'positive dialogue between public and political forces'. Does that mean they were sorry, that things had gone wrong, that the Kabul government had better back off? Or was it another cliché tossed in to make up a paragraph and the lads in the Pul-i-Charki prison were free to carry on with business as normal? When Viktor Chebrikov, then head of the KGB and Najib's mentor, rose at the traditional ceremony for the anniversary of the revolution (the Russian one, not the Afghan) in 1986, 'no one could ever remember having heard such a speech on such an occasion'. Why? He spoke of '*reforms*, instead of the normal *reconstruction, refurbishments, revolutionary transformation* or *changes*'. It sounds tremendous. *Reforms*. But were the audience not equally stupefied the first time that they heard *reconstruction* or *revolutionary transformation*? Did not even *refurbishment* raise a stir? Did KGB staffers rush back to their offices and say: 'By Lenin! He's got it! He's really got it! *Refurbishment!*' And in 1985, in the basements of the Pul-i-Charki, did KHAD interrogators burst into their basement, and clasp their prisoners, and say: 'It's going to be all right! Believe me! Chebrikov just talked about *reform*! Don't worry, we'll have you out of here in no time!'?

[24] Abbas, interview with author.

[25] *Dukh* is army slang for *dukhman* or bandit. Artiom Borovik, *Ogoniok* magazine, Moscow, No. 29, 1987.

CHAPTER 36 RED ELITE

[1] *Nomenklatura*, Michael Voslensky. New York, 1985. Voslensky estimates that: 'The power of the *nomenklatura* in the Soviet Union is exercised by about 250,000 persons, or one thousandth of the population, who are subject neither to election nor rejection by the people, but decide its fate and lay down the people's political line.' P. 91. Include wives, families and dependants and the total for the class approaches three million.

[2] The rouble is worth around £1 or $1.50 at the official rate. Effectively it is worth rather less than a US dollar. By Chinese standards, at least, Russian pay scales are generous. The Chinese conscript gets £1.75 a month.

[3] The average pay of a Soviet office or factory worker is 181 roubles a month with two weeks' paid holiday. Voslensky puts the salary of a typical *nomenklatura* member, the head of a central committee desk, at 450 roubles a month, plus a thirteenth month's pay and a month's free holiday at a Central Committee rest home. On top of this he

gets the *Kremliovka*, either 120 or 90 roubles a month, which is used for food from the Kremlin canteen. In all, Voslensky estimates that he gets eight times the average wage. This is a higher multiple than a senior civil servant would expect in the West, though not overwhelmingly so.

[4] A favourite spot for defence scientists as well as the military. Andrei Sakharov, a father of Soviet nuclear weapons and latterly a leading dissident, had his dacha here. *Russia*, David K. Shipler, New York, 1983; and *The Russians*, Hedrick Smith, London, 1976 edn., give an excellent social context to the Soviet military.

[5] *The Liberators*, Viktor Suvorov, London, 1981, p. 29.

[6] Edward Lozansky, *Tatiana,* qu. Shipler, op. cit.

[7] Aleksei Myagkov, *Inside the KGB*, New York, 1981.

[8] Suvorov, op. cit., pp. 66–7.

[9] Voslensky, op. cit.

[10] Djilas, op. cit.

[11] Only the third career officer to hold the post, after Timoshenko and Vasilevsky.

[12] There is much truth in the old maxim that the Americans make public things that their own interests demand be kept secret, whilst the Russians keep secret things that are already public.

[13] Vladil Lysenko, *A Crime against the World*, London, 1983.

[14] Hedrick Smith, op. cit.

[15] *Soviet Diplomacy and Negotiating Behaviour*, Joseph G. Whelan, Boulder, Colo., 1983, p. 490.

[16] Voslensky, op. cit., p. 107.

[17] Suvorov, op. cit., pp. 114–15. Epishev was head of the Red army's political directorate. Not that the Russians have a monopoly on political tedium. West German TV ran Chancellor Kohl's 1986 New Year's address to the nation in 1987 as well, without most people remarking on it.

[18] Introduction to Voslensky, op. cit.

[19] Shevchenko, *Breaking with Moscow*, New York, 1985.

[20] Though there are examples. Lieutenant General Sivonok of the 20th Guards Army was charged with buying furniture, carpets and a dinner service for his office and taking them home. The head of the Berlin Garrison, Major General Pitkevich, was prematurely retired for selling off food from military stores to East German civilians.

[21] Viktor I. Belenko in *MiG Pilot*, John Barron, *Reader's Digest*, New York, 1980, p. 74.

[22] Suvorov, op. cit., p. 140.

[23] *The Soviet Soldier*, Herbert Goldhammer, Rand Corp., 1975.

[24] *The Ethnic Factor in the Soviet Armed Forces*, S. Enders Wimbush and Alex Alexiev, Rand Corp., 1980.

[25] Goldhammer, op. cit.

CHAPTER 37 THE THREE MILLION

[1] Almost all the officer corps, which accounts for 20 per cent of the srength, are regulars as are 5 per cent of the NCOs.

[2] Hedrick Smith, op. cit., p. 391.

[3] *Voyennyy Vestnik*, October 1971.

[4] 15 July 1972. Qu. Goldhammer, op. cit.

[5] *Military Rituals*, V. Sedykh, Moscow, 1981.

[6] As a reporter in Vietnam, the only all-American aristocrat I met in ground combat

was a Marine lieutenant in Hué who said he had joined up, from UCLA, because he 'wanted to be different'.

[7] The 1979 census total was 262 million, with 137 million ethnic Russians and 42 million Ukrainians.

[8] *Pravada Ukrainy*, qu. Goldhammer, op. cit.

[9] Wimbush and Alexiev, op. cit.

[10] Wimbush and Alexiev, op. cit., p. 51.

[11] Those who look back to Vlasov forget that he commanded a rabble, not a legion, and that French, Dutch, Belgians, Norwegians and Danes also fought for Hitler without it being reckoned much more than an aberration.

[12] Others included A. Khlebystov, who did so three times, and B. Kobzan who apparently rammed luckless German pilots four times.

[13] *Kalendar Viona*, Moskva, Voennoe Izdatelstvo, 1982.

[14] KZ 17.6.72, qu. Goldhammer, op. cit.

[15] Colton, op. cit., p. 184. Commissars were renamed *zampolits* in 1940.

[16] Goldhammer, op. cit.

[17] *Red Star*, May 1981.

[18] December 1979.

[19] 25 East marks is worth about £8 at the official rate of exchange, only £2 on the black market.

[20] *Bild,* 15 January, 1987.

[21] The extreme sensitivity even towards the most faithful satellite, East Germany, is revealing. A dissident in Moscow told the author, 'East Germany has more than one political party. That may mean nothing to you, since the SED is totally dominant. But to us it means plurality and a sort of freedom. The army doesn't want any soldier stumbling on to that kind of idea.'

[22] Not to be confused with that other Katyn, where the Polish officers were massacred, a non-event in the Soviet Union.

[23] Hence the old Red army joke of a private halted by a sergeant at the barrack gate. 'Permission to enter camp, Sergeants!' asks the inebriated infantryman. 'Certainly,' says the sergeant. 'You can both come in.'

[24] *The Guardian*, 8 September 1984. Rybakov's autobiographical novel. *The Burden,* was published by Hutchinson, London, 1984.

[25] *MiG Pilot, the Final Escape of Lieutenant Belenko,* John Barron, Reader's Digest Press. 1980, p. 4.

[26] Robert Gillette, *International Herald Tribune,* 13 September 1982.

[27] *Der Spiegel,* 21 July 1978.

[28] In 1919, 1,761,000 Red army deserters were either caught in raids or appeared voluntarily under amnesties. This does not include the hundreds of thousands who managed to avoid re-entry into the Red army. Whole armies, such as the 11th and 12th Red Armies on the southern front, disintegrated through mass desertion in the spring of 1919. Troop trains, crowded when they pulled out of Moscow or Leningrad, would arrive half empty at the front. In contrast to this Russian tradition, the People's Liberation Army in the harder, longer Chinese civil war had only a few handfuls of deserters. *The Revolutionary Armies,* Jonathan R. Adelman, Connecticut, 1980.

[29] Lieutenant Commander Gregory Young, University of Colorado, *Sea Power* magazine, February 1985.

[30] The boy was murdered by farmers opposed to collectivization. Hedrick Smith, op. cit.

[31] Suvorov, *The Liberators,* op. cit., p. 159.

[32] Erickson, *The Road to Stalingrad,* op. cit., p. 21.

[33] The British army has been involved in warfare or anti-terrorist operations almost every year since the war. British conflicts have included Palestine, Korea, Malaya, Suez, Cyprus, Kenya, Borneo, Aden, Belize, the Falklands and Northern Ireland. The Americans have been engaged in Korea and Vietnam as well as more limited conflicts in the Middle East and Latin America.

CHAPTER 38 ARMY AUDIT

[1] *The Military Balance*, London, 1986.

[2] Christopher Donnelly, *Soviet War Power*, London, 1982, p. 175.

[3] Donnelly, op. cit., p. 229.

[4] Though the bulk of them are outdated T-54, 55 and 62 models. Put another way, to allow for population difference, the Soviets have twenty-five tanks to defend a city with the population of Newcastle. The British have two and a bit – say, the turret.

[5] *The Soviet Army*, Seatons, op. cit., p. 183.

[6] Seatons, op. cit., p. 196.

[7] HEAT (High Explosive Anti Tank) shells are hollow and contain high explosive. When this detonates on striking the target, it implodes on to a cone of copper inside the shell. The cone is shaped to turn into a thin jet of molten copper which streams through armour plate at immense velocity. With a discarding Sabot shell, a tungsten-carbide penetrating core or 'arrow' maintains the initial high velocity of 1,750 metres per second with which it left the muzzle by discarding its outer casing in flight. Almost all the energy of the gun is concentrated on to a small diameter, increasing its penetration.

[8] *The Middle East War*, The Sunday Times, London, 1974, p. 68.

[9] *Middle East War*, op. cit., Appendix.

[10] *The Military Balance*, op. cit., p. 37.

[11] By the late 1980s a new pattern was emerging with more divisions being kept either at full or at minimum strength. A new type of 'second generation' division is being created, which draws its key personnel from the active divisions and uses the older reservists and the most antiquated equipment. It would take several months to mobilize and retrain these 'Dad's Army' divisions. The advantage, of course, is that the younger reservists and better equipment can be concentrated quickly into more efficient divisions.

[12] 1st Guards Tank Army headquartered at Dresden, 2nd Guards Tank and 8th and 20th Guards Armies at Neustrelitz, Erfurt and Bernau, and 3rd Army at Magdeburg. In addition, the 16th Tactical Air Army is under the Group of Soviet Forces Germany command.

[13] In the Moscow, Leningrad, Kiev, Odessa, Byelorussian, Baltic and Carpathian military districts.

[14] How any Russian, with his love of statistics and of sheer size, would be willing captive to these figures! No new dam is properly christened until the cubic metrage of concrete used in its construction, the kilometres of pipe, the volume of water, the kilowattage of electricity produced, are published. Big is beautiful, for the Russians thirst for size, and to be bigger than an American equivalent is poetry. The Peak of Communism is higher than Mount McKinley, the Halo helicopter will outlift any Sikorsky, the Hotel Rossiya outbeds any Holiday Inn. Here, the Soviet Union out-numbers the US in virtually every item of ground equipment. But all of these figures, freely available in Western publications like *The Military Balance* for the equivalent of a few roubles, are classified secrets in the Soviet Union.

[15] Ironically, when Beria looked likely to attempt a coup using MVD troops in Moscow after the death of Stalin, regular troops were brought in to the capital to neutralize them.

[16] James T. Reitz, *Soviet Armed Forces Review*, Vol. VI 1982, p. 296.

CHAPTER 39 RED NAVY

[1] It was a Whiskey-Class submarine that grounded itself in Swedish waters in October 1981 in the 'Whiskey on the Rocks' incident.

[2] The British were impressed enough by the cruiser Khrushchev himself used on a state visit to Britain to send down the frogman Commander Crabbe to examine its hull in Portsmouth Harbour. Crabbe's decapitated body was later washed up along the coast in Chichester Harbour.

[3] A large group of senior officers wrote to the Central Committee to say that they could no longer guarantee the safety of the Soviet Union. The navy was as favourable to the removal of Khrushchev in 1964 as the army.

[4] Mitchell, op. cit., p. 519.

[5] Mitchell, op. cit., p. 531.

[6] Sometimes not too successfully. There have been several collisions, including a Soviet submarine that hit a US carrier off Japan in 1984.

[7] And ex-husband of Elizabeth Taylor.

[8] Sokolovsky, *Soviet Military Strategy*, qu. Fasts, op. cit., p. 172.

[9] *Newsweek*, 20 May 1985.

[10] The CIA attempted to raise one which sank to a depth of five kilometres in mid-Pacific between Hawaii and Midway Island with the specially built salvage ship *Glomar Explorer* in 1974. By 1983 the Russians were themselves able to salvage a Charlie class boat that sank in shallower Pacific waters off the Kamchatka Peninsula.

[11] International Institute for Strategic Studies, *The Military Balance 1986–7*, London. The Russians have an additional 15 missile boats with 39 missiles which do not come under SALT and are assigned theatre missions.

CHAPTER 40 AIR

[1] In those pre-gay days, the MiG-15 was codenamed Fagot by the Americans. US F-86 Sabre pilots achieved a 14 to 1 kill ratio against Chinese and North Korean MiG-15 pilots. Andrew Cockburn, *The Threat*, London, 1983, p. 143.

[2] Cockburn, op. cit., p. 149.

[3] Though that did not save the *Stark* from being hit.

[4] Donnelly, op. cit., p. 113.

[5] Air defence of the border areas was merged with tactical aviation in the early 1980s and about a thousand interceptors were thus transferred to the air force.

[6] Airborne Warning and Control Systems.

CHAPTER 41 SENIOR SERVICE

[1] US Arms Control and Disarmament Agency estimate, 1978, Marshal Ogarkov, *Komunist*, 1981, qu. Holloway, op. cit., pp. 52–3.

[2] Cockburn, op. cit., p. 209.

[3] Air-launched ALCMs are known as 'alkums' to aficionados, sea-launched SLCMs are 'slickums' and ground-launched GLCMs are 'glickums'.

[4] Dr Hans Rushle, MoD, *Crossbow*, April 1985, p. 7.

[5] 'It is reckoned that an effective defence would destroy all but 60 incoming warheads, or around 95 per cent. That, of course, is more acceptable to military and political leaders who could expect to be in hardened command centres than to the general public.

[6] Rushle, op. cit., p. 2.

[7] Cockburn, op. cit., p. 215.

[8] Conventional Arms Control, RAND Corp, Dec 1987.

CHAPTER 42 THE SPIES

[1] The ideological agent is now a rare species.

[2] They may have been warned by the US navy spy John A. Walker Jr, who was sentenced in 1985 for passing naval secrets to the KGB.

[3] Malcolm W. Browne, *International Herald Tribune*, 23 June 1987.

[4] *Le Monde*, 30 March 1985.

[5] Given that Soviet military budgets are grossly underquoted, the actual savings were probably much greater. The official defence budget, for example, may be understated ten times.

[6] *Time* magazine, 11 November 1985.

[7] *Newsweek*, 11 November 1985.

[8] *Newsweek*, 11 November 1985.

[9] *Soviet Military Intelligence*, Viktor Suvorov, London, 1984, p. 23.

[10] Though it was divided into two until after the end of the war.

[11] Suvorov, *Soviet Military Intelligence*, op. cit., p. 29.

[12] In his book *Soviet Military Intelligence*, op. cit., 'Viktor Suvorov's name is well known,' his publishers say coyly, 'though it is not his real name.' He is supposedly a Soviet army officer, now in his early forties, who served with the GRU and who defected to the West.

[13] Consisting of father John, brother Arthur, son Michael and friend Jerry Whitworth and uncovered in 1985.

[14] Op. cit., p. 56.

[15] In addition to the directorates, there are four similar directions. The first of these covers the Moscow area, hoping to ensnare foreign diplomats, attachés and trade representatives working in the capital. The second is responsible for East and West Berlin, the third for national liberation movements and terrorist organizations, such as the PLO. The fourth operates from Cuba against targets that include the US. Suvorov, *Soviet Military Intelligence*, pp. 56–7.

[16] In August 1981.

[17] *High Treason*, Vladimir Sakharov with Umberto Tosi, New York, pp. 84–5.

[18] *L'Exprèss*, 5 November 1982.

[19] Whose members are, according to Suvorov, known as *govnced* or shit-eaters to GRU men. They prefer more straightforward foreigners who sell themselves for money.

[20] By Kurt Wurzbach, secretary of state for defence, November 1986.

CHAPTER 43 WARSAW PACT

[1] East Germany, Poland, Czechoslovakia, Hungary, Rumania and Bulgaria.

[2] *Inside the Soviet Army*, Viktor Suvorov, New York, 1982.

[3] Albania, more remote from Soviet interests, quit the Pact altogether in 1968.

[4] The northern Soviet group is headquartered at Legnica in Poland. The Group of Soviet Forces in East Germany is centred at Zossen-Wünsdorf near Berlin. The centre group in Czechoslovakia is based at Milovice and the southern group in Budapest.

[5] *East European Military Establishments: the Warsaw Pact Northern Tier*, Rand Corporation, 1980.

[6] *The Warsaw Pact Northern Tier*, op. cit.

[7] Nearly 38 million, compared with 23 million in Rumania, 15.6 million in Czechoslovakia, 16.7 million in East Germany, 10 million in Hungary and 9 million in Bulgaria.

[8] *The Warsaw Pact Northern Tier*, op. cit., p. 66.

[9] *Warsaw Pact*, op. cit., pp. 212–13.

[10] *Warsaw Pact*, op. cit., pp. 223–4.

[11] *The Northern Tier*, op. cit., p. 20.

[12] And the Russians ensure that any nationalism does not go too far by constantly reminding East Germans of the past. The old Prussian fortress prison at Spandau in West Berlin, with its 132 cells and for 21 years a solitary prisoner, Hitler's former deputy Rudolf Hess, was kept functioning into 1987 at Soviet insistence. The Japanese equivalent, Sugamo, where Admiral Tojo had been executed, had been closed by the Americans in 1958.

[13] *The Northern Tier*, op. cit., p. 124.

CHAPTER 44 THE METAL EATERS

[1] Luttwak, op. cit., pp. 144–5.

[2] Hedrick, Smith, op. cit.

[3] Luttwak, op. cit., p. 137.

[4] Luttwak, op. cit, p. 144.

[5] Nick Eberstadt, 'The Health Crisis in the USSR', *The New York Review*, 19 February 1981, pp. 23 et seq.

[6] Ibid.

[7] Abel Aganbegyan, director of the Institute of Economics and Management, Siberian department, of the Soviet Academy of Sciences, *Trud*. August 1984. Aganbegyan has subsequently been chosen by Gorbachev as the leading economist of *perestroika*.

[8] The journal of the State Planning Committee criticized the industrial ministries in 1986 for continuing to give priority to new factories rather than modernizing old plant. Only 2 to 3 per cent of machinery is renewed annually compared with an optimal figure of six to eight per cent. *Planovoye Khozyayatvo*, 2/1985, qu. Schmidt-Häuer, op. cit., pp. 184–5.

[9] Eberstadt, op. cit.

[10] *Soviet Military Power*, Washington DC, 1984.

[11] Or so the US Defense Department has estimated. It is, of course, in its interests to do so. Both the Russian and Western military have a vested interest in exaggerating the power of the potential enemy.

[12] Cockburn, op. cit., p. 85.

[13] The F-106 Delta Dart, the F-4 Phantom and the F-15 Eagle.

[14] Cockburn, op. cit., p. 86.
[15] Holloway, op. cit., p. 151.
[16] Holloway, op. cit., p. 126.
[17] Holloway, op. cit., p. 127.
[18] Qu. *Newsweek*, 15 June 1987.

CHAPTER 45 THE RIVAL GENERAL

[1] Khrushchev was directly involved in the Ukrainian retreat of 1941 and much else. Brezhnev was perhaps not the war hero of hagiography, but served as a political commissar, notably with the 18th Army which stopped the German drive in the Caucasus. Andropov set up partisan units on the Finnish front. Chernenko was deeply involved in the resettlement of industry and refugees in Siberia.

[2] *Privolnoye* means 'Liberty' in Russian, the village having been founded by freed serfs in the last century. The name may turn out to be significant or ironic.

[3] Gorbachev is the seventh Soviet leader. He succeeded Lenin (1917–24), Stalin (1924–53), Khrushchev (1953–64), Brezhnev (1964–82), Andropov (1982–4) and Chernenko (1984–5). Of these, all but Khrushchev died in office. A purist might add Malenkov to the list, though his reign in 1953 was only for a few days.

[4] Gorbachev, *Time* Inc., 1989, pp. 45–46.

[5] Later to visit Moscow in different circumstances after the Prague Spring.

[6] *Gorbachev*, Christian Schmidt-Häuer, London, 1986, pp. 86–7.

[7] Schmidt-Häuer, op. cit., p. 104. Ogarkov subsequently regained some influence as C-in-C of the Western sector but retired in 1988.

[8] *The Times*, 19 July 1985. Yepishev was dead within two months.

[9] *The Times*, 26 July 1985.

[10] *The Times*, 12 December 1985.

[11] How many he will find is another matter. 'Today's naval commander must have the qualities of an experienced politician, the willpower of a hardened fighter, the breadth of knowledge of a scientist and the patience of a teacher,' gushed *Red Star*. 'At all times he must be a Bolshevik and a Leninist ... Such a man is Admiral Chernavin.' Such a paragon, indeed, that he might set his periscope on the Kremlin one day.

[12] Seatons, op cit., p. 213.

[13] Richard Owen, *The Times*, 7 May 1985.

[14] Schmidt-Häuer, op. cit., pp. 197–8.

[15] Mark Frankland, *The Observer*, 3 February 1985.

[16] An earlier attempt to kill a leader was made on Lenin by Dora Kaplan in a factory in Moscow in 1918. He survived. It is possible that an attempt was made on Stalin in Red Square in 1938.

[17] Western pressure helped the death sentences passed on two of them to be commuted to fifteen years in labour camps.

CHAPTER 46 *VOYNA*

[1] John Erickson, 'The Chimera of Mutual Deterrence', *Strategic Review*, Spring 1978.

[2] Lieutenant General M. M. Kir'yan, a senior staff member of the Voroshilov Military Academy of the General Staff in Moscow, in his book *Surprise in the Operations of the US Armed Forces*, qu. Nicholas Vaslaf, *Problems of Communism*, May–June 1983, p. 57.

[3] 'The Soviet Conventional Offensive in Europe', Hines and Petersen, *Military Review*, April 1984.

[4] Simon O'Dwyer-Russel, *Sunday Telegraph*, 19 April 1987. NATO has, of course, good lobbying reasons for such a pessimistic valuation. It pressures member governments to beef up conventional strength.

[5] John Erickson, 'Soviet Breakthrough Operations', *RUSIS* Journal, September 1976.

[6] Mark L. Urban, '3rd Shock Army', *Armed Forces*, June 1983, pp. 220 et seq. For another account of a Soviet assault on the central front, see the same author's 'Red Flag over Germany 3', *Armed Forces*, April 1981, pp. 151 et seq.

[7] The Russians do not admit to the existence of any such *operativnaya manevrennaya gruppa* and the only references to them have been by Polish specialists writing about the Red army from 1981.

[8] Ought this to be Frogfeet? NATO will not say.

INDEX

Compiled by Gordon Robinson

Abel, Rudolph, 391
Abramov, Mikhail, 391
Aden naval base, 366
Adenauer, Konrad, 280
Afghanistan
  revolutionary coup, 312
  Soviet occupation, 306–10, 314–19
Aganbegyan, Abel, 251
air defence force, 373–4
  early warning system, 374
air force, Soviet, 369–74
Akhromeyev, Marshal Sergei, 322–3, 404
Albania, post-war communism in, 233–4
Alexander II, 8, 14, 299
Alexandra, Empress, 14, 19, 35
Alksnis, 66, 78
Alliluyeva, Nadezhda (Stalin's wife), 51, 55, 248
  suicide, 63, 72
Alliluyeva, Svetlana (Stalin's daughter), 51, 72, 111, 211
Amin, Asadullah, 308
Amin, Hafizullah, 308, 309, 311, 312, 313
Anders, General, 222, 225
Anderson, Major Rudolf, 261
Andropov, Yuri, xii, 80, 270, 272, 359, 390, 407, 408
  anti-corruption drive, 407
  death, 409
  sponsors Gorbachev, 407
Antonescu, Marshal, 181
Antonov, Colonel G. I., 83–4
Antonov-Ovseenko, 28, 31
Archipov, Colonel V., 344
Ardenne, Baron Manfred von, 243
armed forces operating outside Soviet borders, 330–31, 344–6, 358
Aurora (cruiser), 5, 6

Bach-Zelewski, von dem, 179
Badanov, General, 148
Bagramyan, General I. K., 173, 177
Barabanov, Leonid, 391
Bartha, General Albert, 220
Bata, General Stephen, 221, 269, 270
Batov, General Pavel Ivanovich, 269
Batu, 14fn
Bayerenov, Colonel, 309
Bazhanov, Boris, 58

Beirut, Boleslaw, 179, 224, 225, 226
Belenko, Lieutenant Viktor, 327, 334, 335, 347, 349, 370
Belgrade, liberation of, 184
belief in offensive, Soviet, 419–20
Belkin, Theodore, 220–21
Belyakov, R. A., 402
Beneš, President, 82, 230–31, 232, 233
Berg, Engineer-Admiral, 403
Beria, L. P., 51, 76–7, 79fn, 103, 135, 210–11, 212, 244, 248, 249, 260, 327, 390, 403
Bering, Vitus, 361
Berkman, Alexander, 48–9, 50
Berlin
  airlift, 279–80
  battle for (1945), 195–205
  building of the Wall, 284–5
  post-war partition, 277–8, 280, 282–3
  rising in East Berlin, 280–81
Berman, Jakub, 74, 298, 299
Berzin, Yan, 389
Bialystok, 101
Biriuzov, S. S., 77–8, 87, 227
Blomberg, General Werner von, 60
'Bloody Sunday' at the Winter Palace (1905), 11
Blucher, Marshal, 68, 70, 79fn
Bock, Field Marshal von, 93, 100, 122, 131
Bodnaras, Emil, 229
Bohlen, Charles, 273
Bohr, Niels, 242
Boldin, General, 93–4, 95
Bor-Komorowsky, General, 178, 180
Borodin, 53, 111
Borovik, Artiom, 319
Bowles, Chester, 257
Brauchitsch, Field Marshal, 97, 122
Braun, Eva, 203
Braun, Wernher von, 243fn
Brezhnev, Leonid, xii, 251, 252, 327, 332, 339, 362, 366, 372, 398, 405, 407, 411, 412
  build-up of military strength, 255, 306, 410
  career benefits from Stalin's purges, 80
  Czech crisis, 286, 289, 290, 295–6
  invasion of Afghanistan, 310, 311–12, 313
  threat to Poland, 304
Brusilov, General, 17, 18
Buchanan, Sir George, 20
Bucharest, Soviet occupation of, 182

Budapest
    fall of, 194
    siege of, 185–6
    uprising, 266–7
Budenny, Marshal Semyon, 41, 42, 44, 56, 57, 72–3, 102–3, 107
Bukharin, 61, 62, 67
Bulganin, N. A., 36fn, 211, 212, 326
Bulgaria, post-war Communist takeover, 226–8
Bush, Dr Vannevar, 252
Byong-in, Captain Chung, 408fn

Cam Ranh Bay naval base, 366, 367
Carter, Jimmy, 303, 383
Castro, Fidel, 256, 257, 262
Castro, Raúl, 256
Catherine the Great, 298, 299, 326, 361, 406
Cernik, Oldrich, 286, 291, 292, 295, 296, 297
Chaliapin, Fyodor Ivanovich, 3
Chapin, Selden, 222
Charles II of Sweden, 14fn, 108
Chebrikov, Viktor, 390, 410
Chelomei, V. N., 402
Chernavin, Admiral Vladimir, 368, 409, 410, 411
Chernenko, Konstantin, 80, 332, 409
Cherniakovsky, General I. D., 173, 177, 187, 194–5
Chernov, Victor, 25
Cherny, Lev, 50
Chervonenko, 297
Cherwell, Lord, 247
Chesma, destruction of Turkish fleet at, 361
Chiang Kai-shek, 61, 135
China, border dispute with Soviet, 307fn
Chtcheglov, General, 303
Chuikov, General Vassily, 134, 135, 136, 137, 138, 139, 140, 141, 142–3, 149, 173, 177, 189, 191–2, 195, 198, 202, 203, 204, 251
Churchill, Winston, 23, 40, 83, 87, 127, 161, 162, 173, 179, 180, 185, 192, 193, 196–7, 215, 242
Cienfuegos naval base, Cuba, 365–6, 367
Civil War, Russian, 26–7, 32–50, 55–6
    assault on mutineers at Kronstadt, 48–50
    creation of the Red army by Trotsky, 28–9
    October Rising (1917), 3–7, 28
    Red Terror unleashed, 36
    White Russian offensive, 39–41; retreat, 42–4
Clay, General Lucius, 245, 278
Clementis, Vladimir, 231
climatic conditions in Russia, xvi–xvii
Conrad, Clyde Lee, 421

conscription and the recruits
    desertion, 349
    discipline, 350–51
    drink problem, 334–5, 346–7
    food, 347–8
    informers, 350
    leave, 343–4
    political training, 342–3
    practise of cruelty on raw recruits, 348–9
    racial factors, 340–42
    remote rural postings, 335
creation of the Red army by Trotsky, 28–9
Cuban crisis, 256–62
    Bay of Pigs landing and defeat, 256
    United States blockade, 259–60
Cyril, Grand Duke, 22
Czechoslovakia
    armed forces in the Warsaw Pact, 394
    post-war Communist takeover, 230–33
    Prague Spring (1968), 285–98

Daoud, Mohammed, 311, 312
defence industry and economy of Soviet Union, 397–404
Denikin, General Anton, 17, 34, 37, 39, 40, 41, 43, 69, 161, 248
Djilas, Milovan, 235, 332, 333
Dimitrov, Dr G. M., 227
Dimitrov, Georgi, 226–7, 228
Djugashvili, Yekaterina (Stalin's mother), 51
'Doctors' Plot', 211–12
Donskoi, Dmitri, 114
DOSAAF, 338
drink problems
    armed forces 334–5, 346–7
    civilian, 399
Dubček, Alexander, 285, 286, 287, 288, 289, 290, 291, 292, 294, 295, 296, 297, 298
Dubs, 'Spike', 312, 313
Dukhonin, General, 32
Dulles, Allen, 221
Dulles, John Foster, 268–9, 273
Dumitrescu, General, 144
Dzerzhinsky, Felix, 33, 55
Dzur, General, 286, 287, 297

East Germany
    announces cut in armed forces (1989), 396
    armed forces in Warsaw Pact, 396–7
Eden, Anthony (later Lord Avon), 82, 162
Ehrenburg, Ilya, 42, 195
Eichmann, Adolf, 185
Eisenhower, General, 145, 192, 196, 197, 268, 273, 283
El Alamein, battle of, 145
encirclement, Soviet fear of, 329
Epishev, General, 329

Etsov, Major, 77
Ezhov, Nikolai, 67, 68, 79

Farkas, Michael, 221, 266
Faymondville, Philip R., 66
Fediuninsky, General, 91
Fierlinger, Zdenek, 231
Finland and the Winter War (1939–40), 84–8
    armistice (1944), 83
First World War, 15–19, 32–3
    armistice, 37
    casualties, 17, 18, 19, 24
    continuation by Provisional Government, 24
    defeat at Tannenberg, 16
    retreat from Galicia, 17–19
Frey-Bielecki, General Jan, 300
Frinovsky, General, 406
frontier zones of the Soviet Union, 329
Frunze, Mikhail, xii, 24, 39, 59, 60
Fuchs, Klaus, 245, 246
future war scenario, 419–28

Gagarin, Yuri, 254
Gai, G. D., 71
Gaiour (mujaheddin leader), 319
Gamarnik, I. B., 68
Gdansk, strikes in, 301–2
Gehlen, General Reinhardt, 132, 143, 187, 194
Georgescu, Teohari, 229
Gerasimov, Gennady, 409fn
German War, 91–209
    aid from the Allies, 127–9
    end of the German offensive, 157
    extermination policy of the Germans, in
        retreat, 159–60
    industrial evacuation, 125–7
    partisan warfare, 106, 135, 160, 173–4
    Soviet counter-offensive, 120–23, 144–52,
        158–208
Gerö, Ernö, 266, 268, 270
Gierek, Edward, 301, 302
Glushko, V. P., 252, 402
Goebbels, Josef, 111, 204
Goering, Hermann, 146, 147
Golikov, Lieutenant General, 117
Gomulka, Ladislas, 225, 266, 299, 300, 301
Gorbachev, Andrei, 406
Gorbachev, Mikhail, xii, 62, 64, 80, 249, 250,
    298, 299, 316, 332, 359, 368, 372, 374, 388,
    390, 394, 398, 399, 401, 405, 406, 411–12,
    415
    announces cuts in conventional forces, 322–
        3, 411
    Afghanistan withdrawal, 316, 318, 319
    beginnings, 406–8
    clampdown on drink, 334
    cuts corruption, 339

redeployment of defence industry, 403–4
    removal of rivals, 409–10
    sponsored by Andropov, 407
    succeeds as leader, 409
Gorbachev, Raisa, 407
Gorbachev, Sergei, 406
Gorbatov, General A. V., 75
Gorlikov, General, 144
Gorodnyansky, General, 132
Gorshkov, Admiral Sergei, 362, 363, 365, 368,
    372, 409–10
Gottwald, Klement, 231, 232
Govorov, General Vladimir, 122, 336, 408fn
Grechko, Marshal A. A., 251, 255, 286, 287,
    292, 296, 297, 327
Greene, F. V., 7
Gribkov, General, 304
Gromyko, Andrei, 259, 296, 312, 410
Groves, General Leslie, 245
Groza, Dr Petre, 229, 230
GRU intelligence service, 385, 387–92
    rivalry with KGB, 389–90
    technology espionage, 387–92
Guchkov, Alexander, 24
Guderian, General Heinz, 91, 93, 94, 95, 100,
    102, 105, 106, 107, 108, 109, 110, 112, 114,
    115, 116, 117, 118, 122, 155, 184, 186, 187
Gueidarov, General Arif, 413
Guevara, Che, 256, 257
Gurtiev, Colonel, 140

Haig, General Alexander, 306
Halder, General Franz, 95, 98, 106, 107, 112,
    133, 140
Harriman, Averell, 159
Heinrici, Gotthard, 198
Helfand: articles in Iskra, 30
Helsinki Agreement, 382–3, 384
Hertz, Dr G., 243
Himmler, Heinrich, 179
Hindenburg, Field Marshal Paul von, 16, 19,
    190
Hiroshima bomb, 243
Hitler, Adolf, 14fn, 31, 58, 65, 77, 78, 82, 83,
    218, 243, 393, 420
    appoints himself commander-in-chief, 122
    bomb plot, 178, 181
    issues Commissar Order, 98
    Russian campaign, 91–203, 207
    suicide, 203
Hoeppner, General, 93, 103, 110, 116, 117, 118,
    122
Horthy, Admiral, 82, 184, 185, 218, 221, 272
Hoth, General Hermann, 93, 101, 106, 109, 110,
    111, 116, 117, 131, 133, 146, 148, 154, 156
Hoxha, Enver, 233, 234
Hube, General, 168

Hungary
Red army involvement in post-war Communist takeover, 217–22
uprising (1956), 266–77; deployment of Red army, 274–5
Husak, Gustav, 297–8, 394

Ibragimov, Sultan, 413
Iline, Anatoly, 413
Ilyushin, 65
incentive awards to Red army troops, 334
Ioffe, Abram, 241
Iron Curtain falls, 215, 216
Isaev, A. M., 252
Ivan IV (the Terrible), 15, 22, 50
Ivanov, Captain, 260
Ivanov, Colonel General, 224

Jacob, General Sir Ian, 192, 193
Jagielski, Mieczyslaw, 302
Janin, General, 42
Jankowski, Jan, 224, 225
Jaruzelski, General, 298, 300, 303, 304, 305, 306, 395
Jebb, Gladwyn, 192, 193
John Paul, Pope, 304
Johnson, Louis, 245
Johnson, Lyndon B., 289, 290, 295, 383
Josef Ferdinand, Archduke, 18

Kabul, 307–19
Soviet occupation of, 307–10, 314–19
Kádár, Janos, 265, 273, 275, 276–7, 290
Kaganovich, M. M., 81, 266, 272
Kalinin, Mikhail Ivanovich, 46
Kamenev, Lev, 57, 58, 61, 62, 67
Kampov, Major, 166, 167
Kania, Stanislas, 302, 304
Kantariya, Sergeant, 203
Karasev, Lieutenant Colonel, 348
Kardelj, Edward, 236
Karmal, Babrak, 309, 311, 316, 318
KGB
checks on Red army officers, 327
control of nuclear warheads, 376
involvement in defence industry, 403
rivalry with GRU, 389–90
satellite espionage, 390
technology espionage, 386, 387–8
troops commanded by KGB and GRU, 389–90
Khlan, Sergeant Oleg, 316, 317fn
Khariton, B., 252
Korolev, S. P., 252, 254
Karpov, Vladimir, 104fn
Karpunich-Braven, General I. S., 75
Katyn massacre of Polish officers, 222–4

Kennedy, John F.
Bay of Pigs disaster, 256, 283
Berlin crisis, 256–62
Cuban crisis, 283, 284
Kennedy, Robert, 261
Kerensky, Alexander, 3, 4, 5, 6, 24, 25, 26, 27, 28, 32, 33
Kesselring, Field Marshal Albert, 107
Khabalov, General, 21, 22
Kharkov
liberated and retaken, 151–2
recaptured by Red army, 159
Soviet offensive, 132
Khlan, Oleg, 339, 342
Khozynanov, Andrey, 137–8
Khrushchev, Nikita, xii, 33, 76, 80, 105, 141, 156, 211, 212, 307fn, 311, 326, 327, 340, 388, 403, 409, 413, 419
Berlin crisis, 281, 282, 283, 284
beginnings, 247–8
closing of prison camps, 250
Cuban crisis, 256–62
cuts in conventional forces, 251, 253, 332, 336, 362
death, 251
denounces Stalinism, 249–50, 265–6, 267
deposed, 251, 255, 262, 332
economic failures, 250, 251
expansion of submarine fleet, 362
handling of Hungarian rising, 271–2, 273
personality cult, 251
Polish unrest, 299–300
prime mover in missilry, 247, 251–2, 253–4
succeeds Stalin, 248
kidnapping of German scientists after the war, 243–4
Kiev
attacks on, xx, 14fn
battle of (1941), 107–9
destruction, 209
liberation of, 160–61
Killinger (German ambassador to Rumania), 182
Kiraly, General Bela, 236–7
Kirpichnikov, Sergeant Timofeyev, 23
Kirov, Sergei, 61
murder of, xii, 66–7, 72, 76, 249
Kirponos, General, 103, 108
Kleist, General Ewald von, 93, 102, 103, 108, 112, 131, 132, 148, 149, 169
Klich, Lieutenant General, 103
Klimovskikh, Major General, 103
Kluge, General, 116, 118
Knox, General, 17, 18
Koch, Erich, 105
Kolarov, Vassili, 227
Kolbukhin, 197

Kolchak, Admiral, 34, 37, 39, 40, 42, 43
Koldunov, Air Marshal Alexander, 406, 408
Kolyma prison, 75, 76
Komar, General Wraclaw, 300
Koniev, Marshal I. S., 101, 153, 157, 159, 166,
    167, 168, 169, 178, 187, 188, 189, 191, 196,
    197, 198, 199, 200, 201, 203, 205, 206, 272,
    284, 289
Kopacsi, Alexander, 271
Korean War, 306–7fn
Kornilov, General Lavr, 26, 27, 32, 34, 46
Korolev, S. P., 402
Korsun, battle of, 166–7
Kosygin, Alexei, 80, 288, 407
Kot, Stanislaw, 222
Kovacs, General Bela, 219, 274
Krasnov, General, 27, 34
Kravchenko, General, 206
Krebs, General, 204
Kresty prison, 73
Kronstadt naval mutinies, 12, 22
    attack on mutineers by Trotsky, 44–50
Kropotkin, Peter, 47, 55
Kriukov, Brigade Commander, 80
Krymov, General, 27
Kryuchkov, General Vladimir, 322, 410
Küchler, Marshal von, 165
Kuklinski, Colonel Ryszard, 302, 303, 305
Kulikov, Nikolay, 142
Kulikov, Marshal Viktor, 303, 304, 305, 325,
    404
Kurchatov, Igor, 241, 242, 244
Kurkotkin, General Semen K., 348
Kursk, battle of, 154–7
Kutakhov, Marshal Pavel, 408fn
Kuzichkin, Vladimir, 316
Kuznetsov, Aleksei, 210
Kuznetsov, Admiral N. G., 71–2, 81, 94, 105,
    362
Kuznetsov, General, 122

Larionov, A. N., 250
Leeb, von, 93, 95, 103
Lelyushenko, General, 189
Lenin, xix, 4, 8, 11, 20, 25, 26, 27, 33, 41, 51,
    53, 54, 56, 58, 62, 105, 265, 310–11, 323,
    340
    attempt on his life, 36, 55
    beginnings, 12–13
    death, 58
    exile years, 29, 55, 76
    illness, 57
    launch of Red October, 67
    mistrust of Stalin, 249
    return to Russia, 23
Leningrad, siege of, 108, 109, 111–12, 132, 159,
    165

casualties, 209
    relief of, 166
'Leningrad affair', 210
Liebknecht, Karl, 39
Ligachev, Yegor, 410
Lincoln, Abraham, 361
List, Field Marshal, 131
Litvinov, 53
Liu Shao-chi, 271, 272
Lizichev, General, 409
Lloyd George, David (later Earl), 42
Lobov, General Vladimir, 412
Lodge (US ambassador), 269, 276
Lomsky, General, 286
Lozansky, Edward, 325
Lozovsky, 53
Lubianka prison, Moscow, 74, 225, 327
Ludendorff, General Erich, 16
Lulchev, Kosta, 228
Luxemburg, Rosa, 39
Lvov, 103, 104
    liberation of, 178

McNamara, Robert, 257, 259, 261, 284, 362
Maisky, Ivan, 105
Malenkov, Georgy, 80, 211, 212, 246–7, 248,
    250, 273
Maleter, Colonel Pal, 269, 274, 277
Malinin, General, 273, 274
Malinovsky, Marshal, 168, 169, 181, 182, 184,
    185, 194, 206, 254
Mannerheim, Marshal Gustav, 34, 85, 86
Manstein, Christoph von, 10
Manstein, General, 131, 132, 147, 148, 152, 166,
    169, 172
Manteuffel, General Hasso von, 10, 161, 163
Mao Tse-tung, xxi, 246, 307fn
Marchenko, Valery, 415
Marcks, General, 97
Marshall, General George, 217
Marshall Plan, 217, 220, 231, 279
Martel, General, 66
Marx, Karl, 12
Masaryk, Jan, 231, 233
Matsuoka, 98
Mauriac, François, 277
Maximov, Yuri, 409, 411
May-Maevsky, 42
Medvedev, Roy, 281
Mekhlis, General Lev, 71, 79, 103, 132
Mellenthin, 172
Menon, Krishna, 276
Meretskov, Marshal, 76–7, 206
Michael, King of Rumania, 181–2, 228, 229–
    30
Micunovic, Veljko, 267
Mihailovic, Draza, 235

Mikes, George, 267
Miklos, General Bela, 219
Mikolajczyk, Stanislaw, 179, 225, 226, 227
Mikoyan, 65, 211, 266
Mil, Mikhail, 65, 353
Miller, General, 37, 39, 43
Mindszenty, Cardinal, 221–2, 272, 275, 276
Minsk, destruction of, xix–xx, 209
  liberation, 176
  occupation, 101
Mironov, Filipp, 73
missile-killers
  ABM defence of Soviet, 380
  economic strain, 381
  investment by Soviet, 381
  laser weapons, 379
  US Star Wars programme, 379
missiles, rockets and satellites, Soviet, 244, 251–
  5, 282, 355–6, 358
  cruise missiles, 378–9
  earth orbit, 254
  first cosmonaut, 254
  ICBMs, 375–7, 380, 381
  missile accuracy, 377
  missile sites, xx
  nuclear attack forces, 375–85
  nuclear submarine missiles, 368, 381–2
  reduction agreement with US, 323, 382
  rocket sites, 378
Mlynar, Zdenek, 289, 291–2, 295, 407
Model, Field Marshal, 156, 176, 180
Mohnke, General, 204
Moiseyev, General Mikhail, 323, 412
Molotov, Vyacheslav, 83, 93, 94, 128, 162, 225,
  236, 248, 250, 266, 272, 298
Montgomery, General (later Field Marshal
  Earl), 145, 190, 196
Morozov, Pavel, 65, 350
Moscow, battle of, 109, 111–13, 116–18
Moskalalenko, General, 248
Muklevich, Admiral, 78
Müller, Richard, 388
Munich Agreement, 82–3
Münnich, Ferenc, 273, 275
Mussolini, Benito, 58, 83, 91, 97, 184, 204,
  218
mutinies, naval
  Kronstadt, 12, 22, 45–50
  Potemkin (1905), 12
  Storozhevoy (1975), 349–50

Nadiradize, V. N., 402
Nagy, Ferenc, 219–20
Nagy, Imre, 219, 265, 266, 267, 268, 270, 271,
  272–3, 274, 275, 276, 277, 286
Najib, Major General, 318

Napoleon I, xviii, 14fn, 95, 97, 107, 111, 112,
  114, 123
Nasser, Gamal Abdel, 268
Naumov, Vladislav, 338
Nazi-Soviet pact (1939), 83
Nedelin, M. I., 253
Nekrasov, Viktor, 138
Nevsky, Alexander, 114
Nicholas II, 3, 4, 8, 11, 12, 14, 15, 18, 19, 20,
  21, 28, 43, 399
  abdication, 22, 55
  execution, 35
Nicholas, Grand Duke, 15, 18
Nicholson, Major Arthur, 354
Niedzwiadek-Okulicki, General, 224, 225
Nixon, Richard, 309, 383
Normandy landings, 173
Nosek, Vaclav, 231, 232, 233
Novotny, Antonin, 285
nuclear arms reduction talks
  CSCE in Helsinki, 382–3, 384
  Gorbachev-Reagan agreement, 323
  INF, 384
  MBFR in Vienna, 382, 383
  SALT, 382, 383, 384
  START, 384
nuclear bomb, Soviet drive for, 241, 243–7
  final test, 245–6

Odessa
  bombardment by *Potemkin* mutineers (1905),
    12
  liberation of (1944), 169
officer corps of the Red army, 335–6
  KGB checks on, 327
  political subservience and ignorance, 326–8
  privileges of the high ranking, 323–6
  Stalin's purges of, 67–80
Ogarkov, Marshal Nikolai, 327, 328, 408–9
Ohola, Richard, 73
Oppenheimer, Robert, 242, 246
Orbeli, I., 73
Orlov, Admiral, 78

Pabst, Corporal Helmut, 91, 92, 94, 100, 101,
  102, 105, 111, 114, 119, 123, 127, 130, 142,
  159, 207
Paléologue, 15, 17, 19, 22
Pálffy, Lieutenant General George, 220
Palinkas, Captain, 272
Pankovsky, Yevgeny, 347
Pares, Sir Bernard, 17
Paris summit (1960), 282; chemical warfare
  conference (1989), 354
Patton, General George, 178, 192, 194
Pauker, Anna, 229, 230

Paulus, Field Marshal von, 97, 131, 133, 135, 139, 140, 143, 144, 145, 146, 148, 150
Pavlov, General, 101, 103
Pavlovsky, General Ivan, 287, 290, 293, 313, 314
Peresleni, Sergeant Alexei, 316
Perle, Richard, 388
Pervukhin, 244
Peter the Great, 15, 20, 50, 360–61
Peter, King of Yugoslavia, 184
Peter III, 326
Péter, Gábor, 220, 221
Peter, Imre, 266
Petliakov, V. M., 77
Petöfi, 267
Petrichenko, 50
Petropavlovsk submarine base, 367
Petrov, Nicolai, 227, 228
Petrov, Marshal Vassily, 411
Philby, Kim, 234
Pilsudski, Marshal, 43–4, 82, 299
Pilyugin, A. N., 252
Pimonov, Colonel, 224
Piotrowski, Captain, 306
Piros, Ladislas, 270
Plekhanov, Georgi, 12, 13, 55
Pobedonostsev, 65
Podrabinek, Kirill, 348
Pokryshin, Alexander, 129
Poland
    armed forces in Warsaw Pact, 394–5
    German invasion, 83–4, 222
    massacre of officers at Katyn, 222–4
    post-war Communist takeover and influence of the Red army, 222, 224–6
    state of war imposed by Jaruzelski (1981), 305
    unrest and the Solidarity crisis, 298–306
Polevoi, Boris, 188
Politburo, foundation of, 55
political commissar system reintroduced in Red army, 68
Polkovnikov, Colonel, 5
Popieluszko, Father, 306
Port Arthur, 361, 362
    fall of, 11
Pospelov, 249
Potemkin mutiny (1905), 12
Potsdam conference, 242
Povanitsyn, Sergeant Yuri, 316
Powers, Gary, 281–2
Prague, fall of, 206
    uprising, 285–98
Prchlik, General, 288, 290, 296
Primakov, 69, 70, 71, 74
Prime, Geoffrey, 391
prison camps, Soviet, 74–7

prisoners of war, fate of returning Russian, 209–10, 349
Profumo, John, 260
Purkaev, 206
Putna, General, 67, 71
Puzak, Kazimierz, 225
Puzanov, Alexander M., 312, 313

Radek, Karl, 72
Radescu, General Niculae, 228, 229
Rajk, Laszlo, 265, 266, 267
Rákosi, Matyas, 215, 217–18, 219, 221, 265–6
Rakowski, 306
Rasputin, Gregory, 15, 19
Reagan, Ronald, 303
Red army audit sheet, 351–60
    airborne divisions, 356, 357
    artillery, 354, 355
    aviation, 353
    chemical capability, 354
    civil defence troops, 357
    ground forces, 352
    missiles, 355–6, 358
    tanks, 353–4
Red navy: blue water build-up, 360–68
    aircraft carriers, 365
    minimizing noise from submarines, 385–6
    nuclear missiles, 368, 381–2
    submarine capabilities, 358, 363–4, 366–7, 368, 381–2
Reed, John, 3, 5, 6
Reiff, Ryszard, 305
religion in the Soviet Union, 415
Rennenkampf, General, 16, 17
Revai, Joseph, 218
Revolution, Russian
    abdication of the Tsar, 22
    formation of Provisional Government, 23
    Petrograd rising, 20–22
Riabyshev, Lieutenant General, 104
Ribbentrop, Joachim von, 83, 94
Riehl, Dr N., 243
Rodimtsev, General, 136, 137, 138
Rokossovsky, Marshal Konstantin, 80, 117, 122, 144, 145, 146, 153, 156, 159, 173, 174, 175–6, 177–8, 180, 187, 189, 190, 197, 205, 226, 299, 300
Romanov, Grigori, 409
Romanov, Colonel General Semen, 328
Roosevelt, Franklin D., 161, 162, 192–3, 197, 230, 242
Rotmistrov, General, 157, 166, 168, 251
Rozhdestvensky, Vice-Admiral Zinovy, 11, 12
Rumania, post-war Communist takeover, 228–30
Rundstedt, Field Marshal Karl von, 93, 95, 102
Ruoff, General, 131

Rusk, Dean, 260, 262
Russell, Bertrand (3rd Earl), 243
Russo-Japanese War (1904), 11–12
  (1944), 206–7
Rust, Mathias: his penetration of Soviet air
  defences, 405–6, 419
Rybakov, Vladimir, 347
Rybalko, General, 200
Rychagov, Pavel, 81
Rykov, Igor, 61, 62, 67, 338, 339, 342, 348, 350
Rytir, General Otakar, 286, 296
Ryzhov, Nikolai, 403, 411

Sablin, Captain Valery, 349–50
Sadat, Inwar, 328–9, 366
Sajer, Guy, 160, 161, 183, 194
Sakharov, Andrei, 246, 252
Sakharov, Vladimir, 391
Samsonov, General, 16, 190
Schaal, General, 119
Schulenburg, von, 93
Sebastopol, 92, 132, 170
secret police of the Soviet Union, 70fn
  see also KGB and MVD
Sedyakin, A. I., 66, 78
Semenov, N. N., 241
Semenov, Vladimir, 328
Semyonov, Konstantin, 297
Semyonov, Lieutenant, 104fn
Serov, Colonel General I. A., 243–4, 274
Serpantinka death camp, 75–6
Severodvinsk shipyard, 401
Severomorsk naval base, 367
Shaligin, V., 327
Shaposhnikov, B. M., 70
Sharigin, Vanya, 347
Shchelekov, 359
Shchemenko, General, 289
Shcholokov, General Nikolai, 407
Shehu, General Mehmet, 233–4
Shepilov, Dmitri, 271
Shevchenko, Arkady, 332
Shmushkevich, General, 79
Sholokhov, Mikhail, 37, 39
Shostakovich, Dmitry, 69
show trials, 67, 68–70
Siilasvuo, Colonel Hjalmar, 85, 86
Sikorski, General Wladyslaw, 222
Simeon, King of Bulgaria, 227
Simonov, Konstantin, 119, 124, 139, 182,
  204
Skoblin, General, 68
Skorzeny, Otto, 184–5
Smirnov, Leonid, 387
Smolensk, battle of, 101, 102, 106, 107
  retaken by Red army, 159
Sobolev, Arkady A., 273

Sokolov, Marshal Sergei, xix, 309, 327, 406,
  409, 410
Sokolovsky, Marshal, 278, 287
Solzhenitsyn, Alexander, 104fn, 191, 340
Sorge, Richard, 91, 390
Sourisseau, Bernard, 391
Soviet-Japanese neutrality pact (1941), 97–8
Speer, 146, 191, 243
Stalin, Joseph, 4, 11, 13, 33, 37, 40, 44, 83, 84,
  222, 223, 224, 225, 234, 235, 236, 265, 298,
  306fn, 326, 327, 340, 351–2, 369, 390
  beginnings, 50–55
  Berlin crisis (1948–9), 278–9
  civil war struggles against the Whites, 134
  collectivization policy, 64–5, 406, 420
  death, 212, 248, 249, 280
  denounced by Khrushchev, 249–50, 265–6,
  267
  drive for the nuclear bomb, 241, 244, 245
  exile, 54
  feud with Trotsky, 54, 56–9
  Five Year Plans, 62–3; post-war, 209
  general secretary of Central Committee, 57
  Japanese war (1944), 206–7
  persecution mania, 211
  political killings, xii, 210
  post-war policies, 209–11, 217
  purges of the Red army, 67–80
  re-expansion of the Red army, 217
  revives the Red fleet, 361–2
  Show Trials, 63
  strategy in the German war, 91–208
  treatment of returning prisoners of war, 349
Stalingrad, battle of, 133–50
Standley, Admiral, 128
Standrart, General Hans Henning von, 404
Starinov, Colonel, 77, 94, 103
Stemmermann, General, 166, 167
Stepanovich, Ivan, 344
Stepinac, Mgr, 235
Stetsko, Yaraslav, 413
Stolypin, Peter, 54
strategic materials in USSR, xx
Suez crisis, 268, 273
Sukhomlinov, General Vladimir, 15, 18
Susaikov, General, 229
Suslov, Mikhail, 327
Suvorov, Viktor, 290, 292, 350, 390
Sverdlov, Jacob, 35
Sviridov, General Vadim, 219
Svoboda, General Ludvik, 231, 286, 203–4, 295,
  297
Swaniewicz, Professor Stanislaw, 223
Szalasi, Ferenc, 185
Szasz, Bela, 220–21

Tabolov, Devlet, 348

Taborsky, Professor Edward, 231, 232
Talalikhin, V. V., 342
Talyzin, Nikolai, 403
Tamm, I., 252
tanks, Soviet, 65–6, 353–4
Tannenberg, battle of, 16, 190
Taraki, Nur Mohammed, 311, 312, 313
Taylor, General Maxwell, 256
Teheran conference, 161–2
Teremov, General, 175
terrain of Soviet Union, xvii–xix
Tildy, Zoltan, 219, 221
Timoshenko, Marshal, 42, 94, 102, 106, 108, 132
Tito, Marshal, 183–4, 234, 235, 236, 237, 266, 273
Togo, Admiral, 12
Tokaev, Serge, 244
Tolbukhin, General, 168, 170, 181, 183, 184
Tolubko, Marshal Vladimir, 409
Tombor, Eugene, 220
Tomsky, 61, 62, 67
Tretyak, Alexander Afanasevich, 180
Tretyak, General Ivan, 406
Trotsky, Leon, 3, 4, 5, 6, 11, 13, 22, 25, 27, 52, 53, 60, 61–2, 67, 69, 72, 134, 212
    attack on Kronstadt mutineers, 47–50
    beginnings, 29–32
    command of Red army, 28–9, 32–50, 56
    exile, 29, 31, 62, 76
    feud with Stalin, 54–9
    murder of, xii
    resigns command, 59
    return from exile, 24, 30, 32
    thrown off Politburo, 61
Truman, Harry S., 197, 215, 227, 242, 245, 279
Tsushima, battle of, 12, 361
Tukhachevsky, Marshal Mikhail, 36, 39, 40, 43, 44, 48, 49, 50, 60, 66, 67, 68, 69, 70, 73, 74, 79, 252, 408
Tupolev, Andrei, 65, 369
Tykhy, Oleksy, 415

Uborevich, 69
Ulbricht, Walter, 280, 281, 283
Ulrikh, V., 69
unrest and dissidence in modern Soviet Union, 412–15
Ushakov, Divisional Commander, 75
Ustinov, D. F., 127, 244, 313, 409

Vannikov, B. L., 244
Vas, Zoltan, 219, 220
Vashugin, N. N., 103–4
Vassilevsky, Marshal A. M., 135, 144, 152, 157, 173, 195, 206
Vatsetis, General, 70–71

Vatutin, General N. F., 144, 152, 153, 156, 157, 160–61, 166, 168
Vedenin, Lieutenant General Andrei, 72
Velchev, General, 227
Veres, Peter, 220
Vienna
    arms talks (1973), 382, 383
    Soviet occupation, 198, 362
    summit (1961), 283
Viktorov, Admiral, 78
Vinogradov, Commander, 86
Vitebsk, 101
Vitkovsky, D. P., 74
Vladivostock naval base, 366, 367
Vlasov, General Andrei, 103, 108, 122, 132, 205–6
Voronov, Marshal N. N., 85, 87, 164
Voroshilov, General Kliment, 37, 55–6, 57, 59, 60, 69, 71, 78, 218, 219, 273
Voznesensky, N. A., 125, 128, 210
Vyazma-Bryansk, battle of, 110
Vyshinsky, Andrei, 228–9, 406

Wagner, Walter, 203
Walesa, Lech, 299, 301, 302, 303, 304, 305, 306
Wanner, General Herbert, 392
Ward, Stephen, 260
Warner, John, 363
Warsaw, battle of (1944), 178–80, 188–9
    unrest, 299, 300, 301, 303, 304, 305
Warsaw Pact, 392–7
Weichs, General von, 131
Weidling, General Karl, 198
Weiner, Lieutenant, 141–2
Werth, Alexander, 151, 180
Wilhelm II, 15
Wisniewski, Admiral Jan, 300
Witte, Count, 7
Wrangel, General, 40, 41, 43, 44, 69
Wyszynski, Cardinal, 299, 300

Xoxe, Lieutenant General Koci, 234

Yagoda, G. G., 67, 265
Yakir, Ion, 66, 69, 70, 74
Yakovlev, A. S., 65, 81, 402
Yakovlev, Sergei, 402
Yakubovsky, Marshal, 287, 290
Yalta conference, 192–3
Yangel, M. K., 402
Yazov, Dmitry, xi, xii, xvi, xvii, xviii, xix, xx, xxi, xxii, 329, 336, 376, 392, 396fn, 404, 405, 411
    appointed defence minister, 406, 410
    arms reductions, 322–3
    army audit sheet, 351–60
    controller of the Red army, xi

Yazov Dmitry—*contd.*
  intelligence service, 385
  responsibility, xiii
Yegorov, Sergeant, 203, 278
Yepichev, General Alexei, 287, 313, 409
Yeremenko, Lieutenant General, 108, 144, 145, 146
Yevtushenko, 76
Yezhov, 265
Young Pioneers, 337
Yudenich, General, 37, 39, 40, 41, 56
Yugoslavia
  German occupation, 235
  prewar Communist takeover, 234–7
  Red army presence, 235, 236
  split with Soviet Union, 236–7
Yussupov, Prince Felix, 19

Zahir Shah, King, 311
Zaikov, Lev, 404
Zaitsev, General Mikhail, 409
Zakharov, General G. F., 173, 174, 175, 349
Zapotocky, 274
Zaychenko, Alexander, 323
Zeitzler, General Kurt, 140
Zelenograd, 388
Zelensky, 73
Zhadov, General, 157

Zhdanov, 211
Zholudev, General, 140–41
Zhukov, Marshal Georgy, 42, 123, 130, 138, 140, 144, 147, 152, 157, 158, 168, 169, 173, 187, 196, 204, 205
  appointed Deputy Supreme Commander to Stalin, 135
  arrest of Beria, 248, 327
  beneficiary of Stalin's purge of the Red army, 80, 103fn
  border clashes with Japanese (1939), 84, 98, 103fn
  C.-in-C., Poland, during crisis, 224–5
  commands Red army in battle of Moscow, 103fn, 113–14, 116–18
  death, 327
  defence minister, 271, 273, 276, 326
  demoted by Stalin, 326
  drive for Berlin, 197, 198, 199, 200, 201, 202
  dismissed by Khrushchev, 327, 409
  offensive against the Germans, 174–6, 189, 191
  organizes defence of Leningrad, 103fn, 108, 112
  post-war obscurity, 210
Zinoviev, G. E., 25, 45, 50, 57, 58, 61, 62, 67
Zog, King of Albania, 233
Zorin, Valerian, 232
Zwierzynski, Alexander, 224